VALUING FINANCIAL INSTITUTIONS

VALUING FINANCIAL INSTITUTIONS

Z. Christopher Mercer, ASA, CFA

President
Mercer Capital Management, Inc.

BUSINESS ONE IRWIN Homewood, Illinois 60430

Project editor: *Gladys True*
Production manager: *Irene H. Sotiroff*
Compositor: *Carlisle Communications, Ltd.*
Typeface: *11/13 Century Schoolbook*
Printer: *Arcata Graphics/Kingsport*

Library of Congress Cataloging-in-Publication Data

Mercer, Z. Christopher.
    Valuing financial institutions / Z. Christopher Mercer.
      p.   cm.
    Includes bibliographical references.
    ISBN 1-55623-379-5
    1. Banks and banking—Valuation. 2. Savings banks—Valuation.
  3. Savings and loan associations—Valuation. 4. Financial
institutions—Valuation. I. Title.
HG1708.M47 1992
332.1′068′1—dc20   91–29326

Printed in the United States of America

1 2 3 4 5 6 7 8 9 0 A G K 8 7 6 5 4 3 2 1

To Jane. Thanks.

Preface

Objectives and Scopes

This is a handbook on the financial analysis and valuation of banks and thrifts. It has four basic objectives:

1. To provide a complete educational and reference source for anyone interested in the subject of financial institutions appraisal.
2. To discuss the development of financial institutions valuation concepts within the context of generally accepted valuation theory and practice, and hopefully, to make a contribution to the business appraisal profession in the process.
3. To provide the tools to enable business appraisers with experience in other industries to provide independent valuations of financial institutions.
4. To provide an analytical and valuation framework to help bank and thrift executives understand the critical relationships between bank finacial analysis, bank performance and bank valuation.

No prior knowledge of banking or business appraisal is assumed in the book. The "jargon" of both are defined and explained as terms and concepts are encountered. References to both banking industry and valuation literature are utilized throughout the text, and the bibliography provides additional references for further background or study.

I have attempted to keep the discussion of financial institutions valuation within the mainstream of current business valuation theory and practice. However, where controversies may exist, I have tried to mention the opposing positions and to label my personal opinions as such.

Intended Audience

Valuing Financial Institutions is a book designed for anyone requiring an understanding of how banks and thrifts work, how they are regulated, how they make money, and how they are valued.

Valuing Financial Institutions is a "working" book. It is filled with examples derived from more than fifteen years of valuing and "hands-on" consulting with banks and thrifts. Checklists are provided to assist bankers, appraisers, or other professionals working with banks, as well as students of banking and bank appraisal. These checklists have been developed through experience in valuing and consulting with literally hundreds of institutions.

Several groups should therefore benefit from all or portions of *Valuing Financial Institutions,* including:

1. *Bankers.* With the industry at the beginning phase of the most massive consolidation period in history, bankers need a primer on bank valuation.
2. *Thrift Executives.* Since the process of deregulation began in the 1970s, thrifts have been in the process of becoming more "bank-like." By legislative and regulatory fiat, thrifts are now banks by definition, with only a few rules, primarily regarding asset composition, distinguishing them from banks.
3. *Business Appraisers.* The basic tools of business appraisal are applicable to companies across a wide variety of industries, although it is always important for the business appraiser to understand the factors which make particular industries different from each other, particularly as those differences impact valuation.
4. *Professional Advisors to Banks.* Attorneys, certified public accountants, employee benefits specialists, and other professionals providing services to banks will find the book to be a handy reference source for questions regarding bank operations, structure, or special issues relating to mergers, acquisitions, or shareholder value.
5. *Banking Students.* The book is designed to be a basic or supplemental resource for banking students at the undergraduate or graduate levels. It is filled with analytical examples, practical observations, and checklists designed to help the student (or the banker or appraiser) through the valuation process. The Sample Bank Appraisal incorporates many of the lessons of the book to provide an example of the end product of financial institutions analysis. The book can also be used as a basic or supplementary text by banking schools around the nation.
6. *Bank Regulators.* Banking examiners and other regulators should find that this book provides an interesting and informative overview of the analytical process for reviewing bank performance.

Organization of the Book

The book begins with Part I, "Introduction to Financial Institutions and Their Appraisal," which provides background information (in Chapters 1–7) on both banking and business valuation to set the stage for an industry-specific approach to valuation. Part II, "Bank/Bank Holding Company Financial Analysis," consists of four chapters (Chapters 8–11) focused on the analysis of bank operating and financial performance. Part III, "Bank Valuation," incorporates the preceding two parts of the book into an overview of bank and thrift valuation, and deals with valuation for purposes of Employee Stock Ownership Plans, which are fairly prevalent in banks and thrifts. The six chapters of this section (Chapters 12–17) provide the most comprehensive treatment of financial institutions appraisal available today. Part IV, "Special Issues in Bank Valuation," covers several important topics (in Chapters 18–20) which are unique to banks or particularly relevant to bank valuation today. The final section, Part V, "Conclusion," provides concluding and forward looking comments about the banking industry, as well as the Sample Bank Appraisal.

The book contains many exhibits which illustrate analytical or valuation concepts and provide specific examples of how valuation theory and practice can be combined in a practical sense. Other exhibits provide chapter-specific reference materials. The Appendices provide general valuation reference materials or specific checklists and questionnaires designed for use by bank appraisers or bankers in performing valuations or due diligence for potential mergers or acquisitions.

The bibliography is provided at the end of the book rather than within chapters to facilitate review and research in one place. The bibliography is designed to be helpful for bankers and bank appraisers interested in bank performance, analysis, and valuation. The index is designed to enhance the book's usefulness as an educational and reference source.

Acknowledgments

While I claim responsibility for the idea of writing this book and for preparing the book proposal for the editors at BUSINESS ONE IRWIN, many others have shared in its preparation in critically important ways. Before thanking them, however, let me state the usual and necessary caveat in acknowledgments: whatever assistance has been provided, the responsibility for the final product is mine. More than one of my friends and associates at Mercer Capital and in the business appraisal profession have asked me to consider alternate viewpoints at several places in the text. They, as I, reserve the right to develop and maintain independent opinions in matters of professional judgment.

Special thanks go to the entire staff at Mercer Capital for their assistance and endurance, individually and collectively, throughout the process of writing the book.

Eva M. Lang, CPA, provided research assistance for all phases of the book, wrote the initial drafts of Chapter 5 ("Regulation and Accounting for Banks and Thrifts") and Chapter 7 ("Sources of Comparative Financial and Valuation Data") and is a coauthor of the Sample Bank Appraisal (Chapter 22). Terry S. Brown, AM, prepared the initial draft of Chapter 6 ("Selected Management Issues"), and is a coauthor of the Sample Bank Appraisal. J. Michael Julius, ASA, CFA, prepared drafts of the primary analytical chapters (Chapter 8, "Overview of a Banking Company," Chapter 9, "The Bank Income Statement," Chapter 10, "Analyzing Bank Financial Statements," and Chapter 11, "Holding Company Analysis"), as well as Chapter 19 ("Branch Valuations and Core Deposit Appraisals"). He is also a coauthor of the Sample Bank Appraisal. Special thanks also to Jeff K. Davis CFA, T. Alexander Ivy, CPA, Sandra J. Trobaugh, CPA, Anita A. Redden, Tammy E. Ford, and Rita Jackson, who either proofed chapters, provided research or other assistance, or made it possible for someone else to do the same. Thanks also to Michael J. Mard, ASA, Jim Rigby, CPA, and Erich Sylvester, ASA for their timely proofing and suggestions on the critical valuation chapters, as well as for their encouragement during the process of the book.

I owe a special debt of gratitude to my coauthor (and primary writer) for Chapter 17, "Thrift Stock Valuation." Michael A. Murphy, CFA, Managing Director of Trident Financial Corporation, is one of the leading thrift appraisers in the nation, and his knowledge of and insights into the history, regulation, and operation of thrifts contributed materially to that chapter.

My friend and business partner, Kenneth W. Patton, ASA, assisted with drafting at several places, and served as a sounding board for general content throughout the book and for specific content in quite a few chapters. However, his greatest contributions were in his support, encouragement and unwavering belief that we would finish "The Book," as this volume came to be known at Mercer Capital, and his continuing focus on meeting our ongoing client commitments, particularly as the time dedicated to the process far exceeded my wildest estimates.

Lori A. Mercer, our office manager until she moved from Memphis, kept the entire production process moving and organized once each chapter was drafted. After she left, Barbara A. Walters took over the task of production. In addition to keeping me moving (to the extent that is possible), they both were kind enough to field most of the friendly reminders from my publishers that I had missed yet another deadline!

Several professional associates read one or more of the valuation chapters for content and conformity with current valuation theory. While gratefully acknowledging their assistance, I in no way implicate them with any errors or disagreements regarding emphasis, omissions, or assumptions. Their respective positions with the American Society of Appraisers are indicated following their names and firm affiliations.

David Nicholas, ASA
Ernst & Young,
(Vice Chairman, Business
    Valuation Committee)

Tony S. Leung, ASA, CFA, CPA
Management Advisory Services,
    Inc.
(Editorial Review Board,
    Business Valuation Review)

Wayne C. Jankowske, Ph.D
Associate Professor of Finance
    Xavier University

Brian T. Napier, ASA
Capital Analysts, Inc.
(Chairman, International Board
    of Examiners

Michael A. Murphy, CFA
Trident Financial Corporation

Another professional friend and associate, Shannon Pratt, DBA, FASA, CFA, and author of *Valuing a Business,* also published by BUSINESS ONE IRWIN, served as an ongoing inspiration during the preparation of this book, even though he may not have been aware of his role most of the time. His books' contributions to the field of business appraisal (and to my knowledge) are freely acknowledged both here and in many footnotes throughout this book.

I thank my editors at BUSINESS ONE IRWIN, including Ralph Rieves and Gladys True, for their belief in this book, and for their encouragement along the way to its publication. I also appreciate that they continued to work with me after I missed more deadlines for chapter drafts than I care to recount. I apologize for contributing to their frustrations in dealing with part-time authors (writing on full-time subjects) who cannot always give first priority to their writing efforts.

On a personal note, my wife, Jane, was a constant source of encouragement for me as the momentum for this book ebbed and flowed over more than two years. My son, Zeno, is now sixteen months old. His coming may have slowed progress on the book a bit, but he has certainly been a joy in our lives! A final personal acknowledgment is for my daughter, Amanda, who is now sixteen, who may not yet believe her father can write a book, and who will be surprised at this note when she reads it.

Z. Christopher Mercer

Contents

Diligence Visit: *Interview. Physical Inspection. Evaluation of Management. On-Site Document Review. Documentation of the Interview.* Conclusion.

List of Exhibits

List of Figures

Part I

Introduction to Financial Institutions and their Appraisal

Chapter 1

Introduction to Financial Institution Valuation

. . . One rule which woe betides the banker who fails to heed it . . .
Never lend any money to anybody unless they don't need it.

Ogden Nash

Increasing Requirements for Independent Business Appraisal

Business valuation is relatively new as a profession. Until fairly recently, within the last decade or so, most business valuation requirements were accomplished by investment bankers, accountants, attorneys, or business and financial consultants. However, the confluence of several factors has increased the need for professional, independent appraisal of businesses and financial institutions. Among them are:

1. *Litigation.* Litigation has been one of the growth industries of the last two decades, with litigation over issues relating to the valuation of corporate stock one of the major areas of growth. Litigation includes divorcing couples who hold a significant portion of their marital assets in the shares of closely-held companies or financial institutions.
2. *Regulation.* Regulation is increasing in many areas of society. While financial institutions have always been regulated, all of corporate America has seen increasing regulatory intrusion in recent years. For example, regulations from the Internal Revenue Service (involving gift and estate taxes as well as charitable giving) and the Department of Labor (involving profit sharing plans and Employee Stock Ownership Plans) have generated valuation requirements for many corporations and financial institutions.
3. *Bankruptcy.* The rising trend in business bankruptcies has fueled requirements for business valuation. Needs have ranged from solvency opinions, designed to provide comfort for lenders and other creditors in highly leveraged transactions, to the valuation of equity or debt securities of companies in or near bankruptcy.
4. *Minority Shareholder Awareness.* Tied closely with the growth in litigation has been an increasing awareness of the rights of minority shareholders.
5. *Inflation, Economic Growth, and Time.* The growth in business formations since World War II, combined with more than four decades of relatively high inflation and the passage of time, has created an increasing number of business entities of significant value.

The business valuation profession has begun to develop in response to the rising requirements for independent business appraisal. With the growth of the profession, there is a growing body of knowledge regarding business appraisal.[1] However, there is very little information available dealing with the specific requirements of the appraisal of financial

---

[1]The Bibliography provides a detailed listing of business valuation reference books, as well as numerous articles and other sources of authoritative valuation information.

institutions within the context of current valuation theory and practice. Most books and articles that examine financial institutions have been written by consultants rather than by professional appraisers.

Why a Book on Financial Institutions Appraisal?

Banks are different from most other businesses in several definable ways. The differences require specific knowledge and experience to avoid mistakes in the appraisal process.

Banks and thrifts are regulated businesses. They operate under specific regulations promulgated by myriad state and national agencies. These agencies provide the rules under which banks must operate. Sometimes the rules make sense, and sometimes not. They are, nevertheless, the rules of the game. Appraisers must understand the rules in order to value financial institutions properly.

Banking is an industry in transition. Historically, banks operated under rules that legally provided effective oligopolistic powers in their relevant markets. Thrifts operated in an environment with a legally defined "guaranteed" spread between the "legal maximum allowable" interest they could pay on deposits and the higher rates charged on long-term mortgages.

Both banks and thrifts benefited from a mismatching of the maturity (term) structures of their liabilities, which were and remain generally very short, and their assets, which generally were longer term in nature. In the traditional, historical "rising yield curve" environment, banks and thrifts were almost guaranteed a reasonably profitable level of operations.[2] In fact, there is an old saying that banking was a "3-6-3" business: bankers could borrow (acquire deposits) at 3%, lend at 6%, and play golf at 3 P.M. And everyone has heard the expression *bankers' hours*, which suggests that bankers do not have to work very hard.

The rules have changed, and the nation is in the midst of a profound revolution that will forever change the face of the entire financial institutions industry. The "thrift crisis" of the late 1980s is being followed by the "banking crisis" of the 1990s. Unheard-of failures of financial institutions have left a several hundred billion dollar burden for American taxpayers to repay and are now calling into question the ability of the Federal Deposit Insurance Corporation (FDIC), which guarantees the safety of savings deposited with banks, to cover the known problems in the industry today. A massive restructuring of this nation's financial institutional structure will be the inevitable result. With the industry in such change, appraisers, bankers, regulators, and investors need specific knowledge about bank valuation.

---

[2]In the normal environment, market rates are higher for long-term investment instruments than for short-term instruments of the same nature. The higher yields compensate investors for the additional risk of investing longer term. The process of deregulation that has occurred has allowed banks to pay higher rates on most of their deposits. Rising interest costs, which have been accompanied by increasing competition and lower yields (and shorter repricing terms) on loans and investment securities, have placed banks under spread pressure. These concepts are discussed at length later in the book. However, the reader can equate the concept of spread pressure with lower earnings potential.

Overview of the Banking Industry

The banking industry is huge. As shown in Exhibit 1-1, there are near-ly 13,000 banks and savings banks insured by the FDIC. Collectively, these banks hold over $3.6 trillion in banking assets, have $236 billion in net worth, and employ about 1.5 million people.

Exhibit 1-1

Historical Banking Statistics ($ billions)

FDIC-Insured Commercial Banks (BIF)

Year	Number	Assets	Equity	Net Income
1990	12,342	$3,388	$219	$17
1989	12,713	3,299	205	16
1988	13,139	3,131	197	25
1987	13,699	3,001	181	3
1986	14,200	2,941	182	18
1985	14,404	2,703	169	18
1984	14,477	2,508	154	16
1983	14,460	2,342	140	15

FSLIC-Insured Institutions (SAIF)

Year	Number	Assets	Equity	Net Income
1990	2,519	$1,084	$31	($ 8)
1989	2,878	1,018	40	(9)
1988	2,949	1,351	55	(13)
1987	3,147	1,251	46	(8)
1986	3,220	1,164	52	0
1985	3,246	1,070	47	4
1984	3,136	977	37	1
1983	3,183	815	33	2

FDIC-Insured Savings Banks (BIF)

Year	Number	Assets	Equity	Net Income
1990	471	$261	$17	($2)
1989	487	260	17	(3)
1988	492	284	21	1
1987	484	262	20	2
1986	472	237	18	2
1985	392	205	12	1
1984	291	179	8	0
1983	294	171	8	0

Total—All Institutions

Year	Number	Assets	Equity	Net Income
1990	15,332	$4,733	$267	$ 7
1989	16,078	4,577	262	(4)
1988	16,580	4,766	273	13
1987	17,330	4,514	248	(3)
1986	17,892	4,342	252	20
1985	18,042	3,978	228	23
1984	17,904	3,665	200	17
1983	17,937	3,327	181	17

Sources: *Statistics on Banking,* Federal Deposit Insurance Corporation, 1983–1989 for FDIC-insured commercial banks and savings banks.
Combined Financial Statements of Insured Institutions, Office of Thrift Supervision, 1983–1988 (regulatory basis).
FDIC data compiled by W. C. Ferguson & Company, 1989–1990 for all institutions.
(See Chapters 5 and 17 for more detailed discussions of regulatory and federal insurance structure.)

At the end of 1988, there were nearly 3,000 thrifts insured by the Federal Savings and Loan Insurance Corporation (FSLIC). Those thrifts had assets of $1.4 trillion and regulatory net worth of some $55 billion. By 1990, the number of thrifts had shrunk to 2,500, and thrift assets and net worth had been reduced to $1.1 trillion and $31 billion, respectively. The thrift industry employed nearly 400,000 persons during 1988. Employment in the industry is undoubtedly down given the massive closings of thrifts in 1989 and 1990; nevertheless, the industry remains a major employer nationally.

From the viewpoint of appraisers or investors in community bank stocks, another look at the industry is helpful. Most banks are relatively small, at least when compared with the giant money-center and super-regional banking institutions. Exhibit 1-2 outlines the banking industry distribution by size at the end of 1989.

Exhibit 1-2
FDIC-Insured Commercial Banks as of December 31, 1989 ($ billions)

Asset Size	Total Assets	Total Equity	Total No. Banks	Average Assets/Bank ($ millions)
Less than $25 million	$ 57.1	$ 5.8	3,746	$ 15.2
$25 to $100 million	308.5	26.9	5,982	51.6
$100 million to $1 billion	625.2	46.7	2,607	239.8
More than $1 billion	2,308.2	125.5	378	6,106.4
Totals	$3,299.0	$204.9	12,713	$ 259.5

Source: *Statistics on Banking 1989*, FDIC

Analysis of Exhibit 1-2 indicates that banks of $100 million or more in total assets comprise nearly 90% of industry assets, about 84% of industry equity, and less than 24% of the total number of banks. The 378 banks with assets exceeding $1 billion represent 3% of the nation's banks, 70% of total assets, and 61% of industry equity. The banking industry is not only very large but quite highly concentrated.

While banking commands a great concentration of America's national wealth, there is very little valuation information available about the great majority of banks. A recent issue of *I/B/E/S: The Institutional Brokers Estimate System* showed at least one earnings forecast for only 274 banks and 190 thrifts. *I/B/E/S* is a well-known compendium of coverage of publicly traded stocks by the investment banking community.[3] The coverage afforded banks and thrifts is a clear indication that valuation information is not available on the vast majority of financial institutions.

Trends in Bank Ownership

While it is well known that the banking industry is in a consolidation phase, independent banking is alive and prospering. There are still about 12,800 insured commercial (and savings) banks, down from about 14,800 banks in 1983. The apparent trend, however, may be deceiving. While

---

[3]*I/B/E/S* is published by Lynch, Jones and Ryan, 345 Hudson St., New York, NY 10014.

firm statistics are not available, we believe the actual number of independent banks may be close to holding its own.

In many markets, the sale of the last independent bank motivates organizing groups to start new, independent banks. The number of new bank charters, averaging almost 400 per year in the 1980s, has been greater than the number of bank failures over the period. A substantial portion of the recent decline in the number of banks, then, must be caused largely by bank "closures" resulting from activities of multi-bank holding companies that are consolidating their banks into lead banks or regional banks.

Current regulations encourage diverse ownership of banks by discouraging concentration of ownership in new bank formations. Further, most bank chartering groups realize that a successful community offering of shares is a critical ingredient in tying new shareholders and their banking relationships to a start-up bank.

Most banks have large and diverse shareholder bases. We use the term *quasi-public* to describe the typical ownership structure and market for bank stock. By this we mean that by number of shareholders, many banks are public from the point of view of securities regulation and disclosure, but the market for shares is very limited.

Many banks have been in existence for years. A recent survey, conducted by Mercer Capital Management, Inc., of 38 client banks in nine states revealed an average age of almost 50 years. Observations of hundreds of banks over the last 15 years lead to the conclusion that most banks have fairly large shareholder bases (in relationship to the typical closely-held commercial enterprise) that are multigenerational.

The Mercer survey noted above included banks ranging in size from $14 million in total assets to over $700 million. The average number of shareholders for the 38 banks was 200. About 25% of the banks had 50 or fewer shareholders. Another 25% of the banks had more than 300 shareholders, so about half of the banks had between 50 and 300 shareholders.

Many people who acquired bank stock at some point in their lives have kept it long enough to transfer shares to their children and grandchildren. It is quite common to find banks with shareholders representing two or three generations of families.

Given the trends noted at the outset of this chapter, the absolute size of even the smallest group of financial institutions shown in Exhibit 1-2, whose average stockholders' equity exceeds $1.5 million, and the number and nature of their shareholder bases, the requirements for independent knowledge about valuation are increasing. This is particularly true because active public markets exist for only a relatively small number of banking institutions in the nation.

Focus on Regulation and Litigation

Our society is becoming increasingly litigious. One of the results of this trend is that the fiduciary responsibilities of bank boards of directors and management are being defined by the courts.

Business Judgment Rule Challenged

In the recent case *Smith* v. *Van Gorkom (Trans Union)* [488 A. 2d (Del. 1985)] the Supreme Court of the State of Delaware ruled on the application of the "business judgment rule." The case was a class action suit brought by shareholders of a corporation against the board of directors for its approval of a cash-out merger of the corporation into a new, larger entity. The directors sought insulation from liability under the business judgment rule for exercising normal business judgment in managing corporation affairs.

The court held first that the "Board lacked valuation information adequate to reach an informed business judgment as to the fairness of $55 per share for sale of the Company." Summarizing this holding, the opinion stated: "A substantial premium may provide one reason to recommend a merger, but in the absence of other sound valuation information, the fact of a premium alone does not provide adequate basis upon which to assess the fairness of an offering price." The decision in *Smith* v. *Van Gorkom* held the directors of Trans Union personally liable, leaving them responsible for approximately $13 million in damages above and beyond those covered by liability insurance.

Based on this decision, bank boards should insist that significant transactions be presented in a complete manner and that access be provided to competent experts who can speak to the related legal, valuation, accounting and disclosure issues.

Fiduciary Responsibilities of ESOP Trustees

Recent court decisions are of great importance to companies that have or are contemplating employee stock ownership plans (ESOPs). In *Hines et al.* v. *Rowley and Schlimgen, Inc. et al.* (Western District of Wisconsin Civil Case 85-C-1037-S), the court held ESOP trustees personally liable for their handling of ESOP stock transactions. This should be of particular interest to community banks because management members often serve as trustees for bank ESOPs.

The decision of the court focused heavily on the adequacy of the appraisal and the fiduciary responsibilities of the various parties. The court found there was a breach of fiduciary responsibilities in several important aspects: (1) the administrators failed to act in the best interests of the ESOP participants, and (2) the board of directors of the company failed to properly supervise its "agents," i.e., the administrators who conducted the transactions.

The court further concluded that the business judgment of the trustees of the ESOP "was not in any way directed to the best and sole interest of the participants, which the law requires." Finally, the court concluded that a lower valuation than was used in the pertinent transaction was appropriate and held both the ESOP trustees and the company liable for the difference in the amount, plus costs and attorneys' fees.

Rules and Regulations

Under the Tax Reform Act of 1986, the rules for charitable gifts of non-publicly traded stock became complicated. For gifts of $10,000 or more, a "qualified appraisal" is required. To be acceptable to the IRS, the appraisal should be signed and dated by a "qualified appraiser," be made within 60 days of the date of the contribution, and not involve prohibited fees (i.e., related to a percentage of value). The tax identification number of the appraiser must be provided to the IRS, and an Appraisal Summary (Form 8283) must be signed for each gift. Failure to attach the Appraisal Summary with a filed return may cause a charitable contribution deduction to be disallowed completely by the IRS.

The 1986 Tax Reform Act provided that all ESOPs must have a regular (annual), independent, outside appraisal of company shares held by the ESOP. The ruling applies for any plan year in which there are transactions by the ESOP. Annual appraisals are always necessary for leveraged ESOPs.

On May 17, 1988, the Department of Labor published 29 CFR Part 2510, "Regulation Relating to the Definition of Adequate Consideration: Notice of Proposed Rulemaking," in the *Federal Register*. The proposed regulation clarifies the definition of the term *adequate consideration* provided in the tax code relating to ESOP transactions.

The regulation places responsibility for the determination of adequate consideration in ESOP transactions squarely on the shoulders of a plan's trustee(s). Effectively, the proposed regulation will, for most plan trustees, require the use of independent appraisal services to substantiate ESOP transactions. In addition, the proposed regulation provides specific, detailed requirements for the required written valuations. The proposed regulations are particularly important for bankers and appraisers of banks because of the large number of banks that have installed ESOPs and therefore fall under their guidelines.[4]

Implications for Bank Valuation Requirements

Current trends in several areas are creating increasing requirements on the part of community banks to obtain independent appraisals of their shares. As noted above, the trends include (1) the structure of community bank ownership, (2) court cases relating to responsibilities of boards of directors and ESOP trustees, and (3) changes in tax-related regulations.

Several banking situations are described below. Although fictitious names are used throughout, the situations described are real-life examples of banks that have recently used independent appraisal services to accomplish desired business objectives and to satisfy regulatory or legal requirements.

---

[4]A more detailed discussion of the proposed Department of Labor regulations is found in Chapter 16, and the regulations are reproduced in Exhibit 16-1.

Ownership Consolidation

The Smith family owned controlling interests in three small banks located within 20 miles of one another. Ownership percentages varied with each of the banks, and the nonfamily shareholder bases of each of the banks had little overlap. The banks were run as part of a control group; however, there was little ability to reallocate capital within the group from a better-capitalized bank to a weaker bank.

The Smiths decided to form a multi-bank holding company and place all three banks under one company: Eastern State Holding Company. A merger transaction calling for the exchange of shares by each bank's shareholders for shares in Eastern State was devised. Certain share-holders were given the opportunity to sell their shares, and Eastern State borrowed the funds to accomplish the repurchase.

Several aspects of independent valuation services were required in order to accomplish the mergers. First, each individual bank had to be valued on a stand-alone basis. An exchange ratio for Eastern State stock was then determined, based upon the relative values of the three banks. In order to obtain regulatory approval, the ability to repay the debt created by the stock repurchase had to be shown in the form of financial projections. Finally, a review of the entire transaction was required by the appraisal firm to form an opinion of the fairness of the overall trans-action from the point of view of minority shareholders.

Proxy materials were prepared, reviewed by all appropriate regula-tory bodies, and finally approved by the shareholders. Eastern State was formed, the shares were repurchased from selected shareholders, and a $120 million banking organization came into being.

Since then, Eastern State has formed an ESOP, and the ESOP has been a participant, through the purchase of additional shares, in the ac-quisition of a fourth bank.

Minority Interest Buyout

First State Holding Company owned 82% of First State Bank. The holding company was leveraged and was dependent upon dividend income from First State Bank for cash flow to service its debt. First State Bank, on the other hand, was well capitalized, with equity exceeding 10% of total assets.

Management was involved constantly in dealing with two sets of shareholders and with two sets of shareholder reporting. Estimates of the cost of duplicate reporting were in the range of $15,000 per year.

The holding company board was very cognizant of the fact that 18% of every dividend from First State Bank went to outside shareholders. A special dividend from First State Bank could have reduced the holding company's debt, but given the significant minority interest in First State Bank, no special dividend was ever declared.

The decision was made to engage in a minority "squeeze-out" merger, the effect of which was to require the purchase of the various small blocks of stock making up the 18% minority interest in First State. An appraisal of the fair market value of the minority interests was performed. In addition, the appraisal company made an overall evaluation and issued its opinion that the transaction was fair, from a financial point of view, for the minority shareholders of First State Bank. The transaction was reviewed by all appropriate regulatory bodies and approved by the shareholders. All minority shares were tendered in the offer, and there were no dissenting shareholders.

As a result of the squeeze-out merger, the bank's shareholders received fair consideration for their illiquid minority interests. From the holding company's point of view, it achieved a better utilization of the excess capital in its subsidiary, consolidated its ownership to the 100% level, eliminated the dual level of shareholder reporting, and eliminated the potential capital drain from dividends flowing to outside shareholders of the bank.

Estate Planning

First Delta Bancorp is a one-bank holding company that owns 100% of the outstanding shares of First Delta Bank. Mr. and Mrs. I. M. Lively, now in their late seventies, own 73% of the shares of Bancorp. An appraisal of the Lively's controlling interest in Bancorp was performed for the purpose of a series of gifts to their 20 children and grandchildren. The Livelys' tax advisor has suggested they make regular gifts of shares now, while they are in good health, with the objective of reducing their holdings below the 50% level during their lifetimes. The gifting program is now in place, and each year Mr. and Mrs. Lively give additional shares. If all goes as planned, their estate will be reduced by the substantial amount of several years' annual gifts. Upon Mr. Lively's death, the remaining interest in Bancorp may be valued as a minority interest, further reducing the taxable estate in comparison to the current control valuation.

Employee Stock Ownership Plan 1

Merchants Bank was a high-performance bank in a rural area of its state. The bank was 100% owned by Merchants Bancorp. There was virtually no market for Bancorp's stock; and when the shares traded, the prices reflected the lack of liquidity.

Bancorp's board of directors installed an ESOP with several goals, including: (1) acquiring up to 15% of the holding company's stock over a period of years, (2) providing a limited market for the stock in the local community, and (3) enhancing the bank's employee benefits package. The ESOP operated as planned for several years.

Each year's annual stock appraisal was the basis for ESOP stock purchased that year. Community interest in Bancorp's shares increased over the years as the fair market value appraisals reflected continuing levels of high performance. The annual appraised price came to be the established market price for independent transactions in the stock.

Over several years, the ESOP did acquire the targeted level of 15% ownership, and when Bancorp was acquired by a regional holding company in the state at a price of 2.2 times book value, the employee beneficiaries of the ESOP received a substantial windfall addition to their retirement accounts.

Employee Stock Ownership Plan 2

Community Bancshares, Inc. owns 100% of Community Bank. Because of growth in the area surrounding its suburban location, the bank has grown rapidly over the last few years. During a recent examination, the examiners noted that the bank's capital was below regulatory minimum guidelines and suggested that the bank should develop a capital plan to deal with its growing capital shortfall.

The capital plan prepared by the board of directors included renewed emphasis on cost controls, concerted efforts to control growth, and the establishment of an ESOP by Community Bancshares. Bancshares obtained an independent appraisal of the fair market value of its shares for purposes of the ESOP. The ESOP trustee arranged a loan with a regional correspondent bank to fund the purchase of $500,000 of Bancshares stock. Bancshares then injected the funds into Community Bank as additional equity. The bank's capital shortfall was alleviated, and future contributions to the ESOP will repay the ESOP loan. The capital plan was reviewed favorably in the next regulatory examination.

Annual Control Appraisal

Merchants & Farmers Bank is a successful bank in a bedroom community of a major city. After experiencing severe earnings problems several years ago, the bank has now achieved high-performance status. The board of directors desires, if possible, to operate the bank as an independent community bank for the foreseeable future; however, one by one, its neighboring banks have been acquired by out-of-county institutions.

Realizing that unsolicited offers could be presented to Merchants & Farmers Bank, the board of directors retained a valuation firm several years ago to prepare an annual appraisal on a control basis. The annual appraisal is used by the board of directors as a regular part of the annual business planning process. Based upon the appraisals, the board was able to turn down an unsolicited offer to acquire the bank because they had timely and objective evidence that the proposed consideration was inadequate.

There is a growing realization on the part of the board of directors that one of the state's regional bank-holding companies will probably desire to acquire the bank over the next year or two. Rapid growth in the community is increasing the bank's profile in its metropolitan statistical area. Armed with its periodic appraisals, the board of directors believes it is well prepared to deal effectively with prospective suitors.

Charitable Giving

Peoples Bancshares owns 100% of Peoples Bank, a successful bank with about $200 million in total assets. Bancshares has almost 500 shareholders, but the market in the stock is extremely thin and not considered to be an active public market.

Several members of the board of directors desired to make charitable contributions of appreciated Bancshares stock during December of a recent year. Their tax advisors informed them that charitable gifts of Bancshares stock exceeding $10,000 would require an independent appraisal to substantiate the value of the charitable donations.

Realizing that numerous other stockholders might desire to make similar charitable gifts, the board of directors retained a valuation firm to provide an appraisal of Bancshares stock for purposes of charitable gifts. Shareholders were notified of the pending appraisal and that the appraiser would sign Form 8283, the Appraisal Summary that must accompany the tax return of any shareholder desiring to utilize this opportunity. Several shareholders made charitable gifts that would not have been economical on an individual basis without the shared appraisal result.

Dividend Reinvestment Program

Second Bancorp owns 100% of the outstanding shares of Second National Bank, a growing bank in a sizable market. Growth over recent years has placed Second National under capital pressure.

One of the Bancorp's directors owned shares in a regional bank holding company that had a dividend reinvestment program. He asked whether or not Bancorp, which had a very thinly traded market for its shares among its almost 400 shareholders, could install its own dividend reinvestment program. The director thought that the program could be an important source of capital and that because it would be available to all shareholders, it could be nondilutive to any shareholder who participated.

Research revealed that with proper shareholder disclosure regarding the program, Second Bancorp could indeed have a dividend reinvestment program. Because there was no active public market for the shares, it was necessary to have an independent determination of fair market value for share purchases. An appraisal firm was hired to provide an annual appraisal with quarterly updates of the share prices for purposes of the plan.

Initial response from the shareholders has been favorable. Almost 5% of Bancorp's shareholders, representing about 10% of the outstanding shares, elected to participate during the first year. Because Bancorp usually pays out over one third of earnings in dividends, the effect of the dividend reinvestment plan has been to allow retention of an additional 3% or so of earnings, providing a new and ongoing source of capital for growth, as well as a convenient reinvestment service for shareholders.

Conclusion

Trends in bank ownership, court-defined responsibilities for boards of directors, and regulation suggest that valuation issues are becoming increasingly important for community banks. We offer the following concluding observations for consideration:

4. Management and boards of directors are being held responsible for making informed business decisions in the context of substantial due diligence efforts, which include specific and objective information regarding valuation.

Community bankers will have to become more aware of all the issues relating to the valuation of their banks' shares in a variety of contexts. As is clearly seen in the previous discussion, this awareness requirement far transcends common rules of thumb such as "My bank is work 1.5 or 2.0 times book value." As will be discussed in more detail in later chapters, rules of thumb are out the door in the tumultuous banking environment of the 1990s. Bankers and appraisers of banks need specific valuation information geared to the unique operating, regulatory, and market conditions faced by the financial institutions industry.

Chapter 2

Introduction to Valuation Concepts

The greatest of all gifts is the power to estimate things at their true worth.
LaRochefoucauld

Valuation

Value has many meanings, so it is important to begin with a basic understanding of what we mean when we talk about value, or valuation, as well as the related word *appraisal*. That there has long been confusion regarding the meaning of *value* is confirmed in a quotation from the legal scholar James C. Bonbright, who said:

> As long as common law and statute law persist in using the term "value" as a legal jack-of-all-trades, judges are forced, willy-nilly, to reject the precedent of economists and to follow instead the precedent of Humpty Dumpty (from *Through the Looking Glass*): "When I use a word it means what I choose it to mean—neither more nor less."[1]

We can define *valuation* in the context of financial institutions as: *the process of estimating the worth (value) of an interest (either a portion or the entirety) of a financial institution, or reaching an opinion of its worth, based upon due consideration of the facts and circumstances surrounding the situation, and the exercise of judgment.* Used as a noun, *valuation* becomes the opinion itself. *Appraisal* is another word used to represent the valuation opinion, so valuation and appraisal can be used interchangeably.

Defining Financial Institutions

The term *financial institution* includes several kinds of financial entities, including banks, bank holding companies, savings banks, mutual savings banks, stock-owned thrift institutions, mutual thrift institutions (also called savings and loan associations, or S&Ls), and credit unions. We are *not* dealing here with financially oriented companies lil e insurance companies, brokerage and investment banking firms, and mortgage banking concerns, all of which may offer many services in direct competition with financial institutions.

Financial institutions have several common characteristics:

1. They accept deposits from consumers and/or businesses.
2. The deposits are generally insured by the federal government, at least up to the maximum level for deposit insurance coverage with the FDIC.
3. They are chartered by the federal government or the various states and regulated by agencies of the chartering governments.
4. Financial institutions, through the acceptance of deposits, have the power to "create" money as their loan customers write checks on their deposit accounts.

---

[1]Bonbright, *Valuation of Property* (1937), as quoted in George D. McCarthy and Robert E. Healy, *Valuing a Company: Practices and Procedures* (New York: Ronald Press, 1971), p. 3.

5. They generally deploy the acquired customer deposits by making loans to customers, whether businesses or consumers, making other investments that provide for earnings as well as adequate liquidity, and providing any or all of a wide range of financial services to their customers.[2]

The emphasis of this book will be on the valuation of banks and stock-owned thrift institutions. Except in the case where mutual thrifts and savings banks are converting to stock ownership (see Chapter 17 for detailed treatment of this specialized subject), we will not focus on mutually owned institutions (mutual thrifts and credit unions) because there are no individual equity interests subject to valuation. Nevertheless, many of the analytical techniques found in this book are directly applicable both to mutual thrifts and to credit unions.

The regulatory process and market forces are leading toward greater homogeneity of financial institutions. The financial institutions industry is in the process of a major consolidation that will, we believe, virtually eliminate market and regulatory distinctions between thrifts and banks over the next decade, with banking institutions being the surviving form of operation. Consequently, for the majority of this book we will deal primarily with banks and often will use the terms *bank* and *banking institution* synonymously with *financial institution*.

Why Are Valuations of Financial Institutions Necessary?

"The Market" Values Publicly Traded Banks

There are active, or relatively active, markets for the common stocks of fewer than 800 financial institutions. The remaining stock-owned financial institutions (more than 14,000 at the present time) simply do not have any active market for their shares.

For banks and thrifts with reasonably active markets, the current market price for minority interests is fairly easily determined. Shareholders can look up current market prices in the national or local financial press. The share prices listed are normally reasonable approximations of market value, or the price at which an individual shareholder could sell or acquire shares in the open market at a given time.

However, the shares of many so-called public financial institutions are quite thinly traded. The small number of investment banking firms following these thinly traded stocks do not take large positions in their shares, so the markets are referred to as *workout markets*.[3] A broker

---

[2]Readers are referred to any of several textbooks on the subject of money and banking for a complete discussion of the nature and extent of banking services and of the "sacred trust" held by financial institutions in the protection of customer deposits, as well as their role in the process of creating money in our society. (See the Bibliography for several citations to recent textbooks.)

[3]When an investment banking firm "takes a position" in a stock, it acquires the shares for speculative purposes or for resale. In any event, the firm's capital is at risk when it takes a position in a bank's stock (or any stock). Because the markets for many banks are so thin and so subject to price fluctuation when relatively small amounts of stock are placed on the market for sale or someone desires to accumulate a large block of shares (in relationship to "normal" trading volume), brokers typically refuse to take a position in the shares. Rather, they will purchase or sell those shares that come available in the normal course of business for their customer accounts at normal commission rates, thereby avoiding risk to their capital.

will "work" a customer into or out of a particular block of shares at the rate at which the normal transactions volume will absorb the shares. Stocks with thinly traded markets offer a less reliable indication of market value than those with highly traded markets, and they are more susceptible to large swings in price based upon greater than normal pressure on either the selling or acquiring side of the market.

Shareholders of actively traded banks can generally rely upon the posted price in the financial press as a reasonable indication of market value for purposes of shareholder estate or liquidity planning. The institutions themselves can also rely upon current market prices for purposes of corporate planning and transactions.

Why Financial Institution Valuations Are Necessary

Even the smallest of closely-held, stock-owned financial institutions are substantial economic entities. There are few thrifts (except troubled institutions) and even fewer banks with net worths of less than $1 million. The great majority of financial institutions have net worths (and market values) well in excess of $1 million. Financial institutions (and other corporations) with values in this range develop transactional requirements similar to larger, publicly traded institutions. Both shareholders and the institutions themselves must depend upon independent appraisal for reasonable indications of market value in order to accomplish many normal business transactions.

Figure 2-1 outlines the overall business planning cycle applicable to financial institutions (and other companies as well). The figure highlights an upper loop (solid lines) involving ongoing operations and normal business planning as a continuing process. Unlike most business planning diagrams, however, the figure shows a lower loop (dotted lines) of corporate and shareholder planning that is quite often overlooked by both financial institutions and their shareholders until *after* the needs have become apparent in the normal course of business.

Financial institutions have ongoing responsibilities for shareholder relations and consolidation. They must often consider the estate planning requirements of their shareholders, as well as liquidity planning for their shareholders.

Normal business planning and ongoing operations (the upper loop in Figure 2-1) give rise to many types of transactions involving the stock or debt of financial institutions. These include mergers, acquisitions, and refinancings, as well as fairness opinion requirements for "material" transactions. Upper-loop transactions generate valuation requirements and, in many cases, requirements for independent determinations of value.

Lower-loop requirements present transactions or opportunities that relate more specifically to shareholders, although the financial institutions themselves must often be involved in the planning process. More often than not, lower-loop transactions require independent appraisal

Figure 2-1
The Business Planning Transaction Cycle

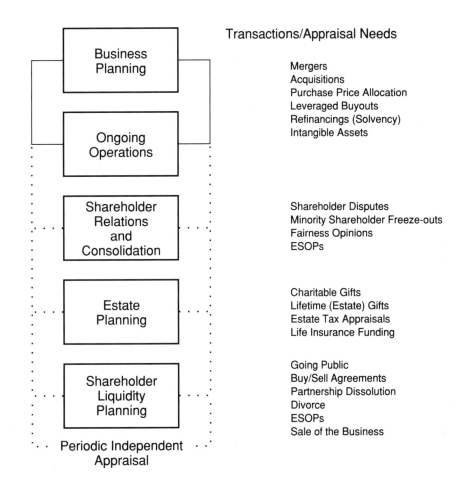

Copyright © 1989 Mercer Capital Management, Inc.

as a basis for satisfactory resolution. At the very least, the transactions and transaction planning are facilitated by knowledge of valuation derived from independent appraisals.

Exhibit 2-1 provides a more detailed analysis of transactions that are typical in the life of virtually every financial institution. The exhibit also indicates when in an institution's life a typical transaction might be encountered and discusses briefly why independent appraisal is needed.

Exhibit 2-1

Business Valuation Requirements for Closely-Held Businesses

Transactions Requiring/ Using Appraisals	When/Why in Company Life?	Why Is Appraisal Needed?
Business Planning/Ongoing Operations		
Mergers	Company is growing Access to capital Liquidity for investors	Set stock exchange ratios Independent opinion of value
Acquisitions	Company is growing	Appraise equity for sale Stock exchange ratios Fairness opinions Value the target
Divestitures	After rapid growth Change in strategy Downsizing Market/competitive changes	Valuation engineering Value the division/subsidiary Pro forma value of remaining equity
ESOPs	Growth phase Employee benefits Shareholder liquidity	Independent valuation required Justify tax deductions Financial advice for ESOP trustees
Purchase Price Allocation	Following acquisitions	Allocate value to tangible and intangible assets
Leveraged Buyouts	Management buyouts, etc.	Lenders may require fairness opinions, solvency opinions
Refinancing	Normal course of business LBOs	Lenders may require solvency opinion; unsecured creditors becoming more militant; establish collateral value of closely-held shares
Intangible Assets	Purchase transactions	Write up identifiable intangible assets for tax deductibility
Fairness Opinions	Sale or other major corporate transactions	Protect rights of minority shareholders (and interests of the board of directors)
Shareholder Relations and Consolidation		
Shareholder Disputes	They happen unexpectedly	Independent valuations help settle disputes over value; sometimes required in dissenting shareholder cases
Minority Shareholder Freeze-outs	Reverse stock splits	Go private; eliminate minority positions
Fairness Opinions	Sale or other major corporate transaction	Protect rights of minority shareholders
Estate Planning		
Charitable Gifts	When gifts made	Appraisal required for gifts of closely-held stock exceeding $10,000
Lifetime (Estate) Gifts	Estate planning	Use $10,000 annual exclusion to shift value to others to avoid estate taxation; file appraisals with gift tax returns
Estate Tax Appraisals	Upon death	Document value of closely-held shares in estate
Life Insurance	When purchasing insurance for buy-sell agreements	Avoid excess coverage; insure adequate coverage

Exhibit 2-1 *(continued)*

Transactions Requiring/ Using Appraisals	When/Why in Company Life?	Why Is Appraisal Needed?
Shareholder Liquidity Planning		
Going Public	When a company needs to raise capital and/or shareholders seek liquidity	Knowledge of pricing factors; negotiate with underwriters
Buy/Sell Agreements	Anytime when have multiple shareholders	Provide independent basis to ensure "fair value" for all parties; establish and update buy-sell agreement values
Partnership Dissolutions	When they occur	Ensure "fair value"
Divorce	When closely-held stock is in marital estate	Ensure "fair value"; prepare for trial; arbitrate value
ESOPs (Partial Sale)	When installed as employee benefit to raise capital or to acquire shares from existing shareholders	Required by law; financial advice for trustee
Sell Business	Prior to sale	Have knowledge; use as negotiating tool
Periodic Independent Appraisal		
Periodic Independent Appraisal	Every couple of years or so; every year for larger firms or firms with large numbers of shareholders or with multiple generations of shareholders	Lifetime planning; business planning; board of director guidance; being ready for unsolicited offers; etc.

Periodic Independent Appraisal

Periodic independent appraisal is a concept that I have advocated for many years. For most successful closely-held companies with significant net worths and market values (and most financial institutions fit this description), the question is not *if* an independent appraisal will be necessary, but *when* it will be required. A review of Figure 2-1 and Exhibit 2-1 will verify this statement.

Institutions obtaining periodic independent appraisals can use the information to inform shareholders for personal planning, for the guidance and/or the measurement of management's performance, and to keep boards of directors focused on valuation and shareholder returns. Independent appraisals, if current, are also helpful for boards of directors if unsolicited offers to acquire control are presented unexpectedly.

Valuation Is a Range Concept

There is no such thing as "the value" for an interest (either for a partial interest or for the entire institution) in a closely-held financial institution. Value is a function of purpose and time and therefore varies with changes in either.

The valuation continuum in Figure 2-2 shows the interrelationships that influence a valuation conclusion in visual form. The figure suggests that for each unique valuation situation there is a reasonable range of values for stock interests in closely-held institutions.[4]

Valuation approaches under the standard of fair market value typically emphasize historical and current financial performance. The orientation for tax-related appraisals is therefore focused primarily upon historical performance, with expectations for the future considered in the direct context of historical performance.

Sellers of financial institutions, however, may have a different set of valuation criteria. The benefit to a purchaser of acquiring a bank is the future stream of economic benefits provided by the potential acquisition target, discounted to the present at the purchaser's discount rate (see the discussion of discounted future benefits in Chapter 14). Sellers hope to convince possible acquirers of the validity of their projections and that the risk of achieving their projections is fairly low. Purchasers must balance the optimism of sellers with their own analysis. Suffice it to say that the focus of most acquisition discussions is on a bank's *expected future performance* and that historical performance is the backdrop for the discussions. Appraisals for sale purposes therefore generally rely heavily upon projections of future performance.

To put the difference between the tax-related and the sale-oriented approaches succinctly, no one wants to pay taxes based upon optimistic projections of how a bank or company might perform in the future; yet every seller desires to capitalize all conceivable future economic benefits into the current valuation and ask the purchaser to pay for them!

Tax-related appraisals attempt to simulate these negotiations through the construct of hypothetical willing buyers and sellers who are fully informed and under no compulsion to act. Few buyers or sellers are, in fact, fully informed. And most are under some compulsion to act when they sell or purchase closely-held companies or their interests. So, in the real world of closely-held transactions, negotiations generally determine the outcome of valuation decisions.

The valuation continuum in Figure 2-2 suggests that valuation is a function of purpose, corporate internal time, and external time. In actual transactions, it is also a function of the relative strength, knowledge, and motivation of sellers and buyers. The appraiser's job in most appraisals is to simulate the negotiation process under the assumptions of full knowledge and lack of compulsion. This suggests that for any valuation situation there is a range of reasonable alternative answers.

Appraisers (or buyers of banks) who forget that valuation conclusions must, in the final analysis, be within the reasonable range, run the danger of excessive advocacy. Future chapters will discuss at length the process for developing a reasonable range of valuation estimates for a financial institution, as well as for testing the reasonableness of the range and the conclusions.

---

[4]Some business appraisers have taken the concept of a reasonable range of values to the extreme of excessive advocacy for their clients' positions in the presentation of their valuation conclusions and, in the process, have provided unreasonable valuation conclusions. (See the discussion related to advocacy in Chapter 20.) On a personal note, the reasonable range for any valuation situation has tended to narrow significantly as I have gotten older.

Figure 2-2
Valuation Continuum

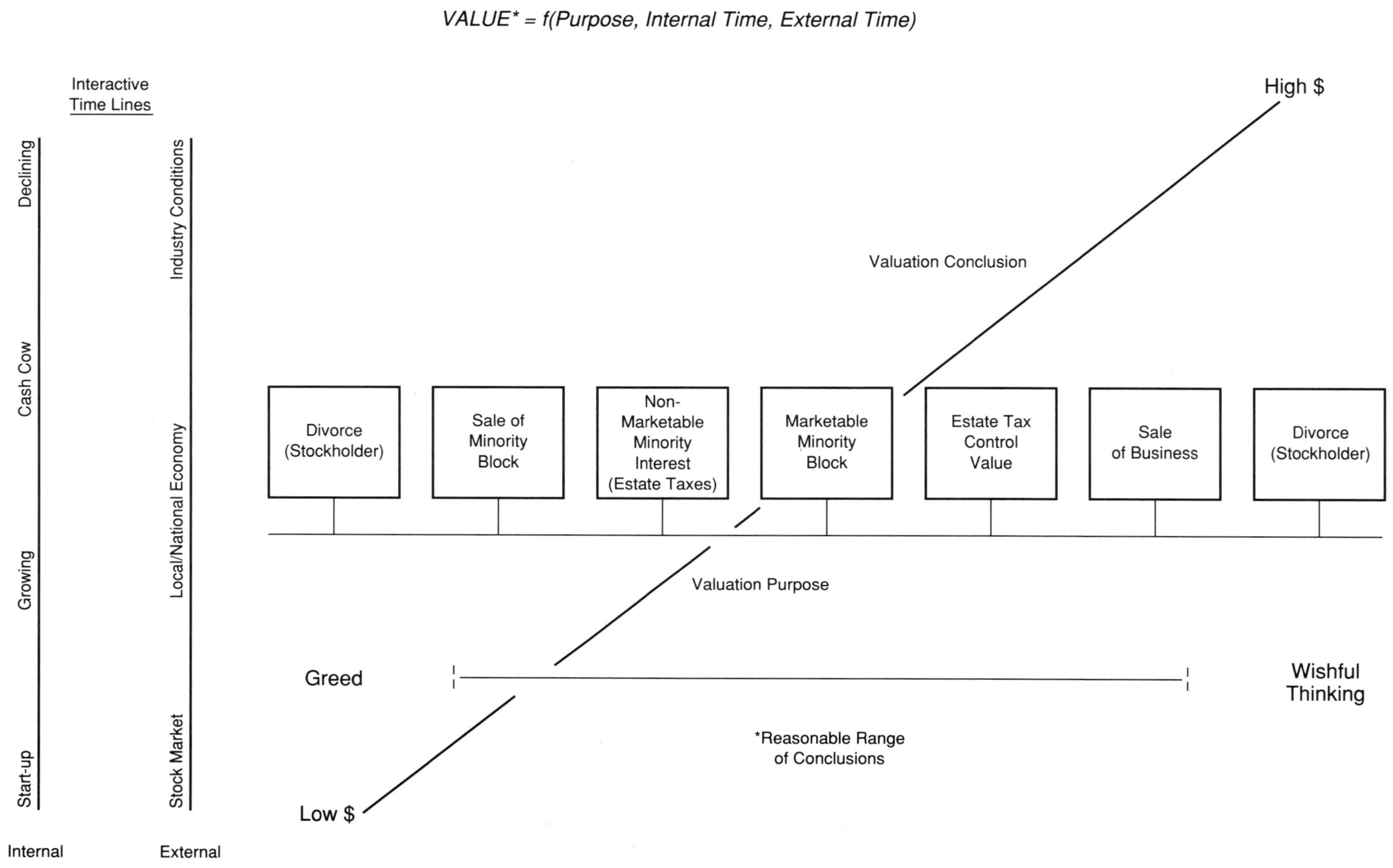

VALUE* = f(Purpose, Internal Time, External Time)

High $

Valuation Conclusion

Divorce
(Stockholder)

Sale
of Business

Estate Tax
Control
Value

Marketable
Minority
Block

Non-
Marketable
Minority
Interest
(Estate Taxes)

Sale of
Minority
Block

Divorce
(Stockholder)

Valuation Purpose

Wishful
Thinking

*Reasonable Range
of Conclusions

Greed

Low $

Interactive
Time Lines

Stock Market

Industry Conditions

Local/National Economy

Growing

Cash Cow

Declining

Start-up

External

Internal

Standards of Value and Related Valuation Concepts

Standards of Value

There are many ways to discuss the concept of value in the context of closely-held financial institutions. It is therefore critical that appraisers, client institutions, and other potential users of valuation reports understand just what concept of value is being considered in an appraisal. Some valuation concepts have evolved to the point of becoming "standards of value." When required, either by law or by agreement with the client, each standard provides a framework, or context, within which the valuation analyst must work.

Two standards of value, *fair market value* and *fair value*, have become reasonably well developed in the valuation literature and in court cases adjudicating valuation issues. Following the introductory discussion of each of these standards of value, several additional concepts of value will be briefly introduced to provide background information. In addition to these standards of value, the Comptroller of the Currency, in dissenting shareholder cases, uses a standard of value that combines market value and investment value (see Exhibit 2-2 on pages 33–37).

Fair Market Value

The most widely recognized and accepted standard of value, fair market value, applies to virtually all federal and state tax valuation matters, including charitable gifts, estate tax issues, and ad valorem taxes, as well as to other tax-related issues. Fair market value is also the applicable standard of value in many bankruptcy cases with valuation issues.

Fair market value has been defined in court cases too numerous to cite, as well as in Internal Revenue Service Revenue Ruling 59-60, which describes fair market value as:

> the price at which the property would change hands between a willing buyer and a willing seller when the former is not under any compulsion to buy and the latter is not under any compulsion to sell, both parties having reasonable knowledge of relevant facts. Court decisions frequently state in addition that the hypothetical buyer and seller are assumed to be able, as well as willing, to trade and to be well informed about the property and concerning the market for such property.[5]

Fair market value is an "arm's length standard" that assumes willing and informed buyers and sellers, neither acting under any compulsion, as well as buyers with the financial capacity to engage in transactions. The majority of independent valuation opinions are issued under the fair market value standard.

There is an implicit assumption that values expressed under the standard of fair market value are cash-equivalent values. Fair market values are adjusted for differences that might arise because of the time value

---

[5]IRS Revenue Ruling 59-60, Section 2.02. See Appendix C for a full reproduction of this very important ruling.

of money between a stated price (or value) and that same value expressed in cash-equivalent terms. In other words, the fair market value standard assumes that any deferred payments in transactions are themselves valued at fair market value.

Finally, the standard of fair market value assumes (as noted in Figure 2-2) that both internal and external conditions influencing a particular financial institution are those *in existence as of the valuation date*. The internal conditions must be determined by examination and investigation. External conditions—including the state of the stock markets, the relevant local, regional, or national economy, and specific industry conditions—must also be determined by appropriate research and investigation.

From the point of view of fair market value, these conditions (and their outlook) "are what they are" as of any specific valuation date. For example, in the early 1980s, bank stocks were typically trading at deep discounts to their book values, often 40% or more. Those market conditions provided much lower valuation conclusions for banks of equivalent performance than did market conditions in the latter 1980s, when typical regional holding company shares were trading at substantial premiums to their book values, often 50% or more.

Revenue Ruling 59-60 suggests that "all available financial data, as well as all relevant factors affecting fair market value, should be considered." Eight specific factors are outlined as fundamental and the subject of required analysis. Virtually every appraisal report recites these factors, which we refer to as the Basic Eight:

1. The nature of the business and the history of the enterprise from its inception.
2. The economic outlook in general and the condition and outlook of the specific industry in particular.
3. The book value of the stock and the financial condition of the business.
4. The earning capacity of the company.
5. The dividend-paying capacity.
6. Whether or not the enterprise has goodwill or other intangible value.
7. Sales of the stock and the size of the block to be valued.
8. The market price of stocks of corporations engaged in the same or a similar line of business having their stocks actively traded in a free and open market, either on an exchange or over-the-counter.

In the context of later chapters, there will be considerable discussion of each of these factors. In any consideration of the Basic Eight, there is considerable room for the exercise of judgment. The Internal Revenue Service recognized this in the following section of RR 59-60:

A determination of fair market value, being a question of fact, will depend upon the circumstances in each case. No formula can be devised that will be generally applicable to the multitude of different valuation issues arising in estate and gift tax cases. Often, an appraiser will find wide differences of opinion as to the fair market value of a particular stock. In resolving such differences, he should maintain a reasonable attitude in recognition of the fact that valuation is not an exact science. A sound valuation will be based upon all the relevant facts, but *the elements of common sense, informed judgment and reasonableness [emphasis added]* must enter into the process of weighing those facts and determining their aggregate significance.

The highlighted elements—common sense, informed judgment, and reasonableness—are referred to as the Critical Three factors. We will focus on these factors, as well as the Basic Eight, in later chapters, for they are essential to develop logical and well-reasoned valuation conclusions.

Fair Value

In nearly all states, fair value is the statutory standard of value applicable to cases involving appraisal rights of dissenting minority shareholders with respect to corporate reorganizations or recapitalizations covered by the various state statutes. However, while the state statutes indicate fair value as the applicable standard of value, we are not aware of any state statute that defines or describes the meaning of fair value in that state. Fair value is generally defined by judicial interpretation of the relevant statute(s). The most well-developed case law has come from Delaware, although there are now fair value cases in many jurisdictions.[6]

Until the early 1980s, the major definition of *fair value* was found in a long line of cases using what is referred to as the Delaware Block method. The Delaware Block requires explicit utilization and explicit weighting of three valuation methods. In many respects, it is similar to the more traditional valuation concept of fair market value noted above. The three valuation methodologies used in the Delaware Block concept of fair value are (1) the market value method, (2) the asset value method, and (3) the earnings (or investment) value method.

Market Value Method

The market value of a share of stock represents the price(s) at which shares of stock in the corporation have exchanged between willing buyers and sellers. Even when a stock is not listed on an exchange and no active market exists for it, a market value estimate can sometimes be determined based upon a limited number of transactions when those transactions were at arm's length. Furthermore, a market value estimate may sometimes be derived as of the valuation date based upon analysis of historical transactions.

Asset Value Method

The asset value method considers the real worth of assets based upon physical appraisals, accurate inventories, realistic allowances for depreciation and obsolescence, and other factors. In essence, the valuation expert must derive a market-adjusted book value, defined as the difference between the current market value of assets and liabilities. Furthermore, asset value should normally be considered in the context of a going concern, not in a liquidation context.

---

[6]See the Bibliography, which provides citations for numerous fair value cases that can influence valuation in various states. This brief discussion will focus on the major themes of interest to appraisers and closely-held institutions in the context of the fair value arena.

Earnings (Investment) Method

The earnings method relates to the earning capacity of a corporation and involves an attempt to predict (and capitalize) its future earnings based primarily on its previous earnings history. In many cases, earnings value has been determined by considering several years of earnings history (usually at least five years, if available). The role of the expert is to examine the historical earnings record, to determine necessary adjustments to earnings for nonrecurring or unusual income and expense items, and to develop an estimate of adjusted earnings. The expert must then capitalize the earnings at a capitalization multiple (e.g., a price/earnings ratio) appropriate for the company given its nature, industry, and historical performance.

The weightings to be placed on the three methods in the Delaware Block are not rigid, but are left initially to the valuation experts, and ultimately to the courts, to determine based upon the unique circumstances of each particular case. Case law provides some guidance in this regard. Companies whose primary purpose is to generate an earnings stream typically receive the greatest weight on the earnings method in this type of analysis. On the other hand, holding companies, whose primary purpose may be to hold assets subject to future appreciation, typically receive the greatest weight on the asset value method. Weightings accorded the market value method are usually assigned based upon an analysis of the nature and extent of activity in the shares for the subject corporation.

So far, the discussion of fair value seems reasonably straightforward. However, there are a number of conflicts in the various legal jurisdictions regarding the further interpretation of fair value statutes:

1. Is fair value a minority interest concept, or is a dissenting shareholder entitled to an enterprise valuation (i.e., a controlling-interest valuation)? Or is fair value something between these two extremes? Fair value is definitely a minority concept in certain jurisdictions; however, other cases suggest some courts are making an interpretation based upon controlling-interest valuation concepts. Still other jurisdictions have no precedent-setting cases, and the issue remains quite murky.

2. Is fair value a historically oriented standard, or can the valuation expert consider future prospects for performance other than those directly embedded in historical earnings performance? In other words, can the appraiser consider earnings projections and such valuation methods as discounted cash flow, or is the standard limited to more traditional capitalization of earnings approaches using an appropriately derived price/earnings ratio? Again, the case law varies from jurisdiction to jurisdiction.

3. Is fair value the same thing as fair market value? In some applications, the two standards seem almost identical. However, the appropriate application of minority interest and marketability discounts can vary under the two standards of value. (See Chapter 12 for a more detailed discussion of these important valuation discounts.) Valuations under the fair market value standard almost always consider—

and use, when appropriate—either one or both of these discounts. The valuation expert must understand the judicial interpretation of the use of marketability or minority discounts in fair value cases.

This discussion is sufficient to suggest that valuation experts who are called upon to render valuation opinions under the fair value standard must be aware of the specific case law applicable to dissenting minority shareholder cases in the state of incorporation of the subject financial institution. Financial institutions should also be aware of this information when engaging in transactions that could trigger dissenters' rights.[7]

Other Valuation Concepts

There are many other valuation concepts. None of these concepts is as generally used as the standards of fair market value and fair value; however, they provide important background information for parties interested in the appraisal of financial institutions. The financial institution's appraiser needs to be familiar with the meaning of these other valuation concepts and to understand the differences between them and the standards of value previously discussed.

Book Value

Perhaps the most familiar "valuation" concept discussed in the financial institutions arena is book value. In reality, however, it is not a valuation concept at all. Book value is an accounting concept that is not even mentioned by its name in many accounting texts! Simply defined, book value is net shareholders' equity. From a balance sheet point of view, it is the sum of all assets, both tangible and recorded intangible, at depreciated historical cost, less all recorded liabilities. Investments in loans and marketable securities are generally stated at their (amortized) acquisition values rather than current market values for financial institutions.

Book value is not the value of a banking institution; however, it is used as a benchmark value with which to compare virtually all other measures of value. Prices of bank shares are almost universally referred to in terms of a multiple of book value, with the multiple expressed either as a numerical multiple or as a percentage. For example, a price equal to double a bank's book value might be expressed as either "two times book value" or "200% of book value."

Going-Concern Value

One implicit assumption of most appraisals is that the opinions consider the subject interests as rendered in the context of a going concern. Simply stated, corporate values are most generally and most favorably realized in viable economic entities, i.e., going concerns. Unless otherwise stated, virtually all appraisals of interests in closely held institutions are rendered under a going-concern assumption. The alternative, in most instances, is liquidation value, either orderly or forced.

---

[7]National banks should specifically be aware that the Office of the Comptroller of the Currency has jurisdiction over dissenting minority shareholder issues for national banks. All parties to dissenting minority shareholder cases involving national banks should therefore make themselves aware of specific procedures, appraisal rights, and methods (see Exhibit 2-2).

Liquidation Value

Liquidation value is generally considered to be the value obtainable through the orderly liquidation of a business enterprise. An *orderly liquidation* is one in which every effort is made to allow the time necessary to realize the best available values for the various assets owned by an entity and in which the expenses of liquidation are managed to avoid consuming the liquidation proceeds with unnecessary expenses. A *forced liquidation* occurs under conditions of duress and seldom achieves the level of value realizable under an orderly liquidation scenario.

In reality, banks are seldom liquidated, except in the case of bank or thrift failures, in which the FDIC or the RTC must liquidate the assets in order to pay off deposits and other liabilities. In any event, specific consideration of liquidation values is not usual in the case of healthy financial institutions.

Investment Value

In his definitive book on business valuation, Shannon Pratt reported on an extensive review of valuation literature related to distinctions between the concepts of investment value and intrinsic value.[8]

Investment value can be defined as that value derived by discounting the expected stream of economic benefits to the present *at a particular investor's relevant discount rate*. If the investor's discount rate coincides with the consensus required rate of return of the relevant market, investment value can be considered to be representative of fair market value. If the investor's discount rate differs from the market consensus, then investment value is not indicative of fair market value. The focus of investment value, however, is on the individual investor and not on the hypothetical willing buyer (or seller) nor, except by way of comparison, on the market.

In the discussion of fair value above, investment value was used as a substitute for the earnings value method of valuation. In the context of fair value appraisals, investment value should focus on consensus capitalization rates and not on individual rates. Problems with confusion over terminology are not very common because investment value is seldom the specified standard of value in actual valuation situations.

Intrinsic or Fundamental Value

Intrinsic (fundamental) value differs from investment value in that it focuses on differences in analytical judgments regarding valuation between various followers of a particular stock, rather than on a particular investor's discount rate. The principles of fundamental analysis espoused by Graham et al. are available for all to use.[9] There may well be, however, differences in opinion among analysts following public companies with respect to the market's recognition of the fundamentals inherent in a given company's performance. These differences relate to the values of underlying assets, the level and growth of expected future earnings, and

[8]Shannon Pratt, *Valuing a Business: The Analysis and Appraisal of Closely Held Companies,* 2d ed. (Homewood, IL: Dow Jones-Irwin, 1989), pp. 25–58. The reader is referred to this source for Dr. Pratt's fuller discussion, upon which these comments are based in part.

[9]Benjamin Graham, David L. Dodd, and Sidney Cottle, *Security Analysis: Principles and Technique* (New York: McGraw-Hill, 1962).

the level and growth of expected future dividends for companies. Fundamental analysts look for the "real," or intrinsic, values in companies that are not yet recognized by the general market.

If the "real" value is considerably greater than the actual value in the market, the fundamental analyst is a "buyer" of the stock; if value is considerably less than actual market value, the analyst is a "seller" of the shares. There is a theoretical relationship between intrinsic value and fair market value (market price for publicly traded stocks). In an efficient market, significant divergences between intrinsic value and the current market price will be recognized by the market and reflected in stock prices over time.

Conclusion

We have defined *valuation* as the process of estimating the worth (value) of an interest (either a portion or the entirety) of a financial institution, or reaching an opinion of its worth, based upon due consideration of the facts and circumstances surrounding the situation and the exercise of judgment. It is clear that in order to accomplish this goal, the financial institution's appraiser must have a thorough knowledge of the relevant standards of value and other common concepts of value. He or she must also become aware of case law relevant to each particular valuation assignment.

In Chapter 3, we will move beyond definitional concepts and outline the critical components of every valuation situation, as well as refer to the contents of a sample engagement letter that should be a useful point of reference for both appraisers and financial institutions.

Exhibit 2-2

BANKING ISSUANCE

Comptroller of the Currency
Administrator of National Banks

Type: Banking Bulletin   Subject: Stock Appraisals

To: Chief Executive Officers of National Banks, Deputy
     Comptrollers (District), Department and Division Heads, and
     Examining Personnel

PURPOSE

This banking bulletin is to inform all national banks of the
valuation methods used by the Office of the Comptroller of the
Currency to estimate the value of a bank's shares when it is
involved in a conversion, merger, or consolidation. The results of
appraisals performed for transactions that were consummated in 1985
and 1986 are also summarized.

References: 12 U.S.C. 214a, 215 and 215a; 12 CFR 11.590 (Item 2)

BACKGROUND

Under 12 U.S.C. Sections 214a, 215 and 215a, any shareholder
dissenting to a conversion, consolidation, or merger involving a
national bank may request from the resulting bank a valuation of
the shares held by the dissenting shareholder. A committee of
three appraisers (a representative of the dissenting shareholder, a
representative of the resulting bank, and a third appraiser
selected by the other two) is then to be formed to appraise the
value of the shares. If the committee is formed and renders an
appraisal that is acceptable to the dissenting shareholder, the
process is complete and the appraised value of the shares is paid
to the dissenting shareholder by the resulting bank. If, for any
reason, the committee is not formed or if it renders an appraisal
that is not acceptable to the dissenting shareholder, an interested
party may request an appraisal by the Office of the Comptroller of
the Currency (OCC).

The above provides only a general overview of the appraisal
process. The specific requirements of the process are set forth in
the statutes themselves.

Exhibit 2-2 *(continued)*

BANKING ISSUANCE

Comptroller of the Currency
Administrator of National Banks

Type: Banking Bulletin   Subject: Stock Appraisals

METHODS OF VALUATION USED

Through its appraisal process, the OCC attempts to arrive at a fair estimate of the value of a bank's shares. After reviewing the particular facts in each case and the available information on a bank's shares, the OCC selects an appropriate valuation method, or combination of methods, to determine a reasonable estimate of the shares' value.

Market Value

The OCC uses various methods to establish the market value of shares being appraised. If sufficient trading in the shares exists and the prices are available from direct quotes from the Wall Street Journal or a market-maker, those quotes are considered in determining the market value. If no market value is readily available, or if the market value available is not well established, other methods of estimating market value can be used, such as the investment value and adjusted book value methods.

Investment Value

Investment value requires an assessment of the value to investors of a share in the future earnings of the target bank. Investment value is estimated by applying an average price/earnings ratio of banks with similar earnings potential to the earnings capacity of the target bank.

The peer group selection is based on location, size, and earnings patterns. If the state in which the subject bank is located provides a sufficient number of comparable banks using location, size and earnings patterns as the criteria for selection, the price/earnings ratios assigned to the banks are applied to the earnings per share estimated for the subject bank. In order to select a reasonable peer group when there are too few comparable independent banks in a location that is comparable to that of the subject bank, the pool of banks from which a peer group is selected is broadened by including one-bank holding company banks in a comparable location, and/or by selecting banks in less comparable locations, including adjacent states, that have earnings patterns similar to the subject bank.

Exhibit 2-2 *(continued)*

BANKING ISSUANCE

Comptroller of the Currency
Administrator of National Banks

Type: Banking Bulletin   Subject: Stock Appraisals

Adjusted Book Value

As a rule, the OCC does not place any weight on "unadjusted book value." While book value is a type of value, it is based on historical acquisition costs of the bank's assets, and does not reflect investors' perceptions of the value of the bank as a going concern. The OCC does consider "adjusted book value." Adjusted book value is calculated by multiplying the book value of the target bank's assets per share times the average market price to book value ratio of comparable banking organizations. The average market price to book value ratio measures the premium or discount to book value which investors attribute to shares of similarly situated banking organizations.

Both the investment value method and the adjusted book value method present appraised values which are based on the target bank's value as a going concern. These techniques provide estimates of the market value of the shares of the subject bank.

OVERALL VALUATION

The OCC may use more than one of the above-described methods in deriving the value of shares of stock. If more than one method is used, varying weights may be applied in reaching an overall valuation. The weight given to the value by a particular valuation method is based on how accurately the given method is believed to represent market value. For example, more weight may be given to a market value representing infrequent trading by shareholders than to the value derived from the investment value method when the subject bank's earnings trend is so irregular that it is considered to be a poor predictor of future earnings.

PURCHASE PREMIUMS

For mergers and consolidations, the OCC recognizes that purchase premiums do exist and may, in some instances, be paid in the purchase of small blocks of shares. However, the payment of purchase premiums depends entirely on the acquisition or control plans of the purchasers, and such payments are not regular or predictable elements

Exhibit 2-2 *(continued)*

BANKING ISSUANCE

Comptroller of the Currency
Administrator of National Banks

Type: Banking Bulletin   Subject: Stock Appraisals

of market value. Consequently, the OCC's valuation methods do not include consideration of purchase premiums in arriving at the value of shares.

STATISTICAL DATA

The chart below lists the results of appraisals performed by the OCC for transactions that were consummated in 1985 and 1986. The statistical data on book value and price/earnings ratios are provided for comparative purposes and are not necessarily relied on by the OCC in determining the value of the banks' shares. These historical data are provided to inform banks and investors about the results of past appraisals and should not be viewed as determinative for future appraisals.

In connection with disclosures given to shareholders under 12 CFR 11.590 (Item 2), banks may provide shareholders a copy of this banking bulletin or disclose the information contained herein, including the past results of OCC appraisals. If the bank discloses the past results of the OCC appraisals, it should advise shareholders that (1) the OCC did not rely on all the information set forth in the chart in performing each appraisal and (2) that the OCC's past appraisals are not necessarily determinative of its future appraisals of a particular bank's shares.

Exhibit 2-2 *(continued)*

BANKING ISSUANCE

Comptroller of the Currency
Administrator of National Banks

Type: Banking Bulletin   Subject: Stock Appraisals

APPRAISAL RESULTS

Appraisal Date *	OCC Appraisal Value	Price Offered	Book Value	Average Price/ Earnings Ratio of Peer Group
1/1/85	107.05	110.00	178.29	5.3
1/2/85	73.16	NA	66.35	6.8
1/15/85	53.41	60.00	83.95	4.8
1/31/85	22.72	20.00	38.49	5.4
2/1/85	30.63	24.00	34.08	5.7
2/25/85	27.74	27.55	41.62	5.9
4/30/85	25.98	35.00	42.21	4.5
7/30/85	3,153.10	2,640.00	6,063.66	NC
9/1/85	17.23	21.00	21.84	4.7
11/22/85	316.74	338.75	519.89	5.0
11/22/85	30.28	NA	34.42	5.9
12/16/85	66.29	77.00	89.64	5.6
12/27/85	60.85	57.00	119.36	5.3
12/31/85	61.77	NA	73.56	5.9
12/31/85	75.79	40.00	58.74	12.1
1/12/86	19.93	NA	26.37	7.0
3/14/86	59.02	200.00	132.20	3.1
4/21/86	40.44	35.00	43.54	6.4
5/2/86	15.50	16.50	23.69	5.0
7/3/86	405.74	NA	612.82	3.9
7/31/86	297.34	600.00	650.63	4.4
8/2/86	103.53	106.67	136.23	NC

* - The "Appraisal Date" is the consummation date for the conversion, consolidation, or merger.

NA - Not Available   NC - Not Computed

Exhibit 2-2 *(continued)*

BANKING ISSUANCE

Comptroller of the Currency
Administrator of National Banks

Type: Banking Bulletin   Subject: Stock Appraisals

For more information regarding the OCC's stock appraisal process, contact the Office of the Comptroller of the Currency, 490 L'Enfant Plaza East, S.W., Washington, D.C. 20219, Director for Corporate Activity, Bank Organization and Structure.

J. Michael Shepherd
Senior Deputy Comptroller

Chapter 3

Defining the
Valuation Assignment

If you don't know where you are going, any road will do.

Unknown

Overview of an Appraisal Assignment

Any valuation assignment can be defined by the answers to a series of definitional questions. Many of the most common and avoidable errors in valuations occur because appraisers fail to specify the assignment properly. While *professional responsibility* is placed upon the appraiser to answer the definitional questions, *practical responsibility* is shared by the client or user of the appraisal product.

Questions 1–6 below relate to the relationship and expectations between the appraiser and the client. Questions 7–11 relate to the specific nature of each appraisal assignment. All 11 questions must be addressed in every appraisal assignment. If a written appraisal report is required, each question should be addressed fully in the report, with the possible exceptions of Questions 4, 5, and 6.

Questions Relative to the Appraiser-Client Relationship

1. Who is the appraiser?
2. Who is the client?
3. What is the nature of the relationship, if any, between the appraiser and the client?
4. What is the fee arrangement, and what indemnifications have been made between the appraiser and the client?
5. What is the nature, form, and extent of the report to be issued by the appraiser?
6. Under what timetable is the appraisal to be delivered?

Questions Relative to the Specific Appraisal Assignment

7. What is the purpose of the appraisal?
8. What is the exact nature of the interest or interests being valued?
9. What is/are the specific date(s) for which the valuation opinions is/are to be applicable?
10. What is the applicable standard of value?
11. What additional requirements, if any, have been placed upon the appraiser, or what specific assumptions have been provided by the client or by the circumstances of the appraisal that further limit or define its conclusion(s)?

The Appraiser-Client Relationship

The Client and the Appraiser

It may seem too obvious to mention that an appraisal report must specify the names of both the client and the appraiser. But what may be obvious to all parties to an appraisal at the time of its issuance may become less clear with the passage of time. Personnel changes at either the client financial institution or the appraisal firm may occur, and the appraisal issued this year may be called into question several years from now. Good documentation at the time of the appraisal will facilitate both current and future use of the appraisal product.

Generally, appraisal firms are retained to provide appraisal opinions, and individual appraisers, as employees or agents of the appraisal firm, perform the actual work. Retention of appraisal firms provides continuity and security for clients in the event that an individual appraiser dies or leaves employment. In those cases, the appraisal firm retains responsibility for the fulfillment of the assignment or later defense of the appraisal and the client's interests are protected.

Appraisers have a fiduciary relationship with their clients and can, under applicable standards of ethics and professional responsibility, release information about an appraisal assignment only to the client or to other parties with the client's permission.[1]

An appraisal report should also describe any previous or existing business or personal relationships between the appraiser and the client. These disclosures are necessary to enable potential readers or users of the report to make their own judgments about the independence of the appraiser with respect to the assignment. For example, an agent of the Internal Revenue Service is likely to discount the independence (and the conclusion) of a gift tax appraisal performed by a bank's chief financial officer on behalf of the president, who owns 45% of the institution's stock!

Fee Arrangement

The fee arrangement should be specified clearly in the engagement letter between the appraiser and the client to avoid any misunderstandings. While specific fee arrangements are seldom described, appraisal reports, prepared in conformity with the standards noted in footnote 1, must state that the independent appraiser's compensation is in no way contingent upon the results of the analysis or the conclusions of the report.

---

[1]The *Uniform Standards of Professional Appraisal Practice* (included as Appendix B) published by The Appraisal Foundation, the Business Valuation Standards of the American Society of Appraisers (Appendix A), and the *Principles of Appraisal Practice and Code of Ethics* of the American Society of Appraisers provide specific guidance to the appraiser regarding the extent of required disclosure of the relationship between the appraiser and clients, as well as the scope of investigation and reporting in the form of written reports.

Indemnifications

Appraisal firms typically require indemnification from clients against the prospect of being made a party to litigation as a result of having prepared an appraisal. The exact nature and extent of indemnifications is often a matter of considerable discussion between appraisers and clients. An indemnification (signed by the client) found in a recent engagement letter stated:

> This indemnification relates only to the assignment described in this engagement letter and is intended to protect [appraiser's name] against being named in any lawsuit arising from this assignment, or as a result of having rendered the contemplated opinion(s). The indemnification would not apply if [appraiser's name] were negligent in carrying out this assignment.

> [Client name] agrees to indemnify [appraiser's name], its officers, employees and agents, and to hold [appraiser's name] harmless from any and all obligations, claims, charges, expenses or costs of any nature whatsoever, including, without limitation, investigation and attorneys' fees arising out of, or in connection with, the performance of the assignment described in this letter.

Appraisal firms typically require an additional indemnification relating to the potential future defense of an appraisal. A sample supplementary indemnification follows:

> If during the course of events, it should become necessary to defend the valuation in any court or legal proceeding, our fees for such work would be at our then prevailing billing rates, plus reasonable out-of-pocket expenses.

The sample indemnification clauses should not be considered as legal advice by any reader. They are intended only to indicate the nature of indemnifications commonly required by appraisal firms. Client companies and financial institutions sometimes require balancing indemnifications, which generally relate to the confidentiality of the client's information; however, the requirement of confidentiality is usually presumed in the nature of professional relationships.

Indemnifications are an important part of the negotiation of any appraisal assignment. Except in the cases of fairness opinions and solvency opinions, however, the existence of indemnification agreements is usually not reflected in written appraisal reports but left as a part of the written record in the appraiser's file.

Form of the Appraisal Report

The appraiser and the client should always agree on the specific nature of the appraisal document. The engagement letter should clearly specify the type of documentation expected for an appraisal. Minimum documentation standards for appraisal reports are set out in the *Uniform Standards of Professional Appraisal Practice* (see Appendix B) and in BVS-II, "Full Written Business Appraisal Report," published June 1991 by the American Society of Appraisers. (See Appendix A and a more detailed discussion of business valuation standards in Chapter 21.)

There are four basic types of valuation reports that may be rendered: (1) the valuation range estimate, (2) the oral report, (3) the letter valuation report, and (4) the stand-alone appraisal report. With the exception of the valuation range estimate, each valuation report type is subject to the minimum appraisal standards referred to above.

Valuation Range Estimates

Clients sometimes retain appraisers to provide a valuation range estimate as part of the planning process for contemplated transactions. The range estimate, normally prepared preliminary to a full report, is useful to determine the feasibility of certain transactions, such as ESOP implementation, gift and estate tax programs, and corporate acquisitions or dispositions. Experienced appraisers giving a range estimate valuation are saying, in effect:

> We have performed the limited due diligence steps noted herein with respect to the subject valuation of ABC Bancorp, Inc. Subject to the accuracy and completeness of the reviewed information, and to the further due diligence necessary to render a more formal valuation opinion, we believe that our conclusion of fair market value of the common stock of ABC Bancorp, Inc., if rendered on a minority interest basis for gift tax purposes, would lie in the range of $10.25–$11.75 per share as of the date of this letter.

Note that a range estimate similar to that for ABC Bancorp, Inc. is not actionable by the client. It cannot be relied upon for gift tax or any other purpose. It is, in short, not an independent valuation opinion, but a set of calculations designed to provide an approximate indication of value based upon limited procedures agreed upon by the appraiser and the client.

Oral Appraisal Report

An oral appraisal report is rendered by an appraiser at the request of a client. Under normal circumstances, an oral report is requested when a client is under extreme time pressure to make a decision related to a valuation issue or in a litigation situation.

We generally do not recommend that oral reports be used because it is too easy for misunderstandings to develop over what was said, the development of the valuation rationale, or even the conclusions presented.

However, appraisers sometimes issue oral reports, usually supported by selected financial tables or exhibits, for presentation of valuation conclusions in courtroom situations. The theory for usage of oral reports in litigation situations is that the "other side" is not given the advantage of having time to review the appraiser's fully developed opinion before trial and is therefore not allowed much time to prepare for cross-examination. Oral reports issued in litigation situations are, however, subject to the same rigorous standards of due diligence as the more formal letter opinions or stand-alone valuation reports.

Letter Valuation Reports

A letter valuation report provides a description of the nature of the appraisal assignment, a listing of documents reviewed and major information sources, a summary of the valuation methodology and rationale, and the valuation conclusion. Letter valuations are sometimes viewed as a cheaper alternative than a full report; however, they are seldom as convincing as fully documented valuation reports.

Unfortunately, letter valuation reports have sometimes been used by appraisers (and their clients) as a substitute for a fully documented valuation opinion when the full due diligence of the latter has not been conducted. This abuse of the letter opinion format, most common in the ESOP area, will be discussed again in Chapter 16.

Stand-alone Valuation Reports

Stand-alone valuation reports are the standard format for rendering independent valuation opinions. Suffice it to say that the reader of a stand-alone valuation report should be able to form his or her own opinion of the scope of the appraiser's: investigation and due diligence, independence with respect to the assignment, qualifications for the particular assignment, and reasonableness of the valuation opinion. (See Appendix A for the requirements of newly issued BVS-II regarding "Full Written Business Report.")

Appraisal Timetable

The timetable for the accumulation of factual information from a client, the due diligence visit(s) by the appraiser, and the preparation and rendering of any draft and final reports should be clearly agreed upon between the appraiser and the client. Timing issues are generally covered in the engagement letter for particular valuation assignments.

Appraisal Assignment Definition Issues

Purpose of the Assignment

Valuation can differ materially with respect to purpose. An estate tax appraisal of a controlling interest in a financial institution may differ from the appraisal of the same interest for purposes of a potential sale. The appraisals differ in time perspective and orientation.

A precise statement of the purpose of an assignment can also enable the reader to form an opinion about the reasonableness of the conclusion. I once reviewed an appraisal opinion related to certain options for the purchase of a significant interest in a publicly traded thrift institution. The valuation was well written and reasoned in many respects; however, all assumptions seemed to minimize value. When I learned the exact purpose of the assignment, which was to value the options for income tax recognition upon transfer from an investment banking firm (which rendered services to the financial institution) to its principals, I became convinced that the appraiser's opinion was biased and that his conclusion was too low to be realistic.

Applicable Standard of Value

There is no such thing as "the value" of anything. As will be discussed throughout this book, value is a function of purpose, time, and applicable standards of value that relate to a particular situation—for example, fair market value or fair value.

Nature of the Interest Being Valued

A fully specified valuation assignment provides a precise definition of (1) the economic entity under consideration, including its state of incorporation, and (2) the particular economic interest being valued in relationship to the entity under consideration.

The need for precise definitions is seen clearly in the arena of financial institutions, where one or more banks or thrifts (and possibly other operating subsidiaries) are owned by a holding company. There are differences in bank and thrift charters; some are federally chartered, and others are state chartered. Subsidiaries may be incorporated in various states.

We have actually seen appraisal reports of financial institutions where the appraiser valued a bank, then took its value and divided by the number of shares in the parent bank holding company to obtain an "opinion" of the value of holding company shares. Chapter 11 discusses the relationships between subsidiary banks and their parent holding companies in more detail. The point here is that the appraiser must clearly specify the economic interest being valued.

Most appraisals do not entail a valuation of the entire economic entity. A particular appraisal assignment should consider:

1. The specific interest of the entity being valued, whether common stock, preferred stock, convertible preferred stock, debt instrument, option, warrant, or any other related interest. The exact number of shares (or bonds or units) must be stated, as well as whether, if voting stock, the shares are to be valued on a minority-interest basis or a controlling-interest basis.
2. Any specific restrictions on the shares being valued. Shares may be subject to restrictive agreements between shareholders, to buy-sell agreements, to voting trust agreements, or other restrictions on their marketability.
3. Any "favorable" restrictions, such as a *put option* to sell shares to a corporation. A put option is a legal option to sell shares to a corporation, subject to the fulfillment of specified conditions, at the holder's option. In the public marketplace, put options are separate securities. In connection with closely-held securities, however, the put may be nonseverable from the exact shares being valued and may serve to increase their marketability and therefore their value.
4. Ownership of the shares being valued, as well as ownership of the remaining shares. The valuation of a specific block of stock can sometimes be influenced by its ownership in relationship to other

blocks of stock. This is particularly true when different family members own shares, which by custom or agreement are voted together, or when a block of stock could provide control to another shareholder or to a group of shareholders acting in concert.

5. Whether the shares being valued are existing or newly issued shares. In the cases of stock offerings or when ESOPs will acquire newly issued shares, the appraiser must consider that issuance of the new shares may have a dilutive (or antidilutive) impact upon existing shareholders.

Failure to specify the precise nature of the valuation subject can cause confusion and error. It is therefore critical that the appraiser and the client agree upon the exact nature of the valuation assignment in the detail noted above.

The As of Date of the Appraisal

It is necessary to specify the precise as of date for every valuation assignment. The as of date establishes the information that is (or was) reasonably available for the appraiser in the conduct of due diligence for a valuation assignment.

For financial institutions, appraisals are generally based upon the most recently available quarterly financial statements. Experienced appraisers prefer quarterly statements filed with the appropriate regulatory agencies and attested to by appropriate members of the board of directors and management over monthly financial statements.

If the appraisal involves approval by one or more regulatory bodies, the financial statements must be current. For example, with valuations requiring approval by the Securities and Exchange Commission (SEC), *current* usually means within 135 days of the close of the most recent quarter for which financial statements are available, which is further interpreted as the most recent quarterly financial statements available. Noncurrent financial statements in a current transaction are often referred to as *stale*.

For appraisers of financial institutions, as well as for their financial institution clients engaged in transactions, the requirement to use current financial statements can create a moving valuation target, particularly as delays in regulatory approval or other normal delays extend the closing of transactions into succeeding quarters.

The appraiser will often be faced with valuation situations with as of dates at some time in the more distant past. Historical valuations are particularly common in the estate tax area and with litigated issues. With historical valuations, the appraiser must exercise judgment in determining what information would reasonably have been available had the appraisal been performed at the time. The need for judgment is not limited, however, to the selection of financial statements; it extends to the selection of all financial, industry, and economic data to be used for any appraisal with a historical as of date. Problems in determining what information should be used with historical valuations are exacerbated when the appraiser is faced with multiple valuation dates.[2]

The as of date is also important because value can change materially over time—and often over fairly short periods of time. "Black Monday"—or October 19, 1987, when the stock market, as represented by the Dow Jones Index, experienced its largest absolute decline in recent history—provides a graphic example of rapidly changing values. The values of many publicly traded securities, including financial institutions, changed materially in a fairly short time as a result of Black Monday.[3] Because valuations of nonpublicly traded financial institutions are often developed in relationship to values of publicly traded securities, it is clear that value can change fairly quickly. Appraisers and financial institutions must be aware of this fact.

Value can also change materially with changes in the fortunes of individual banks, particularly as the underlying fundamentals that may give rise to the valuation shift become known to the investing public (or the appraiser).

Engagement Letters

Engagement letters are based upon detailed discussions between the appraiser and the potential client. Under normal circumstances, the appraiser will have reviewed considerable information about the subject financial institution and discussed the exact purpose and details of the assignment at some length with representatives of the client. The engagement letter is important, then, as the basis for understanding an appraisal engagement by both parties.

Exhibit 3-1 provides a summary of the contents of an engagement letter suggested by the discussion of this chapter. A clear understanding at the beginning of the assignment is essential for both the client and the appraisal firm. Over the course of an appraisal assignment, particularly if circumstances cause unavoidable delays in completion, it is not uncommon for the appraiser or the client to forget the exact specifications of the engagement. The engagement letter provides protection for both parties and minimizes the potential for misunderstandings.

---

[2]Multiple valuation dates often arise in estate tax valuations, where the valuation date may be either the decedent's date of death or the alternative valuation date allowed by tax regulations. They also arise in litigated situations, where the contested issue may involve the appreciation in value of closely-held bank stock over specified periods of time.

[3]For example, the average daily stock price for three well-known banking stocks reflected the following changes in their average daily stock prices as measured two weeks before and two weeks following Black Monday:

	Two Weeks Prior	Two Weeks After	% Change
Citicorp	$29 1/4	$20 1/4	−30.8%
NCNB	$24 1/8	$18 3/8	−23.8%
Wells Fargo	$55 3/8	$43	−22.4%

Exhibit 3-1
Valuation Consultants, Inc.
Contents of an Engagement Letter

Appraiser-Client Relationship
   Who is the client?
   Specification of any previous relationships between the client and the appraiser
   Qualifications of appraisers
   Other background information

Specification of the Assignment
   Exact specification of the entity or interest(s) being valued
      Form of ownership
      State of incorporation
      Description of any restrictive agreements placed upon the interest
   Purpose(s) of the assignment
   Date(s) as of which the appraisal opinion(s) is (are) applicable
   Applicable standard of value
   Any restrictions expected to be placed upon the appraiser

Other Administrative Issues
   Indemnifications, if any
   Specification of the fee arrangement
   Schedule or timetable for delivery of services
   Expected form of the report
   Appropriate signatures
      Appraisal firm
      Client

Conclusion

Assignment definition is a critical part of the appraisal process. Appraisers and clients of appraisers enter into business relationships with each other at mutual peril if they fail to specify the assignment in sufficient detail to avoid confusion or controversy with the passage of time.

Chapter 4

Information Gathering and the Due Diligence Visit

If you haven't been there, you haven't been there.

Z. Christopher Mercer

Why Is the Due Diligence Visit Important?

One critical part of the bank valuation process is referred to as the due diligence visit, the on-site visit, or the management interview. The three terms are used interchangeably in this book. We believe that the due diligence visit is an integral element in the appraisal of financial institutions. This discussion is placed early in the book in order to raise questions for the experienced appraiser or for bankers using this book to assist with acquisition programs. It begins the process of describing the key ways that the valuation of financial institutions differ from other commercial enterprises that continues throughout the book.

Objectives of the Due Diligence Visit

The due diligence visit provides the analyst with an opportunity to integrate many sources of information about a bank into a logical and consistent whole. The visit also helps to complete an overall understanding of how a particular financial institution operates. The process of preparing for and conducting the due diligence visit requires the analyst to develop a command of the facts and circumstances of *this particular valuation case.*

The specific objectives of the due diligence visit include:

1. Reviewing details of documents previously provided by management in order to ensure that all necessary financial and operational disclosure has been obtained and is reasonably understood.
2. Forming an impression of the local economy based upon observation (to help challenge or verify economic statistics or management's overview of the economic situation).
3. Verifying (or questioning) the impressions gained in the management interviews based upon observation of the institution in operation.
4. Identifying those factors or trends that can reasonably be expected to influence the future performance of the institution.
5. Formulating an overall opinion of management's ability to achieve anticipated operating results.

The due diligence visit, if properly conducted, will enable the analyst to gain a more complete perspective of an institution than is possible from reviewing documents alone. For this reason, we believe that the due diligence visit is an essential element in the valuation process for most situations requiring independent appraisal of financial institutions.

Recognition of Importance of Due Diligence Visits

Requirements of Appraisal Practice

The independent appraiser of financial institutions has specific professional responsibilities with respect to due diligence. The American Society of Appraisers has adopted *The Principles of Appraisal Practice and Code of Ethics* (*PAPCE*) for several specific purposes, including:

> **1.31.** Inform those who use the services of appraisers what, in the opinion of the Society, constitutes competent and ethical appraisal practice; and,
>
> **1.32.** Serve as a guide to its own members in achieving competency in appraisal practice and in adhering to ethical standards; and . . . ,
>
> **1.35.** Epitomize those appraisal practices that experience has found to be effective in protecting the public against exploitation.[1]

Paragraph 6.9 of *PAPCE* states that:

> Good appraisal practice requires that the description of the property, tangible or intangible, which is the subject of a valuation, cover adequately (a) identification of the property (b) statement of the legal rights and restrictions comprised in the ownership, and (c) the characteristics of the property which contribute to or detract from its value.

PAPCE goes on to say in Paragraph 7.6 that:

> If an appraiser gives an opinion as to the value, earning power, or estimated cost of a property without having ascertained and weighed *all of the pertinent facts* [*emphasis added*], such opinion, except by an extraordinary coincidence, will be inaccurate. The giving of such offhand opinions tends to belittle the importance of inspection, investigation, and analysis in appraisal procedure and lessens the confidence with which the results of good appraisal practice are received, and therefore, the Society declares the giving of hasty and unconsidered opinions to be unprofessional.

Independent appraisals of financial institutions are required for the many reasons covered in Chapter 2. When rendering valuation opinions, appraisers have a fiduciary relationship with the parties to the transactions for which their appraisals are rendered. Given the requirements of *PAPCE,* the special role of trust played by the independent business appraiser, and common sense, it seems clear that due diligence on the part of an appraiser should include an on-site visit to the subject financial institution whenever possible.

There can always be exceptions to the general rule regarding due diligence visits. Exceptions include litigated situations where on-site visitation is prohibited, and historical valuations, where it may not be possible to visit. Also, it may not be necessary to visit a bank every year when recurring appraisals are being performed, if visits occur every other year or so, and in-depth telephone interviews are conducted in the periods between visits. Nevertheless, we believe that appraisers should make every effort to conduct on-site due diligence visits with management whenever possible.

Support of Opinions in Litigation

Courts determine their opinions of individual appraisers based upon professional qualifications, written work, oral presentations, and their

---

[1]*The Principles of Appraisal Practice and Code of Ethics* (*PAPCE*) is promulgated by the American Society of Appraisers, and all designated members of the society are bound by this document. The American Society of Appraisers is one of eight professional appraisal societies that helped found The Appraisal Foundation, a national self-regulatory organization. The Appraisal Foundation publishes *Uniform Standards of Professional Appraisal Practice* (reproduced in its most current form as Appendix B), which covers many of the same areas of practice as *PAPCE.*

confidence in the due diligence performed by the appraiser in reaching his or her valuation opinion. In certain instances, a court's opinion is swayed by the nature and extent of an appraiser's due diligence effort, including the on-site visit. Certainly, the absence of an on-site visit in cases where there were no arbitrary limitations placed upon the appraiser can tend to call her or his overall opinion into question.[2]

Common Sense

When an independent appraiser is called upon to value a financial institution, there are normally significant economic stakes, either for the bank, for one or more of its shareholders, or for both.

No banker would dream of buying another bank without first talking with the target bank's management, reviewing the loan portfolio, making a detailed investigation into its business practices and reputation in its communities, and conducting much more due diligence. Granted, the scope of due diligence is greater in the normal acquisition than in the typical appraisal situation. Appraisers must usually accept more representations of management without independent verification and detailed investigation than would a purchaser of an entire bank; however, the principles of due diligence remain the same. The due diligence visit is the appraiser's proxy for the extended on-site investigation normally conducted in bank acquisitions. If at all possible, it stands to reason, appraisers should make the on-site visit a normal part of their valuation procedures.

Information Gathering and Preparation for the Due Diligence Visit

Information Request List

At the time a valuation assignment is accepted, the appraiser should provide an information checklist to the bank to facilitate information gathering and to ensure that all necessary data is obtained.

Based upon our firm's experience in providing literally hundreds of appraisals of financial institutions, the successful organization of the information-gathering process is critical to the overall accomplishment

---

[2]See *Nellie I. Brown, TC Memo 1966–92* (Docket No. 4992-64, 4/28/66). This case clearly turned on the experience of the taxpayer's expert, his thorough analysis of a closely-held company, and his particular knowledge of the business based upon his familiarity with the company and its place of business. More recently, I was called upon to defend two bank appraisals that were performed by Mercer Capital during late 1984 and early 1985. A 1985 recapitalization of a one-bank holding company was contested on the basis that the valuation of the underlying bank stock owned by the holding company was undervalued. Two investment bankers were hired by the plaintiffs. Both valued the bank on the order of 50% greater than the original appraisal. Neither expert visited the bank, even though management was substantially the same nearly five years later, and neither reviewed critical period documents that described the bank's troubled immediate past (as of the valuation date). The court sustained the original valuation, in large part because of the quality of the original appraisal, which was bolstered by detailed document reviews and detailed discussions with management regarding the past problems, the then-current state of asset quality, and the outlook for the future. The point of these examples is simple: Due diligence visits can be critical to the credibility of an appraisal and to an analyst's ability to defend it at a later date.

of a timely and well-reasoned valuation.[3] To facilitate data collection, we suggest that the bank designate a contact person to gather and assemble the necessary information that must be obtained from sources around the bank. While a lengthy information request list may at first seem overwhelming or intimidating to a bank client, bank managements almost always are supportive of the effort when properly informed of its necessity for the valuation process. (A sample Financial Institutions Valuation Information Request List for a bank appraisal is included as Appendix D.)

Ideally, all the information on the list should be obtained prior to the due diligence visit. However, time constraints in some appraisal situations will make this impossible. Thus, the appraiser needs to prioritize the data-gathering process for the financial institution and get the minimum information necessary to conduct the interview. Hopefully, the remainder of the information will be developed and ready when the appraiser arrives for the visit. It is important to remember that there is a significant relationship between the early availability of information and the success of the interview and, perhaps, the entire assignment.

Preliminary Analysis of the Data

Upon receipt of the information package, the analyst should begin the analysis to prepare for the valuation interview. Preliminary analysis generally falls into three broad categories: (1) banking industry analysis, (2) analysis of the subject bank and its market area, and (3) financial statement analysis.

The industry analysis should include a current assessment of the banking industry on a national and regional scale; a current assessment of the market performance of financial institution stocks, including the regional holding companies likely to be used in the public comparable analysis; and the general outlook for the banking industry. The objective of this portion of preparation is to become conversant with industry trends and to be able to relate those trends to the particular valuation situation at hand.

The analysis of the subject bank and its market area would include a review of documents relating to the bank's history, ownership, and current organizational structure and management. Economic data for the city, county, and region should be obtained from independent sources as well as from the bank, when available. A preliminary market share analysis should be developed if a current market share study has not been provided by the bank. The objective of this portion of preparation is to be sufficiently familiar with the bank's organization, structure, and market to ask specific clarifying questions.

---

[3]We should note that the information gathered in the process of a bank appraisal is quite similar to that necessary for a successful due diligence effort in a bank acquisition. Obviously, an acquisition due diligence effort will include legal and regulatory inquiries and asset quality investigations beyond the scope of the normal bank appraisal; nevertheless, the Financial Institutions Valuation Information Request List presented in Appendix D is an excellent beginning point for an acquisition due diligence effort. Generally, legal counsel and an acquirer's accounting firm will provide additional, more detailed checklists for the areas not covered in this list.

The preliminary financial analysis should include a detailed financial statement review. The financial exhibits and schedules described in the chapters on financial statement analysis (Chapters 8–11) provide the basis for this analysis. Questions can be developed based upon the trends shown in the statements and schedules as well as from comparisons with the bank's peer group data and with selected publicly traded financial institutions.

The Due Diligence Visit

Interview

The principal objective of the due diligence visit is to obtain the information and form the opinions needed to facilitate the completion of a valuation opinion and the writing of a formal valuation report. It is generally easier to clarify information and to obtain additional documents needed during the course of a visit than at any other time.

A sample Due Diligence Interview Questionnaire is included as Appendix F to this book. It provides a set of generalized questions that can facilitate the interview process. The questionnaire, however, should be augmented with a list of specific questions that the analyst develops based upon his or her preliminary review (see above).

Interviews can be facilitated by careful consideration of the following:

1. Schedule time with appropriate representatives of management. In smaller banks, the CEO may be able to answer virtually all due diligence questions. Nevertheless, if possible, the analyst should be sure to talk with other members of the management team.

2. Be sure to cover topics at an appropriate management level and with an appropriate amount of detail. For example, questions of overall strategy are normally addressed directly with the CEO; detailed financial questions might be discussed with a bank's controller or financial vice president; and the quality and condition of the loan portfolio should be discussed with the bank's senior credit officer.

3. The interview should be paced to allow for good note taking. One of the purposes of the due diligence visit is to document the answers to questions. Memories of conversations fade quickly. Detailed notes provide the basis for good written reports and excellent file documentation.

4. Ask open-ended questions. Try to avoid what seems to be a normal tendency for analysts to volunteer answers to their own questions. Avoid questions that can be answered with a simple yes or no. The point of the interview process is to have bank management answer questions, so phrase questions that require an explanation and that do not suggest answers.

5. Ask specific clarifying questions from the client documents that have been reviewed prior to the date of the visit.

6. Be sure to answer the "catch-all" questions mentioned at the end of the questionnaire. These questions force bank management to reflect over the course of the interview and facilitate frank disclosure

of issues and opportunities that may not have surfaced from the generalized questionnaire or from specific questions based upon reviews of documents.

Interviews that follow a detailed questionnaire supplemented by specific questions developed from document reviews are much more likely to provide the insights into a financial institution's operations necessary to develop a realistic opinion of value than are interviews based upon less structured approaches. Such interviews will *definitely* provide better file documentation than less structured approaches.

Physical Inspection

Part of the due diligence visit should include a tour of the main office, as well as tours of as many branch facilities as time will allow. Experienced analysts can glean a great deal of important information from even a brief tour of operations, including impressions of:

1. The work ethic of the bank.
2. The quality of the bank's main office and branch locations in relationship to its competitors.
3. The adequacy of existing physical facilities for the present and anticipated volume of business.
4. Management's attitude toward organization and documentation.
5. Management's relationships with various levels of employees.

Evaluation of Management

Another primary objective of the due diligence visit is for the analyst to develop an opinion of the quality of management and of the management team's ability to achieve expected financial performance in the foreseeable future. Key questions that must be addressed in the process of the on-site visit include:

1. Is the bank dependent on the knowledge, expertise, contacts, or experience of any one individual?
2. Are there currently any gaps in management that could impact on the bank's ability to achieve expected performance levels?
3. What is the relationship between management and the board of directors? And what is the role of the board of directors in the overall running of the institution?
4. What is management's attitude toward employees? What is the general attitude of employees toward management? How does this interplay influence productivity and the "culture" of the institution?
5. How does the management team communicate with the employees, and how effective is that communication?

The experienced analyst will attempt to develop a "comfort level" with management and an opinion of the adequacy of the management team and the physical facilities to handle expected future growth. The due diligence visit provides an ideal opportunity to accomplish both objectives.

On-site Document Review

An additional objective of the due diligence visit should be to review documents that may not have been provided previously. Documents such as board minutes, strategic plans, internal and state or federal examinations, and loan documentation files may be too cumbersome to forward by mail, and management may believe that such information is too sensitive to be distributed outside the bank. In some cases, it will be necessary for the analyst to allocate time to review documents while on site.

Documentation of the Interview

Every bank valuation should have thorough file documentation. Documentation is important regardless of the reason for an appraisal, although documentation requirements may vary depending upon the purpose and timing of the valuation. The analyst should remember that valuation files should include the information necessary to develop the requested opinion(s). The files should also be sufficiently legible so that another analyst could pick up the file and understand the financial position of the bank.

Conclusion

The due diligence visit is an important part of the bank valuation process. Users of bank valuation reports should inquire into the level of due diligence used by an appraiser to ensure that confidence in the results is warranted. Some appraisers of banking institutions do not visit banks in the normal course of preparing appraisals. In many cases, these appraisers provide fee quotes that are considerably less expensive than other appraisers who follow due diligence procedures similar to those outlined in this chapter. In the case of appraisals of financial institutions, however, as in many other areas of life, cheaper is not always better. *Caveat emptor.*

Chapter 5

Regulation and Accounting for Banks and Thrifts

There have been three great inventions since the beginning of time: fire, the wheel, and central banking.

Will Rogers

Overview

The financial institutions' regulatory structure is in a state of flux. Consequently, it would be impossible to capture every possible change or to discuss all the proposals for bank and regulatory reform. The purpose of this chapter is to provide a broad overview of the banking system and its current regulatory structure and to introduce several important accounting issues.

The regulatory structure of the U.S. banking system is a complex network of federal and state agencies and laws. This structure requires a high degree of cooperation among governmental agencies that often have conflicting goals and policies. An individual financial institution must answer to many masters.

A bank or a savings and loan association (S & L) may operate under either a federal or a state charter. National banks operate under federal charters and are supervised by the Office of the Comptroller of the Currency (OCC). They are required to be members of the Federal Reserve System and to have their deposits insured by the Federal Deposit Insurance Corporation (FDIC). Federal S & Ls are chartered by the Office of Thrift Supervision (OTS) and are insured through the Savings Association Insurance Fund (SAIF) of the FDIC. Banks and federally insured mutual savings banks are insured by the Bank Insurance Fund (BIF) of the FDIC. (See Chapter 17 for a more detailed discussion of current deposit insurance coverage.)

At the state level, banks are chartered by the states and typically supervised by a banking commissioner. Most state banks, however, are still subject to some federal control. A state bank is not required to join the Federal Reserve System or be insured by the FDIC. As a practical matter, however, it is virtually impossible to operate without the deposit insurance offered by the FDIC. If a state bank does elect to become a Federal Reserve member, it must also subscribe to the FDIC. Savings and loan associations also may be chartered by the state. All S & Ls are required to be insured.

Savings and loan associations may be organized as either mutual savings banks or stock associations. Mutual savings associations are owned by their depositors and managed by a board of trustees. Stock associations are organized like other corporations and are owned by stockholders and managed by a board of directors.

Bank stock may be owned by almost any type of company. However, important limitations arise for regulatory purposes if the company is classified as a bank holding company. This occurs once the corporation owns at least 25% of the stock of a bank and/or a bank holding company. Bank holding companies are subject to regulations by the Federal Reserve Board.

Because different regulations apply to the various types of financial institutions, it is important to be precise when referring to a financial entity. Banks differ from bank holding companies, and mutuals differ from stock savings associations in their structure and regulation.

Independent Agencies of the Federal Government

Regulatory Structure Outline

The appropriate federal banking agency with primary supervisory and regulatory authority of the nation's banks, thrifts and their holding companies is outlined in Exhibit 5-1.

Exhibit 5-1
Federal Banking Agencies Regulatory Overview

Office of the Comptroller of the Currency
    National banks
    Banks in the District of Columbia
    Federal branch or agency of a foreign bank

The Federal Reserve Board
    State member insured banks (other than DC)
    Bank holding companies and their subsidiaries

Federal Deposit Insurance Corporation
    State nonmember insured banks
    Foreign banks with insured branches

The Office of Thrift Supervision
    Federal savings associations
    State savings associations
    Savings and loan holding companies

State Banking Departments
    State-chartered banks
    State-chartered savings and loans

Federal Deposit Insurance Corporation (FDIC)

The FDIC was organized as part of the Federal Reserve Act, which was approved on June 16, 1933. In 1950, the FDIC was withdrawn from the authority of the Federal Reserve and its statutes were amended under the Federal Deposit Insurance Act. The FDIC is funded by assessments on deposits held by insured institutions and from interest on the investment of its surplus funds in government securities.

The mission of the Federal Deposit Insurance Corporation is to promote and preserve public confidence in financial institutions and to protect the money supply through insurance coverage for deposits. The FDIC currently insures deposits of up to $100,000 in national banks, in state banks that are members of the Federal Reserve System, and in state banks that apply for federal deposit insurance. In 1989, the Federal Savings and Loan Insurance Corporation (FSLIC) was dissolved, and the FDIC acquired the responsibility of insuring the deposits of federally insured savings associations. The FDIC maintains two separate insurance funds to insure financial institutions: the Bank Insurance Fund (BIF) and the Savings Association Insurance Fund (SAIF), which replaced the FSLIC fund.[1]

The FDIC is governed by a five-member board of directors. One director is the Comptroller of the Currency, and another is the Director of the Office of Thrift Supervision. Two directors are appointed by the President and confirmed by the Senate, and the fifth member serves as the chairperson, who has a very important policy-making role.

The FDIC may make loans to or purchase assets from insured institutions for the protection of depositors. The FDIC acts as a receiver for all failed national banks and for state banks when appointed by state authorities. The FDIC is also the exclusive manager of the Resolution Trust Corporation (RTC) and has sole responsibility for the day-to-day operations of the RTC. The RTC acts as a receiver for all insolvent savings associations. In its capacity as a receiver, the FDIC is not subject to the direction or supervision of any other federal or state agency. However, an institution in conservatorship remains subject to the supervision of its appropriate federal banking agency.

The FDIC requires regular financial reporting on the part of insured banks. Reports required by the FDIC include the following:

1. *Certified Statements.* Must be submitted in January and June of each year showing deposit liabilities.
2. *Consolidated Reports of Condition and Income.* These reports, also referred to as *Call Reports,* must be filed quarterly with the Bank Financial Reporting Section of the FDIC.
3. *Summary of Deposits.* This report on the amount of various types of deposit categories must be filed for each authorized office of an insured bank with branches as of each June 30.
4. *Annual Report of Trust Assets.* Must be filed by February 15 each year by all commercial and savings banks operating trust departments.
5. *Report of Fully Insured Brokered Deposits.* Must be filed for each quarter that fully insured brokered deposits are in excess of a bank's total capital or 5% of total deposits.

Resolution Trust Corporation (RTC)

The RTC was established by the Financial Institutions Reform, Recovery and Enforcement Act (FIRREA) of 1989. The board of directors of the FDIC also serves as the RTC's board of directors. The RTC acts as conservator or receiver for savings associations that are under the direct control of the government or that have failed. The RTC, through the Real Estate Asset Division, develops policies and programs for the management and disposition of all the real property assets under its jurisdiction.

---

[1]At the present time, the FDIC's obligations to protect the integrity of insured deposits exceeds its current financial capabilities by a significant margin. Banks and thrifts are experiencing increases to their FDIC assessments, and various proposals for reform and a return to solvency for the FDIC are being discussed. Suffice it to say that reform will occur and that the proposal(s) adopted will be expensive for both the banking industry and taxpayers.

The mission of the RTC is to manage and resolve financially troubled thrift institutions and to dispose of residual assets in a manner that (1) maximizes returns and minimizes losses to the FDIC insurance fund, (2) minimizes the impact on local real estate and financial markets, and (3) maximizes the preservation of the availability and affordability of residential property for low- and moderate-income individuals.

An Oversight Board establishes overall RTC/FDIC strategy and general policy guidelines. The Oversight Board is composed of the Secretary of the Treasury, the Chair of the Federal Reserve Board, the Secretary of Housing and Urban Development (HUD), and two persons from the private sector who are appointed by the President and confirmed by the Senate. The Oversight Board periodically reviews the work, management activities, and internal controls of the RTC.

Funding to resolve the insolvent savings institutions under RTC conservatorship comes from three sources: the Resolution Funding Corporation, a line of credit from the U.S. Treasury, and unsecured obligations issued by the RTC.

Federal Financial Institutions Examination Council

The Federal Financial Institutions Examination Council was established by Congress in 1978. Its members include the Comptroller of the Currency, the Chair of the FDIC, and a governor of the Board of Governors of the Federal Reserve System.

The mission of the Federal Financial Institutions Examination Council is to promote consistency and progress in federal examination and supervision of financial institutions. The Council has the authority to establish uniform principles, standards, reporting forms, and systems. Uniform Bank Performance Reports are issued by the Federal Financial Institutions Examination Council for every insured bank every quarter. These reports are discussed at length in the chapters on bank analysis.

Federal Reserve System

The Federal Reserve System was established by the Federal Reserve Act of 1913. The Federal Reserve System is the central bank of the United States and is responsible for administering and making policy for the nation's credit and monetary affairs. It also acts as fiscal agent, legal depository, and custodian of funds for the U.S. government. Important functions of the Federal Reserve that affect bank operations include holding the legal reserves of banks and other depository institutions, providing wire transfers of funds, facilitating clearance and collections of checks, examining and supervising state-chartered member banks and bank holding companies, and collecting and disseminating economic data.

The Federal Reserve System consists of six parts: the Board of Governors in Washington, D.C., the 12 Federal Reserve Banks and their 25 branches, the Federal Open Market Committee, the Federal Advisory

Council, the Consumer Advisory Council, and the Thrift Institutions Advisory Council.

The Board of Governors (the Board) is comprised of seven members who are appointed by the President and confirmed by the Senate. The Board has broad supervisory powers to determine general monetary, credit, and operating policies for the system and to formulate the rules and regulations necessary to carry out the provisions of the Federal Reserve Act. The principal duties of the Board of Governors are to monitor monetary conditions and to regulate the amount of credit in the economy.

Under the Bank Holding Company Act of 1956, the Board of Governors has the primary responsibility for supervising and regulating the activities of bank holding companies. A company that seeks to become a bank holding company must first obtain approval from the Federal Reserve. Bank holding companies are required to register with the Federal Reserve within 180 days of becoming a holding company and to file quarterly and annual reports on their operations and financial condition. A bank holding company must obtain the approval of the Federal Reserve if it acquires a subsidiary bank, purchases more than 5% of the equity securities of another bank, purchases substantially all of the assets of another bank, or merges.

The Board has jurisdiction over the admission of banks into membership in the Federal Reserve System, as well as the termination of membership, the establishment of branches, and the approval of mergers and consolidations. The Board has the power to examine all member banks, to require disclosures, and to issue cease-and-desist orders in connection with violations of the law or unsound banking practices. The Board is also the rule-making authority for the Equal Credit Opportunity Act, the Home Mortgage Disclosure Act, and the Fair Credit Billing Act.

The 12 Federal Reserve Banks are located in Atlanta, Boston, Chicago, Cleveland, Dallas, Kansas City (Mo.), Minneapolis, New York, Philadelphia, Richmond, St. Louis, and San Francisco. Branch banks are located in Baltimore, Birmingham, Buffalo, Charlotte, Cincinnati, Denver, Detroit, El Paso, Helena, Houston, Jacksonville, Little Rock, Los Angeles, Louisville, Memphis, Miami, Nashville, New Orleans, Oklahoma City, Omaha, Pittsburgh, Portland, Salt Lake City, San Antonio, and Seattle.

Directors of the Federal Reserve Banks are responsible for supervising and controlling the operations of the Reserve Banks under the general supervision of the Board of Governors. The Federal Reserve Banks receive clearing account deposits of depository institutions and extend short-term adjustment credit to eligible depository institutions to help borrowers meet temporary liquidity requirements. Another function of the Federal Reserve Banks is the issuance of currency in the form of Federal Reserve Notes.

The Federal Open Market Committee consists of the Board of Governors and the presidents of five of the Federal Reserve Banks. The open market operations of the system involve the purchase and sale of securities in the open market to supply monetary reserves to support the credit and money in the economic system.

Three advisory councils meet with the Board of Governors on an irregular basis to provide information on non-bank topics. The Federal Advisory Council, which fields a representative from each Federal Reserve District, acts as an advisor to the Board of Governors on general business conditions. The Consumer Advisory Council is composed of members representing consumer and credit interests and consults with the Board of Governors on the issue of consumer credit protection. The Thrift Institutions Advisory Council includes members from non-bank financial institutions who advise the Board on developments in thrift institutions, as well as in the housing and mortgage industries.

Federal Home Loan Bank System

The Federal Home Bank System was created by authority of the Federal Home Loan Bank Act of 1932 to provide a flexible credit reserve for member savings institutions engaged in home mortgage lending. There are 12 Federal Home Loan Banks, located in Atlanta, Boston, Chicago, Cincinnati, Dallas, Des Moines, Indianapolis, New York, Pittsburgh, San Francisco, Seattle, and Topeka.

Until 1989, the Federal Home Loan Banks were under the supervision of the Federal Home Loan Bank Board. The Financial Institutions Reform, Recovery and Enforcement Act of 1989 created the Federal Housing Finance Board to replace the Federal Home Loan Bank Board as the overseer of the activities of the Federal Home Loan Banks. The Federal Housing Finance Board is an independent agency in the executive branch of the federal government.

Savings associations, insured banks, and insured credit unions with at least 10% of their assets in residential mortgage loans can be members of a Federal Home Loan Bank. Federal Home Loan Banks provide advances to their members as a supplement to savings flows in meeting recurring variations in the supply and demand for residential mortgage credit. Federal Home Loan Bank members are not automatically entitled to advances. The individual institutions must demonstrate a commitment to housing in order to obtain the loans. In addition, the advances must normally be well collateralized.

Offices of the Department of the Treasury

Office of the Comptroller of the Currency (OCC)

The OCC was created in 1863 as part of the national banking system, and it operates as an independent unit within the Department of the Treasury. The Comptroller of the Currency is the chief regulatory officer for national banks and is responsible for governing the operations of national banks. The Comptroller is appointed by the President and confirmed by the Senate for a term of five years.

The OCC periodically examines all national banks to determine their financial condition, soundness of operations, quality of management, and compliance with federal regulations. The Comptroller is also responsible for overseeing the regulation of federally licensed branches and agencies of foreign banks.

Each national bank must submit a quarterly report of the condition of its commercial department to the OCC. These reports are identical to the Call Reports mentioned earlier, which are required to be filed by banks regulated by the FDIC. Other reports filed by national banks include income and dividend reports and information on affiliates, trust departments, and international operations.

One of the most important functions of the OCC is its authority to charter national banks. The National Bank Act of 1864 set forth the framework for chartering national banks and specified the items that the OCC must consider when granting a national bank charter. In addition, the Community Reinvestment Act instructs the Comptroller to review a bank's record of meeting community needs before allowing expansion.

Office of Thrift Supervision (OTS)

The OTS was created in 1989 as part of the FIRREA to replace the Federal Home Loan Bank Board as the primary regulator of savings associations. The OTS administers regulations adopted by the Federal Home Loan Bank Board and the Federal Savings and Loan Insurance Corporation prior to their dissolution. The OTS has responsibility for chartering and regulating federal savings associations and their holding companies and supervising state-chartered savings associations. The OTS, like the OCC, is an autonomous office of the Department of the Treasury.

The Director of the OTS is appointed by the President and confirmed by the Senate for a five-year term. The primary responsibility of the director is to assure the safety and soundness of federally chartered S & Ls and federal savings banks. The agency has the authority to conduct examinations, to issue cease-and-desist orders, and to remove officers of savings associations.

The supervisory and enforcement powers of the OTS are significantly expanded over those possessed by the Federal Home Loan Bank Board. The OTS can issue a cease-and-desist order against any institution-affiliated party, including shareholders, consultants, joint-venture partners, attorneys, accountants, and appraisers who knowingly or recklessly participate in any violation of the law, breach of fiduciary duty, or unsound practice that has an adverse effect on a savings association. The OTS can also use its authority to investigate possible fraud by issuing temporary cease-and-desist orders based on inaccurate or incomplete records. The OTS can proceed against individuals suspected of wrongdoing even if the party is no longer affiliated with the institution.

The functions of the OTS include the regulation of corporate structure, earnings distribution, and lending and investment powers of savings associations, as well as their ability to engage in mergers, conversions, liquidations or dissolutions.

State Banking Departments

Every state has an agency that supervises and monitors state-chartered banks. State-chartered banks are required to file quarterly reports of condition and notices of corporate changes, new branches, and relocations. Many state-chartered institutions are also members of the Federal Reserve System or are insured by the FDIC and are also subject to the regulation of those agencies.

Required Financial Statement Filing Formats

Every national bank, state member bank, and insured state nonmember bank is required to file Consolidated Reports of Condition and Income (Call Reports) as of the close of business on the last calendar day of each calendar quarter. National banks and state nonmember banks submit reports to the FDIC, and state member banks submit their reports to the appropriate Federal Reserve Bank. Reports must be received by the appropriate agency no more than 30 days after the end of the quarter.

The amount of financial disclosure is dependent upon the size of the institution and whether it operates foreign offices. Reports of institutions with no foreign offices and with assets of less than $100 million have the least degree of detail, while institutions of any size with foreign offices are the most detailed. Call Reports generally include financial statements or supplementary exhibits containing detailed information on at least the following items:

1. Income statement.
2. Balance sheet.
3. Changes in equity capital.
4. Charge-offs and recoveries and changes in the allowance for loan and lease losses.
5. Applicable income taxes by taxing authority.
6. Cash and balances due from depository institutions.
7. Securities.
8. Loans and lease-financing receivables.
9. Deposit liabilities.
10. Quarterly average balances.
11. Off-balance sheet items.
12. Past-due and non-accrual loans and leases.
13. Risk-based capital.
14. Supplemental disclosure on significant nonrecurring items or changes of accounting method.

Questions and requests for interpretations of items appearing on the Call Reports should be addressed to an institution's primary supervisory agency. Inquiries are then referred to the Reports Task Force of the Federal Financial Institutions Examination Council. Banks have the option of filing electronically through the collection agent for banking agencies (i.e., CompuServe, Inc.). Call Reports are made available to the public upon request by the federal bank supervisory agencies.

Savings associations are required to file similar, although somewhat less detailed, reports with the Office of Thrift Supervision. Thrift Financial Reports, also filed quarterly, include Statements of Condition, Statements of Operations, listings of troubled assets, commitments and contingencies, and cash flows.

Registration of Securities

Banks subject to the Securities Exchange Act of 1934 usually register their securities and file public disclosure documents with the bank supervisory agencies instead of the Securities Exchange Commission. All banks with registered securities must file quarterly (Form 10-Q) and annual (Form 10-K) reports on their financial condition. Financial institutions subject to the additional filing requirements of the SEC Act of 1934 would include most banks with 500 or more shareholders and those selling securities to the public.

Bank holding companies are chartered as corporations under the laws of their home states. A bank holding company is organized as either one-bank or multi-bank, and its activities may include other related financial services besides banking. Each bank holding company must file a registration statement and an annual report of operations with its district Federal Reserve Bank and the Board of Governors. The reports to be filed are:

1. *Y-6 Annual Report.* Must be filed by all domestic bank holding companies. Includes consolidated and parent-company-only financial statements.
2. *Y-9 Bank Holding Company Financial Supplement.* Required for holding companies with consolidated assets of $50 million or more.
3. *Y-7 Annual Report of Foreign Banking Organizations.* Required to be filed by companies that are organized under the laws of a foreign country.

In order to determine and disclose the holdings of beneficial owners, an acquisition statement must be filed by the purchaser(s) of holding company securities showing the extent of ownership and the source of funds used to purchase the securities. National banks may also be required to file proxies, give notice of tender offers, and make annual reports to security holders. Financial institutions have the option of preparing income statements for these reports using either the Call Report format or the net interest income format prescribed by the SEC.

Accounting for Banks and Thrifts

The accounting practices of banks and savings associations differ from each other and from generally accepted accounting principles as applied to non-financial companies. Generally accepted accounting principles

(GAAP) govern accounting for most internal transactions in banks and thrifts. However, regulatory agencies may require a departure from GAAP in the filing of regulatory reports to meet the special supervisory, regulatory, and economic policy needs served by these reports. Regulatory accounting practices have historically benefited savings institutions, while producing less desirable results for banks. The Competitive Equality Banking Act of 1987 and FIRREA require savings associations to shift from thrift regulatory accounting practices to GAAP. If there is a question about a specific transaction, accounting treatment is determined by an institution's primary federal bank supervisory agency's interpretation of how GAAP should be applied or if a departure from GAAP is justified. (See the more detailed discussion of accounting issues in Chapter 17.)

Under FIRREA, all federal banking agencies are required to establish uniform regulatory accounting standards. Regulatory accounting and reporting standards for thrifts must now be equally stringent for banks. Under GAAP, savings associations discount estimate future proceeds in determining the net realizable value of assets, while banks do not. Banks have traditionally held higher levels of loan loss allowances as a percentage of total loans.

Every savings association is required to have an audit at least once each calendar year, more often if deemed necessary, by auditors approved by the OTS. Thus, the accounting policies, procedures, records, and internal control of the savings institution are subject to a periodic, independent, critical review and evaluation. A copy of the audit, which must include a balance sheet and statement of income, is filed with the OTS. The audit may be conducted either by a public accountant or an internal auditor as long as the auditor is deemed to be qualified and independent by the standards set forth by the OTS.

Banks are not required to have outside audits unless they are subject to the Securities Exchange Act of 1934. Banks that fall under the provisions of the SEC Act of 1934 must have annual audits and include audited financial statements in their annual OCC filings. Most banks, however, do obtain annual independent audits of their financial statements.

Capital Requirements

The Financial Institutions Reform, Recovery and Enforcement Act of 1989 established minimum regulatory capital requirements that will become uniformly applicable to all financial institutions when fully implemented in 1993. Savings associations are required to maintain adequate capital in accordance with three standards: a risk-based capital standard, a leverage standard, and a tangible capital standard.

The risk-based capital standard imposes a higher capital requirement upon those institutions that invest in assets with higher levels of credit risk. The other capital standards are based on the amount of total assets. A savings association's minimum risk-based capital requirement under FIRREA is an increasing percentage of its risk-weighted assets. Until December 30, 1990, the risk-based capital requirement was 6%. For the calendar years 1991 and 1992, the requirement increased to 7%, and after

1992 the requirement will be 8%. Savings associations must maintain core capital of not less than 3% of total assets and tangible capital equal to at least 1.5% of total assets.

The following elements comprise a savings association's core capital:

1. Common stockholders equity including retained earnings.
2. Noncumulative perpetual preferred stock and related earnings.
3. Minority interests in the equity of consolidated subsidiaries.
4. Nonwithdrawable accounts and pledged deposits of mutual savings associations.
5. The remaining goodwill resulting from prior regulatory practices.

National banks are required by the Office of the Comptroller of the Currency to maintain minimum capital standards, and the risk-based capital guidelines are being imposed on the banking industry. More-detailed discussions of bank capital requirements are presented in the next section of the book, and further comparisons between thrift and bank capital requirements are discussed in Chapter 17.

Chapter 6

Selected Management Issues

Without management, a bank is so much scrap, fit only to be liquidated.
George Siemens/Deutsche Bank (ca. 1880)

Overview

Banking is a service business, and most community banks provide the same basic services. As banks grow, the list of services also tends to grow; nevertheless, competitor banks provide the same services. Banking is also a capital business. However, as one banker put it: "My bank's green is the same color as the other bank's green. We have to differentiate ourselves with service to gain attention, respect, and, finally, the business of our customers." Management makes the difference in banking.

Few businesses have as much financial risk directly related to the daily decisions of management as banking. Bankers routinely make decisions that place significant portions of their institutions' capital at risk. As another banker put it: "Anyone can make a loan. It takes a good lender, supported by good loan administration, credit review, and knowledgeable peer loan officer support to collect principal and interest on that loan according to the loan agreement *and* to keep the customer satisfied." Again, management makes the difference in banking.

No appraisal is complete without formulating an opinion about the quality of management. If an appraisal is based solely upon reviews of documents and financial statements, an opinion of management quality must be based upon the trends in operating performance as evidenced in the financial statements. That opinion is strengthened when the appraiser visits directly with management in the bank, hears the management's responses to key operating questions, and observes interaction between management and other bank employees in the context of normal daily operations.

The analyst should focus on at least three specific areas in the process of evaluating bank management: management and organizational structure, information systems, and policies and procedures.

Management and Organizational Structure

Organizational Structure and the Management Team

The organizational concept of a bank must enable the institution to accomplish several basic objectives, including (1) delivering the bank's products and services in an effective and efficient manner, (2) providing timely and accurate recordkeeping, and (3) providing adequate internal controls.

A good place to begin to review a bank's management and organizational structure is with its organization chart. The chart is a good vehicle for discussing the background, knowledge, and experience of the management team in the context of each member's basic area(s) of responsibility.

Organization charts will vary in complexity with the size of the bank. Nevertheless, the typical community bank will generally have an organization along the lines outlined in Figure 6-1, with the organization being described along functional department lines. When reviewing an organization, the analyst should seek to answer several key questions about management and the organizational structure:

1. Is there a current organizational chart? If there is no current chart, are management responsibilities defined with sufficient clarity to avoid confusion over the roles of key personnel?
2. How many persons report directly to the chief executive officer (CEO) and/or the chief operating officer (COO)? Is the span of control unusually narrow, with one reporting to the other, or unusually wide, with many direct reporting relationships to the top officer?
3. Is the chief executive officer directly involved in lending? Depending upon the nature of the loan portfolio, the CEO should probably begin phasing out of direct lending activities (or at least limit participation) as a bank approaches $50 million or so in assets.
4. Is the bank top-heavy with officers? Top-heaviness can have adverse influences on both productivity and morale. Conversely, is the bank too heavily dependent upon the services of any one officer?
5. Who are the bank's key customer groups? Is the bank's organization designed to meet their needs efficiently?
6. Are key positions currently unfilled? How long have the positions been vacant? Why?

Figure 6-1
Organization Chart

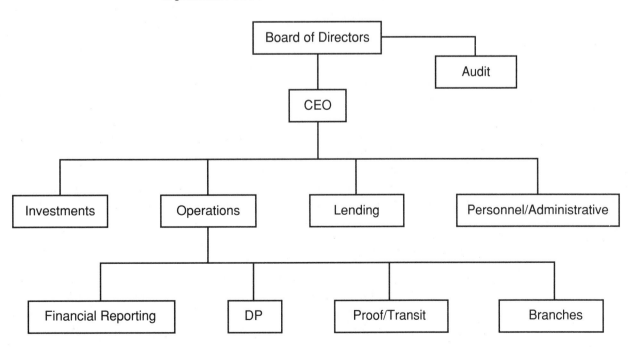

7. Are there any particularly weak managers in the group? The analyst may conclude on her or his own that certain weaknesses exist, but sometimes one or more managers will volunteer this information. If there is a particularly weak manager, is the bank exposed to undue risk as a result?
8. Does the bank "grow its own managers and lenders" internally, or does it go outside to hire needed management and lending talent?
9. Has there been any recent turnover among the key managers of the bank? What was the reason for the change?
10. What is management's general attitude about the bank and its outlook for the future?

These questions asked in the context of the organization chart can help the analyst view the bank from the perspective of management and can, when combined with the general analysis, provide the basis for an opinion of the overall quality of management.

Board of Directors

The role of the board of directors needs to be evaluated in terms of its ability to develop and understand the goals and policies of the bank and to support their execution. A good relationship between bank management and the board of directors is important for the ongoing stability of management and operating performance. Further, an active board can create business opportunities for the bank through the individual efforts of board members. Key questions about the board include:

1. Is the board of directors composed of a cross-section of the community?
2. Are the board members active in their attendance and participation? What board committees exist? What are their purposes, and do they fulfill them?
3. Does the board generally let management manage, or is the group too actively involved in day-to-day operating decisions? Is management comfortable with the board's level of involvement?
4. Is board compensation reasonable?
5. Does the board of directors regularly review sufficient information to make an adequate evaluation of the bank's operating performance? A review of the regular monthly and quarterly board and executive committee reports is the best source of information for this determination.

A review of board minutes over the year or two (or more) preceding the valuation date can be instructive in answering many of these questions.

Management Team

One of the best indicators of the strength of management is found in the level and trend of operating results when measured over time. Consistent and persistent operating performance provides a good indication of management's focus on maintaining profitability and building shareholder value. However, many banks are not currently experiencing stellar operating results; and many others have experienced turnover in one or more key management positions in the recent past. The answers to the following questions, gleaned from the interview process by direct response or by observation, will help the analyst to assess the capabilities of a bank's management team:

1. Does management have a well-developed budgeting process? Is it flexible, and does it provide a system for monitoring and evaluating performance?
2. Is budgeting a participatory process, and has it been communicated to the individuals who will make it happen?
3. Does the bank regularly make comparisons between actual and budgeted performance?
4. Overall, is the budget a useful management tool, and will it assist the analyst in determining the bank's ability to generate ongoing earnings?
5. Has there been continuity of management over the period analyzed? If so, do the profitability trends reflect steady growth? If not, what are the reasons?
6. Have there been breaks or changes in management, and how has this affected growth and profitability?
7. Does management have a transition plan in the event a key officer departs unexpectedly?
8. Is there a formalized, written, long-range business plan that identifies where the bank is, where it wants to go, how it will get there, what needs to be done at least in the next year or so to get there, and who is responsible for making it happen?
9. What is the marketing orientation of the bank, and how does it manifest itself?
10. Is there a marketing profile that establishes current and possible future products or services, and are there customer profiles that reflect the types and frequency of the use of products and services?

These questions are only intended as examples for consideration. The analyst may develop an entirely different set of questions, but the objective is to attempt to assess the element of risk associated with management and the bank's long-range outlook. Management continuity with knowledgeable, committed, and qualified people tends to minimize the risks associated with the ability to generate ongoing earnings and tends to reduce uncertainty in terms of the valuation process.

Information Systems

Another important area of assessment is the bank's internal information system. Appropriate reporting tools indicate that the bank's operations are organized and provide management with the necessary basis for decision making. When referring to systems, we are concerned with the overall management information product (the output) provided by individual areas rather than with particular types of systems.

Data Processing and Systems

Issues related to data processing are often overlooked but can be extremely important. Poor data processing systems can contribute to unnecessarily high operating costs or limitations on a bank's ability to provide new products or services.

Data processing services can be performed in-house or through a service bureau or by combination of the two. Each has unique advantages and disadvantages. The key point is to determine how well the existing system(s) can meet a bank's current and prospective needs. Implementation of a new system is always a major commitment of resources—both financial and people. It can frequently be a process that tests the patience of any organization.

Several questions should be considered in connection with a bank's systems capabilities, including:

1. What types of systems does the bank use? Do they provide the information needed for management decision making?
2. Do the bank's systems provide necessary controls over key areas of risk and provide for regular reconciliation of critical balances?
3. Has the bank had a recent systems evaluation?
4. What back-up support is available? Can the information be obtained by other sources?
5. Does the bank use in-house or service-bureau data processing facilities? If a service bureau is used, does it provide the capability and flexibility to add products that will enable the bank to compete more effectively? Is the in-house system flexible enough to accommodate future growth at reasonable expense?
6. Does the bank have central information file (CIF) capability that allows it to analyze total customer relationships and price products based on functional cost analysis?

In summary, the analyst is assessing whether the bank's current system is adequate to support its current and anticipated needs or whether a major investment in systems will be required in the future.

Management Reporting

There are certain reports common to most banks that management can utilize to make decisions with respect to financial performance, establishing interest rates, investments, and lending policy decisions. Although the exact names of each report may vary among institutions, several key reports and a brief description of each are noted below:

1. *Internal Financial Statements.* Include summary balance sheets and income statements, generally prepared monthly, that may present monthly or yearly comparisons.

2. *Investment Portfolio Summary.* Presents a summary of each type of investment security, average yields, book and market values, maturities, interest rates (yields), and ratings.

3. *Gap Report.* Presents each rate-sensitive asset and liability category by balance, maturity, and gap position. Generally presents cumulative gap and gap as a percentage of total assets. Data input reports on deposit repricing and loan maturities provide important management information.[1]

4. *Budget.* Presents budgeted amounts for each income and expense item by month. Internal financial statements should provide regular comparisons with budgeted performance.

5. *Past-Due List.* Past-due lists should be generated by officer and by category of loan. Timely use of past-due lists can help head off problems.

6. *Problem Loan List.* Classifies known problem loans according to status and balance. Some banks have a "watch list" to facilitate monitoring loans that are known or potential problems.

7. *Loan Loss Allowance Analysis.* Reconciles current loan loss allowance to a targeted amount and recommends adjustments based on potential losses. It should be prepared quarterly.

8. *Schedules of Other Real Estate Owned.* Presents current balances and status of the bank's repossessed real estate.

These management reports are by no means all the regular reports found in most banks. They do, however, provide an overview of the types of management information that should be readily available and frequently referenced by bank management.

Strategic Planning

Evidence of strategic planning is one indication of management's concern for future performance. Good planning and periodic checks on how the bank is performing relative to the plan give the analyst clues as to whether management is in touch with the bank's real position in its market place and industry. Strategic planning is becoming more critical for banks. In the banking environment of the early 1990s, change is rampant. Bankers who are not engaging in some form of long-range planning may be guilty of the ostrich syndrome—placing their heads in the sand while the sands are shifting. The appraiser should know where a subject bank's management stands on planning for the future.

The process of strategic planning generally involves an assessment of a bank's strengths and weaknesses, development of growth assumptions and objectives for the bank for the next several years, development of work plans and budgets required to accomplish objectives, short-term planning, and setting responsibility for specific assignments with specific deadlines.

---

[1]See Chapter 10 for a discussion of the concept of gap.

Policies and Procedures

Good banks are run by the exercise of good policies that are well executed by trained staffs. Banks are required by law to establish a number of policies, including policies regarding loans, investments, and the like. The analyst should obtain and review the following basic policy statements:

1. The *loan review policy* should set forth a procedure for the internal review of the loan portfolio on a continuous basis. The purpose is to monitor credit quality on an ongoing and systematic basis.

2. The *loan policy* provides a basis for conducting lending operations. It generally will establish desirable types of loans, officer loan limits (secured and unsecured, individual and joint), regulatory constraints, credit concentration limits, loan information requirements, file documentation and maintenance systems, and insider loan limitations. It will also establish pricing and collateral requirements and will define past-due loans, set renewal and extension procedures, define action steps for nonaccrual loans, set the charge-off policy, and set procedures for transfers to other real estate, etc. The loan policy may actually be divided into two or more separate policies covering the areas noted above.

3. The *loan loss reserve policy* should provide a system for analyzing the soundness of the loan portfolio and for ensuring that the existing allowance for loan losses is adequate to cover known and reasonably forseeable future losses.

4. The *investment policy* provides guidelines for investing funds not otherwise in use for loan demand. It designates the responsibility and authority for making investment decisions and sets forth acceptable portfolio investments by quality and by maturity.

5. The *asset liability policy* provides objectives for managing the net interest margin within a framework of maintaining adequate liquidity and capital. This policy may also govern deposit pricing in relationship to asset yields. It will set specific objectives with regard to the bank's earnings and asset growth, return on assets, return on equity, the loan-to-deposit ratio, the loan loss reserve ratio, and the net interest margin.

When reviewing a bank's policies and procedures, the analyst needs to ask: (1) Are they current, and how often are they updated? (2) Have they been approved, and do they have the full support of the board of directors? and (3) Does management—and therefore the entire staff—take the bank's policies seriously?

Conclusion

Management has the responsibility for recommending sound operating policies to a bank's board of directors, and then for implementing those policies consistently and persistently over time. Analysis of management is a "soft" part of the analysis of financial institutions. Consequently, many analysts overlook the importance of management in analyzing and valuing banking institutions. In so doing, they place their analyses and valuation conclusions in jeopardy. As will be seen in Parts II and III of this book, management quality is a critical ingredient in the consistency of bank earnings, and in the overall risk assessment influencing the capitalization factors that determine value.

Chapter 7

Sources of Comparative
Financial and Valuation Data

Good intelligence is nine-tenths of any battle.

Napoleon

Overview

The IRS Revenue Ruling 59–60 requires that an appraiser consider "the economic outlook in general and the outlook of the specific industry in particular." Financial institutions do not operate in a vacuum. The fortunes of banks and savings associations are closely tied to changes in the national, regional, and local economies. The sources included here are not intended to be an exhaustive list, but rather a compilation of useful sources that are readily available to the business appraiser.

Fortunately for the appraiser, there is a wealth of information available concerning the banking industry. More articles are written and more statistics compiled for and about the banking industry than almost any other business segment of our economy (except perhaps baseball!). Certainly no other industry has its financial activities so closely scrutinized by the federal government. Because the banking industry is so tightly regulated, privately owned financial institutions are required to make regular, detailed financial disclosures to their regulatory agencies, and these disclosures then become publicly available. Few private companies would consider making this level of disclosure to their shareholders, much less to the public.

On-line (computer-accessed) databases are becoming increasingly popular as sources of business and financial information. Most major libraries now offer database search services to their patrons. As on-line data sources have become cheaper and easier to use, even small companies are finding it time-saving and cost-effective to purchase a modem and subscribe to an on-line data service. Especially popular is the database wholesaler Dialog, which allows access to hundreds of databases using standard commands by dialing one telephone number.

Most sources listed here are available at any major public or university library. Many of the government publications are available free or for a small fee. A local or university library that has been designated a Government Depository Library will usually have most publications that are available from the Superintendent of Documents of the U.S. Government Printing Office.

This chapter briefly describes many data sources for national, regional, area, and local economic data, banking industry information, and bank financial statement data. For ease of reading, the sources usually are not footnoted in great detail. Exhibit 7-1 provides a listing of the data sources cited in this chapter.

Sources of National Economic Data

U.S. Government Publications and Data Sources

U.S. Department of Commerce, Bureau of Economic Analysis

The Bureau of Economic Analysis (BEA) provides information on such issues as national economic growth, inflation, and regional development. Most of BEA's work is presented in the *Survey of Current Business,* a monthly publication that contains estimates and analyses of national economic activity. It also contains an extensive section of current business statistics and business cycle indicators.

Each month, the Bureau of Economic Analysis compiles the "Composite Index of Leading Economic Indicators" (the "Leading Indicators"), based upon 12 leading economic indicators. The "Leading Indicators" appears each month in *Business Conditions Digest,* which tracks cyclical indicators.

For the most current information from "Leading Indicators," BEA makes available recorded telephone messages immediately after data are released. The messages are available 24 hours a day for several days following the release each month. the BEA also tracks other economic indicators on a current basis. For information on:

1. Leading indicators, call 202-898-2450.
2. Gross national product, call 202-898-2451.
3. Personal income and outlays, call 202-898-2452.
4. Balance of trade payments, call 202-898-2453.

The BEA is also a good source for historical economic information. Monthly or quarterly business statistics for the previous five years and annual data dating back to 1961 are available. Publications of the Bureau of Economic Analysis are available from the U.S. Government Printing Office.

Federal Reserve System

The Board of Governors of the Federal Reserve System prepares the *Federal Reserve Bulletin* (the *Bulletin*), a monthly publication that contains national financial and business statistics. The *Bulletin* also features articles on selected topics in economics and domestic and international business activity. Each issue contains approximately 90 pages of statistics on monetary reserves, financial markets, interest rates, housing, and mortgages, as well as international monetary statistics. For each set of statistics, three years of annual historical data are usually presented, and data for the current year are provided in monthly or quarterly units. The statistics that appear each month are collected annually in the *Annual Statistical Digest.* In addition to statistics, each issue of the *Bulletin* contains articles on monetary policy. The *Bulletin* devotes one issue in the first quarter of each year to an analysis of the previous year's economic conditions.

The Federal Reserve also releases weekly statistics on banking activity, capital market developments, interest rates, and foreign exchange. In addition, the Board of Governors periodically publishes Staff Studies, a series of analytical papers on a wide range of subjects related to banking practices and monetary policy.

Each of the 12 Federal Reserve Banks (FRBs) also issues publications, some of which contain national economic statistics. The Federal Reserve Bank of St. Louis publishes *National Economic Trends,* which tracks national employment data, consumer and producer price indexes, industrial production, personal income, retail sales, and GNP. Also available from FRB St. Louis is *U.S. Financial Data,* a compilation of statistics on the money supply, commercial paper and business loans, interest rates, and securities yields. Both of these publications, which can be ordered from FRB St. Louis, are excellent additions to an appraiser's library.

U.S. Council of Economic Advisors

The Council of Economic Advisors publishes the *Economic Report of the President* (the *Economic Report*) each year. The *Economic Report* contains more than 100 pages of economic statistics in such areas as personal income, gross national product, corporate profits by industry, bond yields, and interest rates. The majority of the *Economic Report* is devoted to a lengthy discussion of the state of the economy. The *Economic Report of the President* is available from the U.S. Government Printing Office.

Also available from the Council of Economic Advisors is the monthly summary publication *Economic Indicators.* It contains charts and tables on national output, income, spending, employment, wages, credit, and international statistics.

U.S. Bureau of the Census

The Bureau of the Census publishes the *Statistical Abstract of the United States* (the *Abstract*) annually. The *Abstract* is a summary of social, political, and economic statistics from government and private sources. Housing, employment, and income are only three of the many areas covered by this extensive listing. The *Abstract* is available from the U.S. Government Printing Office.

U.S. Department of Labor

The *Monthly Labor Review* provides articles and statistics on employment, productivity, wages, earnings, prices, wage settlements, and work stoppages. It contains research summaries, book reviews, and 48 tables of current labor statistics. The *Monthly Labor Review* is available on a subscription basis from the U.S. Government Printing Office.

Other Sources of Data on the National Economy

Blue Chip Economic Indicators and *Blue Chip Financial Forecasts* are published monthly by Capitol Publications. *Blue Chip Economic Indicators* contains economic forecasts for 15 variables, including GNP, industrial production, corporate profits, and housing starts. The *Blue Chip Financial Forecasts* focuses on timely interest rate forecasts and analysis.

The Conference Board, a business information service, conducts extensive examinations of management, economic, social, and political trends and issues. Among the publications of the Conference Board are *Across the Board,* a monthly business magazine; *Business Executives' Expectations,* a quarterly poll of CEOs' views on current and prospective economic conditions; and *Economic Road Maps,* a graphic presentation of general economic information. The Conference Board also releases the *Survey of Financial Indicators* twice a year.

The "Selection and Opinion" section of the *Value Line Investment Survey* tracks a variety of price indexes, market measures, and interest rates. Each week, the "Selection and Opinion" section contains an article on the economy and the stock market.

Ibbotson Associates is the authoritative source of historical returns on U.S. and international capital markets. *Stocks, Bonds, Bills and Inflation: 1991 Yearbook* annually provides data on monthly and annual returns on the most important capital asset classes. *Quarterly and Monthly Market Reports* tracks trends in capital markets and includes consensus market forecasts.

The Standard and Poor's Corporation publishes several periodical services that contain information on the national economy. The *Statistical Service* contains monthly data for many economic indicators, and *Trends and Projections* is an excellent source for economic forecasts. The *Outlook* focuses on the stock market and is a source for stock and bond market forecasts.

Congressional Information Services produces a variety of indexes to government publications and congressional activities. The *American Statistics Index,* which includes a separately bound abstracts section, is a compilation of thousands of government statistics. The data are indexed by subject, name, publication title, and agency report number, and the abstracts provide bibliographic data and a description of the subject matter. The *Statistical Reference Index* identifies statistics contained in publications in more than 1,000 sources, including associations, businesses, commercial publishers, state government agencies, and universities.

Wilson & Poole Economics publishes the *Complete Economic and Demographic Data Source.* Although primarily a source of state and local information, this publication also provides 81 statistics on the U.S. economy. Both historical and projected information are included. Historical information is obtained from the U.S. Department of Commerce, and Wilson & Poole makes projections based on this data.

Articles appearing in the various business periodicals are a good source for analysis of economic events. *Business Week* and *Fortune* include capsule articles or forecasts on segments of the economy in every issue. *The Wall Street Journal* regularly publishes statistics on the financial markets and articles on the economy. *Forbes, Business Month, The Economist, Nation's Business,* and *Barron's* are additional sources for articles on the economy. Most business periodicals focus heavily on the economy at the end of each year.

Two indexes that are helpful in locating articles on the economy in the major business publications are the *Business Periodical Index* and *The Wall Street Journal/Barron's Index.* Most larger libraries also have the *Business Index* on microfilm and the electronic index *ABI/Inform.* Predicast's *F&S Index* contains a special section that identifies articles on national economic issues.

Numerous financial institutions collect and publish economic statistics and distribute them free. Two examples are Manufacturers Hanover's weekly newsletter *Financial Digest,* which tracks major economic statistics and contains an article on current economic issues, and Dominion Bankshares' *Economic Update,* a monthly publication that covers 28 key economic indicators.

On-line Data Sources for National Economic Information

The U.S. Department of Commerce operates *The Economic Bulletin Board,* an on-line database of current economic information. *The Economic Bulletin Board* allows access to the latest releases from the Bureau of Economic Analysis, the Bureau of the Census, the Bureau of Labor Statistics, and other federal agencies. It is one of the least expensive databases available.

EconBase, a database available from the WEFA Group, specializes in time series, that is, sets of data corresponding to chronological periods of time. The complete database contains more than 4 million time series covering more than 400 industry sectors in 276 metropolitan areas and 40 nations. Subject areas covered include business conditions, finance, manufacturing, and demographics. This database is also accessible through Dialog.

Many of the aforementioned business periodicals are also indexed on-line. Several databases available through Dialog—including *ABI/Inform* and *PTS Prompt*—index, and sometimes provide the full text of, articles on the national economy.

Other on-line sources that contain information on the national economy are *Donnelley Demographics,* which provides census data and projections for the United States, and *The Information Bank,* an extensive collection of current-affairs abstracts. *Donnelley Demographics* can be accessed through Dialog, and *The Information Bank* is available from the New York Times Information Service.

The *Dow Jones News* database from Dow Jones News Retrieval provides access to late-breaking stories on a variety of financial topics. Full-text articles filed by reporters and destined for *The Wall Street Journal* and *Barron's* are accessible here before the publications are available to the public.

Sources of Regional and Local Economic Information

When valuing community banks, the condition of the local economy may be as relevant as (or more so than) the national outlook. The majority of financial institutions do not have interstate operations, and most do not have branches outside the county or parish where they are headquartered. Several of the sources of national economic data mentioned above also contain information on a regional or local level.

U.S. Government Publications and Data Sources

The U.S. Department of Commerce, Bureau of Economic Analysis (BEA), has a regional economics program that provides estimates, analyses, and projections by region, state, metropolitan statistical area, and county or parish. Regional Reports are released approximately six times a year with summary estimates of state personal income. This information is available on-line on the *Economic Bulletin Board.* Current quarterly state personal-income estimates are reported in the January, April, July, and October issues of the *Survey of Current Business.*

The BEA prepares long-term projections of personal income, employment, and earnings by industry. These projections are prepared every five years for all states and metropolitan statistical areas. The Bureau also tracks gross state product for each state.

The U.S. Bureau of the Census makes available the *City and County Databook* and the *State and Metropolitan Area Databook,* which contain statistics on housing, population, construction activity, and many other economic indicators.

Each of the Federal Reserve Banks compiles economic information for its district. These statistics are often made available in each district's *Economic Review.* The content of the *Economic Review* varies from district to district, but it usually contains one or more articles on an economic issue affecting that region of the country. Some districts devote additional publications to the regional economy, for example, the *Agricultural Letter,* published by the Chicago Federal Reserve Bank, and the *Quarterly Regional Economic Report,* published by the Philadelphia Federal Reserve Bank.

Other Sources of Data on Local and Regional Economies

The Economic and Business Environment Program of the Conference Board publishes a quarterly regional analysis titled *Regional Economies and Markets,* which looks at groups of states in terms of manufacturing production, employment, and income.

The Complete Economic and Demographic Data Source, published by Wilson & Poole Economics, is an excellent source for statistical profiles of metropolitan areas, counties and parishes, and states. Historical as well as projected data are included in this source. Other publications from Wilson & Poole include annual State Profiles and MSA Profiles, which currently include statistical economic data and forecasts through the year 2010.

For larger metropolitan areas, *Metro Insights,* a publication of Data Resources (a unit of Standard and Poor's), provides 10–15 pages of narrative economic discussion well-supported with statistics. This source contains information on the 100 largest metropolitan areas in the United

States. Each area profile includes an economic profile, forecasts for growth, infrastructure evaluation, and construction and demographic data.

Sales and Marketing Management publishes the *Annual Survey of Buying Power.* This publication breaks down demographic and income data by state, metropolitan area, and county or parish. Retail sales data are presented for store groups and merchandise lines. Also included are population and retail sales forecasts for local areas.

Donnelley Demographics, an on-line database service accessed through Dialog, contains demographic statistics for thousands of communities across the United States. This database includes census data, current-year estimates, and five-year projections for all U.S. states, counties or parishes, cities, and ZIP codes, as well as for the United States as a whole.

State and Local Sources of Economic Information

Not surprisingly, the most fruitful sources of local economic data are not the national sources discussed so far, but contacts at the state and local levels. Every state has a department devoted to commerce and economic development. These departments are usually organized to help new businesses and encourage companies to locate in their states, so they compile and distribute a great deal of useful economic data.

Most state departments of economic development publish community profiles for counties or parishes and for local communities. These profiles can be brief summaries of standard demographic and economic data or much longer, in-depth surveys of each segment of the local economy.

Another state agency that provides helpful local information is each state's department of economic security. These departments compile unemployment and labor force statistics by metropolitan area and by county or parish. These statistics are usually published monthly and are available free. Each state's agency can be located in the *National Directory of State Agencies,* published by Cambridge Information Group Directories, or found in the "blue pages" of the phone directory of each state's capital city.

The business schools of many large universities compile and publish local and regional economic information. For example, the College of Business Administration of the University of South Carolina (Columbia) publishes *Business and Economic Review,* a quarterly publication that contains articles on aspects of the regional and national economy, as well as business management issues and regional statistics. The Bureau of Business and Economic Research of Memphis State University publishes *The Memphis Economy,* which tracks Memphis business indicators and calculates a local-business-activity coincident index. Similar publications are available from universities in other regions of the country.

Local Chambers of Commerce are usually the best source for current local demographic and economic data. Many larger Chambers of Commerce have specialized research and/or publication departments that compile and distribute publications about the local economy. For example, the Greater Houston Partnership Chamber of Commerce produces 33 publications (not including audiovisual materials) on the Houston area.

These publications range from a 12-page "Houston Economic Summary" to a 40-page, full-color portrait of Houston titled "Houston: Gateway to the Future."

Chamber of Commerce statistics are usually compiled from state or U.S. Department of Commerce data and are verifiable. However, a local Chamber of Commerce can be such a cheerleader for the community that unfavorable economic information can be glossed over or buried in the back of a report. Analysts must therefore use data obtained from local chambers with some caution.

Local business journals and the business section of local newspapers can be good sources of independent economic information. And reference librarians at most newspaper libraries will field requests from the public for articles on specific topics. In addition, a phone interview with the business editor of a local newspaper or journal can often reveal important information on economic issues and trends that is not yet available in a published source. Other sources of local information include area realty associations, which usually track home construction and sales data, and city or county/parish governments, which release information on building permits issued.

Sources of Banking Industry Information

Industry information is a required part of any bank valuation report, and an understanding of the forces at work in the banking industry is vital to a well-researched report. Many banking industry publications are devoted to bank management or marketing and provide information that is more helpful to bankers than to appraisers of financial institutions. The sources included here focus on the general issues that affect the financial institutions industry.

U.S. Government Publications and Data Sources

In addition to articles on the national economy and monetary policy discussed above, the *Federal Reserve Bulletin,* published by the Board of Governors of the Federal Reserve System, contains articles on banking developments and trends. Also, many of the Federal Reserve Banks produce publications that track the banking industry in their regions, such as *Pieces of Eight,* from the Eighth District Federal Reserve Bank in St. Louis.

The most expedient way to locate articles on banking published by the Federal Reserve System is to consult *Fed in Print,* a cumulative index to all publications of the Federal Reserve Research Departments. This index consists of subject entries referring to periodical articles, working papers, annual reports, conference proceedings, and monographs. *Fed in Print* is published twice a year and is available free from the Federal Reserve Bank of Philadelphia.

The Federal Deposit Insurance Corporation publishes several banking publications that are available free. *FDIC Banking Review* is a periodical containing articles of interest to the banking community. *FDIC Quarterly Banking Profile* is a statistical release of aggregate industry financial data combined with a brief discussion focusing on current developments and trends. *Statistics on Banking* contains year-end statistical data on the banking industry, including data on the number of banks and branches and aggregate information on the assets, income, and liabilities of insured banks.

Also available from the FDIC is *Data Book: Operating Banks and Branches Summary of Deposits in All Commercial and Mutual Savings Banks*. This publication compiles survey results by geographic area in a series of 19 volumes. Each volume includes a national summary containing tables on bank structure and tabulations by class and size of bank, as well as state, metropolitan area, and county/parish tabulations.

Other regulatory agencies publish financial institution data as well. The Office of Thrift Supervision (OTS) produces the *Office of Thrift Supervision Journal*, a quarterly discourse on matters currently affecting the thrift industry. Topics include home ownership, deposit insurance, capital adequacy, accounting, demographics, and economic trends. The Office of the Comptroller of the Currency publishes *Quarterly Journal*, which contains information of interest to the banking industry.

Banking Regulation Sources

Several government agencies have authority to regulate the financial institutions industry (see Chapter 5). Each agency issues regulations and compliance information. The best starting place for an overall look at the authority of the regulatory agencies is Title 12 of the *Code of Federal Regulations*. Title 12 is contained in six volumes (available from the U.S. Government Printing Office) that outline the major regulations each agency is charged with enforcing. The *Code* contains a vast amount of information, from how to charter a national bank to the specific forms required for financial disclosure.

The Office of the Comptroller of the Currency (OCC) produces two manuals, the *Comptroller's Manual for Corporate Activities* and the *Comptroller's Manual for National Banks*. These manuals make available in one place the OCC's policies and procedures for dealing with its interpretative rulings. The OCC also makes available bank examiners' handbooks, which present the policies and procedures for the examination of national banks and national bank trust departments. These manuals and handbooks are only available directly from the Office of the Comptroller of the Currency. They cannot be purchased through the U.S. Government Printing Office.

The Office of Thrift Supervision (OTS) makes available a variety of handbooks that address the major areas of concern to examiners and supervisors regarding compliance with OTS policies on capital adequacy, consumer protection laws, holding company operations, trust activities, and EDP systems. The OTS also periodically releases Thrift Bulletins on practices or events of concern to the thrift industry. These publications are available directly from the Office of Thrift Supervision.

The FDIC collects all its regulations and miscellaneous statutes into a two-volume, loose-leaf publication titled *FDIC Law, Regulations and*

Related Acts. FDIC publications are available from the Corporate Communications Office of the FDIC.

In addition to these government sources, several private companies and associations publish banking regulations.

Selected Banking Periodicals

The American Banker is a national daily banking newspaper covering news about banking developments and industry trends. Articles also appear on pending legislation, bank management issues, national monetary affairs, and other related topics. *The American Banker* also compiles banking statistics and regularly ranks financial institutions. From time to time, it publishes articles that focus on regional banking issues. This publication is available from American Banker–Bond Buyer, New York, and the full text is available on-line through Dialog. Annual statistics from *The American Banker* are compiled into the *American Banker Yearbook.*

Another financial institution newspaper is the weekly *National Mortgage News* (formerly *National Thrift News*). It focuses on national and regional real estate markets, secondary mortgage markets, thrift regulatory issues, and other savings and loan industry topics.

The *ABA Banking Journal* is published monthly by the American Bankers Association. Topics for articles include regulatory developments, community banking issues, and bank operations.

The U.S. League of Savings Institutions publishes the monthly magazine *Savings Institutions,* which features in-depth analyses of the major legislative, regulatory, economic, and technological developments and trends in the savings and loan industry.

United States Banker is another monthly magazine that features articles on issues and developments in the financial services industry.

Several regional banking magazines are published on a monthly or quarterly basis. These publications sometimes provide regional economic information for their readership, as well as articles on the banking industry in the various regions.

Most state banking associations also publish journals, which usually contain articles on regional economic and banking issues. They often profile community banks and their executives and may compile local or regional banking statistics.

Other Sources of Banking Industry Information

Financial institution trade associations compile and publish industry statistics and educational publications and provide various other support services to the industry. The major trade associations are the U.S. League of Savings Institutions and the American Bankers Association.

The U.S. League of Savings Institutions makes available a number of publications to both members and nonmembers. Of special note are the *Regulatory Report,* a monthly, in-depth analysis of current and proposed regulations, and *Savings Institutions Sourcebook,* which contains data on savings, mortgage lending, housing, institution operation, and federal agencies. A catalog listing their many periodicals, books, manuals, and software available can be ordered from the U.S. League of Savings Institutions. The American Bankers Association is a source for similar information on the banking industry.

Other general-interest business publications, such as *Barron's* and *The Wall Street Journal,* also publish articles on the banking industry from time to time. Refer to the national economic source section earlier in this chapter for indexes that track these articles. *Forbes* and *Business Week* both publish special annual issues that review industry groups. These issues always include a profile of the financial institutions industry.

An excellent, concise overview of the banking and S&L industry can be found in *Industry Surveys,* published by Standard and Poor's. This outlook, along with those of several dozen other industries, are updated semiannually. The "Rating and Reports" section of *Value Line* also contains a brief industry analysis of banking, but it is oriented toward larger, publicly traded financial institutions.

Sources of Comparative Bank Financial and Valuation Data

Call Reports

The federal government is a fount of financial data on financial institutions. Every national bank and state member or insured nonmember bank is required to file detailed Consolidated Reports of Condition and Income (also known as Call Reports) with the Federal Deposit Insurance Corporation or appropriate Federal Reserve Bank on a quarterly basis. Reports of Condition of Federal Reserve member banks and national banks (balance sheet only) must be published in the local newspaper where the bank is located.

Call Report data are available to the public through the Freedom of Information Act. A bank analyst can obtain Call Reports directly from client banks. There are also computerized services that allow access to Call Reports on-line or through diskette-based or CD/ROM products. These sources include *Lotus One Source,* which provides data developed by Sheshunoff Information Services, and BankSource, a product of Ferguson and Company. Hard-copy historical summary reports are also available from these sources.

Uniform Bank Performance Reports

The Federal Financial Institutions Examination Council developed the Uniform Bank Performance Report (UBPR) to show, in a convenient format, the impact of management decisions and economic conditions on a bank's performance and balance sheet position. A UBPR is produced each quarter for each commercial bank that is either a Federal Reserve member, is insured by the FDIC, or is supervised by the Office of the Comptroller of the Currency. The reports contain several years of data that are updated quarterly and restated to reflect revised Call Reports filed with the various regulatory agencies. The data used to compute the UBPR are primarily from each institution's Call Reports. Each UBPR also contains peer group information to permit an evaluation of the subject bank relative to other banks of similar size and operations.

Uniform Bank Performance Reports can be ordered from the Federal Financial Institutions Examination Council. Also available are nationwide peer group data and state average peer group data and a user's guide.

Holding Company Performance Reports

Holding Company Performance Reports, similar in format and content to the UBPR, are produced each quarter for each bank holding company supervised by the Federal Reserve Board. These reports are available to the bank analyst from client bank holding companies, or they may be ordered from the Publications Unit of the Federal Reserve System.

Thrift Financial Report

The Office of Thrift Supervision (OTS) requires that thrift institutions file a detailed statement of condition and income that is analogous to the Call Report required of banks. Thrift Financial Reports are filed quarterly with appropriate OTS District Offices. The information in the Thrift Financial Report is also public information. Copies are generally available to analysts from the individual institutions and through the computerized sources listed previously in the Call Reports section.

Other Sources

In addition to the Call Reports, UBPRs, and Thrift Financial Reports required for all financial institutions, publicly owned financial institutions release supplementary information in the form of annual reports to stockholders. Publicly traded financial institutions are covered in the financial press and by the larger investment banking firms.

Moody's Bank and Finance Manual, published by Moody's Investor Service, includes financial information on banks, savings and loan associations, trust companies, and federal credit agencies. Each company profile includes a brief financial history, officers and directors, comparative financial statements, and information on capital stock, dividends, and recent stock prices. Some general industry statistics are also included.

Value Line Investment Surveys (previously mentioned) also contain financial information on individual financial institutions, but only selected larger, widely traded institutions are included.

Standard and Poor's publishes *Security Owner's Stock Guide,* which provides price and earnings information for many public financial institutions on a monthly basis, and *The Daily Stock Price Record,* which provides historical stock prices for publicly traded financial institutions.

National and regional brokerage firms constantly research and publish information on publicly traded financial institutions. Many firms write in-depth analyses of individual institutions as well as discourses on the state of the industry. These publications are often available to banking analysts upon request.

Many bank consulting firms compile and sell financial information on individual institutions. Sheshunoff, SNL Securities, and Swords Associates are just three of the firms that follow the financial institutions market closely and publish financial and market data.

SNL Securities, which provides the most comprehensive array of banks and thrift information products available, offers a number of products and services of interest to the banking analyst. The *Quarterly Bank Digest* and *Quarterly Thrift Digest* contain financial, corporate and market information on publicly traded banks and thrifts. The *Monthly Market Report* and *Bank Securities Monthly* update the quarterly digests. Other specific publications are also available. SNL Securities also maintains databases for both banks and thrifts tracking current and historical GAAP information, current regulatory information and other related financial information.

Merger and Acquisition Information

All Federal Reserve member banks are required to submit applications to effect any change in control to their respective District Federal Reserve Banks. Each district bank publishes a list of those applications in bulletin form. These Application Bulletins are available on a subscription basis from each District Federal Reserve Bank. No financial information is released in these publications. However, financial information is available upon request to review specific acquisition files at each district bank.

Publicly traded financial institutions disclose merger information to their stockholders in annual reports and also in press releases at the time of the announcement.

SNL Securities publishes for thrifts the *Bank Securities Monthly* and the *Monthly Market Report,* which, in addition to financial and market information, include merger data. SNL Securities also publishes a newsletter and maintains a database of bank mergers and acquisitions. *Bank Mergers & Acquisitions* is a newsletter devoted to reporting, analyzing, and interpreting consolidation of the banking industry. *Bank M&A DataSource* tracks private transactions as well as RTC and FDIC deals, branch sales and merger conversions. Other investor-oriented publications, such as *Mergers and Acquisitions* magazine and *MergerStat Review,* track mergers in financial institutions and other industries.

The financial press, especially *The American Banker* and *The Wall Street Journal,* report on mergers nationwide. Predicast's *F&S Index of Corporate Change* indexes articles that have appeared in the financial press about mergers in all industries.

Merger and acquisition information can also be found in on-line databases. Dialog provides access to several databases that contain information on financial institution mergers. Among them are *M&A Filings, IDD M&A Transactions, Businesswire, Moody's Corporate News,* and *PTS Prompt.*

The data sources listed here can be used to create an in-house database that tracks just the information needed. For instance, the database can take the form of market statistics for a group of financial institutions, with merger information compiled to track pricing of acquisitions in a specific geographic area.

Exhibit 7-1

Sources of Information

Sources of National Economic Data and Financial Information

Superintendent of Documents
U.S. Government Printing Office
Washington, DC 20402
(202) 783-3238

U.S. Department of Commerce
Bureau of Economic Analysis
Washington, DC 20230
(202) 523-0777

Board of Governors of the Federal Reserve
  System
Publications Services, MS-138
Washington, DC 20551
(202) 452-3244; (202) 452-3000
(202) 453-3206 for recorded highlights of Fed
  activity

Council of Economic Advisors
Old Executive Office Building
17th St. and Pennsylvania Ave., N.W.
Washington, DC 20500
(202) 395-5034

Capitol Publications
1101 King St., Suite 444
Alexandria, VA 22314
(703) 683-4100

The Conference Board
845 Third Ave.
New York, NY 10022
(212) 759-0900

Value Line, Inc.
711 Third Ave.
New York, NY 10017
(800) 634-3583

Ibbotson Associates
P.O. Box 97837
Chicago, IL 60678-7837
(312) 263-3435

Standard and Poor's Corporation
25 Broadway
New York, NY 10004
(212) 208-8786

Congressional Information Service
4520 East-West Highway, Suite 800
Bethesda, MD 20814-3389
(800) 638-8380

Wilson and Poole Economics, Inc.
1794 Columbia Road, N.W.
Washington, DC 20009
(202) 332-7111

Manufacturer's Hanover Financial Digest
Economics Department, 17th Floor
270 Park Ave.
New York, NY 10017
(212) 270-6000

Dominion Bankshares Corporation Financial
  Group
P.O. Box 13327
Roanoke, VA 24040
(703) 563-7718

On-line Sources of Information

U.S. Department of Commerce
Office of Business Analysis and Economic
  Affairs
"Electronic Bulletin Board"
(202) 377-1986

Dialog Information Services, Inc.
3460 Hillview Ave.
Palo Alto, CA 94304
(800) 334-2564

Local Economic Data

Metro Insights
Data Resources
Attn: F. Orfino
24 Hartwell Ave.
Lexington, MA 02173-9966
(800) 541-9914; (617) 860-6370 in Mass.

Sales and Marketing Management Magazine/
  Annual Survey of Buying Power
Bill Communications, Inc.
633 Third Ave.
New York, NY 10017
(212) 986-4800

Banking Industry Sources

Federal Deposit Insurance Corporation
Office of Corporate Communications
550 17th St., N.W.
Washington, DC 20429-9990
(800) 424-5101; (202) 393-8400

Office of Thrift Supervision
1700 G St., N.W.
Washington, DC 20552
(202) 906-6000

Office of the Comptroller of the Currency
490 L'Enfant Plaza E, S.W.
Washington, DC 20219
(202) 447-1800

American Banker
One State St. Plaza
New York, NY 10004
(212) 943-6700

National Mortgage News
212 West 35th St., 13th Floor
New York, NY 10001
(212) 563-4008

ABA Banking Journal
P.O. Box 466, Village Station
New York, NY 10014-9998
(212) 620-7200

United States Banker
Greenwich Office Park
10 Valley Dr.
Greenwich, CT 06831
(203) 869-8200

U.S. League of Savings Institutions
111 East Wacker Dr.
Chicago, IL 60601
(312) 644-3100

Exhibit 7-1 (*continued*)

American Bankers Association
1120 Connecticut Ave., N.W.
Washington, DC 20036
(202) 663-5000

Sheshunoff Information Services
One Texas Center
505 Barton Springs Road
Austin, TX 78704
(512) 472-2244

Ferguson & Company
Attn: Bonnie Miller
600 E. Las Colinas Blvd.
Irving, TX 75039
(800) 248-8277

Swords Associates
2 Bush Creek Blvd., Suite 100
Kansas City, MO 64112
(816) 753-7440

Federal Financial Institutions Examination
  Council
1776 G St., N.W., Suite 850-B
Washington, DC 20006
(800) 843-1669; (202) 357-0111

Moody's Investor Service
99 Church St.
New York, NY 10007
(212) 553-1677

SNL Securities L.P.
410 E. Main St.
Charlottesville, VA 22902
(201) 963-1000; (804) 977-1600

Federal Reserve Banks
Federal Reserve Bank of Atlanta
104 Marietta St. N.W.
Atlanta, GA 30303-2713
(404) 521-8500

Federal Reserve Bank of Boston
600 Atlantic Ave.
Boston, MA 02106
(617) 973-3000

Federal Reserve Bank of Chicago
P.O. Box 834
Chicago, IL 60690
(312) 322-5322

Federal Reserve Bank of Cleveland
Federal Reserve Bank Building
E. Sixth St. and Superior Ave.
Cleveland, OH 44114
(216) 579-2000

Federal Reserve Bank of Dallas
Station K
Dallas, TX 75222
(214) 651-6111

Federal Reserve Bank of Kansas City
Federal Reserve Station
Kansas City, MO 64198
(816) 881-2000

Federal Reserve Bank of Minneapolis
250 Marquette Ave.
Minneapolis, MN 55480
(612) 340-2345

Federal Reserve Bank of New York
Federal Reserve P.O. Station
New York, NY 10045
(212) 720-5000

Federal Reserve Bank of Philadelphia
Ten Independence Mall
Philadelphia, PA 19106-1574
(215) 574-6000

Federal Reserve Bank of Richmond
701 E. Byrd St.
Richmond, VA 23261
(804) 697-8000

Federal Reserve Bank of San Francisco
P.O. Box 7702
San Francisco, CA 94120
(415) 974-2000

Federal Reserve Bank of St. Louis
P.O. Box 442
St. Louis, MO 63166
(314) 444-8444

Part II

Bank/Bank Holding Company Financial Analysis

Chapter 8

Overview of a Banking Company

*"The time has come," the Walrus said, "to talk of many things: of shoes—
and ships—and sealing wax—of cabbages—and kings."*

Lewis Carroll

Conceptual Model of Bank Performance

Banking companies are financial intermediaries: They are in the business
of bringing savers and borrowers together. Banks take deposits from
savers and make loans to borrowers, the object being for a bank to earn
more interest income on its loans (and other interest-bearing assets) than
it pays out in interest expense on its deposits and other borrowings. Banks
also provide a number of services for which they collect fees: payment
processing via checking accounts, trust services, safety deposit boxes,
etc. The ultimate goal is for the sum of its interest and noninterest income to exceed the sum of its interest expense and overhead (salaries,
rent, and all other expenses) so that a bank can earn a net profit. The
interaction of a bank's balance sheet and its income statement is illustrated in Figure 8-1.

The success or failure of a banking organization is much more closely related to its financial structure than for commercial and industrial
companies. The type, maturity, and riskiness of loans and investments
relative to deposits and other funding sources are key elements in a bank's
ability to earn a net profit. Virtually all aspects of a successful or failing
bank can be linked directly to financial structure as revealed in its financial statements. With non-bank companies, the link between financial
structure and success is less clear, with such issues as marketing and
technological innovation playing a much greater role.

In the following four chapters, we will discuss the financial analysis
of banking institutions in detail. The remainder of Chapter 8 will focus
on defining and describing the components of a bank balance sheet.
Chapter 9 will focus on defining and describing the components of a bank
income statement. Chapter 10 will lay out the important analytical concepts used in bank financial analysis and will provide a framework for
developing an overall evaluation of a bank's financial structure. Chapter
11 will focus on the analysis of bank holding companies.

Balance Sheet Composition

The remainder of this chapter will review the presentation and composition of the typical bank balance sheet. To simplify the analysis, we will
focus on the balance sheet for the bank only and defer discussion of bank
holding companies, parent company balance sheets, and consolidated
balance sheets to a later chapter.

Peer group information is most comparable at the bank level because
the varying parent company capital structures are not present to muddy

Figure 8-1
Balance Sheet and Income Statement Interrelationships

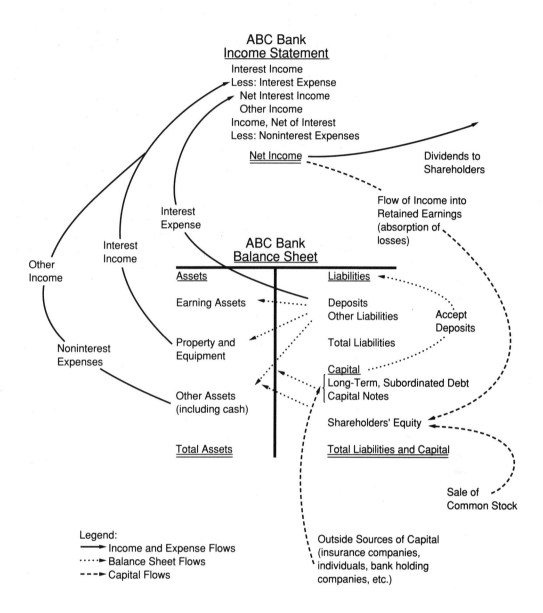

the analytical waters. In addition, actual operations of community banks tend to be concentrated at the bank level; community bank holding companies rarely are more than legal structures to allow additional debt and treasury transactions in the holding company's stock.[1]

We will begin our discussion by comparing a bank balance sheet to that of a typical commercial or industrial company.

---

[1]All nationally chartered banks and most state-chartered banks are prohibited from buying their own stock.

Bank Versus Commercial Company Balance Sheets

A typical balance sheet for a commercial or industrial company is presented in Exhibit 8-1. Exhibit 8-2 is a bank balance sheet following the format typically seen in bank annual reports and a condensed form of the balance sheet appearing in the Call Reports of Condition filed with the OCC or the FDIC. The two exhibits will be used as a basis for making general comparisons between banking institutions and other companies in order to discuss structural similarities and differences.

In many respects, a bank can be viewed as a company whose assets consist primarily of cash and equivalents (vault cash, deposits at other banks, and investment securities) and accounts receivable (loans and Fed Funds sold). On the liability side, a bank can be viewed as a company whose liabilities consist primarily of accounts payable (deposits).

A key difference in balance sheet presentation between banks and commercial companies lies in the absence on bank balance sheets of the distinction between current and long-term assets and liabilities. All loans are usually reported as a single sum with no distinction between loans due in less than one year and those maturing in more than one year.

Exhibit 8-1

Typical Balance Sheet of a Sample Commercial
or Industrial Company as of December 31, 1990

Assets		Amount ($)	Percent of Total Assets
Current assets			
Cash and equivalents		$ 1,700,330	5.0%
Trade accounts receivable		3,850,677	16.4
Inventories		6,088,851	26.0
Prepaid expenses and other		608,885	2.6
Total current assets		11,718,743	50.0
Property and equipment	$13,582,820		
Less accumulated depreciation	− 4,716,564		
Net fixed assets		8,866,256	37.9
Other assets		2,833,657	12.1
Total assets		$23,418,656	100.0%

Liabilities		Amount ($)	Percent of Total Assets
Current liabilities			
Notes payable		$ 796,234	3.4%
Current portion of long-term debt		1,053,840	4.5
Trade accounts payable		4,847,662	20.7
Accrued expenses and other		2,177,935	9.3
Total current liabilities		8,875,671	37.9
Long-term debt		6,486,968	27.7
Deferred taxes		351,280	1.5
Other liabilities		374,698	1.6
Total liabilities		16,088,617	68.7
Total stockholders' equity		7,330,039	31.3
Total liabilities and equity		$23,418,656	100.0%

Exhibit 8-2

Typical Balance Sheet of a Sample Bank as of December 31, 1990

Assets		Amount ($)	Comparisons with Sample Company
Cash and due from banks			Cash and
Non-interest-bearing	$ 14,482,000		marketable
Interest-bearing	3,298,000		investments:
		17,780,000	39% of assets
Federal funds sold		12,000,000	
Securities purchased under			
agreement to resell		7,000,000	
Investment securities (at book)		134,216,000	
Gross loans	250,358,000		Loans or
Less unearned income	– 3,360,000		accounts receivable:
Less reserve for loan losses	– 2,742,000		55% of assets
Net loans		244,256,000	All other assets:
Premises, furniture, and			6% of assets
equipment (net)		14,438,000	
Other real estate owned		3,194,000	
Accrued interest receivable		7,674,000	
Other assets		1,398,000	
Total assets		$441,956,000	

Liabilities		Amount ($)	Comparisons with Sample Company
Demand deposits	$ 46,300,000		Deposits or
Other deposits	337,824,000		accounts payable
Total deposits		384,124,000	87% of assets
Federal funds purchased		11,102,000	Other
Securities sold under			borrowings/
agreements to repurchase		10,000,000	liabilities
Notes payable		1,000,000	6% of assets
Other borrowings		1,000,000	
Accrued interest payable		3,996,000	
Other liabilities		1,884,000	
Total liabilities		413,106,000	
Total stockholders' equity		28,850,000	7% of assets
Total liabilities and equity		$441,956,000	

Securities and time deposit liabilities are treated similarly. Maturity breakdowns for various balance sheet items are typically given in the subsidiary schedules of annual reports and Call Reports of Condition.[2]

The bank in Exhibit 8-2 maintains about 39 percent of assets in cash and marketable securities (although a substantial portion of the securities portfolio is long-term). The company in Exhibit 8-1 held only about 5 percent of assets in cash. Loans, or accounts receivable, comprise about 55 percent of our sample bank's balance sheet, while only 16 percent of the commercial company's assets are in receivables. All other assets, including premises and equipment, total only 6 percent of the bank's assets

---

[2]Call Reports of Condition are regulatory reports filed with the Office of the Comptroller of the Currency by national banks and with the Federal Deposit Insurance Corporation by state-chartered banks. As noted in Chapter 7, detailed bank financial data are available to the public, as well as to the bank analyst under existing disclosure requirements of the Freedom of Information Act. Sources of financial data are detailed in Chapter 7.

versus 79 percent for the company (including inventories of 26 percent and net fixed assets of 38 percent).

Differences between banks and other business enterprises are equally striking on the liability side of the balance sheet. Trade payables comprise 20 percent of the sample company's total assets (or funding sources) compared with the sample bank, which is funded 87 percent by "payables," or deposits.

By most standards, the sample company is relatively highly leveraged, with equity funding only 31 percent of assets. Stated alternatively, each dollar of equity supports $3.19 of assets for this company. The sample bank has equity comprising less than 7 percent of assets, which means that each dollar of equity supports $15.32 of assets!

These comparisons clearly indicate that banks are structurally different from the commercial companies usually seen by business appraisers. We will focus on the unique analytical and valuation characteristics of banks over the next several chapters. These characteristics are of considerable importance to appraisers and bankers, as well as to the many other users of bank financial statements (for example, shareholders, regulators, and professionals dealing with financial institution clients).

Exhibit 8-3 is an analytical presentation of a bank balance sheet. The key change for an analytical presentation is the separation of earning (that is, interest-bearing assets) from nonearning assets. The format is used in the Uniform Bank Performance Report (UBPR), a compilation of Call Report data prepared by the Federal Financial Institutions Examination Council (FFIEC). UBPRs provide multiyear comparative balance sheets and income statements for the subject bank, along with key financial ratios for the bank and its peer group. The FFIEC forms its peer groups using three criteria: asset size, number of branches, and metropolitan versus nonmetropolitan location. Exhibit 8-3 also includes an important concept in analyzing a bank balance sheet: the displaying of the balance of each category as a percentage of total assets.

For a detailed presentation of a bank's financial statements in analytical format—including detailed schedules showing loan and deposit composition and other schedules providing other important perspectives—the reader is referred to Chapter 22 and the appraisal of Sample Bancshares, Inc.

Asset Composition

Earning Assets

Earning assets consist of a bank's interest- or dividend-producing assets. Such assets include loans and lease-financing receivables (net of unearned discounts and the allowance for loan losses), investment securities, Federal Funds sold, securities purchased under agreements to resell, and interest-bearing deposits placed with other banks.

At commercial banks, average earning assets usually range from 85 percent to 95 percent of average total assets. Ratios of average earning

Exhibit 8-3

Sample Bank Analytical Balance Sheet as of December 31, 1990

Assets	Amount ($)	Percent of Total Assets
Earning assets		
Interest-bearing bank deposits	$ 3,298,000	0.7%
Federal Funds sold	12,000,000	2.7
Securities purchased under agreements		0.0
to resell	7,000,000	1.6
Investment securities (at book)	134,216,000	30.4
Gross loans	250,358,000	56.6
Less unearned income	− 3,360,000	0.8
Less reserve for loan losses	− 2,742,000	0.6
Net loans	244,256,000	55.3
Total earning assets	400,770,000	90.7
Nonearning assets		
Cash and non-interest-bearing deposits	14,482,000	3.3
Premises, furniture, and equipment (net)	14,438,000	3.3
Other real estate owned	3,194,000	0.7
Accrued interest receivable	7,674,000	1.7
Other assets	1,398,000	0.3
Total assets	$441,956,000	100.0%

Liabilities	Amount ($)	Percent of Total Assets
Demand deposits	$ 46,300,000	10.5%
Other deposits	337,824,000	76.4
Total deposits	384,124,000	86.9
Federal Funds purchased	11,102,000	2.5
Securities sold under agreements		0.0
to repurchase	10,000,000	2.3
Notes payable	1,000,000	0.2
Other borrowings	1,000,000	0.2
Total acquired funds	407,226,000	92.1
Accrued interest payable	3,996,000	0.9
Other liabilities	1,884,000	0.4
Total liabilities	413,106,000	93.5
Total stockholders' equity	28,850,000	6.5
Total liabilities and equity	$441,956,000	100.0%

assets to average total assets for full fiscal years or on a year-to-date basis are provided in the Uniform Bank Performance Report for any subject bank and its peer group. This ratio can also be calculated using the quarterly average balance sheets given in Schedule RC-K of the Call Report. Daily average balance sheets are also frequently provided in the Reports 10-K and 10-Q of SEC reporting banks required to file financial disclosure documents with the Securities and Exchange Commission.[3]

Other things being equal, the higher the ratio of earning assets to total assets, the better the earning power of the bank will be. Because

[3]Generally, financial institutions with more than 300 shareholders are considered to be public. We refer to banks with 300 or more shareholders and thinly traded markets as quasi-public. Banks in this category, regardless of asset size, may be required to file their financial statements with the SEC (or meet similar disclosure requirements with the FDIC).

most banks derive a substantial portion of their pretax income from net interest income, it is desirable to have the highest possible level of earning assets. A discussion of each category of earning assets follows.

Loans

A key analytical concept is that, other things being equal, the higher the percentage of earning assets represented by net loans, the better. Lending usually provides banks with their best opportunity to earn the highest available yields for any given term to maturity (or repricing). In addition, because most banks lend on relatively short-term repricing schedules, *interest rate risk* tends to be minimized and yields tend to be maximized in lending relative to alternative investments, such as investment securities, which may have maturities ranging from several months to many years.[4]

Lending, however, generally does entail higher credit and liquidity risks than alternative investments. *Credit risk* is the risk that a loan will not be repaid according to the provisions of the loan document, resulting in an outright loss or a reduction in expected yield for the lender. *Liquidity risk* results from loans not being immediately marketable, such that a highly "loaned-up" bank might not be able to pay off maturing deposits with cash raised through the liquidation or maturity of assets.

There are three levels of calculating the balance of a bank's loan portfolio:

1. *Gross Loans:* the aggregate par amount of loans on the books, including unearned discount (also called *unearned income*). Unearned discount is the unamortized dollar amount of interest income on a loan. For example, consider a $5,000 consumer loan priced at 6 percent add-on interest for four years. Interest is $300 per year times four years, or $1,200. The initial accounting entries on the books of the lending bank are:

	Debit	Credit
Consumer loan	$6,200	
Cash		$5,000
Unearned income		$1,200

The unearned discount is a contra (reduction) to the loan account. As the bank receives payments on the loan over its life, interest will be accrued as income (by one of a variety of methods) and the unearned discount will be amortized, along with the "real" loan principal amount of $5,000.

In addition, if a bank sells loan participations to other banks, the portion of any loan "participated out" is deducted from gross loans. Normally, participations are sold without recourse, meaning that the purchasing institution accepts its pro rata share of the credit risk associated with the participation loan.

---

[4]See the discussion on interest rate risk in Chapter 10.

2. *Total Loans:* gross loans net of unearned income (unearned or unaccrued discount). Alternatively, total loans can be defined as the aggregate amortized book basis of a bank's loan portfolio.
3. *Net Loans:* total loans net of the bank's allowance for loan losses. Banks maintain valuation allowances on their loan portfolios as a reserve against potential credit losses. Reserves for loan losses (also called *allowances for loan losses*) generally range from 0.50 percent to 2.00 percent or more of total loans. A discussion of the important concept of loan loss reserve adequacy is presented in Chapter 10.

The total amount of loans on a bank's balance sheet tell only a part of the story. The appraiser needs to understand the composition of the loan portfolio in order to develop an opinion on the future stability of the institution's interest spreads and of the potential for credit risk in the loan portfolio.

Exhibit 8-4, a multiyear analysis of the composition of a bank's loan portfolio, provides the gross dollar amount of each major loan category. Exhibit 8-5 shows each category as a percentage of gross loans. This composition analysis is based on information as presented in the Uniform Bank Performance Report and on Schedule RC-C of the Call Report.

In and of itself, a loan composition analysis may not be very revealing from a valuation standpoint. Although the regulatory reporting requirements provide definitions for each category of loans, classifications do vary from bank to bank. For some banks, one category may represent high-yielding credits, and for another, low-yielding credits. Similarly, for some banks, loans placed in one category may contain above-average risk, while for others, loans in the same category may reflect below-average risk. Also, precise definitions for each category will vary from bank to bank.

The main purpose of a composition analysis is to provide a basis for discussing the character of the loan portfolio with management. The questions for the appraiser relate to the yields and credit risks that are concentrated in each loan type. The loan discussion should also focus on types of loan collateral accepted by the bank, amounts lent against the market value of collateral (loan-to-value ratios), required periodic loan payments versus the borrowers' periodic income (debt service coverage ratios), maximum amounts lent to single or related borrowers, industry concentrations, yields, and maturity/repricing opportunities.

Loans secured by real estate tend to fall into three major categories: construction and development loans, mortgages on 1- to 4-family residential properties, and other real estate mortgages. Construction loans can range from highly speculative loans to developers to well-secured loans on properties with obligated lessees and with commitments for permanent mortgages. Single-family mortgages can range from undercollateralized fixed-rate, second and third mortgages (subordinate liens) on rental properties to adjustable-rate, first liens on owner-occupied houses with low loan-to-value ratios. Other real estate loans generally include commercial property loans (including farmland) with varying interest rate features and degrees of credit risk.

Commercial and industrial loans may be unsecured or secured by equipment, inventories, receivables, corporate stock, or other assets. The

Exhibit 8-4

Sample Bank Loan Portfolio Composition ($ Thousands) as of December 31

Loan Category	1990	1989	1988	1987	1986	1985	Growth Rates 85–90	Growth Rates 89–90
Construction and development	$ 12,192	$ 7,016	$ 7,878	$ 6,038	$ 4,818	$ 3,754	26.6%	73.8%
1–4-family residential	71,840	58,606	43,576	39,446	34,784	26,020	22.5	22.6
Other real estate	68,734	70,306	65,202	57,110	55,608	38,114	12.5	– 2.2
Total real estate	152,766	135,928	116,656	102,594	95,210	67,888	17.6	12.4
Financial institution and bankers' acceptances	1,556	1,894	8,586	0	0	5,188	– 21.4	– 17.8
Agricultural	10,970	8,030	9,626	7,362	9,544	8,848	4.4	36.6
Commercial/industrial	39,710	30,382	22,538	19,258	33,262	33,954	3.2	30.7
Consumer	40,500	37,462	34,274	34,872	40,530	36,540	2.1	8.1
All other	4,856	12,048	13,722	10,940	6,408	10,028	– 13.5	– 59.7
Gross loans	250,358	225,744	205,402	175,026	184,954	162,446	9.0	10.9
Less: unearned income	– 3,360	– 3,144	– 2,860	– 3,412	– 4,380	– 4,476	– 5.6	n.m.*
Total loans net of unearned income	$246,998	$222,600	$202,542	$171,614	$180,574	$157,970	9.4%	11.0%
Total loans net of unearned income/Total assets	55.89%	53.53%	52.33%	48.40%	51.64%	50.02%		
peer group 9/89	58.10%	57.16%	55.19%	54.41%	54.63%	54.21%		
Loan-to-deposit ratio	64.30%	60.78%	59.29%	53.97%	57.99%	56.52%		

*n.m. = not meaningful

Exhibit 8-5

Sample Bank Loan Portfolio Composition as a Percentage of Gross Loans as of December 31

Loan Category	1990	1989	1988	1987	1986	1985	Peer Group 9/90
Construction and development	4.9%	3.1%	3.8%	3.4%	2.6%	2.3%	2.1%
1–4-family residential	28.7	26.0	21.2	22.5	18.8	16.0	28.8
Other real estate	27.5	31.1	31.7	32.6	30.1	23.5	18.2
Total real estate	61.0	60.2	56.8	58.6	51.5	41.8	49.1
Financial institution	0.6	0.8	4.2	0.0	0.0	3.2	0.1
Agricultural	4.4	3.6	4.7	4.2	5.2	5.4	4.1
Commercial/industrial	15.9	13.5	11.0	11.0	18.0	20.9	19.9
Consumer	16.2	16.6	16.7	19.9	21.9	22.5	21.6
All other	1.9	5.3	6.7	6.3	3.5	6.2	5.2
Gross loans	100.0%	100.0%	100.0%	100.0%	100.0%	100.0%	100.0%

SOURCE: Call Reports and Uniform Bank Performance Reports

borrowers may be established businesses or start-up enterprises that need to finance the purchase of fixed assets or that need working capital. Bankers' acceptances (acceptances or BAs) are also usually classified as commercial loans. Acceptances are short-term loans collateralized by readily marketable merchandise and are used to finance international trade. Acceptances are created and guaranteed primarily by money centers and large regional banks and are sold to investors in the secondary market. Acceptances are highly liquid and are considered to entail negligible risk to investors.

Agricultural loans are generally secured by crops or farm equipment, and the borrower's existing debt load and the profitability of his operations are significant in determining the credit quality of the loan. Consumer loans include unsecured "signature" loans and credit card receivables; loans secured by time deposits, automobiles, boats, household appliances, or furniture; and government-guaranteed student loans.

In addition to BAs, banks also purchase loans and pieces of loans called *loan participations* (or participations) from other banks and other sources. Unlike BAs, purchased loans and participations are not of uniformly high quality, nor are they highly liquid. If a bank purchases participations from other banks, or consumer loans (dealer paper) from automobile and other dealers, it is important to discuss such arrangements with management. A large portfolio of loans originated by others (particularly institutions that are out of territory, or far away) may be a red flag indicating the potential for rising credit losses in the future.

Given the diversity of loans falling into each category, it is of primary importance to develop an understanding of the overall character of the subject bank's portfolio. There are several objective means of developing a view of the credit quality of the subject bank's loan portfolio. Exhibit 8-6 is an example of a multiyear reconciliation of a bank's loan loss reserve.

Exhibit 8-6

Sample Bank Multiyear Reconciliation of the Reserve for Loan Losses ($ Thousands)

Loan Loss Reserve Reconciliation	1990	1989	1988	1987	1986	1985
Beginning balance	$2,822	$2,538	$2,752	$1,789	$2,034	$2,004
− Net charge-offs						
Gross loan losses	816	1,088	1,228	3,568	2,446	2,418
+ Recoveries	360	658	338	966	460	546
+/− Other adjustments	0	0	0	0	0	0
= Net charge-offs	456	430	890	2,602	1,986	1,872
+ Provision for loan losses	376	714	676	1,776	3,532	1,902
= Ending reserve balance	2,742	2,822	2,538	963	3,580	2,034
Nonaccrual loans balance	$ 888	$1,428	$1,074	$2,364	$2,468	$1,376
Ending reserve/loans (%)*						
Bank	1.11%	1.27%	1.25%	1.60%	1.98%	1.29%
Peer group 9/90	1.35%	1.32%	1.32%	1.26%	1.17%	1.10%
Net losses/average loans (%)*						
Bank	0.19%	0.20%	0.48%	1.48%	1.17%	1.24%
Peer group 9/90	0.33%	0.40%	0.58%	0.77%	0.72%	0.53%
Provision/average loans (%)*						
Bank	0.16%	0.34%	0.36%	1.01%	2.09%	1.26%
Peer group 9/90	0.40%	0.47%	0.67%	0.90%	0.85%	0.62%
Ending reserve/nonaccrual loans (×)						
Bank	3.09	1.98	2.36	0.41	1.45	1.48
Peer group 9/90	2.69	2.84	2.23	2.12	1.69	2.07
Ending reserve/other real estate (×)						
Bank	0.86	1.64	1.14	0.90	0.87	0.75
Peer group 9/90	3.21	2.64	2.12	2.13	2.38	2.31

*Net of unearned income
Partial-year ratios annualized

SOURCE: Call Reports and Uniform Bank Performance Reports

Gross loan losses, or charge-offs, represent the portion of a loan that management has determined to be uncollectible within the forseeable future. The book value of the loan (or the portion of the loan) is thus written down to management's estimate of that portion that is collectible, and the amount of the loss is deducted from the allowance for loan losses.

Recoveries represent previously charged-off loans that are subsequently repaid in full or in part. Low recoveries (as a percentage of loans previously charged off) may be an indication that management is not working aggressively in this area or that loan charge-offs are delayed until after there is any hope of recovery. Alternatively, and positively, the area could be one to focus on for future earnings improvement.

High net loan losses (charge-offs minus recoveries) are a telltale sign of credit quality problems. A ratio of net losses to average loans exceeding the peer group average by more than a moderate amount is clear evidence of potential credit problems, which may have resulted from overly aggressive lending policies or downturns in the bank's area economy or in the industries in which the bank has concentrated its lending. The bank appraiser should therefore discuss with management the degree of geographic and industry diversification in the loan portfolio.

Another financial indicator of credit risk is the level of nonaccrual (nonperforming) loans. Generally, when a loan is more than 90 days past due, management must stop reflecting its accrual of interest in the bank's income statements. Some banks use a shorter "trigger" to place loans on nonaccrual status as a means of organizational discipline. Generally, nonaccrual status immediately precedes the charge-off of all or part of a credit. Analysis of trends in nonaccrual loans is a key to understanding a bank's current and near-term credit situation.

Investment Securities

Investment securities are essentially loans for which a legal structure has been created to permit active trading among investors. Exhibit 8-7 is derived from Schedule RC-B of the Call Report. Similar schedules are common in the notes to audited financial statements.

Banks maintain detailed listings of their investment portfolios, which are generally updated on a monthly basis (although sometimes quarterly). The portfolio listings typically provide, by major category of security and for each individual security held:

1. Historical cost basis, including accumulated amortization of purchase premiums or accretion of purchase discounts. This is the "book value" of each security and, in total, for the portfolio.
2. Current market pricing for each security, by category of security and for the entire portfolio.
3. Maturity of each security. Weighted average maturities are usually calculated by type of security and for the portfolio.
4. Yield to maturity for each security, by type of security and for the portfolio.
5. Security ratings by recognized rating agencies, or the indication that individual bonds are not rated by any agency.

Exhibit 8-7

Sample Bank Investment Portfolio Composition ($ Thousands) as of December 31, 1990

Type of Security	Book Value	Market Value
U.S. Treasury Securities	$ 39,644	$ 39,712
U.S. Government Agency Obligations		
Guaranteed Mortgage-Backed Securities	4,828	4,688
Other Securities	63,822	63,740
Obligations of States and Political Subdivisions		
Taxable Securities	1,002	1,002
Tax-Free Securities	14,042	13,486
Other Domestic Debt Securities		
Privately Issued Mortgage-Backed Securities	0	0
All Other Domestic Debt Securities	10,496	10,298
Foreign Debt Securities	0	0
Equity Securities		
Marketable Equity Securities		
Investments in Mutual Funds	1,000	850
Other Marketable Equity Securities	0	0
Less Net Unrealized Loss on Marketable Equity Securities	(150)	n.m.*
Other Equity Securities (including Federal Reserve Stock)	382	382
Total	$135,066	$134,158

*n.m. = not meaningful

The bank appraiser should obtain and review this statement as part of the due diligence process. Management's discussion of investment portfolio positioning and strategy can be important to an overall understanding of a bank's liquidity and earning power.

Typical bank investments include:

1. *U.S. Treasury Bills, Notes, and Bonds.* U.S. Treasury securities (Treasuries) are direct obligations of the government of the United States and are considered to be of the highest credit quality. *Treasury bills* pay no coupon interest and have original maturities of one year or less. They provide a return to investors by being issued at a discount to face value. *Treasury notes* have original maturities of one to 10 years, are issued at par value, and pay semiannual interest. *Treasury bonds* are identical to notes, except they have original maturities exceeding 10 years.

    Zero coupon Treasury securities ("zeros") are notes and bonds whose coupons and principal have been separated. Long-term zeros, or "strips," are subject to extreme price volatility as market interest rates change.

2. *U.S. Government Agency Securities.* Agency securities are the debt of government-sponsored corporations, such as the Federal Farm Credit Banks, the Student Loan Marketing Association (SLMA, or Sallie Mae), the Federal Home Loan Banks, the Federal Home Loan Mortgage Corporation (FHLMC, or Freddie Mac), the Federal National Mortgage Association (FNMA, or Fannie Mae), and the Government National Mortgage Association (GNMA, or Ginnie Mae).

    Except for GNMA mortgage pass-through securities, which are backed by the full faith and credit of the U.S. Treasury, agency securities are not obligations of the U.S. government. At best, some of the agencies have the right to borrow directly from the Treasury in a crisis. Nevertheless, there is a perceived moral obligation on the part of Congress and the Treasury to back the debt of government-sponsored corporations, so their securities usually trade at very narrow spreads (premiums in yield) over Treasuries of similar maturity.

Agency securities fall into two major categories: (1) traditional notes and bonds paying semiannual interest and principal at maturity, and (2) mortgage-backed securities (MBS). GNMA, FNMA, and FHLMC all guarantee timely payment of principal and interest from pools of residential mortgages that have been packaged into freely tradable securities. Monthly principal and interest payments are passed through to MBS investors. Mortgage pass-through securities combine the cash flow characteristics of direct mortgage lending with credit guarantees and the ready marketability of other government agency securities.

In addition to guaranteeing pass-through securities, FNMA and FHLMC have issued collateralized mortgage obligations (CMOs) and real estate mortgage investment conduits (REMICs). These securities break up the cash flows from a mortgage pool into several classes with differing maturities. The cash flows of a pool of 30-year, fixed-rate mortgages can support a REMIC with multiple classes of short and long maturities and varying interest rates, thus appealing to a wide variety of investors with different objectives. Banks have frequently purchased the shorter-maturity classes, or "tranches," of CMOs and REMICs, while insurance companies and pension funds have been major buyers of the longer-maturity classes.

FNMA and FHLMC have also issued interest only (I/O) and principal only (P/O) mortgage-backed securities. As the names imply, these securities are mortgage pools whose streams of principal and interest payments have been separated. I/O's and P/O's are subject to substantial price volatility based on changing market yields and unexpected mortgage prepayment experience.

Investment portfolios weighted heavily toward zero coupon bonds, strips, or I/O and P/O securities are subject to greater than normal price fluctuations as market conditions change.

3. *Municipal securities:* Municipal securities (Municipals) are obligations of states, counties, cities, and other political subdivisions. They generally pay interest semiannually and pay principal at maturity; however, zero coupon issues are not uncommon. Municipals fall into two broad categories: general obligation bonds (GOs) and revenue bonds. As the name implies, GOs are direct obligations of the issuer, and the issuer is unconditionally responsible for repayment of principal and interest. Repayment of revenue bonds is derived from the revenues generated by the public project financed by the particular issue. Holders of revenue bonds generally do not have recourse against the general taxing authority of the issuer in the event the project fails to generate adequate revenues to repay the bonds. The credit quality and liquidity of municipal issues can vary widely.

Prior to the Tax Reform Act of 1986, interest on municipal bonds was nearly always exempt from federal income taxes. After 1986, rules changed and new issues deemed by the IRS to be for an essentially private purpose (e.g., public financing of industrial plants) can be denied tax-exempt status. As a result, some municipalities have been issuing taxable municipal securities.

Another effect of the 1986 Tax Reform Act has been to limit the attractiveness of owning tax-free municipal securities. Banks are now denied the deduction of the interest expense ("cost of carry") attributable to funding an investment in any large issue of municipal securities (acquired after 1986), thus offsetting the tax benefit of the tax-free interest income. Banks retain the right to deduct the cost of carry related to new investments in bonds issued by municipalities that issue less than $10 million per year in tax-free securities.

4. *Corporate securities.* The typical community bank is usually not a significant investor in securities issued by commercial and industrial corporations, including short-term commercial paper, notes, and debentures. Notes issued by regional and money center bank holding companies have been more common community bank (or bank holding company) investments. Regulators have tended to criticize investments in corporate securities rated below BBB by Standard and Poor's or Baa by Moody's. So-called private-label CMOs and REMICs—most commonly collateralized by GNMA, FNMA, or FHLMC pass-through securities, but issued by a financing subsidiary of an investment banker or mortgage banker—are often seen in the portfolios of community banks.

5. *Marketable equity securities.* Shares of common or preferred stock and shares of mutual funds are called marketable equity securities. Unlike fixed-income securities, which are carried on the balance sheet at amortized cost, equity securities must be carried at the lower of cost or current market value. Banks are required to mark (i.e., write down) their equity securities to market periodically. If the current market value of an equity security is less than its carrying value (i.e., the bank has an unrealized loss in the investment), the difference is charged to retained earnings and stockholders' equity is reduced accordingly. The mark-to-market of marketable equity securities does not affect current period earnings.

Numerous banks and bank holding companies have been forced to write down their investments in preferred stocks of regional or money center banks and other corporations. Investments of this type should be subjected to the same credit analysis and underwriting standards as other loans of comparable size.

As shown in Exhibit 8-7, banks carry debt securities on their balance sheets at amortized cost—that is, original cost adjusted for the amortization of premiums and the accretion of discounts to par value present in the purchase price. Banks are required, however, to disclose the market value of their securities portfolios on a quarterly basis.

Trading Account Assets

Theoretically, banks are supposed to purchase investment securities with the intent of holding them to maturity. This general intent to hold to maturity is the basis for carrying investment securities at amortized cost. In practice, banks often sell securities prior to maturity for long-term, strategic tax or liquidity purposes or in anticipation of major interest rate movements.

Managements that believe they can profit from short-term trading of securities are usually required by regulators and auditors to set up segregated trading accounts. Trading accounts are marked to market daily, and the resulting gains and losses are reported as other noninterest income or expense on the income statement.

Reserve Accounts

All depository institutions are required by the Federal Reserve Bank to maintain reserves against their transaction account deposit liabilities. At present, the formula for calculating required reserves is 3 percent of the first $4.1 million of transaction accounts and 12 percent of all other transaction accounts. Vault cash and funds on deposit with the Federal Reserve (or indirectly via a pass-through account with a correspondent bank) count as reserves.

Federal Funds

Federal Funds (Fed Funds) are simply unsecured loans of reserve funds. A bank with excess reserves may lend out (sell) Fed Funds to a bank with a deficit of reserves (which is said to buy Fed Funds). There is a very active market for Fed Funds among regional and money center banks. Community banks usually buy and sell Fed Funds via their upstream (larger regional) correspondent banks. Fed Funds are generally lent on a day-to-day basis, being wired back and forth overnight. Fed Funds are sometimes bought and sold for periods of up to six months or more; these transactions are called Term Fed Funds.

Securities Purchased under Agreement to Resell

Securities purchased under agreement to resell (repos) are short-term investment arrangements. A bank buys securities (generally U.S. Treasury or agency bonds) at a specified price and simultaneously agrees to sell the securities back to the seller, who may be a securities dealer, at a specified price on a specified day in the future. Repos are effectively short-term secured loans with terms generally ranging from overnight to six months. To perfect its security interest in the collateral, it is necessary for the bank to either take delivery of the "repo'd" securities or have them placed in safekeeping with a third party. In the early 1980s, a number of banks and other investors who failed to take delivery of collateral suffered substantial losses on repos with bond dealers who had repo'd the same collateral to multiple investors.

Interest-Bearing Deposits at Other Banks

It is not uncommon for banks to invest in the certificates of deposit of other banks. There is an active secondary market for CDs with denominations of $1 million or more from money center banks and large regional banks. Maturities generally range from one to six months, and longer maturities are not uncommon. Banks may also invest in CDs of smaller banks and thrifts who often pay above-market rates to acquire funds for some special purpose. Prudent investing in CDs should entail credit analysis on money center and regional bank issues and the limiting of investments in smaller banks and thrifts to the amount covered by FDIC insurance.

Summary

Earning assets fall into three broad categories: (1) loans, (2) liquidity investments, and (3) long-term securities. In most cases, a bank's credit risk will be concentrated in its loan portfolio, where it has the best opportunity to earn high yields. Liquidity investments are short-term earning assets that can be quickly converted to cash to meet deposit outflows, with minimal risk of loss of principal. Liquidity investments include Treasury and government agency securities maturing in less than one year, Fed Funds sold, repos, CDs of other banks, and bankers' acceptances (which, strictly speaking, are loans). Long-term securities generally serve an intermediate role between loans and liquidity investments, offering higher yields than liquidity investments, lower (or no) risk of principal loss through credit losses, but with greater interest rate risk than either loans or liquidity investments.

Cash and Non-Interest-Bearing Deposits at Other Banks

Banks hold cash in their vaults to meet their depositors' needs and to satisfy reserve requirements. Banks also hold funds on deposit at other banks, either as pass-through accounts to count against reserve requirements or as demand deposits. Larger demand accounts are often used as "compensating balances" to pay for various services at a correspondent bank, such as directors' audits, check clearing, and computer services. The non-interest-bearing balances are placed with the correspondent in lieu of fees. Community banks with relatively large non-interest-bearing deposits with other banks may have elected to forgo potential interest income instead of paying explicit fees for correspondent services. Cash management (often called *float management*) has received increasing scrutiny in recent years as banks have searched for ways to reduce the level of nonearning assets and increase earnings.

Fixed Assets

Fixed assets include the bank's premises, building, improvements, furniture, fixtures, computers, and equipment. Fixed assets are accounted for at cost, net of depreciation. Two aspects of fixed assets have a direct impact on valuation. First, plans to expand or renovate facilities, add new branches or close existing offices, or change computer systems will have an impact on future depreciation expenses and other operating expenses and may have to be considered in the various earnings approaches to valuation. Second, a bank may be holding land for future use that may be both appreciated and unrelated to current operations. In such cases, it may be appropriate to consider the amount of appreciation, net of the implied tax impact, as a valuation adjustment to reported equity. Banks are generally prohibited from holding real estate, other than that related to bank operations, for more than five years.

Investments in Unconsolidated Subsidiaries and Affiliates

A bank may own all or part of a subsidiary offering banking-related services (e.g., mortgage banking, computer processing, etc.) whose balance sheet and income statement are not consolidated with the bank. From a valuation standpoint, it is important to determine the materiality of the subsidiary's operations to the bank and to determine if the bank is using the equity or the cost method to account for its investment. If the equity method is being used, the bank is reflecting its pro rata share of the subsidiary's net earnings and stockholders' equity in its financial statements. Under the cost method, the bank would report its investment at original cost and only reflect dividends received from the subsidiary as income. Whichever method is being used, it is important to determine if the investment in the subsidiary is fairly valued on the balance sheet and if the earnings contributed by the subsidiary are adequately reflected in the income statement; otherwise, adjustments to the bank's net asset value and earning power may be necessary.

Other Nonearning Assets

Other nonearning assets include accrued interest receivable on loans and investments, prepaid expenses, other real estate owned, goodwill, and intangible assets.

Other real estate owned is real estate acquired to satisfy debt, that is, foreclosed properties. Banks are required to have periodic appraisals of other real estate owned and to write down market depreciation via a charge to other noninterest operating expense. Gains recognized on the sale of other real estate owned appear in other noninterest operating income. A high level of other real estate owned puts pressure on a bank's interest margin by reducing the ratio of earning assets to total assets and usually signifies increasing credit risk. Holding other real estate can be an expensive proposition due to such expenses as legal fees, insurance, maintenance, and security. Other real estate (ORE) costs can be a hidden drain on earnings for years as a bank liquidates the properties.

Goodwill is cost in excess of fair value of acquired assets and usually arises in the purchase of a branch of another bank. For instance, if a bank acquires a branch of another bank and pays a premium over the historical cost basis of the premises, equipment, loans, and other tangible assets acquired in the transaction, the premium is reflected as goodwill on the acquiring bank's balance sheet. Goodwill is amortized over an appropriate time period, usually 10 years or more for banks; however, he amortization expense is not deductible for federal income tax purposes. Because goodwill is not an asset separable from the ongoing operations of the bank (i.e., it has no impact on the future economic value of the institution), it is often considered appropriate to subtract goodwill from reported book value as an analytical valuation adjustment to the balance sheet.

Other intangible assets also arise in acquisitions of branches and banks. However, these intangible assets reflect some aspect of the acquired company that confers an identifiable future economic benefit. For example, the core deposit intangible asset reflects the lower risk and below-money-market cost of funds associated with core consumer deposits acquired in the purchase of the branch or bank. (See Chapter 19 for a detailed discussion of core deposit intangible assets.) Similarly, safe-deposit box rental contracts acquired in a branch purchase confer future rental income. The amortization expense related to identifiable intangible assets is deductible for federal income tax purposes. Because intangible assets reflect identified future economic benefits, their presence on a balance sheet may not require a need for valuation adjustments. The analyst will have to decide on a case-by-case basis.

Off-Balance-Sheet Assets

Loan commitments and letters of credit are the most frequent off-balance-sheet assets encountered in valuing banks. A loan commitment is simply an obligation by a bank to fund a loan at some point in the future, subject to certain conditions. In discussing a bank's loan portfolio with management, it is important to cover approved but unfunded loans to identify any major deviations from historical lending policies or changes in mix and concentration. Also, a high level of outstanding loan commitments may imply a much lower than reported level of liquidity.

Letters of credit (LOCs) are essentially guarantees by a bank to third parties that in the event one of its customers defaults on an obligation to a third party, the bank will fund up to a specified amount to satisfy the obligation to the third party. Banks issue letters of credit for fees and often require collateral to support the letter of credit. The credit risk of a letter of credit is no less than that involved in making a loan. It is important to determine that a bank is underwriting its LOCs to the same standards as its loans, is monitoring its expected funding requirements under any outstanding LOCs, and is maintaining appropriate loss reserves.

Liability Composition

Deposits

A bank's deposit liabilities fall into two categories: core deposits and non-core deposits. Core deposits include non-interest-bearing demand accounts, interest-bearing transaction accounts, savings accounts, money market deposit accounts, and certificates of deposit under $100,000. Non-core deposits consist primarily of certificates of deposit over $100,000.

An analysis of deposit composition is shown in Exhibits 8-8 and 8-9.

Exhibit 8-8

Sample Bank Deposit Base Composition ($ Thousands) as of December 31

Deposit Category	1990	1989	1988	1987	1986	1985	Growth Rates 85–90	Growth Rates 89–90
Demand deposits	$ 46,300	$ 44,136	$ 42,548	$ 39,812	$ 35,578	$ 31,854	7.8%	4.9%
Regular savings and NOW	81,942	87,730	83,822	70,376	62,740	70,954	2.9	– 6.6
Time deposits under $100,000	178,126	156,646	143,226	129,992	161,486	123,326	7.6	13.7
MMDA and SuperNOW	26,804	33,708	36,302	46,702	39,120	36,632	– 6.1	– 20.5
Time deposits over $100,000	50,952	44,044	35,722	31,482	12,480	16,718	25.0	15.7
Total deposits	$384,124	$366,264	$341,620	$318,364	$311,404	$279,484	6.6%	4.9%

Exhibit 8-9

Sample Bank Deposit Base Composition as a Percentage of Total Deposits as of December 31

Deposit Category	1990	1989	1988	1987	1986	1985	Peer Group 9/90
Demand deposits	12.1%	12.1%	12.5%	12.5%	11.4%	11.4%	12.6%
Regular savings and NOW	21.3	24.0	24.5	22.1	20.1	25.4	21.8
Time deposits under $100,000	46.4	42.8	41.9	40.8	51.9	44.1	42.0
MMDA and SuperNOW	7.0	9.2	10.6	14.7	12.6	13.1	12.1
Time deposits over $100,000	13.3	12.0	10.5	9.9	4.0	6.0	11.5
Total deposits	100.0%	100.0%	100.0%	100.0%	100.0%	100.0%	100.0%

SOURCE: Call Reports and Uniform Bank Performance Reports

The main differences between core and noncore deposit accounts are interest rate sensitivity and degree of customer loyalty. Certificates of deposit over $100,000 (jumbo CDs) are generally considered to be the most volatile of deposit liabilities because they exceed the FDIC limit (and hence are extremely sensitive to negative information about the solvency of the bank) and are large enough for rate differentials to have a significant effect on the dollar amount of interest earned by investors.

At the other end of the spectrum, demand deposits are the least interest rate sensitive because they bear no interest. Demand deposit relationships tend to be based on convenience, personal relationships with a bank's staff, and fee structure. For other account types, relative interest rates may play an important element in depositors' decisions to retain funds in a particular bank, but this is balanced against such intangibles as convenience, service, and personal relationships. Banks with extensive branch networks tend to have the highest percentage of transaction and savings accounts in their deposit bases. Those with a heavy commercial-lending emphasis and limited branch networks tend to rely most heavily on time deposits.[5]

We will briefly discuss each deposit category listed in Exhibit 8-8.

---

[5]Some banks with a commercial-lending emphasis, however, may have above-normal levels of demand deposits if compensating balances are required in lieu of specific fees for services provided by the bank to its commercial accounts.

Demand Deposits

Demand deposit accounts (often referred to as DDAs) are checking accounts that pay no interest. They may include deposits of individuals, corporations, or government entities. Banks charge fees for account maintenance and transaction processing, or they may require minimum balances in lieu of fees. Corporate or business deposits may, in part, represent compensating balances required in loan agreements. So-called public-funds accounts (accounts of governmental entities) are usually acquired on a bid basis (lowest fees and highest earnings credits given against fees in lieu of interest) and must usually be collateralized with U.S. Treasury securities.

Other things being equal, the higher the portion of total deposits consisting of demand deposits, the better the earning power of the bank. However, other things often are *not* equal. Branch networks are expensive to maintain, and the relatively high service levels and transaction activity related to DDAs may disproportionately increase operating expenses. High percentages of DDA balances comprised of high average account balances with low transactions volume, then, are the keys to maximizing earning power from DDAs.

Interest-Bearing Transaction Accounts

Interest-bearing transaction accounts are generally limited to individuals. These accounts are legally called NOW (negotiable order of withdrawal) accounts. Theoretically, the funds in NOW accounts are not available on demand, but are savings accounts from which third parties can make withdrawals. As a practical matter, NOW accounts are interest-bearing checking accounts, differing from demand accounts only in the payment of interest. Most banks pay relatively low rates on NOW accounts (5.5 percent or less).

Prior to the elimination of Federal Reserve Regulation Q (dealing with deposit rate ceilings), there was a legally distinct category of transaction account called the SuperNOW account. SuperNOWs were accounts with minimum balances over $2,500 that were not subject to rate ceilings. Some banks continue to offer SuperNOW accounts to high-balance depositors, offering a rate above the normal NOW rate. Attempting to match NOW or SuperNOW rates with those available to investors in money market mutual funds can be expensive for banks because these accounts, like demand deposits, are subject to 12 percent reserve requirements (such that only 88 percent of the funds in NOW accounts can be invested in interest-bearing assets).

Savings Accounts

Savings accounts are open-ended accounts with no stated maturity on which checks cannot be drawn. Personal savings accounts are not subject to reserve requirements, and the Federal Reserve recently eliminated the 3 percent reserve requirement on nonpersonal accounts. Most banks pay rates of 5.5 percent or lower on these accounts; however, they are no longer subject to regulatory rate ceilings. Savings accounts tend to be highly insensitive to market interest rates and involve relatively little operating expense per account to the bank. The main operational drawback on savings accounts is that they typically have low average balances, which tend to inflate the operating cost per dollar of deposit.

Money Market Deposit Accounts

Money market deposit accounts (MMDAs) were devised in the early 1980s to allow banks to compete with money market mutual funds during a period when interest rate ceilings were still in force. The accounts have minimum balances of $2,500 and allow depositors to make up to six third-party transfers (of which three can be checks) per month. Like savings accounts, MMDAs are not subject to reserve requirements.

Some banks attempt to compete with money market mutual funds by offering relatively high rates on MMDAs. Others pay only small premiums over their basic savings account rates to MMDA customers. Some banks also elect not to offer checking or third-party transfer options to their MMDA customers, turning the accounts effectively into high-balance savings accounts.

Time Deposits (Certificates of Deposit) Under $100,000

Time deposits are deposits that have specified opening dates and specified maturity dates. Although some banks offer variable-rate certificates and certificates to which additional funds may be added after the initial deposit, most time deposits have a fixed principal amount (i.e., the original amount deposited), a fixed interest rate, and a fixed maturity date.

For most community banks, time deposits under $100,000 (retail CDs) currently account for 50 percent or more of total deposits. Retail CDs normally represent the long-term savings (including individual retirement accounts or IRAs) of its transaction and savings account customers. Maturities typically range from six months to three years. Rates typically approximate those paid on U.S. Treasury securities of similar maturity (reflecting deposit insurance coverage), but rates vary based on local deposit demand and other competitive factors. Most banks have difficulty attracting time deposits with maturities exceeding three years. Certificates of deposit are not subject to reserve requirements.

Time Deposits (Certificates of Deposit) Over $100,000

Jumbo CDs may include deposits of wealthy individuals and of companies, pension plans, and government entities. Public funds usually must be collateralized with U.S. Treasury securities. Banks usually pay a premium over retail CD rates to jumbo CD holders. Jumbo CDs may represent funds deposited by the bank's regular deposit customers or additional funds attracted from outside its normal customer base by offering relatively high rates. Jumbo CDs usually have shorter maturities (one to three months) than retail CDs. The advantage of jumbo CDs— lower operating cost per dollar of deposit—tends to be offset by higher interest expense and greater volatility (because any amount above $100,000 is not insured).

Other Acquired Funds

Banks also can raise interest-bearing funds that are not classed as deposits and that are not covered by federal deposit insurance. Borrowings from the Federal Reserve System would be an important example.

Federal Funds Purchased

Just as community banks can sell Fed Funds, they can also buy Fed Funds to cover seasonal outflows of funds.

Securities Sold Under Agreement to Repurchase

Community banks also have the option of selling securities in their investment portfolio with a simultaneous agreement to repurchase them. This transaction is effectively a collateralized borrowing. The bank does not book a gain or loss on the sale of the securities.

Treasury Tax and Loan Account

Community banks may hold U.S. Treasury funds in the form of interest-bearing collateralized demand notes.

Notes Payable and Mortgages

Like commercial and industrial companies, banks may also elect to issue debt. Debt has the advantage of not being subject to reserve requirements or deposit insurance assessments. Also, fixed-rate debt can be arranged with longer maturities than are usually practical for deposits. Banks also may elect to finance premises and equipment with mortgages or capital leases. Some subordinated notes and subordinated notes convertible to common stock may be counted toward a bank's capital requirements, although under current regulations, regulatory capital is practically limited to common stock, noncumulative preferred stock and the loan loss reserve.

Deferred Taxes

Deferred taxes are generally not an important item for banks because banks do not make heavy investments in hard assets that result in the timing differences between depreciation expense for tax purposes and depreciation expense for financial reporting purposes.

Other Liabilities

Usually, the largest category of other liabilities is accrued-interest payable. Other liabilities also include taxes payable and other accrued expenses.

Contingencies

Appraisers need to inquire about a bank's off-balance-sheet liabilities. Contingencies can include environmental liabilities related to repossessed real estate and lawsuits.

Shareholders' Equity

As with any corporation, shareholders' equity is the difference between total assets and total liabilities. Total equity is the sum of common stock (at par value), preferred stock (if any), surplus, and retained earnings.

Exhibit 8-10 presents a year-to-year reconciliation of a bank's equity account.

Exhibit 8-10
Changes in Equity Capital ($ Thousands) for the Periods Ending December 31

	1990	1989	1988	1987	1986	1985
Beginning equity capital	$27,522	$24,182	$22,528	$21,558	$21,262	$20,410
Net income (loss)	2,618	3,326	2,896	2,400	1,280	1,932
Net sale, conversion, acquisition, retirement of stock:						
Preferred stock	0	0	0	0	0	0
Common stock	0	1600	400	0	0	0
Cash dividends, preferred stock	0	0	0	0	0	0
Cash dividends, common stock	(1,290)	(1,586)	(1,750)	(1,430)	(984)	(800)
Cumulative effect of change in accounting principles	0	0	0	0	0	0
Change in net unrealized loss on marketable equity securities	0	0	0	0	0	0
Other adjustments	0	0	108	0	0	(280)
Ending equity capital	$28,850	$27,522	$24,182	$22,528	$21,558	$21,262

For the typical community bank, the main factors affecting total equity are net income, dividend payout, and adjustments to retained earnings related to unrealized losses in marketable equity securities. Banks are usually prevented from paying out dividends to shareholders in excess of net income in the current period, unless the bank is heavily capitalized. We will defer a discussion of capital adequacy to Chapter 10.

Chapter 9

The Bank Income Statement

Who is a cynic? A man who knows the price of everything, and the value of nothing.

Oscar Wilde

Overview

Income Statement Presentation

This chapter will discuss the various components of a bank's income statement. Exhibit 9-1 presents a detailed income statement presented in the common net interest income format. This format is used for both analysis and for financial reporting purposes.

The main difference between Exhibit 9-1 and income statements found in bank annual reports and Call Reports is that we have included a tax equivalency adjustment for income from municipal loans and municipal securities that is exempt from federal corporation income tax. Such an adjustment also appears in Uniform Bank Performance Reports and is used to enhance the comparability of banks with different levels of tax-free interest income. This presentation is referred to as a fully taxable equivalent (FTE) basis.

Exhibit 9-1 also includes a presentation of the income statement as a percentage of average assets. Because the bulk of bank revenues and expenses is interest and the bulk of a bank's balance sheet consists of interest-earning assets and interest-bearing liabilities, it is common analytical practice to relate the income statement to the asset base.

There are three key elements to the presentation in Exhibit 9-1:

1. Net interest income (interest income minus interest expense).
2. Adjusted gross income (net interest income plus fee income).
3. Basic operating income (adjusted gross income minus noninterest operating expense).

Gains and losses on securities transactions and the provision for loan losses are shown below the basic operating-income line because, for most banks, these items tend to be significantly more volatile than the interest, fee, and overhead components; entail some degree of management discretion; and require specific analytical attention.

Prior to the 1980s, it was common practice to report gains and losses on securities transactions as extraordinary items, calculating a net income from continuing operations before showing securities gains and losses (net of their related income tax effects) on the income statement. From a valuation standpoint, this obsolete accounting practice continues to make a great deal of sense.

Investment securities are theoretically (and by regulation) supposed to be held to maturity or until a strategic repositioning is desired. We have never seen a community bank whose management has been able to generate consistent year-to-year net gains on securities transactions *from a trading portfolio,* although for many years bankers were able to

Exhibit 9-1

Sample Bank Income Statement (Net Interest Income Presentation) for the Year Ending December 31, 1990

Income/Expense Categories	$ Thousands	Percent of Average Total Assets
Interest income		
Taxable loans	$29,754	6.96%
Tax-free loans	396	0.09
Fed Funds sold, resell agreements, and bank deposits	948	0.22
Taxable securities	10,212	2.39
Tax-free securities	1,028	0.24
Other interest income	0	0.00
Estimated tax benefit (FTE adjustment)	734	0.17
Total interest income (FTE)	43,072	10.07
Interest expense		
Time deposits over $100,000	3,892	0.91
Other deposits	20,352	4.76
Fed Funds purchased and repurchase agreements	1,190	0.28
Other interest expense	156	0.04
Total interest expense	25,590	5.99
Net interest income (FTE)	17,482	4.09
Other income		
Service charges on deposit accounts	1,886	0.44
Other operating income	2,274	0.53
Total other income	4,160	0.97
Adjusted gross income (FTE)	21,642	5.06
Noninterest operating expense		
Salaries and benefits	7,858	1.84
Net occupancy	4,124	0.96
Other operating expense	4,200	0.98
Total noninterest operating expense	16,182	3.79
Basic operating income (FTE)	5,460	1.28
Gains/(losses) on securities transactions	116	0.03
Provision for loan and lease losses	376	0.09
Pretax income (FTE)	5,200	1.22
Federal tax equivalency adjustment	734	0.17
Pretax income	4,466	1.04
Income taxes	1,192	0.28
Net income from continuing operations	3,274	0.77
Net extraordinary items	(656)	−0.15
Net income	$ 2,618	0.61%
Total dividends	1,290	
Dividend payout ratio	49.27%	

take seemingly consistent securities gains by cherry-picking their portfolios (i.e., selling only those securities showing gains and "burying" those with losses in the portfolio). The new regulations requiring that trading portfolios be marked-to-market daily have virtually eliminated this practice.

In contrast to securities transactions, some analysts and accountants prefer to show the provision for loan losses just below net interest income, implying that the provision is effectively a reduction in interest income. However, loan loss provisions are generally too volatile from year to year to be considered part of operating income in analyzing the income statement. We prefer to focus on the provision for loan losses separately from the analysis of the basic operating income stream and as part of the overall analysis of credit quality.

Comparisons with a Corporate Income Statement

Exhibit 9-2 is a bank income statement adapted to the format common-ly used for commercial and manufacturing companies. This format is not yet a widely used presentation, but it provides a useful point of reference for readers familiar with nonbank financial statements.

Banks are in the business of buying and selling money, as well as providing services related to the handling or management of money. Thus, a bank's adjusted gross income (net interest income plus fee income) can be considered to be its net revenues or net sales.[1]

Below the line for net sales/adjusted gross income, bank and mer-cantile income statements are generally similar: Bank noninterest operating expense corresponds to general, administrative, and selling expense, while gains and losses on securities transactions and the pro-vision for loan losses correspond to net other income.

Exhibit 9-2
Income Statement ("Net Sales" Presentation) of a Sample Bank
for the Year Ending December 31, 1990

Income/Expense Categories	$ Thousands	Percentage of "Net Sales"
Interest income	$42,338	195.63%
+ Tax equivalency adjustment	734	3.39
= Interest income (FTE)	43,072	199.02
+ Fee income	4,160	19.22
= "Gross sales"	47,232	218.24
− Interest expense	25,590	118.24
= Adjusted gross income ("net sales")	21,642	100.00
− Personnel expense	7,858	36.31
− Occupancy expense	4,124	19.06
− Other expense	4,200	19.41
− Total noninterest operating expense	16,182	74.77
= Basic operating income (FTE)	5,460	25.23
+ Gains/(− losses) on securities transactions	116	0.54
− Provision for loan and lease losses	376	1.74
= Pretax income (FTE)	5,200	24.03
− Tax equivalency adjustment	734	3.39
= Pretax income	4,466	20.64
− Income taxes	1,192	5.51
= Net income from continuing operations	3,274	15.13
+ Net extraordinary items	(656)	− 3.03
= Net income	$ 2,618	12.10%

---

[1] It might be possible to consider interest income as sales and interest expense as the cost of goods sold; however, this approach would eliminate the usefulness of any analysis of margins. The absolute dollar amounts of interest income and interest expense vary greatly as market interest rates move up or down. The fact that a bank generates more *dollars* of interest income from a given loan (or its entire portfolio) when the prime rate is 15 percent than when the prime is 9 percent is essentially irrelevant from a business or analytical point of view. Interest-bearing liabilities cost more in the former rate environment than in the latter. What matters to a bank is the spread it earns between the loan and the corresponding interest-costing liability, or the *net dollars after interest expense*. Net sales for a bank therefore consist of adjusted gross income as defined in the preceding edition.

A brief analysis of Exhibit 9-2 provides some interesting observations about banks:

1. "Gross sales," consisting of total interest income (FTE) plus fee income, are nearly twice as large as "net sales," or adjusted gross income. Banks handle large amounts of gross income dollars to create their usable adjusted gross income. This is possible because of the high degree of leverage in bank balance sheets.
2. Fee income provides a relatively small portion of net sales for most banks (19 percent for the Sample Bank).
3. The Sample Bank generated a 24 percent pretax (FTE) margin on sales during 1990. We will see in Chapter 22 that the Sample Bank is actually a below-average performer. But in comparison to nonbanking corporations, the profit margin *on sales* is quite high, even though the margin *on assets* is relatively low.

These comparisons, together with the balance sheet comparisons in the preceding chapter, indicate that banks are different from the typical manufacturing, distribution, or service company to which bankers lend and that appraisers value. The remainder of this chapter describes the income statement of banks and makes some initial analytical observations. The next chapter builds upon our growing knowledge of bank financial statements to outline and discuss the key analytical concepts necessary to understand how banks work and to place valuation into perspective.

Income Statement Composition

At this point, it is useful to review the individual elements of the income statement.

Interest Income

According to generally accepted financial theory, the required yield necessary to induce investments in particular securities rises with perceived risk. We need to consider the analysis and valuation of banks in the context of this theory.

Banks earn interest income by taking risk in the form of *credit risk, interest rate risk,* and *liquidity risk,* all of which were defined in Chapter 6. The amount of interest income a bank earns will be roughly correlated to the amount of risk it takes. Understanding the way a bank manages the risk inherent in its balance sheet, therefore, leads to an understanding of its income statement.

There are three main questions to consider in understanding the level of interest income:

1. Does the bank lend or invest at fixed rates for long terms? If so, it may take on excessive interest rate risk, because interest income is

defined for long periods while interest expense may rise sharply with rising interest rates, thereby reducing net interest income.

2. Does the bank lend to weak borrowers or invest in low-grade securities? If so, it takes on above-normal levels of credit risk. Note that credit risk does not impact bank earnings until the losses inherent in risky credits are realized.[2]

3. Does the bank keep most of its earning assets in illiquid loans or thinly traded securities? The related question on the liability side of the balance sheet is: Does the bank have too great a portion of its liabilities in jumbo CDs or other short-term, rate-sensitive borrowings? If so, it may be subjecting itself unnecessarily to liquidity risk caused by unexpected funding requirements (e.g., for new loans) or deposit roll-offs (when the deposits were expected to renew upon maturity rather than leave the bank).

If a bank were merely a lender and investor of its own money, the risk profile of its earning assets would serve as a sufficient basis for understanding its operating results; however, risk for a bank is compounded by the fact that it must borrow the money it lends and invests.

Banks are highly leveraged entities, and bankers must manage both the funding and investing sides of the balance sheet. In an environment of rising market interest rates, a bank that funds long-term, fixed-rate assets with short-term, variable-rate deposits suffers not only the lost opportunity of earning higher interest income but also the direct narrowing of its net interest income as its variable-interest expenses rise while its interest income remains relatively fixed.

The situation is worsened if, simultaneously, the bank suffers an unexpected deposit outflow because the bank will either have to borrow at relatively high cost from other banks to replace the funds or take losses on the sale of fixed-rate assets that have depreciated in value.

The previous paragraphs might seem to suggest that bankers should avoid *all* risk and invest only in short-term, liquid, high-credit-quality assets such as Treasury bills and bankers' acceptances. Unfortunately, few banks can adopt such a risk-averse investment profile and remain economically viable. A bank has to earn enough interest income and fee income to offset its interest expense, overhead expenses, and loan loss provisions *and* earn a profit.[3]

Few community banks earn more than 20 percent of "sales" in the form of fee income. Thanks in large part to deregulation and the elimi-

---

[2] As noted in the previous chapter, banks accrue interest on loans until payments required by their corresponding loan agreements are not made in a timely way. Banks engaging in lending with excessive credit risk may then appear, for periods of time, to be performing very well. Park Bank of Florida, located in St. Petersburg, was during the late 1970s and early 1980s one of the fastest growing and most profitable banks in the nation. Yet it failed on Valentine's Day 1986, only a few months after the first public acknowledgment of problems. The bank analyst must be extremely careful in evaluating credit risk, because detailed analysis of loan portfolios is beyond the scope of virtually all appraisals. The clues of future credit problems, however, can often be found by analysis of a bank's historical financial statements.

[3] Several years ago, when banks first began to focus on asset/liability management, a client called to complain that he had bought a computer program from an investment banking firm and had worked almost religiously to eliminate his gap, that is, the mismatch between the maturities of his assets and liabilities. He said he had shortened maturities of assets and had a gap out to one year of virtually zero! In other words, his assets and liabilities maturing within one year repriced almost simultaneously. I told him: "That's great! The only problem is that you can't make any money with your balance sheet in that position." He said, "I know now. That's why I called you."

nation of Regulation Q, deposit rates in most markets are only slightly below (if not above) yields on Treasury bills and bankers' acceptances, so no "spread" is available in these riskless or very low risk assets. To be profitable, bankers must therefore assume some degree of credit, interest rate, and liquidity risk in order to earn an adequate interest rate spread. *The keys to success are found in limiting, balancing, and diversifying risk and, as we will see shortly, in managing noninterest operating expenses.*

In Chapter 6, we discussed the great variety of earning assets that might comprise a given bank's balance sheet. The major classes of earnings assets and their related revenues are outlined in the following sections.

Loan Portfolio

Loans, which are the riskiest assets on a bank's balance sheet, typically provide the highest levels of interest income. In lending, banks assume credit risk directly.[4] The main advantage of lending is that high yields are available without taking on significant interest rate risk. Attractive yields can be obtained on loans with maturities or rate-resetting periods of one month to three years. Marketable securities with comparable maturities generally offer yields only marginally above deposit expenses.

Taxable Securities Portfolio

Taxable securities serve two purposes. Short-term securities such as Treasury bills and short-term federal agency notes enhance a bank's liquidity, but at the same time provide some yield, usually at least minimally above the cost of deposit funds. Longer-term securities are used as a substitute for lending. They fill the gap between the amount of available funds a bank is able or desires to lend and the amount of available funds its management considers necessary to hold in liquid investments.

The higher yields on longer-term securities are a product of the *yield curve.* In most economic environments, market yields rise as the investment term-to-maturity of securities increases. As noted earlier, the marketplace normally compensates investors for taking on interest rate risk.

Banks often substitute credit risk in their loan portfolios for interest rate risk in their securities portfolios, investing in longer-term Treasury and government agency notes and in mortgage-backed securities. As long as these long-term investments (with average lives out to 10 years or more) are "matched" against the base of non-interest-costing equity and demand accounts and the relatively fixed-rate savings and NOW accounts, they can normally be considered to involve modest risk.[5]

Liquidity Investment Categories

Federal funds sold, securities purchased with agreement to resell, and interest-bearing balances at other banks are three categories of investment generally used for liquidity purposes. These categories usually provide yields moderately above U.S. Treasury bills.

---

[4]As noted above, loans are typically illiquid, so banks also assume liquidity risks in lending, except perhaps with residential mortgage loans that are made in conformity with Fannie Mae guidelines, for which there is a ready market.

[5]Alternatively, bankers who invest proceeds from three-month jumbo CDs into 30-year zero coupon bonds are subjecting their institutions to substantial interest rate and liquidity risk.

Tax-Free Securities Portfolio

Municipal securities serve much the same role as other marketable securities. In addition, their after-tax yields can be much higher than their stated yields-to-maturity because of the exemption of their interest from federal income taxes.

Current tax law tends to limit the benefits of investing in municipal securities in two ways. First, if a bank reports sufficient tax-free income that it has an operating loss for federal income tax purposes but shows a book profit in its financial statements, the bank becomes subject to the federal alternative minimum tax (AMT).

Second, the pro rata interest expense attributable to carrying tax-exempt municipal securities issued by governments issuing more than $10 million per year of such securities is not deductible if they were acquired after August 7, 1986. Because of these changes in tax laws, community banks generally reduced their investments in tax-exempt securities during the 1980s.

Fully Taxable Equivalent (FTE) Adjustment

Total interest income is simply the sum of interest income produced by the various categories of earning assets, including interest income earned on trading-account securities. Fully taxable equivalent interest income includes a mathematical adjustment intended to equate the after-tax benefit of interest on tax-exempt municipal securities and loans to municipalities with fully taxable investments.

The formula for converting a tax-exempt municipal yield to its FTE yield is stated as:

$$\text{Tax equivalent yield} = \frac{\text{Tax-exempt yield}}{[1 - \text{Effective (FTE) marginal tax rate}]}$$

This calculation has the effect of "grossing-up" the tax-free yield to the level required of a taxable security (or loan) to provide the same after-tax benefit to the bank as that obtainable from the tax-exempt security.

For analytical purposes, bank income statements are normally prepared on a fully taxable equivalent basis. Analysis on an FTE basis is particularly important when comparing banks, or a given bank with a peer group, because the analyst may never have full knowledge about a bank's history of investment-making decisions. In essence, the FTE adjustment eliminates that concern by placing every bank's income statement on a comparable basis, that is, the earnings that would be realized if all its investments were fully taxable. The analyst then has a realistic method of analyzing the effectiveness of one bank's past strategies in relationship to other banks or to a peer group of banks.

The formula for calculating the dollar tax equivalency adjustment for a bank's interest income, also referred to as the FTE adjustment, is stated as[6]

---

[6]Appendix B, *A User's Guide for the Uniform Bank Performance Report,* published by the Federal Financial Institutions Examination Council, provides an elaborate five-page worksheet for calculating the exact tax equivalency adjustment—that is, the exact tax benefit realized in the period. This worksheet considers, among other elements, the nondeductibility of the cost of carry on most municipal securities acquired after August 7, 1986, the different federal corporation income tax brackets, the alternative minimum tax, and tax loss carryforwards. For most analytical purposes, we consider the simple and easily reproducible calculation shown on page 129 to be adequate.

$$\text{FTE adjustment} = \left[\frac{\text{Tax-free interest}}{(1 - \text{Effective marginal tax rate})} \right] - \text{Tax-free interest}$$

Tax-free interest should include both interest on municipal securities and on loans to municipalities. The current top federal corporate marginal tax rate is 34 percent.

Schedule RI-E of the Call Report provides a breakdown of taxable and tax-exempt municipal interest and includes a memo item showing tax-exempt interest on loans. Application of state income taxes, which are deductible for federal income tax purposes, would raise the effective marginal tax rate by an amount equal to the state tax rate times one minus the federal tax rate, or

State $\% \times (1 - 34\%)$.

The bank analyst should realize that for tax-exempt income to have a fully taxable equivalent benefit, a bank must have taxable income at least equivalent to the taxable equivalent adjustment. Otherwise, lower-yielding tax-exempt securities become just that: lower-yielding securities. In other words, banks must be *profitable* to benefit from the use of tax-exempt securities.

Interest Expense

Banks generally have much less flexibility in managing interest expense than in managing interest income. Historical deposit structures (i.e., the mix of demand, NOW, savings, MMDA, and time deposits) are difficult to change and are often imposed by long-standing community preferences and opinions. Two examples illustrate why deposit patterns may be difficult to shift:

> One bank has a reputation for frequent clerical errors, rude tellers, slow service, and high fees, yet desires to increase its lower-cost deposit account balances. This institution may find it very difficult to gain customers (and dollar balances) in its demand, NOW, and savings account categories without time-consuming and expensive marketing and service improvement programs.
>
> Another bank wishes to shift the bulk of its retail CDs from six-month maturities (a holdover from the money market CDs of the early 1980s, when Regulation Q was still in force) to one-year maturities. The rate differential between the two maturities necessary to induce its customers to change habits may be quite high, especially if the bank must maintain the rates paid on its existing six-month maturity balances to avoid losing customers to other banks. The situation is complicated by competition both from other depository institutions and from nonbank alternatives, such as money market mutual funds.

Deposit interest, mostly interest on certificates of deposit, makes up the bulk of interest expense for community banks.

Jumbo CDs are generally the highest costing deposits because they are so rate sensitive. The main benefit of jumbo CDs is that the dollar amounts are large enough to reduce substantially the operating cost per dollar of deposits.

Deposits of governmental and tax-exempt authorities (public funds) have the added "cost" of requiring government securities as collateral.

In many cases, public funds are obtained on a bid basis, with area banks competing with each other for their "share" of governmental funds. Public funds, other than operating accounts of governmental bodies, are normally acquired in "jumbo" lots.

Regulators are generally concerned about high concentrations of jumbo CDs in a bank's deposit base. Rapid redeployment of jumbo CDs can place a severe liquidity drain on a bank. Further, a relatively high level of jumbo CDs subjects a bank to higher degrees of interest rate risk.

From a valuation point of view, concentrations of jumbo CDs do pose concerns about liquidity risk. Further, as we will see in Chapter 19 in the discussion of core deposit intangible assets, jumbo CDs are simply not worth as much as low-cost and more-stable demand deposits. Many bankers believe their jumbo CDs are really "core deposits." However, the number of readily available investment opportunities (money market mutual funds, CDs from out-of-territory institutions via telephone transactions, etc.), even for loyal customers, call this belief to question.

Retail CDs make up the next highest cost source of funds. Operating cost per dollar of deposits is relatively low because maturities tend to be long—generally six months to three years.

Money market deposit accounts are usually the third highest cost group. Some banks try to compete with money market mutual funds with this account type and pay rates approaching those on CDs; others pay only a slight premium over their basic savings rates. Operating costs on MMDAs tend to be moderate because the minimum balance is usually $2,500 and transaction frequency is low.

Savings accounts typically carry a low interest cost but can be expensive to administer because of low average balances.

NOW accounts usually pay low interest rates, and *demand deposit accounts* pay no interest, but both are subject to reserve requirements, reducing the amount that can be reinvested. Banks usually try to offset the cost of processing demand and NOW accounts by some combination of monthly maintenance fees, transaction fees, and minimum-account balances.

In general, deposits represent the least costly source of funding for community banks because the existence of federal deposit insurance virtually *eliminates credit risk for a bank's customers.*[7]

Net Interest Income

Net interest income is simply the difference between interest income and interest expense. *Net interest income (FTE)* is net interest income adjusted to a fully taxable equivalent basis, reflecting the tax benefit from tax-exempt interest income.

Bank income statements are very much driven by balance sheet composition: The mix of earning assets and funding types and the relative levels of earning assets to total assets and interest-bearing funds to total

---

[7]With FDIC insurance of up to $100,000 *per account* at the current time, the majority of bank customers can "lend" their funds to a bank without concern for credit risk. At the time of this writing, numerous proposals have surfaced that would limit deposit insurance protection available to customers of financial institutions.

assets dominate a bank's profitability. Several measures of interest income, interest expense, and net interest income are helpful in developing an understanding of a bank's performance relative to its peers, relative to its historical results, and to its potential. These measures are shown in Exhibit 9-3 and discussed at some length below.

Interest income as a percentage of average total assets (FTE) reflects the overall efficiency of a bank's asset base because it spreads interest income over both the bank's earning and nonearning assets. Other things being equal, the higher the ratio of earning assets to total assets, the higher the ratio of interest income to total assets.

Interest expense as a percentage of average total assets similarly reflects the interest cost of maintaining the entire balance sheet. Other things being equal, the higher the level of equity and non-interest-costing funds (DDAs, accrued interest payable, etc.), the lower the ratio of interest expense to total assets.

Exhibit 9-3
Relative Spread Measures*

Sample Bank Spread Relationships of Interest Income and Interest Expense for the Years Ending December 31	1990	1989	1988	1987	1986	1985
Bank						
Interest income (FTE)/average assets	10.07%	9.42%	9.27%	9.93%	10.93%	11.44%
Interest expense/average assets	5.99	5.26	4.95	5.61	6.47	7.31
Net interest income (FTE)/average assets	4.09%	4.16%	4.31%	4.32%	4.47%	4.14%
Peer group (9/90)						
Interest income (FTE)/average assets	9.90%	9.90%	9.13%	9.01%	9.71%	10.56%
Interest expense/average assets	5.62	5.62	4.89	4.60	5.04	5.79
Net interest income (FTE)/average assets	4.28%	4.28%	4.24%	4.41%	4.67%	4.77%
Bank						
Yield on average earning assets (FTE)	11.03%	10.25%	10.02%	10.80%	11.81%	12.53%
Cost of interest-bearing funds	7.22	6.32	5.95	6.74	7.82	8.98
Net spread (FTE)	3.82%	3.93%	4.07%	4.06%	3.99%	3.55%
Peer group (9/90)						
Yield on average earning assets (FTE)	10.76%	10.76%	9.97%	9.90%	10.71%	11.64%
Cost of interest-bearing funds	7.23	7.23	6.36	6.00	6.66	7.76
Net spread (FTE)	3.53%	3.53%	3.61%	3.90%	4.05%	3.88%
Bank						
Yield on average earning assets (FTE)	11.03%	10.25%	10.02%	10.80%	11.81%	12.53%
Cost of average earning assets	6.56	5.72	5.36	6.10	6.98	8.00
Net yield on earning assets (FTE)	4.48%	4.53%	4.67%	4.70%	4.83%	4.53%
Peer group (9/90)						
Yield on average earning assets (FTE)	10.76%	10.76%	9.97%	9.90%	10.71%	11.64%
Cost of average earning assets	6.11	6.11	5.33	5.02	5.55	6.40
Net yield on earning assets (FTE)	4.65%	4.65%	4.64%	4.88%	5.16%	5.24%
Average earning assets/average assets	91.31%	91.93%	92.43%	91.98%	92.58%	91.34%
Peer group (9/90)	92.04%	92.04%	91.71%	91.34%	90.90%	90.82%
Average interest-bearing funds/average assets	82.93%	83.19%	83.20%	83.25%	82.70%	81.38%
Peer group (9/90)	77.72%	77.72%	76.80%	76.09%	75.38%	74.61%

SOURCE: Call Reports and Uniform Bank Performance Reports

*Figures may not add because of rounding.

The net interest margin (net interest income as a percentage of average total assets) provides one important measure of the efficiency of a bank's balance sheet in generating a spread that, if of sufficient magnitude, can translate into profitability. A bank with a large net interest margin can support substantial overhead expense or large loan or securities losses and still earn a profit.

The yield on average earning assets eliminates the effect of the level of the bank's nonearning assets and measures the revenues generated by its portfolio of earning assets.[8]

The cost of average earning assets is the ratio of interest expense to average earning assets and measures the cost of carrying the bank's earning asset base. This measure continues to reflect the liability mix and the benefit of having a high level of noncosting liabilities.

The net yield on average earning assets measures the ability of the bank's earning asset base to generate net revenue. This measure reflects the combined effects of changes in asset yields, deposit rates, and funding mix.[9]

The cost of average interest-bearing funds is the ratio of interest expense to interest-bearing liabilities only. The difference between this ratio and the net yield on earning assets is the *net spread,* which reflects absolute rate differentials in a bank's funding and earning asset bases, without the added complication of the impact of nonearning assets and noncosting liabilities. The net spread is the best measure of how management is dealing with changes in market interest rates.

Which is the best overall spread measure? Which measure tells the most about a bank's historical or prospective performance? They all provide important information for the bank analyst. Taken collectively, in conjunction with an entire analysis, they can help the analyst to develop a better understanding of the earnings dynamics of any bank.

Analytical Aside

The prospective or experienced bank analyst (or purchaser of banks or bank stocks) should remember at this juncture that historical performance remains the best predictor of future performance. The previous chapter examined the composition of bank balance sheets. It should be clear that banks are highly leveraged institutions with earnings asset bases comprised of a large number of asset types and literally hundreds or even thousands of individual loan and investment security components.

While many loans reprice frequently, loan agreements have a longer duration. Further, when loan customers experience problems, it is no

---

[8]The term *average earning assets* usually does not exclude nonperforming loans (i.e., past-due loans on which the accrual of interest has ceased) because nonperforming loans are not reported separately from other loans on the balance sheet. Nonperforming loans are identified in footnotes to annual reports or 10-K's of publicly traded institutions and in Schedule RC-N of the Call Report. If a bank has an unusually high level of nonperforming loans, it may be analytically useful to adjust the average earning assets figure by eliminating these loans. Such an adjustment will result in more meaningful calculations of the yield on average earning assets and the ratio of earning assets to total assets. Because this adjustment is not made in the Uniform Bank Performance Reports nor in any other comparable reporting system, to our knowledge, the bank analyst may want to make this adjustment both for a subject bank and for the peer group being used for comparison.

[9]Some analysts use the term *net interest margin* to refer to net interest income as a percentage of average earning assets (i.e., the net yield on earning assets) rather than net interest income as a percentage of average total assets as indicated above.

simple matter to collect the outstanding principal balances in a timely way for replacement by other loans or investments. And many of the securities held by a bank will not mature for years, although some will probably mature within one month, some within a year, and so on.

A bank balance sheet can be likened to so much baggage that a banker is carrying. While he or she might like to throw away the entire balance sheet and start over, this dream will never be realized. A banker must always work *at the margin* of the bank's balance sheet to accomplish financial or operational objectives. Loans are made one at a time. Credit quality is improved one loan at a time. Deposit maturities can be extended, on average, only by adding or replacing deposits, one at a time.

On the down side, what this means to the bank analyst is that, while seeds of destruction may have been planted in a fairly short period if lending controls were lax and aggressive loan growth occurred, the realization of that destruction occurs S-L-O-W-L-Y as the inevitable loan problems surface, usually one at a time.

On the positive side, if a bank is seeking to increase its interest spreads, it can shift earning assets from lower-yielding securities (only as they mature) into higher-yielding loans one at a time—that is, S-L-O-W-L-Y.

Virtually nothing happens quickly in a bank. The analyst who forgets this simple truth will generally underestimate the time required to recover from problems or overestimate the benefit of "new and exciting" strategies or initiatives to improve earnings. In either case, the forgetful analyst will tend to overvalue the institution under study.

Fee Income

Bank fee income is derived from a number of sources. However, for most banks, *service charges on deposit accounts* provide the largest portion of noninterest operating income. Deposit service charges include monthly maintenance and transaction fees on transaction accounts. In addition, penalties for checks written on insufficient-funds balances (not sufficient funds, or NSF, charges), can be a significant source of bank income.

There is some trade-off between interest expense and service charges. Some banks pursue strategies of offering high interest rates on transaction accounts but charge minimal fees and have low minimum-balance requirements. Others offer relatively high rates on transaction accounts but charge high fees or require high minimum balances. Actual pricing policies are usually developed based upon a bank's particular strategy for addressing its competitive situation and for dealing with local consumer preferences or customs.

Other noninterest operating income is derived from a variety of sources. The bank's lending activities may generate closing and documentation fees as well as credit life insurance premiums, particularly on consumer loans.

Banks can also generate fee income through mortgage banking departments that earn fees for originating loans for investors and earn ongoing fees for servicing loans for third parties. More frequently, however, community banks attempt to use their branch and customer networks to originate mortgage loans, which are then sold "servicing-released" into the secondary market. These banks do not build a servicing portfolio, but they do experience a significantly higher level of fee income in good markets for mortgage originations.

Some community banks have active trust departments that make contributions to operating income via fees earned for providing fiduciary services. Other sources of operating income include rental income on safe-deposit boxes and fees charged to provide cashier's checks.

It should be noted that items of a volatile or essentially nonrecurring nature are normally reported as other noninterest income. This would include net income from trading accounts and gains on sales of real estate owned or other assets (except investment portfolio securities). From a valuation standpoint, it is important to obtain a detailed breakdown of other noninterest income and determine if any items that are not fully representative of the bank's ongoing earning power are present.

Adjusted Gross Income (FTE)

Adjusted gross income is the sum of net interest income and noninterest operating income. Analytically, adjusted gross income is usually presented on a fully taxable equivalent basis. It is the best measure of net sales on a bank's income statement, although many, if not most, bankers still do not think in these terms. This measure shows how much overhead expense and provision for loan losses the bank can incur and still break even from operations. In making comparisons between banks and for the same bank over time, adjusted gross income is useful in that it allows meaningful comparisons between management policies that emphasize interest margin maximization with those that focus more strongly on fee generation. From an analytical viewpoint, the dollar level and trend of adjusted gross income is an important indicator of earning power.

Noninterest Operating Expense

Noninterest operating expenses are reported on bank financial statements in three broad categories:

1. *Personnel expenses* include salaries, bonuses, health insurance premiums, and other employee benefits, as well as pension, profit sharing, or employee stock ownership plan expenses.
2. *Occupancy expenses* include depreciation, rent, utilities, local property taxes, housekeeping expenses, and all other expenses related to maintenance and upkeep of fixed assets.
3. *Other noninterest operating expenses* include deposit insurance premiums, net losses from trading-account activities, write-downs and losses on the sale of real estate owned and other assets, state franchise taxes, and professional fees (legal, accounting, and consulting), as well as premiums on fidelity bond and errors-and-omissions insurance policies.

As with noninterest operating income, noninterest operating expenses should be examined in detail to identify any volatile or nonrecurring items (such as gains or losses on sale of real estate owned) to determine if any adjustments to current earnings are required or if changes in a bank's cost structure can be anticipated. Several examples of specific items to consider in the analysis of a bank's cost structure are noted below. While not complete, the listing and accompanying comments provide examples of what to look for.[10]

1. Has the employee stock ownership plan (ESOP) debt been paid off, and will annual contributions to the ESOP be reduced? Or has the bank just installed a leveraged ESOP requiring large contributions to the plan to service debt for the next several years?
2. Has the bank acquired new data processing facilities or switched from in-house to outside processing? What will be the impact on computer and employment expenses?
3. How will changes in the structure of federal deposit insurance affect the bank's deposit insurance premiums?
4. What is the condition of the bank's premises and equipment, and are the facilities adequate for reasonably forseeable growth? Is new capital spending planned that will result in higher depreciation expense? Will the bank lease new facilities or equipment that result in a rise in rental expense?
5. Is the bank involved in litigation resulting in above-normal legal and professional fees or the prospect for favorable or adverse settlements?

These are only a few of the questions that must be raised. These and related questions are necessary in order to estimate the bank's core overhead expense level and its likely rate of growth. Exhibit 9-4 provides a multiyear analysis of noninterest expenses and productivity.

Exhibit 9-4 presents several key measures of productivity that facilitate comparisons of a bank with itself over time and with its peer group. The first measure is *noninterest operating expense as a percentage of average assets* (and, in more detail, personnel, occupancy, and other expenses). Operating expense as a percentage of average assets relates overhead expense to the balance sheet. It shows whether the bank is able to grow and maintain the same overhead per dollar of asset or if growth is followed or preceded by disproportionate increases in operating expense. Also shown in the table are the ratios of *noninterest operating expenses as a percentage of adjusted gross income*. This perspective allows the analyst to examine productivity from a somewhat different vantage point: what the bank is spending per dollar of "sales."

Personnel expense per employee measures relative compensation levels at a bank. A high level of personnel expense may indicate a labor shortage in the local market, excessive management compensation, or high ESOP contributions relative to ESOP debt. Some banks pay higher-than-average salaries but expect more, on average, from their employees. Other banks follow a low-compensation strategy.

---

[10]See the Due Diligence Questionnaire (Appendix F) for a more complete indication of questions relating to the level of noninterest operating expenses.

Exhibit 9-4

	1990 ($000)				Percent of Average Total Assets			Peer Group 9/90
Noninterest Expenses		1990	1989	1988	1987	1986	1985	
Personnel	$ 7,858	1.84%	1.85%	2.03%	2.12%	1.64%	1.58%	1.54%
Occupancy	4,124	0.96	0.92	0.68	0.69	0.69	0.59	0.49
Other	4,200	0.98	0.95	1.28	1.30	1.07	0.94	1.28
Noninterest operating expenses	16,182	3.79	3.72	3.98	4.11	3.40	3.11	3.31
Loan loss provision	376	0.09	0.18	0.18	0.51	1.07	0.63	0.39
Noninterest expenses	$16,558	3.87%	3.90%	4.16%	4.62%	4.48%	3.74%	3.70%
Average assets ($000)		$427,519	$399,912	$377,748	$346,652	$329,402	$303,672	
Noninterest operating expenses ($000)		16,182	14,894	15,050	14,236	11,212	9,444	
Number of employees								
Bank		314	306	334	330	284	266	
Peer group*		229	214	211	206	201	207	
Personnel expenses/employee ($000)								
Bank		25.03	24.20	22.93	22.23	18.99	18.00	
Peer group (9/90)		26.30	26.30	25.26	24.45	23.02	22.47	
Average assets/employee ($000)								
Bank		1,362	1,307	1,131	1,050	1,160	1,142	
Peer group (9/90)		1,870	1,870	1,790	1,680	1,640	1,470	
Fee income/employee ($000)								
Bank		13,248	12,542	10,299	12,073	10,056	9,053	
Peer group (9/90)		16,429	n.a.†	n.a.	n.a.	n.a.	n.a.	
Adjusted gross income/employee ($000)								
Bank		68,922	66,925	59,078	57,495	61,897	56,271	
Peer group (9/90)		96,332	n.a.	n.a.	n.a.	n.a.	n.a.	
Noninterest operating expenses/employee ($000)								
Bank		51,535	48,673	45,060	43,139	39,479	35,504	
Peer group (9/90)		61,794	n.a.	n.a.	n.a.	n.a.	n.a.	
*Equivalent peer bank size based on the bank's average total assets		$427,519	$399,912	$377,748	$346,652	$329,402	$303,672	
Effective tax rate (taxes/pretax income)		26.69%	22.18%	12.02%	7.90%	7.38%	8.61%	

†n.a. = not available

SOURCE: Call Reports and Uniform Bank Performance Reports

Average assets per employee provides one macro measure of the efficiency of a bank's staff. A high level of personnel expense per employee can be offset by a high ratio of assets per employee. Banks with a heavy retail banking focus or with a heavy focus on fee-generating business typically have lower levels of assets per employee.[11]

Exhibit 9-4 also provides two additional ratios: *adjusted gross income per employee,* or sales per employee, and *fee income per employee.* These ratios, in conjunction with the similar comparisons to average assets, can provide additional insight into a bank's productivity trends.

Bankers sometimes overlook the importance of expense control in achieving average or above-average levels of profitability. Bank analysts should not. Assume a bank generates a 5 percent spread on loans, its highest-yielding asset category. Every dollar of "excess" operating expense requires $20 of loans to generate the net interest income necessary to cover the excess.

Banks with above-normal operating expenses, then, are under greater-than-normal pressure to increase their loan portfolios to offset the higher expense levels and generate a "normal" profit. It is just this kind of pressure that can lead to a lowering of credit standards and lay the seeds for future credit losses. Further, the required higher level of loan volume places additional pressure on capital ratios and liquidity.

Basic Operating Income (FTE)

Basic operating income is taxable equivalent pretax income before the provision for loan losses and gains or losses on securities transactions. Alternatively, it can be defined as net interest income plus fee income minus noninterest operating expense.

Basic operating income measures the profitability of a bank's day-to-day operations. From a valuation standpoint, it may be necessary to calculate an adjusted basic operating income figure from which nonrecurring or volatile items (which are otherwise reported as fee income or overhead expense) have been eliminated in order to see the underlying level of earnings generated by ongoing operations.

Securities Transactions

Banks report the net result (gain or loss) of sales of investment securities in each financial reporting period. Theoretically, securities are to be held to maturity (hence, the reporting of investment securities on the balance sheet at amortized cost rather than at current market values). Sales of securities in the investment portfolio should be motivated by strategic factors, such as changes in tax laws, increased loan demand, or changes in interest rate relationships. By their nature, gains and losses on securities transactions will be irregular with respect to their timing and amount.

In our experience, even community bankers who view themselves as talented market players and who view their investment portfolios more as trading accounts are rarely able to make consistently positive con-

---

[11]The number of full-time-equivalent employees is reported in Schedule RI of the Call Report and in the Uniform Bank Performance Report.

tributions to earnings by trading. Additionally, gains taken on the sale of appreciated securities (which are often motivated by the need to offset trading losses) usually result in forgone above-market-rate yields that would have enhanced future interest income.

Provision for Loan Losses

The level of the provision for loan losses in any given fiscal period will be a function of (1) charge-offs in the current period, (2) recoveries of previously charged-off loans, (3) the resolution of existing credit problems, and (4) the identification of new problem credits, all in relation to (5) the level of the loan loss reserve at the beginning of the period.

Over time, the loan loss provision will reflect the amount of credit risk assumed by a bank in its loan portfolio, as well as the quality of its loan administration procedures (front-end credit analysis, ongoing credit reviews, documentation, collateral control, and collection efforts).

Nearly all banks report a periodic provision for loan losses. A *minimum* loan loss provision is necessary to maintain the loan loss reserve at a constant percentage of total loans if the loan portfolio is growing at all. Although we will discuss loan loss reserve adequacy in detail in Chapter 10, it is worth noting here that even community banks with exceptionally well-managed, low-risk portfolios are under constant pressure from regulators (the FDIC, the Comptroller of the Currency, and state banking departments), as well as the market for publicly traded securities, to maintain reserves of more than 1 percent of total loans. As problems in the industry have surfaced in the 1980s, there has been constant upward pressure on this rule-of-thumb minimum loan loss reserve.

We do not use the SEC financial reporting practice of treating the provision for loan losses as a reduction in net interest income because very few banks are able to maintain a provision that is anywhere near as stable as its net interest margin. For instance, year-to-year swings of net interest margin on the order of 0.25 percent (i.e., 25 basis points) are typical. With net interest margins normally ranging from 3.00 percent to 4.50 percent of average assets, this swing represents a proportionate change of 6 percent to 8 percent. Loan loss provisions can more than double from year to year. We believe the loan loss provision requires special analytical attention in conjunction with the overall analysis of the composition and quality of the loan portfolio.

Credit problems and loan growth drive the loan loss provision. How does a well-managed bank control credit risk? The well-managed bank has written underwriting (lending) policies so that the authority and responsibilities of lending officers, credit officers, and directors are made explicit. It follows strict underwriting procedures—requiring committee approval of larger credits—and strict compliance with documentation requirements. The bank maintains ongoing monitoring of the financial position of its commercial borrowers and monitors past-due loans closely.

The well-managed bank requires adequate and consistent documentation proving that borrowers' wealth and/or earnings and collateral are sufficient to repay principal and interest on each loan when due. It maintains proper documentation to ensure that its loans are legally collectible and its claims on collateral are perfected. Its officers have personal contact with borrowers so that they can have some confidence of the borrower's character and his or her ability and willingness to repay his or her debts.

The well-managed bank seeks to minimize concentrations of loans to particular industries and individuals. The community bank limits geographic concentrations to the market area where it is most knowledgeable. Loans concentrated in remote, out-of-market areas are credit time bombs.[12]

Finally, when a loan goes bad, the well-managed bank actively pursues the largest amount of repayment (recovery) possible. A bank with feeble collection practices gives up current income (because the losses are charged to the loan loss reserve and must be replenished through current period loan loss provisions) and may attract abusive borrowers who recognize that recovery efforts by the bank are minimal.

Pretax Income (FTE)

Taxable equivalent pretax income includes the tax equivalency adjustment and is the more useful comparison when levels of tax-exempt interest income vary.

Pretax Income

Pretax income consists of basic operating income plus gains and losses on securities transactions minus the provision for loan losses and the tax equivalency adjustment.

Income Taxes

A bank's income tax provision is a function of the level of taxable income and the prevailing federal corporate tax rates. Tax loss carryforwards arise when taxable income is less than tax-deductible expense. In some cases, a bank's management and accountants may elect to show tax benefits as a reduction in the provision for income taxes. If tax benefits are particularly large in a given reporting period, they may be reported as extraordinary items.

Net Income from Continuing Operations

Net income from continuing operations (also called *net income before extraordinary items*) reflects management's calculation of the residual income remaining after paying out interest expense, paying overhead expense, taking losses or gains on securities transactions, providing for credit losses, and providing for income taxes.

---

[12]Kenneth Patton, Mercer Capital's executive vice president, coined the Fly-Over Rule of credit risk in the 1970s, following experience as National Bank Examiner with the Office of the Comptroller of the Currency and as head of loan administration for a regional bank. Stated simply, credit risk rises exponentially as the number of banks a borrower has to "fly over" to get to a particular lender increases.

Extraordinary Items

Extraordinary items are the income statement results of major events that, in the opinion of management and its accountants, are clearly not part of the bank's normal operations and meet the requirements under generally accepted accounting principles (GAAP) for reporting as extraordinary items.

Some banks report certain tax benefits as extraordinary items. Undisputed examples of extraordinary items would include gains or losses on the sale of a branch or subsidiary, gains or losses on the sale and leaseback of the bank's main office building, and recoveries or payouts in major litigation cases.

From an analytical point of view, most extraordinary items, whether positive or negative, will result in valuation adjustments to the income statement. We should note that the analytical definition of a nonrecurring item, or one subject to adjustment in the valuation process, is not nearly so strict as the requirements under GAAP.

Conclusion

The previous chapter provided a detailed overview of bank balance sheets. This chapter developed a similar overview of bank income statements. Several analytical observations regarding banks were necessary in both chapters to clarify or amplify points of emphasis. The purpose of both chapters, however, has been to lay the groundwork for the specific analytical chapters that follow. They provide the necessary background for bank analysts and investors in bank stocks, as well as for bankers who desire to develop a realistic understanding of bank and financial institutions valuation.

Chapter 10

Analyzing Bank Financial Statements

Knowledge is the only instrument of production that is not subject to diminishing returns.

J. M. Clark

Analyzing Bank Financial Statements

In Chapters 8 and 9, we discussed how a bank works and how it reports its financial condition and operations. With that background, we now proceed to discuss the analysis and evaluation of a bank's performance and condition.

Framework for Analysis

All things are relative in the world of financial analysis. Empirical comparisons are the proper basis for virtually any valuation exercise. Absent comparisons, the financial analyst could observe relatively little that is analytically useful. Investigations for a bank might be limited, for example, to answering such questions as (1) Is net income positive? or (2) Does the bank have a positive net worth?

Even in these simplest of questions, comparisons (with zero or negative numbers) are implied. Comparisons enable analysts to go beyond yes/no observations. Relative comparisons allow the analyst to make both qualitative and quantitative inferences about a business organization.

There are five key comparative approaches for evaluating a bank's financial condition and performance. Comparisons can be made:

1. Relative to the institution itself over time.
2. Relative to a selected peer group, currently and historically.
3. Relative to the bank's budget or business plan.
4. Relative to the subject institution's unique potential.
5. Relative to regulatory expectations or requirements.

Comparisons with an Institution's Own Performance over Time

The first comparative approach requires the preparation of multiyear financial statements (spreads), including balance sheets, income statements, key ratios, and balance sheets and income statements as percentages of average assets or adjusted gross income to provide a picture of what has happened at or to an institution over time. This type of analysis places the bank's current condition and performance in context with its historical results.

The key questions raised by comparisons of an institution with itself over time are: (1) Why is the bank performing differently, either overall or in one component of its balance sheet or income statement, from its historical results? and (2) What seems to be the probability that the present level or direction of performance will continue into the future?

Peer Group Comparisons

The second comparative approach requires the inclusion of peer group averages or medians in the multiyear spreads.[1] Banking is a relatively homogeneous business, and banks of the same asset size often tend to be much more similar than different with regard to their structures and operations, such that significant differences can be very revealing.

The key questions raised by peer group comparisons are (1) Why is the bank performing at variance from the peer group medians, either overall or in the various components of its balance sheets or income statements? and (2) Given the peer group comparisons *and* the historical analysis from above, what seems to be the probability that the present level or direction of performance will continue into the future?

Comparisons with Budgets or Business Plans

Budgets or business plans provide the basis for the third comparative approach. Nearly all banks prepare an annual budget as a basis for performance review and control by management and the board of directors.[2] The bank analyst can learn a great deal from examining current budgets or business plans, as well as similar documents prepared in earlier years.

The key questions raised by comparisons with budgets or business plans are (1) How is the bank performing *this year* relative to its budget? (2) How is the bank performing relative to its multiyear business plan? (3) When looking at historical budgets or business plans, how has the bank performed relative to its previous budgets or business plans? and (4) Based upon the preceding analysis, what seems to be the probability that the bank can achieve budgeted or planned performance for the current and future periods?

Comparisons with an Institution's Unique Potential

The fourth comparative approach proceeds from the first three. It considers the financial impact of such factors as market share, local economic conditions, local salary rates, deposit taking and lending focus, and fixed-asset requirements. Here it is appropriate to balance the bank's operating advantages and disadvantages in the context of its historical performance and the average performance of its peer group. In so doing, the bank analyst can gauge the level of performance a particular bank is capable of attaining and sustaining. Actual or expected performance may fall

---

[1]As discussed in Chapter 7, detailed comparative financial information is available for every banking institution in the nation through the Uniform Bank Performance Reports and Holding Company Performance Reports generated by the Federal Financial Institutions Examination Council. The FFIEC assigns each bank or holding company to a particular peer group based upon asset size and number of branches or banks. It is also possible for the bank analyst to create smaller peer groups using some of the database sources described in Chapter 7.

[2]Given the regulatory protection afforded financial institutions and the existence of federal deposit insurance, we believe that all banks, thrifts, and credit unions should be required to develop and maintain multiyear business plans. The costs to the nation's taxpayers of the thrift crisis that has so painfully unfolded since the mid-1980s and the banking crisis that is developing as we enter the 1990s are simply too great for bankers not to be held to this minimal level of business planning and analysis.

short of or approach this potential, depending upon the effectiveness of previous or present management.

The key questions raised by this comparative approach are (1) What level of performance can a particular bank hope to achieve given the realities of its historical development, competition in its marketplace, the condition of its balance sheet, and the capabilities of its management and staff? (2) How is the bank actually performing in relationship to this potential? and (3) What implications are there for valuation based upon these comparisons?

Comparisons with Regulatory Guidelines

Comparisons under this approach can be based on published guidelines such as capital adequacy requirements, directives on the appropriate levels of interest rate risk, or minimum loan-to-value ratios on real estate loans.[3]

The problem can be illustrated by the story of a young army officer who had been on active duty for about a year. He had received three Officer Efficiency Reports during that year with scores of 93 percent, 95 percent and 97 percent. When he asked the personnel representative from the Department of the Army in Washington, D.C., how he was doing, he was told he ranked in about the middle third of all officers at his level. "With those scores, how can this be possible?" he asked incredulously. The personnel officer's reply told it all: "Well, Lieutenant, you have to understand that in the army, most of our officers are above average."

The bank analyst should never forget the definition of *median* as "that observation in a population *below which and above which* 50 percent of the population lies." It is a fact of life that half of all banks, just like half of all army lieutenants, will be below average (as measured by the median), and half will be above average.

The ideal bank for a cynical bank regulator might be above average with respect to capital adequacy, be above average with respect to asset quality (and below average on credit risk), have back-up management at every position, have less interest rate risk than average, and be more liquid than average.[4]

This ideal bank would also achieve above-average returns on its assets and equity. However, as will be discussed further, there are inherent conflicts in the various risks associated with bank performance, and

[3]Comparisons with regulatory guidelines actually go hand-in-hand with peer group comparisons. In part, regulators establish required capital ratios based upon the performance of the various peer groups. Implicitly, regulators would prefer all banks to perform at *above-average* levels. The only problem with this desire is that it is a statistical impossibility for any given population.

[4]Many bank regulators have good reason to be cynical based upon repeated experience in real life with bankers who "break the rules." It is no small wonder that some regulators may seem to overreact when they see symptoms of abuse of the system. From the regulators' point of view (and perhaps the taxpayers' as well), it may be preferable to put operational restrictions in place first and then, over time, to release them when it is more than apparent that any problem has been taken care of (or even did not exist). Neither this note nor the comments above should be construed as an adverse comment regarding bank regulators, but as a dramatization to make this point: *Bankers and bank analysts need to know the rules as currently promulgated by the regulatory agencies, and bankers need to follow the rules.* No bank we are aware of ever went broke from *not making* loans or from *more-conservative* underwriting standards. There is a great deal of wisdom in the current regulatory tendency to slap controls on first and get the details later. Never forget that regulators are entrusted with responsibility for the integrity of the federal deposit insurance system. Hundreds of thrifts and banks got out in front of the regulators in the 1980s and created problems that have bankrupted the FSLIC and the FDIC.

improvements in one area often come only at the cost of increased risk (or lower comparative performance) in one or more other areas.

Operating a bank "appropriately" within the range between regulatory minimums (or maximums, if risk is measured that way) and the bank supervisor's ideal of above-average (or below-average) performance in all categories is the key to avoiding regulatory restrictions on operations, expansion, or the ability to pay dividends to shareholders. The bank analyst must therefore be sufficiently familiar with regulatory expectations and regulations to assess the actual or potential impact of regulatory problems on a bank's valuation.

Analytical Tools

The detailed, multiyear financial exhibits and schedules accompanying the sample appraisal in Chapter 22 can be characterized as the bank analyst's toolbox. A preview of these financial exhibits was provided in Chapters 8 and 9 during the introduction to a bank's balance sheet and income statement. This chapter goes a step further: to discuss how to use the information in the context of analyzing a bank.

A bank's year-to-year condition and performance, along with relevant peer group averages (median observations), are laid out in a manner that facilitates analysis along the lines discussed in the preceding section. Following this discussion of the tools of analysis, we will present a number of the critical analytical concepts that make bank analysis and appraisal different from other types of business enterprises.

We recommend that the following (or similar) exhibits and schedules be developed as preparation for any bank or thrift appraisal. The references to numbered exhibits and schedules below refer to the corresponding exhibits and schedules in the sample appraisal in Chapter 22. We suggest that readers review the exhibits and schedules to the sample appraisal while reading the sections below that describe each exhibit.

Multiyear Financial Exhibits

Multiyear Balance Sheets (Exhibit 1)
Exhibit 1 presents historical balance sheets for a subject bank, normally for five or more years. The exhibit illustrates overall and line item growth rates, shifts in dollar volume between major line items, and the levels of earning assets relative to total assets and of interest-bearing funds relative to total assets. Exhibit 1 provides indications of general size, balance sheet composition, and growth trends.

Multiyear Percentage Balance Sheets (Exhibit 2)
Exhibit 2 presents the balance sheets of Exhibit 1 in common-size form, that is, with each balance sheet item shown as a percentage of that year's ending total assets. This exhibit provides a means of identifying changes in composition over time (loans versus investments, deposits versus bor-

rowed funds) and of comparing the subject bank's composition to that of its peer group. Additionally, the exhibit shows leverage and capital ratios of the subject bank versus the peer group over time.

This portion of analysis correlates directly with the income statement and the margins the bank earns. For instance, a bank whose base of time deposits (usually the highest-costing major source of funds) is growing faster than its loan portfolio (usually the highest yielding assets) will suffer from narrowing margins unless loan yields can be increased quickly. The upshot will probably be that earnings will not grow as fast as the balance sheet, which in turn may have long-term implications for capital adequacy, dividend capacity, and stock valuation.

Multiyear Income Statements (Exhibit 3)

Exhibit 3 presents historical income statements for a subject bank for the years corresponding to the balance sheets in Exhibit 1. This exhibit tells the analyst where a bank's earnings have come from and where expense dollars have gone. The exhibit also displays the one-year and five-year compound growth rates of each line item. Also shown are dividends paid and dividend payout ratios. This exhibit answers two key valuation questions: (1) How much net income has the bank generated for its shareholders? and (2) Where are its revenues and expenses concentrated?

Multiyear Income Statements as a Percentage of Average Total Assets (Exhibit 4)

Exhibit 4 provides the income statements of Exhibit 3, with each item related to average total assets for the respective years. This exhibit illustrates the relationship between a subject bank's balance sheet and its income statement, both historically and against its peer group. It shows how the key lines of the income statement (net interest income, fee income, other noninterest operating income, basic operating income, the provision for loan losses, and net income) have behaved relative to the balance sheet, and it culminates with return on average assets (or net income divided by average total assets: ROAA or ROA). This type of analysis helps the appraiser measure the level of a subject bank's asset yields, cost of funds, fee income, operating expense, loan losses, and net income relative to a common denominator, average total assets, and then proceed to investigate the causes for any major deviations from the historical tendency or the peer norm.

Loan Portfolio Composition (Schedules 1 and 2)

The loan schedules provide a basis for tracking growth in the particular categories of loans, along with changes in the percentage composition of the loan portfolio. They also provide a basis for discussing with management, in the context of "hard numbers," the details of how a bank's loans are structured. This discussion will help the analyst identify the loan types for which demand is strongest, along with those with the best yields, the highest credit risk, and the highest interest rate risk. Similarly, the bank's asset yields and loan loss experience can be related to changes in loan composition for the bank and its peer group to explain any disparities.

It is helpful for the analyst to have a set of hard numbers to refer to when discussing operating results with management; otherwise, anecdotal and qualitative observations can be taken out of context and lose proper proportion. For example, it is easy for a manager to mistakenly attribute much of an operating improvement or deterioration to a single factor, which in fact loses significance when considered in the larger context. Demand may be very strong for a particular loan product, but its actual and potential overall impact on loan growth and interest income may actually be minor.[5]

Loan Portfolio Quality Analysis (Schedule 3)

Schedule 3 provides a multiyear reconciliation of the loan loss reserve account and thereby illustrates the subject bank's history of loan losses, recoveries of previously charged-off credits, provisions for loan losses, levels of reserves, nonaccrual (nonperforming) loans, and repossessed real estate. Included in the schedule are several key ratios for comparing the bank's loss experience and its level of reserves against its own history and peer group averages.

This presentation helps the analyst focus on two critical aspects of a subject bank's lending practices. First, what is the bank's tendency to make risky loans that ultimately have to be charged off? And second, what is its willingness to reduce current earnings by making provisions to build up reserves against potential loan losses and thereby strengthen its balance sheet and potentially improve future earnings (i.e., reduce earnings when risk is first incurred, rather than wait until the resulting loss is obvious)? The concept of reserve adequacy will be discussed more fully later in this chapter.

Liquid Asset Analysis (Schedules 4 and 5)

The liquid asset schedules describe the composition of the subject bank's liquid assets, historically and in comparison with the peer group. Also shown are the historical levels of market appreciation or depreciation in the bond portfolio in relationship to historical costs. The schedules will serve as a backdrop for a discussion of management's liquidity and portfolio management policies. A historically low level of liquid assets or a level substantially below the peer average may indicate that the subject bank is assuming excessive liquidity risk (i.e., it may be too "loaned-up").

An above-peer-level of cash and non-interest-bearing accounts may indicate that the bank, among other factors, makes heavy use of compensating balances to pay for services from correspondent banks or has a block of volatile commercial clearing-account deposits that must be offset

---

[5]Bankers, like other businesspersons, often lose perspective when confronted with day-to-day operating pressures. Lacking historical figures presented regularly in a comparative format, a banker is likely to believe that the most important factor influencing the institution is the issue she or he has been dealing with this week—or even this afternoon! The banker and the bank analyst need to see performance in perspective in order to differentiate between the trivial, the merely important, and the critical issues facing the bank.

by its own demand accounts at its correspondent banks. Finally, large unrealized gains or losses in the bond portfolio (aside from being typical adjustments to net asset value in valuing the bank's common stock) may indicate that the bank is taking on excessive interest rate risk (i.e., buying securities with excessively long maturities—whose market values tend to be highly volatile).

Deposit Composition (Schedules 6 and 7)

The deposit composition schedules illustrate trends and growth rates in the various deposit categories and the percentage composition of the deposit base, both in comparison to previous years and to the peer median. The main points for discussion here are the trends in cost of funds and the stability and composition of the deposit accounts. Rapid growth in time deposits and a rising percentage of time deposits may explain a rising cost of funds. A high level of demand and savings accounts may explain a relatively low ratio of interest expense to average assets. A rising or above-peer-level of time deposits over $100,000 (which are generally the most volatile and highest cost deposit category) is an important condition to discuss with management, because excessive reliance upon jumbo CDs may imply potentially excessive interest rate and liquidity risks and balance sheet growth that may prove unprofitable in the long run.

Spread Relationships (Schedule 8)

Schedule 8 lays out current and historical interest income and expense as a percentage of average assets, the yield on earning assets, the cost of interest-bearing funds, and the cost of earning assets for both the subject bank and its peer group. Three spread measures are calculated:

1. Net interest margin (ratio of net interest income to average total assets).
2. Net yield on average earning assets (ratio of net interest income to average earning assets).
3. Net spread (the yield on earning assets minus the cost of interest-bearing funds).

These three spread measures are important in determining the success of the core functions of nearly all banks: buying (borrowing) and selling (lending, investing) money and, in the process, taking in more interest income than they pay out. Also included in Schedule 8 are the subject bank's ratios and the peer average ratios of earning assets to total assets and interest-bearing funds to total assets, which are additional significant factors in determining interest margin. The concept of "spread banking" will be discussed at length later in this chapter.

Noninterest Expense and Productivity Analysis (Schedule 9)

Schedule 9 provides multiyear comparisons of several key measures of the bank's noninterest operating expenses. Total personnel expense has three key analytical elements: The average level of salary and benefits expense per employee and the amount of assets per employee determine the ratio of personnel expense per employee. These factors, in combination with the actual number of employees, determine the actual level of personnel expense.

High salaries and a heavy staffing level result in a high ratio of personnel expense to assets. Low salaries and tight staffing result in a low ratio of personnel expense per employee. These relationships for the bank over time and in comparison with its peer group are illustrated in Schedule 9. Occupancy expense and other operating expense as percentages of average assets are also presented.

The more efficiently a bank controls its expenses and the more intensively it employs its personnel, the more profitable it will be able to operate. Schedule 9 provides a basis for discussing operating strategies with management.

Income Statement as a Percentage of "Sales" (Schedule 10)

Schedule 10 provides another approach for measuring the efficiency of a bank's operations. This schedule analyzes the amount of operating expense used to generate a dollar of adjusted gross income (net interest income plus fee income). Schedule 10, in conjunction with Schedule 9, provides valuable insights into how a bank is run.

Return on Equity Analysis (Schedule 11)

Schedule 11 highlights the key components of return on assets (ROA) and return on equity (ROE). ROA is, of course, net income divided by average assets. It is the result of basic operating income (net interest income plus fee income minus noninterest operating expenses) and the potentially more volatile components of the income statement: gains and losses on securities transactions, the provision for loan losses, taxes, and extraordinary items.

ROE is the result of the interplay of the profitability of the bank's asset base as measured in ROA and its leverage ratio. The basic formula showing this relationship is shown below:

$$ROE = ROA \times Leverage$$
$$= \frac{Net\ income}{Assets} \times \frac{Assets}{Equity}$$

The leverage ratio (average assets to average equity) measures the amount of assets supported by the shareholders' equity investment.[6] For a given level of profitability (ROA), returns to shareholders (net income divided by shareholders' equity) rise as leverage rises. At the same time, for a given level of leverage, shareholder returns increase as profitability (ROA) increases. Unfortunately, risk of insolvency rises as financial leverage rises, and there are absolute limits on the amount of leverage regulators or the markets (for bank stock and bank debt) will tolerate.

In summary, Schedule 11 allows the analyst to examine the components of return on equity, especially profitability (ROA) versus financial leverage, over a multiyear period and in comparison with the peer group.

---

[6]Bankers and bank regulators tend to look at leverage in the form of equity/assets, so that, other things being equal, a higher leverage ratio is better than a lower ratio. The bank analyst should recognize both measures of leverage (equity/assets and assets/equity) and use them appropriately.

Reconciliation of the Equity Account (Schedule 12)

Schedule 12 serves an important role, which can be described very simply: It reconciles the bank's equity account, showing the effect of net income, dividend payouts, new stock issues, and special charges to the equity account. Schedule 12 is especially useful in highlighting the impact of a bank's holdings of marketable equity securities, because declines in their market values versus the bank's initial cost basis are charged directly to retained earnings.

Using the Multiyear Spread

If a budget or multiyear business plan is available, a multiyear spread with peer data is invaluable in assessing its validity. There are several key points to probe:

1. How does budgeted performance compare with historical results?
2. How does budgeted performance compare with peer averages?
3. Are budgeted results consistent with shifts in balance sheet composition?
4. Are planned shifts in balance sheet composition or forecast balance sheet growth realistic given local market conditions, past practices and trends, peer group experience, and the bank's capital base?
5. Do projected changes in overhead, fee income, or required loss provisions make sense given the local market, peer experience, management capabilities, and historical tendencies?

Applying these tests to a budget or business plan provides key insights into bank performance and potential. In addition, a budget or business plan can be very helpful in illustrating the quality of management and the direction of the bank.

In sum, a multiyear spread of the subject bank's financial statements allows the analyst to focus on several key ratios (interest margin, fee income, overhead, and loan loss measures) to develop an assessment of its condition and its core earning capacity. Comparisons of the bank's current income statement ratios with its historical results and peer averages, along with its balance sheet composition, provide the analyst with a basis for converting historical trends into likely future performance and for identifying potential risk elements that will affect future performance.

Use of the multiyear spread also serves as the basis for discussing and subsequently understanding the operating structure of the subject bank. The analyst should *never* forget that the *current* operating structure of a bank is largely determinative of its near-term earnings potential. As we have stressed repeatedly, bank structure can be changed only very slowly and at the margin of operations. In other words, at the time of any analysis, a bank is a complex function of past policies, local competition, the local economy, the relative size of the bank, the experience and competence of management, the legal and regulatory environment, and the condition of the banking industry as a whole.

Concept of Nonrecurring Items

The bank analyst must not only understand the current operating structure of a bank, but also those factors that may exist that require adjustment in the valuation process. Valuation, after all, is not determined by *reported earnings* but by the market's judgment (for publicly traded banks) or by the analyst's judgment of recurring or ongoing earning power, potential, or capacity.

According to Shannon P. Pratt, DBA, CFA, FASA, a recognized authority on valuing interests in closely-held businesses:

> In analyzing a company's historical earnings as a guide to estimating the company's earnings base, the analyst should make every reasonable effort to distinguish between past earnings that represent ongoing earning power and those that do not. The analyst should adjust the income statements to eliminate the effects of past items that would tend to distort the company's current and future earning power. Implementation of this analysis requires much judgment.[7]

Historical events that are not indicative of ongoing earning capacity fall into two groups: extraordinary items (a technical term defined by the accounting profession) and other items that can be considered to be nonrecurring by the bank analyst. Extraordinary items are defined in Accounting Principles Board (APB) Opinion No. 30 (1973) as items that must be both *unusual in nature and infrequent in occurrence.*

The detailed text of APB Opinion No. 30 is more restrictive in limiting the classification of events as extraordinary than the analytical concept of nonrecurring events that may require adjustment for valuation purposes. Virtually all items deemed extraordinary under generally accepted accounting principals will be considered as nonrecurring items in valuation. However, many legitimate nonrecurring items used as valuation adjustments will not be considered extraordinary in the bank's financial statements.

Dr. Pratt cites several examples of nonrecurring items that may not be classified as extraordinary items by the accounting profession:

1. Gains or losses on asset sales, including affiliates and segments of the business.
2. Proceeds from or cost of settling lawsuits.
3. Effects of temporary abnormal business conditions.

It is important to look for nonrecurring items in analyzing bank financial statements. Sometimes items of a nonrecurring nature may be hidden in the income statement. For example, gains and losses on asset sales (typically, other real estate owned) are often "buried" in the other noninterest income or other noninterest expense totals.[8] Gains and losses

---

[7]Shannon P. Pratt, *Valuing a Business: The Analysis and Appraisal of Closely Held Companies,* 2d ed. (Homewood, Ill.: Dow Jones-Irwin, 1989), pp. 281–82. Dr. Pratt's book was the first adopted by the Business Valuation Committee of the American Society of Appraisers as an "authoritative reference" in the business valuation field.

[8]For this reason, it is important to obtain *detailed* income statements in order to analyze the components of income and expense for unusual or potentially nonrecurring items.

on securities transactions are listed separately by banks. Most analysts choose to treat securities gains and losses as nonrecurring items in valuing community banks because of the volatility and discretionary nature of this item.

Other events that may make historical earnings noncomparable to likely future income include major changes in the structure of the business. For instance, changes in staffing policy or the elimination or addition of a highly compensated senior management position may have a material and lasting impact on future personnel expense. Large provisions for loan losses related to specific credits and not to systematic deterioration of the loan portfolio may require adjustments. When reviewing historical financial statements with the management of a subject bank, it is vital to look for items that are of a one-time or highly volatile nature or that represent a clear discontinuation or start-up of a revenue or cost stream.

Once actual or potential items are identified and quantified, it is important to make appropriate adjustments to reported earnings as the analyst develops the estimate of current earning power that will be used in the valuation process.

Key Analytical Concepts

In this chapter, we have examined the framework within which banks should be analyzed and we have presented several analytical tools that facilitate analysis and understanding of bank performance. The remainder of this lengthy chapter will focus on the key analytical concepts that must be understood in order to complete the analytical portion of the bank valuation process.

Banking Is a Spread Business

Banks are in the business of lending (selling) and borrowing (buying) money. Interest is the rent earned or paid for the use of money for the terms of related loans, investments, or deposits. The margin, or spread, between interest earned and interest paid is the primary source of earnings for most banks, typically accounting for 80 percent or more of adjusted gross income (or net sales). For a given asset base, the amount of net interest income earned by a bank is determined by the following factors:

1. *Ratio of earning assets to total assets.* The higher the percentage of earning assets in the bank's asset base, other things being equal, the higher the level of interest income. Cash, compensating balances with correspondent banks, buildings, equipment, and other real estate owned do not generate interest income, but they still must be supported by shareholders' equity or other liabilities. The quality of earning assets is also a factor—interest due on nonperforming loans cannot be reflected as current income.

2. *Composition of earning assets.* Loans typically provide higher yields than investments in securities and money market instruments (CDs, BAs, and Fed Funds sold). The bank that maximizes its investment in higher-yielding, reasonable-risk assets will receive relatively high interest income.

3. *Maturities and repricing terms of earning assets.* In most market environments, interest rates rise as the fixed-rate period of an investment lengthens. However, market interest rates fluctuate over time. Banks that do the best job of extending maturities to take advantage of the (normal) upward-sloping yield curve without assuming excessive interest rate risk will receive higher levels of interest income over time.

4. *Yield on earning assets.* The yield on earning assets is largely determined by items 1 through 3 above. Other things being equal, the higher the yield on earning assets, the higher the level of net interest income.

5. *Ratio of interest-bearing funds to average assets.* The higher the ratio of interest-bearing funds to average assets, the higher the level of interest expense and the lower the level of net interest income. Banks with high levels of non-interest-bearing demand accounts or heavily capitalized (underleveraged) banks with a large base of noncosting equity frequently have above-average levels of net interest income.

6. *Composition of interest-bearing funds.* Savings and NOW accounts are generally the lowest-cost source of interest-bearing funds. CDs and money market deposit accounts from retail customers are usually the second cheapest source of funds. Banks funded substantially by these retail core deposits tend to have relatively lower interest expense and therefore higher net interest income. Banks that utilize high-cost jumbo CDs, securities repurchase agreements, Fed Funds purchased, and subordinated debt generally have relatively higher interest expense and thus lower net interest income.

7. *Maturities and repricing terms of interest-bearing liabilities.* Community banks generally have difficulty attracting substantial amounts of fixed-rate deposits with maturities over one year. Flexibility in selecting maturities is thus limited. Nevertheless, the bank that does the best job of anticipating market interest rate fluctuations and of adapting its deposit pricing to the maturity preferences of its customers will have the lowest level of interest expense.

8. *Cost of interest-bearing funds.* The cost of interest-bearing funds is determined by items 7 and 8 above and by the level of competition for deposits in the bank's market territory. Banks in areas with limited competition, favorable deposit composition, and reasonable deposit maturities will generally have the lowest level of interest expense.

9. *GAP management.* Net interest income is maximized by taking those steps that maximize interest income and minimize interest expense. A bank's asset/liability GAP (by time period) is the difference in repricing between its earning assets and its costing liabilities. Because interest rate fluctuations impact both the level of interest income and interest expense, they also affect the level of net interest income. Maximizing net interest income over time requires the coor-

dination of investing and funding decisions in the light of interest rate risk. Investment and funding decisions made separately may both appear to involve reasonable degrees of interest rate risk but, when taken together, may involve a significant risk of reduced net interest income in a volatile interest rate environment because of mismatched maturity/repricing dates.

10. *Liquidity management.* A bank with too many liquid assets is probably invested in too many low-yielding assets. A bank with a low level of liquidity may have to borrow expensive funds to deal with seasonal loan demand or deposit outflows. In addition, a bank with a low level of liquidity may find it necessary to forgo opportunities to lend or invest at especially attractive yields or to service a valuable customer's special borrowing need and thus lose all the customer's business to a competitor. Banks that select the optimal degree of liquidity, given their particular situations, will tend to maximize net interest income over time.

11. *Competition.* The bank's competitive environment will affect all 10 preceding factors and thus have a significant impact on its level of net interest income. Price competition will have a direct bearing on loan yields and deposit costs. In a highly competitive environment, loan yields will tend to be bid down and deposit rates will tend to be bid up. Competition will also affect the bank's assets and funds composition. The GAP position may also be affected: One competitor may aggressively offer long-term, fixed-rate loans, while another bids up short-term deposit rates, creating a market environment in which it is difficult for the subject bank to maintain a balanced GAP position (and a reasonable level of earnings).

Spread management is thus a complex task involving the coordination of many aspects of the bank's operations and financial structure. There are three key measures of a bank's spread position:

1. *Net interest margin.* The net interest margin is net interest income as a percentage of average assets. This measure reflects all of the factors discussed above. The net interest margin gives a good overall picture of how well the bank is managing its net interest income position relative to prior years and to the peer group.

2. *Net yield on earning assets.* The net yield on earning assets is net interest income as a percentage of average earning assets. This spread measure excludes the bank's nonearning asset base and focuses exclusively on how well the bank is managing its earning assets. Because this measure is the same as deducting interest expense as a percentage of earning assets from interest income as a percentage of earning assets, it reflects both the bank's liability composition and its level of noncosting funds. The net yield on earning assets measures how efficiently the bank employs its earning asset base given its funding structure.

3. *Net spread.* The net spread is the difference between the yield on earning assets (interest income to average earning assets) and the cost of interest-bearing funds (interest expense to average interest-bearing funds). This measure eliminates both the impact of the

bank's ratio of earning assets to total assets and the impact of its ratio of interest-bearing funds to total assets. The net spread focuses on the absolute difference in rates earned and rates paid. The net spread is most useful in discussing loan and deposit pricing strategies and in analyzing the impact of the bank's investment and asset/liability management policies.

Spread Management Concepts

A bank's policies regarding the setting of rates and maturities on loans and deposits may be influenced by overriding marketing considerations, which in turn may be independent of conscious spread management decisions. Customer preferences, local competition, the local economy, and the national capital markets may substantially limit a bank's options in managing its spread. Trade-offs in terms of interest rate yield versus maturity, yield versus credit quality, and pricing versus balance sheet growth may limit flexibility.

Managing the net interest margin ultimately becomes a matter of asset/liability, or GAP, management. Although many of the elements that affect net interest income are either determined externally (e.g., loan demand) or require a multiyear effort to change (e.g., loan composition or the maturity structure of the retail time deposit base), maintaining or improving the net interest margin requires management to focus *continuously* on identifying, quantifying, and controlling the interest rate risk related to the structure of its earning asset and interest-bearing liability bases.

The *quality* of net interest income (i.e., its sustainability over the long run) is influenced significantly by the interest rate risk inherent in the bank's asset/liability structure. As will be shown, the quality of net interest income is also influenced by credit risk.

Historically, savings and loan associations earned healthy interest margins by investing in 20- to 30-year fixed-rate mortgages and by funding those investments with passbook savings accounts that were essentially withdrawable on demand.[9] Beginning in 1973, and then again in the later 1970s, when market interest rates both rose sharply and entered periods of extreme volatility, the riskiness of this strategy was driven home when many thrifts simultaneously suffered outflows of deposits (to money market funds and direct investments in Treasury bills) and negative net interest margins.

The introduction of new deposit instruments and the eventual elimination of deposit rate controls curbed the outflow of deposits but did nothing to turn around the thrift industry's negative or severely depressed net interest margins. The thrifts were further damaged because the interest rate environment beginning in the 1970s caused significant rate spread problems as well as a deterioration in the market values of their long-term, fixed-rate loans, such that asset sales made in the course of balance sheet restructuring resulted in enormous reported losses.

---

[9]Thrifts were the prime example of "borrowing short and lending long and getting rich on the difference." Banks, which had more diversified and shorter-term assets also benefited significantly from the mismatching of maturities of assets and liabilities.

Clearly, large repricing differences in earning assets versus costing liabilities can have a catastrophic impact on the net interest margin and ultimately on the solvency of a financial institution. The thrift case makes this abundantly clear. For a bank to have a "high-quality" net interest margin, it needs (1) assets that are of high quality from a credit and liquidity standpoint, (2) a relatively stable deposit base, and (3) a reasonably balanced degree of sensitivity to changes in market interest rates between its earning assets and its interest-bearing liabilities.

An institution whose assets reprice faster (sooner) than its liabilities will suffer a decrease in net interest income in a declining rate market. A bank whose assets reprice more slowly (later) than its liabilities will suffer a decline in net interest income in a rising rate environment.

Ideally, a bank's assets and liabilities would be perfectly matched in terms of maturities or repricing dates such that interest rate risk would be essentially nil; however, given the many factors that affect banks' options in building earning asset and funding structures, the obsessive pursuit of such a policy may result in a net interest margin lower than what a reasonably mismatched GAP position would produce, except in periods of the most extreme interest rate volatility.

The first analytical point from this discussion is that a fully matched GAP position may involve substantial opportunity costs relative to a moderately mismatched position that takes into account the realities of the bank's lending and deposit-gathering opportunities. The second analytical point is that good spread management does not happen by chance! Bank management must be working with these concepts every week, month, and year to build and maintain a quality earnings stream.

Asset/Liability Models

Many banks use computer-driven asset/liability models of varying degrees of sophistication. The models available today fall into three broad methodological categories: (1) maturity/repricing ladder models, (2) simulation models, and (3) duration models.

Maturity/Repricing Ladder Models

Maturity ladder models measure the repricing GAP between assets and liabilities over various periods of time. The repricing dates and amounts of assets and liabilities are scheduled and grouped together in maturity "buckets." For example, if $1 million more of liabilities than assets reprice in the fourth quarter of the fiscal year, that quarter is said to have a negative GAP of $1 million. If $3 million more of assets than liabilities will reprice over the course of the upcoming fiscal year, the bank is said to have a positive cumulative GAP of $3 million for that period. The GAP or cumulative GAP is also expressed as a percentage of total assets, earning assets, or rate-sensitive liabilities.[10]

The main advantage of maturity/pricing models is their relative simplicity: It is fairly easy to schedule all assets and liabilities matur-

---

[10]As a rule of thumb, regulators usually consider a negative (more liabilities repricing than assets) or a positive (more assets repricing than liabilities) cumulative GAP over the upcoming year of greater than 15 percent of total assets (sometimes expressed as 15 percent of earning assets or 15 percent of rate-sensitive liabilities) to be the point at which interest rate risk may begin to be excessive.

ing or repricing within any given period. The main disadvantage of GAP models is that they fail to quantify the potential impact of the mismatch on the bank's income statement or balance sheet.

Banks are required to provide minimal asset/liability repricing information in their quarterly Call Reports (Schedules RC-B, RC-C, and RC-E). This information, while useful, falls short of providing the level of detail necessary for a realistic understanding of a particular bank's GAP position. In order for bankers and bank analysts to understand the degree of interest rate risk in a bank balance sheet, more-powerful simulation tools are necessary. Fortunately, there are several such models available in the market place today.

Simulation Models

Simulation models are essentially budgeting systems that allow the effects of fluctuating market interest rates to be incorporated into budget projections. Banks with simulation models typically will run projections indicating increases and decreases in market interest rates of 1 percent, 2 percent, and 3 percent or more to test the sensitivity of projected net interest income (and net income) to market rate volatility. The simulations are generally made for one- to three-year periods. The degree of interest rate risk is measured by the amount of decrease in net interest income relative to a stable rate projection.

Simulation models not only allow the testing of the bank's present asset/liability position but also allow projections of what-if scenarios involving changes in investment strategies, operating plans, loan pricing policies, and funding sources.

The main advantage of simulation models is that they allow the riskiness of a particular asset/liability management strategy to be quantified with respect to its effects on net interest income. Their disadvantages include complexity and the practical inability to make long-term projections.

Many banks maintain asset/liability projection models. Bank analysts should request copies of current simulation runs from asset/liability models and discuss the output (and the assumptions) with management in the due diligence process.

Duration Models

Duration models are based on the concept of cash flow duration of financial instruments first developed by Frederick Macaulay in 1938.[11] Duration is the present value-weighted average term of the future cash flows generated by a financial instrument. To calculate Macaulay duration, the present value of each cash flow is multiplied by the amount of time remaining until the corresponding cash flow is to be received. These factors are then summed and divided by the current market value (i.e., present value of all the cash flows discounted at an appropriate market interest rate) to obtain the duration factor. Duration measures price volatility relative to changes in interest rates: The longer the duration of an instrument, the more sensitive is its price to changes in interest rates.

---

[11]For a detailed discussion of Macaulay duration and related topics, see Robert W. Kopprasch, "Understanding Duration and Volatility," *The Handbook of Fixed Income Securities*, 2d ed.; ed. Frank J. Fabozzi and Irving M. Pollack (Homewood, Ill.: Dow Jones-Irwin, 1987), pp. 86–120.

The advantage of the duration measure is that it allows meaningful comparisons between instruments with markedly different cash flow characteristics (e.g., high coupon bonds versus zero coupon bonds).

A bank whose earning assets and interest-bearing funds have the same duration has zero interest rate risk from the point of view of the market value of its equity. A bank whose assets have a duration substantially in excess of that of its liabilities has significant risk that the market value of its equity (i.e., the market value of its assets minus the market value of its liabilities) would decline in a rising-rate environment. A bank whose liability duration exceeds its asset duration runs the risk of a decline in the market value of its equity in a falling-rate environment.

With some mathematics, duration models can actually measure the percentage change in the market value of a bank's equity (at least that portion represented by the difference in the market values of its earning assets and costing liabilities) for each one-point change in market interest rates. The advantages of duration models are that they reduce GAP analysis to a couple of meaningful numbers and that they work well for banks with long-term assets and liabilities. The disadvantages of duration models include their complexity and their focus on market value changes. Market value changes do not necessarily correspond to changes in net interest income, particularly in the short run. Duration models are seldom used by community banks because of their complexity. The bank analyst should nevertheless be familiar with the concept of duration, which is just another way to attempt to quantify and predict interest rate risk.

Spread Management Summary

In summary, maximizing net interest income over the long run is a function of making the best use of the bank's available lending, investing, and funding opportunities without incurring excessive interest rate risk. Balancing interest rate risk should be a primary function of the investment portfolio. For example, a bank with a strong demand for three- to five-year, high-yield, fixed-rate amortizing consumer loans and a base of depositors demanding uneconomically high interest rates to extend their CD maturities beyond one year might balance interest rate risk by concentrating on investments in Fed Funds sold and short-term money market instruments. It would be difficult to show that such a strategy was balanced using a maturity ladder model; however, a simulation model or a duration model could be used to fine-tune this balancing.

Adequacy of the Allowance for Loan Losses

Banks' interest spread-generating activities involve taking credit risks, especially in their loan portfolios. Accounting and regulatory conventions require that banks report their loans net of an allowance for known and potential losses. In the event of a (theoretical) liquidation, the aggregate collectible principal balance of a bank's loans as they mature should be no less than the amount of loans, net of the allowance for loan losses, reported on its balance sheet. The allowance for loan losses should represent an amount not less than the difference between the total contractual amount of loans on the bank's books and the amount that management can reasonably expect to collect as they come due.

Maintaining an adequate loan loss reserve is a key factor in properly reporting a bank's financial position and performance. An inadequate loan loss reserve means that historical loan loss provisions have been too low and that historical earnings have been overstated. An inadequate loan loss reserve also means that shareholders' equity is overstated. Failure to make adequate provisions indicates that management may be prone to exaggerating the bank's profitability in the short run or may not be giving sufficient time and effort to monitoring the condition of the loan portfolio.

Watch Lists

Well-managed banks maintain "watch lists" of troubled or potentially troubled loans. Loans are placed on watch lists based on past-due payments, problems revealed in financial statements periodically submitted to the bank under loan agreements, and borrower difficulties discovered via the news media or loan officers' contacts with the borrower or in the community at large. A well-managed bank typically uses its watch list in its loan loss reserve calculation.

Loan Classifications

Loans on the watch list normally are classified as *loss, doubtful,* or *substandard* in conformity with regulatory classifications. The loss classification is applied to loans (or that portion thereof) that management does not expect to collect. The doubtful classification is assigned to loans (or that portion thereof) that management has significant concerns about collecting. Finally, the substandard classification is given to those loans for which there is some defect in either documentation, collateral, or debt service capacity that causes it to fall below the bank's current credit standards for new loans.

Loss reserve ratios are applied to the classified loans to derive the appropriate level for the allowance for loan losses. Typical reserve factors are: 100 percent of loan amounts classified as loss, up to 50 percent or more of loan amounts classified doubtful, and 10 percent of loan amounts classified substandard. To the reserves allocated to adversely classified loans, many banks add a general reserve of 0.50–1.00 percent or more of all loans. The extent of the general reserve is normally developed based upon a historical analysis of loan losses by category.

The process of identifying loans subject to adverse classification is a key component in federal and state regulatory examinations. In most cases, the loan classifications and corresponding loss reserves of a well-managed bank will anticipate those determined by regulators. By the same token, some bankers improperly rely on bank examiners to identify charge-offs and set reserve levels; for these banks, the adequacy of reserve levels reported in their current financial statements may be suspect unless they have recently been examined.[12]

Loan Loss Reserve Analysis

As a practical matter, a loan-by-loan analysis of a bank's loan portfolio is well beyond the scope of the typical stock valuation assignment. As an alternative, the bank analyst must rely upon a careful review of the loan loss experience and reserve level data such as that presented in Schedule 3 of the Sample Bank Valuation Report (see Chapter 22), supplemented by a discussion of that data and the condition of the bank's larger credits and watch list credits with management. Through this process, the appraiser must develop a feel about the risk of unreserved losses in the portfolio and the corresponding likely direction of future loan loss provisions. The loan loss reserve analysis can help to quantify the risks in the loan portfolio and help the analyst establish an objective basis for valuation adjustments. Key points to consider are:

1. *Loan Loss Reserves.* How does the ending reserve as a percentage of total loans (reserve ratio) compare to peer levels and the bank's reserve ratios in prior years? What is the basis for any substantial difference?
2. *Trend in the Loan Loss Reserve.* What is the trend of the period-ending loan loss reserve in relationship to loan growth? A bank must make loan loss provisions each year to account for losses in its *existing* portfolio of loans. Furthermore, additional provisions must be made for anticipated *future losses* in the new loans made during the current year. Banks exhibiting rapidly growing loan portfolios and declining loan loss reserves may be overstating current profitability by failing to provide adequately for current growth in the portfolio. An earnings adjustment may be necessary in the valuation if this condition exists.[13]
3. *Net Loan Losses.* How does the bank's ratio of net charge-offs to average total loans compare with peer medians and its own historical experience? A consistently lower loss ratio may explain a below-peer reserve ratio. If the loss ratio is above the peer median, the need for an above-peer reserve ratio may be indicated unless management has reasonable expectations of a decline in loan losses.

    The analyst may look for "bunching" of charge-offs following regulatory examinations as an indication of management's ability to stay current in its assessment of the loan portfolio.
4. *Nonaccrual Loans.* How does the dollar amount of nonaccrual loans compare with prior periods? How do the ratios of nonaccrual loans to total loans and of reserves to nonaccrual loans compare with peer

---

[12]Even an examination provides no assurance that all of a bank's problem loans have been discovered. Examiners use various dollar-level cutoffs in their examinations. For example, an examining team might specifically look at all loans over $200,000 and apply sampling techniques to smaller loans. Unless problems in a bank are definitely concentrated in one or a *very small* number of loans, it is virtually impossible to identify all of its problems in one review. Purchasers of banks may therefore take too much comfort in recent examination results. Examiners, after all, are concerned with the safety and soundness of the institution and the deposit insurance fund, not with shareholder returns. An examination may be "close enough" for a safety and soundness determination, even if more problems are later discovered. However, those extra problems may mean unsatisfactory investment returns or losses for a bank purchaser!

[13]This is particularly true if a bank's loan growth is outstripping its market's growth and it is gaining market share. Remember, banks compete on the basis of price, service, and quality. Price and service levels tend to equalize for competitive reasons in most markets. So rapid growth often comes only at the sacrifice of quality, which means future charges to earnings. See the further discussion on page 161 on this subject.

averages? What kind of actual losses are expected on the current balance of nonaccrual loans? How many loans are expected to be placed on nonaccrual status within the next two quarters? Have any seriously troubled loans been identified that are not yet on nonaccrual status? A ratio of reserves to nonaccrual loans equal to or in excess of the peer median is normally an indicator of reserve adequacy, unless the bank is slow to put loans on nonaccrual status.

5. *Recoveries.* Does the bank expect to recover significant amounts of previously charged-off loans in the upcoming year? What has been the historical relationship between charge-offs and recoveries? Significant recoveries in the upcoming fiscal periods may tend to reduce the required level of loan loss provisions. A bank that has a high level of recoveries relative to its charge-offs is usually a bank that recognizes problem loans quickly. Some bankers have a tendency to forget about loans once they are charged off. In so doing, they lose a significant potential benefit. Low recoveries may also be an indication of poor quality loan underwriting policies. It is difficult to recover losses on unsecured loans or on loans where collateral interests were not perfected in a timely way.

None of these items is a definitive measure of reserve adequacy. For instance, a high level of nonaccrual loans does not necessarily predict high charge-offs in upcoming quarters—the loans may be well collateralized or simply suffering temporary problems. At the same time, in spite of competent loan review staffs and loan officers, credits can go bad suddenly and without warning and be charged off without ever going on nonaccrual status. That is why banks maintain general loan loss reserves.

Another Caveat on Rapid Growth

A special point of concern lies in the credit quality of rapidly growing loan portfolios. A bank whose loan portfolio is growing at double-digit rates while the national and local economies are growing at single-digit rates requires special scrutiny. Rapid growth suggests that the bank may be acting aggressively to increase local market share, making new types of loans, purchasing loans and loan participations from outside its market territory, or directly originating loans outside its local market.

A rapidly growing bank may be sacrificing credit quality, compromising loan administration capacity, or lending where it has insufficient management knowledge or skill. Rapid growth is often a positive factor in valuing a company's stock; however, for a bank with a rapidly growing loan portfolio, the related risk considerations may offset the potential corresponding improvement in near-term earnings.

Capital Adequacy and Leverage

Banks have to have capital (common equity, preferred equity, loan loss reserves, and long-term debt) to support their assets and their insured deposits. Capital adequacy is necessary to protect the safety and soundness of the banking system. A bank's capital base also serves as a cushion in the event of insolvency to limit the losses that must be covered by the FDIC in making insured depositors whole or in reorganizing the bank.

Comparisons with Other Companies

Compared with commercial and industrial companies, banks are highly leveraged entities. Leverage, measured by the ratio of shareholders' equity to total assets, typically ranges from 6 percent to 10 percent or more for a healthy community bank. This suggests that a dollar of equity in a bank supports from $10 to nearly $17 of banking assets (that is, the ratio of assets to equity ranges from 10x to nearly 17x. A commercial company with an equity-to-assets ratio below 25 percent (depending on the industry) is often considered to be highly leveraged and a potential credit risk. In other words, companies with asset-to-equity ratios of 4x or more are generally thought to be highly leveraged.

Banks are allowed by their regulators and by the markets for bank debt and equity to maintain a relatively high degree of financial leverage for a number of reasons. Banks have high pretax margins as a percentage of revenues (net interest income plus fee income).[14] Banks also have substantial operating leverage. Fixed operating costs are typically low relative to operating income. Their asset bases consist of generally marketable, highly diversified, and frequently collateralized receivables. Banks tend to have relatively stable customer bases: It is much less convenient to change banks as a depositor or borrower than it is to change supermarkets. Finally, banks are subject to government supervision and managements can be ordered to cease and desist from excessively risky activities, provided they are discovered in time.

Concept of Leverage

Leverage is a simple concept. Consider leverage in relationship to a rubber band, whose natural state represents equity. Banks operate by "stretching the equity" and adding deposits and other liabilities. Anyone who has played with a rubber band knows that there is a range within which it will stretch comfortably. Beyond that range, the rubber band begins to tighten, and when stretched too far, the rubber band will break. When things get stretched too far at a bank, things can "break." When that happens, as with a rubber band, it is painful for those holding the pieces.

Relative leverage for banks can be determined by making peer group comparisons. Average equity-to-asset ratios for the various community bank peer groups generally fall in the 7.5 percent to 9.0 percent range. A bank with a below-peer equity-to-asset ratio can be considered to be relatively more highly leveraged. A bank with an above-peer equity-to-asset ratio can be considered to be relatively less highly leveraged.

Although high leverage generally implies a higher degree of financial risk (i.e., the bank can sustain a lower amount of net losses before becoming insolvent), banks with leverage differing from their peer average must be considered in light of their actual operating strategies to obtain an overall assessment of individual financial risk. For instance, a highly leveraged bank with a matched GAP position and conservative

---

[14]Proof of this statement is found in Schedule 10 of the Sample Bank Report in Chapter 22. Bank pretax margins *on sales* are very high in relationship to those of their corporate customers.

lending policies may have an effective overall risk profile below that of an under-leveraged bank with a large negative GAP position and relatively lax lending policies.[15]

Capital Adequacy

Capital adequacy is an increasingly complex area in banking. Capital adequacy is a matter of regulatory compliance (as well as market compliance for publicly traded banks). A bank with inadequate capital may face regulatory limitations or a prohibition on balance sheet growth or on the payment of dividends. The stock market may penalize inadequately capitalized banks with lower stock prices.

Until the introduction of risk-based capital guidelines, the key regulatory ratios for determining capital adequacy were the ratios of equity to total assets and of primary capital to assets. Primary capital is defined as the sum of common equity, noncumulative preferred stock, the reserve for loan losses, and subordinated debt (only in an amount up to 20 percent of the total of the preceding three items). The ratio of primary capital to total assets was a key measure of capital adequacy. Community bank peer groups typically had median primary capital-to-total-asset ratios of 8.0 percent to 9.5 percent.

Risk-Based Capital Requirements

Risk-based capital requirements began to be phased in on December 31, 1990. Effective December 31, 1992, all banks will be required to maintain a risk-based capital ratio of 8 percent.[16] Risk-based capital differs from the preceding measures in that assets are grouped into various risk groupings and the amount of required capital is weighted according to the regulatory perceptions of credit risk for the various categories. Balance sheet assets are each assigned to one of four risk-weighting categories: 0 percent, 20 percent, 50 percent, and 100 percent, based on their relative riskiness from a credit standpoint. Examples of assets falling into each category are provided in Exhibit 10-1.

Risk-based capital guidelines are expected to be modified eventually to include an adjustment for interest rate risk.

Capital as defined under the new regulations will be divided into two tiers. Tier 1, or core capital, is defined as common equity (common stock, surplus, and retained earnings) plus noncumulative perpetual preferred stock minus goodwill and nonqualifying intangible assets. Tier 2, or supplementary capital, consists of cumulative perpetual and limited-life preferred stock, mandatory convertible securities, subordinated debt, and the allowance for loan losses, with some limitations on each category. Tier 2 capital in excess of 100 percent of Tier 1 capital may not be included to meet the regulatory minimums. The capital ratio is calculated

---

[15]Unfortunately, banks that leverage excessively tend to do so in ways that *raise* overall risk levels. A high leverage ratio, for example, might be accompanied by an above peer-level portion of assets in loans (the highest-risk asset category), a below peer-level loan loss reserve, a smaller portion of assets in securities (indicating less liquidity) with maturities concentrated in the longer terms (indicating more interest rate risk), and so on. Leverage also tends to find its way to the income statement, where operating expenses may be higher than peer levels. Often the bank will have recently invested heavily in a new building or renovation program, which increases nonearning assets and increases operating expenses. Bank analysts and shareholders should be aware of the risks associated with these banks.

[16]*Comptroller's Handbook for National Bank Examiners,* Section 303.1, March 1990.

Exhibit 10-1
Summary of Asset Categories by Risk-Weighting
Category Under Risk-Base Capital Guidelines

0% Risk-weighting assets
  Cash
  Securities issued by, or direct claims (loans and leases) on, the U.S. government and other OECD* central governments (including
    balances due from the FRB and FRB stock)
  Portions of claims unconditionally guaranteed by U.S. or OECD central governments (GNMA and SBA)

20% Risk-weighting assets
  Bank deposits (due from U.S. and OECD banks)
  Government agency securities (U.S. and OECD) (Example: FNMA, FHLMC, FFCB, FHLB, etc.)
  Claims collateralized by 0% and 20% risk-weighted assets (CMOs with FNMA, GNMA, or FHLMC pools as collateral)
  General obligation bonds of U.S. and OECD local governments

50% Risk-weighting assets
  First-lien residential, 1–4 family mortgages
  Privately issued mortgage securities (*No* FNMA, FHLMC, GNMA or guarantees)
  U.S. and OECD municipal revenue bonds

100% Risk-weighting assets
  Stripped MBS IO/PO
  MBS and REMIC residuals and subordinated tranches
  Intangibles
  Premises and fixed assets (OREO)
  Industrial revenue bonds
  Private and corporate loans; securities

*Organization of Economic Cooperation and Development, consisting of the United States, Canada, Western European nations, Australia, New Zealand,
and Japan.

by dividing the sum of Tier 1 capital and the includable amount of Tier 2 capital by the risk-weighted asset base.[17]

The weightings cited above imply that banks with substantial investments in government securities, mortgage-backed securities, and mortgage loans could meet the 8 percent risk-weighted minimum with a capital-to-unweighted-asset ratio of well under 4 percent. Bank analysts and bankers can be reasonably assured that minimum leverage ratios resulting in capital well in excess of that implied by the risk weightings will be enforced by the regulators. Historically, community banks with leverage ratios (of equity to assets) below 6 percent have come under intense regulatory scrutiny and have been forced to reduce growth, suspend or reduce dividend payouts, or raise new capital. The imposition of risk-based capital likely means that banks will have to maintain capital levels that the regulators consider to be adequate under *both* the minimum leverage ratio and the risk-based capital ratio standards.

Bank appraisers need to develop an overall impression of the adequacy of a subject bank's capital position because this will have a direct impact on the bank's ability to grow, pay dividends, and avoid being required to sell new stock.

In addition, excess capital, or equity in excess of the expected level for community banks, tends to lower return on equity. Excess capital may therefore not be worth as much as more normally leveraged capital. This concept is developed in Chapter 14.

---

[17]Ibid.

Importance of Market Share

Market share for banks is commonly measured by share of total deposits, loans or assets. Market share data are available on a county-by-county basis (with some time lag) in the *FDIC Databook: Operating Banks and Branches,* pub-lished annually by the FDIC. This publication can be us-ed to determine a subject bank's percentage of total deposits domiciled in the counties in which it has offices. While this measure fails to cap-ture niche information (that is, share of different classes of deposits or share of local loans), it does provide an indication of the amount of market clout a bank can exercise in its market. In most states, the county is a convenient unit for measuring a bank's position in its market territory. Banks interested in more detailed analysis of market share either per-form independent studies, share relevant market data with their com-petitors, or obtain the services of a private marketing consultant.

Market share can have an important influence on bank profitabili-ty. The market leader generally has the power to influence interest rates charged on loans and paid on deposits as well as fees charged for various services. If the competitors are rational, they will usually follow the lead of the market's largest bank. Banks bent on rapid growth or those near-ing insolvency may bid up deposit rates and bid down fees and loan rates, but the larger, well-established banks are in a position to respond and defend their profitability. The larger, well-established banks will general-ly have relationships with the lower-risk borrowers and the less-rate-sensitive depositors in a community.

From a valuation standpoint, market share provides several key con-siderations. A franchise that dominates its market—or at least dominates its niche—will tend to be more profitable over time and less subject to risk than one that does not. If a bank dominates its local market, the question becomes: How strong is the local economy? The dominant bank, provided its loan underwriting has been strong, will be in the best posi-tion to deal with a weak local economy. The level of competition in the market is also a consideration. If no one is bidding down loan rates and service fees or bidding up deposit rates, profitability will be higher. Final-ly, if a market is dominated by two or three well-capitalized, well-managed banks, all with reasonably strong customer loyalty, outsiders may be discouraged from entering the market because of the likelihood of low balance sheet growth relative to the cost of entering the market.

Return Measures

Return on assets is perhaps the most overworked measure of return for a bank. Return on assets (the ratio of net income to average total assets) measures the profitability of a bank's asset base without regard to the amount of equity invested by the bank's shareholders, or to the source of income (whether balance sheet driven or not). Other things being equal, a well-capitalized bank, flush with non-interest-bearing funds from the equity account, will report a higher return on assets than a less well-capitalized bank. Return on assets alone is best used in making comparisons between banks without reference to the value of their common stock. It is used in conjunction with other measures of return in the overall process of analysis and valuation.

Return on equity (net income divided by average total equity) measures the return provided to shareholders on their investment in the bank. This measure is essentially the product of the bank's return on assets and its leverage multiple, average assets to average equity (see Schedule 11 of the Sample Bank Valuation in Chapter 22).

Because the primary purpose (or at least a major one) of any corporation is to produce returns for its shareholders, a dollar invested in the stock of a bank with a high return on equity and a low return on assets will be worth, other things being equal, more than a dollar invested in the stock of a bank with a high return on assets and a low return on equity. A highly leveraged bank with a moderately profitable asset base can provide relatively high returns to its shareholders. On the other hand, an overcapitalized bank with a highly profitable asset base may provide a below-peer-level return to its shareholders.

Although heavy capitalization reduces financial risk, the overcapitalized bank may fail in its obligation to maximize returns to its shareholders, who would be better off (*value judgment!*) receiving dividends that can be invested in other assets.[18] The optimal situation is to maintain the highest degree of leverage consistent with reasonable financial risk and flexibility vis-à-vis government regulators while maximizing the profitability of the bank's asset base (return on assets). Such a strategy will tend to maximize common stock values over the long run.

Management Culture

In valuing a bank, it is important to develop an opinion about its management "culture." Management culture is a determining factor in risk, growth, and the ability to maximize shareholder returns over the long run. Community bank cultures tend to fall into (or between) the following groups:

1. *Go-go.* A go-go bank will typically have several of the following characteristics: double-digit balance sheet and loan growth, low loan rates (priced to ensure getting the business) or high loan rates (for the portion of the local banking market not desired by other competitors), relatively lax credit policies, a reluctance to make loan loss provisions or charge off bad loans, reliance on jumbo CDs and borrowed funds, high deposit rates, below-peer liquidity ratios, high overhead expense levels due to high senior management salaries and

---

[18]Overcapitalization may be the reverse of undercapitalization (overleverage). But like the overleveraged bank, whose stereotypical characteristics were defined in a previous footnote, the overcapitalized bank tends to focus on and be proud of its fairly high return on assets, ignoring the fact that its return on equity is dismally low. In the pursuit of even higher capital ratios, shareholder dividends may be low. Operating expenses may tend to be a bit high (overstaffing may be a problem), and fee income may be somewhat low (so as not to upset the customers). Loan losses are almost nonexistent, which probably means the bank is taking *too little* credit risk. Fixed assets are likely to be well depreciated, and the bank is using outmoded technology for the most part. In short, management fell asleep at the helm and the ship drifts on. Bank analysts and shareholders, beware: The returns and performance for these banks do not justify premium valuations!

heavy staffing in the lower ranks or heavy investments in upscale bricks and mortar, heavy turnover in the investment portfolio (trading), a high dividend-payout ratio, and low capital ratios.

2. *Go-slow.* A go-slow bank will typically have these two characteristics: asset growth at or moderately above the prevailing inflation rate, and a management that attempts to keep all its key performance and balance sheet ratios near its peer group's averages.

3. *No-go (ostrich syndrome).* A no-go bank will have several of the following characteristics: asset growth at or below the prevailing inflation rate, heavy capitalization, low dividend payout, a below-peer loan-to-deposit ratio, above-peer liquidity ratio, restrictive lending policies, high loan rates, low deposit rates, low overhead expense (old facilities, low salaries), and heavy staffing at below-average salaries (bureaucracy).

4. *High performance.* The high performance bank may get there by one of several routes. Consistent high performers, however, tend to build upon the bank's inherent market strengths. Consistent high performers focus on building net interest income, charging fees for appropriate services, and managing overhead expenses well. High-spread banks may have higher levels of expenses than low-spread banks, but both will carefully monitor their expenses in relation to asset and sales growth. High performance banks tend to control credit losses better than other banks. In short, high performance banks tend to understand the wisdom in the simple accounting identity:

Profit = Total revenue − Total costs

Profit is increased in one of only three ways conceptually: (1) by increasing revenues without raising expenses, (2) by lowering expenses without reducing revenues, or, for real impact, (3) by increasing revenues while decreasing expenses. High performance banks tend to look at themselves in light of this tautology and work continually to maintain and increase earnings and shareholder returns.

Management at a go-go institution wants it all—now: high compensation, high profits, high dividends to shareholders, a dominant position (by volume) as a local lender, etc. Unless such an institution has the most skilled management *and* the best of luck, the go-go strategy cannot be sustained. A recession can result in severe losses on marginal credits. Marginal credits may turn sour even in a good economy. A modest decline in loan growth or pressure on the interest margin from increased competition in an environment of uncontrolled overhead expenses will lead to severe pressure on earnings. Except in extraordinary circumstances, the go-go bank is assuming too much risk to sustain profits in the long run. Retrenchment will be the almost inevitable result. Therefore, the bank analyst should take care not to overvalue a go-go bank on the way up. Coming back down can be a long and painful process, and low equity valuations are the inevitable result.

The no-go bank is doing just the opposite of the go-go bank. It is forgoing interest income by staying too liquid and by pursuing an overly strict loan policy. The no-go bank's competitive position may also weaken over time as the institution develops more of an inbred bureaucracy and becomes inattentive to its customers. Low leverage and low profitability (due to a lack of higher-yielding loans in the asset base) lead to low returns on equity for the no-go bank. Relatively low equity valuations tend to be the result of following the no-go strategy.

The go-slow bank may be serving its stockholders reasonably by seeking a reasonable trade-off between risk and return. Average-level returns are achieved at average risk levels. Average equity valuations are the typical result.

High performance banks tend to get that way by focusing on the basics of banking and good business practice. High performance banks can generate exceptional returns for their shareholders at reasonable levels of risk by continually focusing on the basics of banking. An obsession with exceeding peer median performance and balance sheet ratios, however, may not be healthy because such a strategy may push today's high performance bank over into the go-go category. The management that pursues the optimal risk/return trade-off and maintains tight control of overhead expense probably serves its shareholders best. Certainly, this strategy should lead to above-average equity valuations, other things being equal.

If a change in top management becomes necessary due to normal retirement, regulatory insistence, or disappointing returns, changing a bank's culture may be a slow process. Problem loans and problem borrowers tend to take years to resolve. "Junk" in the bond portfolio is often difficult to sell without booking excessive losses. Aside from financial considerations, a bank's officers, staff, depositors, and loan customers may be accustomed to doing business a certain way. Institutional inertia can be an extremely powerful force.

It should be obvious by now that banking is not a get-rich-quick business: Profits are measured in basis points (fractions of a percentage point) relative to total assets. The bank analyst needs to evaluate performance with these concepts in mind.

Conclusion

As the preceding discussion has shown, successful bank management is a balancing act among five key financial parameters, namely, capital requirements, interest rate risk, liquidity, credit risk, and earnings.[19]

It is a bank management's function to select the mix of products and strategies that best achieves the organization's financial and operating goals. Quite often, strategies will have potentially conflicting impact on the five financial parameters. The role of bank management is to select the strategies and products that achieve an institution's earnings goals (quantity of earnings) in the context of a stable and growing net earnings stream (quality of earnings).

The bank analyst's role is to develop an understanding of a bank's products and strategies and to evaluate them in the context of the key financial parameters summarized in the preceding chapters.

---

[19]Kenneth W. Patton and Z. Christopher Mercer, "Asset/Liability Management Today," in *Bank Performance Annual 1987*, ed. Edwin B. Cox (New York: Warren, Gorham & Lamont, Burton, 1987), p. 85.

Chapter 11

Holding Company Analysis

... When you can measure what you are speaking about, and express it in numbers, you know something about it; when you cannot measure it, when you cannot express it in numbers, your knowledge is of a meager and unsatisfactory kind; it may be the beginning of knowledge, but you have scarcely, in your thoughts, advanced to the stage of science. ...

Lord Kelvin

You have to talk to the numbers until the numbers talk to you.

Robert C. Rogers (1975)

Introduction

Bank holding companies do just what the term implies: They hold the stock of banks. The vast majority of bank holding companies own substantial controlling interests in their affiliate banks, in most cases 100 percent of the outstanding stock and rarely less than 80 percent of the stock (in order to be able to file consolidated tax returns). A holding company may own the stock of a single bank, in which case it is called a *one-bank holding company.* If a bank holding company owns the stock of two or more banks, it is called a *multibank holding company.*

One-bank holding companies are normally created in one of two ways. In the first case, shareholders of an existing bank create a holding company structure and then exchange shares in the bank for shares in the bank holding company. The bank holding company becomes the parent company, and the bank becomes its subsidiary. Normally, the objective of the organizing shareholders is to exchange 100 percent of the bank's shares for bank holding company shares, thereby making the bank a 100 percent–owned subsidiary.

In the second case, a bank holding company may be created specifically for the purpose of acquiring the shares of a bank. A group of shareholders form and capitalize a holding company to acquire a bank. Regulatory approval for the acquisition then is sought. If that approval is forthcoming, the holding company normally obtains financing for a portion of the purchase price, offering the shares of the subsidiary bank and perhaps its own shares as collateral for the financing institution.

Bank holding companies enjoy significant flexibility in financial structure and operations relative to independent banks. Holding companies are regulated by the Federal Reserve, and legal restrictions on their activities tend to be less stringent than those on banks. This chapter will discuss some of the special features of holding companies relative to banks and then outline the various methods of holding company financial analysis.

Background on Bank Holding Companies

Special Features of Bank Holding Companies

Holding companies are subject to less stringent regulation than banks, thereby providing management and stockholders with a number of potential advantages over a stand-alone bank. Several of the key features of a bank holding company include:[1]

1. *The legal ability to purchase its own stock.* Virtually all banks are prohibited from buying their own stock. A bank holding company has the ability to provide liquidity to shareholders by making a market in its stock.

    Holding companies have the further option of implementing formal stock repurchase or exchange programs. In a stock repurchase program, a holding company offers to buy back a certain number of shares from its stockholders. A repurchase program can result in higher earnings per share and a higher return on equity for remaining shareholders if excessive prices are not paid. Repurchase programs have the added benefit of concentrating ownership in those shareholders (at no out-of-pocket cost to them) who share an optimistic outlook for the company while at the same time cashing-out those who would prefer to invest elsewhere.

    In an exchange program, the holding company offers notes or preferred stock in exchange for common shares. Those shareholders who accept the offer obtain an investment providing a higher current yield than the common stock. Like a repurchase program, an exchange offer can result in higher earnings per common share, a higher return on common equity, and a concentration of the voting control of the remaining common shareholders. (See Chapter 18 for a more complete treatment of stock repurchase programs.)

2. *The ability to double leverage.* A holding company can borrow from other banks and other lenders (usually pledging the stock of its bank subsidiary as collateral) and then use the borrowed cash to fund an injection of equity into the bank. The additional capital at the bank level can be used to shore up capital ratios in the event of net losses or rapid balance sheet growth.

    Double leveraging has the effect of shifting risk from the federal deposit insurance fund to the company's lenders. Double leveraging is most effective for companies with assets below $150 million, because they do not file consolidated financial statements with the Federal

---

[1]For extensive detail on the special features of bank holding companies, the reader is directed to two unpublished papers: "Executive Summary of Bank Holding Company Course Material from American Bankers Association Stonier Graduate School of Banking," Huggins and Associates, Memphis, Tenn., n.d.; and P. Thomas Parrish, "The Bank Holding Company After FIRREA," Gerrish and McCreary, Memphis, Tenn., 1990.

Reserve. Nevertheless, there are limits to the amount of double leverage the Fed will tolerate, even for smaller companies.[2]

Excessive double leverage may result in pressure from the FDIC, Comptroller of the Currency, or state banking departments being replaced by pressure from the Fed.

3. *Favorable income tax treatment of acquisition and other debt financing.* A holding company owning 80 percent or more of its subsidiary bank can file a consolidated federal income tax return with the subsidiary. The upshot of filing on a consolidated basis is that interest expense on debt at the holding company level is offset by taxable income generated at the bank level. In addition, cash dividends from the bank to the holding company are tax free.

    Under current tax law, individual investors who incur debt to acquire stock are severely limited as to the amount of interest that is deductible from personal taxable income. Acquiring a bank via a holding company (that is, investors capitalizing a holding company, which then borrows the remaining funds to purchase the stock of the target bank) thus involves a significant tax benefit: The acquisition debt can be serviced by the bank's pretax earnings. Interest expense from other leveraged transactions (stock repurchase and exchange programs) is also offset against bank earnings.

4. *The ability to hold investments prohibited to banks.* Holding companies are able to hold assets considered inappropriate for funding by insured deposits. Banks are severely restricted as to the amount and purposes of their real estate holdings.[3]

    No such limits apply to holding companies. A holding company is allowed to lease real and personal property (sale and leaseback). This feature allows a holding company to shore up the capital of a subsidiary with appreciated premises by purchasing the property at current market value and leasing it back to the bank. At the bank level, this transaction results in income (that is, the gain versus the bank's cost basis in its offices) that can flow into its equity position.[4]

    In addition, holding companies are not subject to legal lending limits (regarding loans to one borrower), and if necessary, the needs of a large customer can be met by making a loan at the holding company level. It should be noted that the broader asset powers of a holding company entail higher risks. The regulatory purpose served is to allow banking organizations greater flexibility while isolating riskier investments from the insured deposit base directly to the holding company's shareholders and lenders (which, unfortunately, may be making the loans with insured deposits!).

5. *Geographic diversity.* The holding company structure allowed banking organizations to diversify geographically in states that had

---

[2]See the more detailed discussion below on double leverage.

[3]Most banks may hold real estate only in the form of premises, land for future development (as banking offices), and foreclosed properties (usually subject to a five-year time limit). In some cases, a bank may hold additional real estate but must carry it on its books at zero value. Banks are also limited as to the ratio of real estate assets to total capital, typically no more than 10 percent.

[4]Unfortunately for banks desiring a quick fix to capital problems, any gains on sales involving leasebacks can only be booked over the term of the lease. In other words, sales of this nature are effectively treated as installment sales for book purposes. Basically, under existing accounting rules, the risk of the transfer must be shifted from the seller to the purchaser for a "normal" gain to be booked.

unitary bank laws (one bank, one office) or permitted banks to branch only within a single county, by capitalizing separate banks to meet state branching regulations. This feature of holding companies is less important currently because many states now allow statewide or even interstate branching.

The multibank holding company concept remains valid, however, for combinations of community banks where there is actual or perceived value in maintaining the local character of the subsidiaries and in retaining local management.

6. *The ability to provide additional services and operate nonbank subsidiaries.* Under Federal Reserve Regulation Y, holding companies are allowed to engage in a number of activities considered closely related to and a proper incident to banking. Examples include insurance brokerage, discount stock brokerage, third-party fee appraisals, and third-party data processing.[5]

Operating separate nonbank subsidiaries allows the bank holding company to tailor employee compensation to the economics of different lines of business. Separate subsidiaries also allow market segmentation: A company may want to book higher-risk consumer loans through finance company subsidiaries both to avoid the stricter loan examination criteria at the bank and to segment the customer base.

7. *Multibank, multicompany structure.* The multibank structure not only provides geographic diversity, as described above, but also the potential for economies of scale and greater shareholder liquidity. Several community banks can be merged into a single holding company. Administrative, marketing, data processing, and investment functions can be centralized, potentially cutting overhead without eliminating the local management and character of the member banks.

The consolidation of stockholdings in the member banks into a single holding company can enhance shareholder liquidity by virtue of the increased size of the entity issuing the shares.

Key Differences in Comparison to a Stand-Alone Bank

Three key differences between a bank and a bank holding company can be summarized as follows:

1. Banks are insured depository institutions regulated by the Office of the Comptroller of the Currency (nationally chartered banks) or the Federal Deposit Insurance Corporation and state banking departments (state-chartered banks). A bank holding company is simply a corporation whose primary purpose is the ownership of a controlling

---

[5]Freestanding banks can engage in practically all the activities permitted to holding companies under Regulation Y by setting up bank service corporation subsidiaries. However, given the other advantages of holding companies, few banks have set up service corporations. In the thrift industry, service corporations have been quite common, primarily because the mutual form of ownership once common to savings associations eliminated nearly all of the financial benefits of having a holding company structure.

or significant interest in one or more banks. Bank holding companies are regulated by the Federal Reserve System.

2. Banks are operating entities that offer deposit accounts. Bank holding companies serve mainly as a passive corporate ownership structure. In most cases, nearly all banking operations will occur at the subsidiary bank level, and other business operations will occur at the nonbank subsidiary level.

3. Bank capital requirements are defined by regulation or regulatory interpretation. Banks are dependent upon their own earnings to generate capital internally for growth and to pay dividends to shareholders. Bank holding companies are separate and distinct economic entities with their own capital structures. Because they normally do not have separate operations of their own, they are dependent upon their subsidiary bank(s) to generate capital internally for growth and to upstream dividends, appropriate tax payments and fees, and interest income (if the bank is borrowing from the parent). These funds are necessary to pay holding company direct operating expenses, to service holding company debt, and to pay dividends to the holding company's shareholders.

In other words, bank holding companies entail entirely separate and distinct sets of risk and structural characteristics that must be considered by the bank analyst in the valuation process. Bankers and bank shareholders in small bank holding companies often forget this simple truth in their day-to-day considerations regarding "the bank." The context within which they normally operate is that of the bank, so that is the context within which they think. But the holding company does exist, and the bank analyst cannot overlook it in his or her analysis, even though bankers often do.

Banking companies find the holding company structure to be attractive. According to data provided by the Federal Reserve System, at December 31, 1989, there were 13,201 FDIC-insured banks. On the same date, there were 5,878 one-bank holding companies and 967 multibank holding companies. These statistics suggest that the majority of banks today are owned by bank holding companies. There are now fewer than 1,000 independent banks not owned by a holding company. The primary implication for the bank analyst is that most bank valuation assignments will involve the analysis of a bank holding company.

Parent Company Concept

Bank holding company financial statements may be presented in two ways. The first method is on a consolidated basis. When financial statements are consolidated, all affiliates' assets and liabilities and revenues and expenses are added together and intracompany transactions are eliminated. Consolidation results in a holding company looking much the same as its bank subsidiary, except that holding company debt is reflected on the consolidated balance sheet and holding company interest expense, along with the revenues and expenses of nonbank subsidiaries, if any. Holding companies with consolidated assets of $150 million or more must file consolidated financial statements with the Federal Reserve System.

The other method of presenting holding company financial statements is on a parent company only basis. In a parent company only presentation, assets owned and liabilities owed directly by the holding company are reported on the balance sheet. The holding company's investment in its subsidiary bank(s) and other subsidiaries is shown under the equity method. Under this method, the asset on the holding company's balance sheet represented by its investment in a subsidiary is booked at the current amount of equity reported by the subsidiary times the percentage of the stock of the subsidiary held by the company.[6]

Occasionally, smaller banks do not maintain their parent company books under generally accepted accounting principles. Entries may have been made on the cost basis of accounting or some hybrid method. In those cases, the investment in a subsidiary bank may be grossed-up by goodwill created at the time of the holding company's formation. An analytical adjustment may be necessary to segregate the actual investment, at equity, from goodwill or other items that may be included in the investment. This is particularly true if the use of interim holding company statements is required. At year-end, the bank's accounting firm may make appropriate adjustments for proper financial statement presentation; however, the analyst may be misled in the interim.

Along the same lines, the analyst may underestimate or overestimate interim net income *for the consolidated entity* if all appropriate income tax accruals between the bank(s) and the parent company have not been made in interim financial statements.

Financial Analysis of Bank Holding Companies

Analyzing the consolidated financial statements of a holding company is essentially no different from analyzing a freestanding bank, except that the impact of nonbank subsidiaries, if any, must be taken into account. Analyzing a bank holding company on a parent-only basis involves several new analytical concepts.

Bank Holding Company Performance Report

Holding companies are required to file quarterly reports with the Federal Reserve. Consolidated reports are coded FR Y-9C, while parent-only statements are coded FR Y-9SP. The Fed uses these reports to group holding companies into peer groups based on consolidated asset size and number of subsidiaries and to provide peer group average data. The Fed then produces Bank Holding Company Performance Reports (analogous

---

[6]Usually 100 percent or slightly less. When holding companies are formed, some shareholders refuse to exchange their bank shares for company shares. In such cases, there may be several minority shareholders who continue to hold shares in the subsidiary bank.

to Uniform Bank Performance Reports) for all multibank holding companies and all one-bank holding companies with consolidated assets over $150 million.[7]

The Bank Holding Company Performance Report (BHCPR) includes consolidated and parent company only financial data for both the subject holding company and its peer group. The bank analyst should obtain current copies of available BHCPRs whenever they are available for a subject bank or bank holding company appraisal client, that is, when dealing with a multibank holding company or with a holding company with assets exceeding $150 million.

Capital Ratios

A multiyear parent company only balance sheet, reconciliation of equity, and income statement are provided in Exhibits 5–7 of the Sample Bank Valuation in Chapter 22 for reference.

Capital ratios are used to monitor and evaluate bank and holding company leverage. Leverage at the parent company level is often viewed in two ways: in terms of simple leverage and double leverage. *Simple leverage* is the familiar analytical concept used by analysts to measure the relationships between debt, total liabilities, and total assets. The concept of *double leverage* is used to measure the extent to which leverage at the holding company level is used to further leverage its bank or other subsidiaries.

Several measures of simple and double leverage are commonly calculated. Not all will be relevant for every community bank with a holding company, but several are calculated in the Bank Holding Company Performance Reports. Exhibit 11-1 provides a listing of all ratios in the "Parent Company Analysis—Parts I and II" found in Bank Holding Company Performance Reports.

These ratios are calculated every time a BHCPR is prepared, so the bank analyst should be familiar with them.

Leverage for Small One-Bank Holding Companies

The Fed has published an updated "Policy Statement on Formation of One-Bank Holding Companies.[8] Historically, the Fed has allowed greater leverage for small (under $150 million in assets) one-bank holding companies than for larger bank holding companies. From a policy viewpoint, this has been necessary to facilitate management succession and ownership transfer in small banks. The Fed has focused on the ability of small holding companies to service debt without straining the capital of their subsidiary banks.

The updated policy shifts the regulatory focus from debt repayment to the relationship between debt and equity at the parent company. The minimum downpayment as stated in Appendix B to Regulation Y is 25 percent, that is, acquisition debt should not exceed 75 percent of the pur-

---

[7]See *A User's Guide for the Bank Holding Company Performance Report,* Division of Banking Supervision and Regulation, Board of Governors of the Federal Reserve System, Washington, D.C., 1988.

[8]Appendix B, Regulation Y, "Bank Holding Companies and Change in Bank Control," Code of Federal Regulations, title 12, chapter II, part 225.

Exhibit 11-1

Ratios Presented in the Parent Company Analysis of the Bank Holding Company Performance Reports

<table>
<tr><td>Part I</td><td>Part II</td></tr>
</table>

Part I

Profitability

Net Income/Average Equity Capital
Bank Net Income/Average Equity Investment in Banks
Nonbank Net Income/Average Equity Investment in Nonbanks
Subsidiary Bank Holding Companies Net Income/Average
   Equity Investment in Subsidiary Bank Holding Companies
Bank Net Income/Parent Net Income
Nonbank Net Income/Parent Net Income
Subsidiary Bank Holding Companies Net Income/Parent Net
   Income

Leverage

Total Liabilities/Equity
Total Debt/Equity Capital
Total Debt/(Equity Capital − Excess of Cost Over Fair Value)
Long-Term Debt/Equity Capital
Short-Term Debt/Equity Capital
Current Portion of Long-Term Debt/Equity
Excess of Cost Over Fair Value/Equity Capital
Long-Term Debt/Consolidated Long-Term Debt

Double Leverage

Equity Investment in Subsidiaries/Equity
Total Investment in Subsidiaries/Equity

Double Leverage Payback

(Equity Investment in Subsidiaries − Equity Capital)/
   Net Income ($\times$)
(Equity Investment in Subsidiaries − Equity Capital)/
   Net Income − Dividend ($\times$)

Coverage Analysis

(Operating Income − Tax + Noncash)/Operating
   Expenses + Dividend
(Cash Flow from Operating + Noncash + Operating
   Expenses)/Operating Expenses + Dividend
Adjusted Cash Flow/(Operating Expenses + Repaid Long-
   Term Debt + Dividend)
(Pretax Operating Income + Interest Expenses)/Interest
   Expenses
(Dividend + Interest from Subsidiaries)/
   (Interest Expenses + Dividend)
(Fees + Other Income from Subsidiaries)/(Salaries + Other
   Expenses)
Net Income/(Current Portion of Long-Term Debt + Preferred
   Dividend)

Other Ratios

Net Assets Returned in One Year/Total Assets
Past Due and Nonaccrual as Percent of Loans and Losses:
   90 Days Past Due
   Nonaccrual
      Total
Guaranteed Loans as Percent of Equity Capital:
   to Bank Subsidiaries
   to Nonbank Subsidiaries
   to Subsidiary Bank Holding Companies
      Total

Part II

Payout Ratios—Parent

Dividend Paid/Income before Undistributed Income
Dividend Paid/Net Income
(Net Income − Dividend)/Average Equity

As a Percent of Dividends Paid:
   Dividend Income from Banks
   Dividend Income from Nonbanks
   Dividend Income from Subsidiary Bank Holding
      Companies
         Total Dividends from All Subsidiaries

Payout Ratios—Subsidiaries

As a Percent of Bank Net Income:
   Dividends from Banks
   Interest from Banks
   Management + Service Fees from Banks
   Other Income from Banks
      Total Operating Income from Banks

As a Percent of Nonbank Net Income:
   Dividends from Nonbanks
   Interest from Nonbanks
   Management + Service Fees from Nonbanks
   Other Income from Nonbanks
      Total Operating Income from Nonbanks

As a Percent of Subsidiary Bank Holding Companies Net
   Income:
   Dividends from Subsidiary Bank Holding Companies
   Interest from Subsidiary Bank Holding Companies
   Management + Service Fees from Subsidiary Bank
      Holding Companies
   Other Income from Subsidiary Bank Holding Companies
      Total Operating Income from Subsidiary Bank
         Holding Companies

Dependence on Subsidiaries

As a Percent of Total Operating Income:
   Dividends from Banks
   Interest from Banks
   Management + Service Fees from Banks
   Other Income from Banks
      Operating Income from Banks

   Dividends from Nonbanks
   Interest from Nonbanks
   Management + Service Fees from Nonbanks
   Other Income from Nonbanks
      Operating Income from Nonbanks

   Dividends from Subsidiary Bank Holding Companies
   Interest from Subsidiary Bank Holding Companies
   Management + Service Fees from Subsidiary Bank
      Holding Companies
   Other Income from Subsidiary Bank Holding Companies
      Operating Income from Subsidiary Bank Holding
         Companies

Loans and Advances from Subsidiary/Short-Term Debt
Loans and Advances from Subsidiary/Total Debt

SOURCE: BHCPR, Parent Company Analysis

chase price. This implies a maximum debt-to-equity ratio of 3.00 (see Exhibit 11-2). Under the updated guidelines, applicants for new, leveraged, one-bank holding companies must be able to show that, under reasonable assumptions about future bank performance that correlates with past performance, the parent company debt-to-equity ratio can be reduced to 30 percent over a 12-year period. Projections as shown in Exhibit 11-3 would be required.

While the policy states a minimum equity position of 25 percent, in actual cases at the present time, the Fed is more likely to require an equity position more on the order of 40 percent for new one-bank holding companies. The following discussion of leverage concepts helps place the Fed's current position into perspective.

Simple Leverage

Simple leverage can be expressed as total parent liabilities to total parent assets (including its equity in its subsidiaries) or as interest-bearing debt to total parent assets. It can also be expressed in terms of the various components of the debt structure (short-term, long-term, or total debt) in relationship to equity. Simple leverage ratios can also be developed with primary capital or with tangible equity as the denominator.

Double Leverage

Double leverage measures the relationship between the parent company only (which is identical to consolidated equity) and the investment of the parent company in its subsidiaries. Normally, the double leverage ratio is calculated as:

$$\frac{\text{Investment in Subsidiaries at Equity}}{\substack{\text{Parent Company Only Equity}\\ \text{(or Consolidated Equity)}}}$$

If this ratio is 1.0 (although it is sometimes expressed in percentage terms), there is no double leverage. In other words, the parent has not infused its own borrowings into a subsidiary bank as equity (therefore double leveraging the parent's equity), and bank (or subsidiary) equity equals consolidated equity. To the extent that the double leverage ratio is greater than 1.0, double leverage exists.[9]

Peer Group 06 (multibank holding companies with consolidated assets between $150 million and $300 million) in the Bank Holding Company Performance system can be used to place the double leverage ratio into perspective. The median double leverage ratio for the group at recent year-ends was: 1.53 (1987), 1.43 (1988), and 1.33 (1989). Double leverage is trending downward for this particular group of holding companies; however, the typical holding company does have a significant amount of debt. In the case of the new, one-bank holding company that is allowed to acquire a bank with 40 percent equity (and 60 percent debt that

---

[9]The double leverage ratio begins to present a flawed impression of leverage if the price paid for a bank acquisition rises substantially above its book value. This should be clear, for the denominator—investment in subsidiary *at equity*—will always be the book value of the subsidiary. However, if goodwill is paid in a bank acquisition (that is, purchase price in excess of the fair values of all tangible assets acquired), other things being equal, there is more risk than if no premium is paid.

Exhibit 11-2

Hypothetical Small-Bank Holding Company Double Leverage Ratio Analysis ($ Thousands)

Parent Company Equity 25.0 Percent of Capitalization

Bank Price as Percentage of Book	Bank Price	Goodwill	Parent Equity	Parent Debt	Tangible Equity	Debt/ Equity	Double Leverage	Double Leverage at Cost	Tangible Double Leverage
80%	$4,000	($1,000)	$1,000	$3,000	$2,000	3.00	4.00	4.00	2.50
90	4,500	(500)	1,125	3,375	1,625	3.00	4.00	4.00	3.08
100	5,000	0	1,250	3,750	1,250	3.00	4.00	4.00	4.00
110	5,500	500	1,375	4,125	875	3.00	3.64	4.00	5.71
120	6,000	1,000	1,500	4,500	500	3.00	3.33	4.00	10.00
130	6,500	1,500	1,625	4,875	125	3.00	3.08	4.00	40.00
140	7,000	2,000	1,750	5,250	(250)	3.00	2.86	4.00	−20.00
150	7,500	2,500	1,875	5,625	(625)	3.00	2.67	4.00	−8.00
160	8,000	3,000	2,000	6,000	(1,000)	3.00	2.50	4.00	−5.00

Parent Company Equity 33.3 Percent of Capitalization

Bank Price as Percentage of Book	Bank Price	Goodwill	Parent Equity	Parent Debt	Tangible Equity	Debt/ Equity	Double Leverage	Double Leverage at Cost	Tangible Double Leverage
80%	$4,000	($1,000)	$1,333	$2,667	$2,333	2.00	3.00	3.00	2.14
90	4,500	(500)	1,500	3,000	2,000	2.00	3.00	3.00	2.50
100	5,000	0	1,667	3,333	1,667	2.00	3.00	3.00	3.00
110	5,500	500	1,833	3,667	1,333	2.00	3.00	3.00	3.75
120	6,000	1,000	2,000	4,000	1,000	2.00	2.50	3.00	5.00
130	6,500	1,500	2,167	4,333	667	2.00	2.31	3.00	7.50
140	7,000	2,000	2,333	4,667	333	2.00	2.14	3.00	15.00
150	7,500	2,500	2,500	5,000	0	2.00	2.00	3.00	n.m.*
160	8,000	3,000	2,667	5,333	(333)	2.00	1.88	3.00	−15.00

Parent Company Equity 40.0 Percent of Capitalization

Bank Price as Percentage of Book	Bank Price	Goodwill	Parent Equity	Parent Debt	Tangible Equity	Debt/ Equity	Double Leverage	Double Leverage at Cost	Tangible Double Leverage
80%	$4,000	($1,000)	$1,600	$2,400	$2,600	1.50	2.50	2.50	1.92
90	4,500	(500)	1,800	2,700	2,300	1.50	2.50	2.50	2.17
100	5,000	0	2,000	3,000	2,000	1.50	2.50	2.50	2.50
110	5,500	500	2,200	3,300	1,700	1.50	2.50	2.50	2.94
120	6,000	1,000	2,400	3,600	1,400	1.50	2.08	2.50	3.57
130	6,500	1,500	2,600	3,900	1,100	1.50	1.92	2.50	4.55
140	7,000	2,000	2,800	4,200	800	1.50	1.79	2.50	6.25
150	7,500	2,500	3,000	4,500	500	1.50	1.67	2.50	10.00
160	8,000	3,000	3,200	4,800	200	1.50	1.56	2.50	25.00

*n.m. = not meaningful

is double leveraged), the implied double leverage ratio is 2.5 (or 100 percent/40 percent).

A second double leverage ratio includes any goodwill paid in a bank acquisition in the numerator. The double-leverage-at-cost ratio is:

$$\frac{\text{(Investment in Subsidiaries at Equity + Parent Goodwill)}}{\text{Parent Company Only Equity}}$$

In effect, a holding company's investment in subsidiaries is considered at cost—or, in other words, at equity—plus any unamortized goodwill remaining on the parent company's balance sheet. We call the ratio double-leverage-at-cost. This ratio behaves very much like the double leverage ratio; however, as the price of a bank acquisition rises above book value, unlike the double leverage ratio, it continues to rise, more appropriately reflecting the rising level of leverage and risk.

A third double leverage ratio is even more revealing as leverage increases. It looks at the investment in tangible assets at the subsidiary level in relationship to tangible equity at the parent company. It is called the tangible double leverage ratio:

$$\frac{\text{Investment in Subsidiaries at Equity}}{(\text{Parent Company Only Equity} - \text{Parent Goodwill})}$$

The tangible double leverage ratio and the double leverage ratio are equivalent if there is no goodwill on the parent company balance sheet. However, as goodwill increases, the tangible parent company equity supporting the investment in holding company subsidiaries decreases more than proportionately—again, other factors remaining the same. This ratio rises very rapidly until the point where there is as much goodwill on the balance sheet as equity, at which point the ratio calculation is not meaningful. At still higher levels of leverage, the ratio turns negative.

Double Leverage Analysis

Exhibit 11-2 provides a brief bank holding company double leverage analysis. A hypothetical holding company is used for purposes of the exhibit. It is constructed under three leverage constraints: 25 percent, 33.33 percent, and 40 percent equity capitalization of a one-bank holding company. Various leverage ratios are calculated under acquisition prices for a bank with $5.0 million in equity for each capital structure. The exhibit shows varying acquisition prices as percentages of the bank's book value, goodwill generated by the purchase, and required parent company equity and debt.

Four leverage and double leverage ratios are then calculated: (1) the debt-to-equity ratio (a simple leverage ratio), (2) the double leverage ratio, (3) the double-leverage-at-cost ratio, and (4) the tangible double leverage ratio. A review of Exhibit 11-2 provides several important observations for the bank analyst:

1. The debt-to-equity ratios under the three leverage scenarios look very much like those found in many other kinds of companies.
2. The double leverage ratio suggests that each dollar of equity at the parent level is "stretched" four times (for a 25 percent equity capitalization). This ratio is somewhat like the ratio of total assets to equity, which some analysts use as a leverage measure in corporate analysis. Note also, however, that the double leverage measure tends to decrease if prices for the bank subsidiary exceed 100 percent of book value because the numerator of the ratio is the holding company's investment at equity. This suggests that the ratio is more rele-

vant for holding companies with *de novo* subsidiaries (where no good-will is created on start-up), or for holding companies whose acquisitions were made on a stock-for-stock pooling basis, than as cash purchase acquisitions.

3. The double-leverage-at-cost ratio (defined in the BHCPR as total investment in subsidiaries divided by equity) is constant across a given set of calculations assuming constant holding company capitalization. Note, however, that this ratio exceeds the double leverage ratio at all bank purchase prices exceeding book value. In other words, when there is purchase goodwill on the balance sheet of the parent company, the double-leverage-at-cost ratio is more meaningful than the double leverage ratio.

   Both the double leverage and the double-leverage-at-cost ratios are calculated in the BHCPR reporting system. But neither ratio reveals the true risk impact of premium-priced acquisitions on the underlying tangible capitalization of a holding company nor suggests the true level of risk associated with a highly leveraged holding company with substantial amounts of purchase goodwill on its books.[10]

4. The last ratio in Exhibit 11-2 provides insight into the impact of purchase goodwill on a holding company's risk profile. The tangible double leverage ratio escalates rapidly as the dollar amount of purchase goodwill approaches the level of parent company equity. Because the original purchase prices were presumably justified by the earning power of the subsidiary bank and the holding company's debt was assumed in the purchase (at each purchase price level), the analytical importance of a high tangible double leverage ratio is that the holding company's debt service is extremely vulnerable to any reduction in the subsidiary bank's earning power. The risk profile is only magnified if the tangible double leverage ratio moves into the negative range.

One final observation on Exhibit 11-2 is noteworthy. As noted earlier, the Fed has begun to raise the initial capital requirements for new one-bank holding companies. Capital requirements of 40 percent or more are not uncommon in the current environment. The Fed's rationale can be clearly seen in the exhibit. As the required initial capital increases (from 25 percent to 33.3 percent to 40 percent), the tangible double leverage ratio decreases dramatically. Simply put, the Fed is recognizing that highly leveraged one-bank holding company formations with low starting capitalizations are quite risky. Further still, the higher the price paid for an acquisition (given a level of capitalization), the greater is the risk.

This brief analysis might fall into the category of merely interesting if this were not a book on financial institution valuation. The important analytical point here is that *the Fed, by increasing the capitalization requirements for one-bank holding company formations* (or for recapitaliza-

---

[10]The BHCPR system does include ratios that focus on goodwill (see Exhibit 11-1); however, the included ratios do not get to the point of risk as well as the tangible double leverage ratio.

tion transactions requiring Fed approval) *is decreasing the prices that can be paid for banks in the current market environment.*[11]

Payback Ratios

Payback ratios show how large double leverage is in relation to a holding company's earning power. The first two ratios shown below are given in the BHCPR. A third ratio of interest to analysts is also provided:

1. *Double leverage payback*

    $$\frac{\text{(Equity Investment in Subsidiaries} - \text{Equity Capital)}}{\text{Net Income}}$$

    This ratio measures the time, in years, it would take to "pay off" a holding company's double leverage based upon earnings at the rate of the most recent year.

2. *Double leverage payback (excluding dividends)*

    $$\frac{\text{(Equity Investment in Subsidiaries} - \text{Equity Capital)}}{\text{(Net Income} - \text{Dividends)}}$$

    Bankers do not like to reduce dividends. The second payback ratio measures the time, in years, it would take to pay off a holding company's double leverage based upon the most recent year's retained earnings (net income less dividends). This ratio looks at earnings availability assuming the current dividend will be maintained.

3. *Interest-bearing debt payback*

    $$\frac{\text{Interest-Bearing Debt}}{\text{Net Income}}$$

    This ratio measures the time, in years, it would take for consolidated earnings to pay down all existing interest-bearing debt. Like double leverage payback, this ratio can also be calculated excluding dividends.

The shorter the payback period, from a theoretical viewpoint, the more easily can a bank holding company eliminate double leverage or pay off its debt. Consequently, shorter payback periods are considered less risky, other things being equal, than longer payback periods. If consolidated equity exceeds the investment of equity in banking subsidiaries, the payback ratios may be negative. Generally, if consolidated equity is greater than subsidiary equities, the holding company is considered to be a viable source, without leveraging, of additional capital for the subsidiaries. This position is inherently less risky than a leveraged holding company.

Coverage Ratios and Cash Flow Measures

Coverage ratios measure the ability of the parent company to service its debt and pay shareholder dividends. Cash flow at the parent level

---

[11]This is not a value judgment regarding the Fed's position. The Fed is simply responding to the greater risk now associated with bank earning streams and institutionalizing what the rational market already knows: that today's risky bank earnings are not worth as much as they were during periods when earnings volatility was lower. While the market's perceptions of the risk profile of bank earnings may improve, it is likely that the Fed will only reluctantly lower the holding company capitalization requirements. This suggests that regulatory pressures may place a dampening influence on bank values long after market perceptions of bank earnings risk improve.

consists of dividends from subsidiaries plus net operating income and noncash expenses generated at the parent level. Coverage concepts are designed to measure how well a company's earnings stream (or the portion that might be available) will "cover" particular fixed charges.

Coverage ratios may be calculated for a number of fixed or quasi-fixed charges. The BHCPR lists a number of coverage ratio calculations, all of which highlight varying sensitivities (see Exhibit 11-1). Denominators in the coverage ratios include (1) operating expenses plus dividends, (2) operating expense plus repaid long-term debt plus dividends, and (3) interest expense. From a valuation point of view, it is important to develop an opinion about a subject holding company's ability to service its outside debt (principal and interest) in a timely manner, as well as to maintain shareholder dividends at the parent company level.

Earnings and Return Measures

As with banks, the key return measure for a holding company is return on equity. This measure can be broken out by income component: subsidiary dividends, equity in undistributed earnings in subsidiaries, earnings from operations at the parent company level, and parent company operating expenses. For most holding companies, subsidiary dividends and equity in the undistributed earnings of subsidiaries are the main components of earnings.

Taxes are an important element in earnings, and it is important to understand how taxes are accounted for between the bank and the holding company. Interest and operating expense in excess of parent company income and income provided by subsidiaries will result in a tax benefit on a consolidated basis. As noted above, some banks do not reflect the parent company tax benefit at the bank level during interim financial reporting, while others do. If the company does not produce consolidated statements, it is important to make sure that valuations or projections consider the tax benefit properly, neither double-counting it nor failing to include it in calculating net income.

Special Issues in Multibank Holding Companies

Analyzing a multibank holding company on a consolidated basis may not provide adequate insights, especially if the subsidiaries are geographically diverse and management is decentralized. Balance sheet growth, loan losses, spread pressures, and other factors impacting consolidated earnings may be concentrated in various subsidiaries. Recent acquisitions may not yet reflect the overall management culture of the company. If a problem is isolated at a single subsidiary and management has focused intensively on that problem, it may be easier to solve than a companywide problem.

In smaller bank holding companies, it may be possible to meet with the presidents of the individual banks during the due diligence visit. Whenever possible, this is a good idea, for it provides important impressions about the depth and quality of management. Even if it is not possible to visit all subsidiaries, it is sometimes possible to schedule interviews with key managers of the major subsidiaries at the headquarters location.

As bank holding companies grow in size, it is more appropriate to devote the bulk of analytical time to consolidated analysis. However, we believe it is always a good idea to devote some time to subsidiary analysis in order to focus analytical attention on key problems or areas of opportunity. With larger holding companies, it is always a good idea to examine the lead bank's financials in some detail.

Valuation Methodology

In valuing bank holding companies, the analyst must make decisions with respect to developing and presenting the valuation conclusion. Several possibilities exist:

1. *Consolidated analysis and valuation.* Particularly in the case of large bank holding companies (over $1 billion in total assets in the terminology of this book), many analysts will conduct their entire analysis on the basis of consolidated financial disclosure and then capitalize consolidated earnings in the development of the valuation conclusion. This methodology may also be appropriate for smaller bank holding companies with little or no debt or other holding company activity and where consolidated performance is virtually identical to that of the subsidiary bank.
2. *Subsidiary analysis and consolidated valuation.* The analyst may decide to focus analytical attention primarily on the subsidiary bank(s), with a separate analysis of holding company activities. Based upon conclusions drawn regarding the integration of the bank(s) into the parent, consolidated earnings are then capitalized in the development of the valuation conclusion.
3. *Subsidiary analysis and valuation.* For highly leveraged bank holding companies or for bank holding companies with unusual operating subsidiaries or other assets, it may be appropriate to conduct detailed analyses of the subsidiaries (or other assets) and value the subsidiaries (or other assets) on a stand-alone basis. Then the analyst may create, in effect, a valuation-adjusted parent company only balance sheet to arrive at a preliminary valuation conclusion, followed by appropriate discounts or other adjustments to properly account for the particular risk characteristics or ownership rights of the particular block(s) of stock being valued.

No one approach is always correct or necessarily preferable. The analyst must decide upon the most appropriate presentation based upon her or his own analysis of the circumstances of the appraisal and of the method best suited to facilitate understanding by users of the valuation opinion.

Dealing with Minority Shareholders

The presence of a holding company presents another level of risk to minority shareholders relative to an investment in a stand-alone bank. Holding companies can be substantially more leveraged than a bank. They may hold assets (real estate) and engage in practices (no legal lending limit) significantly riskier than those permitted to banks.

The flexibility of the holding company capital structure also presents opportunities to benefit minority shareholders of the holding company. For example, voluntary tender offers and repurchase/exchange programs may give shareholders in smaller banking companies with no active market for their shares a chance to liquify their investments. Further, minority shareholders who maintain their ownership in bank holding companies that engage in stock repurchase programs stand to benefit from the increase in their relative ownership of the holding company.

Obtaining 100 Percent of the Subsidiary Bank

Sometimes all shareholders of a bank do not swap their shares for holding company stock upon formation. For the holding company formation to work properly, at least 80 percent of the shares in the subsidiary bank must be exchanged for holding company shares to gain consolidated tax return treatment. However, it is inconvenient for a holding company to own less than 100 percent of the stock of its subsidiary. In the worst case, if the company takes on debt to acquire another bank (or to purchase shares of certain of the bank's shareholders) and must rely on a high dividend payout from its subsidiaries to service debt, the remaining bank shareholders receive windfall dividends. This can place a substantial drain on the holding company's potential dividend income from its subsidiaries. From a valuation point of view, however, it can increase the value of the remaining minority interest bank shares because of the required large bank dividend payouts to service holding company debt.

Over time, most bank holding companies seek to acquire the remaining minority interests in their subsidiary banks through purchase offers or exchange offers for holding company securities. In some cases, the subsidiary bank will engage in a freeze-out merger or reverse stock split, the effect of which is to freeze out the bank's remaining minority shareholders, rendering the institution wholly owned by the parent bank holding company.[12]

Reducing the Number of Holding Company Shareholders

In order to reduce the number of shareholders to avoid falling under public company disclosure rules of either the SEC or the FDIC, or for other valid business reasons, a holding company may desire to reduce the number of its shareholders. The holding company may engage in a freeze-out merger or reverse stock split similar to that mentioned above.

Because reverse stock splits entail the mandatory cashing-out of those shareholders who would have fractional shares after the exchange, the valuation of the stock can be a highly contentious matter. Tax liability considerations, the desire to continue to hold stock in the company (or the bank, as noted above), and sheer anger at a forced sale of their stock may cause minority shareholders to litigate for the highest possible price. Most states have laws requiring that minority shareholders (or, technically, those who dissent from the statutory merger event) be paid the *fair value* of their shares. (See Chapter 2 for a discussion on this important standard of value.)

---

[12]Bankers should engage in such transactions only under the advice of experienced counsel. These transactions have implications under the laws of various states, as well as under state and federal securities laws. In addition, such mergers for national banks fall under the jurisdiction of the Office of the Comptroller of the Currency (see Exhibit 2-2).

In our experience, particularly when the buyout prices for reverse stock splits or freeze-out mergers are established by independent appraisal, the transactions are generally conducted smoothly and are perceived as a benefit by all parties. In many instances, the full text of the appraisal opinion is provided to the affected minority shareholders in order to facilitate their understanding of the transaction and of the fairness of the offer being made.

Integrated Parent Company and Bank Analysis

The analysis of a banking company must take into account the needs of both the subsidiary banks and its holding company. The interaction of the company's need to service debt and the tax benefit it provides have a direct impact on the bank's ability to pursue asset growth and maintain adequate capital. In many cases, historical analysis will suffice. Particularly in problem bank situations, it becomes necessary to project future performance in the process of conducting an appraisal.

Exhibit 11-3 provides a fairly simple projection model that integrates a 10-year projection for the Specimen Bank with its parent company, Speciman Bancshares, Inc. The purpose of the projection is to provide an example of the key forecasting elements and of the interrelationships between the bank and its parent. The projection calls for growth at 6 percent at the bank level and maintenance of bank profitability at the level of the first year of the forecast.

In Exhibit 11-3, the Specimen Bank is not a stellar performer, as can be seen on pages 187 and 188. Return on average assets is projected during Year 1 to be 0.76 percent, and return on equity is 10.6 percent. Both measures are projected at essentially flat levels over the projection period. The balance sheet has a ratio of equity to total assets at the end of Year 1 of 7.0 percent, which is maintained for the projection period.

Specimen Bancshares, Inc., is fairly highly leveraged. The double leverage ratio is 1.95, and the tangible double leverage ratio is 2.88. The basic question addressed by the forecast is: Can Specimen Bancshares service its rather substantial debt if Specimen Bank continues to perform at its current levels? Readers can draw their own conclusions.

As noted above, Exhibit 11-3 is a fairly simple, integrated projection model. More complex models, including the addition of quarterly or monthly projections, are required in order to forecast bank performance in more detail. And still further sophistication is required to integrate an employee stock ownership plan into the bank holding company family.

Conclusion

This chapter has developed many of the more important bank holding company analysis tools. Not every ratio is appropriate for every analysis. The bank analyst must exercise judgment in deciding which analytical tools are necessary. This is the final chapter on financial analysis per se. We now must incorporate the background information and financial analysis tools presented in the book to this point into the framework of the theory and practice of current business valuations.

Exhibit 11-3
Specimen Bancshares, Inc.
Multiyear Projections for Years Ended December 31 ($000)

Specimen Bank Balance Sheets	Base Year	Year 1	Year 2	Year 3	Year 4	Year 5	Year 6	Year 7	Year 8	Year 9	Year 10
Earning assets	$319,002	$336,596	$356,677	$378,070	$400,753	$424,798	$450,286	$477,303	$505,942	$536,298	$568,476
Other assets	27,116	28,612	30,319	32,137	34,065	36,109	38,276	40,572	43,007	45,587	48,322
Total assets	$346,119	$365,208	$386,996	$410,207	$434,818	$460,908	$488,562	$517,876	$548,948	$581,885	$616,798
Demand deposits	$ 42,963	$ 45,540	$ 48,273	$ 51,169	$ 54,239	$ 57,494	$ 60,943	$ 64,600	$ 68,476	$ 72,584	$ 76,939
Interest-bearing funds	272,774	289,141	306,489	324,878	344,371	365,033	386,935	410,152	434,761	460,846	488,497
Other liabilities	4,571	4,845	5,136	5,444	5,771	6,117	6,484	6,873	7,285	7,723	8,186
Total liabilities	$320,308	$339,526	$359,898	$381,492	$404,381	$428,644	$454,363	$481,624	$510,522	$541,153	$573,622
Initial equity	25,811	25,811	25,811	25,811	25,811	25,811	25,811	25,811	25,811	25,811	25,811
Retained earnings	0	-129	1,288	2,904	4,627	6,453	8,389	10,441	12,616	14,921	17,365
Total equity	$ 25,811	$ 25,682	$ 27,098	$ 28,715	$ 30,437	$ 32,264	$ 34,199	$ 36,251	$ 38,426	$ 40,732	$ 43,176
Total equity and liabilities	$346,119	$365,208	$386,996	$410,207	$434,818	$460,908	$488,562	$517,876	$548,948	$581,885	$616,798
Assumptions											
Earning assets/total assets		92.2 %	92.2 %	92.2 %	92.2 %	92.2 %	92.2 %	92.2 %	92.2 %	92.2 %	92.2 %
Deposit growth rate		6.0 %	6.0 %	6.0 %	6.0 %	6.0 %	6.0 %	6.0 %	6.0 %	6.0 %	6.0 %
Minimum equity/asset ratio		7.00%	7.00%	7.00%	7.00%	7.00%	7.00%	7.00%	7.00%	7.00%	7.00%
Projection results											
Average earning assets		$327,799	$346,637	$367,374	$389,411	$412,776	$437,542	$463,795	$491,622	$521,120	$552,387
Forecast average earning assets		n.m.*	345,984	366,629	388,618	411,934	436,650	462,849	490,620	520,057	551,261
Average interest-bearing funds		280,957	297,815	315,684	334,625	354,702	375,984	398,544	422,456	447,804	474,672
Average total assets		355,663	376,102	398,602	422,513	447,863	474,735	503,219	533,412	565,417	599,342
Average equity		25,746	26,390	27,907	29,576	31,350	33,231	35,225	37,339	39,579	41,954
Total asset growth		5.5 %	6.0 %	6.0 %	6.0 %	6.0 %	6.0 %	6.0 %	6.0 %	6.0 %	6.0 %
Average earning assets/ average interest-bearing funds		1.167	1.164	1.164	1.164	1.164	1.164	1.164	1.164	1.164	1.164
Ending equity/assets		7.03%	7.00%	7.00%	7.00%	7.00%	7.00%	7.00%	7.00%	7.00%	7.00%

*n.m. = not meaningful

187

Exhibit 11-3 (*continued*)
Specimen Bancshares, Inc.
Multiyear Projections for Years Ended December 31 ($000)

Specimen Bank

Income Statements	Year 1	Year 2	Year 3	Year 4	Year 5	Year 6	Year 7	Year 8	Year 9	Year 10
Interest income	$32,720	$34,535	$36,596	$38,790	$41,118	$43,585	$46,200	$48,972	$51,910	$55,025
Memo: tax-free interest	499	499	499	499	499	499	499	499	499	499
Interest expense	19,122	20,270	21,486	22,775	24,141	25,590	27,125	28,753	30,478	32,307
Net interest income	13,598	14,265	15,110	16,016	16,976	17,995	19,075	20,219	21,432	22,718
Fee income	4,401	4,645	4,923	5,218	5,531	5,863	6,215	6,587	6,983	7,402
Provision for loan losses	2,056	2,170	2,300	2,438	2,584	2,739	2,903	3,078	3,262	3,458
Personnel expense	6,260	6,635	7,033	7,455	7,903	8,377	8,880	9,412	9,977	10,576
Occupancy expense	1,083	1,148	1,217	1,290	1,368	1,450	1,537	1,629	1,727	1,830
OREO losses and expense	525	525	525	525	525	525	525	525	525	525
Other operating expense	4,211	4,463	4,731	5,015	5,316	5,635	5,973	6,331	6,711	7,114
Pretax income	3,864	3,969	4,226	4,510	4,812	5,132	5,472	5,832	6,213	6,617
Memo: taxable pretax income	3,365	3,470	3,727	4,011	4,313	4,634	4,973	5,333	5,714	6,119
Taxes	1,144	1,180	1,267	1,364	1,467	1,575	1,691	1,813	1,943	2,080
Net income	2,720	2,789	2,959	3,146	3,346	3,557	3,781	4,019	4,270	4,537
Dividends to holding company	$ 2,849	$ 1,372	$ 1,342	$ 1,424	$1,519	$ 1,621	$ 1,729	$ 1,843	$ 1,965	$ 2,093
Assumptions										
Yield on earning assets*	9.98%	9.98%	9.98%	9.98%	9.98%	9.98%	9.98%	9.98%	9.98%	9.98%
Cost of interest-bearing funds	6.81%	6.81%	6.81%	6.81%	6.81%	6.81%	6.81%	6.81%	6.81%	6.81%
Loss provision/earning assets*	0.63%	0.63%	0.63%	0.63%	0.63%	0.63%	0.63%	0.63%	0.63%	0.63%
Fee income/earning assets*	1.34%	1.34%	1.34%	1.34%	1.34%	1.34%	1.34%	1.34%	1.34%	1.34%
Personnel expense growth	n.a.†	6.0 %	6.0 %	6.0 %	6.0 %	6.0 %	6.0 %	6.0 %	6.0 %	6.0 %
Occupancy expense growth	n.a.	6.0 %	6.0 %	6.0 %	6.0 %	6.0 %	6.0 %	6.0 %	6.0 %	6.0 %
OREO loss/expense growth	n.a.	0.0 %	0.0 %	0.0 %	0.0 %	0.0 %	0.0 %	0.0 %	0.0 %	0.0 %
Other expense growth	n.a.	6.0 %	6.0 %	6.0 %	6.0 %	6.0 %	6.0 %	6.0 %	6.0 %	6.0 %
Tax rate	34.0%	34.0 %	34.0 %	34.0 %	34.0 %	34.0 %	34.0 %	34.0 %	34.0 %	34.0 %
Projection results										
Total asset growth	5.5 %	6.0 %	6.0 %	6.0 %	6.0 %	6.0 %	6.0 %	6.0 %	6.0 %	6.0 %
Net interest income/average assets	3.82%	3.79%	3.79%	3.79%	3.79%	3.79%	3.79%	3.79%	3.79%	3.79%
Noninterest operating expense/average assets	3.40%	3.40%	3.39%	3.38%	3.38%	3.37%	3.36%	3.36%	3.35%	3.34%
Fee income/average total assets	1.24%	1.24%	1.23%	1.23%	1.23%	1.23%	1.23%	1.23%	1.23%	1.23%
Yield/actual average earning assets	9.98%	9.96%	9.96%	9.96%	9.96%	9.96%	9.96%	9.96%	9.96%	9.96%
Return on average assets	0.76%	0.74%	0.74%	0.74%	0.75%	0.75%	0.75%	0.75%	0.76%	0.76%
Return on average equity	10.56%	10.57%	10.60%	10.64%	10.67%	10.70%	10.73%	10.76%	10.79%	10.81%

*Ratio uses forecast average earning assets
†n.a. = not applicable

Exhibit 11-3 (continued)
Specimen Bancshares, Inc.
Multiyear Projections for Years Ended December 31 ($000)

Specimen Bancshares, Inc. Parent Company Only Balance Sheets

	Base Year	Year 1	Year 2	Year 3	Year 4	Year 5	Year 6	Year 7	Year 8	Year 9	Year 10
Temporary investments	$ 145	$ 145	$ 145	$ 145	$ 145	$ 145	$ 145	$ 145	$ 145	$ 145	$ 145
Loans receivable	257	257	257	257	257	257	257	257	257	257	257
Equity in subsidiaries	25,811	25,682	27,098	28,715	30,437	32,264	34,199	36,251	38,426	40,732	43,176
Goodwill	4,240	3,958	3,675	3,392	3,110	2,827	2,544	2,261	1,979	1,696	1,413
Other assets	123	123	123	123	123	123	123	123	123	123	123
Total assets	$30,576	$30,164	$31,298	$32,632	$34,071	$35,615	$37,268	$39,037	$40,930	$42,953	$45,114
Notes payable	$ 4,988	$ 2,851	$ 1,984	$ 1,001	$ 0	$ 0	$ 0	$ 0	$ 0	$ 0	$ 0
Long-term debt	12,192	12,192	12,192	12,192	11,964	10,446	8,847	7,914	6,821	5,553	4,092
Cashflow operations	0	2,136	867	983	1,229	1,518	1,599	933	1,093	1,268	1,461
New borrowing-calc	0	0	0	0	0	0	0	0	0	0	0
Other borrowing	0	0	0	0	0	0	0	0	0	0	0
Total debt	17,180	15,043	14,177	13,194	11,964	10,446	8,847	7,914	6,821	5,553	4,092
Accrued interest/other	184	184	184	184	184	184	184	184	184	184	184
Total liabilities	17,364	15,227	14,360	13,377	12,148	10,630	9,031	8,098	7,005	5,737	4,275
Initial equity	13,212	13,212	13,212	13,212	13,212	13,212	13,212	13,212	13,212	13,212	13,212
Retained earnings	0	1,725	3,726	6,042	8,711	11,773	15,025	17,728	20,713	24,004	27,626
Total equity	13,212	14,937	16,938	19,254	21,923	24,985	28,237	30,940	33,925	37,216	40,838
Total equity and liabilities	$30,576	$30,164	$31,298	$32,632	$34,071	$35,615	$37,268	$39,037	$40,930	$42,953	$45,114
Assumptions											
Amortization of goodwill	283	283	283	283	283	283	283	283	283	283	283
Projection results											
Double leverage	1.95	1.72	1.60	1.49	1.39	1.29	1.21	1.17	1.13	1.09	1.06
Double leverage at cost	2.27	1.98	1.82	1.67	1.53	1.40	1.30	1.24	1.19	1.14	1.09
Tangible double leverage	2.88	2.34	2.04	1.81	1.62	1.46	1.33	1.26	1.20	1.15	1.10
Double leverage payback (years)	n.m.	6.23	5.08	4.08	3.19	2.38	1.83	1.97	1.51	1.07	0.65
Double leverage + G/W payback	n.m.	8.52	6.92	5.55	4.36	3.30	2.62	2.80	2.17	1.58	1.04
Debt/equity	1.30	1.01	0.84	0.69	0.55	0.42	0.31	0.26	0.20	0.15	0.10
Debt/tangible equity	1.91	1.37	1.07	0.83	0.64	0.47	0.34	0.28	0.21	0.16	0.10
Liabilities/equity	1.31	1.02	0.85	0.69	0.55	0.43	0.32	0.26	0.21	0.15	0.10
Liabilities/tangible equity	1.94	1.39	1.08	0.84	0.65	0.48	0.35	0.28	0.22	0.16	0.11
Interest coverage	n.m.	1.35	1.56	1.75	1.99	2.33	2.83	3.55	4.21	5.18	6.70
Consolidated total assets	$350,883	$369,690	$391,196	$414,123	$438,453	$464,259	$491,631	$520,662	$551,452	$584,106	$618,736

Exhibit 11-3 (concluded)
Specimen Bancshares, Inc.
Multiyear Projections for Years Ended December 31 ($000)

Specimen Bancshares, Inc. Parent Company Only Income Statements	Year 1	Year 2	Year 3	Year 4	Year 5	Year 6	Year 7	Year 8	Year 9	Year 10
Dividends from subsidiary	$ 2,849	$ 1,372	$ 1,342	$ 1,424	$ 1,519	$ 1,621	$ 1,729	$ 1,843	$ 1,965	$ 2,093
Equity in undistributed earnings of subsidiary	− 129	1,416	1,617	1,722	1,826	1,936	2,052	2,175	2,306	2,444
Miscellaneous income	18	19	20	21	23	24	26	27	29	30
Interest on investments	11	11	11	11	11	11	11	11	11	11
Interest on loans receivable	26	26	26	26	26	26	26	26	26	26
Noninterest operating expense	286	303	321	341	361	383	406	430	456	483
Interest on commercial paper	436	249	174	88	0	0	0	0	0	0
Interest on long-term debt	1,189	1,189	1,189	1,189	1,167	1,019	863	772	665	541
Interest on other borrowings	0	0	0	0	0	0	0	0	0	0
Amortization of goodwill	283	283	283	283	283	283	283	283	283	283
Pretax income	581	821	1,049	1,305	1,595	1,934	2,293	2,598	2,932	3,297
Taxable parent income	−1,856	−1,685	−1,627	−1,559	−1,468	−1,340	−1,206	−1,138	−1,055	−957
Bank taxable pretax income	3,365	3,470	3,727	4,011	4,318	4,634	4,973	5,333	5,714	6,119
Consolidated taxable income	1,509	1,785	2,101	2,453	2,846	3,293	3,767	4,195	4,659	5,161
Tax loss carryforwards (NOLs)	13,230	11,721	9,936	7,836	5,383	2,537	0	0	0	0
Adjusted consolidated taxable income	0	0	0	0	0	756	3,767	4,195	4,659	5,161
Consolidated taxes/benefit	0	0	0	0	0	257	1,281	1,426	1,584	1,755
Less bank taxes	−1,144	−1,180	−1,267	−1,364	−1,467	−1,575	−1,691	−1,813	−1,943	−2,080
Net consolidated taxes/benefit	−1,144	−1,180	−1,267	−1,364	−1,467	−1,318	−410	−387	−359	−325
Net income	$ 1,725	$ 2,001	$ 2,317	$ 2,669	$ 3,062	$ 3,252	$ 2,702	$ 2,985	$ 3,291	$ 3,623
Cash flow in parent operations	$ 2,136	$ 867	$ 983	$ 1,229	$ 1,518	$ 1,599	$ 933	$ 1,093	$ 1,268	$ 1,461
Assumptions										
Growth in miscellaneous income	n.m.*	6.0 %	6.0 %	6.0 %	6.0 %	6.0 %	6.0 %	6.0 %	6.0 %	6.0 %
Growth in miscellaneous expense	n.m.	6.0 %	6.0 %	6.0 %	6.0 %	6.0 %	6.0 %	6.0 %	6.0 %	6.0 %
Interest rates										
Notes payable	8.75%	8.75%	8.75%	8.75%	8.75%	8.75%	8.75%	8.75%	8.75%	8.75%
Long-term debt	9.75%	9.75%	9.75%	9.75%	9.75%	9.75%	9.75%	9.75%	9.75%	9.75%
Other borrowings	10.00%	10.00%	10.00%	10.00%	10.00%	10.00%	10.00%	10.00%	10.00%	10.00%
Temporary investments	7.75%	7.75%	7.75%	7.75%	7.75%	7.75%	7.75%	7.75%	7.75%	7.75%
Loans receivable	10.00%	10.00%	10.00%	10.00%	10.00%	10.00%	10.00%	10.00%	10.00%	10.00%
Tax loss carryforwards (NOLs)										
Beginning balance	$13,230	$11,721	$ 9,936	$ 7,836	$ 5,383	$ 2,537	$ 0	$ 0	$ 0	$ 0
Ending balance	$11,721	$ 9,936	$ 7,836	$ 5,383	$ 2,537	$ 0	$ 0	$ 0	$ 0	$ 0
Tax rates	34.0 %	34.0 %	34.0 %	34.0 %	34.0 %	34.0 %	34.0 %	34.0 %	34.0 %	34.0 %
Projection results										
Return on average equity	12.26%	12.55%	12.80%	12.96%	13.05%	12.22%	9.13%	9.20%	9.25%	9.28%
Return on average assets	0.48%	0.53%	0.58%	0.63%	0.68%	0.68%	0.53%	0.56%	0.58%	0.60%

*n.m. = not meaningful

Part III

Bank Valuation

Chapter 12

Valuation Overview

The downfall of a magician is belief in his own magic.

Unknown

This section of the book focuses specifically on bank valuation in the context of the background information on financial institutions and the analytical framework developed in Chapters 1–11. Chapter 12 presents an introduction to the general valuation model. Chapter 13 deals primarily with the development of minority interest valuation methodologies. Chapter 14 deals with the issue of controlling interest appraisals. Chapter 15 then integrates the information in the preceding chapters to discuss the development and presentation of a valuation conclusion. Chapters 16 and 17 deal with specific valuation issues involved with employee stock ownership plans and with thrift institutions.

Context of the Discussion

The entire valuation discussion will focus on the financial and market rationales for various capitalization methodologies in the context of bank valuation. The reader should understand, however, that the concepts discussed in the next few chapters often relate to business valuation generally, not just to the appraisal of financial institutions.

This point is critical because many of the firms and individuals who currently appraise banks are primarily bank consultants, investment bankers, or accountants who may have considerable familiarity with financial institutions but often are not well grounded in current valuation theory and practice.

Introduction to the General Valuation Model

Most bank valuation requirements relate to minority interests in financial institutions. Banks actually change control, on average, about every 7–10 years. However, there are literally millions of individual shareholders in the thousands of banks whose stocks are not actively traded on a public market. Using book value (shareholders' equity) as a crude indicator of market value, the nonpublicly traded banks represent many billions of dollars of total value to their shareholders. It is no small wonder, then, that minority interest valuation needs are much more frequent than requirements for appraisals on a controlling basis.

In simplistic terms, the basic difference between controlling interest and minority interest appraisals of the same entity is that the former are greater (higher) than the latter. Explaining and quantifying the differences between the two extremes of value is a central issue in bank and business appraisal. This chapter outlines a general model to describe, explain, and quantify the differences between controlling interest and minority interest appraisals. The particular model is defined in the context of comparative public market securities analysis, and it relies upon extensive research (cited below) designed to quantify and measure the various explanatory valuation adjustments.

Considerable time has been spent in previous chapters on the understanding and analysis of the earning power of financial institutions. In this chapter, the *general valuation model* is introduced, together with the legal and valuation distinctions between minority interest and controlling interest valuations. We will also discuss the important concepts of valuation premiums and discounts.

The next two chapters will then explore the development of capitalization rates for minority interest and controlling interest valuations, discuss techniques of valuation under each circumstance, and show how the basic valuation model is applied in differing situations.

Basic Earnings Model

To many observers, business (and bank) valuation appears quite straightforward. Value is generally considered to be a function of capitalized earnings, so the basic earnings model can be stated simply as:

Value = Earnings × Capitalization Factor (a multiple), or

$$\text{Value} = \frac{\text{Earnings}}{\text{Capitalization Rate (a divisor)}}$$

We will examine the definitions of some of the above terms later. Suffice it to say, however, that having stated the model, simplicity ends almost immediately in most valuation situations. Earlier chapters have dealt at length with the analysis of financial, economic, management, and other factors necessary to develop a reasonable estimate of earning power for a financial institution. It is clear from the earlier chapters that the estimation of earnings to be capitalized requires training, experience, and skill.

The development of an appropriate capitalization rate for each particular valuation situation also requires experience, training, and skill. Before we consider the direct application of this model in actual valuation situations, however, some further background from current valuation theory is necessary.

Minority Interests versus Controlling Interests

Legal Relationships

There are legal and practical differences between the ownership of a minority interest in a banking company and that of a controlling interest.[1] Powers conferred through the ownership of a majority interest in a company include:

---

[1] The reader is referred to Shannon P. Pratt, *Valuing a Business: The Analysis and Appraisal of Closely Held Companies*, 2d ed. (Homewood, Ill.: Dow Jones-Irwin, 1989), pp. 55–58, 118–121. Dr. Pratt provides a lengthy discussion of the attributes of control and considerations for the analyst in assessing the degree of voting control found in particular valuation situations.

1. Election of directors.
2. Appointment of management and setting of their compensation, bonus systems, and other benefits.
3. Purchase or sale of Treasury shares.
4. Declaration and payment of dividends.
5. Acquisition or disposition of business assets.
6. Establishment of policy and strategic direction for the corporation.
7. Selection of acquisitions.
8. Determination of supplier relationships.
9. Amendment of the articles of incorporation or bylaws.
10. Decisions regarding the sale of the enterprise.
11. Ability to liquidate, dissolve, or recapitalize.

From the list above, it is clear that controlling shareholders have rights not enjoyed by noncontrolling shareholders. In the case of financial institutions, regulatory restrictions may impinge on some of the elements of control. For example, all acquisitions by banking institutions require approval from one or more regulatory agencies. In addition, regulatory requirements related to "safety and soundness" often provide restrictions on management's ability to implement strategies that might conflict with capital, lending, or other regulatory guidelines.

Ownership of 51 percent of the votes in a corporation is often regarded as full control. However, state laws can influence the degree of control represented by a given percentage of ownership. Some states require a "super-majority" vote (usually 66-2/3 percent) for certain actions, such as sale or dissolution of the corporation.

For banking institutions, *full control* might be defined as representing a minimum of 80 percent of the outstanding shares. Acquirers of financial institutions can only obtain the benefits of filing a consolidated federal income tax return if 80 percent or more of a subsidiary bank's shares are held by the acquiring holding company.[2]

Basis of the Appraisal

A *controlling interest* in an enterprise is defined as a block of stock sufficient to exercise control. The term *majority interest* is often substituted for *controlling interest,* and the two are used virtually synonymously. A *minority interest* is defined by the absence of control and represents interests of less than 50 percent. Whether an appraisal is of a controlling interest or of a minority interest is referred to as the *basis* of the appraisal. In other words, the appraisal of a controlling interest is referred to as *prepared on a controlling interest basis.* Correspondingly, a minority interest appraisal is prepared on a minority interest basis.

---

[2] Full control in this instance relates to more than corporate governance. The majority of all banks are owned by holding companies. There are fewer than 1,000 independent banks (defined as *not* owned by a bank holding company) in the United States. There are specific benefits from the holding company form of ownership (see Chapter 11); however, the major benefit comes from being able to file a consolidated federal income tax return with the bank. Leveraged holding companies can therefore effectively deduct the interest expense of their borrowings from the taxable income of the subsidiary bank(s). As a result, virtually every acquisition of a bank involves a holding company.

This conforms with the Uniform Standards of Professional Appraisal Practice (see Appendix B, S.R. 9–2(b)(iii)), which requires that "if the appraisal concerns equity interests in a business, [the appraisal must] consider whether the interests are appraised on a majority or minority basis."

General Valuation Model

Implicit Assumptions

There are several implicit assumptions in the general valuation model that should be stated clearly at the outset:

1. Valuation is an imperfect science, and there may be more than a small element of art involved.
2. The public stock markets provide the only highly visible and ongoing flow of *data* relating to corporate valuation that investors and appraisers must investigate to create decision-making *information.*
3. At any point in time, the public stock markets reflect the prevailing consensus pricing for particular securities (and for the market) of a worldwide group consisting of literally millions of investors.
4. The market may be "right" and it may be "wrong" with respect to its pricing decisions at any moment in time; however, the market is what it is at each moment in time.
5. Based upon financial theory, custom, government regulation, and common sense, business appraisers use information from the public market to help develop capitalization rates (or factors—that is, price/earnings ratios) with which to capitalize the earnings streams of closely-held companies.[3]

We will discuss capitalization rates specifically in the next chapter. We state these implicit assumptions here, however, as necessary background to understand: (1) how the market (and current valuation theory) distinguish between minority and controlling interests, and (2) the general valuation relationships between minority and controlling interest appraisals.

Minority versus Controlling Interests

The important difference between minority and controlling interest valuations is that, all other things being equal, a controlling interest is worth more than a minority interest. A holder of a minority interest generally has a passive investment in a company and, in most cases, must consider the company's capital structure and operations to be given. The minority shareholder cannot initiate the sale of appreciated assets, force a cut in compensation levels, or require a higher dividend payout. In

---

[3]Z. Christopher Mercer, "Do Public Company (Minority) Transactions Yield Controlling Interest or Minority Interest Pricing Data?" *Business Valuation Review,* December 1990, p. 123.

many—if not most—cases, these statements are probably true even if the minority shareholder is an employee of the company.

In determining the earnings value of a minority interest, normalization of earning power most generally involves the elimination of nonrecurring items and the possible discounting of high-risk elements of the earnings stream. In a control situation, normalization logically can go much further because the holder of the interest can influence corporate policy substantially.

In addition to having different sets of normalizing adjustments to reported book value, earnings, and cash flow, controlling interest and minority interest appraisals also involve different sets of public market comparisons. Clearly, applying valuation multiples derived from buyouts of comparable companies (where control changed hands) to a minority interest in a subject company without considering an *appropriate valuation discount for the lack of control* would be unreasonable.

Similarly, applying a price/earnings ratio derived from public market transactions of comparable companies (representing minority interest transactions) to a controlling interest in a subject company would be inappropriate without considering some *appropriate valuation premium for the presence of control.*[4]

Confusion over an appraiser's basis of valuation (minority versus control), either by appraisers or by users of appraisal reports (ESOP trustees, for example), can lead to the placing of inappropriately high or low values on a subject equity interest. The unfortunate result of such errors can include the overpayment of estate taxes, contested estate tax returns, and ESOP transactions that prove uneconomical or unlawful.

It is essential that both business appraisers and the parties using appraisals be aware of the correct basis of valuation and that appropriate methodologies be followed in deriving the conclusion of value for any interest being appraised.

Critical Valuation Terminology

Concepts of Value

Figure 12-1 places minority and controlling interest values in perspective on a conceptual level. The figure is titled "Valuation Relationships: Minority versus Controlling Interests." Three key concepts of value are provided in the chart and discussed below:

1. Controlling interest value.
2. "As-if-freely-tradable" minority interest value.
3. Nonmarketable minority interest value.

---

[4]The "appropriate" premiums and discounts are referred to, respectively, as *control premiums* and *minority interest discounts.* These concepts, together with another appropriate valuation discount called the *marketability discount,* are defined and discussed in the context of Figure 12-1.

Figure 12-1
Valuation Relationships: Minority Controlling Interest

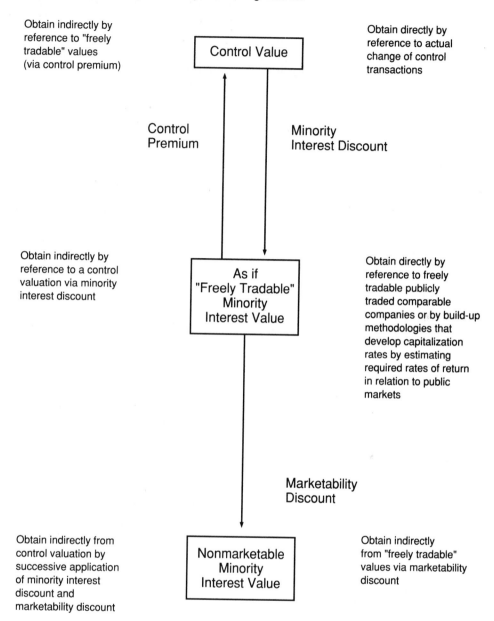

Obtain indirectly by reference to "freely tradable" values (via control premium)

Obtain directly by reference to actual change of control transactions

Control Value

Control Premium

Minority Interest Discount

Obtain indirectly by reference to a control valuation via minority interest discount

As if "Freely Tradable" Minority Interest Value

Obtain directly by reference to freely tradable publicly traded comparable companies or by build-up methodologies that develop capitalization rates by estimating required rates of return in relation to public markets

Marketability Discount

Obtain indirectly from control valuation by successive application of minority interest discount and marketability discount

Nonmarketable Minority Interest Value

Obtain indirectly from "freely tradable" values via marketability discount

The controlling interest value represents the value of the enterprise as a whole. The controlling interest appraisal should therefore encompass the rights, risks, and rewards of having controlling power in a business. *In the context of this discussion, controlling interests in enterprises are considered to be marketable, and a marketability discount is not used.* Some appraisers, however, do apply a discount, which may reflect the costs of brokerage or other factors, to control values.

The as-if-freely-tradable minority-interest value represents the value of a minority interest that is freely tradable in the public marketplace.[5] Stated another way, the valuation does not include any of the valuation elements associated with control, yet the conclusion is not penalized by the absence of liquidity inherent in shares that are not traded in the public markets.

A shareholder's total return from an investment in a security is typically divided into (1) dividend yield, and (2) capital gains or appreciation (or capital losses). A holder of a publicly traded equity security can choose to liquidate his or her investment at will, thereby realizing the capital portion of the return. This may not be possible with a closely-held security because of the absence of a market for the shares.

The nonmarketable minority interest value considers the lower marketability (or liquidity) that is almost always present in closely-held securities (in comparison with publicly traded securities). Reduced levels of liquidity can be due to financial issues, absence of registration for sale on the public stock exchanges, absence of contractual rights to require the purchase or sale of the shares at the holder's will, or other factors. Taken as a whole, however, the illiquidity of closely-held shares represents one of the primary reasons their value is generally below that of freely tradable securities, even if all other factors are similar.

Valuation Adjustment Factors

Three distinct valuation adjustment factors (one premium and two discounts) are presented in Figure 12-1. The factors and their definitions are:[6]

1. *Control premium.* The additional value inherent in the control interest as contrasted to a minority interest that reflects its power of control.
2. *Minority interest discount* (called *minority discount* in the noted source and applied to minority interests of less than 50 percent of the total voting interests of an enterprise). The reduction, from the pro rata share of the value of the entire business, to reflect the absence of the power of control.
3. *Marketability discount.* An amount or percentage deducted from an equity interest to reflect lack of marketability.

These factors will be further discussed and applied in the remainder of this chapter. As noted below and in Chapter 13, however, other ad-

---

[5]*Freely tradable* can be defined for our purposes as the ability to acquire or sell minority interest blocks of stock at will. In other words, the shares are fully marketable. The standard against which the tradability or marketability of shares is gauged is that of a relatively highly capitalized, publicly traded corporation on one of the major stock exchanges or over the counter. Significant minority interest blocks of stock of such corporations (for example, Citicorp or IBM) can be acquired at the market, or at or very close to the price at which the shares are currently being quoted on the New York Stock Exchange. Similarly, they can be sold at the market, and the cash proceeds of the sale, net of brokers' commissions and other transaction costs, will be deposited in the seller's brokerage account in five business days.

[6]See Appendix A, "Definitions of Terms Adopted by the Business Valuation Committee of the American Society of Appraisers."

justments (referred to herein as *fundamental adjustments*) may be necessary to adjust public company, minority interest price/earnings ratios *before* applying the adjustments discussed above.

Control Premiums and Minority Interest Discounts

The existence of control premiums has been documented in numerous studies of publicly traded stocks.[7] For example, in the *Mergerstat Review 1990,* published by Merrill Lynch, the average control premium derived from the acquisition of 185 public companies in 1990 was 42 percent.[8] The *Mergerstat Review* was based on the differences between market prices of each of the publicly traded acquired companies five days prior to buyout announcements and the actual buyout prices.

Based upon the *Mergerstat Review* reports and other studies, control premiums are generally in the range of 20 percent to about 50 percent or more *from the freely tradable base pricing of the public markets.* In other words, control premiums are applied to freely tradable minority interest (or as-if-freely-tradable) valuation bases.

As noted above, a minority interest discount is applied to the value of the enterprise to reflect the absence of control. In other words, the purpose of a minority interest discount is to eliminate the control premium *from a controlling interest valuation base.* An example using a hypothetical bank will explain the relationships.

I. Application of Control Premium

Market Price (freely tradable, minority interest)	$100.00 per share
+ Control Premium (assume 40%)	+ 40.00 per share
= Controlling Interest Price	$140.00 per share

II. Application of a Minority Interest Discount

Controlling Interest Price	$140.00 per share
− Minority Interest Discount [1 − (1 / 1.40)% = 28.6%]	− 40.00 per share
= Minority Interest Price (freely tradable, minority interest)	$100.00 per share

In the first example, we began with the freely tradable minority interest price (for example, the publicly traded price) and added a control premium of 40 percent. The minority interest discount, which in this case is 28.6 percent, is defined as the elimination of the control premium, so it is calculated as shown in the second example. While the relationship between the controlling interest price and the freely tradable minority interest price—and the corollary relationship between the control premium and the minority interest discount—are fairly straightforward,

---

[7]For further references on these concepts, see the Bibliography. In addition, the reader is referred to the extensive bibliography found in Appendix D of Shannon P. Pratt's book *Valuing a Business,* 2d ed. (Homewood, Ill.: Dow Jones-Irwin, 1989), p. 705. Dr. Pratt's staff periodically updates this bibliography as a courtesy to the appraisal profession. These updates are published by the Business Valuation Committee of the American Society of Appraisers in regular issues of *Business Valuation Review,* which is a current source of theoretical and practical articles on topics related to business appraisal.

[8]*Mergerstat Review 1990,* 1991, pp. 100–101. (*Mergerstat Review* was published by W. T. Grimm & Co. until 1987, when it was acquired by Merrill Lynch.) The publication, prepared each year, is a common reference source related to control premiums and other aspects of market transactions.

they are the subject of much confusion by appraisers, courts, and other users of business appraisals.

Marketability Discounts

Readers should not confuse the minority interest discount with the marketability discount. They are separate discounts and are applied to different valuation bases. We have just seen that the minority interest discount is applied to a controlling interest valuation base to eliminate the value attributable to elements of control. The marketability discount is applied to a freely tradable valuation base to penalize a subject valuation interest for its comparative lack of marketability or liquidity.

Theoretically, the marketability discount is that discount necessary to generate a sufficient increment in return to the holder of a minority interest of an entity's closely-held shares to induce the purchaser to make this particular investment, rather than an alternative investment identical in all respects save marketability.[9] Stated alternatively, if predictable and observable returns can be obtained from two similar investments—one in a marketable bank stock and the other in a nonmarketable bank stock—other things being equal, a rational investor will pay somewhat less for the nonmarketable shares than for the freely tradable shares.

Marketability discounts can range from very small (in the range of 5–10 percent) to quite large (60–70 percent or more).[10] The basic logic for the marketability discount lies in illiquidity and the inherent riskiness this implies; therefore, other things being the same, a marketable interest is worth more than a nonmarketable but otherwise identical interest.

Risks associated with illiquidity include the inability to dispose of an interest in the face of deteriorating company or industry conditions, as well as the inability to sell the interest if the investor's personal situation requires liquidity. Illiquidity, then, can pose substantial risks to investors. In addition, most closely-held companies do not pay regular dividends to shareholders. Consequently, the expectation of achieving a reasonable rate of return from an investment in a minority interest of a closely-held company is often extended until ultimate disposition, over which the shareholder has no control. It is no small wonder, then, that marketability discounts can be quite large.

Minority Interest Discount versus the Marketability Discount

This section is written to emphasize that the minority interest discount and the marketability discount are separate and distinct valuation discounts. They are applied to different valuation bases (see Figure 12-1)

---

[9]The marketability discount provides the incremental return (reward) necessary to offset the risks associated with a long or indeterminate holding period until liquidity can be achieved. The concept of developing values based upon comparisons with alternate investments is inherent in the definition of fair market value discussed at length in Chapter 2. The hypothetical willing buyer makes comparisons with alternative investment opportunities before engaging in a transaction. At the same time, the hypothetical willing seller must also make similar comparisons in order to evaluate the reasonableness of an offer for his or her closely-held business interest. Revenue Ruling 59-60, which defines fair market value, outlines several ways that hypothetical investors (and real-life appraisers) can look at alternative investments.

[10]See footnote 7 above for references to literature on marketability discounts.

and are designed to account for different valuation factors. Nevertheless, one of the more common mistakes that appraisers (and, unfortunately, courts) make is to confuse, mix, or combine the two discounts.

There is no such measurable adjustment factor as a "discount for marketability and minority interest." Yet we have seen this mysterious discount in numerous valuations prepared by business appraisers (or would-be business appraisers) and in all too many court decisions.

The use of the minority interest and marketability discounts in combination in the same valuation presumes that the base valuation reference point is a controlling interest value, that a minority interest discount is applied to eliminate the control element in the valuation, and that therefore a marketability discount is applied to derive the value on a nonmarketable minority interest basis. In other words, the discounts are applied successively, as indicated in Figure 12-1.

When discounts are applied in the fashion noted above, it is important for the appraiser to note that they are *successive* and *multiplicative* rather than additive. Following through from the example of discount applications above, the sequential application of the two discounts is shown below, beginning from a controlling interest value base.

III. Application of Successive Minority Interest and Marketability Discounts

Controlling Interest Price (per Example II)	$140.00 per share
− Minority Interest Discount (28.6% discount to eliminate a 40% control premium)	− 40.00 per share
= As-if-freely-tradable price (minority interest basis)	$100.00 per share
− Marketability discount (assume 35% is appropriate)	− 35.00 per share
= Nonmarketable minority interest value	$65.00 per share

The combined discounts total 53.6 percent from the controlling interest base value in the example. The total discount can be calculated in two ways. First, dividing the nonmarketable minority interest discount by the controlling interest price and subtracting from 1 (or 100%) yields a total discount of 53.6 percent, that is,

$$1 - \left(\frac{\$65}{\$140} \right) \% = 53.6\%.$$

Second, the successive and multiplicative nature of the discounts can be seen by the following calculation, which yields the same result. Using the discounts shown above for the minority interest discount (28.6 percent) and the marketability discount (35 percent), the total effective discount is calculated:

$$1 - [(1 - 28.6\%) \times (1 - 35\%)]\% = 53.6\%$$

In the present example, a total discount from the controlling interest base value of well over 50 percent is established after applying successive minority interest discounts (to eliminate control) and marketability discounts (to account for illiquidity). This example is not at all unrealistic and is in the (wide) range of typical discounts for nonmarketable minority interests in relationship to controlling interest values for closely-held business interests.[11]

Are Marketability Discounts Applicable to Controlling Interest Values?

Most studies of marketability discounts make comparisons between freely tradable minority interests in public company shares and shares that are identical with their freely tradable counterparts except for various restrictions on their marketability. In other words, the studies referenced in Note 7 relate to discounts *from the middle block of Figure 12-1*, i.e., from a freely tradable minority interest base.

I know of no objective evidence supporting marketability discounts to be applied to controlling interest values. Companies (or controlling interests therein) do not trade on the New York Stock Exchange, on other exchanges, or over-the-counter. The market for controlling interests in companies is not fluid and freely tradable. It takes time to locate buyers, negotiate price and terms (often including non-compete and employment agreements), arrange financing, perform due diligence, and close a transaction for a controlling interest in a company. Some would say it is therefore obvious that marketability discounts for controlling interests are appropriate.

However, no knowledgeable buyer or seller of companies expects them to be freely tradable. In my experience, the main reason that companies offered for sale do not sell *within a reasonable period of time* (just like houses) is that their offering prices are set at unrealistically high levels, not because they are inherently illiquid or lack marketability.

Further, *during the marketing period, the controlling shareholder(s) have all the rights, privileges and benefits of control*. It therefore seems circular to argue that appraisal value should be penalized because shareholders do not have total liquidity in their investments, when they continue to have the ability to determine the dividend, business and other policies that create the control premiums discussed above. In other words, why would any buyer pay a "full" control price for a company today if, tomorrow, the value of his or her investment would be reduced by a "marketability discount." Rational buyers would lower the price to the level of actual company value (both before and after the transaction).

Adjustments to controlling interest values might be required in certain circumstances to reflect the *net proceeds of a sale* of a controlling interest to its shareholder(s). Two possible adjustments of this type are (1) *transactions costs,* which are sometimes paid by the buyer, absorbed by the selling company during the course of the transaction, or paid directly by the selling shareholders, depending upon negotiations between the buyer and seller(s); and, (2) *taxes,* which we assume will always be paid by selling shareholders to the extent owed. Neither of these adjustments,

---

[11]However, as noted several times in this book, marketability discounts for banks tend to be lower than for closely-held businesses generally, so the total discount from a controlling interest basis to a nonmarketable minority interest basis for a bank or bank holding company may be lower than for similar-sized interests in companies in other industries.

however, affect the *value* of the controlling interest in question, but they clearly may influence the *net proceeds*. Appraisers should therefore be careful not to confuse value with proceeds when appraising controlling interests in companies or banks.

Appraisers sometimes apply "marketability discounts" to controlling interest values (mistakenly, I believe) and arrive at the "right" (or reasonable) conclusions. When this happens, the basic valuation approaches have caused an overvaluation of the business which must be eliminated to derive a reasonable conclusion. In arriving at their reasonable conclusions, appraisers are, in effect, substituting an inappropriate discount, i.e., a "marketability discount," for the sometimes bold fundamental discount(s) that are necessary to compare a subject company with alternative investments of similar risk/reward characteristics. The application of a *subjective* "marketability discount" (since there is no *objective basis* for this type of discount from a controlling interest base) therefore eliminates the fundamental overvaluation, yielding a reasonable result by inappropriate means.

A brief example can illustrate the problem. Assume that a group of publicly traded banks has been selected as a guideline group to value Subject Bank, which has total assets of $50 million. The median price/earnings ratio for the public banks is 12.0x. Subject Bank, however, is an underperformer relative to the guideline companies as well as its peer group.

Using a comparable (guideline) company approach, Appraiser A values Subject Bank's earnings at a multiple of 9.0x, which is the result of applying the *unadjusted* public company median multiple 12.0x to its earnings and then taking a 25% "marketability discount." Appraiser A has made a *totally subjective* adjustment to arrive at her conclusion. The answer in this case is right, but the methodology is wrong.

Appraiser B analyzed Subject Bank relative to the guideline companies in depth and determined that, because of its poor performance and growth prospects, a *fundamental discount* of 40% was necessary to compare Subject Bank's earnings *on a minority interest basis* with the guideline companies. This yielded an adjusted multiple of 7.2x [12.0 × (1 − 40%)]. Appraiser B then applied a control premium of 25% to the adjusted minority interest multiple of 7.2x based upon research relative to control premiums paid for banking institutions. This yielded a price/earnings ratio of 9.0x *on a controlling interest basis* [7.2 × (1 + 25%)]. Appraiser B used his judgment, experience, research and analysis to develop both the fundamental discount and the control premium. There was, therefore, an *objective basis* for his exercise of appraiser's judgment. The answer in this case is right and the methodology is right.

See the discussion above and refer again to Figure 12-1 for the basic logic of Appraiser B's valuation methodology. Chapter 13 deals extensively with the development of capitalization rates (earnings multiples) and with the concept of fundamental discounts relative to comparable (guideline) public companies. In any event, appraisers applying "marketability discounts" from controlling interest values should be clear as to the objective basis for their discounts or run the danger of having their discounts (and valuation conclusions) considered illogical and/or arbitrary.

Conclusion

This chapter defined several important valuation concepts and described what we have called the *general valuation model* (in Figure 12-1). This general model outlines the relationships between the different bases of value (minority interest versus controlling interest) and the further relationship between marketable and nonmarketable minority interests. An understanding of the issues and concepts treated in this chapter is crucial to the further development of minority interest and controlling interest valuation methodologies and techniques discussed in the next two chapters.

Chapter 13

Minority Interest Valuation Methodologies

Every individual endeavors to employ his capital so that its produce may be of greatest value. He generally neither intends to promote the public interest, nor knows how much he is promoting it. He intends only his own security, only his own gain. And he is in this led by an INVISIBLE HAND to promote an end which has no part of his intention. By pursuing his own interest he frequently promotes that of society more effectually than when he really intends to promote it.

Adam Smith, *The Wealth of Nations* (1776)

The Basic Earnings Model

In the last chapter, the basic earnings model was stated as:

Value = Earnings × Capitalization factor (a multiple), or
Value = Earnings ÷ Capitalization rate (a divisor)

To this point in the book, we have focused on the first element in the earnings model: the development of a realistic estimation of ongoing, sustainable earning power for a financial institution. Earning power is a function of many factors, including the interplay between a bank's balance sheet and its income statement, the external operating environment (consisting of local, regional, and national economic conditions and specific industry conditions), and regulatory influences. For purposes of the chapters on valuation methodologies, we will assume the reader has a clear understanding of earning power and how it is developed.

Experience and the Development of Capitalization Rates

Developing capitalization rates and price/earnings ratios is enhanced by the experience and knowledge of the appraiser.

How can an appraiser know that he or she is right when coming to a conclusion with respect to a specific capitalization rate? Experience helps. However, the kind of experience referred to is not simply the passage of time but the recurring involvement in real-life situations where parties at arm's length engage in actual transactions based upon the appraiser's conclusions.[1] Specific examples include:

1. Party *buys a company* at the appraised value or within the appraised range.
2. Party *sells a company* at the appraised value or within the appraised range.
3. Closely-held *entities merge through an exchange of shares* at exchange ratios established by independent appraisal.
4. Parties *enter into binding buy-sell agreements* based upon independent appraisal.

---

[1]*Experience* can be defined loosely as *grappling with issues and growing in the process.* There is a world of difference in the experience of two appraisers, where one has 10 years of grappling and growing and the other has the same year of experience repeated 10 times.

5. Successful *share repurchase programs* involving closely-held entities are based on independent appraisal.
6. Party *elects not to engage in transaction* based upon independent appraisal.
7. *Tax-related appraisals* (for gifting programs or estate tax returns) that have been reviewed and approved (i.e., settled without material adjustment) by the IRS form another aspect of experience, even if one step removed from direct arm's-length negotiations.

In the final analysis, any appraiser must bring to bear her or his best background, knowledge, and experience in the selection of capitalization rates for specific valuation requirements. These factors form the basis for the judgments necessary to the process, regardless of the approach used in the selection of capitalization rates and valuation multiples.

Capitalization Rate Development

Definitions

Earnings are capitalized to develop an estimate of value. *Capitalization* has been defined as *the conversion of income into value.*[2] The same source defines the means of capitalization in the basic earnings model above as:

Capitalization factor: any multiple or divisor used to convert income into value.

Capitalization rate: any divisor (usually expressed as a percentage) that is used to convert income into value.

No Growth Capitalization

In the case of the basic valuation model, earnings can be considered to be an estimate of current earning power or a stream of earnings projected into the future. Capitalization rates, or factors, are applied to current earnings estimates.[3] Recently, capitalization rates have been developed in an inflationary environment; they necessarily include anticipated long-term growth in nominal earnings (which includes both inflationary and real growth components). In the simplest case, where earnings are not expected to grow, value is simply:

I. $\text{Value} = \dfrac{\text{Earnings}}{\text{R}}$

where R = Required rate of return for the subject investment

---

[2]*Definitions of Terms Adopted by the Business Valuation Committee of the American Society of Appraisers.* See Appendix A.

[3]According to financial theory, an estimate of *next year's* earnings is capitalized by application of an appropriate capitalization rate (factor). In valuation practice, it is often *this year's* earnings estimate that is capitalized. As we will see in the discussion of publicly traded banks, the market focuses on *trailing 12-month earnings,* or the most recently reported year's earnings. The source of the analyst's capitalization data and the particular valuation methodology being applied will determine which capitalization rate should be applied to which earnings.

The required rate of return (R) is developed based upon comparisons with alternative investments. For the moment, assume that annual earnings of $100,000 are given and that this earnings stream is not increasing over time. Assume further that R, the required nominal rate of return, is 20 percent. Given these assumptions, value can be determined as:

$$\text{II.} \quad \text{Value} = \frac{\$100,000}{20\%}$$

$$= \$500,000$$

In other words, (R = 20%) is the capitalization rate that "capitalizes" the earnings stream of $100,000 per year so as to provide the value of that stream.

Constant Growth Capitalization

If earnings are growing at a constant rate, however, say at an estimated rate of 5 percent per year, we would develop an inappropriate conclusion of value without considering the impact of that earnings growth. In the present case, we would use the following formula to capitalize the earnings stream of $100,000:

$$\text{III.} \quad \text{Value} = \frac{\text{Earnings}}{\text{R} - \text{G}}$$

where G = Anticipated annual rate of growth of earnings

Therefore,

$$\text{Value} = \frac{\$100,000}{20\% - 5\%}$$

$$= \frac{\$100,000}{15\%}$$

$$= \$666,667$$

The above set of examples illustrates the simple truth that a growing income stream is worth more than one that is not growing, other things being equal.[4]

---

[4]The financially astute reader will know that the formula above is derived from the original Gordon Dividend Discount Model. Finance textbooks often include the mathematical proof that the present value of a perpetual (no growth) income stream is Value = Dividend / k, where k is an appropriate required rate of return *for a dividend income stream*. It can be further proven that if the income stream is growing at a constant percentage rate, the formula reduces to Value = [Dividend × (1 + g)] / (k − g), where g is the constant percentage growth rate to be applied to the initial dividend. If the income stream is changed to Earnings (however defined), this basic formula becomes: Value = [Earnings × (1 + g)] / (R − g), where R is an appropriate required rate of return for the selected earnings stream.

The theory cited above calls for capitalization of *next year's* earnings (or dividends). However, in practice, some appraisers use derived capitalization rates for application to their *current estimate* of earning power. The g in the formula is a long-term growth rate and may bear little resemblance to the actual projection of next year's income, if indeed, a projection exists at all. This follows the convention in the public marketplace of focusing on trailing 12-month earnings, and capitalizes the earnings estimate actually derived by the analyst: [E / (R − g)]. This practice is often more understandable to bankers, clients, judges, juries, and others than the theoretically pure approach: [(E × (1 + g)) / (R − g)].

Theoretical purists sometimes disagree with my preference for this practical simplification of earnings capitalization methodologies. Not inflating earnings by next year's g, which, other things being equal, produces lower answers than so inflating, can be considered to be an element of conservatism, which is sorely needed in many valuations. The alternative assumption is that the analyst, grounded in his or her earnings estimate, assumes that it is applicable to *next year,* from which level, earnings will grow at the assumed g.

Equation III is stated slightly differently from the theoretical standard of Footnote 4, that is, without applying the growth rate to the initial (or current) earnings stream. While theoretically distasteful to some, from a practical viewpoint it is easier to discuss capitalizing the *current level of earning power* rather than next year's earnings, which may be difficult to forecast with accuracy. The *practical solution* to the problem is to select an R, or required rate of return (or capitalization rate), that is appropriate for the earnings stream selected.

Capitalization Factors (Multiples)

In the preceding example, we have used capitalization rates expressed in percentages to develop value indications. Capitalization rates can be converted into capitalization factors (or multiples) by the following relationship:

$$\text{IV. Capitalization factor} = \frac{1}{\text{Capitalization rate}}$$

Therefore, for Equations II and III above, the appropriate capitalization factors (or multiples) are:

$$\text{For II. Multiple} = \frac{1}{20\%}$$

$$= 5.0$$

$$\text{For III. Multiple} = \frac{1}{20\% - 5\%}$$

$$= \frac{1}{15\%}$$

$$= 6.67$$

These examples illustrate two important relationships: (1) Higher capitalization rates imply lower values—that is, higher required rates of return and therefore lower valuation multiples, and (2) Lower capitalization rates imply higher values—that is, lower required rates of return, or higher rates offset by expected future growth of earnings, and therefore, higher valuation multiples.

All this is interesting, but to value banks or other businesses the appraiser must be able to develop capitalization rates, or capitalization multiples, that are appropriate for individual valuation requirements. Fortunately for the bank analyst, there is information available in the public marketplace to assist in the process.

Price/Earnings Ratios

We pointed out in earlier chapters that Revenue Ruling 59–60 requires consideration of the use of comparisons with publicly traded companies in the same or similar lines of business in developing valuation multiples for closely-held businesses. In this section, we will identify the source of such publicly traded valuation multiples and how they relate to the capitalization rates and factors discussed above.

Publicly owned companies, including banks, trade on the national stock exchanges or in the regional or national over-the-counter markets. The public stock markets "value" these companies and banks every day. At the end of each trading day, there is a closing price for all stocks for which there was trading activity during the day.

This information is compared daily in *The Wall Street Journal* and the financial pages of daily newspapers across the nation with *the most recently reported trailing 12-months' earnings per share* for each publicly traded company. The financial press and stock analysts relate the daily stock price and the most recent year's reported earnings to calculate price/earnings ratios.

Relating Price/Earnings Ratios to Capitalization Rates

The discussion and accompanying equations in this section relate the concept of the price/earnings multiple to the previous development of the capitalization rate. For simplicity, we will adopt the following abbreviations: (1) Capitalization rate = CR, (2) Capitalization factor = CF, (3) Price/earnings multiple = P/E. In Equation IV, we saw that the capitalization factor (multiple) was equal to:

$$\text{From IV.} \quad CF = \frac{1}{CR}$$

If the capitalization factor is the multiple by which an earnings stream is capitalized, it is clear, then, that:

$$\text{V.} \quad CF = P/E$$

By substitution,

$$\text{VI.} \quad P/E = \frac{1}{CR}$$

By inversion,

$$\text{VII.} \quad CR = \frac{1}{P/E}$$

Exhibit 10 of the Sample Bank Valuation (in Chapter 22) provides current and historical price/earnings ratios for the group of publicly traded bank holding companies used in the appraisal. The median price/earnings ratio at December 31, 1990, was 7.04x.

Using the median P/E of 7.04x from the Sample Bank Appraisal, we can develop the median market capitalization rate (CR) for the comparable group used in Chapter 22 as:

$$\text{VIII.} \quad CR = \frac{1}{7.04}$$

$$= 14.2\%$$

Financial theory suggests that CR is the result of two components: R, the required rate of return (or, as we will see shortly, *the discount rate*), and G, the expected rate of growth in the bank group's earnings.

By substitution into VII above:

IX. $R - G = \dfrac{1}{P/E}$ $\qquad$ (= CR)

We can estimate the sustainable growth rate (G) for the bank group fairly easily. If we assume that the bank group (or an individual bank) will maintain its capital structure and earnings margins constant from one period to the next and that there will be no infusion of new equity, we can estimate sustainable growth by the following formula:[5]

X. $G = \left(1 - \dfrac{DP}{NI}\right) \times ROE$

Going back to Exhibit 10 in Chapter 22, we find that the median dividend payout ratio for the bank group (DP/NI) is 35.1 percent. The median return on equity (ROE) for the group is 12.50 percent. Substituting in X above:

XI. $G = (1 - 35.1\%) \times 12.50\%$

$\qquad$ $= 8.1\%$

We can estimate an implied sustainable growth rate for the bank group at 8.1 percent based upon its median pricing and returns, combined with current dividend payout practices. The bank analyst should realize that this is simply a point-in-time estimate of growth potential for illustration purposes. However, now that we have an estimate for G, we can go back and relate the P/E we observed from the marketplace to the definition of capitalization rate. Substituting in IX above:

IX. (repeated) $R - G = \dfrac{1}{P/E}$

Therefore,

$R - 8.1\% = \dfrac{1}{7.04}$

$R - 8.1\% = 14.2\%$

and

$R = 22.3\%$

-----

[5]Assume the following abbreviations: (1) Dividend payout = DP, (2) Retained earnings for the current year = RE, (3) Net income = NI, (4) Equity = E, and (5) we know that ROE = NI/E.

$NI = RE + DP$

and, by substitution,

$RE = NI - DP$

now, dividing by NI,

$RE/NI = (NI - DP)/NI$
$RE/NI = (NI/NI) - (DP/NI)$
$RE/NI = 1 - DP/NI$

If we hold the capitalization and profitability of the entity constant (i.e., leverage and profit margins remain unchanged), then we can define sustainable growth, G, as the portion of retained earnings (after dividend payouts) multiplied by the group's (or individual bank's) return on equity. Therefore:

$G = (1 - DP/NI) \times ROE.$

The implied required rate of return for the bank group based upon the analysis above is therefore 22.3%. Given market conditions applicable to the bank group in Chapter 22 (as of December 1990), the analysis thus far suggests that investors were looking for a return on investment in bank stocks on the order of 22 percent at that time. As a practical matter, this relatively high required rate of return is a reflection of the considerable uncertainty with which the market was viewing bank stocks at year-end 1990.[6]

Relating Capitalization Rates to Discount Rates

It should be clear from this discussion that a capitalization rate (CR) is not the same thing as the investor's required rate of return for investing in bank stocks (or the stocks of any other group of publicly traded companies). There is a significant difference between the required rate of return (R) and the capitalization rate (CR), namely the expected growth rate (G). Only in the restrictive case where earnings are not expected to grow will R and CR be identical. Failure to understand this simple truth has caused considerable confusion on the part of appraisers, clients of appraisers, and courts.

When we apply price/earnings ratio analysis in the context of a bank appraisal, the capitalization rate used (i.e., 1 / P/E) is comprised of a market-determined required rate of return and a market-determined growth rate expectation for the public companies examined. *Because neither of these is given in market-derived price/earnings ratios, it is up to the analyst to understand the components of the implied capitalization rate(s) and to consider their implications appropriately in any bank or business appraisal.*

The required rate of return (R) is the rate at which investors would discount a *stream of earnings, or cash flow,* to arrive at a present value, or worth.[7] This required rate of return is often called the *discount rate,* which is defined (see Appendix A) as *a rate of return used to convert a monetary sum, payable or receivable in the future, into present value.*

For practical purposes, we are defining the market investors' required rate of return (R) as the discount rate (DR) at which the market converts expected streams of public company earnings (bank or other) to present value. In the context of the analysis above, the discount rate can be defined as:

XII. DR = CR + G   (DR = R from Formula IX)

It should now be clear that we can observe *capitalization rates* in the public marketplace (see VII), but not *discount rates.* To convert a capitalization rate into a discount rate for a particular closely-held financial institution or other company, we must develop a realistic estimation of the sustainable growth rate embedded in the market pricing information and make any other adjustments necessary for the particular

---

[6]Historical price/earnings ratios as measured at each calendar year-end are shown for the bank group on page 3 of Exhibit 10 of the Sample Bank Appraisal. Clearly, bank P/E's were at their lowest levels in the five years shown in the exhibit.

[7]This distinction has been discussed in several sources, but a clear exposition can be found in: Leung, Tony, "Myths About Capitalization Rates and Risk Premium," *Business Valuation News* (now called *Business Valuation Review* and published by the Business Valuation Committee of the American Society of Appraisers), Vol. 5, no. 1, March 1986, pp. 6–10.

valuation situation. We will come back to the issue of discount rates at the end of this chapter.

Public Stock Markets As a Source of Capitalization Rates

Practical Requirement

Revenue Ruling 59–60 was quoted in Chapter 2, where we discussed the Basic Eight factors that must be considered in every tax-related business appraisal. We quote here the introduction to the section titled "Factors to Consider" and then focus on subparagraph (h), which deals with the use of publicly traded comparables:[8]

> **01.** It is advisable to emphasize that in the valuation of the stock of closely-held corporations or the stock of corporations where market quotations are either lacking or too scarce to be recognized, all available financial data, as well as all relevant factors affecting the fair market value, should be considered. The following factors, although not all-inclusive, are fundamental and require careful analysis in each case:
>
> (a)–(g). See Appendix C.
>
> (h) *The market price of stocks of corporations engaged in the same or a similar line of business having their stocks actively traded in a free and open market, either on an exchange or over-the-counter* (emphasis added).

The advisability and, indeed, the necessity of looking to the public markets for capitalization rate information for tax-related cases was confirmed in *Central Trust Co. vs. United States.*[9] In *Central Trust,* the tax court stressed that appraisals of closely-held companies should rely on as broad a base of comparable companies as possible. Given the number of publicly traded financial institutions of significant size in the United States, there is little reason that comparable guideline companies cannot be used in most appraisals of banking companies.

Public Market for Bank Stocks: Smaller Institutions versus Regional Holding Companies

The markets for the stocks of small banking institutions (defined here generally as institutions with less than $1.0 billion in banking assets) are normally fairly thin and may not meet the requirement of Revenue Ruling 59–60 that they be actively traded in a free and open market. There are several actual or potential problems with using smaller banking institutions as comparables when valuing community banks, including:

1. They are fairly small in terms of market capitalization and normally are fairly thinly traded.
2. Because of this, the pricing data they provide may be unreliable or may be skewed by unusual or even unknown factors.

---

[8]Revenue Ruling 59–60, Section 4.01 (h).
[9]*Central Trust Co.* v. *United States,* 305 F.2d 393 (1962).

3. Small banking institutions may not be required to file financial reports with the Securities and Exchange Commission and often do not provide shareholders and interested parties with financial disclosure considered normal for public companies. In addition, they are seldom followed by the investment and brokerage communities.
4. In spite of being smaller than the regional holding companies, it is normally difficult or impossible to develop a group of banks that are directly comparable with a subject community bank.

Given the limitations above, we generally recommend using a group of regional bank holding companies (defined here generally as institutions with more than $1.0 billion in banking assets) as the basis for developing capitalization rate information (i.e., price/earnings multiples) for the valuation of community banks.[10] Use of regional bank holding companies for comparable groups provides several advantages:

1. The regionals are generally fairly actively traded, at least more so than small banking institutions, and are normally followed regularly by analysts at one or more regional or national brokerage firms.
2. Regionals will almost always satisfy the "actively traded in a free and open market" requirement of Revenue Ruling 59–60.
3. Regionals can normally be selected from fairly broad geographical areas of the country for a particular valuation assignment because the markets tend to paint banking companies with a fairly broad brush and to create fairly identifiable regional pricing differentials.

Peer Group Analysis versus Comparable (Guideline) Company Analysis

Because of the availability of peer group data, bank analysts often spend considerable time in community bank appraisals comparing a subject bank to its peer group in terms of structure and operations. This procedure is analogous to comparing a corporate valuation subject to the best available peer group information, which is normally derived from industry surveys or from publications such as those of Robert Morris Associates.

The bank analyst should be aware, however, that comparisons with community bank peer groups, while providing valid *comparative performance information,* do not provide *direct valuation information.* Community bank peer groups provide no information regarding appropriate capitalization rates. The bank analyst must go to the public markets, either directly or indirectly, or to actual transactions involving sales of bank shares or sales of similar banks, to develop capitalization rate information. It is necessary, then, to consider the relevant fundamental differences between a community bank valuation subject and the comparable group used in the appraisal.

---

[10]It is not uncommon in the valuation of thrift institutions, particularly for purposes of conversion from the mutual form of ownership to the stock form, for analysts to develop a group of "comparable" thrifts that are considerably smaller than $1.0 billion in assets based upon geographical location, balance sheet comparability or business mix, common business strategies, or other common characteristics. However, conversion appraisers also use broad groups of thrifts as the basis for developing market capitalization information.

Exhibits 1–4 and Schedules 1–12 in the Sample Bank Appraisal in Chapter 22 provide historical information relating to the Sample Bank. The exhibits and schedules also contain historical information on the Sample Bank's regulatory peer group. The appraisal report discusses the performance of the Sample Bank in comparison to its peer group.

Exhibits 5–7 of the Sample Bank Appraisal contain information on Sample Bancshares, Inc. This information is also discussed in the report. Exhibit 10 is an eight-page exhibit containing current and historical pricing and performance information on the regional holding companies selected as the publicly traded comparable group for the appraisal. This exhibit also contains comparative performance information for Sample Bancshares in relationship to the comparable group.

Because the publicly traded comparable group is the source of capitalization rate information (i.e., valuation multiples), it is the comparisons between Sample Bancshares and the comparable group that are most directly relevant for the valuation. The other portion of the analysis is used as a basis for understanding, in detail, how the bank has performed in recent years. The bank's peer group provides a convenient context within which to perform this analysis.

Relating P/E's and Other Historical Valuation Approaches to Discounted Cash Flow Methodologies

Discounted cash flow methodologies are, from a theoretical viewpoint, the most correct and precise methods for valuing businesses. After all, what could better describe the value of a business today than the present value (determined at an appropriate discount rate) of all of its future cash flows (or earnings)?

Capitalizing a company's (or a bank's) earnings with a market-derived price/earnings ratio is conceptually the same thing. Market price/earnings ratios are conveniently available and understandable. Current earnings are also usually conveniently available. And current earnings are infinitely more understandable than multi-year projections, which, like Pandora's box, can provide many surprises to the untrained or unwary.

As shown above, market price/earnings ratios contain not only "the market's" required rates of return (or discount rates) but also an implied growth rate. In other words, when the bank analyst capitalizes a bank's earnings with a market-derived price/earnings ratio, the implicit assumption is that the estimate of earning power used will *grow at the rate he or she expects from the base level of earnings established in the appraisal.*[11]

---

[11]From the viewpoint of financial theory, g (or G), the estimate of sustainable growth embedded in market price/earnings ratios, is a very long term growth rate. From a practical viewpoint, one could argue whether the market is always so farsighted, particularly given the pressure for quarterly performance placed on mutual fund money managers and the very high turnover rates in some of their portfolios. In any event, the individual analyst will have to reconcile theoretical expectations and practical considerations in analyzing public market price/earnings ratios for application to closely-held businesses of all types. In the final analysis, valuation remains a business of judgment. We must, however, develop the best possible analytical tools and experience factors to help in the exercise of valuation judgments.

In other words, the business appraiser who uses a price/earnings multiple from the public markets to capitalize a subject company's earnings *is* using a discounted future earnings approach; he or she is capitalizing earnings, which are expected to grow at a constant rate into perpetuity.

In our experience, valuation methodologies based upon capitalizing current or historical earnings more frequently provide realistic and believable valuation conclusions than do approaches utilizing discounted future benefits. That is not to say that discounted future benefits methodologies are not appropriate; in some instances, it is difficult to use any other valuation methodology (for example, start-ups or companies with recent histories of losses and anticipated near-term recoveries).

The issue is of sufficient importance that Shannon Pratt dealt with it in his recent book, *Valuing a Business,* in a short section titled "Generally Accepted Theory," with which we conclude this section:

> A generally accepted theoretical structure underlies the process of valuing a business interest. In theory, the value of an interest in a business depends on the future benefits that will accrue to it, with the value of the future benefits discounted back to a present value at some appropriate discount (capitalization) rate. Thus, the theoretically correct approach is to project the future benefits (usually earnings, cash flow, or dividends) and discount the projected stream back to a present value.
>
> However, while there is general acceptance of a theoretical framework for business valuation, translating it into practice in an uncertain world poses one of the most complex challenges of economic and financial theory and practice. Deviations from the theoretically correct approach to business valuation, however, are not necessarily, or even usually, inconsistent with the underlying theory.
>
> Since the value of a business interest depends on its future benefits, direct implementation of the correct theoretical approach to valuation requires a quantified forecast of the benefits considered relevant in each case, be they earnings, cash flows, dividends, or some other form of return. The discounted future returns approach is applicable in practice only to the extent that the projections and assumptions used are acceptable to the decision maker for whom the business valuation is being prepared.
>
> Such projections may be difficult to make—and even more difficult to get two or more parties with different economic and business expectations to agree on. Therefore, business valuation practitioners have developed various approaches that use historical rather than projected data to arrive at a valuation. In some cases, approaches using historical data tend to be carried out in a somewhat more conservative manner than the discounted future returns approach with respect to reflection of future potential growth. In general, however, approaches using historical data, if properly carried out, should yield a result that is reasonably reconcilable with what a well-implemented discounted future returns approach would derive.[12]

Many business appraisers who make frequent or exclusive use of discounted future benefits methodologies seem to this writer to have a tendency to *underestimate* the discount rate to be applied to projected earnings, which, in turn, *overestimates* the value of those earnings. The

---

[12]Shannon P. Pratt, *Valuing a Business: The Analysis and Appraisal of Closely Held Companies,* 2d ed. (Homewood, Ill.: Dow Jones-Irwin, 1989), pp. 35–36.

end result is that discounted cash flow (DCF) practitioners seem to have a greater propensity to overvalue companies or banks than practitioners of the historical techniques outlined in this chapter. Dr. Pratt's comments above suggest that historical techniques tend to be more conservative than DCF approaches. He appears to be making the same point, although somewhat more cautiously.

Public Market Capitalization Rates for Bank Stocks

Basis of Value

In Chapter 12, we talked at length about the bases of value. Public-market capitalization rates are generally considered to be *minority interest capitalization rates*. In the context of Figure 12-1, the public markets provide as-if-freely-tradable capitalization rates. Another term applied to this concept is that of *marketable minority interest capitalization rates*.

This is an important point for emphasis because it correctly places market-derived capitalization rates into the context of current valuation theory and practice. To develop a controlling interest valuation from a market-derived earnings multiple, for example, it would be necessary to add an appropriate control premium to the multiple to develop a controlling interest valuation estimate.

Alternatively, because the shares of publicly traded banks are freely and actively traded and reported trades are of minority interests, it is necessary to subtract an appropriate marketability discount from an initial value estimate if the shares subject to an appraisal are nonmarketable minority interests.

Price/Earnings Ratios

The derivation of a public average (or median or representative) price/earnings ratio based upon trailing 12-month earnings was discussed above. The ratios are normally calculated based upon the most recently reported trailing 12-month earnings per share in relationship to the current market price. The market price used is normally the daily closing price for shares traded on the major exchanges and the closing bid price for shares traded over the counter. The earnings figure most frequently used is net income (after taxes) from operations (excluding extraordinary items). Price/earnings ratios in *The Wall Street Journal* and the financial press are calculated using these conventions.

The price/earnings ratio is used to capitalize the analyst's estimate of net earning power (adjusted net income). In most bank valuations, the earnings to be capitalized will be earnings reported for the most recent trailing 12-month period, or those earnings as adjusted by the bank analyst in deriving an estimate of current, ongoing earning power. In any event, the analyst should use an earning power estimate that is consistent with the earnings base of the public company group with which comparisons are being made.[13]

Price/earnings ratios can be created in at least two other ways. First, if stock analysts' estimates of earnings are available for the comparable group, a representative P/E can be developed based from the group upon those earnings estimates. If this price/earnings multiple is used, it should be clearly discussed in the appraisal report and applied (with appropriate adjustments) to the analysts' projected earnings for the next year (from a base in time that is comparable to that to which the analysts' estimates apply).

Next, price/earnings multiples can be developed based upon multiple-year averages of earnings for the public comparable group. Multi-year average price/earnings ratios are often helpful at times when bank earnings are fluctuating more than normal. In any event, if a multiple year average P/E is used, it should be clearly developed and discussed and then applied to the analyst's best estimate of earning power for the subject bank based upon the same time period involved in developing the comparable group P/E multiple.

Price/Book-Value Ratios

Another frequently used public market capitalization rate can be developed and applied to the book value of a subject bank. Book value is often considered as a proxy for the net asset value of a bank. Even though it is sometimes only a rough estimate, because of differences between banks in leverage and asset composition, the market does, indeed, capitalize the equity of banks.

As noted in Exhibit 13-1, we are able to derive price/book-value ratios for banking companies from the public markets. The actual calculation of P/B, the price/book-value ratio (or multiple) is:

$$\text{XIII.} \quad \text{P/B} = \frac{\text{Market price per share}}{\text{Most recently reported book value per share}}$$

Price/book multiples will vary between banks because of differences in leverage, perceived differences in asset quality, market position, market growth opportunities, and other factors.

Price/book multiples are often used in the form of rules of thumb related to valuation. Historically, banks were considered to be worth 1.5x to 2.0x book value. This range of values developed because, for years, the median multiples in banking change-of-control transactions were on the order of 1.5x book value or higher in many markets around the nation.[14]

---

[13]Theoretically, the analyst should not only adjust the subject company's earnings but also the earnings of all the companies used in the public comparable group. In practice, particularly if the public comparable group is of sufficient size, the analyst may exclude from the analysis those public companies whose reported earnings appear to be distorted by unusual or nonrecurring events and use the remaining public companies with "normal" earnings as the basis for developing the capitalization rate in a specific appraisal.

[14]Many *potential sellers* of banks still believe their banks are worth a minimum of 1.5x book value. Buyers, on the other hand, have realized that the "new economics" of banking, with higher-risk earnings streams, over-capacity in the industry, increasing capital requirements, less allowable leverage in holding company formations, and capital "penalties" for goodwill on bank balance sheets, require lower valuations to make many potential acquisitions work. The result in the last couple of years has been a slowdown in the rate of transactions. Transactions should begin to pick up over time as sellers adjust to these new economics.

Exhibit 13-1
Regional Bank Holding Companies
Historical Price/Earnings and Price/Book Multiples

P/E Ratios as of December 31

	1990	**1989**	**1988**	**1987**	**1986**
High multiple	9.09 ×	13.67 ×	15.42 ×	13.75 ×	12.95 ×
Low multiple	5.73	6.67	6.89	7.05	8.02
Group average	7.05	9.16	9.49	9.47	10.15
Group median	7.04	8.88	8.70	8.69	10.12

Price/Book Ratios as of December 31

	1990	**1989**	**1988**	**1987**	**1986**
High multiple	1.35 ×	1.78 ×	2.13 ×	2.39 ×	1.70 ×
Low multiple	.51	.84	.89	.73	.87
Group average	.87	1.11	1.12	1.10	1.35
Group median	.89	1.03	1.07	1.07	1.41

SOURCE: Sample Bank Appraisal, Chapter 22, Exhibit 10, pp. 3–4.

Application of the price/book-value method is fairly straightforward given a market-derived price/book-value indication such as that found in Exhibit 13-1. Such a valuation indication is derived in Exhibit 13-2.

Normally, price/book-value ratios are provided in public market sources based upon reported book value per share for publicly traded banking companies. Consequently, if capitalizing the book value of a subject bank, the market multiple (as adjusted, if appropriate) should be applied to the subject bank's reported book value and not to its adjusted asset value.[15]

Sometimes investment banking or research firms publish studies that adjust public banking company assets—for example, bond portfolios or other real estate portfolios—to market values. If such studies are available, or if the analyst conducts a similar study for a comparable group, then the adjusted price/book-value multiples could properly be applied to the similarly adjusted book value for a subject bank.

Dividend Yield Capitalization

It is possible to develop an estimate of bank value by capitalizing the shareholder dividend stream. Calculation of the valuation estimate under the dividend capitalization method calls for the current annual dividend rate for a smaller bank to be divided by the appropriate current market dividend yield for the public comparable group (adjusted, as appropriate). Value estimation is therefore determined by the following formula:

$$\text{XIV.} \quad \text{Value} = \frac{\text{Bank's annual dividend}}{\text{Market dividend yield}}$$

---

[15]Presumably, the same market forces that generate a discount or premium to book values for the public banking companies are operating on the subject bank. Current market pricing effectively adjusts for these factors. Consequently, proper valuation procedure is to apply the market multiple (as adjusted, if appropriate) to the reported (or similarly adjusted) book value of the subject bank.

This method is often *not* used in bank appraisals for several reasons:

1. Many analysts believe that dividend paying capacity is effectively considered in the estimation of overall earning capacity or earning power.
2. Although no banker likes to lower dividends once a given level is established, dividends nevertheless have more potential volatility than the total earnings stream because of regulatory pressures to raise capital ratios.[16]
3. Many leveraged one-bank holding companies and some small multibank holding companies do not pay dividends to their shareholders because of their heavy debt service requirements.

If the dividend capitalization method is used, dividend yields are obtained from the publicly traded comparable banks. The market looks at the *currently indicated annualized dividend* in making yield calculations. In other words, dividend yields are calculated based upon the most recently announced quarterly dividend times four, the annualization factor for quarterly income streams. Dividend announcements are picked up by the financial press immediately and incorporated into the market's pricing of public stocks.

When using the dividend capitalization method, it is important to remember how public dividend yields are calculated. Small banks often pay dividends once a year. The bank analyst should query management regarding the outlook for dividends to ensure that the best estimate of the currently indicated annualized dividend is used for capitalization.[17]

Price/Asset Ratios

Sometimes bank analysts "capitalize" banking assets as an indication of "franchise" value. The price/assets multiple is derived similarly to the price/book value multiple. The question asked by the ratio is: What is a particular bank worth *per dollar of banking assets*? P/A, the price/assets multiple, is calculated as

$$\text{XV.} \quad \text{P/A} = \frac{\substack{\text{Market capitalization} \\ \text{(i.e., Price/share} \times \text{Shares outstanding)}}}{\text{Total assets}}$$

The price/assets ratio can be expressed as a percentage. For example, the median price/asset ratio as of December 31, 1990 for the comparable group in the Sample Bank Appraisal is 4.65 percent. In other words, the median regional bank in the group was worth—based upon market prices at year-end, 1990—4.65 percent of its total assets. Some

---

[16]At this time, numerous public holding companies are actually lowering shareholder dividends as the cheapest available means for raising capital. Why not? With the stocks of many trading below book values, raising capital in the public markets is very unattractive (because of dilution to existing shareholders) or very difficult (since bank stocks have been traded down because of the perceived uncertainty of their earnings streams).

[17]Sometimes, bank management may be less than forthcoming about future dividend policy, particularly in litigated appraisal situations where the analyst represents an interest other than that of the bank. In those cases, the analyst must look to historical dividend policies as reflected in actual dividends paid. If the dividend has been increased 5 percent every year for the last four years and earnings are on course with the past, chances are that the dividend will be increased 5 percent this year.

analysts express the multiple in terms of a price per dollar of assets or per hundred dollars of assets. The median price/assets multiple could therefore be stated as $4.65 per hundred dollars of total assets.

The price/assets ratio takes into consideration, in addition to earning power, factors similar to those noted above for the price/book value multiple, including asset quality, market position or power, leverage and other issues that may be important in particular situations.

Application of the price/assets value method is also fairly straightforward, given a market-derived price/assets value indication such as noted above and as can be found in the Sample Bank Appraisal (Exhibit 10). Such a valuation indication is derived in Exhibit 13-2.

Because of differences in bank profit margins (in relation to adjusted gross income, or "sales"), leverage, and returns between banks, price/asset capitalization is subject to substantial fluctuation between banks. When employed, the measure should be used with care.

Capitalized Deposits (Price/Deposit Multiples)

Some analysts calculate a price/deposits ratio for banking institutions. Normally, this ratio is calculated based upon core deposits, excluding jumbo CDs. This ratio is not found in the Sample Bank Appraisal. It is mentioned here because some analysts do make use of the method. Both the capitalized assets and capitalized deposits multiples attempt to measure the value of the banking franchise as a bundle.

Application of Public Market Capitalization Rates

Many valuation books stop at the theoretical and descriptive discussion in the previous section when discussing public market capitalization rates. In this section, we will discuss public market capitalization rates in the context of the comparable group found in the Sample Bank Appraisal (Chapter 22, Exhibit 10).

Specific Market Capitalization Rates

Exhibit 13-1 provides a summary of public market multiples (or capitalization rates) developed for purposes of the Sample Bank Appraisal. We will not discuss that appraisal specifically here, other than as may be necessary to develop some specific applications related to public market multiples. The valuation methods—that is, the capitalization of earnings and book value using market-derived multiples—will be discussed in more detail below.

For the comparable group in the Sample Bank Appraisal, the median P/E was 7.04 times (7.04x) trailing 12-month earnings as of December 31, 1990. P/E's ranged from 5.73x to 9.09x as of December 31, 1990. The average (mean) P/E multiple was 7.05x, and the median multiple was 7.04x. Looking at the average and median P/E's over the period from 1986 to 1990, it is clear that the multiples have declined considerably, most sharply from 1989 to 1990. Looking at the high and low P/E's over the period since 1986, there has been a considerable variation in the range of multiples.

Similar observations can be made for the price/book value ratios, the dividend yields, or the price/asset ratios in Exhibit 13-1. What lessons can the bank analyst learn from this brief analysis?

1. *At a point in time,* bank stock pricing can vary widely. Examination of Exhibit 10 of the Sample Bank Appraisal indicates that this wide range is derived even after several banks have been excluded from the sample. Had they been included, the range would have been wider still.
2. Bank stock pricing varies widely *over time.* Exhibit 13-1 looks only at year-end observations. More frequent observation points during the period would indicate even wider variability.

It is clear from this brief discussion of Exhibit 13-1 that the bank analyst must exercise considerable judgment in the application of public market capitalization rates in specific valuation situations.

Direct Application of Average Multiples

Business appraisers often calculate several capitalization rates from public market comparable groups, perhaps applying the median multiples to their subject company. They then apply some weighting or average of the valuation indications to develop a conclusion. This methodology, particularly with the application of simple averaging, often does not work well for bank appraisals. The public markets price each banking institution on an individual basis. The various median capitalization multiples would relate appropriately to a subject bank only by chance, which is not a firm basis for appraisal judgment.[18] Exhibit 13-2 applies the me-

Exhibit 13-2
Sample Bancshares, Inc.
Market Capitalization Rate Test ($ Thousands)

Price/earnings ratio		
Adjusted net income	$3,100	
Market median P/E	× 7.04	$21,824
Price/book value		
Reported book value	$30,781	
Median price/book multiple	× 0.89	$27,395
Dividend capitalization		
Indicated 1991 dividend	$1,100	
Median dividend yield	÷ .0561	$19,608
Price/asset ratio		
Consolidated assets	$444,592	
Median price/asset multiple	× 6.02%	$26,764
Unweighted average of methods		$23,898

SOURCE: Exhibit 13-1 for market capitalization rates (medians) and the Sample Bank Appraisal (Chapter 22) for Sample Bancshares' indicated observations for earnings, book value, dividends and total assets.

---

[18]Chapter 15 will discuss the use of weighted averages of valuation observations based upon the analyst's overall analysis as one rational method of overcoming the problems of simple averaging.

dian capitalization multiples of Exhibit 13-1 to Sample Bancshares to illustrate this point.

The median multiples applied to Sample Bancshares' earnings, book value, dividend payout, and asset base developed valuation indications ranging from $19.6 million to $27.4 million. The range can be even greater, particularly for high performance banks, no-go banks, or go-go banks (see the discussion of these terms in Chapter 10).

The reader with a calculator handy will see that, excluding the dividend capitalization method, the average of the other three methods is $25.3 million, or quite close to the prediscount value of $25.2 million developed for Sample Bancshares in Chapter 22. The real lesson from this example is not, however, that one can get a reasonable result by chance, but that the market looks at factors in addition to historical earnings (e.g., asset values, leverage, performance outlook, and the like) in valuing bank stocks, particularly when earnings are depressed.

Adjustments to Market Capitalization Rates

As with the valuation of other commercial enterprises using public comparable groups, it is sometimes necessary to make *fundamental adjustments* to market-derived base capitalization rates in order to make a proper appraisal of a subject bank.

Adjustments are most often required for smaller banks in slow growth markets that may otherwise be average to above-average performers in their peer groups. This seems to contradict the analysis above, which focused on sustainable growth rates for banks. The logic for adjustments in some cases, however, is fairly compelling.

Implicit in sustainable growth analysis is the assumption that there are market opportunities to grow and to maintain leverage ratios *and* profit margins. Assume for the moment that the median public company return on equity is 15 percent and that the median dividend payout ratio is one third.

The sustainable growth calculation (the retained earnings percentage times return on equity) therefore yields a 10 percent growth rate $[(1 - \frac{1}{3}) \times 15$ percent]. These figures are not unusual for good banking organizations in good economic times in good economic markets. When these conditions exist, the public markets normally will be awarding double-digit price/earnings ratios to the public banks (e.g., in 1986 and 1987 in the better regional economies of the nation).

If a subject bank is in a relatively poor economic area with only limited growth opportunities, even if its return on equity and dividend payout match the "good-times" example above, a discount to the market price/earnings ratio (assume it to be in the 11.0x to 12.0x range) will be necessary. Why? Because retained earnings cannot be reinvested in loans and other earning assets to continue to provide the same level of returns, and returns tend to decline over time. Slow growth banks often do not adjust dividend policy to pay out all earnings above a well-capitalized level of equity and tend to become overcapitalized. A fundamental adjustment (in this case, a discount) therefore may be appropriate for slower growth potential in similar cases.[19]

---

[19]Two possible means of quantifying discounts to public market capitalization rates for differences in growth expectations are outlined later in this chapter.

Arguments for Not Adjusting Market Capitalization Rates for Banks

Homogeneity Argument

In some cases, it will not be appropriate to adjust market capitalization rates when applying market median, average, or specifically selected multiples in valuing smaller banks. In "normal times," when banks are not considered to be growth stocks (as they were during the late 1960s and very early 1970s) or when merger mania is not driving stock prices upward (as in the mid-1980s), there may be sufficient similarities between banks to suggest that the market P/E should not be adjusted. If an analyst has derived the "right" public-market price/earnings ratio for a properly selected comparable group of banks, then that multiple may be applied to the earnings of smaller subject banks.

Under this thesis, a dollar of bank earnings is worth a dollar of bank earnings. There are several reasons for the argument:

1. Large publicly traded and small closely-held banks are regulated similarly.
2. There is very little proof that economies of scale exist in banking, although there are nearly always persuasive rationales for *potential economies* in many mergers. If there were economies of scale, then earnings and returns should be better for the large regionals than for small banks. After adjusting for leverage differences, there is little evidence of long-term realization of scale economies in banking. The compensation of bankers seems, at least at the levels of senior management, to increase disproportionately with growth in size. In addition, bureaucracy and inertia can creep into banks just as in many other large institutions. So relative size may not be a reason for discounting market capitalization rates.
3. Lack of management depth is a normal reason for fundamental discounts from public market capitalization rates for many commercial enterprises. However, our firm's experience with literally hundreds of banks and companies in over 200 other industries suggests (without quantifiable proof) that management depth in the typical small bank is better than for typical small companies in other industries.
4. The financial structures of small banks are similar to those of large holding companies in many respects. In fact, on balance, small banks tend to be better capitalized than large institutions.
5. Small banks normally experience a high degree of geographical concentration. In comparison to large publicly traded banks, however, this disadvantage may be offset somewhat by in-depth market knowledge and diversification of the loan portfolio among various types of borrowers within the local economy.
6. Earnings margins and the historical predictability of earnings are often quite similar between small and large banks, and therefore these factors may not be a basis for discounting a market capitalization rate for application to small banks.
7. Closely-held (nonbanking) companies seldom pay dividends to shareholders. A higher capitalization rate (and a lower earnings multiple)

may be necessary when comparisons are made with public companies that pay out a portion of their earnings in cash dividends. Small banks, however, tend to have dividend payout policies similar to those of public banking companies.[20]

Some bank analysts, therefore, tend to value small bank earnings at a market-derived earnings multiple. Other valuation methodologies (e.g., actual transactions in the bank's shares, net asset values, or other appropriate indicators of value) are then used to "balance" the valuation in line with the analyst's perception of how the public markets would treat the subject bank if its stock were actively traded.

Double-Dipping Argument

Fundamental adjustments to market-derived capitalization rates are sometimes called for when a subject company's earnings are temporarily depressed. Because the subject is not performing as well as the public comparables, a fundamental discount may be necessary. But depressed earnings already yield values lower than those flowing from "normal" earnings, given a constant price/earnings multiple. If a further discount to the market-derived multiple is taken for poor but temporary operating performance, an unreasonable, ridiculously low valuation indicator may result.

Interestingly, the public markets tend to respond to temporarily depressed earnings by *raising* the price/earnings multiple. In other words, the market looks beyond the current low level of earnings to the expected higher level of earnings in the next period. The current price/earnings ratio, which is based upon depressed trailing 12-month earnings, is increased in order to maintain the stock's price at a higher level than current earnings would warrant absent the outlook for improvement.

Valuation analysts often deal with the problem of low current earnings (with better earnings expected in the relatively near future) by using historical average earnings, looking at anticipated future earnings, or, if the earnings problem is severe, developing a specific projection of earnings and using a discounted future benefits approach to the valuation.

Fundamental discounts should reflect long-term differences between a valuation subject and a comparable group. In all these instances, the analyst must be careful to develop an appropriate capitalization rate for the earnings estimate(s) used in the analysis.

Transactions in the Stock of the Subject Closely-Held Bank

Market capitalization rates come from stock markets with actively traded shares. However, the bank analyst must be familiar with another kind of "market" capitalization rate. Banks tend to have a considerable number of shareholders, and ownership in many institutions is not concentrated. With their generally aging shareholder bases, a growing number

---

[20]As previously noted, leveraged one-bank holding companies may not pay dividends at all because of the need to make principal and interest payments on holding company debt.

of bank shareholders are beginning to seek liquidity (cash) for their investments in bank stocks. Others gift shares of bank stock to their heirs during their lifetimes, or the shares are distributed at death. These conditions give rise to actual transactions in the shares of most community banks every year, many of which are bona fide arm's-length transactions.

Therefore, the bank analyst should study actual transactions in community bank shares for indications of value. Illiquid though they may be, community stock "markets" sometimes provide valuable information for the analyst. These markets sometimes reflect very real marketability discounts (in relation to marketable minority interests in publicly traded shares).

In addition, indications of current value can sometimes be reconstructed through the use of past transactions. This technique is particularly helpful if a significant number of transactions have occurred in the relatively recent past.

If a past transaction was part of a change of control, it may provide control basis valuation information. In such cases, the bank analyst will need to deflate the control pricing by an appropriate minority interest discount (to eliminate the implied control premium) and then make any appropriate marketability discount if the subject appraisal is of a minority interest.

Further Capitalization Rate Developments

Normally, when valuing a community bank, it will be possible to develop a reasonable group of regional bank holding companies to use as a basis to develop capitalization rates. However, there are particular circumstances in which it may be difficult or impossible to do so, for instance when:

1. The region is devastated economically, or many banks are hit by particular real estate or industry problems (such as the oil depression and the ensuing real estate depression in the Southwest during the mid-to-late-1980s and the real estate depression in the Northeast currently).
2. The subject bank is one of a kind in its asset or funding structure, and it would be inappropriate to compare it with large regionals for valuation purposes.
3. Other unusual circumstances call for an alternative to the normal comparisons with regional bank holding companies for developing realistic capitalization rates.

Build-up Methodologies for Developing Capitalization Rates

Capital Asset Pricing Model

For a number of years, business appraisers have been using "build-up" methods of developing capitalization rates for the valuation of companies for which appropriately comparable groups of public companies could not be identified. These methods are the underlying elements of the capital asset pricing model.[21]

The capital asset pricing model (CAPM) uses three components to develop the expected rate of return for an investment in a diversified portfolio of *publicly traded securities.*[22] The basic CAPM can be expressed as follows:

XVI. $ER = RFR + \beta \times (MR - RFR)$

where

ER = Portfolio's expected return
RFR = Appropriate risk-free rate
 β = Portfolio's beta factor
MR = Appropriate market return measure

Therefore,

MR − RFR = Market's long-run return premium over the risk-free
rate

The capital asset pricing model has many restrictive assumptions. One critical assumption is that investors can, by investing in a diversified portfolio of securities, effectively eliminate specific company (unsystematic) risk from return expectations. CAPM accounts for systematic risk, or the risk of the market, by using the beta factor noted above, where beta measures the volatility relationship of a particular stock's rate of return (or that of a particular portfolio of stocks) relative to that of the return on the market as a whole.

A beta of 1.0 suggests risk for a company (or an industry or a portfolio) equal to that the market, usually described as the return of a broad index of the market (such as the Dow Jones average, the S&P 500, or the Value Line Index). Betas of more than 1.0 suggest greater price volatility than the market or greater relative risk and therefore higher capitalization rates and lower valuations, other things being equal. And betas of less than 1.0 imply lower relative risk and therefore lower capitalization rates and correspondingly higher valuations.

CAPM develops estimates of investors' expected rates of return (ER), or their discount rates for anticipated future benefits to be derived from ownership. There are therefore two basic problems in using the CAPM directly to develop capitalization rates for closely-held businesses, including banks. First, growth (or G, as discussed above) is not directly observable in Equation XVI. And second, CAPM assumes a diversified portfolio of investments such that unsystematic (or specific-company) risks are "diversified away."[23] When valuing the stock of a single closely-held company or financial institution, it is not possible to diversify away the

---

[21]James H. Schilt, "Selection of Capitalization Rates for Valuing a Closely Held Business," *Business Valuation News* (now *Business Valuation Review*), Vol. 1, no. 2, June 1982, p. 2. See also, Shannon P. Pratt, *Valuing Small Businesses and Professional Practices* (Homewood, Ill.: Dow Jones-Irwin, 1986), Chapter 11.

[22]See almost any introductory or advanced finance text for an in-depth discussion of the capital asset pricing model. See also the Bibliography of this book.

[23]This does not mean that specific-company risks do not exist. They do. The theory of diversification (for which there are mathematical and logical proofs) says that in a properly diversified portfolio of publicly traded stocks, the adverse consequences of bad things happening to certain stocks in the portfolio will, on balance, be offset by good things happening to other stocks, leaving the investor with the expected return of the portfolio (risk-adjusted by beta).

specific risks of ownership. Indeed, one purpose of the appraisal process is to identify and quantify those risks to the extent possible. Further, as discussed at some length previously, growth prospects can have a substantial impact on the valuation of a company, so we need a way to consider G specifically in the context of building a capitalization rate.

Adjusted Capital Asset Pricing Model (ACAPM)

Using the work of Schilt and Pratt (cited above) as a base, the analysts at Mercer Capital experimented with the CAPM and other components of value to develop reasonable and explainable capitalization factors in the absence of appropriate comparative public market data. That work was summarized in a recent article published in the *Business Valuation Review*.[24]

ACAPM "builds" a capitalization rate for application to closely-held businesses based upon the theoretical base of CAPM and practical experience in dealing with hundreds of valuation assignments. The model consists of the following components:

1. A "risk-free" rate of return. An intermediate or long-term U.S. Treasury rate is often used as a measure of the opportunity cost of a long-term investment in a closely-held company.
2. A historical premium over the risk-free rate of return attributable to equity securities generally. Measures of this premium can be obtained in research compiled by Ibbotson Associates, Inc.[25] This measure is of (MR − RFR), as noted above in the CAPM. The return measure used here should be reasonably comparable with the term of the risk-free rate used in 1 above. For example, the long-run (1926–1990, as measured by Ibbotson Associates) return on small company stocks (as defined) is 17.1 percent (or MR). The comparable return for long-term government bonds is 4.9 percent (or RFR). Therefore, the current small company stock premium used to provide an estimate of (MR − RFR) using this data series is 12.2 percent (17.1 percent − 4.9 percent). By way of comparison, the common stock return, which is based upon the long-run performance of the S&P 500 Index, was 12.1 percent for the comparable period. The common stock premium over long-term government bonds is therefore 7.2 percent. The common stock premium can also be used to estimate (MR − RFR); however, the small-company stock premium is the more frequently used proxy in valuations of smaller companies using build-up approaches or ACAPM.
3. A specific-company (or bank) risk (SCR) premium. The selection of this risk premium is an abstract concept. Conceptually, a specific com-

---

[24]Z. Christopher Mercer, "The Adjusted Capital Asset Pricing Model for Developing Capitalization Rates: An Extension of Previous 'Build-Up' Methodologies Based upon the Capital Asset Pricing Model," *Business Valuation Review*, Vol. 8, no. 4, December 1989, pp. 147–56 (referred to as the ACAPM article). The ACAPM article makes no claim for mathematical purity, nor does the summary of the concepts in this chapter. ACAPM is presented as a practical tool that works well in the context of the current economic and market conditions.

[25]*Stocks, Bonds, Bills, and Inflation: 1991 Yearbook* (Chicago: Ibbotson Associates, 1991). This annual book provides a variety of measures for estimating the market risk premium (MR − RFR). This discussion will focus primarily on only one of those measures: the small-company stock premium. Other data in Ibbotson regarding larger capitalization stocks (the common stock premium), as well as return measures calculated over differing time periods, extend the usefulness of ACAPM for the experienced analyst.

pany is being compared with a universe of small public companies. Direct comparative data on this universe of stocks are not available, so the analyst must be able to conceptualize the risk profile of the selected universe. Peer group comparisons—such as trade association statistics and ratios compiled by Robert Morris Associates for closely-held companies or the Uniform Bank Performance Reports or other comparative performance services for banks—as well as experience in analyzing public companies in many industries, must provide the basis for the development of specific risk premiums in particular valuation situations.

Since 1982, Ibbotson Associates has used return figures achieved by the 9th- and 10th-decile companies in the Dimensional Fund Advisors (DFA) Small Company Fund, a market value weighted index of the 9th and 10th deciles of the New York Stock Exchange plus similar-sized stocks traded on the American Stock Exchange and in the over-the-counter markets. The minimum market capitalization considered is $10 million. At year-end 1990, the DFA Small Company Fund consisted of approximately 2,200 stocks with a median market capitalization of $26 million (down from $44 million at year-end 1989) and an upper-bound market capitalization of $61 million.

The specific risk factors enumerated in the ACAPM article include: key personnel issues (or management depth); absolute size; financial structure; product, geographical, and customer diversification; earnings margins, stability, and predictability; and other risks associated with a particular company. For multi-million-dollar companies that have been in business for several years, the *total SCR* for all comparisons may run from as low as zero to as high as 8 percent or more.[26] For financial institutions, particularly community banks, the total SCR may range from as low as zero to as high as 7 percent, while for thrifts, the total SCR might be somewhat higher.

The selection of SCR using ACAPM may also include an implicit adjustment to the derived capitalization rate to convert it from one applicable to net income rather than to net cash flow. Alternatively, the analyst may desire to make a specific estimate of this adjustment factor. Exhibit 14-7 refers to this factor as A and provides a (theoretical) means for estimating A. (See also Footnote 30.) We know of no way to measure the adjustment factor (A) empirically, except to say that for a growing business with incremental working capital and capital expenditure requirements, it is a positive component of SCR. This is true because if net cash flow is less than net income (as it would be in this example), a higher capitalization rate (or lower P/E) is necessary to equate the results derived by capitalizing net income as opposed to net cash flow.[27]

---

[26]SCR may be even less than zero for closely-held businesses that are larger than the small capitalization stocks used to develop the small-company stock premium, but smaller than the large capitalization companies in the S&P 500 Index. These observations are based upon direct application of the ACAPM methodology in hundreds of valuations at Mercer Capital in recent years and should not be considered as limits or absolutes.

[27]The selection of the total SCR for a specific valuation assignment requires experience, common sense, and judgment in the context of a detailed analysis of the subject company or bank, as well as a general working knowledge of public-company markets. There is no substitute for experience and repetition of the selection process to develop realistic estimates of SCR. See also the discussion above at "Experience and the Development of Capitalization Rates."

4. The fourth component of ACAPM requires specific consideration of the earnings growth prospects for a subject company or bank. This is an important addition to the CAPM methodology. ACAPM expresses growth in nominal terms. The implied growth forecast is expressed in terms of annual percentage growth and should be reasonably achievable for at least the next 5 to 10 years. If the last five years (or other reasonable period of analysis) of actual or adjusted earnings performance do not specifically support the growth estimate used, the analyst should provide a clear and convincing rationale why the future is expected to differ from the past.[28]

    The growth component is subtracted from the sum of the risk-free rate, the small stock equity premium, and the specific-company risk premium.

5. ACAPM's fifth component is a beta factor. In many cases, beta is assumed to be 1.0 ("the risk of the market"). This is particularly true in the valuation of small businesses or in cases where no group of sufficiently comparable companies is identified by the appraiser and there is no objective basis to estimate beta. However, analysts dealing with diverse industry groups may find that utilization of an industry beta (or a related industry beta, if a directly related group is not available) can be helpful in adjusting capitalization factors for certain industries with known risk profiles. As will be seen below, this is particularly true of the banking industry.

ACAPM Model Stated

Mathematically, the adjusted capital asset pricing model is based upon the capital asset pricing model outlined above and is stated as:

$$\text{XVII.} \quad CR = RFR + \beta \times (MR - RFR) + SCR - G$$

where

  CR = Capitalization rate
  RFR = Appropriate risk-free rate (see above)
    β = Appropriate beta factor, if available (otherwise assume 1.0)[29]
  MR = Appropriate "market return" factor per Ibbotson Associates
  SCR = Analyst's derived specific company risk factor (actually, the total of several possible risk factors). Note that the adjustment factor from net income to net cash flow may be estimated within SCR or separately.
    G = Subject company's long-run growth prospects (in nominal terms)

---

[28]Conceptually, the specific company risk premium and the growth factor should relate to a company under normal operating circumstances. If the analyst overestimates a company's growth potential and uses a high G, he or she has likely invoked a corollary and offsetting increase in the specific company risk factors. While it may be difficult or impossible to measure, there is a covariance between SCR and G, particularly at higher than normal levels of forecasted growth.

As noted previously, G is a very long term concept on theoretical grounds. Some appraisers insist that G should be sustainable for periods of 20 years or more. This writer does not disagree with this *theoretical* position. In *practical* terms, however, the appraiser should be comfortable based upon her or his overall analysis that the G of ACAPM is sustainable for at least a 5- to 10-year (or longer) period. As John Maynard Keynes once said, "In the long run, we'll all be dead."

[29]To be theoretically correct, beta should be applied only to the common stock premium from the Ibbotson Associates data series, rather than to the small company stock premium as implied in Equation XVII. This is particularly true if the beta statistics are based on the historical return of the S&P 500 Index. If beta is assumed to be 1.0, this theoretical distinction becomes moot. Further, if the calculated industry beta hovers in the range of 0.90 to 1.10, as is often the case in practical situations, the impact on CR may be relatively minor.

As defined in the cited ACAPM article, CR is a *growth adjusted, minority interest capitalization rate*. At this point, we normally convert CR into a price/earnings ratio because, per Equation VI above, P/E = 1 / CR. In our experience, capitalization factors expressed as multiples of earnings are more readily understood by judges, clients, and other professionals than when they are expressed as percentage capitalization rates. Some analysts, however, prefer to use capitalization rates directly.

The ACAPM article defines CR (or P/E, as just derived) as applying to the net income of the subject company.[30] And because the components of the Ibbotson Associates series all represent fully marketable investment vehicles, CR is further defined as a *freely marketable minority-interest capitalization rate*. In other words, CR (or P/E), the capitalization factor developed using ACAPM, is defined as representing a viable proxy for the freely marketable minority interest capitalization factors derived directly from public company comparable analysis. Therefore, CR fits in the middle box of Exhibit 12-1. If a particular assignment calls for a minority interest valuation conclusion, an appropriate marketability discount would be applied to the derived P/E. Finally, if a controlling interest valuation conclusion were required, a controlling interest P/E would be developed by applying an appropriate control premium.

ACAPM Model Quantified

The equation for the ACAPM model provides a broad range of price/earnings ratios under varying assumptions regarding specific company risk (SCR) and expected growth (G) for any given set of assumptions with respect to RFR, MR, and industry beta. The ACAPM article provides a valuation matrix of after-tax price/earnings ratios under a variety of assumptions regarding company specific risk and expected growth based upon market conditions as of November 1989.

Exhibit 13-3 provides a similar valuation matrix geared to regional bank stocks as of year-end 1990 to illustrate how the ACAPM model can work. The composite long-term Treasury rate was approximately 8.4 percent at year-end, and the Ibbotson Associates small company risk premium (MR − RFR) was 12.2 percent. A beta of 0.90 was used based upon historical calculations of regional bank betas over several years. The exhibit then provides calculated P/E ratios (using the ACAPM formula from Equation XVII), given the fixed assumptions regarding RFR, MR, and beta and varying the assumptions with respect to SCR and G, or specific company risk and growth.

---

[30]The returns measured by Ibbotson are based on net cash flows, or net free cash flows, to investors. ACAPM has sometimes been criticized on the basis that it should be applied to net free cash flows of subject companies being valued. However, in the case of many small companies, net income may well approximate net free cash flow, particularly in those with minimal or low real growth prospects. In addition, for banks, which do not require large fixed asset investments and whose accounts receivable (loans) are interest bearing, net income is probably a reasonable proxy for realizable cash flow. Further, net free cash flow can be difficult to measure over the short run because, except in the case of the largest companies, fixed asset investments tend to "bunch" and are somewhat unpredictable. As noted in the previous discussion of the specific company risk premium, there is an implicit adjustment as part of SCR that converts the ACAPM capitalization rate to a net income measure. Finally, ACAPM has passed the practical test of developing realistic capitalization rates across a broad range of industries during several years of use by analysts at Mercer Capital. See also Footnote 4 of this chapter for the justification for applying the capitalization rate (or P/E) derived using ACAPM to historical net income or to the analyst's estimate of current earning power.

Exhibit 13-3

Valuation Matrix of After-Tax Price/Earnings Ratios

The following is a valuation matrix of after-tax price/earnings ratios derived using the ACAPM method based upon varying assumptions regarding company specific risk and expected growth.

Assumptions

Composite long-term Treasury rate: 8.40%, year-end 1990
Long-term equity risk premium: 12.2% (per Ibbotson Associates)
Assumed industry beta: 0.90 (historical level for regional banks)
Expected growth rate: see Chart
Appraiser's risk premium: see Chart

Appraiser's Total Specific Company Risk Premium Range

		0%	1%	2%	3%	4%	5%	6%	7%	8%
E X P E C T E D	0%	5.2	4.9	4.7	4.5	4.3	4.1	3.9	3.8	3.7
	1%	5.4	5.2	4.9	4.7	4.5	4.3	4.1	3.9	3.8
	2%	5.8	5.4	5.2	4.9	4.7	4.5	4.3	4.1	3.9
	3%	6.1	5.8	5.4	5.2	4.9	4.7	4.5	4.3	4.1
	4%	6.5	6.1	5.8	5.4	5.2	4.9	4.7	4.5	4.3
	5%	7.0	6.5	6.1	5.8	5.4	5.2	4.9	4.7	4.5
G R O W T H	6%	7.5	7.0	6.5	6.1	5.8	5.4	5.2	4.9	4.7
	7%	8.1	7.5	7.0	6.5	6.1	5.8	5.4	5.2	4.9
	8%	8.8	8.1	7.5	7.0	6.5	6.1	5.8	5.4	5.2
	9%	9.6	8.8	8.1	7.5	7.0	6.5	6.1	5.8	5.4
	10%	10.7	9.6	8.8	8.1	7.5	7.0	6.5	6.1	5.8

banks and regional bank holding companies as of about year-end 1990. Two primary observations can be made based upon an analysis of the data in Exhibit 13-3 in light of the economic and market environments at year-end 1990:[31]

1. Looking first under the 0 percent SCR column, we see a range of derived P/E's from 5.2x to 10.7x, as the assumption for growth increases from 0 percent to 10 percent. In Equation XI, we derived an estimate of sustainable growth of approximately 8.1 percent, based upon the current return on equity of the comparable group of regional bank holding companies found in Exhibit 10 of the Sample Bank Appraisal. Using a G of 8 percent in the exhibit, we see implied P/E multiples of 8.8x, 8.1x, 7.5x, and 7.0x for SCR assumptions of 0 percent, 1 percent, 2 percent, and 3 percent, respectively. For the reader who believes (with the writer) that the stock markets were attributing an additional increment of risk to regional bank stocks based upon perceptions of the then raging thrift and bank crises, it is not difficult to predict a "typical" P/E of somewhat less than 8.0x using the chart. In fact, the median P/E for the comparable group was 7.0x, as noted above and in Chapter 22, the Sample Bank Appraisal.

---

[31]Some readers may tend to believe that the analytical points below are only the result of coincidence. Based upon using the ACAPM model over the past three years, the model has had surprising explanatory and predictive power when used to examine groups of public companies in numerous industries. Like any other model that attempts to simplify a complex world, however, it does not always work so cleanly.

2. While the median estimate of G was about 8 percent for the comparable group, banks in some areas (e.g., Mississippi and Arkansas) are generally considered to have slower growth opportunities based upon the current economic outlook. If the earnings growth sustainable in a market is limited to inflation only, growth on the order of 4 percent to 5 percent might be expected. Looking across from 0 percent to 2 percent under assumptions for SCR, we see implied P/E multiples in the range of 5.8x to 7.0x. Because the median P/E for the comparable group is 7.0x, half of the group's P/E's are below 7.0x, and the lowest P/E in the group is 5.7x.

We have found the ACAPM model to be a valuable tool for developing capitalization rates (and thus, P/E multiples) for closely-held companies, as well as for banks and thrifts. The model is particularly useful in helping (or forcing) the appraiser to understand the critical relationships between specific company risks—which, in the final analysis, must be determined with an element of subjectivity in combination with as much objective information as possible—and expected growth, which can have such a dramatic impact on valuation.

Based upon this presentation of the ACAPM model, as well as the ACAPM article cited above, the adjusted capital asset pricing model can be used as an important tool to assist the business or bank appraiser in selecting capitalization rates for valuations in the absence of good public comparable data. However, because every appraisal is grounded in its particular facts and circumstances, including time (as of date) and purpose, the methodology is certainly no substitute for the exercise of good valuation judgment. It is simply one more tool to be used by the appraiser in the exercise of good judgment and experience.

Using the ACAPM to Estimate Fundamental Discounts from Public Comparable Groups

Business and bank appraisers face a difficult task in developing capitalization rates in situations where they are unable to identify a comparable group of public companies to use as a foundation. The ACAPM model provides some assistance in this regard.

But the analyst sometimes faces an equally imponderable task in assessing where, relative to a public comparable group, to "price" the earnings of a valuation subject. The analytical question is straightforward: How can the analyst justify a significant discount to the P/E multiples derived from public comparables even when it seems obvious that the subject company should command a considerably lower multiple?

While a public company comparable group provides an objective basis for comparing a subject company's results, either with measures of the group average (such as the mean or median) or with regard to the performance of specific companies in the group, appraisers often end up applying what amounts to a large judgmental discount to the comparable average (e.g., . . . "on the order of 50 percent based upon our detailed analysis") to obtain a correct (i.e., more reasonable and realistic) valuation multiple to be applied to the subject company.

ACAPM can help the appraiser reduce the element of judgment and quantify a discount from a public comparable group price/earnings multiple. The general case is shown below. Assume that a carefully selected public comparable group comprised of small capitalization stocks has a median P/E of 11.0x. The corresponding capitalization rate, the reciprocal of this factor, is 9.1 percent. We know from the preceding analysis that there is an implicit growth rate, G, implied by the market's capitalization factor. ACAPM can help the appraiser estimate the comparable group's G, which in turn can be used as input in the valuation process for a closely-held business. We can estimate G for the assumed comparable group as follows:

Long-term Treasury rate	8.0%	Per *The Wall Street Journal*
Ibbotson small-stock premium	12.2%	Per *1990 Yearbook*
Base capitalization rate	20.2%	beta assumed to be 1.0
Less public-company capitalization rate	− 9.1%	CR = (1 / P/E) = (1 / 11.0)
Implied G for public group	11.1%	

The implied growth rate from the ACAPM model for the public comparable group described above is about 11 percent. In actual circumstances, this sort of calculation can be tested by examining brokerage company analysts' projections of earnings for the individual companies in a group or by analysis of historical earnings growth for the public group.[32]

Now assume that the analyst's study of a closely-held company suggests a long-run growth expectation in the range of 8.0 pecent. If we assume no specific company risk premium, we find that, other things being equal, if expected growth is 8.0 percent rather than 11.1 percent, a P/E on the order of 8.0x rather than 11.1x is warranted.

Long-term Treasury rate	8.0%	Per *The Wall Street Journal*
Ibbotson small-stock premium	12.2%	Per *1990 Yearbook*
Base capitalization rate	20.2%	beta assumed to be 1.0
Less subject company G	− 8.0%	Per analyst's study
Implied CR for small company	12.2%	
Implied P/E for small company	8.2 ×	P/E = (1 / CR) = (1 / 12.2%)

By comparing the P/E of the comparable group (11.1x) with the growth-adjusted P/E for the small company being valued using ACAPM, the analyst can justify a fundamental discount on the order of 25 percent from the public comparable group P/E on the basis of growth differentials alone (1 − [8.2 / 11.1] = 26 percent).[33]

---

[32]This methodology yields a reasonable approximation of public-company growth expectations in a surprising number of circumstances. If the public companies are large capitalization stocks, it may be appropriate to use Ibbotson's common stock premium rather than the small-stock premium. Further, it may be necessary to adjust the analysis by an appropriate industry beta.

[33]In reality, this exercise is another example of the "magic" of compound interest at work. Assume that an investor's target rate of return is 20.2 percent, which is the long-run small-stock return per Ibbotson (i.e., the 12.2 percent premium discussed above plus the current government bond rate of 8.0 percent from the examples above). The investor is considering each of two investments with earnings streams beginning at $1.00 in the first year. Investment A is expected to grow at 11.1 percent per year into perpetuity, and Investment B is expected to grow at 8.0 percent. Based upon these assumptions, Investment A is worth $10.99 (or $1.00 / [.202 − .111]), and Investment B is worth $8.20 (or $1.00 / [.202 − .08]). If Investment A is the "base" value, it is clear that the value of Investment B should be discounted by about 25 percent relative to Investment A for the investor to achieve the target return of 20.2 percent on either investment (i.e., [1 − $8.20 / $10.99]). The ACAPM model simply provides a convenient vehicle for estimating the public-company G and for conducting this comparative valuation exercise.

In the context of the banking industry analysis presented in Exhibit 13-3, the impact of growth rate differentials upon the valuation multiples can be seen quite clearly. Referring back to the 0 percent SCR column, the ACAPM model predicts a P/E of 10.7x for a bank (operating in the environment suggested by the assumptions) with an expected growth rate of 10 percent. Other things being equal, a bank with expected growth of 7 percent warrants a P/E of only 8.1x. The difference in growth expectations for these two hypothetical banks with differing growth expectations calls for a valuation differential of approximately 24 percent, or (1 − 8.1 / 10.7).

This brief section reinforces two important points for appraisers. First, growth expectations are a critical valuation driver. And second, if the public markets are expecting rapid growth for a particular industry and an analyst's subject company or bank has considerably lower growth prospects, the result should be a lower relative valuation for the closely-held entity. This seems to be a particularly difficult concept for appraisers who are confronted with high P/E multiples (and high growth expectations) in a public comparable group. The lesson is simple: If the expected growth level required by the public markets (for the comparable group to achieve market multiples) is not present for a subject closely-held bank or business, the valuation should reflect an appropriate discount for its lower growth prospects.

Using the Adjusted Capital Asset Pricing Model to Develop Discount Rates

In the next chapter, we will discuss the use of discounted future benefits methodologies for the valuation of banks. As will be seen, the selection of the appropriate discount rate is one of the most critical components of discounted future benefits valuation methodologies. As a prelude to the broader discussion, this section looks at one method for deriving discount rates within the framework of the adjusted capital asset pricing model.

Market Observable Discount Rates

Using Equation IX, we developed an estimate of R, or the discount rate, for the comparable group of banking companies in the Sample Bank Appraisal as of year-end 1990. Recalling that equation:

$$\text{IX. (repeated)} \quad R - G = \left(\frac{1}{P/E} \right) = (CR)$$

We estimated G, or the sustainable growth rate for the group, as 8.1 percent (in Equation XI above). We also observed that, with a median P/E of 7.4x, the implied capitalization rate (1 / P/E) was 14.2 percent. Substituting our estimate of G and the derived capitalization rate of 14.2 percent, we derived R, or the market's implied median required rate of return for the group as:

$$R - 8.1\% = 14.2\%$$

Therefore,

$$R = 14.2\% + 8.1\%$$
$$= 22.3\%$$

The discount rate derived above has the advantage of being indirectly observable in the marketplace, or market observable. As indicated at the outset of the discussion of the ACAPM model, the bank or business valuation analyst often needs to develop capitalization rates (or discount rates) in the absence of good comparative market information. The basic ACAPM model was designed to derive capitalization rates, or P/E multiples. We now want to examine the development of discount rates using ACAPM in the context of the present market observable example in order to validate a methodology for developing discount rates when market observations are not readily available.

Validating the Market Observable Discount Rate

We should be able to validate, at least approximately, the market-observable discount rate of 22.3 percent derived above using the ACAPM model.[34] Exhibit 13-4 provides the basic outline of the methodology to reconcile to the observable 22.3 percent discount rate. The methodology begins in a manner similar to the process of building capitalization rates. The sources for the exhibit are the same as those cited for Exhibit 13-3.

Exhibit 13-4

Discount Rates Using the ACAPM Model Reconciling
the Market's Implied Discount Rate as of December 1990

		Discount Rate
Long-term Treasuries		8.4%
Ibbotson small-stock premium	12.2%	
Assumed beta	× .90	
Risk-adjusted industry return		11.0%
Temporary industry risk		2.9%
Discount rate		22.0%

In Exhibit 13-4, a long-term beta for regional bank stocks of 0.90 has been assumed. In order to reconcile the model to the market, an additional factor called *temporary industry risk* has been added. In the alternative, one might assume a temporary higher beta statistic (on the order of 1.10) to reconcile the market with the model. The point is that the market prices of bank stocks were under substantial pressure during the third and fourth quarters of 1990. This pricing pressure was the result of concerns over credit problems from real estate loans and loans to highly leveraged companies amidst prospects of an economic recession of unknown depth and magnitude. At the time of this writing (mid-1991), we have the benefit of hindsight and know that bank stocks recovered

---

[34]As has been stated throughout this discussion of the ACAPM model, it is by no means a perfect tool. As in every area of business or financial institutions appraisal, it will be necessary for the analyst to exercise judgment based on experience. This is particularly true in the development of discount rates. The model will present a framework for discussing the important elements of required rates of return. Because the methodology is presented as one means of developing substitutes for market-observable discount rates, it will always be important that the analyst be grounded in current industry, market, and economic conditions.

strongly in the first quarter of 1991. In fact, the median price/earnings multiple had increased to 8.5x for the same group of banks by mid-year 1991.[35]

Developing Capitalization Rates for Specific Companies Using ACAPM

Exhibit 13-4 attempted to use the framework of the adjusted capital asset pricing model to validate the public market's implied discount rate for one group of banks at year-end 1990. For the examples in Exhibit 13-5, assume that the subject bank happens to be located in an area where the majority of publicly traded banking companies have experienced severe earnings pressures. Price/earnings ratios developed from regional banking companies are either not meaningful (for those banks experiencing losses) or abnormally high (for those banks with sharply lower earnings). Subject Bank, which has approximately $100 million in total assets and is capitalized at 7.0 percent of assets (i.e., shareholders equity is $7.0 million) has just recovered from isolated, unique problems of its own. It is expected to earn about $1.0 million this year, and earnings should reasonably grow at about 8.0 percent, based upon a detailed analysis of the bank and its potential. There are specific opportunities to increase earnings through fee income enhancement and expense reductions until the overall area is expected to recover, after which the growth rate should be sustainable.

Exhibit 13-5
Discount Rates Using the ACAPM Model
Developing a Specific Discount Rate as of May 1991

	Variation 1		Variation 2	
Long-term Treasuries		8.2%		8.2%
Ibbotson small-stock premium	12.2%		7.2%	
Ibbotson common stock premium				
Assumed beta	× .90		× .90	
Risk-adjusted industry return		11.0%		6.5%
Area ecomonic risk factor		1.0%		1.0%
Specific-company risk (2%–3%)*		2.5%		2.5%
Discount rates		22.7%		18.2%
Implied P/E [1 / (DR − 8.0%)]		6.8×		9.8×
Current earnings		$1,000M		$1,000M
Implied value†		$6,800M		$9,800M
Implied price/book multiple		97%		140%

*See the discussion in the text.
†Per the discussion in the text, this value is a minority interest marketable value in the context of Exhibit 12-1.

Exhibit 13-5 provides two variations on the derivation of a discount rate for Subject Bank in the context of the ACAPM model. The purpose of showing two variations is to indicate, at least partially, the extent of the range of judgment in developing discount rates, as well as to introduce

---

[35]No simple model can explain all the complexities of industry, market, and economic forces that go into the pricing of bank or other stocks all the time.

the reader to some of the many alternatives available in developing capitalization and discount rates within the context of the adjusted capital asset pricing model.

Note that the exhibit adds a factor called an *area economic risk factor* of 1.0 percent. The analyst suggesting this factor determined that there was risk associated with owning bank stocks in this area of the country that transcended the risks quantified in the Ibbotson premiums or in the specific company risk assessment.

Based upon the analysis of Subject Bank, the analyst concluded that a specific company risk premium in the range of 2–3 percent was appropriate based upon the bank's historical earnings trends and recent losses, as well as uncertainties associated with new management coming on board. He used a midpoint estimate of 2.5 percent for the specific risk premium.

A beta statistic of 0.90 was derived from a study of a national group of regional holding companies at the time of the appraisal, as well as historical studies of bank betas available to the analyst.

Variation 1 in Exhibit 13-5 uses the Ibbotson small-stock premium as the estimate for the market's premium return over long-term government bonds (MR − RFR). As previously discussed, this is the current long-term premium return for the small-stock series found in the Ibbotson Associates *1991 Yearbook*. Applying the assumed beta to the 12.2 percent small-stock premium and adding the other components of the ACAPM yields a discount rate of 22.7 percent.

Variation 2 in the exhibit uses the Ibbotson common stock premium, which is based upon the Standard and Poor's Composite Index. The common stock premium over long-term government bonds since 1926 has been 7.2 percent. The larger capitalization stocks comprising the S&P Composite Index are generally considered to be less risky than the smaller capitalization stocks. Some analysts use this measure routinely in developing discount or capitalization rates under variations of the adjusted capital asset pricing model.[36] However, at the very least it is appropriate to use higher estimates of SCR when using the common stock premium because the basis of comparison was shifted from the smaller capitalization to the larger capitalization universe. Variation 2, as shown with an apparent mistake in the selection of the analyst's estimate of SCR, derives a discount rate of 18.2 percent.

Variation 1 yields an implied valuation indication of $6.8 million, or 97 percent of book value, with a 6.8x P/E multiple. Variation 2 yields an implied valuation indication of $9.8 million, or 140 percent of book value, with a 9.8x P/E multiple. In the current market environment (as described above for this example), Variation 1 provides a much more appropriate indication of value (before considerations of marketability) than

---

[36]Variation 2 is provided here not to suggest that the Ibbotson common stock premium is the appropriate market premium measure for the valuation of community bank stocks, but to introduce it as one more market premium measure available to the analyst in appropriate circumstances and to show the impact of its use, without compensating adjustments, relative to the small-stock premium. In fact, the common stock premium may be quite appropriate for use in the valuation of very large financial institutions or large closely-held businesses. Further, in certain circumstances, the valuation analyst might develop a rationale for a market premium somewhere between the two measures most commonly quoted from the Ibbotson study. In addition, Ibbotson yearbook provides historical data series that can allow the analyst to derive her or his own market return measure for time periods other than the 1926-to-current-year series that are frequently quoted.

Variation 2 because it considers what this writer believes to be the risks of owning minority interests in community bank stocks in relationship to alternative investments available in the public stock markets.

Implications of the ACAPM Discount Rate

As with any capitalization factor, we must know to which earnings stream a derived discount rate applies and the basis of value that it develops. We stated the opinion that price/earnings multiples (or capitalization rates) developed using the ACAPM model can be applied to the net income of a subject valuation company as determined on a current, ongoing basis by the appraiser. We believe similarly that the discount rate derived using the ACAPM model should be applied to the projected net income of subject valuation companies. The implications of this decision will be discussed in Chapter 14, in the section on discounted future benefits methodologies.

We stated the opinion that capitalization rates (or price/earnings multiples) derived using the ACAPM should be considered to be minority interest marketable, or as-if-freely-traded in character. In other words, the P/E multiples of Exhibit 13-3 are considered to be substitutes for similar multiples developed from the public stock markets when appropriate comparable information is available. Similarly, the discount rates derived using the ACAPM can be considered to be minority interest marketable discount rates and to yield minority interest marketable conclusions. In other words, the conclusions developed using ACAPM discount rates should fit into the middle box of Figure 12-1. The analyst should then give appropriate consideration to the use of control premiums (for controlling interest appraisals) or marketability discounts (for non-marketable minority interest appraisals).

Conclusion

The bank analyst may derive capitalization rates based upon the analysis of public company comparable (guideline) groups of banks, by using alternative means such as build-up methodologies based upon the Capital Asset Pricing Model (or the Adjusted Capital Asset Pricing Model as described in this chapter), or both. Regardless of approach, the objective is always to develop reasonable and believable valuation multiples to be applied to the earnings of a subject bank. An analyst may be theoretically correct and absolutely wrong. He or she may also be on target (by chance or otherwise) but with methodologies so far outside the realm of current financial theory and practice as to be worthless. Good valuation requires a reasonable blend of theory, practice, experience and judgment.

Chapter 14

Controlling Interest
Valuation Methodologies

Through the alterations in the income streams provided by loans or sales, the marginal degrees of impatience for all individuals in the market are brought into equality with each other and the market rate of interest.

Irving Fisher
The Theory of Interest

Introduction

Chapter 13 dealt with valuation approaches designed to develop *minority interest* valuation conclusions. This chapter will present five approaches often used to prepare *controlling interest* valuation conclusions for banking institutions, including:

1. Payback analysis.
2. Public market comparisons.
3. Analysis of comparable transactions.
4. Dilution analysis.
5. Discounted future benefits.

In valuing banks on a controlling interest basis, experienced analysts will often use one or more of these approaches.

Prior to discussing specific controlling interest valuation approaches, however, it is important to discuss two concepts related to the differences between cash values for controlling interests in banks and values based upon acquisitions made through tax-free exchanges of shares. The concepts are those of relative pricing (from the viewpoint of acquirers of banks) and risk-adjusted pricing (from the viewpoint of sellers).

Relative Pricing from a Buyer's Viewpoint

In "hot markets" for bank stocks, analysts or bankers using the public market comparative approach often overvalue individual community banks *in relationship to valuation approaches based upon cash returns.* Sellers of banks also tend to develop inflated concepts of value in relation to pricing justified solely based upon the direct earnings of the subject bank.

When bank markets are attractively priced—when market multiples, expressed in terms of book value, trade in the range of 140–150 percent of book value or higher—large banks with actively traded shares tend to be more acquisition minded than when their shares are trading at lower multiples. In the high-priced environment, public banks have four basic options for financing their acquisitions:

1. Borrow the funds and leverage their balance sheets. Given leverage constraints, this option provides limited opportunities for growth by acquisition for even the largest banks.

2. Sell newly issued stock to the public at current (high) prices, and use the cash to finance cash purchases.
3. Sell newly issued shares to the shareholders of acquisition targets by effecting acquisitions via stock exchanges.
4. Some combination of the first three options.

When their shares are attractively priced, large public banks tend to make more stock acquisitions than cash acquisitions. Cash acquisitions tend to be more dilutive of earnings and book value than similarly priced stock acquisitions.[1]

High priced public bank shares therefore tend to yield high priced acquisitions, particularly when the acquisition values (based upon share exchanges) are denominated in dollar terms. In other words, it is normally less dilutive for existing shareholders of a regional holding company to pay a premium price of, say, 200 percent of book value for a community bank with stock valued at 150 percent of book value or more than to pay a cash price of 200 percent of book value.

The *relative premium* paid is actually much lower in the case of the stock acquisition. From the point of view of the acquirer, a simplistic analysis can illustrate this point. The regional bank that paid 200 percent of book value in cash for a community bank paid a cash premium of 100 percent of the acquired bank's equity. In the stock acquisition at a similar price, the acquiring bank issued equity (new shares) for the entire price. The *effective* premium can be measured by the relative pricing of the acquisition and the acquirer's shares. Because the acquirer's shares in this example are trading at 150 percent of book value and a price of 200 percent of book value was paid, the relative premium paid was only 133 percent (i.e., 200 percent / 150 percent). A relative pricing of 133 percent of book value in a stock acquisition is considerably less dilutive, other things being equal, than a cash pricing of 200 percent of book value.

Risk-Adjusted Pricing from the Seller's Viewpoint

Sellers of banks should be aware that there is a significant difference between cash sales and stock-for-stock exchanges. While it may seem obvious, the main difference is that the selling shareholders receive *cash* for their shares in cash sales. They are responsible for their individual ordinary income taxes or capital gains taxes on gains (or losses). Whatever proceeds are left are then available to the individual sellers on an after-tax basis.

When banks are sold in stock-for-stock exchanges, sellers normally receive marketable shares in the acquiring company in the form of a tax-free exchange. In theory, each selling shareholder has the opportunity to liquidate shares into the open market, pay capital gains taxes, and

---

[1]This concept will be clarified in the discussion of dilution analysis, which focuses on the impact of acquisition pricing on postacquisition estimates of earnings per share, book value per share, and market pricing.

have after-tax proceeds of the remainder. In practice, many selling shareholders retain their newly acquired shares, in many instances to avoid paying capital gains taxes. In so doing, they incur the *risk* of holding the newly acquired securities.

The concept of the relative premium for the acquirer can be related to the risk-adjusted price for the seller. Bank A and Bank B are similar in most respects and are equally attractive to potential acquirers. Both banks have book values of $10 per share. Assume that Shareholder A owns 1,000 shares of Bank A and Shareholder B owns 1,000 shares of Bank B. Both shareholders inherited their shares and have a tax basis of $2 per share, or $2,000 for their individual blocks. Both shareholders have a combined marginal tax rate (federal and state) of 30 percent. Two examples illustrate the concept of risk-adjusted pricing:

Bank A was sold to a small bank holding company in an adjacent county for a cash price of $13.33 per share, or 133 percent of book value. Shareholder A received cash proceeds of $13,330 and reported a taxable gain of $11,330 ($13,330 − $2,000). She therefore paid capital gains taxes totalling $3,399 (30 percent × $11,330) and had after-tax proceeds from the sale of $9,931 ($13,330 − $3,399). Shareholder A then reinvested her after-tax proceeds into a money market mutual fund while she made a longer-term decision regarding their use.

Bank B was sold to Regional Bancshares at approximately the same time for a price of $20 per share in a tax-free exchange of shares. Shareholder B, who knew Shareholder A, silently gloated at the much better price he received for his shares. Because Regional Bancshares stock was trading at $20 per share (which was 150 percent of its book value of $13.33 per share at the time), Shareholder B received 1,000 shares of Regional in exchange for his shares of Bank B, or $20,000 of stock at the then current market price. Shareholder B considered selling his shares immediately, but he decided not to sell in order to avoid paying capital gains taxes of $5,400 on his paper gain of $18,000 ($20,000 − $2,000), even though he was pleased to note that his proceeds after taxes would have been $14,600 ($20,000 − $5,400). He therefore placed his shares into his safe deposit box. Unfortunately, Regional announced in the next quarter a sharp downturn in earnings caused by unexpected loan losses, and its stock fell in value to $15 per share. This concerned Shareholder B, but he thought that Regional's shares would recover in the near term. Unfortunately, the very next quarter was October 1987, and bank shares in general fell sharply in price along with the general market following Black Monday. Regional's shares drifted down to $11 per share over the next few months. Just a few short months following Bank B's premium sale, the market value of Shareholder B's stock is now only $11,000 (with an after-tax value to Shareholder B, if sold, of $8,300).

Shareholder B learned the meaning of risk-adjusted pricing during the several months following the sale of his bank.

The important caveat for the bank analyst from this and the preceding section is that it is important to make a clear distinction in any controlling interest valuation conclusion between valuation indications based upon cash transactions and those dependent, either particularly or in their entirety, upon the exchange of shares.

Payback and Rate-of-Return Analysis

The first control basis valuation technique described in this chapter is called *payback and rate-of-return analysis* or simply *payback analysis*. In some respects, this is the simplest and most straightforward valuation technique. It approximates the approach used by many purchasers of banks, particularly of single banks through the use of one-bank holding companies.

Payback analysis calls for the following:

1. A detailed investigation of the subject bank is required in order to begin to understand its potential for future performance.
2. The bank's prospective performance should be modeled, or forecast, under a variety of assumptions about the local economy, national economic conditions, and the level and direction of interest rates, as well as fundamental operating characteristics. The expected rate of growth of banking assets is a critical assumption in this analysis. Exhibit 11-1 provided a summary example of a forecasting model for a bank. In an actual valuation situation, the analyst should either develop a more detailed model for the subject bank or be able to translate specific changes that might impact the bank's future performance in terms of a simple bank model such as that presented in Exhibit 11-1.
3. The bank performance forecast should then be incorporated into the context of a one-bank holding company forecasting model (or into an existing holding company) in order to observe performance on an incremental basis under a range of assumptions regarding potential pricing of the subject bank. Again, Exhibit 11-1 provides an example of an integrated bank/holding-company forecasting model.
4. In order to value the bank using payback analysis, the analyst must make an explicit assumption concerning the down payment that will be required by the Federal Reserve and an assumption about the terms and conditions of possible financing for the acquisition. Given each assumption of a bank purchase price, the forecasting model should (a) "capitalize" the holding company with the required down payment, (b) book any goodwill (excess of purchase price over the fair values of assets to be acquired), (c) "finance" the remainder of the purchase price with debt at the holding company level under realistic assumptions regarding pricing and terms, and (4) make an assumption about the minimum required level of capital at the subsidiary bank level, which will determine its ability, given the assumptions made about bank performance, to upstream dividends to the parent company to finance acquisition debt.
5. The analyst should then run the model and observe how the assumed performance will service the required principal and interest on the holding company debt. If the debt can be serviced according to its terms, calculations of the rate of return to be expected from an investment in the subject bank under each set of assumptions about

performance and pricing can be made. In this case, an assumption about the value of the bank at the end of the forecast period must be made in order to calculate expected returns.

6. Finally, based upon an analysis of the sensitivity of payback ability and anticipated rates of return on initial equity investments in the model one-bank holding company, the analyst can develop a matrix of reasonably achievable pricing and returns.

With the exception of the rate-of-return calculations, this methodology is similar to the analysis that the Federal Reserve would make of a one-bank holding company application to acquire the subject bank (see Chapter 11). The methodology therefore simulates regulatory scrutiny in addition to examining potential rates of return in relationship to the expected risk of investing in a leveraged one-bank holding company.

Exhibits 14-1 and 14-2 provide examples of the use of payback analysis to value a bank under two different assumptions regarding its future performance. The exhibits summarize projection data from a model similar to that found in Exhibit 11-1.

The major limiting assumptions of Exhibits 14-1 and 14-2 are:

1. The Fed will require that 40 percent of the purchase price be financed with equity in the holding company.
2. The remainder of the purchase price is financed at a 10.5 percent fixed rate with interest-only payments due for Year 1 and then level amortization of principal and interest over the next 11 years.
3. The bank is projected to grow at 6.0 percent per year for the forecast period in Exhibit 14-1 and at 4.0 percent per year in Exhibit 14-2.
4. The minimum equity constraint at the bank level is set at 8.0 percent of total assets, and all equity over that level is upstreamed to the holding company at the end of each year to service debt.
5. The holding company owns 100 percent of the bank and files a consolidated federal income tax return, thereby taking advantage of the tax deductibility of the original acquisition debt.

In Exhibit 11-1, Specimen Bank is projected to earn a return on average assets in the range of 1.25–1.30 percent for the forecast period. The model was run at various levels of pricing, expressed in terms of the price/book multiple, to find the maximum pricing assumption under which the bank's earnings would comfortably cover the debt service requirements of the acquisition debt. In Exhibit 14-1, that level of pricing was approximately 1.40x book value. Various measures of bank and holding company performance are summarized in the exhibit.

The model calculates the expected rate of return for the shareholders of Specimen Bancshares assuming that the bank is sold at the end of Year 10 of the projection. Given the assumptions outlined above (for the cash inflows and outflows at the bottom of Exhibit 14-1), the investors' rate of return on their investment in Specimen Bancshares would be approximately 15.3 percent.

Exhibit 14-2 provides an analysis under assumptions similar to those in Exhibit 14-1, except that the bank's performance, in terms of return on average assets, is projected in the range of 1.01–1.10 percent. The

Exhibit 14-1
Specimen Bancshares, Inc.
Payback/Rate-of-Return Analysis for Acquisition of Specimen Bank ($ Thousands)

Specimen Bancshares, Inc.

Price/book multiple paid for bank	1.40
Dollar price paid for bank	$11,200
Regulatory required equity %	40.00%
Initial required equity capital	$4,480
Holding company acquisition debt	$6,720
Interest only Year 1	
Then amortize over term of	11 years

Specimen Bank

Net worth	$8,000
Total assets	$100,000
Return on assets	1.25%
Return on equity	15.67%
Beginning equity/assets	8.00%
Minimum equity/assets for projection	8.00%
Estimated growth rate	6.00%

Projection Summary	Year 1	Year 2	Year 3	Year 4	Year 5	Year 6	Year 7	Year 8	Year 9	Year 10
Negotiated Debt Terms										
Beginning debt	6720	6720	6367	5977	5546	5070	4544	3962	3320	2609
Scheduled total payment	706	1059	1059	1059	1059	1059	1059	1059	1059	1059
Scheduled interest	706	706	669	628	582	532	477	416	349	274
Scheduled principal	0	353	390	431	476	526	581	643	710	785
Ending debt	6720	6367	5977	5546	5070	4544	3962	3320	2609	1825
Ending debt per projection	6552	6272	5938	5542	5079	4541	3921	3209	2397	1476
+ / – relative to terms	168	95	39	4	–9	2	41	110	212	349
Bank Performance										
Net income	1291	1430	1507	1589	1677	1769	1867	1971	2081	2198
Return on assets	1.25%	1.31%	1.30%	1.30%	1.29%	1.28%	1.28%	1.27%	1.27%	1.26%
Return on equity	15.67%	16.37%	16.28%	16.20%	16.12%	16.04%	15.97%	15.91%	15.85%	15.79%
Ending equity	8480	8989	9528	10100	10706	11348	12029	12751	13516	14327
Ending total assets	106000	112360	119102	126248	133823	141852	150363	159385	168948	179085
Ending equity/total assets	8.00%	8.00%	8.00%	8.00%	8.00%	8.00%	8.00%	8.00%	8.00%	8.00%
Dividend to parent company	811	921	968	1018	1071	1127	1186	1249	1316	1387
Holding Company Performance										
Net income	435	575	660	754	856	967	1088	1220	1363	1519
Cash flow from operations	168	279	334	396	463	538	621	712	812	922
Ending equity	4915	5490	6150	6904	7760	8727	9815	11035	12398	13918
Double leverage ratio	1.73	1.64	1.55	1.46	1.38	1.30	1.23	1.16	1.09	1.03
Tangible double leverage	4.40	3.31	2.65	2.22	1.90	1.67	1.48	1.34	1.22	1.11
Debt/equity	1.33	1.14	0.97	0.80	0.65	0.52	0.40	0.29	0.19	0.11
Valuation Information										
Bank value at acquired multiple	11872	12584	13339	14140	14988	15887	16841	17851	18922	20057
Less holding company debt	–6552	–6272	–5938	–5542	–5079	–4541	–3921	–3209	–2397	–1476
Implied value of holding company	5320	6312	7401	8597	9909	11346	12920	14642	16525	18582
Annual change in value	18.76%	18.64%	17.26%	16.16%	15.26%	14.51%	13.87%	13.33%	12.86%	12.45%
Rate of Return Analysis										
Cash –out/+in	–4480									+18582
(Assuming sale at end of Year 10)										
Internal rate of return	15.29%									

249

Exhibit 14-2

Specimen Bancshares, Inc.

Payback/Rate-of-Return Analysis for Acquisition of Specimen Bank ($ Thousands)

Specimen Bancshares, Inc.

Price/book multiple paid for bank	1.20
Dollar price paid for bank	$9,600
Regulatory required equity %	40.00%
Initial required equity capital	$3,840
Holding company acquisition debt	$5,760
Interest only Year 1	
Then amortize over term of	11 years

Specimen Bank

Net worth	$8,000
Total assets	$100,000
Return on assets	1.01%
Return on equity	12.59%
Beginning equity/assets	8.00%
Minimum equity/assets for projection	8.00%
Estimated growth rate	4.00%

Projection Summary	Year 1	Year 2	Year 3	Year 4	Year 5	Year 6	Year 7	Year 8	Year 9	Year 10
Negotiated Debt Terms										
Beginning debt	5760	5760	5457	5123	4754	4346	3894	3396	2845	2237
Scheduled total payment	605	907	907	907	907	907	907	907	907	907
Scheduled interest	605	605	573	538	499	456	409	357	299	235
Scheduled principal	0	303	334	369	408	451	498	551	609	672
Ending debt	5760	5457	5123	4754	4346	3894	3396	2845	2237	1564
Ending debt per projection	5629	5364	5060	4713	4319	3875	3376	2817	2193	1499
+/− relative to terms	131	93	63	41	26	19	20	28	43	65
Bank Performance										
Net income	1027	1172	1213	1256	1301	1348	1396	1447	1499	1554
Return on assets	1.01%	1.10%	1.10%	1.10%	1.09%	1.09%	1.08%	1.08%	1.07%	1.07%
Return on equity	12.59%	13.81%	13.75%	13.69%	13.63%	13.58%	13.52%	13.47%	13.42%	13.38%
Ending equity	8320	8653	8999	9359	9733	10123	10527	10949	11386	11842
Ending total assets	104000	108160	112486	116986	121665	126532	131593	136857	142331	148024
Ending equity/total assets	8.00%	8.00%	8.00%	8.00%	8.00%	8.00%	8.00%	8.00%	8.00%	8.00%
Dividend to parent company	707	839	867	897	927	959	991	1026	1061	1098
Holding Company Performance										
Net income	344	491	544	600	661	727	797	873	955	1043
Cash flow from operations	131	265	304	347	393	444	499	559	624	695
Ending equity	4184	4676	5219	5819	6480	7207	8004	8878	9833	10876
Double leverage ratio	1.99	1.85	1.72	1.61	1.50	1.40	1.32	1.23	1.16	1.09
Tangible double leverage	3.09	2.63	2.28	2.01	1.80	1.62	1.47	1.35	1.24	1.14
Debt/equity	1.35	1.15	0.97	0.81	0.67	0.54	0.42	0.32	0.22	0.14
Valuation Information										
Bank value at acquired multiple	9984	10383	10799	11231	11680	12147	12633	13138	13664	14210
Less holding company debt	−5629	−5364	−5060	−4713	−4319	−3875	−3376	−2817	−2193	−1499
Implied value of holding company	4355	5019	5739	6518	7360	8272	9257	10321	11470	12711
Annual change in value	13.41%	15.26%	14.34%	13.57%	12.93%	12.38%	11.91%	11.50%	11.14%	10.82%
Rate of Return Analysis										
Cash −out/+in	−3840									+12711
(Assuming sale at end of Year 10)										
Internal rate of return	12.72%									

derived pricing for the bank, under the requirement that the holding company should be able to service its acquisition debt according to its original terms, is 1.20x book value. The investors' internal rate of return in Exhibit 14-2 is approximately 12.7 percent.

In this simple comparison, lower expected returns and growth at the bank level generated both lower pricing for the bank and lower expected returns for investors in the holding company.

Exhibit 14-3 provides a broader use of payback analysis by summarizing information with respect to investors' potential rates of return for investing in a bank through the vehicle of a one-bank holding company, as well as information about the "bankability" of transactions under varying assumptions regarding regulatory minimum capital requirements and relative bank pricing (in terms of the price/book value multiple).

The assumptions underlying Exhibit 14-3 are identical to those found in Exhibit 14-1. Exhibit 14-3 shows that there is a fairly clear relationship between leverage, bank pricing, and bankability. The interaction between the Fed's minimum equity requirements and the requirements of bank stock lenders that an acquiring holding company be able to service its acquisition debt according to original terms are both combining, in the present banking and regulatory environments, to decrease leverage and prices paid for banks in cash acquisitions.

In valuing a bank using payback analysis, the analyst would normally develop a range of pricing under varying assumptions regarding expected growth and operating performance of the bank to be acquired or valued.

Specimen Bank is projected to earn an ROA of 1.25–1.30 percent for the next 10 years. Its equity/total-assets ratio is 8.0 percent at the date of purchase, and that level of capital is maintained for the 10-year forecast period. Specimen Bank is projected to grow at 6.0 percent per year. The model focuses on investor rates of return under varying assumptions

Exhibit 14-3
Specimen Bank
Impact of Regulatory Leverage Requirements on Bank Pricing and Investor Rates of Return
If Purchase Is Accomplished with a Newly Formed One-Bank Holding Company

	Assumed Fed Equity Requirement						
	Projected Internal Rates of Return at Various Multiples of Book Value						
	1.00	**1.10**	**1.20**	**1.30**	**1.40**	**1.50**	**1.60**
25%	21.7%(a)	20.8%(a)	19.9%(b)	19.2%(c)	18.5%(c)	17.9%(c)	17.3%(c)
30%	20.6 (a)	19.3 (a)	18.5 (a)	17.8 (b)	17.2 (c)	16.6 (c)	16.1 (c)
35%	19.9 (a)	18.7 (a)	17.4 (a)	16.7 (a)	16.1 (b)	15.6 (c)	15.1 (c)
40%	19.5 (a)	18.1 (a)	17.0 (a)	15.8 (a)	15.3 (a)	14.8 (b)	14.3 (c)
45%	18.1 (a)	17.8 (a)	16.6 (a)	15.6 (a)	14.6 (a)	14.1 (a)	13.7 (b)
50%	18.0 (a)	16.5 (a)	16.3 (a)	15.2 (a)	14.3 (a)	13.6 (a)	13.2 (a)

(a) Services debt or generates some surplus cash (bankable)
(b) Shortfall by Year 10 between $1,000 and $1,000,000 (marginally bankable)
(c) Shortfall greater than $1,000,000 in debt service ability (probably not bankable)

about the Fed's minimum equity investment required in a one-bank holding company formation and varying price/book multiples, assuming: (1) no dividends are paid to shareholders of the holding company until the acquisition debt is paid off, and (2) the bank is sold at the end of Year 10 at the same multiple of book value at which it was purchased.

Payback analysis develops a cash price for a bank because it begins with a cash down payment and proceeds to examine the cash flows generated by the subject bank and the cash returns to be expected from an ultimate sale of the investment. The method is particularly well suited for the valuation of community banks in rural locations not being targeted by larger, publicly traded holding companies. The methodology may "undervalue" a bank if it is a candidate for inclusion in the portfolio of a larger holding company where the perceived risk profile of the investment may be lower, or where the required rate of return of potential purchasers may be lower than for investors in leveraged one-bank holding companies. Nevertheless, payback analysis can provide a solid analytical and valuation tool for the bank analyst seeking to value banks on a controlling interest basis.

Public Market Comparisons

Traditional theory suggests that transactions in shares of actively traded, public companies provide minority interest valuation data (see Chapters 12 and 13). Exhibit 12-1 indicates that we can develop a controlling interest price/earnings multiple by adding an appropriate control premium to the freely tradable minority interest multiple derived from analysis of an appropriate group of comparable publicly traded companies.

If this approach is used, it is critical to adjust the base price/earnings multiples for fundamental differences between the subject bank and the larger, publicly traded companies before adding any control premium. As discussed at length in Chapter 13, fundamental differences for factors such as growth and risk can require significant adjustments to the base multiples for appropriate application to a community bank.

Analysts using public market comparisons to develop controlling interest valuation indications may use multiples of earnings, book value, deposits, or assets. The control premium studies cited in Chapter 12 provide some objective evidence of the appropriate range of control premiums to be applied to multiples of earnings. According to *Mergerstat Review 1990*, the average premium paid over the preannouncement minority interest prices for financial services companies has been in the range of 31.2 percent (1987) to 43.9 percent (1986) for the 1986–1990 period. The average premiums over market paid for financial services companies were about 41 percent in both 1989 and 1990.[2]

Using the example of Specimen Bank in Exhibit 14-1 as a base, we can see how the public market comparison approach can be used to deter-

---

[2]*Mergerstat Review 1990* (Merrill Lynch, 1991), p. 91.

mine an estimate of value on a controlling interest basis. Because the information is not provided in Exhibit 14-1, assume that trailing 12-month earnings for Specimen Bank are $1.2 million and that there are no adjustments to be made to earnings based upon an analysis of the bank. Assume further that, based upon a review of an appropriate group of comparable bank holding companies, the median price/earnings multiple for the group is 8.0x trailing 12-month earnings.

Based upon a study of the hypothetical Specimen Bank, an analyst determined that its earnings should be valued at a discount of approximately 15 percent to the median multiple of the comparable group. The valuation indication of Specimen Bank provided by public market comparisons is provided in Exhibit 14-4.

Exhibit 14-4
Specimen Bank
Valuation Estimate Using Public Market Comparisons as of June 30, 1991 ($ Thousands)

Median P/E as of June 30, 1991		8.0 ×
Fundamental adjustment (15%, per text)		− 1.2
Adjusted minority/marketable P/E		6.8 ×
Control premium range (30% to 40%, per text)	30%	40%
Controlling interest P/E range	8.8	9.5
Specimen Bank ongoing earnings	$1,200	$1,200
Valuation range	$10,560	$11,400
Implied price/book multiples	1.32 ×	1.43 ×

The analyst should exercise caution in the use of public market price/earnings (or price/book) multiples directly in the valuation of banking institutions on a controlling interest basis. There is a tendency to use unadjusted public market multiples plus a control premium when using this technique. As discussed at length in Chapter 13, appropriate adjustments must be made to the base public multiples for fundamental factors *prior to the application of any control premium* in order to avoid overstating (or understating) the derived multiple of earnings and therefore overstating (or understating) the derived *controlling interest* valuation conclusion. Recall from Chapter 13 that in *minority interest* valuations, analysts sometimes use the unadjusted base public price/earnings multiple and, effectively, make necessary adjustments by weighting other valuation approaches in the conclusion. The use of public market comparisons to derive a controlling interest valuation indication should probably be used in conjunction with other methods.

Comparative Transactions Approach

In Chapter 13, we discussed the market approach to developing minority interest indications of valuation. The market approach calls for investigating the market for minority interests in a subject bank's shares. In developing controlling interest valuations, the market approach calls for comparisons, not with transactions in the subject's shares, but with control sales of other banks. By making appropriate comparisons with other control sales, the bank analyst can develop indications of the current value of a subject bank.

Necessary Comparisons

In developing an indication of value using comparative transactions analysis, it is important for the analyst to make comparisons between the subject bank and the comparable sale transactions used as a basis for pricing. Appropriate comparisons might include:

1. *Geographical proximity.* Ideally, comparisons should be made with banks in reasonable proximity to each other. Adjustments may have to be made for transactions in markets of differing attractiveness or growth potential.
2. *Similarity of market position.* Other things being equal, acquirers will tend to pay more for banks controlling large market shares of deposits and loans than for smaller institutions in a given market. The analyst may need to consider the impact of market share on the pricing of acquisitions in order to draw appropriate conclusions from particular comparative transactions.
3. *Proximity in time.* While there is some empirical evidence that enterprise values are not as volatile as minority interest values in the public stock markets, values for business enterprises can change significantly over fairly short periods of time. Comparisons with other transactions should therefore be made over time (to discern any trends in pricing), and as close to the actual valuation date as possible (to determine current levels of pricing).
4. *Similarity of terms.* Transactions involving exchanges for stock should be analyzed separately from those involving cash and other forms of consideration. The terms of transactions should be analyzed to place all transactions on a cash-equivalent basis. In other words, notes, contracts, and other forms of purchase price should be analyzed, if possible, to ensure comparability and that cash-equivalent calculations have been made in the estimates of total consideration for the transactions.
5. *Structural characteristics.* Comparisons of the balance sheets of comparable transactions should be made. Adjustments may be necessary to reflect differences in leverage, asset composition, or deposit structure to ensure comparability. Further, it is important to note whether the pricing of comparable transactions is based upon the sale of leveraged or unleveraged holding companies. The implied pricing of the subsidiary bank may be significantly different from the apparent pricing of a leveraged holding company.
6. *Performance characteristics.* The analyst should examine historical performance trends and returns in order to ensure comparability with a subject bank. Adjustments may have to be made to ensure comparability.
7. *Other relevant comparisons.* Ideally, the analyst would make appropriate adjustments for any other significant points of difference between a subject bank and the institutions used for comparative pricing analysis.

In the ideal situation, the bank analyst would make all the relevant comparisons noted above between a subject bank and the banks selected for comparative pricing analysis. There are, however, several problems that can arise in the process of comparative analysis. The first problem arises in the availability of comparative information. In most cases, the analyst simply will not have information in sufficient detail to make many of the comparisons outlined above.

Information Limitations

Theoretically, detailed disclosure information is available in disclosure documents filed with the various Federal Reserve Banks for virtually every acquisition. However, unless the analyst personally goes to the pertinent Federal Reserve Bank(s) and studies the transaction documents on file, there may be considerable uncertainty regarding important aspects of the historical transactions.[3] In any event, the more "macro" the data used for comparison purposes, the further is the analyst from knowledge about the underlying fundamentals of the comparative institutions and the less reliable the data become for specific comparative analysis.

Another problem with comparative transactions analysis is that there are almost always too few comparable sales in the same general geographic area at approximately the same time for realistic analysis. This problem is further compounded by the time it takes for banking sales to be consummated. Time lags of several months between the announcement of a sale and its ultimate regulatory approvals and consummation create further problems with comparative transactions analysis. Bank sales often close in an entirely different market environment than in which they were announced.

The *announcement market* for bank acquisitions may provide a more up-to-date indication of the current pricing of bank sales than does the *closing market*. However, announced bank acquisitions do not always close, so announcements provide only a current indication of pricing. Further, less information is available regarding the actual pricing, structure, and terms of announced deals than is available regarding closed deals.

This discussion of comparative transactions underscores two major limitations about valuation using this method. The first limitation is relative to time. Value today is a function of current market conditions and the outlook for the future of a particular bank. Because comparable transactions analysis is historically oriented and the actual (closed) transactions available today were, in the most favorable instance, announced a minimum of several months ago, it is important for the analyst to maintain appropriate focus on both current market conditions and historical transactions. The second significant limitation to comparative transactions analysis relates to the availability of reliable information about historical transactions in sufficient detail for meaningful valuation comparisons.

---

[3]A sampling by Mercer Capital of available services that summarize transactions data based upon physical examinations at the various Federal Reserve Banks suggests that errors in summarizing important information about transactions, historical performance, or operating data regarding the acquired banks or confusion in the reports between the acquired bank or bank holding company occur more frequently than desirable.

Adjustments for Excess Equity

The previous discussion has indicated that many adjustments may be necessary to develop the current value of a subject bank based upon comparative transactions analysis. One critical adjustment often made by acquirers of banks relates to excess equity. *Excess equity* can be defined in a regulatory context as *capital accumulated above the level viewed as "normal" by the regulatory agencies.*

If a bank maintains an equity/asset ratio of 13 percent in a regulatory enviroment calling for a minimum ratio of 6 percent and a peer group median ratio of 8 percent, at least that level of capital above the level of 8 percent might be considered to be excess equity. That capital is available for additional leveraging, or, in an acquisition environment, it may be available as a special dividend (with regulatory approval if necessary) that can be paid to shareholders prior to an acquisition or upstreamed to a new parent holding company to reduce acquisition debt. In other words, in this case, the median level of capitalization is considered to be *fully leveraged.* An acquirer, however, might have a different definition of fully leverages than a bank's median capital ratios.

Simply put, it is not economic to pay a market premium for equity that will either be leveraged as result of the acquirer's efforts or used to pay down acquisition debt. Rational purchasers are increasingly viewing excess equity as worth "dollar for dollar" rather than worth a market multiple.

Exhibit 14-5 provides an analysis of how excess equity might be treated in a bank valuation (or in a real-life negotiation). The exhibit provides values for hypothetical banks with specific levels of leverage (as measured by the ratio of equity/total assets) and returns (as measured by ROA and ROE). The exhibit assumes that fully leveraged equity is at the 7.5 percent level of equity/total assets. For two levels of ROA (0.95 percent and 1.05 percent) and for three controlling interest price/earnings multiples (9.0x, 10.0x, and 11.0x), the exhibit provides the implied price/book-value ratio at various levels of capitalization ranging from 6 percent (considered to be regulatory minimum levels in the table) up to 14 percent.

The price/book value (P/B) ratios indicated in Exhibit 14-5 are calculated assuming that fully leveraged equity (i.e., up to 7.5 percent equity/total assets) receives a full-market multiple of earnings and of book value. In the middle column, for example, with an indicated market control P/E of 10.0x, a fully leveraged bank earning an ROA of 0.95 percent would achieve a P/B multiple of 1.27x. More highly capitalized banks (with higher equity/asset ratios) would achieve successively lower P/B ratios because excess equity is valued at dollar for dollar. For clarification of the calculations in Exhibit 14-5, assume the fully leveraged bank has equity of $7.5 million and total assets of $100 million. It is earning $950,000 per year (ROA of 0.95 percent) and its ROE is 12.67 percent. The table suggests that at 10x earnings, the bank is worth $9.5 million (10 × $950,000). The implied P/B multiple is therefore 1.27 × ($9.5 million / $7.5 million).

The implied price/book ratios are calculated such that at higher levels of capitalization, the "value" of the bank is equal to the market multiple of earnings plus excess equity. Moving down the middle column of

Exhibit 14-5

Control Valuation Matrix Relating Leverage, Returns, and the Implied "Value" of Bank Equity in Terms of the Price/Book Multiple

ROE, ROA, and leverage (EQ/TA) assumed to be as reported by bank to be acquired.
Assume rational acquirer pays full valuation multiple for "fully leveraged" equity/total assets of 7.50 percent.
"Excess equity" valued dollar for dollar implies lower P/B if > 7.50 percent EQ/TA.

Market Control P/E = 9.00

ROE	ROA	EQ/TA	P/B
15.83%	0.95%	6.00%	1.43
14.62%	0.95%	6.50%	1.32
13.57%	0.95%	7.00%	1.22
12.67%	0.95%	**7.50%**	1.14
11.87%	0.95%	8.00%	1.13
11.18%	0.95%	8.50%	1.12
10.56%	0.95%	9.00%	1.12
10.00%	0.95%	9.50%	1.11
9.50%	0.95%	10.00%	1.11
9.05%	0.95%	10.50%	1.10
8.64%	0.95%	11.00%	1.10
8.26%	0.95%	11.50%	1.09
7.92%	0.95%	12.00%	1.09
7.60%	0.95%	12.50%	1.08
7.31%	0.95%	13.00%	1.08
7.04%	0.95%	13.50%	1.08
6.79%	0.95%	14.00%	1.08

Market Control P/E = 10.00

ROE	ROA	EQ/TA	P/B
15.83%	0.95%	6.00%	1.58
14.62%	0.95%	6.50%	1.46
13.57%	0.95%	7.00%	1.36
12.67%	0.95%	**7.50%**	1.27
11.87%	0.95%	8.00%	1.25
11.18%	0.95%	8.50%	1.24
10.56%	0.95%	9.00%	1.22
10.00%	0.95%	9.50%	1.21
9.50%	0.95%	10.00%	1.20
9.05%	0.95%	10.50%	1.19
8.64%	0.95%	11.00%	1.18
8.26%	0.95%	11.50%	1.17
7.92%	0.95%	12.00%	1.17
7.60%	0.95%	12.50%	1.16
7.31%	0.95%	13.00%	1.15
7.04%	0.95%	13.50%	1.15
6.79%	0.95%	14.00%	1.14

Market Control P/E = 11.00

ROE	ROA	EQ/TA	P/B
15.83%	0.95%	6.00%	1.74
14.62%	0.95%	6.50%	1.61
13.57%	0.95%	7.00%	1.49
12.67%	0.95%	**7.50%**	1.39
11.87%	0.95%	8.00%	1.37
11.18%	0.95%	8.50%	1.35
10.56%	0.95%	9.00%	1.33
10.00%	0.95%	9.50%	1.31
9.50%	0.95%	10.00%	1.29
9.05%	0.95%	10.50%	1.28
8.64%	0.95%	11.00%	1.27
8.26%	0.95%	11.50%	1.26
7.92%	0.95%	12.00%	1.25
7.60%	0.95%	12.50%	1.24
7.31%	0.95%	13.00%	1.23
7.04%	0.95%	13.50%	1.22
6.79%	0.95%	14.00%	1.21

Market Control P/E = 9.00

ROE	ROA	EQ/TA	P/B
17.50%	1.05%	6.00%	1.58
16.15%	1.05%	6.50%	1.45
15.00%	1.05%	7.00%	1.35
14.00%	1.05%	**7.50%**	1.26
13.13%	1.05%	8.00%	1.24
12.35%	1.05%	8.50%	1.23
11.67%	1.05%	9.00%	1.22
11.05%	1.05%	9.50%	1.21
10.50%	1.05%	10.00%	1.20
10.00%	1.05%	10.50%	1.19
9.55%	1.05%	11.00%	1.18
9.13%	1.05%	11.50%	1.17
8.75%	1.05%	12.00%	1.16
8.40%	1.05%	12.50%	1.16
8.08%	1.05%	13.00%	1.15
7.78%	1.05%	13.50%	1.14
7.50%	1.05%	14.00%	1.14

Market Control P/E = 10.00

ROE	ROA	EQ/TA	P/B
17.50%	1.05%	6.00%	1.75
16.15%	1.05%	6.50%	1.62
15.00%	1.05%	7.00%	1.50
14.00%	1.05%	**7.50%**	1.40
13.13%	1.05%	8.00%	1.38
12.35%	1.05%	8.50%	1.35
11.67%	1.05%	9.00%	1.33
11.05%	1.05%	9.50%	1.32
10.50%	1.05%	10.00%	1.30
10.00%	1.05%	10.50%	1.29
9.55%	1.05%	11.00%	1.27
9.13%	1.05%	11.50%	1.26
8.75%	1.05%	12.00%	1.25
8.40%	1.05%	12.50%	1.24
8.08%	1.05%	13.00%	1.23
7.78%	1.05%	13.50%	1.22
7.50%	1.05%	14.00%	1.21

Market Control P/E = 11.00

ROE	ROA	EQ/TA	P/B
17.50%	1.05%	6.00%	1.93
16.15%	1.05%	6.50%	1.78
15.00%	1.05%	7.00%	1.65
14.00%	1.05%	**7.50%**	1.54
13.13%	1.05%	8.00%	1.51
12.35%	1.05%	8.50%	1.48
11.67%	1.05%	9.00%	1.45
11.05%	1.05%	9.50%	1.43
10.50%	1.05%	10.00%	1.41
10.00%	1.05%	10.50%	1.39
9.55%	1.05%	11.00%	1.37
9.13%	1.05%	11.50%	1.35
8.75%	1.05%	12.00%	1.34
8.40%	1.05%	12.50%	1.32
8.08%	1.05%	13.00%	1.31
7.78%	1.05%	13.50%	1.30
7.50%	1.05%	14.00%	1.29

Exhibit 14-5, we see that if the equity/total-asset ratio for a $100-million-total-asset bank were 11.00 percent, its ROE would be 8.64 percent if it earned an ROA of 0.95 percent.

According to Exhibit 14-5, this bank is "worth" $13 million. Excess equity is ([11% − 7.5%] × $100 million), or $3.5 million. Earnings are worth a multiple of 10.0x, so the "value" of the capitalized earnings is (10 × $950,000), or $9.5 million. The total value of the bank is therefore the sum of capitalized earnings ($9.5 million) and excess equity ($3.5 million), or $13.0 million. (Even lower values would be developed if the earnings stream for highly capitalized banks were penalized for the fact that excess equity is earning at current money market rates).

Exhibit 14-5 is not provided as a formula for valuation but as an illustration of how acquirers and bank analysts might look at excess equity. The implication for heavily capitalized banks is fairly clear: Substantial accumulations of excess equity in community banks will likely cause downward pressure on acquisition multiples (at least, as expressed in terms of book value).

Concluding Comments on Comparative Transactions Analysis

Comparative transactions analysis can be a useful approach for developing an indication of the current control value of a bank. However, like other approaches, it requires thoughtful analysis and is best applied in conjunction with one or more other valuation approaches.

Discounted Future Benefits

Discounted future benefits (DFB) is a general term applied to valuation approaches deriving indications of value based upon calculations of the present value of anticipated (or projected) flows of income. The most frequently used variation of the discounted future benefits family is called *discounted cash flow* (DCF). Another frequently used variation is referred to as *discounted future earnings* (DFE).

Discounted future benefits is an approach used to determine the net present value of future income flows. As such, it is the flip side of the concept of compound interest. We learn in school that a dollar invested "at interest" will grow over time, and that a dollar regularly (or periodically) invested at interest will grow even faster. Normally, then, we begin with the investment and determine what it will be worth at some point in the future.

With discounted future benefits, we begin with the future stream of benefits and ask what is the *present value* of that stream of benefits. In order to answer the question, we must *discount* the expected future benefits to the present at an appropriate discount rate.

Discounted Future Benefits Valuation

Discounted future benefits valuation approaches are at once theoretically sound, fairly straightforward in terms of concept, and extremely sensitive to the underlying assumptions of the analysis. The basic methodology requires three elements:

1. A forecast of the expected future benefits. Generally, analysts develop forecasts of earnings and/or cash flows for periods ranging from 5 to 10 years or more.
2. A determination of the *terminal value,* or the value of all income flows beyond the immediate forecast period.
3. The selection of an appropriate discount rate with which to "discount" the forecasted stream of benefits to the present. The sum of the present values of all the future flows is called the *net present value,* or the present value of the expected flows.

Exhibit 14-6 provides an example of how the discounted future benefits concept works. The notes below the exhibit provide brief comments about how the elements are created and/or why the various elements of the methodology work the way they do. Several brief sections will address issues and problems involved with the use of discounted future benefits approaches. Then a discounted future earnings approach will be used to develop valuation indications for a bank.

Selection of the Discount Rate

In Chapter 13, we suggested the use of the adjusted capital asset pricing model (ACAPM) for developing minority interest marketable discount rates. In that discussion, we further suggested that the specific company risk (SCR) component of ACAPM may include the adjustment factor necessary to convert discount rates developed using the capital asset pricing model, which many analysts believe relate to the net cash flows (rather

Exhibit 14-6
Example of Discounted Future Benefits Approach ($ Thousands)

Assume a Discount Rate of 20%[1]

	Earnings Forecast by Year					
	1	2	3	4	5	6
"Earnings"[2]	100	124	119	130	145	150[3]
Terminal growth rate[4]						8%
Terminal value[5]					$1,250	
Present-value factors[6]	.833	.694	.579	.482	.402	
Present values of earnings of terminal value	83.3	86.1	68.9	62.7		
Sum of all present values			861.6			

[1]Assume that the discount rate is appropriate for the earnings that are forecasted. See additional comments in text.
[2]The earnings have been forecasted by an experienced analyst and are accompanied by detailed forecasts of balance sheets, income statements, and cash flows.
[3]Even though this is a five-year forecast, a sixth year of earnings is projected. This convention flows from the earnings discount model discussed at length in Chapter 13.
[4]The analyst believes that this income stream will grow at 8 percent into perpetuity, or at least for a very long time.
[5]The terminal value is calculated using Year 6's earnings, but is discounted from the last year of the forecast. The formula is:

Terminal value (end of Year 5) = (Year 6 projected earnings) / [Discount rate (R) − Perpetuity growth rate (G)]

See comment 3 above.
[6]The present value factors can be derived from present value tables for a discount rate of 20 percent, or by using hand-held or desktop computers. In many presentations, the present value factors are not shown.

than to net income) of business enterprises to discount rates appropriate for application to net income. Exhibit 14-7 provides a more detailed rationale for this position generally, but especially in the context of the valuation of financial institutions. For purposes of the remainder of this discussion, then, we will use discount rates developed using the ACAPM methodology of Chapter 13 to apply to the net income of financial institutions.

Requirements of Discounted Future Benefits Forecasts

Analysts should not use discounted future benefits (DFB) valuation approaches as wholesale substitutes for comparable company analysis or other legitimate valuation approaches. Based upon experience with valuations performed by Mercer Capital analysts, as well as opportunities to review reports of many other analysts from around the nation, I would offer several general comments on each of the three key elements of DFB valuation approaches, i.e., the earnings forecast, the terminal value calculation, and the discount rate.

1. *Earnings forecast.* Ideally, the earnings forecast should be accompanied by a forecast of income statements, balance sheets, and cash flow statements. Critical assumptions of the forecast (relating to margins, growth, required capital expenditures, debt amortization, and other factors) should be made clear to the reader of the forecasts. A ratio analysis showing indicators of performance, activity, leverage, and growth should be provided. All these factors help prove the reasonableness of the forecast.

   The analyst should also perform a market analysis to determine if the projected growth is reasonably achievable given the overall size of the relevant market, the entity's ability to develop new products, and the existence of established competitors in the marketplace. If multiple forecasts are not provided, the analyst should be able to discuss the sensitivity of the forecast to changes in critical assumptions and to explain clearly why the assumptions of her or his forecast are reasonable under the circumstances. Finally, for existing companies or financial institutions, the analyst must bridge the gap between actual historical performance and projected future performance. Great leaps of faith may be appropriate in a religious context but they are never appropriate in the context of a valuation report!

2. *Terminal value.* In a discounted future benefits (DFB) valuation approach, the analyst must make an assumption about the terminal value for the forecast. Exhibit 14-4 provided one means of estimating the terminal value of a DFB valuation approach. In bank reports and in valuations of other companies, other estimates are sometimes used. Effectively, the terminal value calculation is a "valuation" of the entity at the appropriate future time—that is, a valuation of all remaining cash flows not captured in the basic forecast. Analysts sometimes apply a price/earnings multiple to earnings or a price/book multiple to book value, or they use book value or some other proxy of value at the end of the forecast period. In many instances, analysts will use a slower growth assumption for the years beyond the basic forecast than for the basic forecast period.

The assumption regarding the terminal value has a critical impact on the overall valuation. In Exhibit 14-4, for example, the terminal value contributes nearly 60 percent of the total value of the entity under consideration. In a 10-year forecast, the terminal value will seldom account for less than 25 percent of the total value of the entity. The message is clear: With so much of a current valuation riding on "valuations" made five or more years into the future, the analyst should be very careful about the basic assumptions of any forecast and the development of the terminal value assumption.

3. *Discount rate.* The analyst must first decide how to derive the discount rate. It is clear from the discussion of both the adjusted capital asset pricing model and the capital asset pricing model that *risk assessment* is a critical element of the process of developing discount rates. Many practitioners tend to *underestimate risk.* In so doing, they *underestimate the discount rate* and therefore *overestimate value.*[4]

As noted above, we believe the discount rates derived using the ACAPM or the CAPM methodologies are minority interest marketable-discount rates. This assumption flows from the fact that the return measures tracked by Ibbotson and Associates relate to minority interests in freely tradable shares of publicly traded companies. Therefore, it may be appropriate to use control premium studies such as *Mergerstat Review 1990* as a basis for deriving control premiums to be applied to base level minority interest marketable values derived using DFB valuation methodologies. However, analysts sometimes make control adjustments to earnings in developing their earnings forecasts. In such cases, it may be appropriate to utilize lower control premiums than normally found in the studies (or no control premium at all) because the earnings are already "marked up" to reflect what a controlling shareholder could do. The analyst must make appropriate decisions regarding adjustments to DFB valuations from minority interest levels to control levels based upon the overall analysis.

---

[4]In a recent conversation with Shannon Pratt on this subject, I asked if I would be misquoting him to suggest he agreed with me that analysts using discounted future benefits methodologies tend to overvalue companies relative to analysts using more historically based valuation approaches. He said I would not be misquoting him. He then went on to suggest that in his experience the ratio of overvaluations to undervaluations, regardless of techniques utilized, seemed to be on the order of 4:1! The message is clear to the bank analyst using DFB techniques or any other valuation techniques.

Exhibit 14-7
Elaboration upon Discount Rates Used in Discounted Future Benefits Valuations

As noted in both Chapters 13 and 14, many analysts believe that discount rates developed using the capital asset pricing model (CAPM) are appropriately applicable to the net cash flows of business enterprises rather than to other levels of the income statement, such as net income.[1] Pratt suggests that discount rates developed using CAPM, arbitrage pricing theory (APT), or the dividend discount model should apply to the cash flows of business enterprises because the returns to investors using such methods represent dividend income plus capital appreciation, or investors' cash flow. Pratt goes on to say that, in practice, there is considerable variation in the definition of cash flow (DCF) to which such discount rates should be applied. This suggests that there can be considerable variation in the answers developed using DCF methodologies.

Pratt then suggests an alternate method to derive a discount rate to apply to projected net income (DFE) rather than to cash flow (DCF). That method is the earnings growth model discussed in Chapter 13.

Because there has been some controversy over my suggestion that discount rates developed using the ACAPM should be applied to projected net earnings rather than to projected cash flows (of whatever variety), it is appropriate to attempt to reconcile the two positions.

Practical Considerations in Benefit Stream Selection

The first effort at reconciliation is based upon practical observation. In the case of many smaller, closely-held businesses that are not experiencing rapid growth, there may be very little difference between net income and net cash flow for extended periods of time. In cases such as these, which account for a large portion of the valuation assignments of many appraisers, the distinction between net income and net cash flow becomes moot.

In the case of financial institutions, where "cash flow" can be generated almost at will by the assumption of incremental deposit liabilities, defining the cash flow to be capitalized becomes even more difficult than for other types of business enterprises. Banks do not have to sell products, collect the principal of loans, or liquidate assets to generate cash over considerable periods of time. Consequently, we believe that the appropriate stream of future benefits to be capitalized in DFB approaches for banks is net income.

The last practical argument for the application of ACAPM discount rates to net income rather than to net cash flow relates to Mercer Capital's experience in developing what I believe to be reasonable valuation conclusions using this approach. That experience relates directly to the discussion at the beginning of Chapter 13 in "Experience and the Development of Capitalization Rates." The fact that many independent parties have engaged in real-life transactions with very real financial consequences based upon Mercer Capital appraisals using these methods adds an element of realism to the practical observation.

Theoretical Considerations in Benefit Stream Selection

The model used by many appraisers to discuss the relationships between earnings and cash flow consists of the following:

---

[1]See in particular "DCF or DFE? Matching the Return Stream with the Discount Rate," Shannon P. Pratt, *Valuing a Business: The Analysis and Appraisal of Closely Held Companies,* 2d ed. (Homewood, Ill.: Dow Jones-Irwin, 1989), pp. 83–84.

Exhibit 14-7 (*continued*)

> Net income (after taxes)
> \+ Noncash charges (depreciation and amortization)
> − Net capital expenditures (new purchases of fixed assets less net disposals)
> +/− Incremental changes in working capital
> +/− Net changes in long-term debt
> = Net free cash flow

In a growing company, net capital expenditures are often greater than current (historical) depreciation and amortization charges, and if earnings margins, balance sheet ratios, and capitalization remain constant, incremental changes in working capital requirements and net changes in long-term debt are normally negative (or reductions of free cash). The result of the calculation is that net free cash flow for growing companies is often less than net income. If this is the case, then the discount rate to be applied to net free cash flow must be lower than the discount rate to be applied to the net income of the same company in order to yield the same valuation result.

Relationship Between Net Income and Net Free Cash Flow Discount Rates

The relationship between net income and net free cash flow discount rates was stated clearly in a recent article in *Business Valuation Review.* The abbreviations shown below have been changed from the article to conform with those used in this book.[2]

> | | + RFR | Risk-free rate of return |
> | + (MR | − RFR) | Additional rate of return needed for equity investments (equity risk premium) |
> | | + SCR | Company-specific rate-of-return premium |
> | | = R_{cf} | Discount rate for net free cash flow |
> | | + A | Additional rate of return required for after-tax earnings versus cash (i.e., net free cash flow) |
> | | = R_{ni} | Discount rate for earnings (net income) |

Gilbert suggests that selection of SCR "falls back to appraiser experience and expert interpretation of the economic-industry-company-financial analysis done in the appraisal." This is entirely consistent with the discussion of SCR in Chapter 13. Gilbert also states that his research did not find (nor did mine) any available studies to measure A, the adjustment factor for the additional rate of return necessary to convert from net free cash flow discount rates to net income discount rates.

The discussion in Chapter 13 suggests that any specific adjustment required in particular discount rate determinations may be included in the selection of SCR by the appraiser using the ACAPM. Now it only remains to be shown that A is not a large number in many appraisal situations and that it can reasonably be included as an element of SCR (or estimated separately if the analyst so desires).

---

[2]Gregory A. Gilbert, "Discount Rates and Capitalization Rates—Where Are We?" *Business Valuation Review,* Dec. 1990, pp. 108–13.

Exhibit 14-7 (*continued*)

Estimating the Adjustment Factor

We can estimate A, the adjustment factor to convert a cash flow discount rate to one applicable to net income for a hypothetical company, Signal Company, Inc. (Signal), as follows:

Assume for the moment that the capital asset pricing model (and the adjusted capital asset pricing model) develops a discount rate applicable to net free cash flow, or R_{cf}. Then:

$$R_{cf} = RFR + \beta \times (MR - RFR) + SCR$$

From the discussion in Chapter 13, we know that R_{cf}, if applied to all the expected future cash flows of Signal Company, would generate a value of that business, which we call V_{cf} below. Define CF as current period net free cash flow, and we can define V_{cf} as:

$$V_{cf} = \frac{CF \times (1 + G)}{R_{cf} - G}$$

From the discussion above, we know that the earnings growth model incorporates a discount rate, R_{ni}, which is appropriate to be applied to the net income of business entities. Define Signal's current period net income as NI. We further know that we can derive V_{ni}, which is a value of Signal Company, from the earnings growth model:

$$V_{ni} = \frac{NI \times (1 + G)}{R_{ni} - G}$$

For the sake of simplicity, assume that Signal Company has no debt. Reason suggests that over any extended period the growth rates of Signal's earnings and net free cash flow should be substantially the same. V_{cf} and V_{ni} are valuation indications of the same company and therefore must be equal. If $V_{cf} = V_{ni}$,

$$\frac{CF \times (1 + G)}{(R_{cf} - G)} = \frac{NI \times (1 + G)}{(R_{ni} - G)}$$

Dividing by $(1 + G)$ yields:

$$\frac{CF}{R_{cf} - G} = \frac{NI}{R_{ni} - G}$$

Inverting the equations, we get:

$$\frac{R_{cf} - G}{CF} = \frac{R_{ni} - G}{NI}$$

Multiplying both equations by NI yie

$$\frac{NI}{CF} \times (R_{cf} - G) = R_{ni} - G$$

Therefore, solving for R_{ni} yields:

$$R_{ni} = \frac{NI}{CF} \times (R_{cf} - G) + G$$

Exhibit 14-7 (*continued*)

For a given company, then, the relationship between R_{ni} and R_{cf} can be seen to be a function of the relationship between net income and net free cash flow. If NI = CF, then, as suggested in the discussion above, the last equation collapses such that $R_{ni} = R_{cf}$.

But what happens if net income and net free cash flow are not identical? The table included with this exhibit provides calculations for A, the adjustment factor implied by this analysis, for assumed levels of R_{cf} of 15 percent, 20 percent, and 25 percent, a range that encompasses the normal levels of discount rates developed using ACAPM or CAPM in the current market environment.

If NI/CF is less than or equal to 110 percent, which suggests that net free cash flow is 90 percent or more of net income, and expected growth is in the general range of 4 percent (assumed inflation) to 10 percent, the calculations in the table below suggest that A, the factor necessary to adjust R_{cf} to a level applicable to net income, or to R_{ni}, would be on the order of 2 percent at the highest. The magnitude of A decreases rapidly as the level of anticipated cash flow begins to approximate anticipated net income. As R_{cf} rises (holding G and NI/CF constant), the magnitude of A rises. Interestingly, the magnitude of A diminishes rapidly as the expected growth rate increases.

For most smaller, closely-held businesses, A would appear to be on the order of 2 percent or less based upon this analysis. From a practical viewpoint, the analyst can estimate A specifically or, as suggested in Chapter 13, simply embed A into the overall SCR adustment factor for specific company risk.

Adjustment Factor for Financial Institutions

For the reasons stated in Chapters 13 and 14, we believe that net income is the best available income statement measure available for valuations of banks using discounted future benefits valuation methodologies. Fixed asset and traditional working capital requirements are minimal for most banks for significant periods of time. Consequently, we believe that the A factor necessary to adjust a cash flow–based discount rate to one applicable to net income is minimal. We therefore suggest the use of ACAPM to develop discount rates as described in Chapter 13. We further suggest that for banks the derived discount rates are applicable to projected net income.

Concluding Comments Regarding Discount Rates

It is a fact of life that when valuing income streams the business or bank appraiser must determine either a capitalization rate, the inverse of which is a price/earnings multiple, or a discount rate with which to relate expected future income to present-day value.

The CAPM and ACAPM, both of which have been discussed in Chapters 13 and 14, provide organized frameworks within which the experienced analyst can develop valuation multiples or discount rates. It is important to understand the theoretical underpinnings of the frame-works, as well as their inherent limitations. In the final analysis, there is no substitute for solid analysis combined with the benefits of experience and common sense. The basic objective of the valuation process, after all, is typically to simulate arm's length negotiations between parties who probably know nothing about CAPM or ACAPM. The result of the valuation process should be well-developed, well-

Exhibit 14-7 (*concluded*)

reasoned, and reasonable valuation opinions that are logically presented so that nonexpert readers can understand and take action based upon them.

Estimation of Adjustment Factors Relating Discount Rates Applicable to Net Income and Net Free Cash Flow

BASIC EQUATION	$R_{ni} = NI/CF \times [R_{cf} - G] + G$
	$\quad\ = NI/CF \times R_{cf} - (NI/CF \times G) + G$
	$A = R_{ni} - R_{cf}$

R_{cf} = 25.0%

(G) Growth	Calculated Adjustment Factors (A) Given Various Values of NI/CF					
	125.0%	120.0%	115.0%	110.0%	105.0%	100.0%
2.0%	5.8%	4.6%	3.4%	2.3%	1.1%	0.0%
4.0%	5.3%	4.2%	3.1%	2.1%	1.0%	0.0%
6.0%	4.8%	3.8%	2.8%	1.9%	0.9%	0.0%
8.0%	4.3%	3.4%	2.5%	1.7%	0.8%	0.0%
10.0%	3.8%	3.0%	2.2%	1.5%	0.7%	0.0%
12.0%	3.3%	2.6%	1.9%	1.3%	0.6%	0.0%
14.0%	2.8%	2.2%	1.6%	1.1%	0.5%	0.0%

R_{cf} = 20.0%

(G) Growth	Calculated Adjustment Factors (A) Given Various Values of NI/CF					
	125.0%	120.0%	115.0%	110.0%	105.0%	100.0%
2.0%	4.5%	3.6%	2.7%	1.8%	0.9%	0.0%
4.0%	4.0%	3.2%	2.4%	1.6%	0.8%	0.0%
6.0%	3.5%	2.8%	2.1%	1.4%	0.7%	0.0%
8.0%	3.0%	2.4%	1.8%	1.2%	0.6%	0.0%
10.0%	2.5%	2.0%	1.5%	1.0%	0.5%	0.0%
12.0%	2.0%	1.6%	1.2%	0.8%	0.4%	0.0%
14.0%	1.5%	1.2%	0.9%	0.6%	0.3%	0.0%

R_{cf} = 15.0%

(G) Growth	Calculated Adjustment Factors (A) Given Various Values of NI/CF					
	125.0%	120.0%	115.0%	110.0%	105.0%	100.0%
2.0%	3.3%	2.6%	1.9%	1.3%	0.6%	0.0%
4.0%	2.8%	2.2%	1.6%	1.1%	0.5%	0.0%
6.0%	2.3%	1.8%	1.3%	0.9%	0.4%	0.0%
8.0%	1.8%	1.4%	1.0%	0.7%	0.3%	0.0%
10.0%	1.2%	1.0%	0.7%	0.5%	0.2%	0.0%
12.0%	0.7%	0.6%	0.4%	0.3%	0.1%	0.0%
14.0%	0.2%	0.2%	0.1%	0.1%	0.0%	0.0%

Exhibit 14-8
Specimen Bank Controlling Interest Valuation Estimate Using Discounted Future Earnings Analysis

Net worth	$8,000	Trailing 12-month earnings $1,200
Total assets	$100,000	Assumed beta 0.90
Return on assets	1.25%	Risk-free rate 8.20%
Return on equity	15.67%	Small-stock premium
Beginning equity/assets	8.00%	Beta-adjusted premium 10.98%
Minimum equity/assets for projection	8.00%	Specific-company risk 2.00%
Estimated growth rate	6.00%	Discount rate 21.18%
Terminal growth rate	4.00%	12.20% (Ibbotson)

Projection Summary	Year 1	Year 2	Year 3	Year 4	Year 5	Year 6	Year 7	Year 8	Year 9	Year 10	Year 11
Bank Performance											
Net income	$1,291	$1,430	$1,507	$1,589	$1,677	$1,769	$1,867	$1,971	$2,081	$2,198	$2,321
Return on assets	1.25%	1.31%	1.30%	1.30%	1.29%	1.28%	1.28%	1.27%	1.27%	1.26%	1.26%
Return on equity	15.67%	16.37%	16.28%	16.20%	16.12%	16.04%	15.97%	15.91%	15.85%	15.79%	15.73%
Ending equity	$8,480	$8,989	$9,528	$10,100	$10,706	$11,348	$12,029	$12,751	$13,516	$14,327	$15,186
Ending total assets	$106,000	$112,360	$119,102	$126,248	$133,823	$141,852	$150,363	$159,385	$168,948	$179,085	$189,830
Ending equity/total assets	8.00%	8.00%	8.00%	8.00%	8.00%	8.00%	8.00%	8.00%	8.00%	8.00%	8.00%
Dividend potential	$811	$921	$968	$1,018	$1,071	$1,127	$1,186	$1,249	$1,316	$1,387	$1,462
DFE Analysis 21.79%											
Net income	$1,291	$1,430	$1,507	$1,589	$1,677	$1,769	$1,867	$1,971	$2,081	$2,198	$2,321
Discount rate	21.18%										
Present value			$6,425								
Terminal value										$13,512	
Present value			$1,979								
Marketable minority value			$8,404								
Control premium range %		30.00%		40.00%							
Control premium range $		$2,521		$3,361							
Implied control value		$10,925		$11,765							
Average (rounded)			$11,300								
Implied price/book multiple		1.37	1.41	1.47							
Implied price/earnings ratio		9.10	9.42	9.80							

267

Exhibit 14-9
Specimen Bank Controlling Interest Valuation Estimate Using Discounted Future Earnings Analysis

Net worth	$8,000
Total assets	$100,000
Return on assets	1.01%
Return on equity	12.59%
Beginning equity/assets	8.00%
Minimum equity/assets for projection	8.00%
Estimated growth rate	4.00%
Terminal growth rate	4.00%

Trailing 12-month earnings	$950
Assumed beta	0.90
Risk-free rate	8.20%
Small-stock premium	12.20% (Ibbotson)
Beta-adjusted premium	10.98%
Specific-company risk	1.50%
Discount rate	20.68%

Projection Summary	Year 1	Year 2	Year 3	Year 4	Year 5	Year 6	Year 7	Year 8	Year 9	Year 10	Year 11
Bank Performance											
Net income	$1,027	$1,172	$1,213	$1,256	$1,301	$1,348	$1,396	$1,447	$1,499	$1,554	$1,610
Return on assets	1.01%	1.10%	1.10%	1.10%	1.09%	1.09%	1.08%	1.08%	1.07%	1.07%	1.07%
Return on equity	12.59%	13.81%	13.75%	13.69%	13.63%	13.58%	13.52%	13.47%	13.42%	13.38%	13.33%
Ending equity	$8,320	$8,653	$8,999	$9,359	$9,733	$10,123	$10,527	$10,949	$11,386	$11,842	$12,316
Ending total assets	$104,000	$108,160	$112,486	$116,986	$121,665	$126,532	$131,593	$136,857	$142,331	$148,024	$153,945
Ending equity/total assets	8.00%	8.00%	8.00%	8.00%	8.00%	8.00%	8.00%	8.00%	8.00%	8.00%	8.00%
Dividend potential	$707	$839	$867	$897	$927	$959	$991	$1,026	$1,061	$1,098	$1,137
DFE Analysis											
Net income	$1,027	$1,172	$1,213	$1,256	$1,301	$1,348	$1,396	$1,447	$1,499	$1,554	$1,610
Discount rate	20.68%										
Present value			$5,093								
Terminal value										$9,655	$9,655
Present value			$1,474								
Marketable minority value			$6,566								
Control premium range %		30.00%		40.00%							
Control premium range $		$1,970		$2,627							
Implied control value		$8,536		$9,193							
Average (rounded)			$8,900								
Implied price/book multiple		1.07	1.11	1.15							
Implied price/earnings ratio		8.99	9.37	9.68							

Using Discounted Future Benefits to Value Banks

Exhibits 14-8 and 14-9 provide valuation indications for Specimen Bank under two different assumptions regarding expected future performance. The basic assumptions are essentially the same as provided in Exhibits 14-1 and 14-2, which relate to payback analysis. For the reasons outlined above and in Exhibit 14-7, we utilize a discounted future earnings approach in this analysis rather than a discounted cash flow approach.

Once again, the projections utilized in Exhibit 14-8 and 14-9 are based upon a model similar to that provided in Exhibit 11-1. The valuation indications in the exhibits are developed by applying the techniques outlined in Exhibit 14-4 to the sets of assumptions outlined in the exhibits.

In Exhibit 14-8, Specimen Bank is projected to earn in the range of 1.25–1.31 percent of average assets over the forecast period and to grow at a 6 percent rate through Year 10. The discount rate of 21.2 percent is developed using the ACAPM methodology of Chapter 13. The implicit assumption of the analysis is that the bank is acquired by an equity investment.

Because no adjustments were made to reported earnings in the analysis, control premiums in the range of 30–40 percent (as discussed above for financial institutions) were considered. The midpoint value using the analysis as described was $11.3 million, which represented a price/book value multiple of 1.41x and a price/earnings multiple of 9.4x the most recently reported trailing 12-month earnings. This value corresponds fairly closely to the value derived using payback analysis under similar assumptions found in Exhibit 14-1.

Exhibit 14-9 provides a valuation indication of Specimen Bank under the assumption it will earn between 1.00 percent and 1.10 percent of average assets over the forecast period and will grow at the fairly modest rate of 4 percent during the years of the forecast and beyond. The midpoint value is $8.9 million, representing a multiple to book value of 1.11x. Lower earnings and slower expected growth account for the difference in values in the two situations.

Concluding Comments Regarding Discounted Future Benefits

Discounted future benefits methodologies should be used carefully and in appropriate valuation situations. They should be considered as a supplement to other valuation methodologies, not as a substitute.

Dilution Analysis as a Valuation Tool

Publicly traded regional bank holding companies have provided a considerable portion of "the market" for controlling interests in banking organizations in recent years. Under the assumption that the larger regional holding companies will continue over time to acquire community banks, a form of *dilution analysis* can be a helpful valuation tool. The objective is to determine the approximate levels of controlling interest pricing that the regionals can pay without suffering "excessive" dilution to existing shareholders in stock-for-stock acquisitions of community banks.

In performing a dilution analysis, the objective is to estimate the impact of a stock-for-stock merger upon the acquirer and the seller in a bank merger. Individual acquirers make this type of analysis instinctively by asking such questions as:

1. If we pay X dollars for Specimen Bank and issue shares, how many shares will we have to issue?
2. What will be the impact on our reported earnings per share and book value per share under reasonable assumptions about the Specimen Bank's performance?
3. What will happen to our dividend payout ratio if we maintain our current dividend to shareholders after the acquisition?
4. What will the impact of the expected future growth of the Specimen Bank be on our future earnings per share?
5. What will be the likely impact on our stock price if we pay X dollars for Specimen Bank?

In addition to opinions from valuation experts and chief financial officers about the worth of particular acquisitions, regional bank managers are (or should be) concerned about the reaction of the investment banking community to their acquisitions. If the bank analysts following a regional bank believe it is engaging in excessively dilutive transactions, chances are their opinions of that bank's management—and, consequently, about the prospects for its future performance—will be diminished.

There are no rules to determine the level at which acquisition dilution becomes excessive. However, the message of the markets is clear: Excessive perceived dilution translates to lower stock prices. Significant acquisitions, representing asset increments of 20 percent or more, or entry into higher growth markets may justify dilution of earnings per share on the order of 2–4 percent; higher levels of dilution in today's market environment are generally viewed with skepticism in the absence of a compelling strategic rationale. For relatively small or nonstrategic acquisitions, even lower levels of dilution are expected by bank stock analysts and investors.

A summary form of a dilution analysis is presented in Exhibit 14-10. In the exhibit, Specimen Bancshares, Inc., a publicly traded bank holding company, is analyzing the impact of an acquisition of Target Bank in a stock-for-stock, pooling-of-interests merger. Target Bank is considered to be an attractive merger candidate; however, in the terms of the preceding paragraph, its acquisition is clearly nonstrategic in nature. The model is set up to determine the impact of a pro forma pooling of Specimen and Target. It was run to determine the maximum price that could be paid for Target assuming that the merger would be no more than nominally dilutive of existing shareholders of Specimen.

In Exhibit 14-10, Specimen Bancshares can pay approximately $10.2 million for Target Bank, which has a current net worth of $8.0 million, and maintain pro forma earnings at Specimen's current level of $2.28 per share. In other words, at this pricing of the acquisition, it would be nondilutive with respect to earnings per share. Because a premium to Target's book value is being paid, the acquisition would be moderately

Exhibit 14-10
Dilution Analysis Stock-for-Stock Pooling Acquisition ($ Thousands)

Buyer is: Specimen Bancshares, Inc.
Seller is: Target Bank

	Buyer	Seller	Simple combined	Pro forma pooling	Transaction Pricing Data	
Basic Information						
Total assets	$1,000,000	$100,000	$1,100,000	$1,100,000	Price/book value	1.28
Stockholders' equity	$65,000	$8,000	$73,000	$73,000	Dollar value of deal	$10,240
Trailing 12-month earnings	$9,100	$1,200	$10,300	$10,300	Price per share	$25.60
Buyer's anticipated economies		$0			Price/earnings ratio	8.53
Current annual dividends	$3,200	$275	$3,475	$3,610	Price/asset ratio	10.2%
Number shares outstanding	4,000	400	n.m.	4,512		
Equity/assets	6.5%	8.0%	6.6 %	6.6%		
Return on assets	0.91%	1.25%	0.94 %	0.94%		
Return on equity	14.0%	15.0%	14.1 %	14.1%		
Dividend payout ratio	35.16%	22.92%	33.74 %	35.04%	Implied % change in dividend payout for buyer to maintain dividend P/S	– 0.3%
Per Share/Market Information						
Earnings per share	$2.28	$3.00	n.m.	$2.28	Impact on buyer's EPS	0.3%
Dividends per share	$0.80	$0.69	n.m.	$0.80	Maintain buyer's dividend	
Book value per share	$16.25	$20.00	n.m.	$16.18	Impact of buyer's book/share	– 0.4%
Market price per share	$20.00	$20.00	n.m.	$19.99	Average of pretransaction P/E × EPS and P/B × BV for buyer's shares	– 0.0%
Price/book ratio	1.23	1.00				
Price/earnings ratio	8.79	6.67				
Dividend yield	4.0%	3.4%				
Price/assets	8.00%	8.00%				
Postmerger Analysis						
Shares outstanding/to be issued	4,000.000	512.000				
Earnings per issued share	$2.28	$2.34				
Seller's dividends (per new shares)		$0.54		$0.80	Pick-up (– decrease)	48.1%
Seller's book value (per new shares)		$15.63		$16.18	Pick-up (– decrease)	3.5%
Buyer's aggregate market value dilution			($37)			
Year's seller's earnings to "recover"			0.0			

	Year	Buyer growth 8.0%	Seller growth 6.0%				Based on EPS dilution (with same market multiple)
Projected Dilution Analysis							
Estimated impact of relative growth rates on projected earnings per share							
	1	$2.46	$2.48	Not dilutive			
	2	$2.65	$2.63	Dilutive			
	3	$2.87	$2.79	Dilutive			
	4	$3.10	$2.96	Dilutive			
	5	$3.34	$3.14	Dilutive			
	6	$3.61	$3.32	Dilutive			
	7	$3.90	$3.52	Dilutive			
	8	$4.21	$3.74	Dilutive			
	9	$4.55	$3.96	Dilutive			
	10	$4.91	$4.20	Dilutive			

n.m. = not meaningful

dilutive of book value, which would fall from $16.25 per share to $16.18 per share on a pro forma basis. Assuming that the market considers capitalized earnings and capitalized book value equally in pricing this regional bank's shares, the market price might be unaffected by the acquisition. Under the actual calculation in the exhibit, the projected price based upon the pro forma pooling was basically unchanged from the current $20.00 per share price.[5]

In a section in Exhibit 14-10 called "Projected Dilution Analysis," assumptions are made regarding the relative growth rates expected for Specimen and Target. In the exhibit, with longer term growth rate expectations of 8 percent and 6 percent for Specimen and Target, respectively, we see that—while the transaction as priced (at 128 percent of book value) is not immediately dilutive of Specimen's earnings per share—it may become dilutive of future earnings per share unless some economies can be brought to bear as result of the merger. The bank analyst or chief financial officer would want to consider this factor in some fashion in an overall assessment of value.

The dilution analysis of Exhibit 14-10 also provides information of interest to the shareholders of Target Bank in addition to the indicated pricing. Assuming Specimen Bancshares maintains its current dividend of $0.80 per share per year, Target shareholders would realize a 48 percent increase in dividends on their new holdings of Specimen compared to Target's previous dividend policy. In addition, Target's shareholders would experience a 3.5 percent increase in effective book value per share after the transaction.

We should note that the analysis of Exhibit 14-10 does not constitute an appraisal of Target Bank per se. In the context of the presentation thus far, it is a tool for a potential acquirer. However, given knowledge of the kind of analysis described, it is possible for the bank analyst to estimate, for one or more selected publicly traded regional banking companies, the range of rational pricing for a particular bank on the basis of publicly available information.

By carefully selecting a group of potential acquirers in a particular valuation situation, the analyst can conduct pro forma "mergers" similar to the one shown in Exhibit 14-10 between a subject bank and the selected regional holding companies. The analysis can be performed based upon reported earnings. It can be enhanced by using analysts' projections of earnings for the various holding companies. In the process of conducting the pro forma mergers, a range of valuations can be developed based upon the analyst's assumptions regarding the amount of dilution, if any, that makes sense for the acquirers given an overall assessment of the attractiveness of the subject bank for the individual acquirers. The results of the dilution analysis can then be incorporated into the overall valuation analysis using other techniques.

---

[5]Specimen Bancshares stock is trading at $20.00 per share, or 123 percent of book value in Exhibit 14-10. The topside pricing under the assumptions of the exhibit is $10.2 million, or 128 percent of Target's book value. If all other factors remain the same and we assume that Specimen's shares are trading at $24.00 per share, or 148 percent of book value, then the topside, nondilutive, dollar-denominated pricing for the acquisition of Target would be $12.4 million, or 155 percent of book value. In other words, the higher the pricing of the acquirer's stock price, other things being equal, the higher the price that can be paid for the same bank and achieve nondilutive results.

Chapter 15

Developing and Presenting a Valuation Conclusion

It is important to make certain that our efforts are directed at the decisive core of the problem, and not on distracting side issues. The more complex the difficulties we face, the more important it becomes to bear this in mind, for it is human nature to try to evade what we cannot cope with.

Bernard Baruch

Introduction

A substantial portion of Chapters 1 to 14 has dealt with building the components of a bank valuation, while the remainder has presented background information necessary to place the valuation components into proper perspective and in relationship with banks and other business enterprises.

Chapter 22 provides a Sample Bank Appraisal and presents a valuation of Sample Bancshares using the principles and methods discussed in the book. This chapter will therefore focus on important issues of report development and presentation for consideration by bank analysts and users of bank valuation reports. We will also refer to (and provide copies of) current standards for valuation reports promulgated by the Appraisal Foundation and the American Society of Appraisers. Practical information on report development, as well as a listing of common errors or problems with valuation report presentation, will also be discussed. Finally, the use of a Summary Appraisal Review Checklist is discussed, and a sample checklist is provided.

There is a considerable focus in this chapter, either directly or by implication, on what not to do. This is not meant to suggest that many bank and business analysts make the mistakes or errors discussed. But, the problems encountered in valuation reports are at least inconvenient and can be costly for those who depend upon the reports. So the focus of this "negative" discussion is to direct the thinking of analysts and users of valuation opinions to problem areas. By being aware of potential problems, either in the preparation of valuation reports or in their use, we can avoid the problems or take steps to mitigate their impact. Fortunately, we do not have to make mistakes ourselves in order to learn from those of others.

The Valuation Conclusion and the Valuation Process

A sound valuation process is critical to developing sound valuation opinions. Opinions should be presented in well-written, organized form and must, if delivered by appraisers credentialed by the American Society of Appraisers, meet minimum standards for written reports promulgated by the Appraisal Foundation and the American Society of Appraisers.

Valuation Process

Bank analysts and users of bank valuation reports should consider that developing valuation conclusions is part of an overall valuation process. An overview of the process will help place valuation conclusions into proper perspective. The bank valuation process requires communication and coordination between the appraiser and the client bank at several steps and requires additional steps on the part of the bank analyst. At a macro level, the bank valuation process involves:

1. Data collection. A good information questionnaire facilitates communication and coordination between the analyst and the client institution. (See Appendixes E and F for sample checklists for bank appraisal assignments.)
2. A detailed review of all information received from the bank by the bank analyst.
3. Preparation of detailed financial statement spreadsheets to place the bank or bank holding company into historical perspective. (See the exhibits and schedules of the Sample Bank Appraisal in Chapter 22 for examples.)
4. Identification of all key changes in the financial statements indicated on the spreadsheets and preparation of an outline analysis of the bank based upon the review of the financial statements and other documents received.
5. Development of a list of specific questions or issues to be covered in the valuation interview based upon the outline analysis and reviews noted above.
6. Use of a generalized questionnaire to ensure that all other likely questions and issues are addressed in the course of the valuation interview. (See Appendix F for a sample interview questionnaire for banks.)
7. Discussions within the valuation firm between the primary analyst and partners or peers when appropriate to ensure that the key valuation issues are being addressed.
8. Development of the valuation conclusion for the purpose at hand.
9. Outline and draft of the valuation report.
10. Internal review of the draft report at the valuation firm to ensure that the report meets the firm's standards and those of the Uniform Standards of Professional Appraisal Practice, as well as any other standards applicable to the valuation opinion.
11. Presentation of the draft report to the client for review and comments regarding questions or misunderstandings related to factual matters. Discussion with the client about the draft and its conclusion(s).
12. Preparation and signing of the final report and delivery to the client. (See the Sample Bank Appraisal in Chapter 22.)

It is important to review the valuation process in this chapter because problems occur with valuation reports if the bank analyst tries to shorten the process.

Members of the American Society of Appraisers are required to prepare written valuation reports that comply with the requirements of the Uniform Standards of Professional Appraisal Practice. In addition, the Business Valuation Committee of the American Society of Appraisers has adopted a standard for written valuation reports that includes by reference the requirements of the Uniform Standards of Professional Appraisal Practice, standards promulgated by the American Society of Appraisers, and the Principles of Appraisal Practice and Code of Ethics of the American Society of Appraisers.[1]

The Preamble of BVS-II, which is excerpted below and reproduced in its entirety in Appendix G, states:

A. To enhance and maintain the quality of business valuation reports for the benefit of the business valuation profession and users of business valuation reports, the American Society of Appraisers, through its Business Valuation Committee, has adopted this standard. This standard is required to be followed in the preparation of full, written business valuation reports by all members of the American Society of Appraisers, be they candidate, accredited, or senior members.

B. The purpose of this standard is to define and describe the requirements for the written communication of the results of a business valuation, analysis, or opinion, but not the conduct thereof.

C. The present standard provides minimum criteria to be followed by business appraisers in the preparation of full, written valuation reports.

D. Written reports must meet the requirements of the present standard unless, in the opinion of the appraiser, circumstances dictate a departure from the standard; if so, such a departure must be disclosed in the report.

A review of BVS-II in Appendix G provides an overview of the minimum requirements for a full, written valuation report.

Comments on Revenue Ruling 59–60

There are numerous references to Revenue Ruling 59–60 in this book, including a reproduction of the ruling as Appendix C. One section of the ruling dealing with the use of multiple valuation approaches has created problems for some analysts. That section is quoted and discussed below:

07.   AVERAGE OF FACTORS. Because valuations cannot be made on the basis of a prescribed formula, there is no means whereby the various applicable factors in a particular case can be assigned mathematical weights in deriving fair market value. For this reason, no useful purpose is served by taking an average of several factors (for example, book value, capitalized earnings, and capitalized dividends) and basing the valuation on the result. Such a process excludes active consideration of other pertinent fac-

---

[1]Business Valuation Standard BVS-II, "Full, Written Business Valuation Reports," adopted by the Business Valuation Committee of the American Society of Appraisers.

tors, and the end result cannot be supported by a realistic application of the significant facts in the case except by mere chance.

This section of Revenue Ruling 59–60 suggests that a process using an average of various valuation approaches, or a weighted average of approaches, "excludes active consideration of other pertinent factors." More correctly, an appropriately selected set of weights may be necessary in order to develop a reasonable valuation opinion and may be the process whereby "all relevant factors" are brought together into a unified valuation conclusion.

Many analysts, including those who work at Mercer Capital and many other appraisal firms, as well as those who work for the government, utilize averages or weighted averages of valuation approaches. Regardless of the valuation approach(es), however, it remains the reponsibility of the analyst not to exclude pertinent factors and, indeed, to consider all relevant factors in the process of developing valuation conclusions.

Valuation Report Organization

There is no prescribed order for organization of an appraisal report. Different analysts bring different organizational concepts to their reports, and a given analyst may present reports in varying formats, depending upon the relative importance of issues and background information.

We believe that written valuation reports are enhanced by the presentation of a table of contents, exhibits, and appendixes. The table of contents normally includes each major and minor subheading found in the report, together with page references. A good table of contents provides the reader of a valuation report with an overview of content and organization and facilitates cross-referencing within the report. (See the Sample Bank Appraisal in Chapter 22 for an example of a table of contents for a bank appraisal.)

Historical versus Current Appraisals

Many valuation reports are written "as of the present time, as of a present date." In such cases, the reader and the appraiser are viewing a subject bank or other company from the same vantage point. There is little question regarding the availability of financial statements, public stock market information, or economic conditions. Both the appraiser and the client are standing at the same point in time and are able to view the uncertain future with a common set of facts and information.

Perspective on Historical Appraisals

Many other valuation requirements, however, relate to historical dates. Historical appraisals can be said to be written as of the present time, as of a historical date. Estate tax appraisals of substantial interests in closely-held businesses are often required following the deaths of their owners. Historical valuations of business interests are also frequently needed in litigation situations.

Regarding historical valuations, whether or not financial statements, public stock information, and economic or industry data was available *as of the valuation date* is not always so clear as with present-day appraisals.

Further, with many historical appraisals, none of the parties interested in the valuation result is generally standing on common ground looking at an uncertain future. Most of the time, the various parties know "what will happen" following the valuation date because, in many instances, it has already happened!

When conducting historical appraisals, the appraiser should attempt to obtain the financial statements and other information that reasonably would have been available if the appraisal had been conducted at the historical date. The appraiser should be aware of several potential issues with historical appraisals. An as-of date of December 31, 1985, for a bank appraisal conducted in late 1991 is used here to discuss some of them. As of December 31, 1985:

1. What financial information was available for the bank? Realistically, full-year financials were not available as of December 31, 1985; however, by common practice, full-year statements, which were not available until late January 1986, and the audited financial statements, which were not issued until March 1986, will normally be considered appropriate. Why? Because that information was "reasonably knowable" as of the valuation date, even though it was not physically prepared until later. In my experience, those financial statements, and all supporting schedules relating to them, will almost always be admitted into evidence if the valuation is at issue in a court of law or arbitration proceeding.

2. What financial information was available for public comparable companies? Public companies report financial information according to rules set down by the Securities and Exchange Commission. As of the date of the valuation, the analyst should normally consider only that information that was actually available to the public, which means released to the SEC and reported to the public financial markets. When using public comparable groups, appraisers should be quite familiar with the process by which information on public companies becomes public (is disseminated to the public). However, from a practical viewpoint, full-year earnings are often used for year-end bank appraisals, because most regional banking companies release earnings reports within two to four weeks of year-end. This convention, if used, corresponds to the use of full-year earnings for the subject bank.

3. What industry information was available? By researching publications that would have been in print and distributed as of the valuation date, the analyst can develop industry information that would have been available as of the valuation date.

4. What economic data was available? The analyst's research should include those forecasts and analyses that would have been in print and distributed as of the valuation date. Keep in mind that most na-

tional economic statistics are announced with a lag of one or more months, so it is not always acceptable to take year-end data from a later publication.

5. What information was available regarding interest rates? Interest rates quotations are available daily, and rates for government bills, notes, and bonds, as well as many corporate securities, can be found in *The Wall Street Journal* and other publications. Information for the stock and bond markets published as of December 31, 1985, in the January 2, 1986, issue of *The Wall Street Journal* is normally considered available as of year-end because the market was open that day.

6. What other information was available as of December 31, 1985? The appraiser will have to exercise judgment in decisions made regarding the availability of other internal or external information that could have an impact on the valuation conclusion.

Perspective on Current Appraisals

One of the best arguments for the careful documentation of *current* valuation reports, in addition to the import of the requirements noted above, is that, over the course of time, it may be necessary to defend their conclusions. (This argument applies to *all* current opinions, because it is simply impossible to know which reports will later have to be defended.) The "tail" on appraisals can be very long, indeed, particularly for tax-related appraisals or for appraisals used as a basis for transactions.

Appraisers may find themselves defending valuation reports prepared three to five years ago (or even more). Rest assured, any appraiser brought in to prepare a historical appraisal as of the date of the original report will have the benefit of hindsight, as will everyone else in court the day the issue goes to trial. The appraiser's job today, in a current valuation, is to lay the groundwork, through research, work papers, and in the presentation of the actual report, so that the judge or jury down the road will not be swayed by subsequent events in their consideration of the original appraisal.[2]

Is Hindsight Always "20-20"?

A recent example from our files illustrates the importance of well-documented current appraisals very well. In late 1984 and early 1985, Mercer Capital issued valuation opinions related to a bank and its parent holding company. Although the valuations were accepted by the affected parties in the original transactions, the appraisals were called into question because of other, later litigation related to the ownership of the parent holding company. The bank had been a problem bank and had been totally recapitalized in 1983. There were substantive questions about credit quality and earning power as of the original valuation dates, and those questions were reflected in the original appraisals, which valued the bank on a controlling interest basis at approximately its book value at the time.

---

[2]Note that in litigated situations, subsequent events are almost always adverse to the original appraisal, otherwise the issue would likely not have arisen in the first place. Further, despite the fact that information on subsequent events should not be admitted into evidence pertaining to a historical appraisal, that evidence will nearly always find its way into the record!

In late 1989, when the issue went to trial, evidence was tendered to the court (and accepted) that showed that the bank's earnings had substantially exceeded the Mercer Capital projections. Because of this evidence, it was argued, the original valuation was too low. That argument was buttressed by opinions of analysts from two regional investment banking firms active in following banking stocks, both of whom concluded that the early 1985 appraisal should have been about 150 percent of book value.

Fortunately, our files were well documented, considerable on-site due diligence was performed, and the valuation reports were comprehensive and well written. Furthermore, sophisticated parties at arm's length had accepted the original valuations. However, the issues, as well as all the valuations, were the subject of a hotly contested, several-day trial.

In the final analysis, the court held that the appropriate value for the bank was the value established by the original appraisals. Paraphrasing the court's opinion related to this discussion, the presiding judge wrote that he was not going to second-guess the judgment of the appraiser who was on the spot at the time looking at the facts as they looked at the time.[3] Hindsight need not be "20-20" if the appraiser properly documents and presents current appraisals realizing that they may one day be historical appraisals without the benefit of hindsight.

ABZs of Solid Valuation Conclusions and Reports

A couple of years ago, I prepared an internal training memo on "the ABZs" of reaching solid conclusions and preparing well-documented reports. That memo fits nicely into the progression of this chapter and serves to summarize much of the analytical discussion of the earlier chapters.

Because it was written in the second person, we will depart briefly from the basic writing style of this book. Although the memo did not relate specifically to banks, it is applicable to bank valuations almost in its entirety. With no apologies for any redundancies, the ABZs go like this:

A. Get command of the numbers. Read your spreads to be sure they make sense. If things seem out of line or unusual, verify to source documents or raise questions for answering in interviews.

B. Make sure you have considered all the obvious income statement adjustments (nonrecurring items, owner compensation, accelerated versus straight-line depreciation, LIFO to FIFO, etc.). Lay them all out on a valuation worksheet for consideration before eliminating them. Whether you use them or not, you must know what they are! If there are NOLs available that may shelter income in the future, be sure you get an immediate handle on the amounts and expira-

---

[3]Interestingly, during the trial, the bank became aware of a substantial loan loss that wiped out nearly a year's earnings and brought cumulative earnings, as reported from 1985 to 1989, to within a few thousand dollars of the original projections for the same period!

tions. Be sure your investigation picks up the adjustments that are less than obvious. Ask the necessary questions to find the potential adjustments.[4]

C. Make sure you have considered all the obvious balance sheet adjustments (LIFO reserve, appreciated real estate or other assets, appreciated investments, condition of receivables and inventory, intangible assets, etc.), and the appropriate tax-effecting of these adjustments. If you see early on that there are appreciated assets for consideration, initiate steps to get more information (appraisals, management estimates of value, etc.). As with the income statement, be sure to ask the questions that will reveal balance sheet adjustments that are not so obvious. Remember the other asset of $5,267 on a client's balance sheet that turned out to be the cost of shares of Wal-Mart stock purchased shortly after the initial public offering, which had a market value, after splits, of nearly $800,000 in 1989!

D. If there is a budget or business plan, be sure it is considered in the valuation worksheet, and be sure you have an opinion about its reasonableness or achievability.

E. Be sure you come to grips *early on* with the comparable group and that you have an opinion about the subject case in relationship to the comparable group. Immediately begin to form your opinion about the appropriate capitalization rate(s) in light of the comparable data.

F. If there is no comparable group, *immediately begin to form your own opinion about an appropriate capitalization rate by an alternative method.* Get the appropriate data for a build-up rate, or devise some other method that seems reasonable to you (and at least two more of us).

G. Be sure you know everything there is to know about actual transactions in a company's stock. The financial statements often provide evidence of transactions (related to treasury transactions, ESOPs, buy-sell agreements, stock options, etc.) if they have occurred. Be absolutely persistent in getting transactions data *in detail* from clients.

H. If you realize there is information from an unusual source that can help solve a valuation problem, move heaven and earth to get it ASAP. Don't wait until your back is to the wall when you know the answer is out there. Go get it!

I. Be sure you know the particulars of state corporate tax rates or other tax considerations affecting the company.

J. Regarding information, be sure you know what you have and what you need. Figure this out *when information comes in,* so if there are shortfalls, you can call or write for what is missing. Don't put yourself in the position of being short on critical data at the time you have to commit to a conclusion or finish a report.

K. When valuing multicompany holding companies, *always be sure to obtain consolidating statements!* These statements provide clues

---

[4]Terms not discussed in this book to any extent include depreciation methods, including the last-in, first-out (LIFO) and the first-in, first-out (FIFO) methods. See an introductory accounting text for a more complete discussion of these concepts. NOLs are net operating loss carryforwards that may be available to shelter income taxes.

regarding intercompany relationships, show how a company is really financed, and provide a parent company only statement that is necessary to come to an opinion of consolidated value.

L. Immediately after a client visit (whether or not you went on the visit), initiate all necessary follow-up to ensure that what you will need is available when you will need it.

M. Immediately after a client visit, force yourself to value the company. If you have all necessary information, you can reach a preliminary conclusion. Otherwise, attempting to reach a conclusion should force you to recognize any information shortfalls or issues that need to be addressed.

N. When you start to value a company, *never stop until you have a conclusion or know what you need to get to a conclusion!*

O. If a company's numbers are "moving around," be sure you understand why. If you go on the interview, be sure to ask why. If you don't go, be sure to specify the questions for the interviewer and have the answers recorded. If, after the interview, you still do not know the answers, immediately get back in touch with the company to have them help you figure out what's going on. You cannot value a company until you understand the numbers. Document your answers in a workpaper to save the rest of us from the problem if we later have to look into the file.

P. Outline your draft before you begin to write. Get a clear mental picture of what you are trying to say at the outset, and you will save *hours* every time. If you do not make conscious decisions about drafting, skeletons may force you into spending hours that have no impact on your conclusion, add nothing to the quality of the final report, and have little to do with what you consider really important in the case.[5]

Q. Read your draft with pencil in hand before you ask someone else to read it. If possible, allow yourself time to set a draft aside for a couple of days or more, and then review your own work. Not only will you catch most of your obvious mistakes, you will learn how to draft better on the first try—if you habitually read your own work! You cannot improve your analytical thinking or your writing skills by hoping someone else will catch your problems and fix them for you. While the firm's credibility is on the line when the report goes out the door, your personal credibility is on the line internally.

R. Outline your draft before you begin to write. Read your outline to see if it makes sense in light of your knowledge of the case, the budget, the deadline, and the product we have promised to the client.

S. Force yourself to come to your own conclusions (opinions) before asking someone else. Then you are testing, validating, affirming, and learning. You gain confidence in reaching conclusions by practice, not by asking someone else what he or she thinks.

T. If you come to a valuation committee meeting with a valuation conclusion, present the conclusion with confidence. If you don't do that, aggressive people like Mercer (or clients) will realize you lack confidence and proceed immediately to develop their own conclusions—in

---

[5]At Mercer Capital, a *skeleton* is a detailed report outline that provides a basic structure within which to draft a report. It is designed to provide some similarity of report structure and to facilitate thinking about what should be in a particular draft, not to determine what should be in it. The analyst must make these decisions in every case.

which they have confidence. If you have followed the steps above, there is no reason you and others should not have confidence in your conclusions.

U. If a conclusion other than yours is suggested, do not allow the change unless you understand why and are convinced of its superiority. Changes can result from finding errors of fact, omission, overemphasis, underemphasis, interpretation, mathematics, judgment, etc. Now is the time—before your report is finalized and out the door—to catch these problems and to internalize the process by which they were identified.

V. Force yourself to draft each report immediately after the client visit. Our collective knowledge is seldom enhanced by the passage of time; in fact, it tends to dim with time unless we are actively working on the file over an extended period. So don't wait until you or the visiting analyst cannot remember details. Draft immediately according to your outline!

W. Be sure to stay in regular touch with the client(s) during the course of an engagement. Clients desire and deserve to have the perception of substantial effort on their behalf during the course of an engagement. Regular contact is the only way to ensure the reality and, therefore, the possibility of the perception. Clients do not generally become disturbed if problems (whether involving data, interpretations of documents, or issues) arise during the course of an engagement; they become disturbed if we ignore them when these problems arise and then surprise them with their impact on the engagement!

X. If you will have to use an acquisition model or a discounted future earnings model, either as a validation of a valuation conclusion or as a primary methodology, be doubly sure you have command of the historical numbers as well as any projections available from the client. Do not wait until the last minute to get these methods set up. Templates can provide the structure for many models, but you must supply the command of the numbers and the critical link between historical and forecasted results.[6]

Y. Outline your report before you start. It is an investment of time that will save you time every time and will improve the quality of your writing.

Z. Always keep client deadlines in mind when you work on a report. We promise drafts to clients within 30 days of our on-site visit in most of our engagement letters. That means you should have the draft done within about three weeks to allow for review, redrafting, or any other problems that might spring up at the end, as well as delivery time to the client.

The topic of this chapter is developing and presenting a valuation conclusion. This section suggests that the bank analyst should develop a command of a subject bank's numbers and other information, ask the

---

[6]Templates are basic spreadsheet models designed to forecast income statements, balance sheets, and cash flows for companies or banks. The templates can be modified by the analyst to fit the particular facts and circumstances of an appraisal situation, and they are designed as a starting point to save time and to avoid repetitive modeling steps. For example, Exhibit 11-1, which forecasts bank and bank holding company earnings, dividends, debt service requirements, and the like, was developed from a basic template.

questions necessary to clarify issues raised by the information, and focus analytical attention on the process of valuation. He or she should also outline the report to ensure not only the inclusion of appropriate information in the draft, but also the logical and orderly progression of its presentation, and then draft (write) the report accordingly. After a reasonable wait, the analyst should then review (i.e., critically edit and make the necessary changes or corrections) to his or her own work. By following this procedure, chances are that the report is off to a good start. Most valuation firms then have additional review procedures which check for quality, completeness, reasonableness and conformity with applicable appraisal standards. (For example, see Exhibit 15-2.)

The ABCs focus analytical attention and encourage clear thinking about valuation issues. They provide a good start toward developing and presenting a valuation conclusion. By avoiding common errors in report presentation, the analyst can increase the probability of having a well-written, well-organized, understandable, and reasonable valuation opinion.

Common Problems with Valuation Reports

Over the course of the last 15 years, I have had the opportunity to review hundreds of valuation reports, the majority of which were prepared by analysts of Mercer Capital (normally in draft form), but a large number of which have been prepared by analysts from other firms from around the nation. In reviewing these reports, I detected two types of problems that influence their readability, credibility, and reasonableness. These problems are discussed below as general and specific problems with valuation reports.

General Problems with Valuation Reports

General problems with valuation reports seem to develop as result of inadequate planning on the part of the responsible analyst(s). General problems include:

1. Failure to understand the valuation objective—that is, what is being valued, why it is being valued, and the valuation as-of date. If the valuation objective is not clear from the outset to the conclusion of a report, the report can be seriously flawed. Confusion over these issues creeps into a surprising number of valuation reports.
2. Failure to perform an adequate financial analysis of the bank or the company and to recognize the key analytical issues involved prior to drafting. I have seen valuation reports where the entire financial analysis of substantial companies or banks has consisted of no more than a paragraph. Interestingly, analysts making this error often fail to include sufficient historical financial information in their reports to allow the reader to perform an independent analysis.
3. Failure to understand the nature of the business being valued or of the industry or industries in which it operates. This might seem dif-

ficult in the valuation of financial institutions, but inexperienced analysts can easily make mistakes.

4. Failure to develop the valuation rationale sufficiently early to influence the content and tone of a report. It is always interesting to read reports with a neutral or negative tone and find a wildly optimistic valuation conclusion (or the reverse).

These general problems with valuation reports can be avoided by following the steps of the valuation process outlined above, as well as the report standards in Appendix B (Uniform Standards of Professional Appraisal Practice) and Appendix G (the existing business valuation standards of the American Society of Appraisers, or BSV-I BVS-II, as well as additional standards proposed by the Business Valuation Committee which are in the final approval process of the American Society of Appraisers.[7]

Specific Problems with Valuation Reports

In no particular order, several specific problems that appear in valuation reports are noted and discussed briefly below.

Great Leaps of Faith

Great leaps of faith (or merely leaps of faith) can occur in many places in a valuation report. They all have one thing in common: The reader simply cannot get to the conclusion (or subconclusion) based upon the information presented in the report. With blatant leaps of faith, the reader of a report can make some judgment regarding the credibility of the report. Other leaps of faith, however, are more insidious and can fool all but the most wary reader.

I recently reviewed an appraisal of a small, retail consumer electronics wholesaler. The report was well written, presented a good analysis of the company and the industry, included detailed exhibits with full financial information, and, in every respect except one, was an impressive document. The only problem was that, in a very brief paragraph, the analyst derived a price/earnings multiple of more than 12x by reference to the S&P Stock Index. The company's historical performance—combined with an industry situation with major competitors such as Circuit City and Silo cutting rapidly into its market share, and an immediate change in top management—would not justify a multiple above the range of 5x to 7x earnings.

---

[7]The proposed standards include: (1) additions to the BVS-I Terminology standard to define certain terms; (2) BVS-III General Performance Requirements for Business Valuation, (3) BVS-IV Asset Based Approach to Business Valuation, and (4) BVS-V The Guideline Company Valuation Method.

This book was substantially written prior to the passage of the proposed standards by the Business Valuation Committee (BVC). As a consequence, even though I was a member of the BVC approving the standards, some portions of this text may not totally embrace the new terms as defined or introduced. However, the book is in substantive compliance with the proposed standards. It will take some time for appraisers to become accustomed to the new terms.

The terminology standards include specific definitions of "valuation approaches" and "valuation methods," which have heretofore been used synonymously by many appraisers (and occasionally in this text!). Without referencing them specifically, this book is in conformity with proposed BVS-III General Performance Requirements for Business Valuation and proposed BVS-IV Asset Based Approach to Business Valuation. The book and the Sample Bank Appraisal of Chapter 22 are in conformity with the methodological content of proposed BVS-V The Guideline Company Valuation Method, however, much of the language in the text refers to "comparable companies" rather than to "guideline companies," the proposed terminology of BVS-V.

This great leap of faith, although hidden in an otherwise impressive report, had a material impact on the conclusion that rendered it inappropriate for its intended purpose. Great leaps of faith can occur as a result of factual or intellectual carelessness on the part of an appraiser. Readers of valuation reports should beware of great leaps of faith.

Reconciling the Past with the Outlook for the Future (The Great Leap Forward)

Too often, valuation reports fail to explain the progression from a company's historical performance to projections for the future. There are two main forms of this reconciliation problem, which can be subtitled *the great leap forward.*

Analysts using discounted cash flow or discounted future earnings projections often provide no bridge in the report between the spotty (or cyclical) past and the expected glorious future. First year profit margins projections often exceed anything accomplished in recent years and then improve from there. Sales (adjusted gross income for banks), which have been up and down or stagnant in recent years, begin to grow at a prodigious rate. In its most extreme form, the perpetrator of this great leap forward will not even provide historical financial statements, presumably on the premise that they would only confuse the reader. Analysts using discounted future benefits methodologies have a responsibility to the users of their reports to explain their projections in the context of historical performance and to reconcile any significant variations between the two.

Analysts are often guilty of another, more subtle form of the great leap forward. The use of a capitalization rate that embodies an inadequate risk premium and, implicitly, a growth projection that far outstrips the subject company's historical growth pattern effectively makes the same mistake as noted in the preceding paragraph. This form of the great leap forward was noted above in the discussion of great leaps of faith.

Standard of Value

Analysts sometimes show some confusion in the application of the appropriate standard of value. The standard of value applicable to a particular valuation should be provided and defined at the outset of a valuation report. See the more detailed discussion of this issue in Chapter 2.

Failure to Cite Sources

Analysts should cite information sources in their reports. Well-known sources that are accepted references in valuation reports are often cited generally. However, nonstandard sources should be cited specifically so that the reader can identify and locate them if desired.

Rationale for Approaches Used

One or more valuation approaches are contained in every valuation report. The analyst should explain clearly why the particular approaches found in a report are appropriate under the circumstances. Further, it may be appropriate to mention other approaches and the reasons they were not used in the report. For example, in a tax-related valuation report based upon direct reference to Revenue Ruling 59–60 (which requires consideration of comparisons with public companies in the same or similar lines of business), it is probably necessary to explain why an alternative method of developing a capitalization rate was used and why a guideline (comparable) company approach was not used.

Rationale for Weighting of Approaches

Recalling the admonition in Revenue Ruling 59–60 regarding the use of averages of approaches, it is desirable that the analyst provide his or her specific rationale for the weighting of approaches leading to a valuation conclusion. In using multiple approaches, the analyst is attempting to simulate the kind of thinking that the market would perform or the considerations of fully informed buyers and sellers. It is therefore helpful that the rationale for weightings be explained for readers of valuation reports.

Disproportionate Coverage in the Report

Valuation reports should contain a reasonable balance between boiler-plate (definitions and basic materials to provide report structure) and analysis. I reviewed a report several years ago that contained more than 10 pages discussing the general concept of the use of discounted cash flow. In less than one page, the entire forecast, including assumptions, the development of the discount rate, and the valuation conclusion were presented.

Along the same lines, I reviewed a bank valuation report containing more than 70 pages of text. The review of the industry consumed more than 30 pages, and the national and regional economic overview was more than 20 pages long. The financial analysis and background on the subject bank contained about three pages, and the valuation was presented in two paragraphs.

The elements that are important in the development of a valuation conclusion should be given appropriate weight in the presentation of the text.

Failure to Use Comparative or Comparable Data Properly

Comparative data are available for many valuations. Comparative data may be related to similar closely-held businesses (such as found in the Uniform Bank Performance Reports or publications of Robert Morris Associates) or from similar publicly traded companies.

Analysts should search diligently for comparable information and should use it to the extent possible in developing financial analyses and valuation rationales. We do live in a comparative world, our financial theory is one of alternative (comparative) investments, and our legislation and case law almost uniformly suggest the use of comparable information whenever possible.

If You Can't Understand It, Don't Stand for It

My first valuation client was the chairman and majority shareholder of a successful manufacturing company. For several years prior to our meeting, he had obtained an annual independent appraisal of his company. He retained the investment banking company I worked for at the time to provide a second valuation opinion that year. The next year, he dropped the first firm, and we obtained the annual assignment.

He later told me why he had made the change of appraisers, and I have never forgotten what he said: "When I read your report, I recognized my company."

Valuation reports are written for users who are not typically valuation experts. Valuation reports should therefore be understandable to bankers, company executives, judges, attorneys, accountants, and other users.

Terminology needs to be defined, explained, and consistently applied. The same applies to valuation methodologies. It is often appropriate to place complex theoretical discussions in an exhibit or appendix of a report and to bring forward to the main body that portion of the analysis necessary for the reader to understand the logical flow of the developing valuation rationale. Successful appraisers can explain the use of complex theories in terms understandable to users, both in written reports and in oral communications related to their conclusions.

"Proving" the Reasonableness of Valuation Conclusions

All too many valuation reports simply conclude by stating words to this effect:

> Based upon our analysis of all the relevant factors related to American Bancshares, Inc., it is our opinion that the fair market value of American's common stock is $42 per share. This conclusion is rendered for estate tax purposes on a minority interest basis as of December 31, 1990.

Such a conclusion, while technically proper, omits an important step that can help the reader of appraisal reports (and other appraisers) understand the overall reasonableness of appraisal conclusions. In my judgment, appraisal conclusions should include a "proof" of the reasonableness of the appraiser's opinion. The proof can consist of simple comparisons with comparative reference points, including:

1. The price/earnings multiple or range of the selected comparable (guideline) group.
2. The price/book-value multiple or range of the comparable group.
3. Other market multiples developed from the comparable group, including price/sales ratios, price/assets, dividend yields, price/pretax-income multiples, price/cash flow multiples, etc.
4. Comparisons with actual transactions in the company's stock.
5. Comparisons with transactions multiples involving similar companies.
6. Other comparisons that can help the reader understand the reasonableness of the conclusion(s).

Comparisons such as these help the reader and the appraiser place the conclusion of the report into a context that both should be familiar with after reading the report. If the valuation conclusion stands out by way of relative comparison as particularly high or low, the appraiser and the reader should be comfortable that this relative comparison is reasonable in light of the total analysis of the report.

When appraisers provide recurring valuations of the same company, (e.g., for employee stock ownership plans or for gift tax purposes), it is equally important to relate the current conclusion with the prior conclusion(s). In addition to "proving" the reasonableness of the current appraisal in relationship to the market or other familiar contexts, the appraiser should also "prove" its reasonableness in comparison to previous appraisal(s). Exhibit 15-1 reproduces a brief article I wrote for the *Business Valuation Review* to illustrate this point.

Summary Appraisal Review Checklist

Exhibit 15-2 provides a Summary Appraisal Review Checklist as a means of summarizing much of the discussion on report development and presentation. The checklist asks questions relating to the major areas of a valuation report. It can be used both by appraisers and users of appraisal reports.[8]

Sample Appraisal Report

Chapter 22 provides a sample appraisal report related to the hypothetical Sample Bancshares, Inc. The appraisal is not intended to be patterned after any particular bank but is used as a vehicle to illustrate many of the elements of analysis and report presentation discussed in Chapters 1 to 15. The report provides one illustration of how these elements can be combined into a valuation analysis and report. Other appraisers may develop different organizational patterns to achieve the same result, which is, hopefully, a well-written, well-developed, well-reasoned, and reasonable conclusion of value of the common stock of Sample Bancshares, Inc., for the purpose stated in the report.

---

[8]Readers are referred to a publication of the National Association of Review Appraisers and Mortgage Underwriters titled "Reviewing a Business Appraisal Report" for further information on appraisal review. The publication, written by Shannon P. Pratt, can be obtained from the NARA/MU, 8383 East Evans Road, Scottsdale, Arizona 85260-3614.

Exhibit 15-1

===
LETTER TO THE EDITOR
===

Issues In Recurring Valuations:
Methodological Comparisons From Year-to-Year

October, 1988

Dear Editor:

In the last issue of this publication, one author suggested a procedure for recurring ESOP appraisals which tracks valuation **conclusions** from year to year, thereby forcing the analyst to discuss or reconcile the reasonableness of the current conclusion in light of previous years' results ("Tracking A Company's ESOP Value," Jeffrey P. Wright, ASA, CFA, BUSINESS VALUATION REVIEW, September, 1988, p. 124). This procedure would be a welcome addition to many appraisal reports. However, it deals only with the conclusions themselves, **not with how the analyst reached them**.

We believe a further procedure is necessary with recurring valuation assignments to: 1) insure the intellectual honesty of the analyst (and the firm); 2) allow the reader to understand the basis for significant methodological shifts; and 3) provide the perspective a reader needs to anchor the reasonableness of the current conclusion, not only today, but in light of historical results.

The current year methodology is summarized in a table in the report. The table includes all methodologies considered, valuation indicators derived, and weights assigned to each. All discounts or premiums to market multiples applied in the various methodologies are disclosed in the table, as are all marketability or minority interest discounts. The prior year conclusions (one or two years) are then displayed next to the current year data, and changes are noted. Finally, comparative data such as the effective price/earnings, price/sales or price/book value ratios implied by the conclusions, and relevant public market comparisons are included.

The procedure requires the analyst to discuss specific reasons for significant metho-dological shifts, changes in weightings applied to methodologies, or changes in fundamental comparisons, or marketability/minority discounts. While consistency has been called "the hobgoblin of little minds," **this methodology requires careful consideration and justification of methodological changes and weighting shifts.**

When this procedure is applied consistently within a firm, it will inevitably and appropriately **highlight "outlier" conclusions, and will, over time, help develop consistency of procedures and conservatism of results. In addition, the procedure adds credibility to the conclusions in the current report, in discussions with clients, and occasionally, in courtroom testimony regarding the valuations.**

Sample Of Methodology: XYZ Banking Company (see Table 1)

The regional bank stock market, from which the base capitalization rate was derived, was down 15% from the prior year-end in the aftermath of "Black Monday" in October, 1987. The fundamental discount applied to the earnings stream of this bank, in relationship to the public comparable group, was lowered from 20% to 15% because of improving operating fundamentals that appeared to be sustainable. The rise in adjusted earnings more than offset the decline in the adjusted capitalization rate, and the earnings value observation rose 22%.

There were no market transactions in the bank's stock during either year, so no value obser-

Exhibit 15-1 (*continued*)

vation was derived. Net asset value, adjusted primarily for losses in the bank's securities portfolio, was virtually unchanged from year-to-year. Earnings and net assets were weighted 60% to 40%, respectively, in each year. The initial weighted value rose 13% overall, to $3.5 million, dampened by the small decline in net asset value.

The marketability discount remained unchanged for reasons discussed above. The final conclusion of fair market value per share, after considering the dilutive effect of the marketability discount and the ESOP contributions, rose 11% from $14.71 per share in 1986 to $16.31 per share at year-end, 1987.

The current conclusion appears reasonable in light of the current year's analysis and in comparison with the prior year. The ratio of market price to adjusted earnings fell from 7.6x to 6.4x, primarily because of the market decline; however, the price/book value ratio improved from 104% to 109%. Both conclusions were also reasonable, in our opinion, when compared to the same ratios for the publicly traded comparable group shown in Table 1 and discussed previously in the text.

Z. Christopher Mercer, ASA, CFA

TABLE 1: XYZ BANKING COMPANY

Comparison of Valuation Conclusions as of December 31, 1987 and 1986

Valuation Component	12/31/87	12/31/86	Change
Base Price/Book Ratio*	1.28x	1.48x	−13.5%
Base Cap. Rate*	8.85x	10.42x	−15.1%
Fundamental Discount	15%	20%	Down 5%
Adj. Cap. Rate	7.52x	8.34x	−9.8%
Adjusted Earnings	$519,113	$385,000	+34.8%
Earnings Value	$3,903,730	$3,210,900	+21.6%
Market Transactions	none–n/a	none–n/a	
Net Asset Value	$2,815,826	$2,850,442	−1.2%
Earnings Weight	60%	60%	No Change
Market Trans Weight	0%	0%	No Change
Net Asset Weight	40%	40%	No Change
Initial Weighted Value	$3,468,568	$3,066,717	+13.1%
Marketability Discount	5%	5%	No Change
ESOP Contribution	$68,810	$147,542	
Initial Shares O/S	197,848	188,000	
Shares Issued to ESOP	4,219	10,028	
Fully Diluted Shares O/S	202,067	198,028	
Per Share Conclusion of Fair Market Value	$16.31	$14.71	+10.9%
Fully Diluted: Price/Book Value	109%	104%	
Price/Adj. Earnings	6.4x	7.6x	

*Developed from Public Market Comparisons

Mr. Mercer is President of Mercer Capital Management, Inc., Memphis, Tennessee.
He holds Senior status in business valuation, and is president of the West Tennessee Chapter of the ASA.

This letter was published originally in the Business Valuation Review, December 1988, pages 171-173.

Exhibit 15-2
Summary Appraisal Review Checklist

Note: Items identified by Roman numerals I–VIII are the "Basic Eight" factors required for consideration by Revenue Ruling 59–60 plus additional factors required by the proposed regulations on adequate consideration relating to ESOP appraisals.

I. Description of the Valuation Subject and Purpose

1. Is the party retaining the appraiser identified?
2. Is the interest being valued defined in relationship to a specific entity?
3. What is the form of ownership (C or S corporation, partnership, etc.)?
4. Is the state of legal incorporation or registration provided?
5. Are the legal rights and/or restrictions of ownership detailed, if they are not obvious?
6. Is a description of the classes and distribution of ownership of the entity's securities provided?
7. What is the purpose of the appraisal?
8. Is the standard of value identified, with appropriate statutory references, if applicable?
9. Is/are the date(s) for which the valuation is applicable identified?
10. Is there a statement of contingent and limiting conditions to which the appraisal values are subject, including limitations of the use of hypothetical, fractional, or preliminary appraisals?

II. Appraiser Qualifications and Independence

1. Is there a transmittal letter with signatures of responsible parties?
2. Does the report provide evidence of appraisal experience on the part of the appraisers and/or the appraisal firm?
3. Is there a statement of the appraiser's disinterestedness in the valuation result?
4. Has the appraiser made a physical inspection and/or visited with management and conducted an interview at the subject's location?

III. Qualitative Factors about the Business

Are there discussions related to the following factors:

1. THE NATURE AND HISTORY OF THE ENTERPRISE SINCE INCEPTION?
2. The entity's products, services, and business mix?
3. Industries, markets, and customers served?
4. Competitors and the competitive environment?
5. Description of the entity's physical facilities?
6. General discussion of the general flow of operations, if applicable?
7. Description of management and key personnel?
8. Organizational structure, including subsidiaries and affiliates?
9. Related parties and entities and the extent of the relationships, particularly if the relationships could influence valuation conclusions?
10. NATIONAL ECONOMIC CONDITIONS?
11. INDUSTRY ANALYSIS AND OUTLOOK?
12. LOCAL OR REGIONAL ECONOMIC OUTLOOK?
13. Information sources provided that are verifiable by the reader?

Exhibit 15-2 (*continued*)

IV. Financial Position and Performance

Does the appraisal contain discussions relating to or contain:

1. The composition of the entity's balance sheet, including assets, liabilities, and capital structure?
2. BOOK VALUE AND FINANCIAL CONDITION, including liquidity considerations and leverage?
3. EXISTENCE OF GOODWILL OR OTHER INTANGIBLE VALUE?
4. Financial performance, including discussions of revenue, expenses, and profit margins (historical, current, and expected future performance) and nonrecurring or extraordinary items during the period of analysis?
5. EARNING CAPACITY?
6. DIVIDEND-PAYING CAPACITY, HISTORY, AND PROSPECTS?
7. Historical financial statements, preferably spread in a logical fashion to facilitate comparisons over time of key balance sheet and income statement values, margins, significant ratios, trends, etc.?
8. The number of shares outstanding and the number of shares being valued?

V. Valuation Approaches and Methods

Does the appraisal report contain or discuss:

1. Description and explanation of the appraisal approaches and method(s) used? If certain approaches or methods are expected and not used, are the reasons for exclusion explained?
2. Proper support and justification for the valuation approaches and methods used?
3. Financial statement adjustments that are reasonable and well documented?
4. Discussion of SALES OF STOCK AND THE SIZE OF THE BLOCK TO BE VALUED?
5. MARKET PRICES OF SIMILAR COMPANIES WHOSE STOCKS ARE PUBLICLY TRADED?
6. Clear criteria and selection procedures of comparative (guideline) companies, if used, and sufficient explanation if not used?
7. Develop reasonable capitalization rate/factor or discount rate based upon comparisons of subject company with the public comparable group, if this approach is utilized?
8. Clear and convincing connection between historical and projected performance, if projections are utilized?
9. Projections in sufficient detail, with critical assumptions shown, to enable reader to understand the dynamics of expected future performance (including income statements, balance sheets, cash flows, and ratios)?
10. If a method other than public comparables was used for developing the capitalization rate, is it explained and understandable and does it yield a reasonable capitalization rate or discount rate?
11. Proper use of minority interest discounts, if appropriate?
12. Proper consideration of control premiums, if appropriate?
13. WOULD AN INDEPENDENT THIRD PARTY PAY A CONTROL PREMIUM UNDER THE CIRCUMSTANCES OF THE APPRAISAL (for ESOP appraisals)?
14. SPECIFIC FACTORS RELATIVE TO THE ESOP THAT COULD HAVE AN IMPACT ON VALUATION (for ESOP appraisals)?

Exhibit 15-2 (*continued*)

15. Consideration of the marketability of the securities being valued and use of a marketability discount, if appropriate?

VI. Valuation Analysis and Conclusion(s)

1. Is there a clear statement of the valuation conclusion(s) with specific reference to the as-of date(s) and the interest(s) being valued?
2. Is/are the conclusion(s) logical and reasonable in light of the presentation of the report?
3. Is there proper support and justification for the conclusion(s) in the report?
4. Can the conclusion(s) be replicated by the reader based upon the information provided?
5. Does the report provide reconciliations with prior appraisals (e.g., in case of recurring ESOP appraisals), if any?

VII. General Report Presentation Issues

1. Does the overall layout, organization, and appearance of the report make it "readable"?
2. Is terminology in the report well defined and consistently applied?
3. Is the analysis in the report internally consistent?
4. Is the reader required to make "great leaps of faith" at any point in the analysis leading to the conclusion(s)?
5. Is there a reasonable balance between boilerplate materials and actual analysis in the report?
6. Is the overall analysis of sufficient quality and quantity to convince the reader of the reasonableness of the conclusion(s)?
7. Could a businessperson without valuation training read and understand the report?

VIII. Compliance with Relevant Standards

1. Does the report comply with Standards 9 and 10 of the Uniform Standards of Professional Appraisal Practice?
2. Does the report comply with Business Valuation Standard II (BVS-II) of the American Society of Appraisers related to full, written business valuation reports as well as to any other applicable standards?

Chapter 16

Employee Stock Ownership Plans

We are witnessing the most significant attempt in recent history to expand worker ownership in American society. For nearly fifteen years, employee ownership and participation have been heralded as a premier form of labor-management cooperation as well as the solution to America's lagging competitiveness. The most popular method for fostering worker ownership in individual firms is the Employee Stock Ownership Plan, or ESOP. Quite simply, an ESOP is a means by which employees can own stock in the companies where they work. It is a form of worker ownership and participation designed for taxpaying corporations and encouraged by federal law.

Joseph R. Blasi, *Employee Ownership: Revolution or Ripoff?*

Introduction

Employee stock ownership plans (ESOPs) have been widely publicized in the business press. Nevertheless, misconceptions and misunderstandings abound. This chapter cannot answer every question about ESOPs and their appraisal. However, it does provide an overview of their major benefits and disadvantages, as well as an introduction to many of the valuation issues presented by ESOPs generally and by bank ESOPs specifically. Unfortunately, there are no clear-cut answers to many of the valuation issues discussed, so the need for appraiser judgment noted throughout this book is heightened in the area of ESOP appraisal.[1]

What Is an ESOP?

An employee stock ownership plan is a qualified retirement plan designed to invest primarily in the securities of companies (employer securities), thereby providing an indirect means for employees of the companies to obtain an ownership stake in those companies.[2] ESOPs were statutorily created by the Employee Retirement Income Security Act of 1974 (ERISA), and have been enhanced in subsequent legislation.[3]

Banks considering the installation of an ESOP should be certain to employ competent legal, accounting, and administration experts to ensure compliance with regulations of both the Internal Revenue Service (regarding tax deductibility) and the Department of Labor (regarding employee retirement plan requirements).

ESOP Benefits

At the present time, the primary benefits provided by ESOPs include the following:

---

[1]The title of a recent article validates this statement: Mark P. Pagano, "Uniform Appraisal Practices Are Needed in Leveraged ESOP Valuations," *Business Valuation Review*, March 1991, p. 21.

[2]ESOPs are sometimes referred to as employee stock ownership trusts (ESOTs). For the purposes of this book, ESOPs and ESOTs are treated as identical.

[3]This is a nontechnical discussion of ESOPs, which have many very technical aspects. See the Bibliography for a selection of books and articles that provide more-detailed and -technical discussions of ESOPs. One recent article that discusses many of the technical aspects of ESOPs in understandable language is David Ackerman, "Innovative Uses of Employee Stock Ownership Plans for Private Companies," *DePaul Business Law Journal*, Vol. 2, no. 2 (Spring 1990), pp. 227–54.

1. An ESOP is a wealth-distributing vehicle that allows employees to develop, at least potentially, substantial ownership stakes in the equity securities of their employers.
2. ESOPs provide a vehicle to enable shareholders of companies and financial institutions to achieve liquidity for their investments in closely-held entities. In other words, ESOPs can purchase stock directly from shareholders. In so doing, an ESOP can create at least a partial market for corporate stock.
3. If an ESOP acquires as much as 30 percent of the stock of a nonpublic company, shareholders selling their stock to the ESOP are eligible for a tax-free rollover reinvestment of the proceeds into qualifying securities. If the rollover investments are held until the selling shareholder's death, the estate can achieve a stepped-up basis for the securities, enabling the avoidance of capital gains tax on the proceeds from the sale to the ESOP.
4. If an ESOP owns at least 50 percent of the shares of an employer, half of the interest on loans made to the ESOP by qualifying financial institutions is tax free.
5. ESOP contributions are tax deductible for employers just like contributions to any other retirement plan, and the contributions are subject to less stringent limitations than other plans.
6. Dividends received on shares owned by an ESOP are tax deductible to the employer if (1) they are flowed through as direct cash benefits to the plan participants, or (2) they are used to amortize ESOP debt incurred by the ESOP to purchase those securities.
7. ESOPs can be leveraged, and contributions made to amortize principal and interest are tax deductible. Contributions are tax deductible up to 25 percent of eligible payroll (for principal reduction) plus interest expense associated with ESOP debt.
8. ESOPs can purchase newly issued shares of the employer and generate new capital for the enterprise on a tax-deductible basis.
9. ESOPs can be an important tool for employee motivation and for productivity enhancement.

From the list of ESOP benefits above, it is clear that ESOPs are a unique employee retirement benefit. ESOPs can also be an important corporate financing tool. It is estimated that there are approximately 9,000 ESOPs in the United States today. Although no firm statistics are available, I believe that the banking industry has more ESOPs than any other industry. Banks have used ESOPs to augment existing retirement plans, to replace retirement plans, to encourage employee productivity, to make markets in their shares, and to raise capital.

Actual and Potential Disadvantages of ESOPs

ESOPS have certain actual or potential disadvantages that should be considered by any company or financial institution prior to installation:

1. *Dilution.* If ESOPs are used to raise capital—that is, if an ESOP acquires newly issued shares through a direct contribution by a bank or through a leveraged purchase—the ownership interests of the remaining shareholders will be diluted. The equity ownership positions

of the remaining shareholders will be reduced pro rata based upon the number of shares issued to the ESOP and value per share will be diluted as well. If the ESOP works as desired, these forms of dilution can be overcome by increased productivity on the part of employees.

2. *Repurchase liability.* ESOPs are normally required by law to have a put option (see the discussion below), which enables departing employees of nonpublic companies with vested shares to put their shares, either to the company or to the ESOP, in order to provide them with an option for liquidity.[4] This repurchase liability is sometimes referred to as an emerging liability because it grows over time as shares vest with employees and as the value of the employer securities (hopefully) grows. Repurchase liability has not become a general problem for bank ESOPs to date, although it is sometimes necessary to anticipate retirements of key employees and to plan for the availability of funds to meet specific liabilities. Most banks have been able to meet their repurchase liabilities on a pay-as-they-go basis. Occasionally, however, a bank will need to borrow funds to be repaid from future ESOP contributions to meet specific repurchase requirements.

3. *Valuation.* There is a requirement that ESOPs be valued annually and as of the date of certain transactions or contributions. See the discussion below regarding valuation issues.

4. *Lack of diversification.* An ESOP is a qualified retirement plan that is not subject to the diversification rules of profit-sharing and pension plans. ESOPs are designed to invest primarily in employer securities and are, by definition, not diversified. If the employer experiences financial difficulties and the value of its securities declines, ESOP participants will experience a decline in the value of their retirement benefits. Effective January 1, 1987, ESOP participants over age 55 were provided the opportunity to diversify their holdings in ESOPs subject to certain limitations.

5. *Alternative minimum tax.* ESOP companies utilizing the deductibility of dividends paid on ESOP shares can experience problems with alternate minimum tax issues.

6. *Fiduciary liability.* An ESOP must have one or more trustees responsible for the operation of the plan for the exclusive benefit of the employee participants. For this reason, many attorneys recommend that independent fiduciaries be appointed as trustees of ESOPs. In real life, however, key managers or employees are often placed in the position of ESOP trustee. There are very real opportunities for conflicts of interest between the ESOP, the company or bank, and shareholders who might desire to sell their shares to the ESOP.

7. *Stock performance.* If things work as designed, the value of employer securities owned by an ESOP will appreciate over time. As noted above, however, companies can encounter problems, experience financial distress, and see their share values decline. Further, share

---

[4]Although the put option is a right and not a requirement, employees virtually always exercise their put rights on departure.

values can decline even when a company experiences improving performance because of stock market declines that are independent of that company, yet influence its value indirectly.[5] Declining values in the face of improving performance can have a negative impact on employee morale.

8. *Administrative cost and complexity.* ESOPs are more complex and more expensive to operate than many other retirement plan types. Most companies engage the services of an independent administration firm to handle ESOP accounting, which is normally more time consuming (and expensive) than for profit-sharing plans. In addition, there is a requirement for an annual independent appraisal under normal circumstances and more frequent appraisal requirements if the ESOP engages in transactions with "insiders."

The discussion thus far has only touched upon the features, advantages, and disadvantages of ESOPs. A more extensive treatment is beyond the scope of this book; however, the discussion does outline many of the major issues facing ESOP companies, including banks and thrifts.

Types of ESOPs

There are two types of ESOPs: unleveraged and leveraged. Unleveraged ESOPs, at least in concept, are relatively straightforward creatures, but leveraged ESOPs can be more complex.

Unleveraged ESOP

An unleveraged ESOP works fairly simply. If ABC Bancorp, Inc. (ABC), establishes an ESOP, it can then make annual contributions to the trust, either in cash or in ABC common stock. In either event, ABC's contributions are tax deductible, and the employee beneficiaries begin to acquire an ownership interest, through the ESOP, in ABC. Figure 16-1 provides an illustration of the operation of the unleveraged ESOP at ABC. If cash contributions are made, shares of ABC can be acquired from existing shareholders. The shares are acquired at or below prices determined by independent appraisal of ABC.

ESOP accounting is a fairly complex process. At the most simple level, however, each eligible employee of ABC will have an account in the ESOP. Normally, full-time employees with one year or more of service are eligible for participation in the ESOP. Generally, when banks or other companies have preexisting retirement plans, employees are allowed to carry their preexisting vesting status into the ESOP. Ownership in ABC shares will vest according to the vesting schedule established in the ESOP document. Contributions, either in cash or stock, accumulate in the ESOP until an employee quits, is fired, dies, or retires.[6]

---

[5] In fact, this is exactly what happened in the Sample Bank Appraisal found in Chapter 22.
[6] Some appraisers and other ESOP practitioners use the acronym *QFDR* for those ESOP participants who "Quit, are Fired, Die, or Retire" during a given plan year.

Figure 16-1

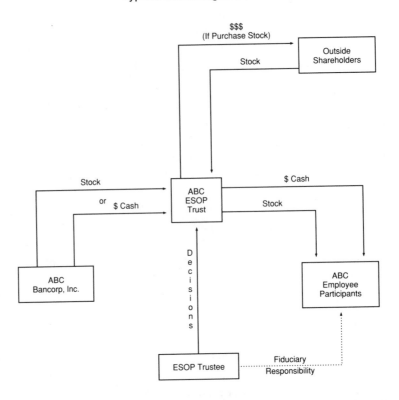

ABC Bancorp, Inc.
Typical Unleveraged ESOP

Upon departure from employment, the ESOP participant has the right to receive ABC stock equivalent in value to her or his vested interest. In virtually all cases, ESOP participants will exercise their option to "put" their shares back to ABC or the ESOP and to receive cash for the shares. If shares are tendered back to ABC, the ESOP participant will normally receive cash at the most recently appraised value of ABC stock. In some cases, ESOP documents allow for the payment of shares by issuing an interest-bearing note.[7]

At this point, we should mention one issue that will be discussed more fully later. The structure of the put option in an ESOP can have an impact on the appraiser's decision regarding the extent of any marketability discount in the annual valuation. Cash distributions upon departure (if an employee exercises the put option) are most favorable from the viewpoints of both the participant and valuation.

The last "player" in the unleveraged (or any) ESOP is the ESOP trustee. Most diagrams of ESOPs leave out a box for the trustee. However, the trustee's role is critical to the successful and lawful operation of an ESOP and should be remembered explicitly. See the discussion below regarding proposed regulations of the Department of Labor and the responsibilities of the ESOP trustee.

---

[7]The terms of distribution of an ESOP participant's benefits must generally begin no later than the last day of the plan year following the plan year of departure from employment, or the fifth year following the year of departure. If a note is provided to an ESOP participant, it must provide for an interest rate approximating market rates and be repaid within a period of five years, unless the participant agrees otherwise.

Figure 16-2

DEF Bancorp, Inc.
Leveraged ESOP for Purchase of Newly Issued Shares

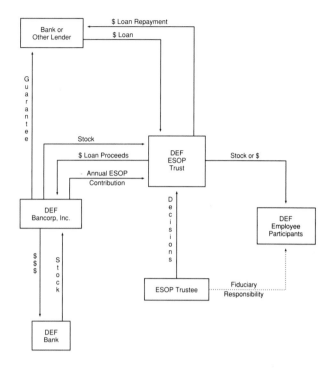

Leveraged ESOP

Leveraged ESOPs are more complicated than unleveraged ESOPs. Figures 16-2 and 16-3 provide examples of how DEF Bancorp, Inc., might establish a leveraged ESOP to inject additional capital into DEF Bank (Figure 16-2) or to acquire a substantial block of stock from an existing shareholder (Figure 16-3). The structures shown in the figures are fairly basic. In real life, leveraged ESOP structures can become quite complex.

Both examples introduce a lending institution. In most cases, the lender would be an upstream correspondent bank servicing a community bank, but other institutional lenders such as insurance companies sometimes make ESOP loans.[8]

Figure 16-2 illustrates the case where DEF Bancorp desires to use a leveraged ESOP to acquire funds to inject (invest) new capital into DEF Bank. As is normal in similar situations, the lender has required a guaranty from DEF as the sponsoring entity. Because of this guaranty and the fact that the ESOP loan's successful amortization is a function of DEF's annual contributions to the DEF ESOP, the ESOP debt is reflected as a liability on the DEF Bancorp's balance sheet in accordance with generally accepted accounting principles and regulatory accounting requirements.[9]

---

[8]For simplicity, Figures 16-2 and 16-3 indicate that the lending financial institution makes a loan directly to the ESOP. In reality, the loan is often made directly to the bank or company sponsoring the ESOP, which then makes a "mirror loan" on the same terms and conditions to the ESOP. In any event, it is the sponsoring entity's annual contributions that are expected to amortize the loan.

[9]See FAS 76-3 of the American Institute of Certified Public Accountants, "Accounting Practices for Certain Employee Stock Ownership Plans," for a discussion of current accounting practices with respect to ESOPs.

Figure 16-3

DEF Bancorp, Inc.
Leveraged ESOP to Purchase Existing Shares

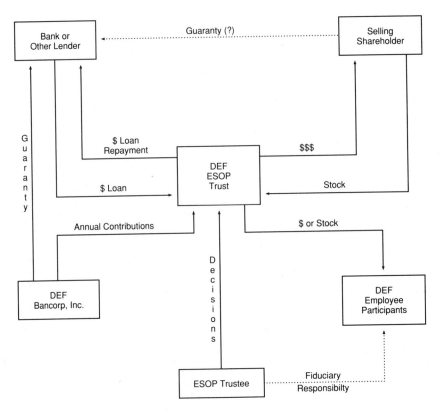

As in the case of ABC Bancorp's unleveraged ESOP, participants will accrue benefits in their ESOP accounts according to DEF's vesting schedule. However, leveraged ESOPs are subject to another complicating factor. Although debt is outstanding on ESOP shares, they are held in what is known as a *suspense account* and are not available to plan participants. Shares are released from the suspense account according to allowable procedures as the ESOP debt is repaid. So an employee's benefits under a leveraged ESOP are subject to a release schedule related to debt amortization as well as to the vesting schedule.

In Figure 16-3, DEF's ESOP acquires shares from existing shareholders using a leveraged ESOP. Instead of purchasing newly issued shares from DEF as in Figure 16-2, the ESOP makes the purchase from one or more existing shareholders. The borrowed funds are used to make the stock acquisition, and DEF's future ESOP contributions will be used to amortize the ESOP debt. A dotted line is shown from the selling shareholder(s) to reflect that, under some circumstances, the financing bank may require a guaranty from them as well as from DEF Bancorp.

The examples of the unleveraged and the leveraged ESOPs are simplified for illustration purposes. The examples do serve, however, to show the basics of how ESOPs work. They also suggest that there is sufficient complexity to ESOPs that banks or other companies considering implementing an ESOP should do so only with competent legal, accounting, and valuation advisors.

Valuation Requirements for ESOPs

The Congress, in the enabling ERISA and tax regulations for ESOPs, has mandated that ESOPs in closely-held entities can only engage in transactions in employer securities when the transaction prices are based upon independent appraisal of the underlying stock. ERISA states in Section 3(18) that fair market value for ESOP transactions should be determined in good faith "and in accordance with regulations promulgated by the Secretary [of Labor]."

Proposed Department of Labor Regulations on Adequate Consideration

In the May 17, 1988, issue of the *Federal Register,* the Department of Labor published proposed regulations that discuss the minimum requirements for the determination of "adequate consideration" in ESOP transactions.[10] The proposed regulation is provided in its entirety as Exhibit 16-1.

While the proposed regulation is not final, most ESOP professionals consider it to represent the current state of thinking of the Department of Labor with respect to valuation issues. While I am not an attorney and this statement does not reflect a legal opinion, it would seem very foolish from a business point of view to engage in ESOP transactions that were inconsistent with the guidance found in the proposed regulation on adequate consideration!

Because of the importance of the proposed regulation, Section B.1., "General Rule and Scope," from the supplementary information prior to the actual proposed regulation, is quoted in its entirety:

> Proposed § 2510.1-18(b)(1)(i) essentially follows the language of section 3(18)(B) of the Act and section 8477(a)(2)(B) of FERSA and states that, in the case of a plan asset other than a security for which there is a generally recognized market, the term "adequate consideration" means the fair market value of the asset as determined in good faith by the trustee or named fiduciary (or, in the case of FERSA, a fiduciary) pursuant to the terms of the plan and in accordance with regulations promulgated by the Secretary of Labor. Proposed § 2510.3-18(b)(1)(ii) delineates the scope of this regulation by establishing two criteria, both of which must be met for a valid determination of adequate consideration. First, the value assigned to an asset must reflect its fair market value as determined pursuant to proposed § 2510.3-18(b)(2). Second, the value assigned to an asset must be the product of a determination made by the fiduciary in good faith as defined in proposed §2510.3-18(b)(3). The Department will consider that a fiduciary has determined adequate consideration in accordance with section 3(18)(B) of the Act or section 8477(a)(2)(B) of FERSA only if both of these requirements are satisfied.
>
> The Department has proposed this two-part test for several reasons. First, Congress incorporated the concept of fair market value into the definition

---

[10]"Proposed Regulation Relating to the Definition of Adequate Consideration, 2510.3-18 Adequate Consideration." Although issuance of final regulations has been expected since 1989, it is unlikely that the final regulations will be issued before mid-1992.

Exhibit 16-1

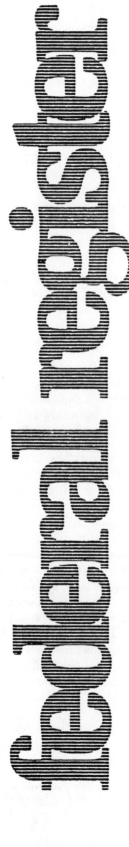

Tuesday
May 17, 1988

Part VI

Department of Labor

Pension and Welfare Benefits
Administration

29 CFR Part 2510
Regulation Relating to the Definition of
Adequate Consideration; Notice of
Proposed Rulemaking

Exhibit 16-1 *(continued)*

DEPARTMENT OF LABOR

Pension and Welfare Benefits Administration

29 CFR Part 2510

Proposed Regulation Relating to the Definition of Adequate Consideration

AGENCY: Pension and Welfare Benefits Administration, Department of Labor.

ACTION: Notice of proposed rulemaking.

SUMMARY: This document contains a notice of a proposed regulation under the Employee Retirement Income Security Act of 1974 (the Act or ERISA) and the Federal Employees' Retirement System Act of 1986 (FERSA). The proposal clarifies the definition of the term "adequate consideration" provided in section 3(18)(B) of the Act and section 8477(a)(2)(B) of FERSA for assets other than securities for which there is a generally recognized market. Section 3(18)(B) and section 8477(a)(2)(B) provide that the term "adequate consideration" for such assets means the fair market value of the asset as determined in good faith by the trustee or named fiduciary (or, in the case of FERSA, a fiduciary) pursuant to the terms of the plan and in accordance with regulations promulgated by the Secretary of Labor. Because valuation questions of this nature arise in a variety of contexts, the Department is proposing this regulation in order to provide the certainty necessary for plan fiduciaries to fulfill their statutory duties. If adopted, the regulation would affect plans investing in assets other than securities for which there is a generally recognized market.

DATES: Written comments on the proposed regulation must be received by July 18, 1988. If adopted, the regulation will be effective for transactions taking place after the date 30 days following publication of the regulation in final form.

ADDRESS: Written comments on the proposed regulation (preferably three copies) should be submitted to: Office of Regulations and Interpretations, Pension and Welfare Benefits Administration, Room N–5671, U.S. Department of Labor, 200 Constitution Avenue NW., Washington, DC 20216, Attention: Adequate Consideration Proposal. All written comments will be available for public inspection at the Public Disclosure Room, Pension and Welfare Benefits Administration, U.S. Department of Labor, Room N–5507, 200 Constitution Avenue NW., Washington, DC.

FOR FURTHER INFORMATION CONTACT: Daniel J. Maguire, Esq., Plan Benefits Security Division, Office of the Solicitor, U.S. Department of Labor, Washington, DC 20210, (202) 523–9596 (not a toll-free number) or Mark A. Greenstein, Office of Regulations and Interpretations, Pension and Welfare Benefits Administration, (202) 523–7901 (not a toll-free number).

SUPPLEMENTARY INFORMATION:

A. Background

Notice is hereby given of a proposed regulation under section 3(18)(B) of the Act and section 8477(a)(2)(B) of FERSA. Section 3(18) of the Act provides the definition for the term "adequate consideration," and states:

The term "adequate consideration" when used in part 4 of subtitle B means (A) in the case of a security for which there is a generally recognized market, either (i) the price of the security prevailing on a national securities exchange which is registered under section 6 of the Securities Exchange Act of 1934, or (ii) if the security is not traded on such a national securities exchange, a price not less favorable to the plan than the offering price for the security as established by the current bid and asked prices quoted by persons independent of the issuer and of any party in interest; and (B) in the case of an asset other than a security for which there is a generally recognized market, the fair market value of the asset as determined in good faith by the trustee or named fiduciary pursuant to the terms of the plan and in accordance with regulations promulgated by the Secretary.

The term "adequate consideration" appears four times in part 4 of subtitle B of Title I of the Act, and each time represents a central requirement for a statutory exemption from the prohibited transaction restrictions of the Act. Under section 408(b)(5), a plan may purchase insurance contracts from certain parties in interest if, among other conditions, the plan pays no more than adequate consideration. Section 408(b)(7) provides that the prohibited transaction provisions of section 406 shall not apply to the exercise of a privilege to convert securities, to the extent provided in regulations of the Secretary of Labor, only if the plan receives no less than adequate consideration pursuant to such conversion. Section 408(e) of the Act provides that the prohibitions in sections 406 and 407(a) of the Act shall not apply to the acquisition or sale by a plan of qualifying employer securities, or the acquisition, sale or lease by a plan of qualifying employer real property if, among other conditions, the acquisition, sale or lease is for adequate consideration. Section 414(c)(5) of the Act states that sections 406 and 407(a)

of the Act shall not apply to the sale, exchange, or other disposition of property which is owned by a plan on June 30, 1974, and all times thereafter, to a party in interest, if such plan is required to dispose of the property in order to comply with the provisions of section 407(a) (relating to the prohibition against holding excess employer securities and employer real property), and if the plan receives not less than adequate consideration.

Public utilization of these statutory exemptions requires a determination of "adequate consideration" in accordance with the definition contained in section 3(18) of the Act. Guidance is especially important in this area because many of the transactions covered by these statutory exemptions involve plan dealings with the plan sponsor. A fiduciary's determination of the adequacy of consideration paid under such circumstances represents a major safeguard for plans against the potential for abuse inherent in such transactions.

The Federal Employees' Retirement System Act of 1986 (FERSA) established the Federal Retirement Thrift Investment Board whose members act as fiduciaries with regard to the assets of the Thrift Savings Fund. In general, FERSA contains fiduciary obligation and prohibited transaction provisions similar to ERISA. However, unlike ERISA, FERSA prohibits party in interest transactions similar to those described in section 406(a) of ERISA only in those circumstances where adequate consideration is not exchanged between the Fund and the party in interest. Specifically, section 8477(c)(1) of FERSA provides that, except in exchange for adequate consideration, a fiduciary shall not permit the Thrift Savings Fund to engage in: transfers of its assets to, acquisition of property from or sales of property to, or transfers or exchanges of services with any person the fiduciary knows or should know to be a party in interest. Section 8477(a)(2) provides the FERSA definition for the term "adequate consideration" which is virtually identical to that contained in section 3(18) of ERISA. Thus, the proposal would apply to both section 3(18) of ERISA and section 8477(a)(2) of FERSA.

When the asset being valued is a security for which there is a generally recognized market, the plan fiduciary must determine "adequate consideration" by reference to the provisions of section 3(18)(A) of the Act (or with regard to FERSA, section 8477(a)(2)(A)). Section 3(18)(A) and section 8477(a)(2)(A) provide detailed reference points for the valuation of

Exhibit 16-1 *(continued)*

securities within its coverage, and in effect provides that adequate consideration for such securities is the prevailing market price. It is not the Department's intention to analyze the requirements of section 3(18)(A) or 8477(a)(2)(A) in this proposal. Fiduciaries must, however, determine whether a security is subject to the specific provisions of section 3(18)(A) (or section 8477(a)(2)(A) of FERSA) or the more general requirements of section 3(18)(B) (or section 8477(a)(2)(B)) as interpreted in this proposal. The question of whether a security is one for which there is a generally recognized market requires a factual determination in light of the character of the security and the nature and extent of market activity with regard to the security. Generally, the Department will examine whether a security is being actively traded so as to provide the benchmarks Congress intended. Isolated trading activity, or trades between related parties, generally will not be sufficient to show the existence of a generally recognized market for the purposes of section 3(18)(A) or section 8477(a)(2)(A).

In the case of all assets other than securities for which there is a generally recognized market, fiduciaries must determine adequate consideration pursuant to section 3(18)(B) of the Act (or, in the case of FERSA, section 8477(a)(2)(B)). Because it is designed to deal with all but a narrow class of assets, section 3(18)(B) and section 8477(a)(2)(B) are by their nature more general than section 3(18)(A) or section 8477(a)(2)(A). Although the Department has indicated that it will not issue advisory opinions stating whether certain stated consideration is "adequate consideration" for the purposes of section 3(18), ERISA Procedure 76-1, § 5.02(a) (41 FR 36281, 36282, August 27, 1976), the Department recognizes that plan fiduciaries have a need for guidance in valuing assets, and that standards to guide fiduciaries in this area may be particularly elusive with respect to assets other than securities for which there is a generally recognized market. *See*, for example, *Donovan v. Cunningham*, 716 F.2d 1455 (5th Cir. 1983) (court encourages the Department to adopt regulations under section 3(18)(B)). The Department has therefore determined to propose a regulation only under section 3(18)(B) and section 8477(a)(2)(B). This proposal is described more fully below.

It should be noted that it is not the Department's intention by this proposed regulation to relieve fiduciaries of the responsibility for making the required determinations of "adequate

consideration" where applicable under the Act or FERSA. Nothing in the proposal should be construed as justifying a fiduciary's failure to take into account all relevant facts and circumstances in determining adequate consideration. Rather, the proposal is designed to provide a framework within which fiduciaries can fulfill their statutory duties. Further, fiduciaries should be aware that, even where a determination of adequate consideration comports with the requirements of section 3(18)(B) (or section 8477(a)(2)(B) of FERSA) and any regulation adopted thereunder, the investment of plan assets made pursuant to such determination will still be subject to the fiduciary requirements of Part 4 of Subtitle B of Title I of the Act, including the provisions of sections 403 and 404 of the Act, or the fiduciary responsibility provisions of FERSA.

B. Description of the Proposal

Proposed regulation 29 CFR 2510.3-18(b) is divided into four major parts. Proposed § 2510.3-18(b)(1) states the general rule and delineates the scope of the regulation. Proposed § 2510.3-18(b)(2) addresses the concept of fair market value as it relates to a determination of "adequate consideration" under section 3(18)(B) of the Act. Proposed § 2510.3-18(b)(3) deals with the requirement in section 3(18)(B) that valuing fiduciary act in good faith, and specifically discusses the use of an independent appraisal in connection with the determination of good faith. Proposed § 2510.3-18(b)(4) sets forth the content requirements for written valuations used as the basis for a determination of fair market value, with a special rule for the valuation of securities other than securities for which there is a generally recognized market. Each subsection is discussed in detail below.

1. General Rule and Scope.

Proposed § 2510.3-18(b)(1)(i) essentially follows the language of section 3(18)(B) of the Act and section 8477(a)(2)(B) of FERSA and states that, in the case of a plan asset other than a security for which there is a generally recognized market, the term "adequate consideration" means the fair market value of the asset as determined in good faith by the trustee or named fiduciary (or, in the case of FERSA, a fiduciary) pursuant to the terms of the plan and in accordance with regulations promulgated by the Secretary of Labor. Proposed § 2510.3-18(b)(1)(ii) delineates the scope of this regulation by establishing two criteria, both of which must be met for a valid determination of

adequate consideration. First, the value assigned to an asset must reflect its fair market value as determined pursuant to proposed § 2510.3-18(b)(2). Second, the value assigned to an asset must be the product of a determination made by the fiduciary in good faith as defined in proposed § 2510.3-18(b)(3). The Department will consider that a fiduciary has determined adequate consideration in accordance with section 3(18)(B) of the Act or section 8477(a)(2)(B) of FERSA only if both of these requirements are satisfied.

The Department has proposed this two part test for several reasons. First, Congress incorporated the concept of fair market value into the definition of adequate consideration. As explained more fully below, fair market value is an often used concept having an established meaning in the field of asset valuation. By reference to this term, it would appear that Congress did not intend to allow parties to a transaction to set an arbitrary value for the assets involved. Therefore, a valuation determination which fails to reflect the market forces embodied in the concept of fair market value would also fail to meet the requirements of section 3(18)(B) of the Act or section 8477(a)(2)(B) of FERSA.

Second, it would appear that Congress intended to allow a fiduciary a limited degree of latitude so long as that fiduciary acted in good faith. However, a fiduciary would clearly fail to fulfill the fiduciary duties delineated in Part 4 of Subtitle B of Title I of the Act if that fiduciary acted solely on the basis of naive or uninformed good intentions. *See Donovan v. Cunningham, supra,* 716 F.2d at 1467 ("[A] pure heart and an empty head are not enough.") The Department has therefore proposed standards for a determination of a fiduciary's good faith which must be satisfied in order to meet the requirements of section 3(18)(B) or section 8477(a)(2)(B) of FERSA.

Third, even if a fiduciary were to meet the good faith standards contained in this proposed regulation, there may be circumstances in which good faith alone fails to insure an equitable result. For example, errors in calculation or honest failure to consider certain information could produce valuation figures outside of the range of acceptable valuations of a given asset. Because the determination of adequate consideration is a central requirement of the statutory exemptions discussed above, the Department believes it must assure that such exemptions are made available only for those transactions possessing all the external safeguards envisioned by

Exhibit 16-1 (*continued*)

17634   Federal Register / Vol. 53, No. 95 / Tuesday, May 17, 1988 / Proposed Rules

Congress. To achieve this end, the Department's proposed regulation links the fair market value and good faith requirements to assure that the resulting valuation reflects market considerations and is the product of a valuation process conducted in good faith.

2. Fair Market Value

The first part of the Department's proposed two part test under section 3(18)(B) and section 8477(a)(2)(B) requires that a determination of adequate consideration reflect the asset's fair market value. The term "fair market value" is defined in proposed § 2510.3–18(b)(2)(i) as the price at which an asset would change hands between a willing buyer and a willing seller when the former is not under any compulsion to buy and the latter is not under any compulsion to sell, and both parties are able, as well as willing, to trade and are well-informed about the asset and the market for that asset. This proposed definition essentially reflects the well-established meaning of this term in the area of asset valuation. *See,* for example, 26 CFR 20.2031–1 (estate tax regulations); Rev. Rul. 59–60, 1959–1 Cum. Bull. 237; *United States v. Cartwright*, 411 U.S. 546, 551 (1973); *Estate of Bright v. United States*, 658 F.2d 999, 1005 (5th Cir. 1981). It should specifically be noted that comparable valuations reflecting transactions resulting from other than free and equal negotiations (*e.g.,* a distress sale) will fail to establish fair market value. *See Hooker Industries, Inc. v. Commissioner*, 3 EBC 1849, 1854–55 (T.C. June 24, 1982). Similarly, the extent to which the Department will view a valuation as reflecting fair market value will be affected by an assessment of the level of expertise demonstrated by the parties making the valuation. *See Donovan v. Cunningham, supra,* 716 F.2d at 1468 (failure to apply sound business principles of evaluation, for whatever reason, may result in a valuation that does not reflect fair market value).[1]

The Department is aware that the fair market value of an asset will ordinarily be identified by a range of valuations rather than a specific, set figure. It is not the Department's intention that only one valuation figure will be acceptable as the fair market value of a specified asset. Rather, this proposal would require that the valuation assigned to an asset must reflect a figure within an acceptable range of valuations for that asset.

In addition to this general formulation of the definition of fair market value, the Department is proposing two specific requirements for the determination of fair market value for the purposes of section 3(18)(B) and section 8477(a)(2)(B). First, proposed § 2510.3–18(b)(2)(ii) requires that fair market value must be determined as of the date of the transaction involving that asset. This requirement is designed to prevent situations such as arose in *Donovan v. Cunningham, supra.* In that case, the plan fiduciaries relied on a 1975 appraisal to set the value of employer securities purchased by an ESOP during 1976 and thereafter, and failed to take into account significant changes in the company's business condition in the interim. The court found that this reliance was unwarranted, and therefore the fiduciaries' valuation failed to reflect adequate consideration under section 3(18)(B). *Id.* at 1468–69.

Second, proposed § 2510.3–18(b)(2)(iii) states that the determination of fair market value must be reflected in written documentation of valuation [2] meeting the content requirements set forth in § 2510.3–18(b)(4). (The valuation content requirements are discussed below.) The Department has proposed this requirement in light of the role the adequate consideration requirement plays in a number of statutory exemptions from the prohibited transaction provisions of the Act. In determining whether a statutory exemption applies to a particular transaction, the burden of proof is upon the party seeking to make use of the statutory exemption to show that all the requirements of the provision are met. *Donovan v. Cunningham, supra,* 716 F.2d

at 1467 n.27. In the Department's view, written documentation relating to the valuation is necessary for a determination of how, and on what basis, an asset was valued, and therefore whether that valuation reflected an asset's fair market value. In addition, the Department believes that it would be contrary to prudent business practices for a fiduciary to act in the absence of such written documentation of fair market value.

3. Good Faith

The second part of the Department's proposed two-part test under section 3(18)(B) and section 8477(a)(2)(B) requires that an assessment of adequate consideration be the product of a determination made in good faith by the plan trustee or named fiduciary (or under FERSA, a fiduciary). Proposed § 2510.3–18(b)(3)(i) states that as a general matter this good faith requirement establishes an objective standard of conduct, rather than mandating an inquiry into the intent or state of mind of the plan trustee or named fiduciary. In this regard, the proposal is consistent with the opinion in *Donovan v. Cunningham, supra,* where the court stated that the good faith requirement in section 3(18)(B):

is not a search for subjective good faith * * * The statutory reference to good faith in Section 3(18) must be read in light of the overriding duties of Section 404.

716 F.2d at 1467. The inquiry into good faith under the proposal therefore focuses on the fiduciary's conduct in determining fair market value. An examination of all relevant facts and circumstances is necessary for a determination of whether a fiduciary has met this objective good faith standard.

Proposed § 2510.3–18(b)(3)(ii) focuses on two factors which must be present in order for the Department to be satisfied that the fiduciary has acted in good faith. First, this section would require a fiduciary to apply sound business principles of evaluation and to conduct a prudent investigation of the circumstances prevailing at the time of the valuation. This requirement reflects the *Cunningham* court's emphasis on the use of prudent business practices in valuing plan assets.

Second, this section states that either the fiduciary making the valuation must itself be independent of all the parties to the transaction (other than the plan), or the fiduciary must rely on the report of an appraiser who is independent of all the parties to the transaction (other than the plan). (The criteria for determining

---

[1] Whether in any particular transaction a plan fiduciary is in fact well-informed about the asset in question and the market for that asset, including any specific circumstances which may affect the value of the asset, will be determined on a facts and circumstances basis. If, however, the fiduciary negotiating on behalf of the plan has or should have specific knowledge concerning either the particular asset or the market for that asset, it is the view of the Department that the fiduciary must take into account that specific knowledge in negotiating the price of the asset in order to meet the fair market value standard of this regulation. For example, a sale of plan-owned real estate at a negotiated price consistent with valuations of comparable property will not be a sale for adequate consideration if the negotiating fiduciary does not take into account any special knowledge which he has or should have about the asset or its market, *e.g.,* that the

property's value should reflect a premium due to a certain developer's specific land development plans.

[2] It should be noted that the written valuation required by this section of the proposal need not be a written report of an independent appraiser. Rather, it should be documentation sufficient to allow the Department to determine whether the content requirements of § 2510.3–18(b)(4) have been satisfied. The use of an independent appraiser may be relevant to a determination of good faith, as discussed with regard to proposed § 2510.3–18(b)(3), *infra,* but it is not required to satisfy the fair market value criterion in § 2510.3–18(b)(2)(i).

Exhibit 16-1 (*continued*)

independence are discussed below.) As noted above, under ERISA, the determination of adequate consideration is a central safeguard in many statutory exemptions applicable to plan transactions with the plan sponsor. The close relationship between the plan and the plan sponsor in such situations raises a significant potential for conflicts of interest as the fiduciary values assets which are the subject of transactions between the plan and the plan sponsor. In light of this possibility, the Department believes that good faith may only be demonstrated when the valuation is made by persons independent of the parties to the transaction (other than the plan), *i.e.*, a valuation made by an independent fiduciary or by a fiduciary acting pursuant to the report of an independent appraiser.

The Department emphasizes that the two requirements of proposed § 2510.3–18(b)(3)(ii) are designed to work in concert. For example, a plan fiduciary charged with valuation may be independent of all the parties to a transaction and may, in light of the requirement of proposed § 2510.3–18(b)(3)(ii)(B), decide to undertake the valuation process itself. However, if the independent fiduciary has neither the experience, facilities nor expertise to make the type of valuation under consideration, the decision by that fiduciary to make the valuation would fail to meet the prudent investigation and sound business principles requirement of proposed § 2510.3–18(b)(3)(ii)(A).

Proposed § 2510.3–18(b)(3)(iii) defines the circumstances under which a fiduciary or an appraiser will be deemed to be independent for the purposes of subparagraph (3)(ii)(B), above. The proposal notes that the fiduciary or the appraiser must in fact be independent of all parties participating in the transaction other than the plan. The proposal also notes that a determination of independence must be made in light of all relevant facts and circumstances, and then delineates certain circumstances under which this independence will be lacking. These circumstances reflect the definitions of the terms "affiliate" and "control" in Departmental regulation 29 CFR 2510.3–21(e) (defining the circumstances under which an investment adviser is a fiduciary). It should be noted that, under these proposed provisions, an appraiser will be considered independent of all parties to a transaction (other than the plan) only if a plan fiduciary has chosen the appraiser and has the right to terminate that appointment, and the

plan is thereby established as the appraiser's client.[3] Absent such circumstances, the appraiser may be unable to be completely neutral in the exercise of his function.[4]

4. Valuation Content—General

Proposed § 2510.3–18(b)(4)(i) sets the content requirements for the written documentation of valuation required for a determination of fair market value under proposed § 2510.3–18(b)(2)(iii). The proposal follows to a large extent the requirements of Rev. Proc. 66–49, 1966–2 C.B. 1257, which sets forth the format required by the IRS for the valuation of donated property. The Department believes that this format is a familiar one, and will therefore facilitate compliance. Several additions to the IRS requirements merit brief explanation.

First, proposed paragraph (b)(4)(i)(E) requires a statement of the purpose for which the valuation was made. A valuation undertaken, for example, for a yearly financial report may prove an inadequate basis for any sale of the asset in question. This requirement is intended to facilitate review of the valuation in the correct context.

Second, proposed paragraph (b)(4)(i)(F) requires a statement as to the relative weight accorded to relevant valuation methodologies. The Department's experience in this area indicates that there are a number of different methodologies used within the appraisal industry. By varying the treatment given and emphasis accorded relevant information, these methodologies directly affect the result of the appraiser's analysis. It is the Department's understanding that appraisers will often use different methodologies to cross-check their results. A statement of the method or methods used would allow for a more accurate assessment of the validity of the valuation.

---

[3] The independence of an appraiser will not be affected solely because the plan sponsor pays the appraiser's fee.

[4] With regard to this independence requirement the Department notes that new section 401(a)(28) of the Code (added by section 1175(a) of the Tax Reform Act of 1986) requires that, in the case of an employee stock ownership plan, employer securities which are not readily tradable on established securities markets must be valued by an independent appraiser. New section 401(a)(28)(C) states that the term "independent appraiser" means an appraiser meeting requirements similar to the requirements of regulations under section 170(a)(1) of the Code (relating to IRS verification of the value assigned for deduction purposes to assets donated to charitable organizations). The Department notes that the requirements of proposed regulation § 2510.3–18(b)(3)(iii) are not the same as the requirements of the regulations issued by the IRS under section 170(a)(1) of the Code. The IRS has not yet promulgated rules under Code section 401(a)(28).

Finally, proposed subparagraph (b)(4)(i)(G) requires a statement of the valuation's effective date. This reflects the requirement in proposed § 2510.3–18(b)(ii) that fair market value must be determined as of the date of the transaction in question.

5. Valuation Content—Special Rule

Proposed § 2510.3–18(b)(4)(ii) establishes additional content requirements for written documentation of valuation when the asset being appraised is a security other than a security for which there is a generally recognized market. In other words, the requirements of the proposed special rule supplement, rather than supplant, the requirements of paragraph (b)(4)(i). The proposed special rule establishes a nonexclusive list of factors to be considered when the asset being valued is a security not covered by section 3(18)(A) of the Act or section 8477(a)(2)(A) of FERSA. Such securities pose special valuation problems because they are not traded or are so thinly traded that it is difficult to assess the effect on such securities of the market forces usually considered in determining fair market value. The Internal Revenue Service has had occasion to address the valuation problems posed by one type of such securities—securities issued by closely held corporations. Rev. Rul. 59–60, 1959–1 Cum. Bull. 237, lists a variety of factors to be considered when valuing securities of closely held corporations for tax purposes.[5] The Department's experience indicates that Rev. Rul. 59–60 is familiar to plan fiduciaries, plan sponsors and the corporate community in general. The Department has, therefore, modeled this proposed special rule after Rev. Rul. 59–60 with certain additions and changes discussed below. It should be emphasized, however, that this is a non-exclusive list of factors to be considered. Certain of the factors listed may not be relevant to every valuation inquiry, although the fiduciary will bear the burden of demonstrating such irrelevance. Similarly, reliance on this list will not relieve fiduciaries from the duty to consider all relevant facts and circumstances when valuing such securities. The purpose of the proposed

---

[5] Rev. Rul. 59–60 was modified by Rev. Rul. 65–193 (1965–2 C.B. 370) regarding the valuation of tangible and intangible corporate assets. The provisions of Rev. Rul. 59–60, as modified, were extended to the valuation of corporate securities for income and other tax purposes by Rev. Rul. 68–609 (1968–2 C.B. 327). In addition, Rev. Rul. 77–287 (1977–2 C.B. 319). amplified. Rev. Rul. 59–60 by indicating the ways in which the factors listed in Rev. Rul. 59–60 should be applied when valuing restricted securities.

Exhibit 16-1 (*continued*)

17636   Federal Register / Vol. 53, No. 95 / Tuesday, May 17, 1988 / Proposed Rules

list is to guide fiduciaries in the course of their inquiry.

Several of the factors listed in proposed § 2510.3–18(b)(4)(ii) merit special comment and explanation. Proposed subparagraph (G) states that the fair market value of securities other than those for which there is a generally recognized market may be established by reference to the market price of similar securities of corporations engaged in the same or a similar line of business whose securities are actively traded in a free and open market, either on an exchange or over the counter. The Department intends that the degree of comparability must be assessed in order to approximate as closely as possible the market forces at work with regard to the corporation issuing the securities in question.

Proposed subparagraph (H) requires an assessment of the effect of the securities' marketability or lack thereof. Rev. Rul. 59–60 does not explicitly require such an assessment, but the Department believes that the marketability of these types of securities will directly affect their price. In this regard, the Department is aware that, especially in situations involving employee stock ownership plans (ESOPs),[6] the employer securities held by the ESOP will provide a "put" option whereby individual participants may upon retirement sell their shares back to the employer.[7] It has been argued that some kinds of "put" options may diminish the need to discount the value of the securities due to lack of marketability. The Department believes that the existence of the "put" option should be considered for valuation purposes only to the extent it is enforceable and the employer has and may reasonably be expected to continue to have, adequate resources to meet its obligations. Thus, the Department proposes to require that the plan fiduciary assess whether these "put" rights are actually enforceable, and whether the employer will be able to pay for the securities when and if the "put" is exercised.

Finally, proposed subparagraph (I) deals with the role of control premiums in valuing securities other than those for

which there is a generally recognized market. The Department proposes that a plan purchasing control may pay a control premium, and a plan selling control should receive a control premium. Specifically, the Department proposes that a plan may pay such a premium only to the extent a third party would pay a control premium. In this regard, the Department's position is that the payment of a control premium is unwarranted unless the plan obtains both voting control and control in fact. The Department will therefore carefully scrutinize situations to ascertain whether the transaction involving payment of such a premium actually results in the passing of control to the plan. For example, it may be difficult to determine that a plan paying a control premium has received control in fact where it is reasonable to assume at the time of acquisition that distribution of shares to plan participants will cause the plan's control of the company to be dissipated within a short period of time subsequent to acquisition.[8] In the Department's view, however, a plan would not fail to receive control merely because individuals who were previously officers, directors or shareholders of the corporation continue as plan fiduciaries or corporate officials after the plan has acquired the securities. Nonetheless, the retention of management and the utilization of corporate officials as plan fiduciaries, when viewed in conjunction with other facts, may indicate that actual control has not passed to the plan within the meaning of paragraph (b)(4)(ii)(I) of the proposed regulation. Similarly, if the plan purchases employer securities in small increments pursuant to an understanding with the employer that the employer will eventually sell a controlling portion of shares to the plan, a control premium would be warranted only to the extent that the understanding with the employer was actually a binding agreement obligating the employer to pass control within a reasonable time. *See Donovan* v. *Cunningham, supra,* 716 F.2d at 1472–74 (mere intention to transfer control not sufficient).

6. Service Arrangements Subject to FERSA

Section 8477(c)(1)(C) of FERSA permits the exchange of services between the Thrift Savings Fund and a party in interest only in exchange for adequate consideration. In this context, the proposal defines the term "adequate consideration as "reasonable compensation", as that term is described in sections 408(b)(2) and 408(c)(2) of ERISA and the regulations promulgated thereunder. By so doing, the proposal would establish a consistent standard of exemptive relief for both ERISA and FERSA with regard to what otherwise would be prohibited service arrangements.

Regulatory Flexibility Act

The Department has determined that this regulation would not have a significant economic effect on small plans. In conducting the analysis required under the Regulatory Flexibility Act, it was estimated that approximately 6,250 small plans may be affected by the regulation. The total additional cost to these plans, over and above the costs already being incurred under established valuation practices, are estimated not to exceed $875,000 per year, or $140 per plan for small plans choosing to engage in otherwise prohibited transactions that are exempted under the statute conditioned on a finding of adequate consideration.

Executive Order 12291

The Department has determined that the proposed regulatory action would not constitute a "major rule" as that term is used in Executive Order 12291 because the action would not result in: an annual effect on the economy of $100 million; a major increase in costs of prices for consumers, individual industries, government agencies, or geographical regions; or significant adverse effects on competition, employment, investment, productivity, innovation, or on the ability of United States based enterprises to compete with foreign based enterprises in domestic or export markets.

Paperwork Reduction Act

This proposed regulation contains several paperwork requirements. The regulation has been forwarded for approval to the Office of Management and Budget under the provisions of the Paperwork Reduction Act of 1980 (Pub. L. 96–511). A control number has not yet been assigned.

---

[6] The definition of the term "adequate consideration" under ERISA is of particular importance to the establishment and maintenance of ESOPs because, pursuant to section 408(e) of the Act, an ESOP may acquire employer securities from a party in interest only under certain conditions, including that the plan pay no more than adequate consideration for the securities.

[7] Regulation 29 CFR 2550.408b–(j) requires such a put option in order for a loan from a party in interest to the ESOP to qualify for the statutory exemption in section 408(b)(3) of ERISA from the prohibited transactions provisions of ERISA.

---

[8] However, the Department notes that the mere pass-through of voting rights to participants would not in itself affect a determination that a plan has received control in fact, notwithstanding the existence of participant voting rights, if the plan fiduciaries having control over plan assets ordinarily may resell the shares to a third party and command a control premium, without the need to secure the approval of the plan participants.

Exhibit 16-1 (*continued*)

Federal Register / Vol. 53, No. 95 / Tuesday, May 17, 1988 / Proposed Rules   **17637**

Statutory Authority

This regulation is proposed under section 3(18) and 505 of the Act (29 U.S.C. 1003(18) and 1135); Secretary of Labor's Order No. 1–87; and sections 8477(a)(2)(B) and 8477(f) of FERSA.

List of Subjects in 29 CFR Part 2510

Employee benefit plans, Employee Retirement Income Security Act, Pensions, Pension and Welfare Benefit Administration.

Proposed Regulation

For the reasons set out in the preamble, the Department proposes to amend Part 2510 of Chapter XXV of Title 29 of the Code of Federal Regulations as follows:

PART 2510—[AMENDED]

1. The authority for Part 2510 is revised to read as follows:

Authority: Sec. 3(2), 111(c), 505, Pub. L. 93–406, 88 Stat. 852, 894, (29 U.S.C. 1002(2), 1031, 1135); Secretary of Labor's Order No. 27–74, 1–86, 1–87, and Labor Management Services Administration Order No. 2–6.

Section 2510.3–18 is also issued under sec. 3(18) of the Act (29 U.S.C. 1003(18)) and secs. 8477(a)(2)(B) and (f) of FERSA (5 U.S.C. 8477)

Section 2510.3–101 is also issued under sec. 102 of Reorganization Plan No. 4 of 1978 (43 FR 47713, October 17, 1978), effective December 31, 1978 (44 FR 1065, January 3, 1978); 3 CFR 1978 Comp. 332, and sec. 11018(d) of Pub. L. 99–272, 100 Stat. 82.

Section 2510.3–102 is also issued under sec. 102 of Reorganization Plan No. 4 of 1978 (43 FR 47713, October 17, 1978), effective December 31, 1978 (44 FR 1065, January 3, 1978), and 3 CFR 1978 Comp. 332.

2. Section 2510.3–18 is added to read as follows:

§ 2510.3–18 Adequate Consideration

(a) [Reserved]

(b)(1)(i) *General.* (A) Section 3(18)(B) of the Employee Retirement Income Security Act of 1974 (the Act) provides that, in the case of a plan asset other than a security for which there is a generally recognized market, the term "adequate consideration" when used in Part 4 of Subtitle B of Title I of the Act means the fair market value of the asset as determined in good faith by the trustee or named fiduciary pursuant to the terms of the plan and in accordance with regulations promulgated by the Secretary of Labor.

(B) Section 8477(a)(2)(B) of the Federal Employees' Retirement System Act of 1986 (FERSA) provides that, in the case of an asset other than a security for which there is a generally recognized market, the term "adequate consideration" means the fair market value of the asset as determined in good

faith by a fiduciary or fiduciaries in accordance with regulations prescribed by the Secretary of Labor.

(ii) *Scope.* The requirements of section 3(18)(B) of the Act and section 8477(a)(2)(B) of FERSA will not be met unless the value assigned to a plan asset both reflects the asset's fair market value as defined in paragraph (b)(2) of this section and results from a determination made by the plan trustee or named fiduciary (or, in the case of FERSA, a fiduciary) in good faith as described in paragraph (b)(3) of this section. Paragraph (b)(5) of this section contains a special rule for service contracts subject to FERSA.

(2) *Fair Market Value.* (i) Except as otherwise specified in this section, the term "fair market value" as used in section 3(18)(B) of the Act and section 8477(a)(2)(B) of FERSA means the price at which an asset would change hands between a willing buyer and a willing seller when the former is not under any compulsion to buy and the latter is not under any compulsion to sell, and both parties are able, as well as willing, to trade and are well informed about the asset and the market for such asset.

(ii) The fair market value of an asset for the purposes of section 3(18)(B) of the Act and section 8477(a)(2)(B) of FERSA must be determined as of the date of the transaction involving that asset.

(iii) The fair market value of an asset for the purposes of section 3(18)(B) of the Act and section 8477(a)(2)(B) of FERSA must be reflected in written documentation of valuation meeting the requirements set forth in paragraph (b)(4), of this section.

(3) *Good Faith—*(i) *General Rule.* The requirement in section 3(18)(B) of the Act and section 8477(a)(2)(B) of FERSA that the fiduciary must determine fair market value in good faith establishes an objective, rather than a subjective, standard of conduct. Subject to the conditions in paragraphs (b)(3) (ii) and (iii) of this section, an assessment of whether the fiduciary has acted in good faith will be made in light of all relevant facts and circumstances.

(ii) In considering all relevant facts and circumstances, the Department will not view a fiduciary as having acted in good faith unless

(A) The fiduciary has arrived at a determination of fair market value by way of a prudent investigation of circumstances prevailing at the time of the valuation, and the application of sound business principles of evaluation; and

(B) The fiduciary making the valuation either,

(1) Is independent of all parties to the transaction (other than the plan), or

(2) Relies on the report of an appraiser who is independent of all parties to the transaction (other than the plan).

(iii) In order to satisfy the independence requirement of paragraph (b)(3)(ii)(B), of this section, a person must in fact be independent of all parties (other than the plan) participating in the transaction. For the purposes of this section, an assessment of independence will be made in light of all relevant facts and circumstances. However, a person will not be considered to be independent of all parties to the transaction if that person—

(1) Is directly or indirectly, through one or more intermediaries, controlling, controlled by, or under common control with any of the parties to the transaction (other than the plan);

(2) Is an officer, director, partner, employee, employer or relative (as defined in section 3(15) of the Act, and including siblings) of any such parties (other than the plan);

(3) Is a corporation or partnership of which any such party (other than the plan) is an officer, director or partner.

For the purposes of this subparagraph, the term "control," in connection with a person other than an individual, means the power to exercise a controlling influence over the management or policies of that person.

(4) *Valuation Content.* (i) In order to comply with the requirement in paragraph (b)(2)(iii), of this section, that the determination of fair market value be reflected in written documentation of valuation, such written documentation must contain, at a minimum, the following information:

(A) A summary of the qualifications to evaluate assets of the type being valued of the person or persons making the valuation;

(B) A statement of the asset's value, a statement of the methods used in determining that value, and the reasons for the valuation in light of those methods;

(C) A full description of the asset being valued;

(D) The factors taken into account in making the valuation, including any restrictions, understandings, agreements or obligations limiting the use or disposition of the property;

(E) The purpose for which the valuation was made;

(F) The relevance or significance accorded to the valuation methodologies taken into account;

(G) The effective date of the valuation; and

Exhibit 16-1 *(continued)*

(H) In cases where a valuation report has been prepared, the signature of the person making the valuation and the date the report was signed.

(ii) *Special Rule.* When the asset being valued is a security other than a security covered by section 3(18)(A) of the Act or section 8477(a)(2)(A) of FERSA, the written valuation required by paragraph (b)(2)(iii) of this section, must contain the information required in paragraph (b)(4)(i) of this section, and must include, in addition to an assessment of all other relevant factors, an assessment of the factors listed below:

(A) The nature of the business and the history of the enterprise from its inception;

(B) The economic outlook in general, and the condition and outlook of the specific industry in particular;

(C) The book value of the securities and the financial condition of the business;

(D) The earning capacity of the company;

(E) The dividend-paying capacity of the company;

(F) Whether or not the enterprise has goodwill or other intangible value;

(G) The market price of securities of corporations engaged in the same or a similar line of business, which are actively traded in a free and open market, either on an exchange or over-the-counter;

(H) The marketability, or lack thereof, of the securities. Where the plan is the purchaser of securities that are subject to "put" rights and such rights are taken into account in reducing the discount for lack of marketability, such assessment shall include consideration of the extent to which such rights are enforceable, as well as the company's ability to meet its obligations with respect to the "put" rights (taking into account the company's financial strength and liquidity);

(I) Whether or not the seller would be able to obtain a control premium from an unrelated third party with regard to the block of securities being valued, provided that in cases where a control premium is taken into account:

(1) Actual control (both in form and in substance) is passed to the purchaser with the sale, or will be passed to the purchaser within a reasonable time pursuant to a binding agreement in effect at the time of the sale, and

(2) It is reasonable to assume that the purchaser's control will not be dissipated within a short period of time subsequent to acquisition.

(5) *Service Arrangements Subject to FERSA.* For purposes of determinations pursuant to section 8477(c)(1)(C) of FERSA (relating to the provision of services) the term "adequate consideration" under section 8477(a)(2)(B) of FERSA means "reasonable compensation" as defined in sections 408(b)(2) and 408(c)(2) of the Act and §§ 2550.408b–2(d) and 2550.408c–2 of this chapter.

(6) *Effective Date.* This section will be effective for transactions taking place after the date 30 days following publication of the final regulation in the Federal Register.

Signed in Washington, DC, this 11th day of May 1988.

David M. Walker,

Assistant Secretary, Pension and Welfare Benefits Administration, U.S. Department of Labor.

[FR Doc. 88–10934 Filed 5–16–88; 8:45 am]

BILLING CODE 4510–29–M

of adequate consideration. As explained more fully below, fair market value is an often used concept having an established meaning in the field of asset valuation. By reference to this term, it would appear that Congress did not intend to allow parties to a transaction to set an arbitrary value for the assets involved. Therefore, a valuation determination which fails to reflect the market forces embodied in the concept of fair market value would also fail to meet the requirements of section 3(18)(B) of the Act or section 8477(a)(2)(B) of FERSA.

Second, it would appear that Congress intended to allow a fiduciary a limited degree of latitude so long as that fiduciary acted in good faith. However, a fiduciary would clearly fail to fulfill the fiduciary duties delineated in Part 4 of Subtitle B of Title I of the Act if that fiduciary acted solely on the basis of naive or uninformed good intentions. See *Donavan v. Cunningham, supra,* 716 F2d at 1467 ("[A] pure heart and an empty head are not enough.") The Department has therefore proposed standards for a determination of a fiduciary's good faith which must be satisfied in order to meet the requirements of section 3(18)(B) or section 8477(a)(2)(B) of FERSA.

Third, even if a fiduciary were to meet the good-faith standards contained in this proposed regulation, there may be circumstances in which good faith alone fails to ensure an equitable result. For example, errors in calculation or honest failure to consider certain information could produce valuation figures outside of the range of acceptable valuations of a given asset. Because the determination of adequate consideration is a central requirement of the statutory exemptions discussed above, the Department believes it must assure that such exemptions are made available only for those transactions possessing all the external safeguards envisioned by Congress. *To achieve this end, the Department's proposed regulation links the fair market value and good-faith requirements to assure that the resulting valuation reflects market considerations and is the product of a valuation process conducted in good faith [emphasis added].*

The Department of Labor recognizes the clear potential for conflict between ESOP fiduciaries, many of which are the key officers or employees, the interests of the bank or company, and ESOP employee beneficiaries. In another portion of the supplementary information, the Department suggests the responsibility of the ESOP fiduciary to *negotiate* on behalf of the ESOP in transactions with all information available to the fiduciary:

Whether in any particular transaction a plan fiduciary is in fact well-informed about the asset in question and the market for that asset, including any specific circumstances which may affect the value of the asset, will be determined on a facts and circumstances basis; if, however, the fiduciary negotiating on behalf of the plan has or should have specific knowledge concerning either the particular asset or the market for that asset, it is the view of the Department that *the fiduciary must take into account that specific knowledge in negotiating the price of the asset in order to meet the fair market value standard of this regulation* [emphasis added].

The proposed regulation addresses several other key issues relative to the issue of valuation, including:

1. Qualifications of appraisers for ESOP valuations. Basically, the requirement for qualifications falls back to tax regulations related to valuation qualifications for charitable gifts. These regulations state that a qualified appraiser is one who (a) customarily holds himself or herself out to the public as an appraiser, (b) can state he or she is qualified to make the subject appraisal, (c) is adequately independent with respect to the transaction to render an opinion (and a reasonable person reviewing the situation would reach the same conclusion), and (d) understands the implications of a false or fraudulent overstatement of the value of the subject property. (See also the section below titled "Qualifications of Appraisers.")

2. Documentation requirements for ESOP valuations. The proposed regulation does not explicitly require that a written appraisal report be prepared to justify ESOP transactions, but it would be virtually impossible to meet the requirements for consideration (and to be able to document that consideration) without the preparation of a fully documented valuation report.

3. Regarding timing of required appraisals, the proposed regulation states that valuations involving insiders must be *as of the date of such transactions.* In practical usage, most ESOPs obtain annual independent appraisal as of their plan year-ends and separate appraisals as of the date of prohibited transactions that may occur between annual appraisals.

4. Additional factors that must be considered in a determination of adequate consideration, and therefore in an ESOP appraisal, that relate to the ESOP itself. These issues relate specifically to the questions of whether an ESOP can pay a control premium, the circumstances

influencing the extent of any necessary marketability discount in valuation, and the impact of an ESOP's emerging repurchase liability upon the appraisal.

5. As noted above, the proposed regulation also provides guidance relative to the requirement for a determination of adequate consideration in good faith.

The reader is encouraged to read the full text of the proposed regulation on adequate consideration, including the supplementary information, found in Exhibit 16-1.

Formula Appraisals

Current regulations call for annual independent appraisal for ESOPs. Occasionally, an ESOP company might desire to use the methodology of an initial appraisal as a formula for future appraisals. Others have considered the use of an industry rule of thumb.

The ESOP Association Valuation Advisory Committee first published a booklet titled "Valuing ESOP Shares" in 1986; it was reissued in 1989.[11] Because the subject of formula appraisals often comes up with respect to ESOP appraisals, a section on this specific subject is quoted below:

> Formula appraisals are totally unacceptable because they will often result in an insupportable appraisal. The many variables that must be considered in the proper appraisal of a business interest are far too complex to be reduced to a formula that will lose validity as the underlying economic, industry, and company circumstances change over time. While reasonable consistency of appraisal approaches is desirable (as long as the approaches remain valid), the appraisal practitioner must use informed judgment to evaluate the approaches at each appraisal date and institute any changes in approach that are more appropriate in light of newer circumstances.
>
> Canned computer programs do not provide for analysis of subjective factors and should only be used as a supporting analytical tool. A computer program by itself is not a satisfactory valuation method. [*The reader may wish to substitute the term "rules of thumb" for "formula appraisals."*]

Appraisal Requirements

Effective with the Tax Reform Act of 1986, annual ESOP appraisals are required from qualified independent appraisers for all ESOPs of nonpublicly traded companies and banks. The term *qualified independent appraiser* relates to regulations concerning charitable gifts and was previously discussed.

ESOP appraisals are required at several points in an ESOP's life:

1. Upon formation of the plan and the initial acquisition of stock for the ESOP.

---

[11]"Valuing ESOP Shares," rev. ed. (Washington, D.C.: The ESOP Association, 1989).

2. Thereafter, appraisals are required at least annually. Some ESOP companies have their stock appraised semiannually, and a growing number of financial institutions, particularly those with assets exceeding about $250 million, have an appraisal on a quarterly basis.

3. If, between annual appraisals, the ESOP engages in a prohibited transaction with an insider, it is necessary to obtain a current appraisal *as of the date of the transaction.*

4. Finally, it is necessary to obtain an independent appraisal at the time an ESOP is terminated or if an ESOP liquidates a significant portion of its holdings. It is also prudent to retain an independent financial advisor if the sponsoring entity is the subject of an acquisition attempt or tender offer.

Figures 16-1, 16-2, and 16-3 show that there are several parties to every ESOP. What the figures do not show is that the various parties reflected in the boxes sometimes play multiple roles. The potential for conflicts of interest abound, particularly as they relate to the issue of ESOP valuation.

The U.S. Congress established fair market value as the standard of value for ESOP transactions. Fair market value is an arm's-length standard. In other words, it is designed to simulate the negotiations of arm's-length parties even when, in reality, they are not independent of each other. The appraiser's role can therefore be likened to "the arm" in the negotiating process involving ESOP valuation. The appraisal document provides a summary of the items of "negotiation" and leaves a record of that "negotiation." It should be clear from the proposed regulation, however, that the appraiser's primary responsibility is to the ESOP trustee and, through the trustee, to the employee beneficiaries of the ESOP.

ESOP Economics

ESOPs come in two forms, leveraged and unleveraged, and their ownership positions can be described in two ways, minority interests and controlling interests. This section on ESOP economics introduces the forms and ownership interest positions of ESOPs and raises a number of issues related to valuation as a result.

Economics of an Unleveraged ESOP

Contributions can be made to an unleveraged ESOP in the form of cash or stock of the employer. In either case, the appraiser must understand the impact of the contribution on overall value and reflect that understanding appropriately in the ESOP appraisal.

One-Time Contribution of Shares

Stock contributions to an unleveraged ESOP can increase after-tax cash flow to a bank or other company. The benefit relates to the tax shelter resulting from the tax deductibility of the ESOP contribution. Assume, for example, that a company earning at the current rate of $2.0 million (pretax) makes a one-time contribution of shares of $2.0 million to an ESOP. The company's earnings and addition to equity for the period, with and without the ESOP contribution, appear as:

	With ESOP	Without ESOP
Pretax income	2,000,000	2,000,000
Less ESOP contribution	− 2,000,000	− 0
Pretax income		2,000,000
Less assumed taxes @ 40%		− 800,000
Net income		1,200,000
Plus ESOP contribution to equity	+ 2,000,000	+ 0
Net addition to equity	$2,000,000	$1,200,000

If a company can increase equity by the difference between $2.0 million and $1.2 million, or $800,000, by making a tax-deductible contribution to an ESOP, why would every company or bank not want to do this?

Assume further that the company in the present example has 1.0 million shares outstanding and that the company's pre-ESOP value, on a minority interest basis, is $10.0 million (i.e., a multiple of five times pretax income, before considering the ESOP). Assume further that the $800,000 after-tax benefit of the ESOP adds directly to the minority interest value of the company post-ESOP.

We need to look at the impact of the $2.0 million contribution in question *on the non-ESOP shareholders* to better understand the economics of unleveraged ESOPs:

	Before ESOP	After ESOP
Minority interest value	10,000,000	10,000,000
Plus ESOP tax benefit	+ 0	800,000
Less ESOP's value	− 0	− 2,000,000
Value of non-ESOP shares	10,000,000	8,800,000
Non-ESOP shares outstanding	1,000,000	1,000,000
Value per share of non-ESOP shares	$10.00	$8.80

A wise observer of the stock markets once said, "There's no such thing as a free lunch in the markets." There is also no such thing as a free lunch when tax benefits are concerned. If the value of the non-ESOP shares after the ESOP falls from $10.00 per share pre-ESOP to $8.80 per share post-ESOP, then the ESOP must receive shares valued at $8.80 per share.

Because the contribution was $2.0 million, the ESOP must receive 227,273 shares ($2,000,000 / $8.80). After the ESOP, there will be 1,227,273 shares outstanding. Because non-ESOP shareholders own 1,000,000 shares, their holdings now represent 81.5 percent of the now outstanding shares and the ESOP owns the remaining 18.5 percent.

We can observe and infer three important characteristics of unleveraged ESOPs using stock contributions from the present example:

1. Non-ESOP shareholders will be diluted to the extent that the rise in value from the contribution is less than the full dollar amount of the contribution. In the present example, value was assumed to rise by the amount of the tax benefit. If the pre-ESOP value was substantially in excess of asset values, some appraisers would argue that the company's value would not rise at all *until the new capital is successfully deployed in the enterprise,* in which case, dilution would be greater.

2. In this case, non-ESOP shareholders were diluted from 100 percent of the outstanding shares to 81.5 percent of the stock, or 18.5 percentage points of ownership. On a per share basis, value declined from $10.00 per share to $8.80 per share, or 12 percent. Non-ESOP shareholders must hope that the combination of the new capital from the ESOP contribution and the benefits to be derived from increased productivity and motivation on the part of the entity's employees will, in the fairly short run, more than offset the initial decline in per share values.

3. We can infer from the example that the higher the initial valuation of the company, the lower will be the dilution, both in terms of percentage ownership and value per share, for non-ESOP shareholders. For example, if the pre-ESOP valuation had been $20.0 million above, pre-ESOP value of $20.00 per share would have declined to $18.80 per share, or only 6.0 percent. Only 106,383 shares would therefore be issued to the ESOP, providing it with 9.6 percent of the outstanding shares, compared with 18.5 percent of the stock in the actual example. Because of the financial implications of overvaluation to the ESOP and the other shareholders, it is therefore critical that the appraiser be independent.

Impact of Dilution

The mechanics of the example above can be summarized in two equations.[12] The first equation takes the dilution impact of the stock contribution into effect and ensures that the fair market value of the ESOP shares after the contribution are the same as the fair market value of the non-ESOP shares after the contribution, which becomes the fully diluted fair market value per share.

$$\frac{\$ \text{ Stock contribution to ESOP}}{\text{Number of shares issued to ESOP}} = \frac{\text{Aggregate fair market value of company's shares}}{\text{Number of pre-ESOP shares} + \text{Number of shares issued to ESOP}}$$

The second equation, an algebraic rearrangement of the first, simplifies to:

$$\frac{\text{Fair market value per share}}{} = \frac{\text{Aggregate fair market value of company's shares} - \$ \text{ Value of stock contribution to ESOP}}{\text{Number of pre-ESOP shares}}$$

---

[12]Ibid., pp. 12–13.

Inserting the appropriate values from the initial example into the second formula, we can verify the calculations provided:

$$\text{Fair market value} \atop \text{per share} = \frac{\$10,800,000 - \$2,000,000}{1,000,000 \text{ shares}}$$

$$= \frac{\$8,800,000}{1,000,000 \text{ shares}}$$

$$= \$8.80 \text{ per share}$$

In many instances, an appraiser's valuation report will have been obtained prior to the actual contribution of shares. This often occurs when the company or bank desires to know the conclusion before determining the exact amount of the contribution. In these cases, the ESOP trustee and the company need to ensure that the formula considering dilution is used to determine the fair market value per share so that the appropriate number of shares can then be calculated for the contribution. The appraiser is sometimes asked to make this calculation after the fact for purposes of documentation relative to the ESOP transaction.

Recurring Cash and Stock Contributions

The example thus far has considered only a large, one-time stock contribution to an unleveraged ESOP. In this instance, an effective valuation adjustment to earnings was made for the entire amount of the ESOP contribution.

Cash contributions to unleveraged ESOPs are normally made to acquire shares from existing shareholders or to provide liquidity for plans to fund their put option liabilities to reacquire shares from departing shareholders. Normally, cash contributions of the magnitude in the example above are not made.

Recurring contributions to ESOPs, whether in cash or stock, can have an impact on ESOP valuation. Most appraisers make the basic assumption that ESOP companies, in the absence of an ESOP (or in addition to it), would have some other form of retirement benefit plan. Adjustments to earnings are therefore considered for levels of ESOP contributions *above that of "normal" retirement plan contribution levels.* There can be considerable judgment in determining what is a normal level of retirement plan contributions. Adjustments of this type—to the extent determined appropriate by the appraiser based upon the facts and circumstances of the appraisal situation—would add back a portion of the ESOP contribution to earnings to be capitalized in an appraisal and would tend to increase value and reduce the extent of resulting dilution for non-ESOP shareholders. However, if it is determined that above-normal ESOP contributions represent a *permanent claim* on a company's earning power, the appraiser may elect not to make an earnings adjustment.

Economics of Leveraged ESOPs

Leveraging an ESOP adds another level of complexity to the valuation process. For purposes of discussion, we will divide leveraged ESOPs into two types: those owning a minority interest in the ownership of the employer (i.e., ownership of less than 50 percent) and those owning a controlling interest in the ESOP (or ownership of more than 50 percent). We know of only one majority-owned bank ESOP: Phelps County Bank in Rolla, Missouri.[13]

Minority-Interest Leveraged ESOPs

The most common use of leveraged ESOPs in financial institutions is for the acquisition of existing common stock. It is often necessary to borrow funds to acquire significant blocks of stock when they become available. With companies, the most common new ESOP formations we have seen in the last few years have been for the acquisition of at least a 30 percent block of stock, which enables the selling shareholders to take advantage of the tax-free rollover provisions in the tax law discussed above. With banks, however, 30 percent ESOPs are still fairly rare.[14]

I made a presentation at the 1990 Annual Convention of the ESOP Association titled "ESOP Valuation Concepts: What Happens to Value after the Leveraged ESOP Transaction?"[15] This presentation looked at leveraged ESOPs acquiring 30 percent, 51 percent, and 100 percent of target companies and summarized the results of extensive financial modeling of the hypothetical companies under three different assumptions about post-ESOP performance in relationship to pre-ESOP performance (even, improving, and declining).

The point of the presentation as it related to a 30 percent minority interest acquired by a leveraged ESOP is that posttransaction value will probably decline. This possibility exists with the acquisition by an ESOP of any significant (10–20 percent or more) block of a company's shares. The findings of the projection analysis for a 30 percent leveraged ESOP are summarized for further discussion below:

Performance Even with Pre-ESOP Performance

1. ESOP debt amortization reduces earnings during the amortization period.
2. Repurchase liability puts further long-term pressure on earnings.
3. Repurchase liability after the amortization period, to the extent greater than the level of employee benefits contributions embedded in the initial valuation, may represent a permanent claim on a portion of earnings.
4. Leverage factor can cause a decrease in the effective valuation multiple after the ESOP is installed.
5. Value is reduced in the next period (after the transaction) and "recovers" as debt is paid, up to the level of permanent impairment (from ongoing repurchase liability), if any.

Improving Performance

1. Keep in mind that we expect a certain level of growth embedded in the capitalization rate of the initial valuation.

---

[13]"Case Study: Phelps County Bank," *Employee Ownership Report,* National Center for Employee Ownership 11, no. 2 (March/April 1991), p. 4. See the following discussion.
[14]There is a regulatory and psychological hurdle to cross when an ESOP acquires 25 percent of a bank holding company's shares. At that point, the ESOP itself becomes a separately regulated bank holding company. In addition, because of capital constraints, bank ESOPs tend to accumulate ownership more slowly than other corporate ESOPs.
[15]Z. Christopher Mercer, "ESOPs: Building Equity and Growth for America's Future," *Proceedings of the 13th Annual Convention of the ESOP Association,* 1990, pp. 495–500.

2. Improving performance can come from more-rapid growth than anticipated (unlikely in the case of banks), improved margins, or a combination of the two, and can offset the decline in posttransaction value.

3. In most 30 percent leveraged situations, it will take at least 2–3 years to offset the adverse impact of lower earnings plus the repurchase liability.

Declining Performance

Expect the adverse impact of increased ESOP contributions and increased leverage to be magnified if fundamental performance deteriorates.

General Comments Regarding the Projection Analysis

1. Appraisers have sometimes mistakenly tried to "hold" the value, or to satisfy management's erroneous assumption that value should automatically increase.

2. There is a growing realization on the part of appraisers of the need for (a) more comparative knowledge about employee benefits levels of "comparable" public companies, and (b) ongoing analysis of emerging liability faced by ESOPs and the identification of sources of funding to meet it.

3. Unless there is an offset, the minority interest leveraged ESOP may result in a permanent increase in compensation expense that can permanently diminish value *on a minority interest basis.*

4. Watch out for a "debt-free" approach to valuation, which can overlook the impact of increased financial risk on the newly leveraged company.

The major point of the 1990 presentation and of this discussion is that adding significant leverage to a company or a bank can have an adverse impact on post-ESOP value. If a significantly leveraged ESOP transaction is considered in the content of a treasury stock transaction of similar size, it is not surprising that value can decline. For example:

1. In a treasury transaction, where 30 percent of an entity's outstanding shares are acquired, the number of outstanding shares is reduced. Overall entity value will be reduced; however, depending upon the price actually paid, value per share for the remaining shareholders may increase. (See the discussion on stock repurchase programs in Chapter 18.)

2. Debt assumed to acquire shares in a treasury transaction must be amortized on an after-tax basis. Interest expense is tax deductible, but principal must be repaid with after-tax earnings. When the debt is repaid, there is no further liability with respect to the transaction.

3. Debt assumed with an ESOP can be amortized, principal and interest, with pretax dollars. Favorable tax treatment and the employee benefit and motivational aspects of an ESOP are critical positive factors *from a company's point of view.*

4. When an ESOP's debt is fully repaid, there will be a continuing liability related to the ESOP's repurchase requirements as employees leave the sponsoring entity. Consequently, at least a portion of the initial

claim on earnings represented by contributions to amortize ESOP debt must be considered to be *permanent* because the repurchase liabilities will be realized when vested employees quit, are fired, die, or retire.

The benefits of an ESOP must be considered in the context of the facts and circumstances affecting all the parties to potential ESOP transactions, including the bank or company, the employee beneficiaries, the ESOP trust and trustee, the selling shareholders, and any other stakeholders, including management. But the benefits should not be considered naively or in the absence of quantitative and qualitative information supporting the decision, nor should they be considered without consulting expert legal, accounting, and valuation advisors.

Controlling-Interest Leveraged ESOPs

Given the existence of regulatory leverage constraints, it would be virtually impossible for an ESOP to acquire a banking institution in a single leveraged transaction. The decapitalization of the holding company's balance sheet resulting from booking the ESOP's debt liability in accordance with FAS 76-3 would almost certainly create regulatory capital and approval problems.

In the example of Phelps County Bank noted above, the ESOP acquired its 68 percent interest over a period of years. A total of 8 percent of the shares was acquired from the controlling shareholder by the ESOP in 1980. By 1986, the ESOP's ownership position had risen to 13 percent, when the controlling shareholder sold another 19 percent of the bank's shares to the ESOP in a leveraged transaction, bringing its stake to 32 percent of the bank. For the next several years, the bank grew slowly and repaid ESOP debt. In 1991, the ESOP acquired another 36 percent of the bank's shares, bringing its total ownership to 68 percent.

There are several basic questions that must be asked when considering valuation of a controlling interest in a leveraged ESOP.

1. When can an ESOP pay a control premium, or a controlling interest price, for shares of a financial institution? This question is addressed in the next section under "Other ESOP Valuation Issues."
2. Should an ESOP that owns control of a banking institution be valued on a controlling interest basis or a minority interest basis? This question is critical from the point of view of plan administration. While the ESOP may own a controlling interest of the bank, the cumulative ownership benefits of individual employees will almost always be minority interests.

    There are arguments for either position; however, it is our position that the question is not one for the appraiser to determine. It must be answered by plan documents in the portions related to appraisal requirements and plan administration. As an appraisal firm, we look to the ESOP trustee for direction regarding the appropriate basis for the appraisal. Based on informal conversations with appraisers around the nation, this position is held by a number of ESOP appraisal firms.
3. Should a controlling interest in a bank ESOP be valued on a basis that considers the ESOP's debt as outstanding, or should the ESOP

be valued on a debt-free basis? This question also has important implications for plan administration.

One view suggests that the valuation should consider the ESOP's debt as outstanding and that it should be subtracted from the entity's value prior to developing a per share value for ESOP purposes. If the ESOP is leveraged and this practice is followed, employees departing prior to the full repayment of the debt will be penalized relative to those who remain until after its extinction. If the ESOP's objective is to reward those employees who are on board after the period of debt repayment, this view may be favored.

The contrary view suggests that the valuation should consider the value of the entity on a debt-free basis (i.e., excluding only the ESOP's debt), and this value is used to determine the per share value for ESOP purposes. Under this scenario, employees with vested benefits who depart prior to the debt's full repayment will be rewarded at full-enterprise value. Those employees who remain must bear the economic risks of the remaining debt as well as any additional debt required to provide liquidity for those who departed early. However, these risks may be offset by the ongoing benefits of the ESOP for remaining participants.

We take the same position on the question of debt treatment as we do with the selection of the basis (minority interest or control) of the appraisal: It is an issue to be treated by the plan documents. We look for direction from the ESOP trustee on this issue as well.

4. Should the economic benefits of the ESOP be considered in the appraisal of a controlling interest of a bank or bank holding company? This issue is one of appraiser judgment. In controlling interest valuations for leveraged ESOP transactions, some valuation practitioners advocate a procedure calling for a valuation free of the ESOP's debt, then subtracting the ESOP debt and *adding the present value of expected future benefits of the ESOP.*

The expected future benefits from the ESOP are the streams of cost savings from below-market interest rates on ESOP debt (available only if the ESOP acquires more than 50 percent of the stock) plus the benefit of being able to repay the ESOP debt principal with pretax dollars. The net present value of those streams of cost savings is called something like *ESOP-related benefits* and is added to the enterprise value reduced by the ESOP's debt.[16]

This position appears to be an attempt by some appraisers to split the difference between the polar value positions (including and excluding ESOP debt) described in paragraph 3 immediately above.

At this time, I prefer to think of tax benefits in a controlling interest ESOP appraisal as being the result of a *financing decision*

---

[16]James H. Zukin, *Financial Valuation: Business and Business Interests* (New York: Maxwell Macmillan, 1990), pp. 8-8, 8-9. The discount rate used in the cited example is 15 percent, which, if the methodology is appropriate, is probably too low. In any event, we believe that appraisers considering the present value of expected future tax benefits as an increment to value should use a discount rate that is considerably higher than that applied to underlying equity. Consideration of the present value of future tax benefits is extremely risky business. Tax laws change. Most recently, the marginal corporate tax rate was reduced in stages from 48 percent in 1986 to the present level of 34 percent. We know that the *marginal corporate tax rate* is a subject for possible change in the tax laws in the future. Further, while a particular deal's tax benefits may be grandfathered, future legislation can impact the basic tax-deductible benefits for ESOPs we now take for granted.

wherein the use of an ESOP was selected. Presumably, a controlling shareholder will make decisions to obtain the lowest cost financing available given the chosen structure of a deal. The structure of financing neither adds nor subtracts value from the enterprise. It is selected based upon the controlling shareholder's available options at the time of a deal. In this case, the ESOP's financing is different from, for example, below-market debt existing on a company's balance sheet at the time of a particular appraisal, in which case a valuation adjustment might be appropriate.

5. Other issues related to multi-investor leveraged ESOP transactions, such as equity allocation, are beyond the scope of this chapter. In addition, as noted above, such transactions involving a financial institution would be rare.

If anything is clear with respect to controlling interest ESOP appraisals, it is that everything is not clear. Some of these issues will undoubtedly be clarified by future regulations or judicial decisions in ESOP cases. The Valuation Advisory Committee of the ESOP Association is currently working to develop a position paper on issues related to controlling interest ESOP appraisals. The Business Valuation Committee of the American Society of Appraisers can also be expected to develop an ESOP valuation standard. In the meantime, however, there is considerable room for appraiser judgment in developing controlling interest ESOP valuation conclusions. Appraisers must, as always, exercise that judgment in the context of the facts and circumstances of each valuation situation.

Other ESOP Valuation Issues

There are a number of other valuation issues related to ESOPs that are not clearly resolved by existing or proposed regulations of the Internal Revenue Service or the Department of Labor and where there may be some level of disagreement, or at least some room for judgment in application, among business appraisers. Several of these issues are briefly discussed below.

Earnings Base to Capitalize

In Chapter 13, the concept of ongoing earnings was developed. In ESOP appraisals, as with other valuations, it is important to develop an appropriate base of earnings for capitalization. The earnings base might be net cash flow, net income, pretax income, or some other level of the income statement. Earnings might be actual earnings, as reported for the most recent year or most recent trailing 12 months, a simple average of earnings, a weighted average of earnings, or some other derived estimate of ongoing earning power.

Appropriate Capitalization Rate

Whichever earnings base is selected in an appraisal, the appraiser must develop a reasonable and supportable capitalization rate (factor) with which to capitalize the earnings base. The capitalization rate selected for an ESOP appraisal should be appropriate for the selected earnings base.

Adjustments to Earnings for ESOP Contributions

In the preceding discussion, we briefly mentioned the possibility of adjusting earnings for all or a portion of the ESOP contribution in ESOP appraisals. We need to look at the question of ESOP contribution adjustments through two sets of filters. The first filter deals with the recurring nature of the contributions, and the second concerns the basis of the appraisal (minority interest versus controlling interest).

Recurring versus Nonrecurring Contributions

First, ESOP contributions can be recurring or nonrecurring. Typically, if a large, one-time contribution of stock is made to an ESOP (as in the detailed example above), the most common treatment is to add back the contribution in its entirety to the earnings stream in the valuation.

If ESOP contributions are recurring but vary considerably from year to year, the analyst may want to consider an averaging process or a smoothing process and adjust current earnings appropriately.

Finally, if ESOP contributions are fairly steady and recurring, it may be appropriate to consider adjustments, as noted above, for contribution levels in excess of "normal" levels of employee benefit plan contributions for comparable companies. On the other hand, if the recurring contributions represent a *permanent level* of ESOP expense, it may not be appropriate to make any adjustment to earnings because of the permanent nature of the ongoing expense.

Minority Interest versus Controlling Interest Appraisals

The question of adjustments for recurring ESOP contributions is further filtered by asking if the appraisal is on a minority interest or a controlling interest basis. We have found that in minority interest appraisals there is a low likelihood that ESOP contributions will warrant specific adjustment, other than adjustments related to smoothing or averaging related to fluctuating contribution levels.

With controlling interest ESOPs, the question of whether an adjustment is appropriate for ESOP contributions will be answered as the appraiser deals with the questions above, under the section "Controlling Interest Leveraged ESOPs."

Adjustments for Excess Compensation

The issue of adjustments for "excess" management compensation often comes up in minority interest ESOP appraisal situations. Most commonly, one or more key managers are part of a group seeking to sell shares to an ESOP. Historically, the insider-shareholders may have paid themselves above-market salaries and bonuses.

We have taken a position that, for most ESOP appraisals, we will make a positive adjustment to a pretransaction ESOP valuation based upon above-normal salaries only if we have the company's commitment that, posttransaction, salaries will be reduced to the approximate "normal" level used in the adjustment. Absent this consideration, the selling shareholders could receive the double benefit of capitalizing the adjustment into their share values and then continuing to receive the ongoing earnings that just had been capitalized.

Minority Interest versus Controlling Interest Valuations

If an ESOP owns a minority interest of a company, it is clear that the ESOP appraisal should be performed on a minority interest basis. If the ESOP owns a controlling interest in a company, the plan documents should determine whether the appraisal is to be prepared on a minority interest or a controlling interest basis. As discussed at some length above, we do not believe that this question is appropriately answered by the appraiser.

We now must confront the question of *when* an ESOP can pay a control premium for shares. This question is addressed directly by the proposed Department of Labor regulations in a list of requirements that must be considered in the valuation process, including[17]

> (I) Whether or not the seller would be able to obtain a control premium from an unrelated party with regard to the block of securities being valued, provided that in cases where a control premium is taken into account:
>   (1) Actual control (both in form and in substance) is passed to the purchaser with the sale, or will be passed to the purchaser within a reasonable time pursuant to a binding agreement in effect at the time of the sale, and
>   (2) It is reasonable to assume that the purchaser's control will not be dissipated within a short period of time subsequent to acquisition.

According to the proposed regulation, an ESOP can pay a control premium if (1) someone else could reasonably get a premium for the same block of shares, (2) control passes *in fact* (or is promised to pass pursuant to a binding agreement within a reasonable period, which many appraisers assume to be within five years or less), and (3) control will not be lost by reasonably forseeable events, such as a required recapitalization, management incentive stock option programs, or other events that can be anticipated.

ESOP Is a Minority Interest Participant in a Change-of-Control Transaction

Many appraisers would agree that an ESOP *should* be able to pay a control premium if it is a minority interest participant in a change-of-control transaction along with one or more other participants. This is particularly true if none of the other participants acquires a controlling interest in

---

[17]See Exhibit 16-1: "Proposed Regulation Relating to the Definition of Adequate Consideration."

the acquired entity, but it becomes less clear if there is a controlling shareholder other than the ESOP. The rationale for this belief is simple: Groups of minority interest shareholders often join forces to acquire control of companies and become, posttransaction, individual minority interest shareholders. However, it would appear that ESOP trustees should engage in such transactions only upon the advice of qualified ESOP counsel, if at all. The language of the proposed regulation simply does not appear to allow for this kind of transaction.

Marketability Discounts in ESOP Appraisals

The valuation standard for ESOP appraisals in fair market value, which, by reference to Revenue Ruling 59–60 and to the proposed Department of Labor adequate consideration regulations, requires consideration of comparisons with publicly traded companies whose shares are actively traded. Capitalization rates developed using direct public-market comparisons, the capital asset pricing model, or the adjusted capital asset pricing model are generally considered to be "as if freely tradable on a minority-interest basis." In other words, such capitalization rates are in the middle box of Figure 12-1. (See also the discussion of capitalization rates in Chapter 13.)

To arrive at a valuation conclusion for an ESOP, the appraiser must develop an appropriate marketability discount from an as-if-freely-tradable valuation base. Under normal circumstances, marketability discounts can be substantial, on the order of 30–50 percent or more. However, the put option of an ESOP is designed to provide liquidity or marketability for ESOP plan participants upon departure.

In order to develop a marketability discount, it is necessary to examine the put option from two standpoints: the timing of distribution and the form of payment. The standard for comparison for marketability is that of the sale of actively traded public company shares, where liquidity (cash) can be realized in five business days after placing a sale order with a broker.

Some ESOP put options are exercisable within a relatively short time following an employee's departure from employment. In such cases, marketability discounts are normally fairly small, on the order of 5–10 percent. The availability of excess cash in an ESOP (or at a company) to handle put requirements, as well as a history of redeeming shares quickly, has a major bearing on the marketability discount. The better the redemption record, other things being equal, the lower the marketability discount. Some appraisers have taken the position that the put opinion, financial capacity on the part of the ESOP, and a record of timely redemptions can eliminate the marketability discount entirely. However, many (if not most) experienced ESOP appraisers normally utilize a marketability discount that is greater than 0 percent.

If an ESOP document allows for the deferral of payment under the put option, or for payment in the form of a note at interest, and this feature is commonly used in practice, the comparison begins to depart from "cash in five days," which is the standard of marketability from the public stock markets. Marketability discounts of 10–20 percent or more are not uncommon in such cases. In the case of ESOP valuations on a controlling interest basis, marketability discounts are not normally applied.

Impact of Repurchase Liability on ESOP Valuation

There are two ways to consider repurchase liability in an ESOP appraisal. Some appraisers believe that if an ESOP or its sponsoring entity lacks the financial capacity to meet the ESOP's emerging repurchase liability, this lack of capacity should be reflected by raising the marketability discount to a level where the liability can be met. The problem with this approach is that it is difficult to quantify in a specific way.

Other appraisers try to consider the repurchase liability as a direct and ongoing liability chargeable directly against a company's earnings stream. This can be done if the company has a current repurchase liability study, or the charge to earnings related to the repurchase liability can be otherwise estimated based upon discussions with management regarding employee turnover.[18]

Posttransaction ESOP Value

As discussed above, it is quite possible that the valuation of a company or a bank for ESOP purposes will be lower immediately after a leveraged transaction than immediately prior to one. This happens because the ESOP has a going-forward impact on an entity's earning power that must be reflected in the appraisal.

While the posttransaction drop in value is a predictable event, some ESOPs report the pretransaction value to their employee beneficiaries as the initial valuation. Employees then tend to be disappointed or surprised when the next annual appraisal reflects a lower value.

One way to deal with this situation is to have the appraiser provide, at the time of the transaction, a posttransaction value that considers the going-forward impact of the new ESOP on value. This lower, posttransaction value is also provided to employees as the baseline valuation. Subsequent valuations are then comparable because they are prepared on a similar basis.

Special Problems with Bank ESOPs

There are a number of potential problems with bank or bank holding company ESOPs that require consideration by appraisers, bankers, and advisors to financial institutions.

---

[18]Assume, for example, that the total vested benefits related to employer securities have a current value of $1.0 million, that there is no remaining debt on the ESOP's shares, and that the ESOP has not yet accumulated significant liquid assets other than the shares owned. If a study of employee turnover indicates a turnover rate of 8–10 years, it is reasonably predictable that ESOP contributions of between $100,000 ($1,000,000 / 10 years) and $125,000 ($1,000,000 / 8 years) will be required to meet the ESOP's repurchase liability. If a contribution in this range were not being made in such a case, the appraiser might consider adjusting the earning power base downward to reflect an ongoing charge in this range.

What Is Meant by "Not Readily Tradable"

According to current regulations, trustees of ESOPs holding actively, or readily tradable, securities may rely upon the quoted market prices of the employer's securities as an appropriate indicator of fair market value.

In cases where employer securities are not readily tradable, the ESOP trustee must make an independent determination of fair market value in good faith. Most trustees meet this obligation by relying upon appraisals performed by qualified independent appraisers (as defined above).

The real question for ESOP trustees is this: What constitutes an employer security that is not readily tradable? Financial institutions with what we term *quasi-public markets* often assert that their shares are readily tradable and consequently that independent appraisals are not required for their ESOPs. *This is a very high risk assertion for ESOP trustees that, in my opinion, is not objectively supportable.*

The proposed Department of Labor regulations state that the question of whether there is a recognized market for a security must be determined in light of the security's trading characteristics. Isolated trading activity is generally not sufficient to show the existence of a recognized market.

A recent letter ruling by the Internal Revenue Service helps clarify the tradability issue.[19] The letter ruling held that the market for a company's shares, where prices were quoted in a local newspaper by a local brokerage firm, were not readily tradable for ESOP purposes.

There are few banking institutions under about $1.0 billion in total assets that we would consider readily tradable. ESOP trustees who rely upon inactively traded market quotes or price indications for purposes of ESOP transactions are effectively making an affirmative statement that the institution's shares are readily tradable. That position is not objectively supportable in the absence of active trading on the national or regional stock exchanges or NASDAQ. It would appear that the only safe harbor for ESOP trustees to meet their responsibility to determine fair market value in good faith is through reliance upon independent appraisal.

Controlling Interest Valuations Under the Guise of Minority Interest Appraisals

The majority of bank ESOPs own a minority interest in their sponsoring institution's shares. Nevertheless, we have seen a number of minority interest bank ESOP valuations that could only be described as having controlling interest conclusions.

Based on more than 15 years of experience in valuing banking institutions in a variety of external market environments, I have seen only a couple of minority interest bank ESOP appraisals with a legitimate

---

[19]LTR 8910067, dated December 14, 1988.

valuation conclusion as high as 1.2x to 1.25x book value. A few highly leveraged one-bank holding company ESOP appraisals have had higher price/book-value ratios based upon the holding company's book value, but that multiple was the result of holding company leverage where there may have been some factors mitigating the risk of the leverage and not a higher valuation on the underlying bank subsidiary.

The lower degree of leverage in community banks relative to the regional banking companies with which they are compared—together with lower growth prospects and, in many cases, lower returns on equity—are the major limiting factors creating what has been an effective ceiling on community bank minority interest ESOP appraisals.

Appraisers reaching higher conclusions than noted above should at least question their methodology and conclusions. ESOP trustees presented with conclusions above the noted range should seek comfort from the appraiser that the conclusion is reasonable and supportable and, perhaps, a review of the appraisal by another qualified bank appraiser.

Using ESOPs to Raise Capital for Problem Banks

A number of consultants around the country have advocated the use of ESOPs to raise capital for problem banks. A brief discussion of the two basic ways ESOPs have been used as capital generators is appropriate.

First, leveraged ESOPs have been used by one-bank holding companies to borrow funds, acquire stock of the parent holding company, and then to inject the newly acquired capital into the subsidiary bank (see Figure 16-2). In the past, bank regulators may have overlooked the leverage of the parent holding company in their examinations of a subsidiary bank. Further, prior to recent modifications to FAS 76-3, bank accountants often did not reflect the ESOP debt as a liability of the subsidiary bank, rather showing the debt on the parent company statement or not at all.

However, if the bank's earnings are the only source of repayment for the holding company's debt, there is a logical argument to require the booking of the ESOP's liability as a reduction of equity at the bank level and as a corresponding liability.

The point is that equity raised through the use of leveraged ESOPs has a fairly low probability of being considered to be new capital for regulatory purposes in problem bank situations.

The second way that leveraged ESOPs are used in problem bank situations is in combination with the termination of a pension or profit-sharing plan and the subsequent rollover of preexisting retirement benefits of individual employees into the ESOP.[20] In this fashion, the rollover funds are new equity. The ESOP trustee should be extremely careful in this situation. Employees are being asked to make decisions to move funds from a retirement plan required by law to have a reasonable degree of diversification of its assets to a nondiversified plan designed to invest in the securities of one company, the employer, that is known to have

---

[20]This can only be done with proper disclosure to employees and without coercion of any kind. Institutions considering such a program should definitely seek special employee benefits, tax, and securities law counsel.

financial problems. The standard of due diligence should be quite high for all parties to this type of transaction.

Cheaper Is Not Necessarily Better

A few U.S. firms have quoted extremely low prices on bank ESOP appraisals. Efficiency is to be applauded, and competition is the name of the game. But ESOP trustees confronted with widely divergent fee quotations should ask a number of questions to ensure that the selection decision considers not only the dollar amount of the fee quote, but also whether the work process and work product are similar ("apples-to-apples") and will satisfy the fiduciary responsibilities mandated by the Department of Labor. These requirements suggest that a bank ESOP appraisal is not a generic thing but a custom-crafted appraisal of a particular institution at a point in time. See Exhibit 16-2 for a list of questions to ask of appraisers generally and of ESOP appraisers in particular.

In my experience, to perform a bank ESOP appraisal that meets (1) the requirements of Revenue Ruling 59–60 and the proposed Department of Labor regulations, (2) the Uniform Standards of Professional Appraisal Practice, and (3) the standards of the American Society of Appraisers, requires a minimum of at least 35–45 hours of professional time and perhaps more time for initial appraisals or if there are special valuation issues requiring specific treatment.[21]

It is not uncommon for appraisers to make quotations for ESOP appraisals on a multiyear basis. Appraisers sometimes provide an initial-year fee quote and a lower quote for subsequent-year reappraisals. Other appraisers, in reliance upon a multiyear agreement, provide a fixed annual quote for the term of the agreement. In either event, the ESOP trustee should ensure that the subsequent-year work process and valuation reports continue to meet the standards of the initial year. The proposed Department of Labor regulations make no distinction between an initial appraisal and subsequent appraisals. The trustee's responsibility is the same every year.

While there are some areas for efficiencies in annual reappraisals, they can easily be overstated. It is occasionally possible to conduct the management interview by telephone, for example, and there are benefits to having background information and historical financial statements in word processing or spreadsheet files. However, these potential efficiencies are often offset by new issues requiring consideration and professional time and judgment each year. The ESOP trustee should require that the appraisal budget allow for a fresh look at the bank each year.

If all other things about two appraisal firms—including experience, professional credentials, and the other characteristics indicated by the

---

[21]One way to test a fee quote is to divide the quoted annual professional fee by, say, 40 hours as a good minimum and to compare the implied hourly billing rate with that of the attorneys, accountants, and other professionals the bank customarily relies upon for specialized advice. If the implied hourly billing rate is materially below what the bank normally pays for specialized professional services, several possibilities are suggested: (1) the appraiser is not worth a market billing rate for professional services, (2) less qualified personnel will actually be doing the work, (3) the appraiser does not plan to put in anywhere near 40 hours of professional time in the conduct of the appraisal, or (4) I have simply overestimated the time required to perform a bank ESOP appraisal (see Chapter 22).

questions of Exhibit 16-2—are approximately similar and the trustee is satisfied that the valuation report work products to be received are of comparable quality and ability to satisfy his or her (or the employing institution's) fiduciary responsibilities, and if one of the two firms provides a fee quotation that is materially lower than the other, then price is a good basis upon which to make the selection of appraisers.

A quotation by John Ruskin often seen on wall plaques in businesses provides a fitting close to this discussion:

> It's unwise to pay too much, but it's worse to pay too little. When you pay too much you lose a little money—that is all. When you pay too little, you sometimes lose everything, because the thing you bought was incapable of doing the thing it was bought to do. The common law of business balance prohibits paying a little and getting a lot—it can't be done. If you deal with the lowest bidder, it is well to add something for the risk you run. And if you do that, you will have enough to pay for something better.

Qualifications of Appraisers

It is appropriate to end this chapter on ESOPs with a brief discussion of bank appraiser qualifications generally and ESOP appraiser qualifications specifically.

Educational Background

Appraisers generally have undergraduate degrees in business-related fields, including economics, accounting, marketing, finance, or other business majors, although there are always successful exceptions to this pattern. The majority of business appraisers, at least in the larger appraisal firms, seem to have advanced degrees in accounting, business, law, or finance. Again, there are always successful exceptions. The point is that business and financial institutions appraisal is heavily dependent upon an understanding of the business disciplines of economics, finance, accounting, and marketing.

Professional Credentials

There are two generally recognized professional credentialing organizations offering programs of study and examinations leading to professional credentials that are directly applicable to the discipline of business appraisal. These are the American Society of Appraisers and the Association for Investment Management and Research.

The Association for Investment Management and Research, a professional association comprised of the Financial Analysts Federation and the Institute of Chartered Financial Analysts, provides a three-year program of organized study and examinations leading to the professional designation Chartered Financial Analyst (CFA).

The CFA designation is the leading professional designation in the money management and investment banking fields. Required areas of study include ethical and professional standards, financial accounting, quantitative analysis, economics, fixed-income securities analysis, equity securities analysis, and portfolio management. A number of CFAs have evolved into the business appraisal field, and many current appraisers are seeking, or have earned, the CFA designation.

CFAs can be identified by consulting the *1991 Membership Directory* (published annually) of the Association for Investment Management and Research, Charlottesville, Virginia.

The American Society of Appraisers (ASA) is a multidisciplinary professional organization promoting the education and credentialing of appraisers in several fields, including business appraisal. The ASA offers two levels of professional credentials in the business valuation field. With two years of full-time business appraisal experience, the passing of a series of examinations in four 4-day courses of study (or the passing of a comprehensive examination covering the material of the course of study), verification of educational requirements, and approval of two appraisal reports by the International Board of Examiners, a candidate can earn the AM designation, indicating that he or she is an Accredited Member of the American Society of Appraisers. There is also a five-year full-time experience requirement to achieve the Accredited Senior Appraiser (ASA) designation.

Credentialled members of the American Society of Appraisers can be found in *Accredited Business Appraisal Experts International Directory* published each year by the ASA. Readers can obtain a current copy of this directory by calling the American Society of Appraisers (1-800-ASA-VALU).

A number of certified public accountants (CPAs) have also entered the business appraisal field, and many are highly qualified. In fact, several of the professionals at Mercer Capital are certified public accountants. I should point out, however, that the CPA designation is not a professional designation in business appraisal, although it does provide excellent background for those who desire to pursue business appraisal. The course of study leading to the CPA designation does not cover business appraisal issues.

Many CPAs who are serious about the business appraisal field either have obtained or are currently seeking designation by the American Society of Appraisers. Others have attended one or more of the business valuation courses sponsored by the American Society of Appraisers for specific training in the business appraisal field.

Other Professional Organizations

The ESOP Association is a national nonprofit association of companies with employee stock ownership plans and practitioners with a professional commitment to ESOPs. Based in Washington, D.C., the ESOP Association is actively involved in lobbying efforts to maintain favorable ESOP legislation and also communicates with federal regulatory agencies on issues affecting ESOPs. The association publishes a variety of materials on specific ESOP subjects, including the monthly ESOP Report. Standing committees on administration, banking, communication, legislative and regulatory affairs, public relations, and valuation provide detailed analyses of specific ESOP issues.

The ESOP Association conducts its annual convention in Washington, D.C., and it is attended by ESOP company representatives as well as professionals in the various fields who support ESOPs, including representatives from law firms, accounting firms, administration firms, lenders, valuation firms, and others. In addition, the ESOP Association conducts a variety of regional seminars promoting ESOPs each year.

The National Center for Employee Ownership (NCEO) is a private, nonprofit information and research organization that focuses on ESOPs. The NCEO has published numerous academic studies on employee ownership and regularly conducts surveys of ESOP companies. A variety of publications and studies are available for companies desiring specific background information on ESOPs. The NCEO also publishes the bimonthly *Employee Ownership Report,* which provides survey results, articles on ESOPs, and current information on the state of ESOPs.

Both the ESOP Association and the NCEO publish directories of ESOP professionals who are active in the various areas in which ESOPs require support, including valuation. Most valuation firms who are serious about remaining current with ESOP valuation issues are members of one or both of these organizations.

Questions for Your Appraiser

Exhibit 16-2 provides a list of questions to ask potential appraisers generally and ESOP appraisers specifically. The answers to the questions can help in selecting appraisal firms for specific assignments.

Exhibit 16-2
Questions to Ask of Your Bank or Business Appraisal Firm

1. Does the firm require its appraisers to be active members of the American Society of Appraisers (ASA) Business Valuation Division?
2. Do a majority of the appraisers have one or more advanced professional credentials, such as Accredited Senior Appraiser (ASA), Accredited Member (AM), Chartered Financial Analyst (CFA), or Certified Public Accountant (CPA), as well as other advanced degrees?
3. Are the firm's appraisers experienced as business appraisal expert witnesses in the federal and state court systems?
4. Will the appraisal firm meet both legal and perceptual independence requirements? Will your firm's attorney or other outside party perceive that the appraiser is totally independent and ob-jective re-garding the appraisal because the appraiser or the firm does not or will not provide significant other nonappraisal services to your firm (e.g., auditing, investment banking, business brokerage, etc.)?
5. Does the firm have access to the most current comparative information by regularly accessing the available business computer databases and hard-copy information sources?
6. Does the firm have experience in performing business valuations for a variety of purposes?
7. Does the firm provide financial advisory services related to business valuation issues?
8. How many business appraisal assignments has the firm completed in the last 5–10 years?
9. Has the firm performed business valuations for a broad cross-section of industries?
10. Does the firm work exclusively in the area of appraisals? (Some firms may be more interested in investment banking, pension or ESOP administration, ESOP promotion, or insurance sales.)
11. Does the firm have enough full-time appraisers to provide a well-rounded work environment and support for most unique appraisal situations?
12. Can the firm realistically provide for timely completion of projects?

Exhibit 16-2 (*continued*)

13. Does the firm require annual continuing education in busines valuation for its appraisers?
14. Does the firm's staff teach seminars for recognized professional and/or trade associations?
15. Do the firm's professionals publish articles on subjects related to business appraisal? Articles of general interest to businesses and supporting professionals? Articles focused on specific industries? Articles for professional business valuation publications?
16. Does the appraisal firm prepare all valuation reports in conformity with the Uniform Standards of Professional Appraisal Practice promulgated by the Appraisal Foundation and the Business Valuation Standards established by the American Society of Appraisers?
17. Does the firm represent itself as a qualified independent appraiser in the context of the proposed Department of Labor regulations for ESOPs?
18. How many ESOP appraisals does the firm currently provide *annually*?
19. Does the firm recognize its responsibility to the ESOP trustee in its proposal letters and valuation reports?
20. Is the firm a member or associate member of organizations—such as the ESOP Association or the National Center for Employee Ownership (NCEO)—that promote ESOPs and the dissemination of current information on ESOPs?

Chapter 17

Thrift Stock Valuation[1]

---

[1]Michael A. Murphy, CFA, is the primary writer and coauthor of this chapter. Mr. Murphy is a managing director of Trident Financial Corporation, one of the leading appraisers of thrift institutions in the United States. He is Director of Trident's Corporate Finance Group, which is responsible for merger and acquisition advisory services, business valuation, financial institutions research, and consulting. Prior to joining Trident, Mr. Murphy was a management consultant and an officer in the U.S. Navy. He is a frequent writer and speaker on topics of valuation, mergers and acquisitions, and capital raising.

Mr. Murphy earned his B.A. degree from the University of Virginia. He holds an M.A. degree from Webster College and an M.B.A. degree from the University of North Carolina at Chapel Hill. He is a Chartered Financial Analyst and a member of the North Carolina Society of Financial Analysts.

There is nothing permanent except change.

Heraclitus (501 BC)

Introduction

In previous chapters, we focused attention primarily on commercial banks. In this chapter, we will concentrate on thrift institutions: savings and loan associations, savings banks, and savings and loan holding companies.

The basic mission of thrift institutions is financing home ownership. At the end of 1990, thrift institutions controlled approximately $1.3 trillion of assets and $1.0 trillion of deposits. This equals more than 25 percent of combined bank-thrift assets and deposits, so thrifts are a very significant segment of the financial services industry.[2]

When the four major classes of financial intermediaries were originally formed, each had a limited purpose.[3] Commercial banks existed to serve merchants, manufacturers, and other large providers and users of capital. Mutual savings banks (today's state-chartered, BIF-insured savings banks) were chartered to meet the savings needs of the wage-earning classes. These institutions originally invested only in federal and state securities and did not make loans. It was not until the end of the 19th century that mutual savings banks began to make mortgage loans. The first mutual savings banks, the Philadelphia Savings Fund Society and the Provident Institution for Savings in Boston, were chartered in 1816. The earliest building and loan associations (today's savings and loans) were created to assist savers in purchasing homes. Although the form of ownership of savings and loans has undergone numerous changes since 1831, when the Oxford Provident Building Association was organized in Frankford, Pennsylvania, their primary investments remain home mortgage loans.

At December 31, 1990, there were 2,341 savings and loans (not including the more than 400 failed thrifts controlled by the Resolution Trust Corporation) and 453 savings banks.

Finally, credit unions were formed to provide consumer credit to workers. The first U.S. credit union, the St. Mary's Cooperative Credit Association, was organized in new Hampshire in 1909. Credit unions retain their basic mission today, although in recent years they have begun of offer home mortgage loans as well. Because the "equity" of credit unions is owned mutually by their customers, the valuation of credit unions is not treated in this book. However, the techniques of analysis of financial institutions mentioned throughout the book are highly applicable to credit unions.

---

[2]OTS and FDIC data at December 31, 1990.

[3]For an excellent discussion of the history of financial intermediaries, see "Historical Overview of Financial Institutions," by Ronald Paul Auerbach, published by the FDIC.

Thrift Industry Structure

Thrifts can be classified according to charter, type of deposit insurance, and form of ownership. Like banks, thrift institutions can be either federally or state chartered. Thrift deposits can be insured either by the Savings Association Insurance Fund (SAIF), formerly the Federal Savings and Loan Insurance Corporation (FSLIC), or by the Bank Insurance Fund (BIF). The SAIF and the BIF are separate funds of the Federal Deposit Insurance Corporation (FDIC). As part of the Financial Institutions Reform, Recovery and Enforcement Act of 1989 (FIRREA), the FSLIC was dissolved and replaced by the SAIF, a separate fund of the now larger and reorganized FDIC. The BIF is the new name for the pre-existing FDIC. As a result, both SAIF- and BIF-insured institutions can now advertise that they are insured by the FDIC.

Under FIRREA, the Federal Home Loan Bank Board (FHLBB), the national chartering and regulatory agency and operating head of the FSLIC, was replaced by the Office of Thrift Supervision (OTS), a division of the United States Department of the Treasury. Thus, the FHLBB's chartering and supervisory duties were separated from its deposit insurance responsibilities. FIRREA also created the Resolution Trust Corporation (RTC) to manage and sell failed thrifts and their assets, a function formerly performed by the FSLIC. Unless otherwise noted, this chapter will not address RTC-controlled thrifts. All federally chartered thrifts are SAIF-insured. State chartered thrifts can be insured by the SAIF or the BIF, depending on state law. At December 31, 1990, approximately two thirds of SAIF-insured thrift institutions were federally chartered. As of July 1, 1991, SAIF- and BIF-insured institutions both pay the same level of deposit insurance premium (0.23 percent of deposits).

The distinction between savings and loan associations and savings banks has largely disappeared in recent years. In fact, many federal savings and loan associations converted to a federal savings bank charter for marketing reasons, without making any changes in operations. However, in some states, notably in the Northeast and the Northwest, there exists a special class of state-chartered, FDIC-insured thrifts. These thrifts, which are insured by either fund of the FDIC, are not regulated by the OTS, but rather by the various states, and enjoy greater operating flexibility. They are also subject to a less stringent qualified thrift lender test.

Traditionally, thrift institutions have been mutually owned. That is, they were owned by their depositors and borrowers, as are all credit unions and many insurance companies. Although most thrift institutions remain mutual, the vast majority of thrift assets are owned by stock companies. At year-end 1990, approximately 44 percent of SAIF-insured thrifts and 35 percent of BIF-insured thrifts were stock companies. However, stock companies account for approximately 75 percent of assets for SAIF-insured thrifts and 68 percent of the assets of BIF-insured thrifts.

Exhibit 17-1 is a breakdown of the thrift industry by type of ownership and by asset size. Although the vast majority of thrifts have less than $500 million of assets, the few thrifts larger than $500 million control the majority of assets. Hence, the industry is two-tiered. The first tier consists of the few large stock thrifts that control most of the assets. The second tier is made up of many smaller thrifts that hold only a minority of the assets. Exhibit 17-2 provides a comparison of the average size of SAIF-insured and BIF-insured thrifts (broken down by type of ownership), commercial banks, and bank holding companies. Stock thrifts tend to be nearly four times the size of mutuals, and bank holding companies dominate banking assets.

Exhibit 17-1

Thrift Industry Classified According to Assets at December 31, 1990

| | SAIF-Insured Thrifts* | | | | | |
| | Stock | | Mutual | | Total | |
Bank Assets ($ Millions)	No.	%	No.	%	No.	%
Less than $25	77	7.5%	175	13.3%	252	10.8%
$25 to $49	137	13.4	250	19.0	387	16.5
$50 to $99	215	21.0	333	25.3	548	23.4
$100 to $249	236	23.0	347	26.4	583	24.9
$250 to $499	137	13.4	116	8.8	253	10.8
$500 to $999	86	8.4	51	3.9	137	5.9
$1,000 to $2,499	70	6.8	36	2.7	106	4.5
$2,500 to $4,999	42	4.1	5	0.4	47	2.0
$5,000 to $9,999	16	1.6	2	0.2	18	0.8
$10,000 or more	10	1.0	0	0.0	10	0.4
Totals	1,026	100.0%	1,315	100.0%	2,341	100.0%

| | BIF-Insured Savings Banks | | | | | |
| | Stock | | Mutual | | Total | |
Bank Assets ($ Millions)	No.	%	No.	%	No.	%
Less than $25	4	2.5%	16	5.4%	20	4.4%
$25 to $49	4	2.5	38	12.9	42	9.3
$50 to $99	10	6.3	58	19.7	68	15.0
$100 to $249	33	20.9	107	36.3	140	30.9
$250 to $499	30	19.0	42	14.2	72	15.9
$500 to $999	36	22.8	21	7.1	57	12.6
$1,000 to $2,499	25	15.8	11	3.7	36	7.9
$2,500 to $4,999	10	6.3	1	0.3	11	2.4
$5,000 to $9,999	6	3.8	1	0.3	7	1.5
$10,000 or more	0	0.0	0	0.0	0	0.0
Totals	158	100.0%	295	100.0%	453	100.0%

*Excludes RTC-controlled companies.

SOURCE: OTS and FDIC data compiled by W. C. Ferguson and Company.

Exhibit 17-2
Average Size of Thrifts and Banks at December 31, 1990

	Total Assets ($ Billions)		Institutions		Average Assets/Institution
SAIF-insured thrifts*	Assets	%	No.	%	($ Millions)
Mutual	$ 249.5	24.8%	1,315	56.2%	$ 189.8
Stock	755.4	75.2	1,026	43.8	736.2
Total	1,004.9	100.0	2,341	100.0	429.3
BIF-insured savings banks					
Mutual	74.1	32.2	295	65.1	251.3
Stock	156.0	67.8	158	34.9	987.2
Total	230.1	100.0%	453	100.0%	508.0
Commercial banks	3,388.5		12,342		274.5
Bank holding companies†	$3,755.2		1,588		$2,364.7

*Excludes RTC-controlled companies.
†Includes foreign operations; to be included must have $150 billion of assets or own more than one subsidiary bank.

SOURCE: OTS, FDIC, and Federal Reserve Board data compiled by W. C. Ferguson and Company.

State of the Thrift Industry

The thrift industry (and increasingly, the banking industry) has been subject to a torrent of bad publicity in recent years. The industry has been characterized by some as being infected with incompetence and dishonesty. Clearly, there have been plenty of these characteristics to go around, but the true causes of the problems run much deeper.

Roots of Current Industry Problems

The current state of the thrift industry has its roots in the high interest rates of the late 1970s and early 1980s and the accompanying deregulation of deposit accounts and assets. Interest rates skyrocketed in the 1970s, which resulted in massive deposit outflows as consumers moved their funds out of low-yielding, insured savings accounts into uninsured money market mutual funds and other investments, a process called disintermediation. In order to provide relief from disintermediation, Congress passed the Deposit Institutions Deregulation and Monetary Control Act in 1980. This act authorized NOW accounts and the phaseout of interest rate ceilings and minimum-balance requirements on savings products, resulting in a return of funds to thrifts and banks, but at a much higher cost because funds were priced at market rates.

Thrifts suffered huge operating losses as interest rates on deposits rose much more rapidly than the yields on earning assets since the primary assets of thrift institutions were long-term mortgage loans whose yields did not adjust in line with the cost of deposits. This mismatch resulted in the cost of funds actually exceeding the yield on assets for most thrifts during the early 1980s.

Legislated "Relief"

In 1982, Congress passed the Garn–St. Germain Depository Institutions Act, which granted additional lending and other operating powers to thrifts in order to promote a more competitive environment and to allow increased diversification. This provided the opportunity for ill-equipped thrift managers to enter into new and riskier lines of business. It also provided the avenue for some unscrupulous individuals and groups to acquire control of a significant number of thrifts that subsequently grew too rapidly and invested in overly risky assets. Meanwhile, real estate values escalated through the mid-1980s in several key areas of the nation, including the Southwest and areas of the West. The real estate markets then crashed when supply far outstripped demand and the tax laws that promoted overbuilding were changed in 1986.

By 1987, the FSLIC was insolvent and needed recapitalization. Congress responded with the Competitive Equality Banking Act (CEBA). CEBA provided $10 billion of funds to recapitalize the FSLIC and put the brakes on some of the more abusive accounting practices. Unfortunately, CEBA was an example of legislation that could be described as "too little, too late."

Congress again applied itself to the task of providing funds to insure deposits at failed thrifts and reregulating the thrift industry by passing FIRREA in 1989. The act provided new funding for deposit insurance, mandated increased capital requirements in line with national banks, redefined the qualified thrift lender test (see below), applied restrictions on nonresidential lending and loans to one borrower, ended non-GAAP financial reporting, allowed bank holding companies to acquire healthy thrifts, and reconfigured the regulatory and deposit insurance bureaucracy.

The magnitude of the thrift crisis seemingly has no limits. At December 31, 1990, the RTC controlled 421 thrifts with aggregate deposits of nearly $68 billion. Between August 1989 and May 1991, the RTC resolved nearly 380 thrift failures with $130 billion of affected deposits. Many experts have suggested that the eventual cost to taxpayers for insuring thrift deposits will be more than $500 billion.

Not All Thrifts Are Problems

Despite all of the problems of the thrift industry, there remain many healthy and profitable thrifts. Most of the healthier thrifts are relatively small and have stuck to the fundamentals, avoiding higher-risk investments and strategies. Exhibit 17-3 stratifies the industry by ownership and level of equity at December 31, 1990. At that date, approximately 53 percent of the SAIF-insured companies (which accounted for only 29 percent of industry assets) had equity of 6 percent of assets or more. The average size of this segment of the industry was only $230 million, little more than half of the size of the average SAIF-insured thrift. Among BIF-insured thrifts, nearly 83 percent had equity of 6 percent or greater, which accounted for 66 percent of assets. These BIF-insured thrifts had average assets of $405 million.

Exhibit 17-3

Thrift Industry Classified According to Equity Capital as a Percentage of Assets at December 31, 1990

	SAIF-Insured Thrifts*					
	Stock		Mutual		Total	
Equity Capital (% of Assets)	No.	%	No.	%	No.	%
Under 0%	17	1.7%	43	3.3%	60	2.6%
0% to 1.9%	58	5.7	69	5.2	127	5.4
2.0% to 3.9%	152	14.8	124	9.4	276	11.8
4.0% to 5.9%	351	34.2	293	22.3	644	27.5
6.0% to 7.9%	203	19.8	325	24.7	528	22.6
8.0% to 9.9%	99	9.6	217	16.5	316	13.5
10.0% to 11.9%	58	5.7	130	9.9	188	8.0
12.0% to 14.9%	49	4.8	84	6.4	133	5.7
15% or more	39	3.8	30	2.3	69	2.9
Total	1,026	100.0%	1,315	100.0%	2,341	100.0%

	BIF-Insured Savings Banks					
	Stock		Mutual		Total	
Equity Capital (% of Assets)	No.	%	No.	%	No.	%
Under 0%	5	3.2%	2	0.7%	7	1.5%
0% to 1.9%	5	3.2	3	1.0	8	1.8
2.0% to 3.9%	10	6.3	9	3.1	19	4.2
4.0% to 5.9%	24	15.2	21	7.1	45	9.9
6.0% to 7.9%	42	26.6	87	29.5	129	28.5
8.0% to 9.9%	28	17.7	102	34.6	130	28.7
10.0% to 11.9%	21	13.3	45	15.3	66	14.6
12.0% to 14.9%	15	9.5	21	7.1	36	7.9
15% or more	8	5.1	5	1.7	13	2.9
Total	158	100.0%	295	100.0%	453	100.0%

*Excludes RTC-controlled companies.

SOURCE: OTS and FDIC data compiled by W. C. Ferguson and Company.

Thrift Industry Outlook

Thrifts can continue to be a viable form of financial intermediary. However, because mortgage lending is, by nature, a relatively low margin business, successful thrifts must pay close attention to operating costs and avoid risks. Market area and the nature of competition are also very important variables. Thrifts that operate in relatively noncompetitive or rural markets tend to be better performers, despite what are probably less attractive demographics. Thrifts operating in metropolitan areas experience severe competition, which drives down loan yields and increases deposit and operating costs.

The 1989 passage of FIRREA set the financial services industry on an irreversible path toward consolidation. For the first time, bank holding companies were authorized to acquire healthy thrifts. As of mid-1991, however, most of the bank-thrift merger activity had centered on RTC-assisted transactions. In addition, banks in regions of the country with large numbers of healthy mutual thrifts had focused their efforts on acquiring these thrifts in merger conversions (see below). The acquisition of stockholder-owned thrifts by bank holding companies has been relatively slow thus far, as bank holding companies have sought to take advantage of the opportunities presented by RTC-assisted transactions and merger conversions.

When acquired, most thrifts will be merged into the acquiring bank (and thus converted to a commercial bank charter) rather than held as a separate thrift subsidiary of a bank holding company. Converting to a bank charter will trigger recapture of the bad-debt reserve for taxes (see "Qualified Thrift Lender Test," later in this chapter) and create an immediate tax liability that will significantly reduce the acquired thrift's equity. Although actual payment of the taxes may take place over a number of years, the liability must be recognized immediately for GAAP purposes. Despite the heavy economic cost of converting charters, many industry observers believe most acquired thrifts will be converted to banks. Conversion will allow an acquired thrift to diversify into more profitable commercial and consumer lending.[4]

The thrift industry of the future will be smaller. Many thrifts will be acquired by commercial bank holding companies, some thrifts will voluntarily convert to bank charters, thrift-thrift acquisitions will continue to occur, quite a few thrifts will fail, and a few new thrifts will be formed. The remaining thrifts will probably evolve into community bank–like operations, serving their local communities with a variety of deposit products and consumer and real estate lending services.

Thrift Holding Companies

Numerous stock thrifts are owned by holding companies. This is particularly true among the larger thrifts. Of the publicly-traded thrifts, 65 percent are owned by holding companies. The holding company form has a number of significant advantages over traditional savings and loan associations or savings banks. Chapter 11 discusses the basic advantages of the holding company form of organization. Thrift holding companies are classified as either unitary or multiple and as either diversified or nondiversified.

Unitary thrift holding companies own only one savings institution. Other institutions may be acquired, but they must be merged into the existing thrift unit. Unitary thrift holding companies may engage in virtually any lawful line of business without limitation, as long as the subsidiary thrift is operated in a safe and sound manner and continues as a "qualified thrift lender" (see "Qualified Thrift Lender Test," later in this chapter.)

---

[4]Under FIRREA, there is no requirement for a thrift acquired by a bank to convert deposit insurance from SAIF to BIF. In fact, healthy thrifts are prohibited from transferring deposit insurance until 1994 (except for small transfers, such as with branch acquisitions). When allowed to transfer from SAIF to BIF, insured deposits must exit SAIF and pay an exit fee and enter BIF and pay an entrance fee. These fees are stiff, and BIF insurance currently offers no rate advantage to SAIF (beginning in July 1991). Consequently, given the stiff exit and entrance fees and the lack of a spread between BIF and SAIF deposit insurance rates, it appears unlikely that the deposit insurance of many acquired thrifts will be transferred from SAIF to BIF.

Multiple holding companies own more than one institution. Multiple holding company activities are generally restricted to providing management services to subsidiary thrifts, owning an insurance agency or escrow business, holding and managing repossessed assets or other properties owned by or acquired from the subsidiary thrifts, acting as a trustee for deeds of trust, engaging in thrift-related activities as are permitted service corporations of federal associations, and other activities authorized by the Federal Reserve Board for bank holding companies.

Nondiversified holding companies are companies in which more than 50 percent of net worth comes from subsidiary thrifts. Debt issues of nondiversified holding companies must receive prior approval of the OTS. If less than 50 percent of a holding company's net worth is accounted for by its ownership of a thrift, then the company is classified as diversified. Diversified holding companies are permitted to issue debt without approval of the OTS. Examples of diversified thrift holding companies include Sears and the Ford Motor Company.

Public Market for Thrift Stocks

Only a handful of the larger thrifts have what can be termed a liquid trading market for their stock. A survey of market conditions in early June 1991 illustrates this point. Somewhat more than 40 percent of all thrifts are stock companies. Of the stock companies, only 367 had sufficient trading activity to warrant listing on NASDAQ or an exchange. The "publicly traded" thrifts represent only about 30 percent of the stock companies and about 48 percent of total thrift industry assets. However, being listed does not ensure an active trading market. The listed companies had an aggregate market capitalization (market price per share times shares outstanding) of $18.1 billion. The median market capitalization for a listed thrift was only $14.1 million, and it generally had only two or three market makers. The 23 thrifts listed on the New York Stock Exchange accounted for 50 percent of the total market capitalization of the publicly traded thrifts. Nearly 90 percent of listed thrifts are traded on NASDAQ. The American Stock Exchange listed but 14 thrifts, accounting for less than 3 percent of aggregate market capitalization.

At the same time (June 1991), 382 banks and bank holding companies were listed on NASDAQ or on an exchange, just 15 more than thrifts. However, the aggregate market capitalization for the banks was $168 billion, more than nine times that of thrifts. The median market capitalization was $78 million, 5.5 times that of the median thrift. Only about 3.1 percent of all banks are listed, but that figure increases to 24 percent of bank holding companies. The listed banks and bank holding companies accounted for more than 75 percent of the total banking industry assets.

Most thrifts are community financial institutions with limited market appeal outside of their local markets. The National Daily Quotation Service (the Pink Sheets) published by the National Quotation Bureau, Inc., lists dozens of additional thrifts, but that market is largely a "workout" market where brokers attempt to match buy and sell orders only when the need arises. Many thrifts do not trade at all or trade only over their presidents' desks.

Historically, thrift stock pricing ratios have been roughly one half those of bank stocks. Lower relative pricing is caused by a variety of factors, including more irregular earnings, lower dividend yields, concerns over credit quality, and, of course, thinner trading markets. However, despite the relatively illiquid nature of even the listed thrift stocks, we believe there is still enough market evidence to provide guideline indicators for capitalization factors for thrift valuations.

Figure 17-1 illustrates the movement of relative stock prices for publicly traded thrifts between May 1986 and June 1991. Stock prices are indexed to March 31, 1984, and the index is market value weighted. As seen on the graph, thrift stock prices peaked in early 1987. At that time, the typical thrift traded for more than book value. In April of that year, interest rates rose, dropping thrift stock prices nearly 20 percent. When the stock market crash of October 1987 occurred, thrift stock prices fell 30 percent, roughly in line with the market as a whole. Thrift stocks slowly rose 44 percent between late 1987 and late 1989, shortly after FIRREA was passed. As the impact of FIRREA was assessed and asset quality deteriorated, thrift stocks fell 62 percent between late 1989 and late 1990 before turning up again. Between late 1990 and June 1991, prices rose more than 60 percent (but starting from a lower base), as general stock market conditions improved and interest rates fell.

Figure 17-1
Thrift Price Index

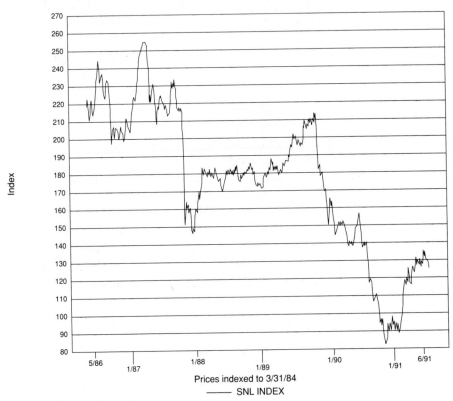

Prices indexed to 3/31/84
—— SNL INDEX

SOURCE: SNL Securities, L.P.

Anatomy of a Thrift

To the layperson, banks and thrifts appear to be very similar. However, they are different in a number of important ways. For example, thrifts are largely in the home financing business, while commercial banks are more diversified. Banks have higher yield/cost spreads and net interest margins, but thrifts have lower operating expenses. Thrifts tend to have lower levels of general loan loss reserves. The customer base of thrifts tends to be either seniors with large savings balances or young people needing home loans, while banks have a wide diversity of customers.

Exhibit 17-4 is a normalized comparison of the asset composition of SAIF-insured thrifts, BIF-insured thrifts, and commercial banks at December 31, 1990.[5] The discussion that follows will focus on SAIF-insured thrifts. BIF-insured savings banks, while having slightly different investment powers and operating limitations (as set by the various states), are quite similar to SAIF-insured thrifts.

Every company is unique; therefore, the industry information discussed below is provided merely for reader perspective. Economic conditions vary from year to year, as well as from region to region. Because the industry data is a composite, it is highly influenced by the larger companies, many of which are not particularly healthy.

Thrift Assets

Exhibit 17-4 provides a comparison of thrift and banking industry asset structures. The following discussion focuses on the key differences between the two.

Cash and Investments

Thrifts tend to be less liquid than banks. Most banks have 20–30 percent of their assets invested in various investment securities, while thrifts tend to have only about half that level. In recent years, with the slowdown in real estate lending activity nationwide (and the continuing amortization of thrift mortgage-related assets), the liquidity of most thrifts has increased.

Thrifts are required to maintain a minimum amount of cash, U.S. government securities, and certain other short-term investment securities equal to 5 percent of deposits and short-term borrowings. In addition, they are required to have short-term liquid assets equal to 1 percent of deposits plus the current portion of debt. Thrifts have lower liquidity needs than banks because they do not have significant commercial checking accounts or lines of credit, making their cash needs more predictable. They are able to borrow funds easily from their Federal Home Loan

---

[5]The statistics cited in this section's discussion come from OTS and FDIC data compiled by W. C. Ferguson and Company. Information concerning SAIF-insured thrifts excludes RTC-controlled companies. Balance sheet items, unless otherwise noted, are as of December 31, 1990. Income statement items are for the year ending December 31, 1990.

Exhibit 17-4

Thrifts versus Banks†

Asset Composition as a Percentage of Assets as of December 31, 1990

	SAIF-Insured Thrifts (%)‡	BIF-Insured Thrifts (%)	Commercial Banks (%)
Cash, deposits, and investment securities			
Cash and cash equivalents	1.3%	1.5%	6.4%
U.S. government and federal agency securities	4.3	3.9	6.6
Interest-earning deposits	2.0	1.0	3.0
Federal Funds sold	1.0	2.0	4.3
Mortgage-derivative securities	1.9	0.6	1.6
Other debt securities	2.4	6.0	5.0
Equity securities	0.3	1.7	0.3
Assets held in trading accounts	n.a.*	0.3	1.4
Adjustments	−0.1	−0.2	0.0
Net cash, deposits, and investment securities	13.1	16.8	28.6
Mortgage pool securities	14.5	8.7	4.3
Loans			
Real estate loans			
Construction	2.5	3.2	n.a.
Permanent mortgage			
1 to 4–family dwellings	42.9	40.8	n.a.
Multifamily	6.2	6.2	n.a.
Nonresidential	6.3	10.8	n.a.
Land	1.1	n.a.	n.a.
Total real estate loans	59.0	61.0	24.5
Nonmortgage loans			
Commercial and industrial loans	2.2	4.0	18.2
Consumer loans	4.4	4.0	11.9
Other loans	0.0	0.8	8.1
Total nonmortgage loans	6.6	8.8	38.2
Adjustments	−1.5	−0.3	−0.5
Reserves	−0.7	−1.1	−1.6
Net loans	63.4	68.4	60.6
Other assets			
Repossessed assets	2.1	1.7	0.6
Real estate held for investment	0.2	n.a.	n.a.
Investment in subsidiaries	1.2	0.4	0.1
Office premises and equipment	1.1	1.2	1.5
Accrued interest receivable	0.8	0.5	0.6
Capitalized loan servicing	0.4	0.1	0.1
Goodwill and other intangibles	1.1	0.6	0.3
Other	2.1	1.6	3.3
Net other assets	9.0	6.1	6.5
Total assets	100.0%	100.0%	100.0%

*n.a. = not applicable.
†Composite industry data.
‡Does not include RTC-controlled companies.

SOURCE: OTS and FDIC data compiled by W. C. Ferguson and Company.

Bank. Additionally, because the mortgage lending business has lower margins than other forms of lending, thrifts generally minimize their holdings of lower yielding investment securities.

Most investment securities are carried on thrift balance sheets at amortized cost. Mutual fund shares and other marketable equity securities are shown at the lower of cost or market. Any unrealized losses in the value of mutual funds or other marketable equity securities are accounted for as direct valuation reserves against equity. Later, if these securities rise in value, their carrying values are adjusted upward and the reserves against equity are reduced. Securities can never be valued in excess of amortized cost. Only if securities are sold does any gain or loss flow through the income statement. Under FIRREA, thrifts are required to divest any "high-yield" or "junk" bonds prior to August 1994. As a result, any junk bonds maturing after August 1994 are carried at the lower of cost or market.

SAIF-insured institutions are required to own stock in their regional Federal Home Loan Bank (FHLB). The amount of required stock is a function of the amount of residential mortgage loans held and the amount of money borrowed from the FHLB by a thrift. FHLB stock is shown on the balance sheet under "Cash and investments," "Other assets," or as a separate line item. FHLB shares are purchased from the FHLB and are occasionally sold back to the FHLB at par value. There is no trading market for FHLB stock. The FHLBs pay dividends to stockholders, generally in the form of stock, and the dividends are exempt from federal taxation. Under FIRREA, the various FHLBs are required to pay a portion of the resolution costs of failed thrifts; consequently, FHLB dividends have been reduced during the last couple of years.

Mortgage Pool Securities

Mortgage pool, or mortgage-backed, securities are interests in pools of mortgages bought and held by a variety of secondary mortgage market agencies, including the Federal Home Loan Mortgage Corporation (Freddie Mac), Federal National Mortgage Association (Fannie Mae), and Government National Mortgage Association (Ginnie Mae). Freddie Mac, Fannie Mae, and Ginnie Mae are government-sponsored agencies. Their securities are generally considered to have little credit risk. However, because they are merely securitized mortgage loans, largely fixed-rate, they possess the same level of interest rate risk as do long-term, fixed-rate mortgage loans. Some mortgage-backed securities are adjustable-rate in nature. Unlike other debt securities, mortgage-backed securities pay principal and interest monthly. For many thrifts, their investment in mortgage-backed securities represents securities backed by their own mortgage loans. There is an active market for these securities, and they are easily marked to market.

Banks classify mortgage pool securities as investment securities, whereas thrifts classify them as loans. Thrifts are larger investors in mortgage-backed securities than banks.

Loans

As discussed earlier, thrifts are mainly mortgage lenders and banks are more diversified lenders. In addition, thrifts tend to have a greater percentage of their balance sheets invested in loans than do banks. At December 31, 1990, nearly 78 percent of all SAIF-insured thrift assets were loans (including mortgage pool securities), compared to 65 percent for banks.

Real Estate Loans

More than 90 percent of loans made by thrifts are real estate loans (including mortgage pool securities). Banks generally devote less than 40 percent of loans to real estate. Of thrift real estate loans, more than 80 percent are for the construction or purchase of single-family dwelling units (actually 1–4-family dwelling units). Approximately 9 percent of thrift real estate loans are for the construction or purchase of multifamily dwellings (largely condominiums and apartments), and another 9 percent are secured by nonresidential real estate (churches, shopping centers, office buildings, etc.). Less than 2 percent of real estate loans are for the purchase of raw land. Approximately 3 percent of SAIF-insured thrift loans are for new construction. BIF-insured thrifts have slightly greater percentages of construction and nonresidential loans and lower levels of single-family loans and mortgage-backed securities.

Most thrifts will lend up to about 80 percent of the appraised value of the real estate securing a loan. The loan-to-value ratio can be increased to as much as 95 percent for a single-family loan insured with private mortgage insurance (PMI). The secondary mortgage market agencies (Ginnie Mae, Fannie Mae, and Freddie Mac) also have size, income, and documentation requirements for loans eligible for their programs. Most thrifts have adopted these national market requirements for their own underwriting criteria.

The typical residential mortgage loan has a 15- to 30-year term. However, because of fluctuating interest rates and because homeowners move periodically, the effective term for most home mortgages is 8–10 years. The prepayment rate varies from locale to locale due to local economic conditions and demographics. Residential mortgage loans generally have a due-on-sale clause and no prepayment penalty for paying off a mortgage loan before it matures. Multifamily and nonresidential mortgage loans generally have shorter terms or incorporate balloon payments.

Historically, most thrift mortgage loans have been fixed rate in nature. Beginning in the early 1980s, thrifts began offering adjustable-rate mortgage loans, called ARMs, under a variety of programs. The interest rates on ARM loans adjust periodically to offer some measure of protection to lenders against rising interest rates. The majority of ARMs adjust annually, although some adjust every six months, three years, or five years. Most ARMs also incorporate annual and lifetime interest rate caps. The standard is a 2 percent maximum annual change (cap) and 6 percent maximum lifetime change (cap) from the original rate. There are also 2 percent annual and 5 percent lifetime ARMs and 1 percent annual and 4 percent lifetime ARMs.

Most ARMs are priced against an index, such as the U.S. Treasury one-year constant-maturity index. There are a number of other indexes as well. The interest rate on an ARM is the sum of the index and the margin. The typical margin for a one-year ARM, indexed on the one-year U.S. Treasury constant-maturity index, is 2.75 percent—that is, if the index is 8 percent and the margin is 2.75 percent, then the fully indexed interest rate is 10.75 percent.

In competitive markets, most lenders offer a "teaser rate" for the first year of the loan. For example, a given lender may offer a one-year ARM for 8.75 percent for the first year, even though the fully indexed rate is 10.75 percent. The following year, the lender is able to adjust the interest rate, according to the index, up to a maximum of 2 percent (usually). If interest rates remain unchanged during the year, the teaser loan will adjust upward 2 percent to 10.75 percent and thus be in line with the market. If rates drop 1 percent during the next year, then the teaser ARM would only adjust 1 percent to 9.75 percent, as the rate on the ARM cannot exceed the fully indexed rate. On the other hand, if interest rates rise 1 percent during the next year, this ARM loan will adjust up the maximum 2 percent to 10.75 percent, but still be 1 percent below the fully indexed rate of 11.75 percent. Of course, rate adjustments can be downward as well.

The ARM loan was created to minimize the impact of rising interest rates on the earnings of thrifts. However, most consumers prefer fixed-rate mortgage loans. This is because many homeowners fear that upward adjustments in interest rates will increase the possibility that they will be unable to make their monthly mortgage payments. Therefore, when interest rates drop, ARM borrowers often refinance their mortgage loans for cheaper fixed-rate loans.[6]

Few thrifts located in competitive markets are able to make a significant number of ARMs in low interest-rate environments because borrowers know their payments will rise. During higher rate periods, ARMs are popular because they offer the prospect of reduced mortgage payments when interest rates fall. They are also popular during higher rate times because they are often offered with a teaser rate, usually below that offered for a fixed-rate mortgage loan. Consequently, many ARM lenders, particularly in competitive metropolitan markets, receive lower average interest rates over the lives of the average ARM loan than they would have if they had made fixed-rate loans at prevailing market rates over time.

At December 31,1990, approximately 60 percent of all mortgage loans at SAIF-insured thrifts were ARMs. About 58 percent of single-family mortgage loans were adjustable, as were more than 70 percent of multifamily and nonresidential mortgage loans. Construction, multifamily, and nonresidential loans usually adjust with the prime lending rate. Commercial banks, on the other hand, tend not to lend "long" with a fixed rate. About 50 percent of all bank loans are floating-rate in nature. At December 31, 1990, only about 35 percent of all bank loans mature or reprice beyond the one-year horizon. Only 12 percent mature or reprice beyond five years.

Construction, multifamily, and nonresidential mortgage lending entails significantly more credit risk than does relatively safe single-family mortgage lending. Under FIRREA, thrifts' nonresidential lending is limited to 400 percent of capital. Formerly, up to 40 percent of thrift assets were allowed to be nonresidential loans.

Non-Real Estate Lending

The majority of commercial bank loans are not real estate related. Approximately 60 percent of bank loans are for commercial, consumer, or

---

[6] The result is that ARM lenders are often "stuck" with what amount to fixed-rate mortgage loans with low coupons.

other borrowers (other financial institutions, agricultural, political subdivisions, etc.). On the other hand, only about 10 percent of thrift loans
are commercial or consumer loans. BIF-insured savings banks tend to
have a slightly greater level of nonmortgage loans. Until the early 1980s,
few SAIF-insured thrifts engaged in a material amount of consumer or
commercial lending. Many thrifts, however, see consumer lending as the
major growth area for the future. In fact, more consumer loans are
originated annually than mortgage loans at many thrifts. Only about
one third of nonmortgage thrift loans are commercial loans.

Thrift commercial loans are usually made with inventories, accounts
receivable, equipment, vehicles, securities, or crops and livestock as collateral. Many thrifts insist on real estate as additional collateral as well.
Secured commercial loans usually have a fairly low loan-to-value ratio,
typically 50 percent. However, more than 40 percent of thrift commercial loans are unsecured. Commercial loans generally adjust using the
prime lending rate as the index. Federally chartered thrifts are permitted to invest up to 10 percent of assets in commercial loans.

Thrift consumer loans are secured by deposits, second mortgages,
automobiles, recreational vehicles, boats, mobile homes, and a variety
of other types of collateral. Most thrifts lend between 80 percent and 90
percent against the value of the collateral when making a consumer loan.
Less than 15 percent of thrift consumer loans are unsecured. Federally
chartered thrifts are allowed to invest up to 30 percent of their assets
in consumer loans, not including home improvement and loans on
deposits. Consumer loans at thrifts tend to have five-year or shorter terms
(except second mortgages, which can have terms up to 15 years) and can
be either fixed- or adjustable-rate in nature. They also have higher yields
than mortgage loans. The combination of shorter terms and higher yields
make nonmortgage loans attractive to thrifts.

Loan Loss Reserves

Thrifts have historically added to loan loss reserves only when specific
problems came to light, rather than adding to general reserves on a
regular basis as do most banks. Consequently, reserve levels are usually much lower at thrifts. In recent years, thrifts have been required by
their regulators to begin establishing general reserves. It should be noted,
however, that thrifts generally do not require the same degree of reserve
coverage as banks. Because the vast majority of thrift loans are relatively
safe single-family mortgage loans, thrifts typically are able to operate
with lower reserve levels than banks.

When testing for the adequacy of reserves, many analysts apply
reserve factors (based on experience and the relative risks of each general
category of loans) to the various types of loans at a thrift to estimate
reasonable loan loss reserve levels. A thrift's actual reserve level is then
compared to this estimated required level to assess the adequacy of the
current loan loss reserves.

Loans to One Borrower

Loan concentrations are a major area of risk for financial institutions.
Thrifts were formerly allowed to lend to one borrower, or groups of affiliated borrowers, an amount equal to regulatory capital. In 1986, the

FHLBB proposed limiting that maximum amount to 25 percent of regulatory capital. That proposal was never implemented, but when FIRREA was passed in 1989, loans to one borrower were limited to the greater of $500,000 or 15 percent of capital (calculated according to the lowest of the three regulatory capital requirements). This level is in line with the limitations imposed on commercial banks. Thrifts are allowed to lend up to an additional 10 percent of capital for loans fully collateralized by readily marketable collateral. Also, thrifts are allowed to lend up to the lesser of $30 million or 30 percent of capital for certain types of housing development loans.

The imposition of FIRREA's loan to one borrower restrictions caused considerable problems for lenders and borrowers alike. As a result, a transition rule was passed. For those thrifts meeting their fully phased-in capital requirements, up to 30 percent of capital is allowed to be lent to a single borrower. The transition rule is due to expire on December 31, 1991. Loans that were granted prior to the enactment of FIRREA are grandfathered and therefore exempt from the limitations. However, lenders are not allowed to extend, increase, or otherwise modify grandfathered loans if doing so results in the new loan exceeding the new limitation.

Participation Loans

Because economic conditions vary throughout the country, many thrifts and banks in capital-surplus regions have sought to make loans in capital-deficient regions through participation lending. Typically, however, a lender may seek to make a local loan that is beyond its legal or internal loan limit. The lead lender contacts other lenders in capital-surplus areas to solicit participants for the loan. A participation loan is originated by the lead lender, and "pieces" of the loan are sold to participants. The lead lender underwrites and services the loan on behalf of the participating lenders and generally retains a small percentage of the loan (typically 10 percent). As noted in Chapter 8, commercial banks also originate and/or purchase participation loans.

Participation lending is a perfectly valid method of diversifying geographical risk as well as reducing excess liquidity. Unfortunately, many thrifts (and commercial banks) have not underwritten their participation loans as carefully as their local loans. Too often, they have relied upon lead lenders to investigate and document the creditworthiness of the projects and the borrowers. In addition, participants do not know the market area of participation loans as well as they know their own areas. As a consequence, many thrifts have suffered severe losses as a result of poor underwriting of participation loans.

Qualified Thrift Lender (QTL) Test

Thrift institutions enjoy a tax preference because home ownership is considered to be in the national interest. For many years, thrifts, like credit unions, did not pay income taxes. Later, taxes were levied, but a large percentage of thrift income was shielded from taxation. During the years immediately prior to 1986, thrifts were allowed to deduct 40 percent of their pretax earnings before determining their taxable income. This untaxed portion of retained earnings was set aside as a reserve for bad debts. In 1986, the bad debt deduction was reduced to 8 percent of income, but the corporate tax rate fell to 34 percent at the same time, resulting in no change to the effective federal tax rate of 31.28 percent.[7]

In order to retain this tax preference, thrifts must invest a large percentage of their balance sheets in assets related to home ownership. Prior to passage of FIRREA, thrifts had to maintain 60 percent of assets in qualifying loans, investments, and other assets. FIRREA increased the qualifying loan percentage to 70 percent of portfolio assets. The calculation of the qualifying loan percentage is called the qualified thrift lender (QTL) test.

Qualifying assets for the QTL test include: residential mortgage loans; manufactured-housing loans; home equity loans; mortgage-backed securities; certain obligations to the FDIC, FSLIC, and RTC; investments in service corporations (thrift subsidiaries) involved in housing; church, school, nursing home, and hospital loans; 5 percent of consumer loans; and an amount equal to 200 percent of low-to-moderate-income housing loans. Not included in portfolio assets are goodwill and other intangible assets, office premises, and liquid assets up to 10 percent of assets.

Thrifts that fail the QTL test can be required to convert to a national bank and be limited to the investments and operations allowed to national banks in the state of domicile. More importantly, they will be liable to pay taxes on the amount of income previously untaxed. Many analysts believe that FIRREA's imposition of a stricter QTL standard will make it much more difficult for thrifts to improve earnings and build or attract capital. By requiring thrifts to concentrate further in mortgage lending, an inherently low margin business, additional failures may result.

Other Assets

Thrifts tend to have a greater level of non-interest-earning (other) assets than banks. Other assets include all assets that are not cash, investment securities, or loans. Thrifts have larger investments in subsidiary service corporations and intangible assets, while banks have greater investments in their offices. Of course, the level of repossessed assets varies from institution to institution and from period to period, depending on local economic conditions and the underwriting standards of individual institutions.

Thrift subsidiaries (called *service corporations*) are often involved in real estate development and management, discount brokerage, sales of insurance and annuities, and mortgage banking. Thrifts may invest up to 2 percent of assets in their service corporations and an additional 1 percent of assets for community and inner-city development purposes. Assets repossessed from borrowers are often transferred to service corporations.

---

[7]The 31.28 percent effective federal tax rate is calculated as follows: Assume a thrift had net income before taxes of $100. The bad-debt deduction allows the thrift to deduct 8 percent, or $8 in this case, resulting in adjusted pretax income of $92. Applying the 34 percent corporate tax rate to the $92 results in taxes of $31.28 and thus an effective tax rate of 31.28 percent.

Banks tend to invest more heavily in their offices and facilities than do thrifts because they are much more transaction oriented than thrifts. Thrifts do not have as many checking accounts or make as many consumer or commercial loans. Consequently, many thrift offices do not have drive-up facilities or automatic teller machines. They also tend to have smaller lobbies and fewer private offices for bankers to meet with customers.

Intangible assets include goodwill, unamortized premiums paid for deposits, and capitalized loan servicing. Thrifts have traditionally acquired other thrifts with cash, rather than issuing stock, so the thrift industry has a much higher percentage of goodwill on its balance sheet than does the commercial banking industry. Pre-FIRREA, thrifts were also able to count goodwill as part of regulatory capital, whereas banks could not. In fact, even though the thrift industry is only about one third the size of the banking industry, it actually has more total goodwill and other intangibles on its composite balance sheet than does the banking industry ($10.8 billion versus $9.0 billion). Goodwill amortization is not deductible for tax purposes, but amortization of deposit premia are deductible. As a result, banks have made an effort to allocate as much of the purchase price for other banks as possible to deposit premia, rather than goodwill. (See Chapter 19's discussion of core deposit intangible assets.)

When loans are sold to a secondary mortgage market agency or to other financial institutions, the seller normally continues to service the loans for a fee. Servicing fees are usually 0.375 percent of the outstanding loan balance for single-family, fixed-rate loans and 0.5 percent for ARMs. Servicing responsibilities include collecting payments from borrowers, remitting payments to the owners of the loans, inspecting properties securing the loans, setting up escrow accounts and paying taxes and insurance on secured properties, and collecting late payments and working with delinquent borrowers. Capitalized mortgage servicing rights include the acquisition price of servicing rights purchased from others, an allocation of the purchase price of other financial institutions, as well as gains from excess servicing spreads on loans sold.

The valuation of mortgage servicing rights can be tricky. Value is a function of several factors, including the current level of interest rates compared to the average coupon rates of the loans, expected prepayment rates, the average age of the loans being serviced, the average loan size, the incremental cost of servicing the loans, and the expected rate of inflation. If any of these assumptions is incorrect, the value of the servicing may be understated or overstated. A large component of the value of mortgage servicing rights relates to the ability of the servicer to hold non-interest-bearing (or low-interest-bearing) escrow deposits. These deposits are funds collected monthly from borrowers to be held for the payment of annual property taxes and insurance premiums. Consequently, escrow funds build up during the course of the year until the servicer pays the borrowers' annual property taxes and insurance premiums. While escrow funds are held by a servicer, they are invested in interest-earning assets. Because escrow deposits are non-interest bearing (or low-interest bearing), the servicer is able to earn a wide spread on the funds.

Under GAAP, financial institutions are required to verify the book value of loan servicing rights annually. The book value of the capitalized servicing rights is amortized over the life of the loans being serviced. For many thrifts, the value of loans serviced for others is an off balance sheet asset because self-created servicing has no cost basis and therefore does not appear on the balance sheet. This accounting treatment is analogous to that of the treatment of core deposit intangible assets for banks and thrifts.

Thrift Liabilities

We now turn our attention to the liability and equity side of the balance sheet. Although banks and thrifts are both in the business of accepting deposits, the composition of the deposits varies considerably between the two. Exhibit 17-5 compares the composite liabilities and equity of thrifts versus banks.

Exhibit 17-5

Liability and Equity Composition As a Percentage of Assets
Thrifts versus Banks† as of December 31, 1990

	SAIF-Insured Thrifts (%)‡	BIF-Insured Thrifts (%)	Commercial Banks (%)
Deposits			
Domestic			
Passbook accounts	6.5%	15.3%	5.9%
Transaction accounts			
Demand deposit accounts	n.a.*	2.5	13.7
Other transaction accounts	n.a.	3.7	6.4
Total transaction accounts	5.1	6.2	20.1
Money market deposit accounts	8.0	9.8	11.2
Fixed-maturity certificates	56.8	51.2	32.3
Foreign			
Non-interest-bearing	n.a.	n.a.	0.4
Interest-bearing	n.a.	n.a.	8.3
Total deposits	76.4	82.5	78.2
Borrowings			
Federal Home Loan Bank advances	8.9	n.a.	n.a.
Reverse repurchase agreements	4.0	n.a.	n.a.
Mortgage-backed securities	0.7	n.a.	n.a.
Federal Funds purchased	n.a.	2.7	7.2
Subordinated debt	0.4	0.2	0.7
Other borrowings	2.7	6.5	4.8
Total borrowings	16.7	9.4	12.7
Other liabilities	1.8	1.1	2.6
Total liabilities	94.9	93.0	93.5
Equity	5.1	7.0	6.5
Total liabilities and equity	100.0%	100.0%	100.0%

*n.a. = not applicable or not available.
†Composite industry data.
‡Does not include RTC-controlled companies.

SOURCE: OTS and FDIC data compiled by W. C. Ferguson and Company.

Deposits

Banks cater to the transaction needs of businesses and individuals. Thrifts, on the other hand, have focused on the savings market. Only during the last 10 years have thrifts offered checking type accounts. Because interest rate ceilings were removed in 1980, banks and thrifts have seen a progressive shift of funds away from low interest rate passbook accounts to market rate paying certificate accounts. In addition, various types of interest-paying checking accounts began to be offered.

As illustrated in Exhibit 17-5, SAIF-insured thrifts and commercial banks fund only about 6 percent of assets with passbook accounts. BIF-insured savings banks have done a better job of attracting and retaining these accounts, probably because savings banks are concentrated in the Northeast, where large ethnic populations tend to hold savings in passbook accounts. Compared to banks, thrifts have much lower levels of transaction accounts, such as checking accounts, negotiable orders of withdrawal (NOW accounts), and Super-NOW accounts (which pay slightly higher rates). Just under 1.5 percent of SAIF-insured thrift deposits are non-interest-bearing (3 percent for BIF-insured savings banks), whereas more than 18 percent of commercial bank deposits are non-interest-bearing. Banks also have a greater percentage of money market demand accounts (limited checking accounts), which are also a lower cost account type.

Thrifts fund the majority of their operations with various types of time deposits. Nearly 75 percent of thrift deposits are fixed maturity time deposits. Time deposits at banks, however, account for only about 40 percent of deposits. Most time deposits are fairly short term, so they are quite rate sensitive. More than 60 percent of thrift time deposits have maturities of one year or less. More than 80 percent of bank time deposits mature or reprice at least annually.

Thrifts tend to rely less heavily on jumbo deposits (over $100,000) than do banks. At December 31, 1990, more than 14 percent of bank deposits were classified as jumbo deposits, primarily because of large corporate and governmental cash balances held by banks. Jumbo deposits represented about 11 percent of total deposits for SAIF-insured thrifts and about 8 percent for BIF-insured savings banks. SAIF-insured thrifts had somewhat more brokered deposits than commercial banks or BIF-insured savings banks. Nearly 4 percent of SAIF-insured deposits were brokered, compared to less than 3 percent for BIF-insured savings banks and commercial banks. Jumbo and brokered deposits tend to be more rate sensitive than other deposits, so they present interest rate and liquidity issues to banks and thrifts.

Partially as a result of their large percentage of transaction accounts, particularly non-interest-bearing accounts, banks tend to have a lower cost of funds and a much higher net interest spread than do thrifts (see Chapters 9 and 10). On the other hand, thrifts generally have lower levels of non-interest operating expenses than do commercial banks. On the liability side of the balance sheet, processing savings accounts is less costly than processing transaction accounts. And on the asset side of the balance sheet, mortgage loan processing is generally more standardized and efficient than commercial loan processing.

Borrowings

SAIF-insured thrifts tend to be larger borrowers of nondeposit funds than BIF-insured thrifts or commercial banks, partially because thrifts have enjoyed easy access to a variety of advances through their memberships in the Federal Home Loan Bank system (all SAIF-insured thrifts are required to be members of the FHLB system) and partially because thrifts have suffered large deposit outflows as a result of negative publicity in recent years. The various Federal Home Loan Banks serve as a central credit facility for thrifts desiring to supplement their deposits to fund asset growth or for short-term cash needs. There are 12 regional FHLBs, and each bank determines its own lending rates. The FHLB system borrows funds from the public as a consolidated system, rather than individually. After passage of FIRREA, commercial banks, savings banks, and credit unions have been allowed to join the FHLB system if they meet certain minimum requirements.

Approximately 54 percent of thrift borrowings were FHLB advances at December 31, 1990. FHLB advances can be either secured or unsecured and short- or long-term, depending on the needs of the borrowing thrift. Each of the regional FHLBs sets its own lending limit, but borrowing limits tend to be around 25 percent of assets for individual thrifts.

The second largest source of borrowed funds for thrifts is reverse repurchase agreements (reverse repos) or agreements in which a thrift sells a security (usually a U.S. Treasury, federal agency, or mortgage-backed security) to a securities dealer and agrees to repurchase the same or similar security at a later date for a greater price (which includes the interest return to the purchaser). In essence, reverse repos are a form of secured borrowings that are generally short-term.

To a lesser degree, thrifts also borrow funds from other financial institutions or arrange collateralized borrowings by issuing mortgage-backed securities or collateralized mortgage obligations (CMOs). BIF-insured savings banks tend to borrow less than SAIF-insured thrifts because they are not all members of the FHLB system. The largest source of borrowed funds for banks are federal funds purchased.

Equity

SAIF-insured thrifts as a group are less well capitalized than either BIF-insured thrifts or commercial banks. Equity, as measured under generally accepted accounting principles (GAAP), was approximately 5.1 percent of total assets for SAIF-insured thrifts at December 31, 1990, compared to 7.0 of assets for BIF-insured thrifts and 6.5 percent of assets for commercial banks. Reducing equity by goodwill results in tangible net worth to assets ratios of 4.0 percent (SAIF), 6.4 percent (BIF), and 6.2 percent (banks). Equity at BIF-insured thrifts is higher than at SAIF-insured thrifts and commercial banks, primarily because of the large number of BIF-insured savings banks that converted to the stock form in 1986 and 1987 at the height of the market for thrift shares. Savings banks converting during that period were able to raise two or three times their preconversion net worth in conversion offerings. Historically, BIF-insured thrifts have also been more profitable than SAIF-insured thrifts.

During the last 20 years, thrifts have been subject to a variety of minimum capital requirements. Until 1989, thrift regulatory capital was supplemented by a variety of non-GAAP accounting conventions. FIRREA mandated that thrifts adhere to GAAP and required them to meet the capital standards of national banks. As a result, beginning in late 1989, thrift capital standards were revised upward. The new standards mandated that thrifts be able to meet requirements for tangible capital, core capital (leverage), and risk-based capital.

The tangible capital requirement was set at 1.5 percent, the core capital requirement at 3 percent and the risked-based requirement at 6.4 percent of risk-weighted assets. Beginning on January 1, 1991, the risked-based capital requirement was increased to 7.2 percent of risk-weighted assets and is scheduled to increase again to 8.0 percent on January 1, 1993. The OCC increased core capital requirements for certain national banks in 1990, which will result in higher core capital requirements for thrifts. As of October 1991, the revised core capital requirements for thrifts had not been issued. However, the OTS-proposed core capital rules suggest that thrifts with the highest examination rating will be allowed to retain a 3 percent core capital requirement. All other thrifts will be required to have core capital ratios of 4 to 5 percent, to be set on a case-by-case basis.[8]

Core capital for thrifts is generally defined as GAAP equity, less intangibles (including capitalized mortgage servicing rights) plus qualifying supervisory goodwill plus 90 percent of the book value of purchased mortgage servicing rights (up to 50 percent of core capital) plus noncumulative preferred stock. Tangible capital is defined as total capital less all intangibles (except the purchased mortgage servicing rights).

In order to determine compliance with risk-based capital requirements, both risk-based capital and risk-weighted assets must be computed. Risk-based capital is defined as core capital plus general valuation allowances, certain types of preferred stock, and subordinated debt. To calculate risk-weighted assets, thrift assets are divided into five risk categories, ranging from 0 percent (for risk-free assets, such as U.S. Treasury securities) to 200 percent (for high risk assets, such as repossessed assets and delinquent loans). Most single- and multifamily mortgage loans, because of their low risk, are placed in the 50 percent risk category. Mortgage-backed securities are placed into either the 0 percent category (Ginnie Mae) or 20 percent risk category (Freddie Mac and Fannie Mae). Assets placed into the 100 percent risk category include consumer and commercial loans, nonresidential loans, construction and land loans, home equity loans, fixed assets, qualifying supervisory goodwill, purchased mortgage loan servicing rights, and certain nonperforming single-family and multifamily loans. If all assets were in the 100 percent risk category, then risk-weighted assets would equal total assets. However, because of thrifts' large investments in home mortgage loans,

---

[8]In addition to the three capital standards discussed above, the OTS has proposed an interest rate risk component to the capital requirements. The regulation under consideration would require thrifts to maintain capital equal to 50 percent of the estimated decline in the market value of the thrift's portfolio equity that would result from an immediate and permanent 200 basis point change in interest rates. As of mid-1991, it was not clear how the OTS intended to implement this requirement or when or even if it would take effect.

the average risk-weighted assets to total assets ratio was 54 percent at December 31, 1990.

Of the 2,341 SAIF-insured institutions, 422 thrifts (or 18 percent of all thrifts) did not meet the three capital requirements in effect at December 31, 1990. If the requirements were increased to 4 percent for core capital (the probable minimum for most thrifts) and 8 percent for risk-based capital (the fully phased-in level) at the same date, 659 thrifts (or 28 percent) would fail the test. Finally, if a 5 percent core capital requirement had been imposed at December 31, 1990, then only 1,447 thrifts (or 62 percent) would meet the test. Clearly, many thrifts must increase earnings dramatically, raise additional capital, or merge with capital surplus institutions in order to meet the new capital requirements.

Thrift Income Statements

The examination of the comparative balance sheets of thrifts and banks discussed above gives many clues to the relative profitability of each type of institution. Exhibit 17-6 is an analysis of 1990 profitability by type of institution. As shown in the exhibit, approximately 73 percent of SAIF-insured thrifts were at least marginally profitable. Approximately 60 percent of BIF-insured thrifts were profitable, as were 87 percent of commercial banks. However, the thrift industry as a whole lost money (see Exhibit 17-7). The magnitude of losses by the unprofitable companies overshadowed the income of the profitable companies for both SAIF-insured and BIF-insured thrifts. Only 10 percent of SAIF-insured thrifts and 6 percent of BIF-insured thrifts earned a return on assets (ROA) of more than 1 percent during 1990. On the other hand, 46 percent of commercial banks earned an ROA exceeding 1 percent. On the loss side, 11 percent of SAIF-insured thrifts lost in excess of 1 percent of average assets while only 7 percent of commercial banks performed as poorly. Nearly 31 percent of BIF-insured savings banks lost more than 1 percent on assets. BIF-insured thrifts were especially hurt by poor economic conditions in the Northeast in 1989 and 1990.

All three types of institutions have shown a decline in industry earnings during the three years ending in 1990. Industry earnings have been adversely affected by deteriorating asset quality and the flat or inverted yield curve that was prevalent in 1989. Earnings were also hurt by the implementation of Financial Accounting Standard (FAS) 91, which required banks and thrifts to defer net loan origination fees over the life of loans as an adjustment to yield, rather than being recognized when the loans are originated. In the long term, FAS 91 will result in smoother reported earnings for thrifts, but it has significantly reduced reported earnings in the short term. The net amount of uncredited loan fees is shown on the balance sheet as unearned income, a contra asset.

Exhibit 17-7 is a composite, normalized income statement for SAIF-insured thrifts, BIF-insured savings banks, and commercial banks. Although 1990 was a poor year for all three types of financial intermediaries, the general characteristics of the individual components of the income statement can be discerned from the results shown.

Exhibit 17-6

Financial Institution Profitability as a Percentage of Average Assets 1990*

Return on Average Assets	SAIF-Insured Thrifts†		BIF-Insured Thrifts		Commercial Banks	
	No.	%	No.	%	No.	%
Losses						
1.00% or more	265	11.3%	108	23.8%	846	6.9%
.99% to .50%	126	5.4	27	6.0	282	2.3
.49% to .25%	107	4.6	25	5.5	208	1.7
.24% to .00%	113	4.8	19	4.2	221	1.8
Profits						
.00% to .25%	308	13.2	58	12.8	525	4.3
.26% to .50%	431	18.4	69	15.2	866	7.0
.51% to .75%	465	19.9	67	14.8	1,497	12.1
.76% to 1.00%	285	12.2	50	11.0	2,259	18.3
1.01% to 1.50%	192	8.2	20	4.4	4,128	33.4
1.51% or more	49	2.1	10	2.2	1,510	12.2
Total	2,341	100.0%	453	100.0%	12,342	100.0%

*Composite industry data.
†Excludes RTC-controlled companies.

SOURCE: OTS and FDIC data compiled by W. C. Ferguson and Company.

Exhibit 17-7

Income Statement as a Percentage of Average Assets Thrifts versus Banks 1990*

Income Statement	SAIF-Insured Thrifts (%)†	BIF-Insured Thrifts (%)	Commercial Banks (%)
Interest income	9.14%	9.34%	9.67%
Interest expense	7.25	6.77	6.18
Net interest income	1.89	2.57	3.49
Noninterest income	0.57	0.54	1.66
Adjusted gross income	2.46	3.11	5.15
Noninterest operating expense	2.09	2.47	3.49
Basic operating income	0.37	0.64	1.66
Provision for loan losses	−0.54	−1.23	−0.96
Net gain on sale of assets	0.11	−0.02	0.01
Pretax income	−0.06	−0.61	0.71
Income taxes	0.12	0.08	0.24
Net income before extraordinary items	−0.18	−0.69	0.47
Extraordinary items, net of taxes	0.01	0.00	0.02
Net income	−0.17	−0.69	0.49
Total assets ($ billions)	$1,005	$230	$3,389
Employees	268,075	69,583	1,517,456
Assets per employee ($ million)	$3.7	$3.3	$2.2
Compensation per employee	$30,680	$33,089	$34,093

*Composite industry data.
†Excludes RTC-controlled companies.

SOURCE: OTS and FDIC data compiled by W. C. Ferguson and Company.

Net Interest Income

Banks enjoy a much higher level of net interest income than thrifts. This results from a number of factors affecting banks more favorably than thrifts, including: a higher ratio of interest-earning assets to interest-bearing liabilities (because of lower levels of nonearning assets and higher levels of non-interest-bearing deposits), higher yields on loans (because mortgage loans have lower yields than consumer or commercial loans), and lower cost of funds (because of the more attractive deposit composition). During the four years ending in 1990, SAIF-insured thrifts had an average level of net interest income as a percentage of average assets of 1.86 percent, compared to 2.74 percent for BIF-insured savings banks and 3.53 percent for commercial banks. In addition to achieving generally higher levels of net interest income, bank performance in this category has tended to be more consistent from year to year.

Noninterest Income

Most thrifts have limited sources of noninterest income, particularly after FAS 91 was implemented in 1988. Nearly 50 percent of thrift noninterest income is comprised of fees from servicing loans as well as late fees, minimum balance fees and NSF charges. Thrifts also derive noninterest income from operating real estate, earning service corporation profits (a net loss in 1990), and other sources. Like thrifts, banks earn fees from service charges, but they also generate fee income from trust services, credit cards, and other sources. Typically, a bank earns about three times the level of noninterest income as does a thrift. Noninterest income at thrifts averaged between 50 and 60 basis points, compared with 166 basis points (1.66 percent) of average assets for the commercial banks during 1990.

Adjusted Gross Income

Adjusted gross income (AGI)—the sum of net interest income and noninterest income, or sales—for thrifts is much lower in terms of average assets than for commercial banks. AGI as a percentage of average assets was 2.46 percent for SAIF-insured thrifts and 3.11 percent for BIF-insured thrifts in 1990, compared with 5.15 percent for commercial banks. Lower AGI per dollar of assets is the direct result of the considerably lower net interest income and noninterest income factors outlined above.

Noninterest Operating Expenses

The area in which thrifts most frequently outperform banks is that of noninterest operating expenses. Banks operate at approximately 150 percent of the cost level of thrifts. Of course, banks offer more services and bank facilities tend to be larger and offer greater customer convenience than thrifts. Banks invest more in advertising and marketing as well. Most importantly, banks have more employees and pay them better than do thrifts. At December 31, 1990, the assets-per-employee ratio for SAIF-insured thrifts was $3.7 million. The corresponding figures for BIF-insured savings banks and commercial banks were $3.3 million and $2.2 million, respectively. Average compensation was $30,670 per employee for SAIF-insured thrifts in 1990, $33,089 for BIF-insured savings banks, and $34,093 for commercial banks.

Basic Operating Income

The comparisons between banks and thrifts above indicate clearly that the basic operating income of thrifts is considerably lower than for banks. SAIF-insured thrifts had basic operating income of 0.37 percent of assets in 1990, compared with similar ratios for BIF-insured thrifts and commercial banks of 0.54 percent and 1.66 percent, respectively. These comparisons of basic operating income show, on the negative side, the wide discrepancy that exists between the underlying profitability of banks and thrifts. On the more positive side, however, the comparisons indicate that the thrift industry is exhibiting positive operating income. If the industry can weather its remaining credit problems, there would appear to be an income stream from which profitability can be nurtured and grown. Nevertheless, the basic operating income of the thrift industry can best be described as anemic at the present time.

Provision for Loan Losses

The magnitude of loan loss provisions taken by financial institutions in 1990 gives an indication of the severity of the real estate depression that has affected most regions of the country. This is particularly true for the Northeast, the primary operating area of BIF-insured thrifts. Although SAIF-insured thrifts reserved a much lower level than did commercial banks, it is probably a relatively greater amount when one considers that nearly 70 percent of thrift loans are secured by single-family housing. All three types of institutions have significantly increased loan loss provisions in recent years.

The provision for loan losses as a percentage of average assets totaled 0.54 percent for SAIF-insured thrifts in 1990. The comparable ratios for BIF-insured thrifts, which are mostly concentrated in the Northeast, and commercial banks were 1.23 percent and 0.96 percent. Suffice it to say that credit losses of the magnitude to require loan loss provisions at the 1990 levels have a devastating impact on the profitability of the financial institution industry as a whole.

Net Gains on Sale of Assets

Because thrifts have been under so much pressure to report earnings and build capital, many have sold selective assets at a profit, even though analysts do not consider nonrecurring gains on asset sales to be core income. During the four years ending 1990, thrifts have reported an average net gain on sale of assets of 0.15 percent, as compared to 0.06 percent for savings banks and 0.03 percent for commercial banks. Unfortunately, when a financial institution sells assets at a gain, the proceeds from the sale are normally reinvested at lower rates, thus reducing future pro-fitability and lowering the overall portfolio yield on the remaining assets.

Taxes

Both SAIF- and BIF-insured thrifts reported pretax losses in 1990, but both groups provided for income taxes because most loan loss provisions are not tax deductible unless the credit is actually charged off. However, providing for taxes in a loss year will reduce taxes in a profitable year. Thrifts have an effective federal tax rate of 31.28 percent. The banking industry reported an effective (average) combined federal and state tax rate of 33 percent. Taxes on bank earnings are reduced because of the large amount of tax-free income received from municipal and state-issued securities held by banks.

Pretax Income (Loss)

SAIF-insured thrifts experienced a pretax loss of 0.06 percent of average assets in 1990. BIF-insured savings banks, battered by real estate–related losses in the Northeast, experienced a pretax loss of 0.61 percent of average assets. Commercial banks recorded a pretax income of 0.71 per-cent of average assets during the same year, which was the second-worst earnings performance in the last decade (following a pretax ROAA of 0.27 percent in 1987).

These figures serve to illustrate several significant points about thrift earnings relative to bank earnings, in addition to the fact that relative earnings performance is significantly lower for thrifts than for banks:

1. Interest rate spreads are low and under continuing pressure.
2. Noninterest income is low because of lower numbers of transactions accounts and other fee income generating businesses relative to banks.
3. Thrift noninterest operating expenses, although low relative to banks, will be under pressure as thrifts seek to add services, to become more competitive with banks, and to survive.

In summary, most thrifts are generally less profitable than commer-cial banks. Thrift income comparisons suffer from lower asset yields and higher funding costs. Mortgage loans do not provide yields as high as do commercial and consumer loans, and time deposits are more expen-sive than checking accounts. Thrifts also have a lower level of earning assets relative to costing liabilities. The higher level of net interest in-come for banks more than overcomes the more favorable noninterest margin (noninterest income less noninterest expense) reported by thrifts.

Interest Rate Risk

Yields on earning assets at thrifts are far less responsive to changes in interest rates than are the costs of deposit liabilities. Consequently, dur-ing periods of generally rising interest rates, thrift industry earnings decline as deposit costs increase more rapidly than yields on loans. Bank earnings, because of the more interest-sensitive nature of commercial lending, are somewhat less vulnerable to earnings fluctuations resulting from changing interest rates. When an institution has more rate-sensitive assets than rate-sensitive liabilities during a given period, it is said to have a positive "gap." Such institutions experience improving earnings during periods of rising interest rates and lower earnings during periods of declining interest rates. This is the situation at some commercial banks. On the other hand, thrifts are usually negatively gapped and tend to be more negatively gapped than commercial banks. The basic thrift industry structure requires the funding of long-term assets with short-term liabilities. Even ARM loans are not particularly rate sensitive because most adjust only annually and annual adjustments are limited by annual and lifetime caps.

When valuing a thrift, the analyst must consider the amount of interest rate risk inherent in the subject company. This is a difficult task because there is no universally accepted method of measuring interest rate risk. In addition, there is no single source of raw data available to the public to allow a complete independent analysis. The OTS and FDIC do not release maturity and repricing data in sufficient detail to allow for more than a cursory observation about interest rate risk concerning the industry as a whole. Publicly traded companies release data about their one-year gaps, but the measurement of the gap is not consistently performed from company to company. In addition, publicly traded thrifts represent but 16 percent of all thrift institutions. Only a few very large thrifts regularly produce their own analysis of interest rate risk. The typical thrift reports a one-year gap (adjusted for loan prepayments and deposit runoffs) of between −5 percent and −15 percent of total assets.[9]

Fortunately, even small thrifts now receive quarterly reports concerning interest rate risk, although the reports are not generally available to the public. These reports are generated by the OTS, the thrift's FHLB, or an outside service, and they usually provide three measurements: the one-year asset/liability maturity gap, changes to projected net interest income resulting from changes in interest rates, and changes in the market value of portfolio equity resulting from changes in interest rates. In addition to providing information on the subject institution, the gap reports also provide comparable data for various peer groups. Although these measurements are far from perfect—indeed the results vary significantly from period to period and from one report provider to another—they do provide a basis for assessing relative interest rate risk.

Asset Quality

Two of the most important areas of risk that an analyst must consider are credit risk and asset quality. The poor quality of thrift assets and bank assets have been well publicized by the media. Many companies have reported sharply lower earnings in recent years, largely because of unusually large loan loss provisions (see Exhibit 17-7). Most analysts consider the ratio of nonperforming assets as a percentage of total assets

---

[9]The one-year gap is calculated by subtracting liabilities maturing or repricing within one year from assets maturing or repricing within one year and dividing that amount by total assets.

to be one reasonable indicator of asset quality. For thrifts, nonperforming assets are usually defined as the sum of repossessed assets, loans delinquent more than 90 days but still accruing interest, nonaccruing loans, and restructured troubled debt. At December 31, 1990, SAIF-insured thrifts reported nonperforming assets of 5.1 percent of total assets. The comparable figures for BIF-insured savings banks and commercial banks were 5.6 percent and 3.2 percent of assets, respectively.

Nonperforming assets place a current charge against earnings in the form of forgone interest income on nonearning or underperforming loans. They are also the source of potential future charges to earnings. Therefore, when appraising a thrift, the analyst must consider not only the levels of nonperforming assets and loss reserves, but also the prospect for future additions to both. The quality of loan underwriting must be evaluated, as well as the degree of exposure to single borrowers, geographic locations or industries, the method used by the company to evaluate loss exposure, and its charge-off experience. Based on the continuing credit losses reported by the financial industry, it must be concluded that many banks and thrifts have been optimistic when reporting quarterly results. It is not uncommon for an institution to report much higher loan loss reserves as part of its annual independent audit than in its quarterly earnings announcements, resulting in a fairly high number of required corrections to previously filed regulatory financial statements.[10]

Valuation of Stock Thrifts

The valuation process for stock thrifts is very similar to that for commercial banks. In general, the same approaches and methodologies apply. However, the application of the various techniques must account for the operational differences between banks and thrifts.

As previously noted, thrift capitalization factors (i.e., price/earnings multiples, price/book-value ratios or price/assets ratios) tend to be significantly lower than those for banks. This occurs because of a variety of factors, including greater interest rate risk, credit risk (thrifts tend to reserve for specific loan losses rather than maintaining an adequate general loan loss reserve), and prepayment risk (for mortgage-related assets) for thrifts relative to banks. Hence, thrift earnings tend to be more variable from period to period than bank earnings. Earnings multiples therefore tend to be lower, reflecting these risks. In addition, because of the long-term, fixed-rate nature of thrift assets, historical cost accounting tends to overstate thrift book values, relative to the market values of the underlying assets, so thrift price/book-value ratios tend to be lower than those of banks.

When appraising a thrift converting from the mutual to the stock form of ownership, the appraiser employs a slightly different technique. In a mutual-to-stock conversion, the appraiser must determine the pro forma fair market value of the converting thrift. This requires account-

---

[10]As a consequence, it is important to ensure that sources of regulatory financial data used by the thrift analyst, whether hard-copy reports from the subject institution or publicly available data sources, include the most recently amended regulatory financial statements for the periods under consideration.

ing for the addition of the new capital resulting from the conversion and the pro forma earnings on the net conversion proceeds. In addition, the appraiser may apply an appropriate discount to reflect the lack of a previous trading market for the shares of the converting thrift, commonly known as the *new issue discount*. This methodology is explained in the following sections.

Mutual-to-Stock Conversions

Mutual-to-stock conversions are a relatively recent development. In 1948, only three states permitted stock savings and loan associations and there were no federal stock charters. Between 1948 and 1955, only a limited number of stock conversions occurred under a variety of conversion plans. Between 1955 and 1962, the FHLBB imposed a conversion moratorium until a comprehensive set of conversion regulations could be formulated. The 1961 regulations called for a free distribution of a converting association's accumulated net worth.

In 1963, however, the FHLBB implemented a second moratorium on conversions because of inequities that had developed in the process. Insiders at many converting institutions had convinced the account holders to sell their interests in the converting association's net worth at a discount. The insiders suggested that the conversion stock would have little value and that there would be no market for the securities. Thus, windfall profits accrued to the insiders of the converting institutions. There was also concern that depositors would shift their funds from association to association seeking a windfall from the free stock distribution.

The 1963 moratorium lasted until 1976, during which time eight test case conversions were approved by the FHLBB. Also during this period, after numerous studies and false starts, as well as severe congressional criticism, the FHLBB adopted a sale-of-stock approach to conversions. Under this approach, depositors were given first right of refusal, on a priority basis, to purchase conversion stock in an amount proportionate to their deposits on a given record date. Any shares not purchased by the depositors would be offered to management and the public. The amount of stock issued would be equal to the pro forma fair market value of the converting association. At this time, the need for an independent appraisal in the conversion process was born.

The sale-of-stock approach was subject to lawsuits during the late 1970s. However, these challenges were ultimately defeated.[11] Exhibit 17-8 shows conversion activity among SAIF-insured thrifts between 1975 and 1991. Since 1975, more than 800 SAIF-insured thrifts have converted to stock, raising approximately $12 billion of capital. Billions more have been raised by BIF-insured savings banks. The peak of conversion activity occurred between 1983 and 1987, when 473 savings and loans raised more than $9 billion of new capital.

---

[11]For a discussion of the history of mutual-to-stock conversions, see Julie L. Williams, et al., "Mutual-to-Stock Conversions: New Capitalization Opportunities and Post-Conversion Control Developments," *Legal Bulletin*, May 1987.

Exhibit 17-8
Mutual-to-Stock Conversions*

Year	Number of Transactions	Proceeds ($ millions)
1975	1	$ 1.3
1976	14	50.9
1977	14	29.6
1978	5	13.5
1979	16	114.4
1980	15	141.4
1981	37	126.6
1982	31	123.0
1983	83	2,740.7
1984	96	714.9
1985	78	1,385.0
1986	86	2,482.2
1987	130	1,957.3
1988	98	767.1
1989	35	351.4
1990	69	774.4
1991†	21	78.2
Totals	829	$11,851.9

*Includes all types of conversions (SAIF-insured thrifts only).
†Through April 1991.

SOURCE: OTS.

Historically, thrifts have not been as well capitalized as commercial banks. In recent years, regulations and laws have been implemented to encourage thrift institutions to raise additional capital. FIRREA, enacted in 1989, requires that thrifts adhere to the same capital requirements as are applicable to national banks. As a result, hundreds of thrifts do not meet their new capital standards and will need to raise capital. In addition, most analysts believe the mutual form of organization is dying, because one of the primary benefits to conversion is being able to attract good management. Mutuals will be unable to draw new managers without the incentives from stock options or ESOPs. Consequently, as the current generation of mutual managers retires, there will be increasing pressure to convert. As a result, conversion activity is expected to continue for a number of years.

At December 31, 1990, there were more than 1,600 mutual thrifts. Of this number, less than half are candidates for a standard conversion during the next five years. Approximately 25 percent of the mutuals will fail or will undertake a nonstandard conversion (discussed later in this chapter). The remainder may retain mutual status for some years to come; but eventually, they, too, will probably convert.

Mutual-to-Stock Conversion Process

The conversion regulations effective in mid-1991 were implemented in 1983, with some minor amendments in 1985 and 1986.[12] These conversion regulations apply to all SAIF-insured thrifts, regardless of charter. In addition, the OTS has issued guidelines to appraisers submitting ap-

---

[12]The OTS conversion regulations are set forth in 12 C.F.R., part 563b.

praisal reports in connection with conversions.[13] The conversion of BIF-insured thrifts is regulated by the various states. State conversion rules are very similar, if not identical, to the federal conversion regulations.

The conceptual basis for conversion rests on a number of key points, including:

1. The converting thrift's members (depositors and borrowers) receive the right of first refusal to subscribe for the purchase of the conversion stock. These rights are nontransferable.
2. The stock is sold at fair market value, as determined by an independent appraiser. Independence refers to independence from the converting thrift, not from an underwriter. Appraisals are reviewed by the OTS (or the state) to determine reasonableness.
3. Postconversion windfalls are precluded by limiting the amount of stock that can be acquired by an individual, group, or entity. Generally, the maximum purchase limitation is 5 percent of the offered stock.
4. The ability to acquire control of a recently converted thrift is limited. Purchases by insiders (management and directors) in the conversion are limited to a total of between 25 percent and 34 percent of the offering, depending upon the size of the institution. No third party is allowed to acquire more than 10 percent of the shares during the three years following conversion without permission from the appropriate regulators. This antitakeover protection can be shortened with the cooperation of the thrift.
5. The rights of the mutual members are protected through the establishment of a "liquidation account." In the event the thrift is voluntarily liquidated, the mutual members would receive a preference ahead of the stockholders in an amount equal to the net worth of the thrift immediately prior to conversion. The liquidation account is reduced over time as preconversion members withdraw funds from their deposit accounts. Voluntary liquidation is most uncommon, and a merger or acquisition does not trigger a liquidation.

Conversion Process

The mutual-to-stock conversion process involves six steps, as outlined below:

1. Adoption of a plan of conversion (a resolution by the board of directors that outlines the process by which the thrift will convert).
2. Submission of the application for conversion (Form AC) to the appropriate regulators (contains the plan of conversion, proxy statement/offering circular or proxy statement/prospectus for holding companies, and appraisal).
3. Review and approval of the application and appraisal by the regulators.
4. Holding of the special meeting of the members to approve the plan of conversion.
5. Holding of the subscription offering in which stock is offered to members.

---

[13]"Guidelines for Appraisal Reports for the Valuation of Savings and Loan Associations and Savings Banks Converting from Mutual to Stock Form of Organization" (Washington, D.C.: Federal Home Loan Bank Board, Office of Policy and Economic Research, October 1983).

6. Holding of the public offering in which any stock unsold after the subscription offering is offered to the public.

As shown above (step 2), the conversion appraisal is submitted to the proper regulator for review at the time the application for conversion is filed. The review process examines the appraisal to ensure that the value is neither too high nor too low. The regulatory concern is that too high a value will result in the stock price dropping after completion of the offering and too low a price will result in a windfall to shareholders. The reviewer may request additional information from the appraiser during the review period.

Valuation Is a Moving Target

Elapsed time between the valuation date and final closing of the conversion offering can be many months. Consequently, conversion appraisals are updated at least once and possibly more often. The appraiser should confirm the valuation just prior to the stock offering itself to ensure that the market has not moved up or down materially or that the thrift has not experienced a change in its operations. If there have been changes, the appraiser must file a brief appraisal update justifying the change in circumstances and value. If there is no need for a change in the value, then no update is generally filed. At the end of the offering, however, the appraiser must file an update to confirm to the OTS (or the state) that the amount of stock sold was equal to the pro forma market value. All updates include a discussion of changes in the market as well as results of operations at the converting company since the appraisal was filed. The final update must also discuss the results of the stock offering and show the final pricing ratios.

The appraiser submits a range of values in a conversion appraisal. Typically, the appraiser expresses the value as a midpoint with a 15 percent range above and below. For example, if the appraiser determined that the value of a converting thrift was $10 million, then the range of value would be from $8.5 million to $11.5 million. Ultimately, it is the responsibility of the board of directors of the converting thrift to determine how much stock is to be sold. However, the amount sold must be within the approved valuation range and must be justified in light of changes to the market and the thrift since the original appraisal was filed.

Occasionally, circumstances occur during the course of the stock offering period that require a change in the valuation. When this happens, the stock purchasers must be presented with amended offering materials and asked to confirm or change their orders. It should be noted that during periods in which the market for thrift equities is robust, more orders for stock are often received than shares available in the offering. Because there is no established market for the converting thrift's shares and because the offering period lasts a minimum of 20 days, there is no way for the public to gauge the popularity of the stock during the offering period. Thus, orders may not be in line with the value. Therefore, some orders may have to be returned or reduced in accordance with the allocation scheme that is part of the plan of conversion, assuming there has been no change in the fundamental value of the thrift. The reverse is also true. Not enough orders may be received to reach the minimum offering size. In that situation, the offering is generally extended. The point is that the aggregate amount of stock ordered is not necessarily synonymous with the value of the converting thrift.

In practice, most conversion offerings incorporate a community offering simultaneously with the subscription offering. In a community offering, the stock is sold directly by the thrift to members of the local community without using an underwriter to resell stock in a public offering. This encourages local ownership and results in new customers for the converting thrift. For small or medium-sized offerings, a subscription and community offering is generally all that is required to sell the stock.

Conversion Team

A conversion offering is a highly complex process involving a team of professionals. It requires careful planning and skillful execution in order to avoid a failed conversion. In addition to the management and directors of the converting thrift, the conversion team includes a special conversion counsel (an attorney or law firm experienced in securities matters), an appraiser, an independent auditor to help prepare the necessary financial disclosure, a financial printer, a data processing company to help determine the membership, and often an investment banker to assist in selling the stock in either a community or a public offering. Most conversions take four to six months—sometimes longer—from adoption of the plan of conversion to selling of the stock to completion.

Converting thrifts also may elect to convert as part of a holding company. In this case, the stock sold is that of a newly formed holding company rather than the thrift itself. Usually the holding company's major asset is its ownership of the thrift. This type of conversion is more expensive because it requires additional applications, and it is somewhat more complex and time consuming because the registration statement is also reviewed by the SEC. On the other hand, the holding company form is more flexible, allows additional liability protection to directors and officers from shareholders (as determined by state law), and has tax advantages if the holding company decides to repurchase stock in the secondary market after conversion.

Merger Conversions

A *merger conversion,* also known as a *conversion merger,* is the simultaneous conversion of a mutual thrift and merger with a stock thrift or, as recently allowed by FIRREA, with a bank holding company. As in the case of the holding company conversion, the stock offered in a merger conversion is that of the stock company, not the converting thrift. Merger conversions can involve healthy as well as capital-deficient mutuals. They can be structured so that the mutual can be merged directly into the stock company or operated as a separate company within a holding company structure.

Issues

Merger conversions involving healthy thrifts are extremely attractive for the acquirer because they are priced at or near the price at which the thrift would convert on its own. Thus, no control premium is paid. Actually, the mutual is acquired free and the stock company raises additional capital. In mid-1991, the typical mutual converted to stock at approximately 40–45 percent of pro forma book value or 4–6 times pro forma earnings. If pooling of interests accounting is used, the acquiring entity therefore gets $100 of capital for every $40–$45 of stock issued (without accounting for expenses). In contrast, the acquisition of a stock thrift might be priced in excess of 100 percent of book value. Acquisition prices for commercial banks are even higher.

Mutuals can benefit from a merger conversion because they have more control over the selection of a compatible long-term partner. The acquiring company is generally larger, so that it can take over some of the administrative tasks of the mutual. Thus, the former mutual can devote its efforts to its business and not to administration. Frequently, the acquiring company is publicly traded, whereas the mutual may be too small to develop an active market for its stock.

A criticism of merger conversions is that the mutual gives up the opportunity to convert to stock at, say, 45 percent of pro forma book value (in the market environment of mid-1991) and later to sell out at a premium to book value. However, the mutual may still be able to participate in the consolidation of the financial services industry if the acquiring institution is later acquired. Thus, mutual depositors involved in a merger conversion do not completely give up the opportunity to cash out at a future higher price.

Merger Conversion Example

Exhibit 17-9 illustrates the financial aspects of a merger conversion. In the example, ABC Federal (the mutual) is entering into a merger conversion with XYZ Federal. XYZ Federal is trading for $11 per share, or approximately 56 percent of book value and 7 times core earnings (as defined in Exhibit 17-9). ABC Federal is appraised for $4.0 million, which is approximately 47 percent of pro forma book value and 5–6 times pro forma earnings. As a result of the merger conversion, XYZ Federal was able to increase book value and earnings per share, because XYZ Federal was trading at a relatively higher price (i.e., at higher price/earnings and price/book multiples) than the price at which ABC Federal converted. (See the discussion of dilution analysis in Chapter 18.)

Merger conversions are financially attractive to acquirers, so mutuals can be very elusive and have considerable negotiating power. Because the price is determined by independent appraisal, merger negotiations tend to focus on benefits to the management and employees of the mutual, such as employment agreements, salaries, retirement benefits, stock options, and restricted stock awards. The OTS will examine the benefits package to ensure that the management and directors have not "sold" control of a mutual institution in exchange for personal benefits. However, the acquiring company can easily afford to make the transaction attractive to the mutual's management and board of directors.

Preferential Pricing for Members

The other major negotiating issue is whether to offer the mutual's membership the opportunity to buy the acquirer's stock in the merger conversion at a discount to the market, typically 5 percent. The aggre-

Exhibit 17-9
Merger/Conversion Analysis

Stock: XYZ Federal
Mutual: ABC Federal

	XYZ Federal 12/90	%	ABC Federal 12/90	%	Pro Forma Combined Balance Sheet	%
Assets		%		%		%
Cash and investments	$10,000	6.0	$9,000	9.3	$22,550	8.4
Loans	150,000	89.3	82,500	85.1	232,500	86.6
REO (foreclosure)	1,500	0.9	1,000	1.0	2,500	0.9
REO (investment)	500	0.3	500	0.5	1,000	0.4
Fixed assets	2,500	1.5	1,500	1.5	4,000	1.5
Goodwill	0	0.0	0	0.0	0	0.0
Other assets	3,500	2.1	2,500	2.6	6,000	2.2
Total assets	$168,000	100.0%	$97,000	100.0%	$268,550	100.0%
Liabilities and equity		%		%		%
Deposits	$135,000	80.4	$90,000	92.8	$225,000	83.8
Borrowings	18,500	11.0	1,500	1.5	20,000	7.4
Other liabilities	2,500	1.5	500	0.5	3,000	1.1
Total liabilities	156,000	92.9	92,000	94.8	248,000	92.3
Equity	12,000	7.1	5,000	5.2	20,550	7.7
Total liabilities and equity	$168,000	100.0%	$97,000	100.0%	$268,550	100.0%
Reported net income	$890		$520		$1,641	
Core net income*	$977		$523		$1,731	
Adjusted net income†	$850		$429		$1,510	
Dividends	$248					
as a percentage of core net income	25%					
Shares outstanding	621,042				984,678	
Book value per share	$19.32				$20.87	
Tangible book value per share	$19.32				$20.87	
Earnings per share (core)	$1.57				$1.76	
Dividends per share	$0.40				$0.45	
Share price	$11.00					
Price/earnings (reported)	7.68 ×		5.33 ×		6.60 ×	
Price/earnings (core)	6.99 ×		5.31 ×		6.26 ×	
Price/earnings (adjusted)	8.04 ×		6.06 ×		7.17 ×	
Price/book value	56.93%		46.78%		52.71%	
Price/tangible book value	56.93%		46.78%		52.71%	
Price/assets	4.07%		3.98%		4.03%	
Dividend yield	3.64%				4.06%	
Change in book value/share					8.0 %	
Change in tangible book/share					8.0 %	
Change in pro forma core earnings per share					11.7%	

Conversion Offering Information

Gross offering	$4,000
Expenses	$450
Net proceeds	$3,550
Shares issued	363,636
Earnings rate on net proceeds (ATX)	6.50%

*Core income is equal to reported income before taxes less gains, losses, and loan loss provisions, taxed at a 35 percent rate.
†Adjusted income is equal to reported income before taxes less gains and losses, taxed at a 35 percent rate.

371

gate amount of stock sold must still equal the pro forma fair market value, but the individual shares can be sold for slightly less than the market price. Generally, the discount is only offered to the thrift's members, not to the public at large. For example, if the appraised value of the mutual is $10 million and the price of the stock company is $20 per share, then 500,000 shares would be sold in the merger conversion. However, if a 5 percent discount is offered (allowing members to pay $19 per share), then more shares of stock will have to be sold in order to equal the appraised value. If the members subscribe for 275,000 shares at the discount price of $19 per share, they will raise $5.2 million in the offering. Because an additional $4.8 million must be raised from the public (to equal the $10 million valuation), 238,750 shares must be sold at the public offering price of $20 per share. Thus, by offering the 5 percent discount to members, the acquirer had to sell a total of 513,750 shares, or 13,750 shares more than necessary at the appraised offering price, and the public shareholders are moderately diluted.

Merger Conversion Economics Can Impact Value

Although merger conversions are generally priced at or near the price at which the thrift would convert on its own, there is a unique appraisal issue. The appraisal must not only determine the pro forma fair market value of the converting thrift but also consider the added value that the merger creates. Therefore, two values are derived: the value of the thrift as if it were converting on its own and the incremental increase in the value of the acquiring stock company as a result of the merger. The OTS will require that stock be sold in an amount equal to the higher of the two values.

The incremental increase approach recognizes the value of various synergies, such as closing overlapping offices or entering new markets. On the other hand, if the mutual merges with a larger institution with a more liquid stock, the discount for an illiquid stock may be decreased or eliminated. In some cases, merging with a much larger company with a liquid stock can even create a premium relative to the comparable companies for liquidity of the stock. In practice, the two values tend to be very close.

Prior to 1989, merger conversions were relatively unusual transactions. After passage of FIRREA that year, however, bank holding companies were allowed to acquire healthy thrifts for the first time. Banks have been very aggressive in courting mutuals. FIRREA also imposed stricter operating and capital standards on thrifts, which has encouraged many mutuals to enter into merger conversions. Consequently, merger conversions have become quite common, particularly with bank holding companies, and are expected to increase in popularity during the next five years.

Conversion Appraisal Issues

As suggested earlier, valuing a stock thrift is similar to valuing a bank. However, when appraising a mutual undertaking a conversion, a few adjustments to the standard valuation methodology must be made. First, the valuation is on a pro forma basis. In other words, it must incorporate retention of the conversion proceeds (when utilizing price/book value multiples and price/assets multiples) as well as pro forma earnings on the net proceeds (when using price/earnings multiples). Second, appraisers generally apply a discount to the value of the converting mutual relative to the comparable companies because the stock is a new issue.

The preferred method for valuing equities is usually the price/earnings (capitalization of earnings) approach. However, because of extreme volatility in the earnings performance of the thrift industry, achieving meaningful results using an earnings based methodology can be difficult. As a result, other methodologies that are less sensitive to current earnings levels take on increasing importance. Appraisers commonly use the price/book value method and the price/assets method as supplements.

In fact, the most popular technique of valuing a thrift is the price/book value method. Although this method suffers from a variety of shortfalls, as discussed in other chapters, it tends to be the most common methodology, probably because the denominator (book value) tends to be more stable than earnings. On the other hand, the price/assets approach tends to be the least used methodology. It can suffer from manipulation because the balance sheet of a thrift can be inflated easily with borrowings. It also does not consider the institution's financial condition or operations. However, it is often used when the subject company is unprofitable, has little capital or is over-capitalized.

Conversion Mathematics

When using either the price/book value or price/assets methods, the appraiser must determine the capitalization factor as well as the proper book value or asset base. The capitalization factor is determined through a comparative analysis of the subject company versus a comparable group, as discussed in Chapter 13. The book value or asset base must include not only the preconversion base but also the net proceeds resulting from the conversion in order to be on par with the comparable companies.

The valuation equation using the price/book value method can be expressed as:

Value = Price/book value factor × Book value

In the conversion context, book value is the sum of the preconversion book value plus the net conversion proceeds, as shown below:

Value = Price/book value factor × (Preconversion book value + Net conversion proceeds)

Symbolically, this is expressed as:

Equation 17-1 $\quad V = P/B \times [B + (V - X)]$

where
$\quad\quad V = $ Value
$\quad P/B = $ Price/book value factor
$\quad\quad B = $ Preconversion book value
$\quad\quad X = $ Conversion expenses

Solving for V results in:

Equation 17-2 $V = \dfrac{P/B \times (B - X)}{1 - P/B}$

Therefore, once the appraiser determines the proper price/book value factor, the value can be derived easily from Equation 17-2.

Similar logic applies when using the price/assets approach. Equation 17-3 is very similar to that used in the price/book value method but substitutes assets for book value.

Equation 17-3 $V = P/A \times [A + (V - X)]$

where

P/A = Price/assets factor
A = Preconversion assets

Again, solving for V yields:

Equation 17-4 $V = \dfrac{P/A \times (A - X)}{1 - P/A}$

Using the price/earnings approach requires the appraiser to consider the earnings impact the net conversion proceeds will have on the converting company. This is done in order to maintain comparability between the converting thrift and those that are already trading. The basic relationship is as follows:

Value = Price/earnings ratio × Earnings base

In a conversion scenario, the earnings base includes not only the preconversion earnings but also the expected annualized earnings on the conversion proceeds, as shown below:

Value = Price/earnings ratio × [Preconversion earnings base + (Rate of return on net proceeds × Net conversion proceeds)]

Algebraically, the expression above reduces to:

Equation 17-5 $V = P/E \times (Y + [R \times (V - X)])$

where

P/E = Price/earnings ratio
Y = Preconversion earnings base
R = Rate of return on net conversion proceeds (after tax)

Finally, solving Equation 17-6 for V results in:

Equation 17-6 $V = \dfrac{P/E \times [Y - (R \times X)]}{1 - (P/E \times R)}$

Thus, the mathematics of conversions is slightly different than that of valuing stock companies. The OTS appraisal guidelines require the appraiser to show these calculations explicitly on a worksheet similar to Exhibit 17-10. In this case, ABC Federal, a $250 million thrift, has preconversion equity of $12.5 million and annual earnings of $1.625 million. The conversion is expected to cost the issuer $1.3 million, and

Exhibit 17-10
ABC Federal Savings and Loan Association Pro Forma Analysis Sheet

Date of Appraisal Report to the Board: June 1, 1991
Date of Comparative Prices Used in the Appraisal Report: June 1, 1991

	Symbols	Substitutes	Public Group Comparatives		All Public Thrifts	
			Mean	Median	Mean	Median
Pro forma value after conversion	V					
Price-earnings ratio assumed	P/E	5.00–6.00 ×	6.94	6.84	8.53	6.81
Price-book value assumed	P/B	45.0–50.0%	51.41	50.00	48.83	43.60
Price-assets ratio assumed	P/A	4.00–4.50%	4.47	4.77	3.80	3.01
Preconversion earnings base*	Y	$1,625,000				
Preconversion book value	B	$12,500,000				
Preconversion total assets	A	$250,000,000				
Incremental return on new money	R	6.5%				
Estimated fixed expenses	X	$1,300,000				

Calculation of Pro Forma Value after Conversion
1. Price to earnings

$$V = \frac{P/E \times [Y - (R \times X)]}{1 - (P/E \times R)}$$

   $V = \$11,411,111$ to $\$15,152,459$ $\qquad \bar{V} = \$13,281,785$

2. Price to book

$$V = \frac{P/B \times (B - X)}{1 - P/B}$$

   $V = \$9,163,636$ to $\$11,200,000$ $\qquad \bar{V} = \$10,181,818$

3. Price to assets

$$V = \frac{P/A \times (A - X)}{1 - P/A}$$

   $V = \$10,362,500$ to $\$11,718,848$ $\qquad \bar{V} = \$11,030,674$

Conclusion

	Total Shares	Value Per Share
Total Estimated Value at 06/01/91		
$12,000,000	1,200,000	$10.00
Recommended Range of Value		
$10,200,000	1,020,000	$10.00
$13,800,000	1,380,000	$10.00

Allowable Range of Value   Total Estimated Value
   $12,000,000 × 0.85 = $10,200,000
   $12,000,000 × 1.15 = $13,800,000

*Core net income for the 12 months ending March 31, 1991.

the converting company ought to be able to earn 6.5 percent (after taxes) on the net proceeds. Applying Equations 17-2, 17-4, and 17-6 develops values ranging from approximately $9.2 million to $15.2 million. Of course, some methods are more relevant than others, so the range can be narrowed by selecting and justifying the most relevant methodology (as discussed in Chapters 13 and 14).

It should be noted that in some circumstances one of the pro forma valuation formulas will not yield a meaningful result (namely, when the price/book value ratio approaches 1.0x or when the product of the price/earnings multiple and the rate of return on net conversion proceeds approaches 1.0x). In this case, the appraiser must rely on one of the other two pricing methods. In any event, it is up to the appraiser to determine the most appropriate methodology(ies) and to derive a reasonable pro forma conversion value.

Exhibit 17-11
ABC Federal Savings and Loan Association Pro Forma Effect of Conversion Proceeds

Conversion Proceeds

Pro forma market value (Midpoint of conversion value range)	$12,000,000
Less estimated offering expenses	1,300,000
Conversion proceeds	$10,700,000

Estimated Additional Income from Conversion Proceeds

Conversion proceeds	$10,700,000
Times estimated incremental rate of return (after tax)	6.50%
	$695,500

Pro Forma Earnings, 12 Months Ending March 31, 1991

	Reported Earnings	Adjusted Earnings	Core Earnings
Before conversion	$1,290,000	$1,150,000	$1,625,000
After conversion	$1,985,500	$1,845,500	$2,320,500
Preconversion price/earnings	9.30	10.43	7.38
Price to pro forma earnings	6.04	6.50	5.17
	Pro Forma Net Worth	**Pro Forma Tangible Net Worth**	**Pro Forma Assets**
Before conversion	$12,500,000	$12,500,000	$250,000,000
Conversion proceeds	$10,700,000	$10,700,000	$10,700,000
After conversion	$23,200,000	$23,200,000	$260,700,000
Preconversion price to net worth	96.00%		
Price to pro forma net worth	51.72%		
Preconversion price to tangible net worth		96.00%	
Price to pro forma tangible net worth		51.72%	
Preconversion price to assets			4.80%
Price to pro forma assets			4.60%

After reconciling the pricing methods to determine the final value, the appraiser should then calculate the final pricing ratios for the selected value. Again, the pricing ratios are determined on a pro forma basis. Exhibit 17-11, also a required exhibit to be submitted with a conversion appraisal, illustrates the mathematics of calculating the final pricing ratios.

Initial Issue Discounts

In addition to the mathematics of conversions, the second difference between appraising a stock company and a converting thrift is the need to incorporate a discount relative to the comparable group to reflect the fact that the stock offering is an initial public offering. There are four reasons for incorporating this discount:

1. The issuer does not have a track record as a public company, and investors do not know how the company will react in adverse times or how much information the company will release about its operations after the conversion. Often, there is little information readily available to the public about the company prior to its conversion.

2. Conversion stock offerings last at least 20 days, possibly much longer. Investors will have their money tied up during the offering period.
3. All of the stock is sold at one time, rather than in small blocks. Just as in real estate—where the price per acre of land is lower for large tracts than for quarter-acre lots, when all of the stock of a company is sold at one time—the price must often be reduced in order to ensure a successful sale.
4. Finally, investors must have an incentive to liquidate other investments or reduce cash holdings in order to invest in a new stock issue with unknown characteristics.

Investment bankers have traditionally applied a new issue discount to initial public offerings. Although it is difficult to isolate the magnitude of the discount against changes in the market as a whole, many investment bankers suggest that new issue discounts tend to average roughly 15 percent. During hot periods in the market, the new issue discount may be small or even nonexistent. On the other hand, new issue discounts may need to be 30 percent or more during declining or uncertain markets. As an aid to determining the magnitude of the new issue discount, appraisers should analyze the pricing of other recent conversion issues compared to the market as a whole.

Nonstandard Conversions

The previous discussion refers to conversions of relatively healthy thrifts that will be able to sell stock to the public successfully and be able to meet all capital requirements. These types of conversions are known as *standard conversions*. Of course, it is difficult for an undercapitalized and unprofitable thrift to sell stock successfully and to convert. In order to sell stock successfully, the issuing company must present an attractive investment opportunity. Hence, it is often the profitable and well capitalized companies, many of which do not really need the capital, that are able to convert successfully. Because of this paradox, the conversion regulations allow for special types of conversions to promote capital formation for insolvent or capital-deficient thrifts. These special types of transactions are voluntary supervisory conversions and modified conversions.

Voluntary supervisory conversions allow for the acquisition of an insolvent mutual savings association by a single entity or individual. In this situation, because the thrift is insolvent, the depositors have no residual rights and no right to purchase stock. Therefore, there is no stock offering. There is also no requirement for a conversion appraisal. In return for 100 percent control, the acquiring entity acquires the company with a direct capital infusion sufficient to enable the thrift to meet its capital requirements. To qualify for this treatment, the thrift must be insolvent according to GAAP.[14] According to OTS records, more than 100 supervisory conversions were completed between 1984 and 1990.

A *modified conversion* is a hybrid of a standard and a supervisory conversion. It involves a stock offering to the members, as well as a sale

---

[14]In practice, a thrift with a tangible capital-to-total assets ratio of 1 percent or less may qualify.

of control to an outside party. In order to qualify for a modified conversion, a thrift must be unable to meet its capital requirements, even after adding the amount of capital it could reasonably expect to raise in a standard conversion offering. Because the thrift is not yet insolvent, depositors still have a residual interest, albeit a small one. Therefore, stock is offered to the depositors, but they have no right to vote on the plan of conversion. The amount of stock offered to the members can be limited depending on the severity of the thrift's capital situation. The outside party acquiring control of the thrift must pay a control premium (see Figure 12-1 and the related discussion) in excess of the pro forma market value of the converting thrift. Because there is a stock offering, there is also a need for an appraisal. The appraisal must support not only the pro forma market value but also the magnitude of the control premium. It must also document that the thrift would be unable to meet its capital requirements, even after raising capital in a standard conversion. Less than two dozen modified conversions have been completed to date.

Figure 17-2
Mutual Holding Companies

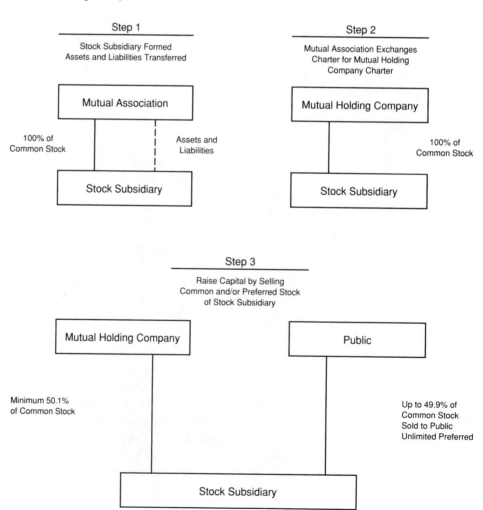

Mutual Holding Companies

The most recent development in conversions is that of mutual holding company conversions. Mutual holding companies were first authorized in the CEBA legislation. A number of states also authorize mutual holding companies. The OTS issued proposed mutual holding company conversion regulations in January 1991, with final regulations expected to be issued during the second half of 1991.

Formation of a mutual holding company is a two-step process. First, the mutual thrift charters a new stock savings association, wholly owned by the mutual, and transfers its assets and liabilities to the stock subsidiary. Second, the mutual thrift exchanges its mutual savings and loan charter for that of a mutual holding company.

The new mutual holding company, controlled by the depositors and borrowers of the thrift, can then elect to raise capital by selling less than a majority of the shares of the stock subsidiary. It can also raise capital by selling an unlimited amount of preferred stock or by borrowing at the holding company level. There is no requirement to sell any stock to the public. Figure 17-2 illustrates the steps in organizing a mutual holding company. Full conversion to a 100 percent publicly owned thrift at a later time is permissible. Such a conversion would be governed by the conversion regulations in effect at the time of the conversion.

The mutual holding company format provides an opportunity to raise capital while remaining a mutual. This structure allows for nearly absolute antitakeover protection because the mutual holding company retains ownership of more than 50 percent of the shares of the stock subsidiary. This organizational structure also allows for the sale of stock over time and in small increments. This is important for a well capitalized thrift that would be unable to earn a market return on equity because it would be overcapitalized if it effected a standard conversion. It also allows for a more orderly and considered investment of the proceeds. Mutual holding companies can also facilitate various corporate actions such as mergers and acquisitions. Mutual holding companies afford an opportunity for management and employees to share in the future success of the company through stock options, ESOPs, and other benefits similar to those available in standard conversions.

If a mutual holding company sells shares of the subsidiary stock association to the public, it must be appraised as in any standard conversion. The appraiser determines the value of the subsidiary as a whole and the company sells only a portion of the shares to the public. For example, if ABC Federal (the stock subsidiary, not the mutual holding company) is appraised for $50 million and the parent mutual holding company desires to sell 49 percent of the stock, then only $24.5 million of stock will be offered. The remaining $25.5 million worth of shares is retained by the mutual holding company.

There are a number of valuation issues involved in mutual holding company conversions. There is probably less takeover value in the stock of a mutual holding company subsidiary than in most other thrifts because mutual holding companies are formed for control reasons more than profit reasons. In order to attract investors, mutual holding companies tend to pay significant dividends. The shares of the stock subsidiary therefore tend to trade like a noncallable preferred stock, at yields discounted somewhat from comparable long-term bonds (with the discounts depending on the level of expected dividend growth). Also, because management and the board of directors determine the size of dividends, they have an unusual level of control over the stock price. Obviously, if the dividend is cut or omitted, the value of the stock will drop precipitously.

To date only one thrift has converted to a mutual holding company and sold stock to the public. One other thrift has effected the conversion without electing to sell stock to the public. After the OTS issues its final rules governing mutual holding companies, it is likely that a number of well capitalized thrifts will convert to mutual holding companies. A significant number of mutual holding companies will probably not elect to offer stock to the public.

Data Sources and Accounting Conventions

There is no lack of financial information about the banking and thrift industries. There are two basic types of information sources: industry financial data and market pricing data. Industry financial data are available from a variety of vendors or directly from the OTS or the FDIC.[15] Industry data are updated quarterly and are derived from quarterly regulatory financial statements submitted by the various thrifts to the OTS or the FDIC. These data are generally available to the public about four months after the end of the quarter. Market pricing data on actively traded thrifts, including less-detailed financial statements, are available in a variety of formats, including quarterly books, monthly summaries, and even daily computer downloads.[16] The analyst must convert *data* into *information* in the context of individual appraisal assignments. The information must always be interpreted by the analyst in the valuation process before appropriate conclusions can be developed.

GAAP versus RAP Accounting

Between 1982 and 1989, many thrifts employed certain accounting methods that were not in accordance with GAAP. These methods, called *regulatory accounting principles* (RAP), involved a variety of treatments that were created to bolster the apparent capital position of insolvent or nearly insolvent thrifts. Although data beginning in 1990 conform closely to GAAP, historical financial data may utilize RAP accounting.

---

[15]The major private vendors of industry financial data are W. C. Ferguson and Company (Irving, Texas) and Sheshunoff Information Services Inc. (Austin, Texas). See also the more extensive discussion of data sources cited in Chapter 7.

[16]The most specialized source of market pricing information for banks and thrifts is SNL Securities, L. P., of Charlottesville, Virginia.

The user of historical data from regulatory financial statements may therefore need to make adjustments for comparability before using that information. Most of the vendors of regulatory financial data attempt to adjust certain line items to GAAP (or show enough detail to allow adjustment by the analyst). However, certain adjustments can only be estimated, as the necessary detail cannot be discerned from the data. This problem mostly affects mutuals because stock thrifts are required to report to shareholders using GAAP.

Adjusting the subject company to GAAP is relatively simple if the analyst has access to the company's audited financial statements. Independent auditors qualify their audit opinions for RAP-reporting companies and include a footnote that details the balance sheet and income statement differences between RAP and GAAP. The problem for the analyst is in making similar adjustments to peer groups or to companies for which no audited financial statements are available.

The major difference between RAP and GAAP was caused by the practice of allowing thrifts to sell low coupon loans at a loss and then to amortize that loss over the expected life of the loans sold, rather than recognizing the entire loss at the time of the sale. The amount of the loss is found on the balance sheet under "Other assets" and is known as a "deferred loan loss." This RAP practice caused an overstatement of capital at the expense of future income. After a loan sale at an institution, the deferred loss was amortized, creating an expense that reduced income. Like depreciation, deferred loan loss amortization is not a cash expense. When adjusting RAP statements to GAAP, the amount of the deferred loan loss must be deducted from assets and from retained earnings and the amount of annual amortization must be added to income.

The second largest source of RAP-GAAP divergence was appraised equity capital. During most of the 1970s and 1980s, inflation drove up the value of real estate. Appraised equity capital was nothing more than the result of marking an institution's office facilities to current market (appraised) values, thus recognizing the increased value of the real estate (under RAP). Current market value was determined by appraisal. Of course, this partial mark-to-market methodology recognized only the positive influence of inflation and ignored the major negative influence of the period: higher interest rates. While real estate values were higher, the value of portfolio loans was lower; however, the reduced market value of loans was not recognized under RAP. Appraised equity (i.e., the net difference between the appraised value of selected real estate assets and their historical cost bases) was added to fixed assets, thus overstating equity. There was no income effect. To adjust to GAAP, the analyst must simply reduce fixed assets and retained earnings by the amount of the appraised equity capital.

Other differences between GAAP and RAP included the method by which loan fees were recognized and the existence of various "capital" certificates such as net worth certificates, mutual capital certificates, or income capital certificates. Loan fees under RAP were generally allowed to be recognized more rapidly than allowable under GAAP, which overstated income and net worth. There is no way to determine the amount of the RAP-to-GAAP adjustment for loan fees without consulting the company's audited financial statements. The "capital" certificates were nothing more than promissory notes issued by the FSLIC to under-capitalized institutions. Of course, these notes had no true value because the final creditor of an insolvent thrift was the FSLIC. The face value of these certificates must be deducted from assets and capital when adjusting historical statements to GAAP.

The industry financial data released by the OTS contain only cursory information about asset quality and interest rate risk at the present time. The OTS does not release information concerning classified assets or asset/liability maturity mismatches. However, it does release information about repossessed assets and delinquent and nonaccrual loans, as well as information about overall levels of adjustable-rate mortgage loans. Thrift industry financial reporting requirements and the resulting quality of financial statement disclosure have not been as extensive as for banks. We expect the quality of thrift financial data to improve under the current regulatory framework.

Although using industry data derived from regulatory statements has its drawbacks, it does provide useful information to the analyst, such as indicating the composition of a given company's loan portfolio versus that of a peer group or the industry as a whole. This information is also available for every thrift, mutual, or stock, so it is often used for preliminary merger analysis or other valuation needs.

Thrifts that employed RAP accounting and later decided to convert to the stock form must restate past financial statements in accordance with GAAP. In addition, all thrifts that are traded on NASDAQ or an exchange also report their statements under GAAP. Therefore, there is no need to adjust the financial statements of actively traded comparable companies to GAAP when valuing a thrift using a comparable-company analysis.

The accounting profession and the various regulatory bodies are clearly moving toward market value accounting for financial institutions. This accounting convention would require thrifts and banks to mark all assets and liabilities to current market values. By one school of thought, income for a period would merely be the difference in net asset value of a thrift or bank from one period to the next. Currently, the market value of investment and mortgage-backed securities is disclosed annually as a footnote to thrift audited financial statements. FDIC-insured savings banks and commercial banks report the market value of investment securities quarterly in their call reports.

While it is not a difficult task to mark most investment and mortgage-backed securities to market, valuing loans and other assets is much more difficult. The factors to be considered include term to maturity, prepayment expectations for mortgage-related assets, credit quality, liquidity, type of loan, and type of collateral. Before implementing market value accounting, numerous valuation techniques and standards must be agreed upon by the accounting and regulatory communities. Market value accounting will be a burden to smaller thrifts and banks that do not have the expertise to monitor and calculate market values on a regular basis.

Conclusion

This chapter discussed the state of the thrift industry as well as specialized valuation issues related to thrifts. Thrift valuations will take on increased importance as the industry continues to consolidate. Many industry observers believe bank holding companies will eventually absorb much of the thrift industry. The methodology used to value stock thrifts is largely the same as employed when valuing banks. When valuing mutual thrifts converting to the stock form of organization, however, certain changes to the valuation equations must be made in order to account for retention of net conversion proceeds and additional earnings to be derived from the additional capital.

Part IV

Special Issues in Bank Valuation

Chapter 18

Special Issues in Bank and Financial Institution Valuation

Former Student: Professor, this is the same examination that you gave to my class when I was a student twenty years ago. Don't you ever change the questions?
Professor: The questions don't change, just the answers.

Bank Merger and Liquidity Considerations

The Need for Liquidity

The need for liquidity is inherent in all investments. Liquidity is present in an investment when that interest (e.g., shares in a financial institution) can readily be converted to cash without loss of value within a reasonable time. The vast majority of community banks have sufficiently small shareholder bases and relatively limited transactions volume to cause their shares to have only limited liquidity. While generally more liquid than the typical closely-held business, the marketability of minority interests of community bank stock can still be a problem.

The options for providing liquidity in the shares of a community bank are relatively straightforward. Absent a sale of an entire institution, the most commonly used means for *achieving* liquidity (from a shareholder's point of view) or *providing for* liquidity (from the institution's viewpoint) are:

1. *Stock repurchase plans.* Although banks are prohibited from engaging in transactions in their own shares, bank holding companies do not operate under this regulatory restriction. Some bank holding companies have regular share repurchase programs, while others engage in such programs infrequently, if ever.
2. *Employee stock ownership plans.* An ESOP can be used to help "make a market" in the shares of a banking institution (see Chapter 16 and the discussion below). Some banks have used their ESOPs to provide an increased level of liquidity for their shareholders.
3. *Irregular efforts to interest local brokers in placing the stock.* Some banks try to establish relationships with local brokers, or with the local offices of national brokerage operations, to encourage them to make a market in their shares. These efforts rarely achieve any real increase in liquidity for a bank's shares. In most cases, the brokerage offices only match buyers and sellers and do not take the positions in the stocks necessary to develop markets.
4. *Irregular efforts to match sellers and buyers.* Bank presidents have historically assisted in matching buyers and sellers of their institutions' shares.
5. *Sale of the institution.* Shareholders have the opportunity to achieve liquidity when the entire institution is sold.

If management is unsuccessful in creating liquidity for the shareholders on a minority interest basis, then the pressure to sell the entire institution may increase. This is particularly true for banks with aging and multigenerational shareholder bases. This pressure is natural and evolutionary in closely-held companies of all types as their shareholder bases diversify. Further, if the financial performance of a bank slips, the pressure for liquidity may intensify as shareholders desire to "cut their losses" and achieve financial diversification from the troubled situation.

Liquidity from the Minority Interest Perspective

The two most common methods for creating shareholder liquidity, the share repurchase plan and the ESOP, warrant further discussion at this point.

Employee Stock Ownership Plans

As noted previously, an ESOP can be used to make a market in the shares of a financial institution. In so doing, the ESOP can help provide limited liquidity for minority shareholders of a bank. Properly administered and with sufficient funding—either through direct contributions from a banking institution or through borrowing funds that will be repaid through future contributions—an ESOP can make a limited market in a bank's shares. In other words, if shares are offered to the ESOP by existing shareholders, the ESOP can make purchases for the benefit of its employee beneficiaries.

The ESOP can also contribute to minority shareholder liquidity indirectly. The existence of an ESOP that makes regular purchases of existing shares can help establish the "market price" for a bank's shares and can encourage other shareholders to engage in transactions at the market price. Shareholders generally know that ESOP share prices are established by independent appraisal. If the appraisal firm and the appraisals have credibility over time, arm's-length transactions tend to occur at many banks at or near the appraised share values. Thus, ESOPs may help encourage the development of independent transactions between shareholders, thereby creating more liquidity for minority shareholders than would be possible from their own direct purchases of shares.

By fairly common practice, many ESOP trustees simply make all purchases at the most recently appraised price, thus helping to set the market price for the bank's shares at the appraised price. However, trustees—who have an obligation to pay not more than the appraised price for shares—may also have an obligation to obtain the *best possible price* on behalf of the ESOP in individual transactions. The implication is that the trustee of an ESOP may have an obligation to negotiate the best possible price for each ESOP purchase made. We are not aware of any complaints filed by the Department of Labor relative to ESOP purchases at prices determined by timely, independent appraisal. We nevertheless mention this issue for consideration by bankers, ESOP trustees, and other professionals working with banking clients.[1]

Stock Repurchase Plans

Because of restrictions in state and federal laws, most banks cannot purchase their own shares; however, a bank holding company may do so within certain limitations. The potential advantages of a share repurchase program are numerous. Earnings per share and the relative owner-

---

[1] See Chapter 16 for a more detailed discussion of ESOPs and ESOP appraisal issues.

ship positions of the remaining shareholders may both improve. The repurchase plan may also provide a floor price for the stock that enhances shareholder perceptions of value.[2] The following reasons for the potential attractiveness of a stock repurchase plan were listed in the cited article by Huggins:

1. Earnings per share and return on equity may increase immediately.
2. Current tax laws favor debt over equity because of the deductibility of interest as opposed to the nondeductibility of dividends.
3. Current tax laws do not favor reinvesting cash into fixed assets.
4. The cost of incurring debt to retire equity is relatively low because of interest rates.
5. Repurchase plans communicate to the market that management is optimistic about a firm's future and feels that the stock is undervalued.
6. Stock repurchases support stock prices by stabilizing the market and providing a floor, or minimum price, for stock.
7. These plans can act as (a) an antitakeover device, (b) a way to go private (drop the number of shareholders below the SEC reporting requirement of 300 shareholders), and (c) a way to consolidate ownership around a long-term core group of shareholders, such as directors, large shareholders, and management.
8. The cost of obtaining stock for stock options, ESOPs, and dividend reinvestment plans may be reduced by buying in the open market rather than using authorized but unissued stock.
9. Many financial institutions may well have excess capital as a result of the new risk-based capital guidelines under the Financial Institutions Reform, Recovery, and Enforcement Act of 1989.
10. Pressure from major shareholders for management to pass on the financial benefits of a firm's previous financial success may be a reason to institute a stock repurchase plan.

Exhibit 18-1 provides an analysis of the impact of a stock repurchase plan for a hypothetical $60 million bank holding company, Exchange Bancorp, Inc., which has no assets other than its ownership of its wholly owned subsidiary, Exchange Bank. Exchange Bancorp is considering a buyback of up to 10 percent of its outstanding shares. The bank has arranged a credit facility with an upstream correspondent bank to finance the program. The other assumptions of the analysis are summarized at the top of the exhibit. Repurchase prices ranging from 50 percent of book value to 150 percent of book value are considered in Exhibit 18-1, which indicates:

1. Pro forma earnings per share increase across the entire range of potential prices. For example, if the repurchase occurred at book value, or $50.00 per share, earnings per share would increase 5.7 percent, from $7.00 per share to $7.40 per share.

---

[2] A more detailed discussion of shareholder repurchase plans can be found in Stanley M. Huggins, "Bank Consolidation: Buy, Sell, or Stay Put?" *The Bankers Magazine*, Vol. 173, no. 3, May/June 1990, pp. 56–63.

Exhibit 18-1
Exchange Bancorp, Inc.
Financial Impact of Buyback Program

Assumptions

Assets	$60,000,000	Current "market price" = $50.00 per share	
Equity	$5,000,000		
Equity/assets ratio	8.33%		
Earnings	$700,000		
Number of shares	100,000		
Return on equity (ROE)	14.00%		
Book value per share	$50.00		
Earnings per share (EPS)	$7.00		
Shares repurchased	10,000	Assume a 10% share repurchase program	
Interest rate	11.00%		
Tax rate (state and federal)	38.00%		

Offering Price		Pro Forma Values						
Price/ Book (%)	Share Price	Debt Assumed	Earnings	EPS	Book Value	Book Value/ Share	ROE (%)	Equity/ TA (%)
50.0	$25.00	$250,000	$682,950	$7.59	$4,750,000	$52.78	14.38	7.95
60.0	$30.00	$300,000	$679,540	$7.55	$4,700,000	$52.22	14.46	7.87
70.0	$35.00	$350,000	$676,130	$7.51	$4,650,000	$51.67	14.54	7.80
80.0	$40.00	$400,000	$672,720	$7.47	$4,600,000	$51.11	14.62	7.72
90.0	$45.00	$450,000	$669,310	$7.44	$4,550,000	$50.56	14.71	7.64
100.0	$50.00	$500,000	$665,900	$7.40	$4,500,000	$50.00	14.80	7.56
110.0	$55.00	$550,000	$662,490	$7.36	$4,450,000	$49.44	14.89	7.49
120.0	$60.00	$600,000	$659,080	$7.32	$4,400,000	$48.89	14.98	7.41
130.0	$65.00	$650,000	$655,670	$7.29	$4,350,000	$48.33	15.07	7.33
140.0	$70.00	$700,000	$652,260	$7.25	$4,300,000	$47.78	15.17	7.25
150.0	$75.00	$750,000	$648,850	$7.21	$4,250,000	$47.22	15.27	7.17

2. Pro forma book value in *dollar terms* decreases by the amount of the debt assumed. Generally accepted accounting principles require that treasury transactions be recorded as reductions of equity.
3. Pro forma book value *per share* increases if the repurchase price is below book value, and the transaction is *antidilutive* with respect to book value per share. Book value per share decreases if the repurchase price is above book value, so in those instances, the transaction would be *dilutive* with respect to book value per share.
4. Pro forma return on equity rises following the share repurchase program in all cases shown. Since ROE continues to rise as the repurchase price increases, it might seem that the higher price paid, the better. However, the increments of return are decreasing at higher prices, and leverage, and therefore the risk of the remaining shareholders, is increasing.

What has all this to do with valuation? Assume that the "market price" of Exchange Bancorp's shares in its limited market was $50.00 per share before the transaction, which occurred at $50.00 per share. Pro forma earnings rise 5.7 percent to $7.40 per share. If the market is rational and does not perceive that management has increased overall risk much, it may maintain the original price/earnings ratio on the bank's earnings of 7.14x ($50.00 / $7.00 per share) and increase the market price of the shares to $52.75–$53.00 per share (i.e., 7.14 × $7.40 per share).

At the pricing noted, Exchange Bancorp would have borrowed $500,000 and increased the market value of its remaining shares by about half that amount, or $250,000. In other words, there are 90,000 shares outstanding following the repurchase program, revalued at from $2.75–$3.00 per share higher, for a total rise in market value *for the remaining shareholders* of about $250,000.[3]

From the perspective of return on equity, the buyback program will be successful so long as the after-tax cost of debt incurred to buy the stock is less than the rate of return on the core earnings of the bank. From the perspective of earnings per share, there does come a point at which the absolute cost of interest exceeds the relative benefit of the lower number of shares (which did not happen in the pricing range shown in Exhibit 18-1).

Although the analysis of Exhibit 18-1 is somewhat oversimplified, it does present the concepts and the benefits of a stock repurchase plan. There are, however, two major risks to share repurchase plans. First, by their very nature, repurchase plans increase leverage. The extent of leverage can and should be evaluated prior to implementing any stock repurchase plan. The second risk is less obvious: Once capital has been used in a stock repurchase plan, it is not available for other opportunities or problems. So stock repurchase plans should not be entered into without an overall evaluation of a bank's strategic alternatives.

Liquidity from the Perspective of the Controlling Shareholder(s)

History of Bank Mergers and Acquisitions

Banking has been in a state of consolidation for a number of years. However, the pace of mergers quickened in the mid-1980s as the prices of publicly traded banks soared. As stock prices moved well above book values, many of the regional and superregional banking companies had cheaper "currency," which allowed them to purchase other banks at substantial premiums to book value without inflicting unacceptable degrees of dilution on their shareholders.

As the merger wave reached its peak in 1988–89, even the discipline of dilution began to give way as acquirers made acquisitions for numerous strategic reasons. Lower stock prices in 1990 slowed the consolidation phase significantly, except for the thrift industry, where consolidation has been forced by regulatory takeover and resale of institutions or large portions of branch networks. Acquirers could no longer afford to pay high prices, and sellers believed that prices were unreasonably low.

New factors are likely to renew the trend toward consolidation in the 1990s, even if bank stock prices do not recover to their peak levels

---

[3]This is true even though total market value declined by a similar amount. When any company engages in a significant treasury purchase, it decapitalizes itself by the dollar amount of the purchase. If accomplished within prudent ranges, however, market values for the remaining shareholders may increase, as in the example above. Such is the magic of share repurchase plans.

of the 1980s. Earnings are under pressure from problem assets, rising federal deposit insurance premiums, and cost pressures in general. At the same time, regulatory agencies continue to raise capital requirements. Given the fundamental rule of economics that capital always seeks a satisfactory rate of return, banks are going to be under increasing pressure to find ways to improve earnings and therefore shareholder returns. One of the most direct means will be to seek a merger partner, which will allow the elimination of redundant expenses. At the very least, there are opportunities to consolidate back-office and administrative functions in most mergers.

In summary, the merger wave of the 1980s was fueled by the "carrot" of high stock prices. We believe the trend of the 1990s will be driven by the "stick" of earnings pressure and the need to improve shareholder returns.

Impact of Capital Rules

The regulatory approach to assessing capital adequacy creates a dilemma for mergers and acquisitions in the 1990s. It is currently difficult to use stock to acquire a bank because of low prices (and a lagging memory of higher prices among potential sellers), yet the use of cash is also difficult if excessive goodwill is created. The latter is true because goodwill is treated as an intangible asset that is deducted from the capital account before the capital adequacy rules are applied. If the use of cash is limited, then it is likely that more creative stock deals will be forthcoming.

Sale/Merger Concepts

The decision to buy or sell a bank is among the most important ever made by managements and boards of directors. The question of independent ownership versus consolidation with another banking organization should be resolved through a comprehensive, ongoing strategic or business planning process. A number of factors are vitally important in reaching the decision. A full discussion of these elements is outside the scope of this book, but the more important among them are the bank's marketplace, its financial and managerial strength, its products and services, its operational needs, and the desires of its shareholder base regarding liquidity. (See the discussion near the end of this chapter in the section "Capital/Business/Strategic Planning for Community Banks and Thrifts.")

Valuation Engineering

Banks are similar to other businesses with respect to the decision to sell.[4] The impetus to act is often based upon short-term criteria. However, shareholders are better served if management and the board of directors focus on value from a different, longer-term perspective, which we call *valuation engineering*.[5]

---

[4]Banks are different with respect to the *implementation* of a decision to sell. Regulatory and shareholder approvals for transactions involving financial institutions typically take months longer than comparable transactions among unregulated industries.

[5]We first saw the term *valuation engineering* in a recent article: Robert F. Reilly, "Value Enhancement Through a Valuation Engineering Analysis," *The Journal of Technical Valuation* 4, no. 2 (Aug. 1990), pp. 41–48. We have long advocated strategies for using the tools and knowledge of valuation to *build value* over the long term in business and banking, and we currently use the term *valuation engineering* for this concept.

We define valuation engineering as the develoment of strategies and tactics to maximize the value of business interests using the tools and knowledge gained in the valuation process. Valuation engineering should be clearly contrasted with the traditional concept of "window dressing" a business immediately prior to sale. Window dressing involves tinkering with a business balance sheet in the short run, painting and fixing those things that make a first impression on potential buyers.

Valuation engineering is a long-term, ongoing philosophy of operations designed to enhance value. Although it takes time and effort, the end result will almost always be an easier sale at a better price *when the shareholders are ready to sell.*

The techniques of valuation engineering are straightforward: Improve the *fundamentals* of the balance sheet and the income statement and therefore improve the basis for any potential sale. In addition, valuation engineering continually builds on the important nonfinancial areas that can directly influence value.

The nonfinancial areas, although not necessarily obvious, are quite important in valuation engineering. Management depth should be created to minimize dependency on a key person. Information systems should be built that give the potential buyer confidence in the entity's financial and operational data. A solid business plan should be in place as a guide for future operations. Ownership should be simplified or rationalized if necessary—that is, get the bank's shares into the hands of those who share a common philosophy about the future of the organization.

The financial areas for work are more readily apparent: (1) improve the quality and quantity of earnings, and (2) increase capital while building reserves and reducing credit risk. The income statement can be improved in a variety of ways, including, possibly, raising prices, reducing costs, increasing fee income, lowering deposit costs, and so on. The key point is that valuation engineering is a long-term concept designed to be implemented over a number of years. Valuation engineering is the antithesis of a crash program to improve the financial picture of a bank. Over time, however, managements who focus on building value in their institutions will develop more valuable and more marketable equity for their shareholders.

Cash versus Stock Transactions

The structure of a deal always revolves around the consideration offered. The composition of consideration—whether cash, stock, deferred payments, or a combination—is important to buyers and sellers, often for different reasons. Selling shareholders must determine their needs and appetite for liquidity (cash), longer-term investment potential and tax deferral (stock), and reduction of risk (cash).

In an all-cash transaction, sellers receive cash in exchange for their shares and pay capital gains tax based upon the difference between the sale price and their tax basis in the shares. They can then reinvest the fully liquid cash in any alternative investment.

Sellers who receive stock may have another set of decisions. Sellers receiving stock in another banking institution in exchange for their bank's stock may be subject to restrictions on the sale of the shares, particularly if they are deemed to be "insiders." If the shares received are not legally restricted, there may be practical restrictions on their sale, at least in bulk, because of the nature and activity of the market for the acquiring institution's shares.

Sellers of banks who receive stock in exchange should realize that an often unrecognized role reversal takes place at closing: The "sellers" become the "buyers."[6] Because they will own stock of the acquiring corporation (often subject to various resale provisions for some time), the need for a serious inquiry into the financial condition and structure of the buyer easily becomes among the most important issues of the deal.

Yet it has been our experience that sellers sometimes assume that the shares of the acquirer reflect below-average risk and above-average appreciation potential. The key point to recognize is that all aspects of the transaction should be analyzed very carefully.

Purchase versus Pooling Accounting

Two accounting conventions are directly applicable to bank merger structures. Acquisitions are normally accounted for either on the purchase basis or on the pooling basis. Each method has several derivations and different implications for tax purposes as well as for financial reporting purposes.

Expert advice is needed to select the appropriate accounting treatment. It is important to recognize, however, that the required accounting treatments may not mesh with the needs and desires of the parties. For example, a seller who desires an all-cash sale (which would trigger purchase accounting for the buyer) may well have irreconcilable differences with a buyer who is only willing to offer stock (which permits treatment as a pooling of interests).

Two sample transactions are outlined below to illustrate the differences between purchase and pooling of interests accounting. The transactions have been simplified for discussion purposes. For example, appraisals of tangible assets or specifically identifiable intangible assets (core deposits) might lower the amount of goodwill booked in the first transaction.

Simplistically, in purchase accounting, the net assets of the acquired institution, valued at their fair values as of the date of the acquisition, are added to the assets of the acquiring bank or holding company. Any portion of the purchase price in excess of the fair values of assets acquired is booked as goodwill on the acquiring institution's balance sheet, unless one or more specifically identifiable intangible assets can be valued to absorb the unidentified intangible, that is, the goodwill.[7]

---

[6]Recently, our firm was representing a fairly large community bank in its sale to a regional bank holding company. During the due diligence process, our questions often seemed to make the buyer's management uncomfortable. After all, they were assuming all the risk and buying our firm's client! However, when it was pointed out to them that, *for a day,* the shareholders of our client would be this holding company's largest single shareholder (in that we would be "buying" about 15 percent of their postmerger shares), they became more open and cooperative. Needless to say, *on the day after the merger,* our client's share positions became just several hundred more minority interests in the acquiring company.

[7]See Chapter 19 and the detailed discussion on bank core deposit intangible assets for a more complete discussion of the distinction between goodwill and other identified intangible assets.

Purchase accounting can be devastating to an acquirer's capital ratios if a significant premium to book value (or fair market value of the assets) is paid in an acquisition. Consider the following oversimplified example:

Exhibit 18-2
Sample Acquisition
Purchase Accounting Method ($ Millions)

	Acquirer	Target	Combined
Total assets	$1,000	$100	$1,100
Reported equity (book value)	75	8	75
Purchase price		12	
Goodwill paid	4		
Tangible equity	75	8	71
Tangible assets	1,000	100	1,096
Equity/assets	7.5%	8.0%	6.5%

In Exhibit 18-2, the acquirer paid a cash price of $12 million, or 150 percent of book value of $8 million, for the target bank. The acquiring bank was 10 times larger than the target. With the acquisition accounted for as a purchase, consolidated assets after the merger are $1.1 billion (the sum of the assets of both institutions).

Reported equity after the deal remains at $75 million. *Tangible equity,* however, falls to $71 million following the acquisition because the new asset, $4 million of goodwill, is *subtracted from* reported equity in its calculation. This is of critical importance because regulatory (and market) calculations of capital adequacy are often based upon tangible equity (and tangible assets). The ratio of equity to total assets therefore falls from a comfortable level of 7.5 percent preacquisition to a more marginal level of 6.5 percent postacquisition. This acquiring institution's acquisition days are over until it can raise more capital!

A pooling transaction looks considerably different. For an acquisition to be treated as a pooling of interests, several requirements must be met.[8] The same transaction is now considered under a pooling of interests accounting treatment in Exhibit 18-3.

In Exhibit 18-3, the acquirer paid the same *nominal price* as in Exhibit 18-2, that is, $12 million, or 150 percent of the acquired institution's book value of $8 million. However, the currency paid in the second example consisted not of cash but of common stock of the acquiring bank. In the pooling of interests acquisition, the balance sheets (and income statements) of the two institutions are simply added together (although the goodwill is treated as a contra-equity entry so that the sum of the individual equities will be consolidated equity).

---

[8]See Accounting Principles Board (APB) No. 16. There are, in fact, 12 requirements that must be met in a merger for it to be accounted for as a pooling of interests for financial reporting purposes. Whether those requirements are met in a given case will be determined by the independent accounting firm of the acquiring institution. Needless to say, the accountants should be consulted early in any acquisition process. Pooling for tax purposes is critical from the viewpoint of the seller. If an acquisition is treated as a pooling, the seller may exchange shares for shares of the acquirer, transfer the tax basis of the old shares to the new shares, and defer capital gains taxation until the later sale of the new shares. Most banks engaging in a merger calling for the exchange of shares obtain a tax opinion from qualified tax counsel that their transaction will be treated as a tax-free exchange.

Exhibit 18-3
Sample Acquisition
Pooling of Interests Method ($ Millions)

	Acquirer	Target	Combined
Total assets	$1,000	$100	$1,100
Reported equity (book value)	75	8	83
Purchase price		12	
Premium paid	4		
Tangible equity	75	8	83
Equity/assets	7.5%	8.0%	7.5%

The acquirer issued $12 million of common stock, but only $8 million of equity is added in the combined company. The premium of $4 million paid in common stock is treated as a reduction of a retained earnings account, essentially diluting the equity of the other shareholders. Combined reported equity and combined tangible equity are both now $83 million. Given total combined assets of $1.1 billion, the ratio of equity to total assets remains at 7.5 percent.[9]

This institution remains well capitalized and may be on the lookout for future acquisition opportunities when the present acquisition is absorbed from management and operational perspectives.

The reader should remember that actual merger situations are never as simple as the one just presented. There are real limitations on the prices that can be paid, even in stock-for-stock exchanges. These limitations arise from the relative earning power of the acquiring and acquired institutions as well as the nominal price paid. In other words, no analysis of a pooling of interests merger would be complete without a detailed analysis of the dilutive (or antidilutive) impact of the merger with respect to earnings per share, book value per share, dividends per share, and the potential reception of the deal by the public stock markets. (See Chapter 14 for a more detailed discussion of dilution analysis.)

The form of a banking transaction (cash versus stock) may have a significant impact on shareholder liquidity. Cash transactions yield liquidity—that is, cash. However, cash transactions, because of the nature of purchase accounting and regulatory capital rules, may yield lower prices than share exchange transactions. Bank shareholders must look to the consideration received to determine the level of liquidity a particular transaction structure may offer.

Expected Trends in Bank Merger Activity

The trend toward bank consolidation in the 1980s is expected to intensify during the 1990s, although for at least two different reasons. The first relates to cost pressures. Community banks are facing the same pressures on profitability that larger banks are. Consequently, there will

---

[9]The actual improvement of the ratio to 7.54 percent from 7.50 percent is masked by the rounding in the Exhibit 18-3.

be a growing need to control operating costs. The second reason for *increasing* consolidation among community banks relates, oddly enough, to a *decreasing demand* for them by the larger entities.

Cost Pressures Lead to Intramarket Mergers

We believe that many community banks will consider *intramarket mergers,* a route that was often seen as impossible just a few years ago because of potential regulatory constraints related to market concentration, as well as normal business and competitive reasons. In the present troubled banking environment, concentration of market power is much less frequently a reason for not approving a merger of financial institutions. The competitive issues, however, have lingered. We define intramarket mergers as involving banks in the same town or county. In addition, intramarket mergers include mergers of rural banks within a reasonable drive, even if they are not, strictly speaking, in the same market.

Community banks have frequently enjoyed a measure of friendly competition. However, it is also true that long-standing family and business relationships, which seemingly made it impossible to consider a merger with a community bank competitor, may have to be overcome in the face of economic self-interest. Intramarket mergers may become the only viable means to improve earnings and returns on invested capital for some community banks. In addition, the banks that started up in the 1980s, as well as smaller urban financial institutions, are facing the same difficulties and may have to seek the same solution.

Declining Interest in Rural Small Banks

The potential for intramarket mergers is enhanced for another reason. Many of the larger regional holding companies already have banking offices in the attractive markets of their regions. As a result, a significant factor in the current (1990–91) slowdown in bank acquisitions is the declining interest of the larger holding companies in owning more community banks at almost any price. As a result, the number of buyers of community banks, particularly rural banks, is shrinking as the larger institutions divert their attention to new markets and seek larger acquisition targets, often using failed banks or savings and loans as the vehicle for entry.

The larger bank holding companies are also (or soon will be) more focused on the basic businesses that they desire to be in for the long term. All of this is leading to a declining interest in the smaller banks. There should continue to be interest in community banks in small towns surrounding urban centers or for the dominant banks in attractive rural markets. However, this analysis still leaves thousands of banks for which there will be limited demand.

Two-Step Method of Achieving Liquidity

One strategy that we believe will be followed increasingly by community banks will involve mergers of one or more institutions to form, over time, more sizable and noticeable banking companies covering significant rural geographic areas. Most of these mergers or consolidations, we believe, will occur at relatively nonpremium pricing levels. In other words, two or more banks or bank holding companies may exchange shares for shares in a surviving holding company or in a new holding company formed for the purpose. The exchanges will be based upon nondilutive or minimally dilutive pricing or valuation structures that reflect only fundamental valuation differences between the merging institutions, rather than arbitrary, automatic, or negotiated premiums.

Examples of multibank combinations without customary acquisition premiums are occurring with increasing frequency.[10] The logic for these intramarket mergers is fairly clear. First, the larger institutions have opportunities to spread overhead over a broader base of banking assets, thereby providing opportunities to enhance profitability. Second, the larger institutions become significant economic entities with prospects for the evolution of more active markets for their shares. And third, the larger institutions will inevitably be more attractive as acquisition candidates by the larger regional banking companies when bank stocks recover from their current cyclical lows, thereby increasing the potential for a sale at a later date at premium pricing levels.

From the point of view of shareholders, then, a two-step process may be necessary for liquidity at premium prices to be achieved. In the first step, through intramarket mergers, larger banking entities are created and operated for a period of time, perhaps even several years. In the second step, the larger entities are sold, hopefully at premium pricing levels, to regional holding companies seeking to consolidate operations within specific geographic territories.

Perspectives on Bank Mergers/Sales

The following sections address a variety of perspectives relating to achieving shareholder liquidity through the sale of a banking institution.

Sale Team

There are a number of players on the team when a sale transaction is contemplated. The roles of the attorneys and accountants are well documented. The valuation consultant may be employed to help establish a price as well as opine on the fairness of the financial aspects of the transaction. We will not delve into all aspects of a merger negotiation. However, one point seems worth remembering: We have seen too many instances where the appropriate professionals were brought into the process too late to help the client prevent a problem or strike a better deal.[11]

---

[10]For example, at the time of this writing, our firm is providing valuation services and fairness opinions with respect to three intramarket mergers involving postmerger institutions with assets of approximately $80 million, $200 million, and $225 million. Several other similar mergers are being contemplated by institutions within our contact sphere. Prior ot 1990, transactions of this nature were a rarity.

[11]Our firm was retained to provide a transaction fairness opinion by one small bank *after* it had signed a letter of intent to be acquired by a regional holding company in a stock-for-stock exchange. The bank was in an extremely rural location and had experienced earnings problems, though largely related to a single credit that had been cleared out and written off at the time of the negotiations. The pricing of the deal, however, did not reflect the improving earnings performance that resulted from the resolution of that problem. Based upon our due diligence, it was our opinion that the deal pricing was inadequate. The price was renegotiated and the deal closed, with a fairness opinion based upon the new pricing level.

Purchasers of banks have a distinct advantage over sellers. Absent a serious mistake that limits future flexibility, purchasers can learn from experience. Large regional bank holding companies actively involved in acquisitions get to "practice" the acquisition process over and over. Most active acquirers have developed acquisition teams to coordinate the process. Additionally, there are always other banks to acquire if a particular negotiation does not succeed.

Sellers, on the other hand, do not get to practice. Once a bank is sold, it is sold for good. Why, then, do sellers repeatedly allow buyers to stack the odds against them? First, they are not in the business of selling banks; they run them. Second, sellers often do not realize they are sellers until they are in the midst of active negotiations. And third, sellers seldom assemble their "sale team" ahead of time.

The sale team should include appropriate board and/or management representation. Accounting and tax expertise is critical in analyzing offers or in setting guidelines for structural negotiations. Legal expertise is necessary in the negotiation and documentation of definitive sales or merger agreements. In addition, valuation expertise should be utilized to establish the range of rational price expectations, to determine the reasonableness of offers, to provide focus on positive valuation elements, and to evaluate securities or notes offered as consideration.

Buyer's Perspective

A buyer's motivations can greatly affect perceptions of value. Banks or branches will have pure *financial values* based upon required rates of return of various purchasers. Pricing above financial values is often justified for *strategic reasons,* such as market share consolidation, new-market penetration, or additional product lines. Also at work are more-emotional reasons, such as size for the sake of size, keeping a competitor out of a specific market, and "if we don't get it, someone else will." Shareholders should always remember that management is generally compensated on the basis of institutional size, which can create a poor incentive to acquire another institution. Strategic reasons can be used to rationalize almost any price, particularly in the heat of negotiations.

Another note of caution for buyers relates to the opportunity to buy a failed institution. The bid process occurs rapidly, often with only a few days to do the necessary pricing and due diligence work. The heat of competitive bidding can produce unusual results as prosective buyers bid aggressively. Once again, the objective advice of an outside party can be invaluable in helping to set pricing.

Seller's Perspective

Unlike most buyers, the seller is engaging in a one-time affair. For that reason, the buyer's representatives generally have far more experience in negotiating transactions. A smart seller will quickly find a way to put a team together that at least equals the buyer in knowledge and experience. Sellers like to remember high levels of bank pricing, and they may not pay close attention to the actual market for controlling interests. This can lead to selling too cheaply in a rising market and frustration at the absence of a deal in a falling market. It is the valuation professional's job to know the market. Once again, the valuation professional can be of greatest assistance when brought into the process as early as possible.

The seller's need for assistance can be compounded when an institution becomes the subject of an unsolicited approach and offer. In such cases, bank managements, often the primary negotiators for the bank, may well be negotiating with their future employers. The interests of the shareholders and management are not always totally in line. Therefore, it may well serve to protect both management and the shareholders by having an outside influence present in the negotiations.

Acquisition by a Large Regional Bank

After the parties to an acquisition of a community bank by a larger institution have agreed that a stock-for-stock arrangement is satisfactory, it is necessary to establish the price. *The price can be expressed as a dollar amount, a specific number of shares, or a formula.* The formula approach is often expressed as a multiple of book value. It is important to remember that the seller is generally receiving a control price, while the buyer is delivering shares that represent minority interests.

Each of the above pricing methods raises a number of issues. A fixed number of shares exposes the seller to a reduced nominal purchase price if the price of the buyer's shares declines between the date of the initial agreement and the closing date. However, it protects the buyer in that the maximum level of dilution, if any, is fully defined.

A fixed dollar price, which may translate into a varying number of shares, will have just the opposite effect. The seller is protected because the dollar value received is fixed. However, the potential dilution incurred by the buyer could be unacceptable if share prices fall significantly between the date of agreement and the date of closing.

Formula pricing generates its own set of issues. First and foremost, it is critical that all the terms in the formula agreement be carefully defined. However, formulas can be particularly troublesome if market conditions change during the due diligence and regulatory approval periods prior to closing.

A variety of arrangements are used to protect both buyers and sellers from price fluctuations. Sometimes known as "collar-and-cuff" agreements, they set a maximum and minimum number of shares to be paid by the buyer in the event of price fluctuations in his or her stock. Note that each party to the transaction has relative incentives to suggest a collar-and-cuff structure. For example, the seller may find it useful to define a minimum number of shares, particularly if the lower end of the pricing range is still very acceptable. On the other hand, the buyer will definitely want to set a maximum number of shares in order to be able to control the potential dilutive impact of an acquisition.

Another form of formula pricing is based upon a multiple of book value. For example, the dollar pricing may be agreed upon as "1.4 times book value of the bank at the month-end immediately prior to closing." Sellers often agree to a dollar price based upon a book value during the approval phase, which may take up to nine months or more. This can be quite expensive.[12]

Merger of Equals

The stock-for-stock exchange in a merger of equals presents a somewhat different set of issues. Banks may choose to merge based upon their relative fair market values determined on a similar basis, such as control values. They may also choose to merge simply on the basis of book values, if their financial performances are very similar. The key point is that neither party is receiving a premium for its shares relative to the other. This is the form of merger that we expect to see in many intramarket mergers of community banks during the 1990s.

To be effective, mergers involving equals must be carefully considered and well structured. Hard decisions must be made regarding simple questions, including: (1) Who is going to run the institution? (2) Where will headquarters be located? and (3) Will the banks merge or continue to operate autonomously? There were a number of well-publicized "mergers of equals" during the 1980s where these questions were not addressed adequately prior to merger. The result has been disappointing performance for those institutions. We expect that market discipline and the need to improve performance will increase the focus of merger candidates on the key issues that will determine subsequent performance.

Dividend Pickup

Key questions for the seller are the amount and security of the dividend on the buyer's shares. From the seller's point of view, there is a good probability in a merger with a large regional bank that there will be a dividend pickup as result of the merger. Most community banks are owned by holding companies, many of which are leveraged. While their subsidiary banks may have dividend payout ratios in the normal range for public banks of 35–40 percent, all or a portion of the dividends may be used by their holding companies for debt service, leaving relatively lower payout ratios for the shareholders of the community bank holding companies. There are important valuation implications from potential dividend pickups. Expectation of higher cash dividends provides value

---

[12]Consider a $60 million bank with $5 million in equity. A dollar price of $7.0 million could be negotiated based upon a 1.4x multiple of book value. If the bank is earning $700,000 per year (14 percent return on equity) and regulatory approval requires six months, book value at closing will be $5.35 million. If the bank negotiates a constant multiple based upon closing equity, it would achieve a total pricing of $7.49 million, or a full 7 percent higher price than the price on the announcement date. At the other extreme, a formula based upon a multiple of book value can protect the buyer if significant adjustments to the selling bank's book value are created by unexpected loan losses, required writedowns by regulators, or adjustments necessitated by a due diligence audit.

to be considered in evaluating the total package. The security and stability of the dividend are also vitally important, as well as the likelihood of dividend increases. It may also be true that shareholders in a bank that is not considered to be extremely attractive, and hence does not receive high-priced offers, could benefit greatly from the increased level of cash flow from dividends on the purchaser's stock, thereby offsetting a lower initial purchase price.

Fairness Opinions

The final aspect of the merger/sale process is the fairness opinion. A fairness opinion is provided by an independent financial advisor to the board of directors of selling banks in most transactions today. In cases where the transaction is considered to be "material" for the acquiring bank, a fairness opinion from a different financial advisor is sometimes obtained on its behalf.

A fairness opinion involves a total review of a transaction from a financial point of view. The financial advisor must look at pricing, terms, and consideration received in the context of the market for similar institutions. The advisor then opines that the transaction is fair, from a financial point of view and from the perspective of minority shareholders.

Why is a fairness opinion important? While there are no specific guidelines as to when to obtain a fairness opinion, it is important to recognize that the board of directors is endeavoring to demonstrate that it is acting in the best interest of all the shareholders by seeking outside assurance that its actions are prudent.

The facts of any particular arrangement often lead reasonable (or unreasonable) people to conclude that a number of perhaps preferable alternatives to the proposed transaction are present. A fairness opinion from a qualified financial advisor can minimize the risks of disagreement among shareholders and misunderstandings about a deal, as well as litigation that can kill transactions.

Although the following is not a complete list, consideration should be given to obtaining a fairness opinion if one or more of these situations are present:

1. Competing bids have been received that are different in price or structure, thereby leading to an interpretation as to the exact terms being offered.
2. Insiders or other affiliated parties are involved in the transaction.
3. The bank has experienced a recent history of poor financial performance.
4. The offer is hostile or unsolicited.
5. There is lack of agreement among the directors as to the adequacy of the offer.
6. There is concern that the shareholders fully understand that considerable efforts were expended to assure fairness to all parties.

7. The board desires additional information about the investment characteristics of the acquiring bank.
8. Varying offers are made to different classes of shareholders.
9. There is only one bid for the bank, and competing bids have not been solicited.

Bank directors have a legal fiduciary responsibility to the shareholders known as the *business judgment rule*. In general, directors and management are given broad discretion in directing the affairs of a business. Directors are expected to act in good faith based upon the care that an ordinary person would take in supervising the affairs of the business. Inherent in this rule is the requirement that the board of directors be informed about the basis for major decisions prior to reaching a conclusion. In essence, there is an expectation that the proper decision will be made in the proper way.

Smith v. Van Gorkom

In the landmark case *Smith* v. *Van Gorkom, (Trans Union),* (488 A. 2d Del. 1985), the Delaware Supreme Court expanded the concept of the business judgment rule to encompass a requirement for informed decisions. The process by which a board goes about reaching a decision can be just as important as the decision itself. While the Delaware court decision is applicable only to Delaware, the wide influence of Delaware law on business law in general makes the case very important. We have noticed a number of situations where the attorneys in other states were well aware of the case and felt that attention should be devoted to its requirements. Because of the importance of the case, we believe that is useful to review it in some detail.

Trans Union, a diversified holding company publicly traded on the New York Stock Exchange, had difficulty generating sufficient taxable income to take advantage of accumulating investment tax credits. In August 1980, Jerome Van Gorkom, Trans Union's chief executive officer, began to discuss the possibility of selling the company to a larger entity that could use the tax credits. After some internal financial study, he approached Jay A. Pritzker with the sale of Trans Union for $55 per share 45 percent higher than the current market price of $38 per share at the time the proposed merger was signed. Within a week, a special session of the board was called for (September 20, 1980), and the transaction was approved upon hearing an oral presentation by Van Gorkom.

At the meeting, Van Gorkom did not furnish written copies of the proposed merger agreement and failed to explain the methodology by which he arrived at the $55 per share price or to discuss the price negotiations. No other estimates of value were presented and no outside professional was present to speak to valuation issues. The board meeting lasted approximately two hours, and the directors accepted the proposal, ostensibly reserving the right to accept a better offer, if made.

After reviewing the facts, the important business implications of the court's decision were as follows:

1. Taken alone, the presence of a premium in the merger price, as compared to the market price, was not a sufficient reason to approve the

merger. The directors were obligated to seek other sound valuation advice.

2. The board made efforts that were believed to have a curative effect on any shortcomings at the September 20th meeting. These efforts included hiring a well-known investment banker to seek competitive bids. In addition, the overwhelming support of the shareholders was deemed to be evidence of fairness.

3. The Delaware court ruled that negligence had occurred because the procedure for reaching the decisions of the board had been inadequate.

4. The directors were held personally liable for a multimillion dollar judgment (beyond insurance coverage) for breach of their fiduciary responsibilities.

In summary, the lessons of *Smith* v. *Gorkom* should cause directors to insist that significant transactions be presented in a complete manner and that access be provided to competent experts who can speak to the related legal, valuation, and disclosure issues. The standard of care required of directors has been increased with this decision. Its specific application is, of course, a matter of legal judgment. Expert legal counsel should be sought to assure that a board of directors involved in merger activities is complying fully with all state and federal statutes and related court decisions.

Fairness Considerations

The fairness opinion is a short document, typically a letter. The supporting work behind the fairness opinion letter is substantial, however. A well-developed fairness opinion will be based upon at least the following five considerations:

1. Financial performance and factors impacting earnings.
2. Dividend-paying history and capacity.
3. Pricing of similar transactions.
4. A review of the investment characteristics of the acquiring bank.
5. A review of the merger agreement and its terms.

Due diligence work is crucial to the development of the fairness opinion. The financial advisor must take steps to develop an opinion of the value of the selling bank and the investment prospects of the buyer (when selling for stock). We believe that it is prudent to visit the selling bank, conduct extensive reviews of documentation, and interview management.

A similar process should be performed with respect to the buying bank. If the purchaser is a public company, it is imperative that all recent public financial disclosure documents (10-K's, 10-Q's, etc.) be reviewed. It is also helpful to talk with financial analysts who routinely follow the purchasing bank in the public markets.

Quotes from two recent court decisions provide an indication that the standards of due diligence and independence of financial advisors are rising and that the fuller disclosure of fairness considerations in shareholder proxy materials may become the norm in the future.

Howing Co. v. *Nationwide Corp.*, 927 F.2d 263 (6th Circuit, 1991): "In our earlier opinion, we found that the defendant corporations in their going-private offer to the minority public shareholders had violated Item 8 required under Rule 13e-3 by making no effort to state, discuss or explain in reasonable detail the net book value, the going concern value or the liquidation value of the company whose minority interests were purchased. On remand, the District Court concluded that such a discussion would not have provided a shareholder with information of 'material' value under the legal standard of 'materiality' in securities transactions. . . . The District Court therefore granted summary judgment for the defendant corporations which were responsible for the proxy statement we had previously found defective under Item 8 of Rule 13e-3. . . . The facts do not justify the grant of summary judgment on the ground that a reasonable investor would not find an explanation of book, going concern, and liquidation value of any significance. . . . Where a defendent does base its 'fairness' opinion in part on a comparison of book value to the cash out price, it should discuss in reasonable detail the multiplier used and why that multiplier is appropriate."

Sandberg v. *Virginia Bankshares, Inc.* 891 F.2d 1112 (1989): "The proxy statement also stated that First American Bankshares, Inc., had hired Keefe Bruyette and Woods 'to pass on the fairness of the merger from a financial point of view,' although whether KBW's opinion focused on fairness to Bankshares or to the minority stockholders is disputed. It is admitted that KBW relied only on the market price to set a value on the stock, and Sandberg's expert witness was able to show that the actual value was considerably higher. . . . That KBW's $42 valuation was something less than the product of a completely independent analysis was a question of fact. The representation in the proxy statement that it was such an independent determination could certainly have been found to be a material misrepresentation."

A sample fairness opinion relative to the pending (hypothetical) merger of Specimen Bancorp, Inc., and Sample Bancshares, Inc., is provided as Exhibit 18-4. The letter is addressed to the board of directors of Specimen Bancorp and deals with the issues outlined above. The reader is cautioned that this is only a sample opinion. Valuation firms and investment banking firms may approach their fairness opinion letters in greater or lesser detail. The sample fairness opinion does, however, provide an example letter for purposes of illustration and discussion.

If the trends noted in *Howing Co.* and *Sandberg* continue, even fuller disclosure of the factors involved in developing fairness opinions may have to be included for opinions placed in public company proxy statements. These trends would then filter down to quasi-public entities, such as most financial institutions.

Directors' Memorandum

A fairness opinion may be supplemented with additional documentation for board review. As noted above, this documentation may be required in the opinion itself in the future. A report or memorandum that discusses the factors referenced in the fairness opinion in greater detail may be suggested by a bank's special counsel for the merger. If prepared, it would include a detailed discussion of the due diligence efforts and a list of documents reviewed. The fairness memorandum may be discussed in depth in a meeting of the board of directors called for that purpose. Specific items for documentation could include:

Exhibit 18-4

Sample Bank
Sample Fairness Opinion

July 8, 1991

Board of Directors of Specimen Bancorp, Inc.
P.O. Box 987
Sometown, Tennessee 38000

RE: **Fairness Opinion Relative to Pending Agreement of Specimen Bancorp, Inc., Sometown, Tennessee, to Merge with and into Sample Bancshares, Inc., Anytown, Tennessee.**

Gentlemen:

The Board of Directors of Specimen Bancorp, Inc. (Specimen, or, the Company), has retained Valuation Experts, Inc. (Valuation Experts), in its capacity as a financial valuation and consulting firm to render its opinion of the fairness, from a financial viewpoint, of the pending merger of the Company with and into Sample Bancshares, Inc. (Sample), Anytown, Tennessee. Other than the present assignment, we have no present, past, or contemplated future business interest with either Specimen or Sample.

As outlined in our engagement letter dated April 1, 1991, our approach to this assignment has been to consider:

1. A review of the financial performance of the Company and the valuation of its stock in the proposed merger;
2. A review and evaluation of the stock of Sample;
3. A review of information regarding recent comparable mergers in Tennessee;
4. A review of the current market prices of the common stocks of regional bank holding companies headquartered in Tennessee and neighboring states;
5. A review and evaluation of the investment characteristics of the common shares of the Company and Sample;
6. A review of the Form S-4 dated May 1, 1991, filed by Sample Bancshares, Inc., with the Securities and Exchange Commission (including the draft Joint Proxy Statement of Specimen Bancorp, Inc., and Sample Bancshares, Inc.);
7. A review of the Agreement of Mergers by and between Sample Bancshares, Inc., and Specimen Bancorp, Inc., dated March 1, 1991; and
8. An evaluation of such other factors as were considered necessary to render this opinion.

Exhibit 18-4 (*continued*)

Board of Directors
July 8, 1991
Page Two

It is our understanding that the law firm of Rehnquist, O'Connor, Scalia, Kennedy & Souter, P.C., Washington, D.C., has issued an opinion that the merger and resulting exchange of the stock of Specimen Bancorp, Inc., for shares of common stock of Sample Bancshares, Inc., constitute a non-taxable reorganization for federal income tax purposes. Our assumption, for purposes of this opinion, is that the Rehnquist, O'Connor, Scalia, Kennedy & Souter tax opinion will be upheld by the Internal Revenue Service and that the exchange of shares will therefore entail no federal tax liability for the stockholders of Specimen Bancorp, Inc.

DUE DILIGENCE REVIEW PROCESS

In performing this engagement, we have reviewed the documents specifically outlined in Exhibit 1 (pertaining to the Company) and in Exhibit 2 (pertaining to Sample). We have developed internally and/or reviewed information pertaining to recent community bank control transactions in Tennessee and the pricing of minority interests in regional bank holding companies headquartered in Tennessee and neighboring states. In addition, we have reviewed such other public documents and internal records pertaining to Specimen and Sample as were deemed necessary to render this opinion.

Review of Specimen Bancorp, Inc.

We visited with management of Specimen in Sometown, Tennessee, and discussed its operations in detail. During the interviews, we discussed questions regarding the current financial position and performance of Specimen and its operating subsidiary, Specimen State Bank & Trust Company, its outlook for the future, and other pertinent issues.

Review of Sample Bancshares, Inc.

We visited with management of Sample in Anytown, Tennessee, during the course of this engagement. During the interview, we discussed questions regarding the current financial position and performance of Sample and its operating subsidiary, Sample Bank, NA, the outlook for the future, and other pertinent issues.

Merger Documentation

We have reviewed the Agreement of Merger by and between Specimen Bancorp, Inc., and Sample Bancshares, Inc., dated March 1, 1991. We have discussed appropriate aspects of this agreement with management and counsel for the Company.

We have relied upon the above referenced information, which was obtained from or developed by sources that we consider to be reliable, without independent verification.

Exhibit 18-4 (*continued*)

Board of Directors
July 8, 1991
Page Three

MAJOR CONSIDERATIONS OF THE OPINION

Numerous factors were considered in our overall review of the proposed merger. Our review process included considerations regarding Specimen, Sample, and the proposed merger. Important considerations regarding each facet of our review are summarized below.

Regarding Specimen Bancorp, Inc.

- Historical financial performance and dividend record;
- Outlook for future performance and ongoing capacity to earn profits;
- Economic conditions in Some County, Tennessee;
- The level of competition for banking services in Specimen's market territory;
- Comparisons with comparable banks and bank holding companies;
- History of recent banking company control sale transactions in Tennessee;
- Current market prices of minority blocks of the common stock of regional bank holding companies headquartered in Tennessee and neighboring states;
- The current balance sheet position and income performance;
- Potential levels of risk in the loan portfolio;
- The amount of goodwill at the holding company level;
- The amount of debt at the holding company level and Specimen's capacity to service its debt;
- Historical stock prices, transactions volume, and the general degree of liquidity of minority shares;
- Historical shareholder dividend policy; and
- Such other factors as were considered necessary to render this opinion.

Regarding Sample Bancshares, Inc.

- Historical financial performance and dividend record;
- Outlook for future performance and ongoing capacity to earn profits;
- Economic conditions in Any County, Tennessee;
- The level of competition for banking services in Sample's market territory;
- Comparisons with comparable banks and bank holding companies;
- History of recent banking company control sale transactions in Tennessee;
- Current market prices of minority blocks of the common stock of regional bank holding companies headquartered in Tennessee and neighboring states;
- Sample's current balance sheet position and income performance;
- Potential levels of risk in the loan portfolio;
- The amount of goodwill at the holding company level;
- The amount of debt at the holding company level and Sample's capacity to service its debt;
- Historical stock prices, transactions volume, and the general degree of liquidity of minority shares;
- Historical shareholder dividend policy; and
- Such other factors as were considered necessary to render this opinion.

Exhibit 18-4 (*continued*)

Board of Directors
July 8, 1991
Page Four

Regarding the Merger

• The merger agreement and its terms;
• The specific pricing of the merger;
• Adequacy of the consideration to be paid to Specimen's shareholders;
• The assumption that the tax opinion regarding the tax-free nature of the share exchange will be upheld;
• The future earnings potential of Specimen and the impact on the earnings of Sample;
• The amount of debt and goodwill on the balance sheet of Specimen and the impact on Sample's liquidity and capital positions;
• The historical dividend policy of Sample and the likely impact on dividend income on exchanged shares to Specimen's shareholders;
• The pricing of recent control sale transactions in Tennessee;
• Current pricing of minority blocks of the common stocks of regional bank holding companies head-quartered in Tennessee and neighboring states; and
• Such other factors as were considered necessary to render this opinion.

FAIRNESS OPINION

Based upon our overall evaluation of the proposed merger of Specimen Bancorp, Inc., with and into Sample Bancshares, Inc., it is our opinion that the proposed transaction is fair from a financial view-point from the perspective of shareholders of Specimen Bancorp, Inc.

Sincerely yours,

Valuation Experts, Inc.

Attachment(s)
    Exhibit 1: Sample Bancshares, Inc.
    Exhibit 2: Specimen Bancorp, Inc.

Exhibit 18-4 *(continued)*

Exhibit 1
Specimen Bancorp, Inc.
Documents Review

_____

1. Agreement of Merger by and between Specimen Bancorp, Inc., and Sample Bancshares, Inc., dated March 1, 1991;
2. Form S-4 filed with the Securities and Exchange Commission by Sample Bancshares, Inc., on May 1, 1991 (including Joint Proxy Statement of Specimen Bancorp, Inc., and Sample Bancshares, Inc.);
3. Audited Financial Statements of Specimen Bancorp, Inc., for the years ending December 31, 1984–1990, prepared by Ernst & Anderson, Memphis, Tennessee;
4. Uniform Bank Performance Reports of Specimen State Bank & Trust Company as of December 31, 1988–1990;
5. Call Reports filed with the Federal Deposit Insurance Corporation by Specimen State Bank & Trust Company as of December 31, 1984–1990;
6. Minutes of the Board of Directors of Specimen Bancorp, Inc., and of Specimen State Bank & Trust Company from January 1, 1989, to April 30, 1990;
7. Report of Examination of Specimen State Bank & Trust Company by the Federal Deposit Insurance Corporation, as of October 31, 1990;
8. Report of Examination of Specimen Bancorp, Inc., by the Federal Reserve Bank of St. Louis, as of June 30, 1990; and
9. Additional pertinent financial information and other information deemed necessary to render this opinion.

Exhibit 2
Sample Bancshares, Inc.
Documents Review

_____

1. Agreement of Merger by and between Specimen Bancorp, Inc., and Sample Bancshares, Inc., dated March 1, 1991;
2. Form S-4 filed with the Securities and Exchange Commission by Sample Bancshares, Inc., on May 1, 1991 (including Joint Proxy Statement of Specimen Bancorp, Inc., and Sample Bancshares, Inc.);
3. Audited Financial Statements of Sample Bancshares, Inc., for the years ending December 31, 1984–1985, prepared by Coopers & Touche Company, Chattanooga, Tennessee, and for the years ending December 31, 1986–1990, prepared by Peat & Price Associates, Nashville, Tennessee;
4. Uniform Bank Performance Reports of Sample Bank, NA, as of December 31, 1989–1990;
5. Call Reports filed with the Office of the Comptroller of the Currency by Sample Bank, NA, as of December 31, 1984–1990;
6. Minutes of the Board of Directors of Sample Bancshares, Inc., and of Sample Bank, NA, from January 1, 1989, to April 30, 1990;
7. Report of Examination of Sample Bank, NA, by the Office of the Comptroller of the Currency, as of September 30, 1990;
8. Report of Examination of Sample Bancshares, Inc., by the Federal Reserve Bank of Atlanta, as of May 31, 1990; and
9. Additional pertinent financial information and other information deemed necessary to render this opinion.

1. Summary of discussions with executive managements of both the buyer and seller.
2. Review of historical financial performance and dividend record.
3. Outlook for future earnings for both the buyer (if a stock-for-stock deal) and seller.
4. Valuation ranges for the seller and the buyer (if a stock-for-stock deal).
5. Economic conditions (national and local or regional).
6. Comparisons with peer-size banks.
7. Review of control sale transactions over a relevant time and area.
8. Potential levels of risk in the loan portfolio.
9. Historical stock prices, transactions volume, and general degree of liquidity for minority shareholders.
10. Unique risks, such as litigation.
11. Other factors unique to a particular acquisition.

If the trend toward increasing disclosure continues, fairness opinions may become more like valuation reports. The directors' memorandum described above would then become something of an outline for the development of fairness opinions in bank merger situations.

Bank Capital and Capital Adequacy Revisited

Capital adequacy is an issue of extreme importance in banking because of the visibility and regulated nature of banking companies. It is not a simplistic issue, however, because of the difficulties in defining capital and then assessing its adequacy in the context of the industry in general and of specific banks in particular. Earlier portions of this text have discussed the more common definitions of bank capital, including shareholders' equity, primary capital, and risk-based capital.

Capital serves a variety of purposes in a financial institution, including (1) acting as a buffer to protect uninsured depositors from loss, (2) creating a sense of public confidence, (3) providing funds for operations, and (4) protecting the federal deposit insurance funds from loss. Banks usually augment their capital accounts through retained earnings. From time to time, however, it is necessary to raise capital externally to support future growth or to replenish the capital base.

Why Raise Capital?

In essence, there are only two reasons to raise capital from the marketplace. The first is to support future growth, and the second is to cure an existing deficiency. The motivation behind the sale of new capital is very important. If the new equity is to support future growth, then earnings can be expected to increase by the earnings on the invested capital *and* the net earnings on the additional assets acquired as a result of leveraging the new capital. The ability to leverage new equity can normally enable a bank to maintain or improve its return on equity. The value of the institution can therefore be enhanced by new (growth) capital.

If the new equity only cures a capital deficiency, then earnings will increase only by the direct earnings of the new funds infused into the capital account. The inability to leverage new equity (because of capital deficiencies) will drive the total return on equity down. It may also require existing shareholders to accept substantial dilution, because new investors will want an appropriate rate of return on their investment. If this requires the earnings from the new capital and a portion of the previously existing earnings stream, then the current shareholders will obviously suffer dilution.

When to Raise Capital

I learned a very simple rule about raising capital many years ago when I worked for the chief financial officer of a Tennessee bank holding company. He always said that the *best time to raise capital is before it is needed*. Institutions raising capital prior to an immediate need have much greater flexibility with respect to the actual timing of an offering or placement and the terms under which it is raised. Institutions having to raise capital under duress may find that their flexibility for timing and terms is virtually nonexistent.

The corollary to my initial lesson on capital is that banking institutions should always be in the mode of raising capital. This position will be clarified as we discuss ways to raise capital.

Ways to Raise Capital

There are three ways to raise capital in a banking institution. While the methods may seem obvious, it is useful to discuss each one briefly. Net new dollars of capital can be raised for a particular banking institution by:

1. Increasing earnings.
2. Decreasing the dividend-payout ratio.
3. Selling new equity securities or qualifying debt securities.

Capital can be "raised" in two other ways. First, if total assets are reduced, and other things remain the same for the bank, capital measures will show improvement. If, however, earning assets must be sacrificed as a bank shrinks its asset base, the benefit of the shrinkage must be weighed against the forgone earnings from the liquidated assets. Capital can also be "raised" by slowing the rate of growth of assets to below the earnings retention rate. In such cases, capital ratios will improve over time from the relative improvement in earnings retention.

Earnings: The Primary Source of Bank Capital

Earnings are the primary source of bank capital. Two studies performed by analysts at Irving Bank (which was acquired by Bank of New York several years ago) provide an interesting verification of this point:

> During the decade of the 1970s, it was estimated by an Irving Bank research department study that 80 percent of all capital added to the commercial banking industry, regardless of size or type of banking institutions, was in

the form of retained earnings. Ten percent of the increase in capital in the banking industry was in the form of subordinated notes or debentures, and 10 percent was added through debt and equity securities. This research study was replicated in 1985, covering the years 1980–1984, and the Irving Bank study indicated again clearly that 80 percent of all capital added to the banking industry in the early 1980s was from profitability and not from outside sources of capital, either through debt or equity securities. Since larger commercial banks and bank holding companies have far greater access to regional and national securities markets, it can be inferred that community banking organizations would have a larger percentage of their total capital infused through earnings, not through debt or equity securities, or other esoteric forms of capital infusion.[13]

If 80 percent or more of capital raised by community banks is in the form of retained earnings, it stands to reason that capital-hungry entities like commercial banks and thrifts should continually focus on maintaining and improving earnings. Unfortunately, bankers, like managers in other industries, often overlook the basics when looking for ways to increase earnings. And the basics are just that—basic. Consider the accounting identity:

Profit (P) = Total revenue (TR) − Total costs (TC)

If profit, indeed, is equal to total revenues less total costs, there are only three ways to increase profits:

1. Increase TR and hold TC constant.
2. Hold TR constant and reduce TC.
3. Increase TR *and* decrease TC.

The simple truth of these statements is clarified in Exhibit 18-5, where the examples relate to the comments immediately above. To give the example a banking flavor, assume that TR is adjusted gross income (AGI), or "sales," and that TC equals noninterest operating expenses (NIOE). The difference between AGI and NIOE is basic operating income (BOI). (See Chapter 9 for a review of these terms.)

A reading of the Sample Bank Appraisal in Chapter 22 will indicate that Sample Bank is performing substantially below peer group levels in terms of earnings, and that its capital ratios are also below peer group levels. In other words, Sample Bank could face serious capital problems if it encountered material loan losses or grew faster than expected. However, because of its relatively poor earnings performance, it is not likely to be able to raise capital on favorable terms.[14] Exhibit 18-5 therefore focuses on the potential for improving earnings as a source of capital for the bank.

In Example One of Exhibit 18-5, it is assumed first that Sample Bank can increase adjusted gross income by 5 percent—not 50 percent, but 5 percent. The means to accomplish this might include loan pricing reviews,

---

[13]Douglas V. Austin, *Capital Planning for the Community Bank* (Rolling Meadows, Ill.: Bank Administration Institute, 1989), p. 53.

[14]For purposes of this example, we are assuming that Sample Bank is an independent bank and that there is no holding company, contrary to the report in Chapter 22, which actually provides a valuation of Sample Bancshares, Inc.

pricing policy adjustments, deposit pricing policy adjustments, increases in fees for services, new charges for services previously offered free, and so on. Such a strategy, successfully implemented, would increase basic operating income from $5.5 million to $6.5 million, or nearly 20 percent. So for every one percentage point increase in adjusted gross income, operating income will increase about 4 percent (20 percent ÷ 5 percent). The bank's profit margin, or basic operating income as a percentage of adjusted gross income, would rise from 25.2 percent to 28.8 percent.

Exhibit 18-5

Sample Bank Focus on Opportunities to Raise Capital
through Increased Earnings ($ Thousands)

As of December 31, 1990

Total assets	$441,956
Total equity	$28,850
Equity/assets %	6.5%
Peer group median equity/assets %	7.1%
Equity shortfall to peer group %	$2,652 ([7.1% − 6.5%] × Total assets)

	AGI	− NIOE	= BOI	Profit Margin (BOI / AGI)	% Change from Base
Base level	$21,642	$16,182	$5,460	25.2%	n.m.*
Peer group median				35.9	
Example One					
Increase AGI 5%	22,724	16,182	6,542	28.8	19.8
Decrease NIOE 5%	21,642	15,373	6,269	29.0	14.8
Combine the above	$22,724	$15,373	$7,351	32.3%	34.6%
Example Two					
Increase AGI 5%	22,724	16,182	6,542	28.8	19.8
Decrease NIOE 10%	21,642	14,564	7,078	32.7	29.6
Combine the above	$22,724	$14,564	$8,160	35.9%	49.5%

*n.m. = not meaningful
SOURCE: Chapter 22.

If Sample Bank held adjusted gross income constant and reduced non-interest operating expenses by 5 percent, basic operating income would rise to $6.3 million, or about 15 percent from the 1990 base level of performance.

"Margin magic" occurs if the bank can combine the 5 percent increase in adjusted gross income with the 5 percent decrease in operating expenses. Basic operating income bounds 35 percent from the base level to $7.4 million, and the profit margin rises to 32.3 percent, or two thirds of the way to the peer group level.

There is overlooked operating leverage to increase profitability in many, if not most, banks. This operating leverage is a function of the hefty profit margins on sales combined with substantial balance sheet leverage. (See Chapters 8, 9, and 10.)

Had the bank operated with combined higher income and lower expenses as shown in Example One during 1990, basic operating income would have been $1,891 thousand higher than actually reported ($7,351 − $5,460). If we assume that Sample Bank's marginal tax rate (combined state and federal) is 38 percent and that all other factors remained the same, net income would have been $1,172 thousand higher than reported ($1,891 × [1 − 38%]).

While the discussion is theoretical in nature, the $1,172 thousand of forgone income (assuming further that the dollar amount of dividends was unchanged) represents about 44 percent of the total capital shortfall to the peer group average ($2,652 thousand) noted in Exhibit 18-5. In other words, with just over two years of earnings following measures taken to moderately increase income and decrease operating expenses, Sample Bank's capital shortfall could be eliminated.

Example Two is provided to show what would be necessary to bring Sample Bank's profit margin up to the peer group median level of 35.9 percent. It assumes the 5 percent increase in adjusted gross income from Example One combined with a more Draconian 10 percent decrease in noninterest operating expenses. This combination, if successfully implemented, would increase basic operating income by $2.7 million, or about 50 percent, to $8.2 million and would increase the profit margin to the peer group level of 35.9 percent of adjusted gross income. The increased earnings would provide an after-tax increase of $1.7 million, or about 63 percent of the capital shortfall in one year.

Earnings provide over 80 percent of incremental capital to the banking system. For individual banks, however, earnings may be the only practical means of raising capital. This discussion simply reiterates the importance of focusing on the little things that can increase income or decrease expenses so that banks can maximize their earnings potential and value and self-generate their capital requirements.

Dividend Policy

We have said that earnings are the primary source of bank capital. More appropriately, we should say that *retained earnings*—net income less dividends paid to shareholders—are the primary capital source. Over the last several years, banks have paid about 35 percent of their earnings in shareholder dividends. Industrial companies typically pay dividends in the range of 45–50 percent of earnings. Bank stocks have also typically traded at discounted multiples relative to the broad market averages.

Banks need to be careful in establishing and communicating their dividend policies because such policies can have an impact on share values.

Bank shareholders expect to obtain a reasonable rate of return for their investments in bank stocks. Shareholder returns come in the form of dividends, or current income flowing from ownership, and from (hopefully) capital gains upon ultimate disposition of shares. Relatively low dividends in the stock market are typically associated with "growth companies." When the market expects that a company can reinvest retained earnings and generate a higher future benefit than could individual shareholders, the market "trades" current income for expected future growth.

Banks able to generate an above-average return on equity that also have reinvestment and growth opportunities can realistically justify a below-normal dividend payout ratio, in the range of 15–25 percent. It might be a mistake for such a bank to *reduce* its dividend because that might indicate to the market that management's expectation for future growth has dimmed. However, if a bank is in the fortunate circumstance of already having a relatively low dividend payout, it should probably avoid the temptation to increase it, thereby retaining this important source of incremental capital.

Banks with a below normal return on equity and below normal growth opportunities should consider raising dividends to the higher end of the normal range, perhaps on the order of 40–50 percent of earnings. In so doing, they will reward shareholders with current income and avoid the accumulation of excess (underperforming) equity.

Some banks have instituted a dividend policy consisting of a fairly low regular dividend, perhaps 15–20 percent of earnings. This dividend is then supplemented with an annual special dividend based upon the board's evaluation of the year's performance, capital requirements, and outlook.

When a bank needs capital the most—when earnings are depressed or nonexistent—it may be prudent for the board of directors to reduce the dividend or eliminate it entirely. Unfortunately, lowering the dividend in this instance is not much of a source of capital because the basic earnings stream is impaired, which leads back to the discussion of earnings in the preceding section. Further, if a bank is experiencing earnings and/or capital problems, its primary regulatory agency may simply mandate that dividends be eliminated until the problems are corrected.

There is another problem with eliminating dividends: It is tantamount to admitting that the outlook for future earnings is fairly bleak. Creating this perception among shareholders can only serve to reduce share liquidity and values. If the bank is experiencing severe problems, this may be happening anyway. However, it is probably not a prudent policy for a healthy bank with a normal or near normal return on equity to eliminate its dividend in order to raise capital. Such a policy might signal entirely the wrong message to the shareholders and the market, and those perceptions can be difficult to overcome.

In the case of many community banks, however, where there is virtually no market for their shares anyway, lowering dividends might be an effective means of raising capital. If there is no market for the shares, a banker might ask what difference it makes, since the market cannot penalize their value. However, intangible factors related to community perceptions can create business problems, and shareholders' ill will should not be stirred up lightly.

Community banks can use dividend policy to help preserve capital in several ways. First, if there is a choice between being somewhat over normal or somewhat under normal with dividend payouts, it may be good to consider the latter posture. Second, the dividend payout ratio can be adjusted over time by lagging the growth of dividends below that of the growth of earnings. And third, a bank can consider the use of the special-dividend concept to segregate a lower, regular dividend from the higher actual payout in the minds of the shareholders. Banks using such a policy have the luxury of forgoing the special dividends when circumstances warrant, while preserving the regular dividend. This policy should be clearly communicated to shareholders if it is used.

Selling Equity

Banks can raise capital by selling newly issued shares to the public or to private investors. Because there are no established markets for many community banks, they lack the access to the capital markets that is afforded to larger, regional bank holding companies. Stock in community banks is normally sold in one of three basic ways: (1) through community offerings of shares, (2) through placement of shares with insiders, normally directors, and (3) through the private placement of shares with outside investors.

In all three cases, the actual pricing of the shares is critical to the success of the offering. Pricing for bank share offerings occurs in several ways. Share offering prices are often set by the board of directors for community offerings. Prices can sometimes be set relatively favorably if the bank has a good reputation and presence in the community. However, independent appraisal is sometimes used by banks as a basis for establishing offering prices.

Prices must be negotiated if shares are placed with insiders or outsiders. If insiders purchase shares, the board has a fiduciary duty to other shareholders to ensure that the pricing is fair and not excessively or inappropriately dilutive of the interests of minority shareholders. In such instances, independent appraisal is more frequently used as a basis for establishing share prices. Additionally, the financial advisor or valuation firm is often asked to provide a fairness opinion relative to the interests of the minority shareholders. (See the discussion above.)

Independent appraisal is also frequently used to establish negotiating ranges for private placements of bank shares with outside parties. The appraisal becomes a basis for communicating a bank's financial position and outlook in terms that investors can understand and for establishing the reasonableness of the negotiating range. Again, fairness opinions are sometimes obtained to help ensure that the placement pricing and terms are fair from a financial point of view to the minority shareholders.

Issues in Raising Capital

There are several actual or potential issues that can impede or prevent the raising of capital funds for banking institutions. Several of these issues are discussed in the following sections.

Publicly Traded Banks

The difficulties in raising capital that confront publicly traded banks are somewhat different from those faced by the community banks. Public bank holding companies have greater access to the capital markets and generally have greater interest from the investment community in helping them access capital. Interest may be heightened when the stocks are followed on a regular basis by securities analysts.

The publicly traded companies also face greater sensitivity to the trends of the stock market in general, the attitude of institutional investors, and wider perceptions about the stability of the nation's banking system. Any of these factors can be positive or negative for raising capital.

Community Banks

Raising capital in the community bank presents a different set of issues. By definition, the capital is generally raised within the local community, providing a much smaller pool of potential funds than the financial markets in general. The stock offering to capitalize a new bank is frequently spread relatively widely within a community. Subsequent stock offerings, however, tend to be far more concentrated, often among the directors or other closely-knit groups of shareholders.

Community bank stock offerings tend to be less susceptible to the influences of the larger markets. There is still a mystique about owning community bank stock that exercises a powerful draw for capital. On the other hand, a large pool of funds may just not be present in a given area.

A community bank has a decided advantage over its public counterparts when raising capital in a financially troubled situation. The amount of equity (generally less than $3.0 million) to be raised is small enough that a group of wealthy individuals can accomplish it. In so doing, they may achieve effective control of an institution. Publicly traded banks are typically much larger in asset size and consequently need much larger amounts of capital. Placing a larger block of stock can be much more difficult when the offering has to pass the analytical requirements of institutional investors and stock analysts and when it is virtually certain that postinfusion management and board leadership (which created the problems causing the capital deficiency) will remain in place.

Issues Common to All Banks

Banks are like other companies in that depressed share prices in the public markets make it more difficult to raise new equity capital without diluting the ownership of the existing shareholders.

One proposition is axiomatic for virtually all banks: It is difficult to raise capital when you need it. Capital is best obtained when its need is not apparent. The market does not normally provide capital as a cure for past problems without extracting a heavy price (in terms of dilution) from the existing shareholders. As a result, capital raised in times of trouble is likely to be far more expensive than if raised during times of positive operations.

One final note is that banks that need equity capital need equity capital. Debt instruments and leveraged employee stock ownership plans, for example, have their place, but it is very difficult to use them to overcome capital problems. The benefits are often illusory and may well be nonexistent in a troubled bank situation.

Loan Loss Reserve (Allowance) Revisited

Almost no valuation assignments call for an independent valuation of the loan portfolio from either a credit risk or mark-to-market perspective. The marketplace, however, is implicitly valuing the portfolios of publicly-traded banks from both perspectives. From the earlier discussion, it is clear that the value of the loan portfolio is crucial to the value of the bank.

The adequacy of the allowance for loan losses is frequently the major factor in determining when capital is adequate. Once the proper level of the reserve is measured, the need for a provision for loan losses to augment to the reserve is then determined. The impact on earnings then has a direct impact on capital. The provision for loan losses is a subjective, yet crucial element in determining capital adequacy.

Dramatic changes in bank earnings and capital (and value) occur most frequently when there is a realization that a significant deterioration in the loan portfolio has occurred. The valuation consultant should be alert to the events that trigger these types of announcements, particularly the completion of a bank examination. Although the specific components of the exam are confidential by law, it is always prudent to learn the results and the impact on earnings and capital if an examination is underway. Remember that while management and the examiners' views may well differ widely, the regulators are almost certain to prevail in any disagreement.

Capital/Business/Strategic Planning for Community Banks and Thrifts

The business planning process is sometimes referred to as the strategic planning process, although the "strategic planning" language of the 1970s and early 1980s has generally given way to "business planning" terminology. Regardless of terminology, however, capital planning for banks is an integral part of the overall business or strategic planning process.

We consider the *business planning process* as requiring a multiyear examination of a bank's position and outlook. Emphasis should be placed on the word *process*. Too often, bankers and other businesspersons engage in a planning exercise, develop a document, put it on a shelf, and refer to it only when visitors come by. Business planning, to be effective, must be an ongoing process.

Figure 18-1 provides a startegic planning model to illustrate the process. The figure is relatively self-explanatory, so the discussion here will be brief. The point is that all banks *should* engage in an ongoing, forward-looking business planning process. Several years ago, only a relatively

Figure 18-1
Mercer Capital
Strategic Planning Model

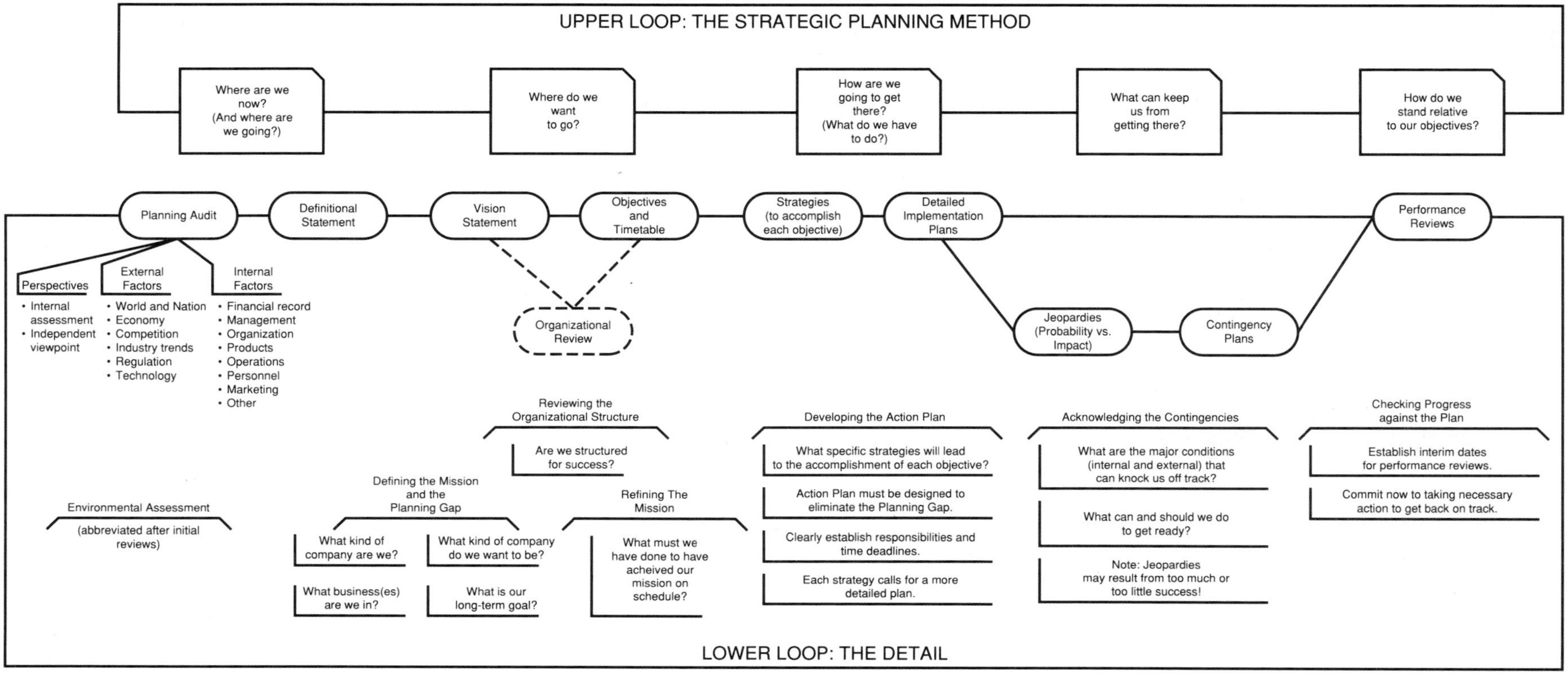

UPPER LOOP: THE STRATEGIC PLANNING METHOD

LOWER LOOP: THE DETAIL

421

small handful of banks and thrifts engaged in some form of active business or capital planning process. Increasingly, however, bankers are focusing on capital planning and on the implications of growth and profitability on their banks' compliance with regulatory capital guidelines. Sometimes these planning efforts result in the creation of formal documents, and sometimes they do not.

Increasingly, however, bank and thrift regulators are requiring that banks develop written capital plans. In late 1989, for example, all thrifts not meeting new capital guidelines established pursuant to the Financial Institutions Reform, Recovery and Enforcement Act (FIRREA) of 1989 were required to develop current capital plans *prior to January 8, 1990.*[15]

Thrift Bulletin 36a, "Capital Adequacy," was issued March 8, 1990, to clarify the original TB 36 (November 1989) on the same subject.[16] The bulletin applied to institutions not meeting new FIRREA capital guidelines; however, several sections provide an interesting perspective on capital planning for banks and thrifts. Quoting from the summary of the bulletin: "The Director of OTS shall treat as an unsafe and unsound practice any failure by a savings association to file an acceptable capital plan and to comply with the guidelines set forth below."

The general requirements, set forth in FIRREA for any capital plan, are outlined in TB 36a as:

1. Address the savings association's need for increased capital.
2. Describe the manner in which the savings association will increase its capital so as to achieve compliance with capital standards.
3. Specify the types and levels of activities in which the savings association will engage.
4. Require any increase in assets to be accompanied by an increase in tangible capital not less in percentage amount than the leverage limit then applicable.
5. Require any increase in assets to be accompanied by an increase in capital, as defined under a risk-based capital rule as adopted, not less in percentage amount than required under the risk-based capital standard then applicable.

In other words, the contents of a capital plan should include a consideration of those factors that both healthy and troubled financial institutions (whether bank or thrift) should be considering on an ongoing basis in the ordinary course of business.

TB 36a goes on to describe the contents of a capital plan:

The capital plan should explain in detail the proposed strategies for raising capital and for accomplishing the overall objectives of the savings association. *Over-reliance on consultants by the board of directors and management*

---

[15]This requirement was received by U.S. thrift executives whose institutions were not in compliance with new capital guidelines based upon June 30, 1989, financial statements. The letters, dated in mid-November 1989, required the development for acceptance by the Office of Thrift Supervision of "capital restoration plans." Needless to say, the deadline was impossible for institutions to meet unless they already had an ongoing business planning process underway.

[16]Office of Thrift Supervision, Thrift Bulletin TB 36a, published for *Thrift Activities Handbook,* Section 320, Subject: Capital Adequacy, subtitled "Guidelines for FIRREA Capital Plans, Exemptions, and Exceptions," March 8, 1990.

for the preparation of the plan is discouraged and may raise a supervisory issue with respect to managerial competence. [Emphasis added. Consultants can facilitate, but management and the directors must plan and implement the strategies called for in the plan.] An acceptable capital plan must be accepted by the board of directors of the savings association.

The capital plan should not be merely a budget of projected operations. It must be a comprehensive plan that is the result of strategic, in-depth planning on the part of the savings association's board of directors and management. The plan should describe a set of strategies and assumptions that have been made after a careful assessment of the available alternatives. All capital plans should include an analysis of the available strategies and a written summary as to why the selected strategies were chosen. Capital plans based upon projections regarding the ability to raise capital through the sale of stock will be rejected if not fully supported by objective data acceptable to the District Director.

In other words—overlooking the compliance aspects of the preceding paragraphs—a thrift's capital plan should be developed as a result of an ongoing business planning process similar to that outlined in Figure 18-1. The bulletin also recognizes the difficulties discussed concerning raising capital for troubled financial institutions. Similar requirements are being placed by the Office of the Comptroller of the Currency, the FDIC, and state bank regulators upon banks failing to comply with current capital guidelines. The upshot is an increasing focus on capital by bankers and thrift executives.

What is the relevance of this discussion on business and capital planning in a book on valuing financial institutions? For all practical purposes, the capital referred to in capital planning requirements is the shareholders' equity of community banks and thrifts. The value of that equity is the object of examination in most bank or thrift appraisals. We believe that value is created through the business and capital planning process and the subsequent execution of business plan strategies. In the final analysis, banks that engage in a healthy, ongoing business planning process, on average, will be worth more than those that do not.

Chapter 19

Branch Valuations and Core Deposit Appraisals

Democracy is the recurrent suspicion that more than half the people are right more than half the time.

E. B. White

Introduction

When individual branches or branch networks are sold, two types of assignments for bank valuation experts arise. The first assignment is the proper valuation of the branch as a going concern for negotiation purposes between the buyer and seller. The second assignment is the independent appraisal of the intangible asset consisting of the branch's core deposit base for tax and financial reporting purposes.

A core deposit base consists of the specific account relationships existing at the time of the sale. Given that those specific account holders will eventually die, relocate, move their accounts to a competitor, or otherwise terminate their business with the branch, the core deposit base can be described as having a *limited life*. Core deposits are usually defined as all deposits, *except* brokered deposits and certificates of deposit over $100,000, or those deposit types where considerations such as service, convenience, and long-standing relationships are typically important in the mind of the customer.

The value of a core deposit base results from its being a more stable and lower-cost source of funds than the market alternatives (e.g., brokered deposits, commercial paper, Fed Funds, and debt). Because the base of relationships providing the stream of revenues (i.e., the cost savings versus the next best alternative) has a limited life, the intangible asset representing the present value of the stream of revenues correspondingly is a *wasting asset*. Because the core deposit intangible asset is both a wasting asset and a reflection of a quantifiable expected future economic benefit, it receives tax and regulatory treatments that differ from that of general goodwill.[1]

A branch operation is not a wasting asset, and under normal circumstances it is a going concern. In contrast to the appraisal of a purchased core deposit base, which hinges on the amount of income attributable to the particular set of account relationships acquired by the purchaser and the rate at which those relationships are expected to terminate, the valuation of a branch involves such considerations as deposit growth (both in dollar balances and number of accounts), potential staffing changes, changes in fee structures, condition of fixed assets, and so on. Branch valuations are often prepared in the context of acting as financial advisor for a buyer or a seller.

---

[1] On July 25, 1991, Congressman Dan Rostenkowski introduced H. R. 3035 in the House of Representatives. The bill provides for the amortization of purchased goodwill and other intangible assets, including core deposit intangible assets. The proposal as written is considered "revenue neutral" and is supported by the Department of the Treasury. H. R. 3035 would provide a single asset life (14 years) for all qualifying purchased intangible assets. If passed, the uniform amortization period would reduce current tax controversies regarding the deductibility of intangible assets, including core deposit intangibles and goodwill, and would substantially eliminate uncertainties related to the tax consequences of many transactions. If H. R. 3035 is enacted substantially as proposed, the need for independent valuations of core deposit intangible assets will disappear.

Given this brief introduction to the branch valuation process and the valuation of acquired core deposit intangible assets, we will discuss the two topics in detail.

Valuing a Branch

As stated above, branch valuations are most commonly performed in the context of acting as a financial advisor to a buyer or seller. The purpose is to assist the client in staking out a negotiating position. The question to consider is "What can we do with this branch?" or "What can *they* do with this branch?" The driving assumptions tend to become rather specific to the parties in the negotiation.

Settlement of a Branch Sale

Branches are typically sold at the market values of their fixed assets (land, buildings, furniture, and fixtures) plus a premium for the acquired deposits. The size of the premium is generally based on the relative attractiveness and earnings potential of the branch. In some cases, loans and other earning assets domiciled at the branch are also acquired by the purchaser. If the buyer does not take any earning assets from the seller, the seller must fund the transaction with cash by remitting to the purchaser the difference between the total deposits assumed and the amount owed the seller for the premium and the fixed assets.

The amount of cash a seller must provide is reduced by the amount of earning assets the buyer is willing to accept. For example, if a branch has total deposits of $25 million and the purchaser has agreed to pay a premium of $1.5 million, to pay $1.8 million for the fixed assets, and to accept $10 million in earning assets, the seller would have to provide $11.7 million to balance the deal. Exhibit 19-1 provides an illustration of how this transaction looks at settlement from the purchaser's viewpoint.

Exhibit 19-1

Hypothetical Branch Settlement Analysis from Purchasers' Viewpoint

Assets		Liabilities	
Fixed assets	$ 1,800	Deposits acquired	$25,000
Earning assets	10,000		
Branch premium	1,500		
Cash settlement from seller	11,700		
	$25,000		

Assets acquired = Liabilities assumed

Branch sales can allow branch sellers to reduce total balance sheet footings rapidly, but they can also be a major drain on liquidity. Although the potential gain from the sale of a branch can look attractive, the liquidity costs can sometimes offset the potential benefits for some sellers.

Branch Valuation Model

The easiest way to discuss the process of valuing a branch is to work through an example. Exhibit 19-2 is a moderately detailed model designed for valuing a branch. In this case, the branch is the 399 Park Avenue Branch of Specimen Bank, which has approximately $23 million in deposits.

Schedule A of the exhibit shows the net present values and internal rates of return that result from the acquirer's initial investment in the deposit premium and fixed assets of the branch given the various balance sheet and income statement assumptions. This model treats the purchaser's cost basis in the deposit premium and fixed assets as the equity in the deal, and the acquired deposits are assumed to be reinvested 100 percent in earning assets (i.e., Earning assets + Fixed assets + Premium = Acquired deposits + Equity).[2] The model is conservative, with a 10-year investment horizon and the assumption of liquidation at the end of the period.

Schedule A of Exhibit 19-2 shows various return on investment measures based on the earnings generated by the branch during the 10-year period and its terminal equity. Returns based on net income, dividends, cash flow, and pretax income are shown. In this particular version of the model, the key return measure is dividends plus terminal value because the balance sheet has been set up to pay dividends to the parent bank equal to 100 percent of the branch's projected net income plus the amortization of the deposit premium. The present value of the dividend stream plus the terminal equity discounted at 15 percent is $2.382 million, or slightly less than the $2.488 investment in fixed assets and deposit premium. Correspondingly, the internal rate of return resulting from the initial investment in fixed assets and the deposit premium plus the returns represented by dividends and terminal equity is 14.07 percent. If terminal equity is adjusted for 6 percent annual appreciation in the value of fixed assets, the internal rate of return rises to 15.26 percent. The analysis in Schedule A allows the buyer and/or seller to test the sensitivities of the projected returns to various balance sheet and income statement assumptions and pricing levels.

Schedules B and C are summary projected balance sheets and income statements, respectively. Assumptions underlying Schedules B and C are summarized in Schedule D. The key balance sheet assumption in this projection is a 30 percent runoff of deposits in the first year after the purchase, followed by zero growth in the second year, 3 percent growth in the third year, and 6 percent annual growth thereafter. This deposit pattern is considered to represent a situation in which the branch's customers react negatively to the change in ownership. The acquired deposits are assumed to be reinvested in a generic pool of earning assets

---

[2] A branch purchase may be modeled in the manner in which they are actually settled (i.e., Earning assets + Fixed assets + Premium = Acquired deposits), but such a presentation implies 100 percent leverage and thus precludes the calculation of meaningful return on investment ratios. Exhibit 19-2 is set up as a consultant's tool rather than to determine an opinion of fair market value. It is designed to assist a branch purchaser or seller to establish negotiating positions. Consequently, its presentation should not be considered to be inconsistent with the earlier discussion of valuations using discounted future benefits methodologies.

Exhibit 19-2a
Specimen Bank
399 Park Avenue Branch
Acquisition Analysis ($ Thousands)

Core deposit premium	$1,148	Premium as % of deposits	5.00%	Annual rate of appreciation of
Fair market values		% of premium that will		market value of fixed assets 6.00%
Land	965	be tax deductible	80.0%	
Building	300	Purchased loans	0	
Equipment	75	Initial cash investment	$2,488	
Total investment in				
nonearning assets	$2,488			

Various Measures of Projected Earning Power	Over a Ten-Year Investment Horizon Discounted Present Values at					Over a Ten-Year Investment Horizon Assume FMV of Fixed Assets Appreciates Discounted Present Values at				
	10.00%	15.00%	20.00%	25.00%	30.00%	10.00%	15.00%	20.00%	25.00%	30.00%
Net income	$1,827	$1,474	$1,220	$1,031	$ 889	$1,827	$1,474	$1,220	$1,031	$ 889
+ Terminal equity	516	331	216	144	97	786	504	329	219	148
Total return	$2,343	$1,805	$1,436	$1,175	$ 986	$2,613	$1,978	$1,549	$1,250	$1,036
Dividends	$2,532	$2,050	$1,701	$1,441	$1,243	$2,532	$2,050	$1,701	$1,441	$1,243
+ Terminal equity	516	331	216	144	97	786	504	329	219	148
Total return	$3,049	$2,382	$1,918	$1,585	$1,341	$3,318	$2,554	$2,030	$1,660	$1,391
Cash flow	$2,710	$2,196	$1,822	$1,545	$1,333	$2,710	$2,196	$1,822	$1,545	$1,333
+ Terminal equity	516	331	216	144	97	786	504	329	219	148
Total return	$3,226	$2,527	$2,039	$1,688	$1,430	$3,496	$2,699	$2,152	$1,764	$1,481
Pretax income	$2,840	$2,293	$1,898	$1,605	$1,383	$2,840	$2,293	$1,898	$1,605	$1,383
+ Terminal equity	516	331	216	144	97	786	504	329	219	148
Total return	$3,357	$2,624	$2,114	$1,749	$1,480	$3,626	$2,797	$2,227	$1,824	$1,531

Projected Internal Rates of Return Based On:

Equity injection, net income, terminal equity	8.94%	10.48%
Equity injection, dividends, terminal equity	14.07%	15.26%
Equity injection, cash flow, terminal equity	15.34%	16.46%
Equity injection, pretax income, terminal equity	16.18%	17.23%

Exhibit 19-2b
Specimen Bank
399 Park Avenue Branch
Multiyear Balance Sheets ($ Thousands)

Years Ending December 31

Balance Sheets	Initial	1991	1992	1993	1994	1995	1996	1997	1998	1999	2000
Purchased loans	0	0	0	0	0	0	0	0	0	0	0
Other earning assets	$21,826	$15,259	$15,259	$15,719	$16,666	$17,670	$18,734	$19,862	$21,057	$22,325	$23,668
Building	364	364	364	364	364	364	364	364	364	364	364
Equipment	75	75	75	75	75	75	75	75	75	75	75
Land	965	965	965	965	965	965	965	965	965	965	965
Core deposit premium	1,148	1,033	919	804	689	574	459	344	230	115	0
Reserve requirement	1,074	751	751	774	820	870	922	977	1,036	1,098	1,164
Other assets	0	0	0	0	0	0	0	0	0	0	0
Total assets	$25,452	$18,448	$18,333	$18,700	$19,579	$20,517	$21,518	$22,587	$23,726	$24,941	$26,235
Demand deposits	$ 6,876	$ 4,813	$ 4,813	$ 4,958	$ 5,255	$ 5,570	$ 5,905	$ 6,259	$ 6,634	$ 7,032	$ 7,454
NOW and SuperNOW	2,070	1,449	1,449	1,492	1,582	1,677	1,778	1,884	1,997	2,117	2,244
MMDA	3,642	2,549	2,549	2,626	2,783	2,950	3,127	3,315	3,514	3,725	3,948
Savings	3,992	2,794	2,794	2,878	3,051	3,234	3,428	3,634	3,852	4,083	4,328
Time deposits	6,384	4,469	4,469	4,603	4,879	5,172	5,482	5,811	6,160	6,529	6,921
Other liabilities	0	0	0	0	0	0	0	0	0	0	0
Total liabilities	$22,964	$16,075	$16,075	$16,557	$17,550	$18,603	$19,720	$20,903	$22,157	$23,486	$24,896
Initial equity	$ 2,488	$ 2,488	$ 2,488	$ 2,488	$ 2,488	$ 2,488	$ 2,488	$ 2,488	$ 2,488	$ 2,488	$ 2,488
Retained earnings	0	-115	-230	-344	-459	-574	-689	-804	-919	-1,033	-1,148
Total equity	$ 2,488	$ 2,373	$ 2,258	$ 2,143	$ 2,028	$ 1,914	$ 1,799	$ 1,684	$ 1,569	$ 1,454	$ 1,339
Total equity and liabilities	$25,452	$18,448	$18,333	$18,700	$19,579	$20,517	$21,518	$22,587	$23,726	$24,941	$26,235
Equity/assets (%)	9.77	12.86	12.32	11.46	10.36	9.33	8.36	7.46	6.61	5.83	5.11
Earning assets/total assets (%)	85.76	82.72	83.23	84.06	85.12	86.12	87.06	87.93	88.75	89.51	90.21
Interest-bearing funds/total assets (%)	63.21	61.05	61.43	62.03	62.80	63.52	64.20	64.83	65.42	65.97	66.48
Total earning asset growth (%)		-30.1	0.0	3.0	6.0	6.0	6.0	6.0	6.0	6.0	6.0
Total asset growth (%)		-27.5	-0.6	2.0	4.7	4.8	4.9	5.0	5.0	5.1	5.2
Total deposit growth (%)		-30.0	0.0	3.0	6.0	6.0	6.0	6.0	6.0	6.0	6.0
Total liability growth (%)		-30.0	0.0	3.0	6.0	6.0	6.0	6.0	6.0	6.0	6.0
Total equity growth (%)		-4.6	-4.8	-5.1	-5.4	-5.7	-6.0	-6.4	-6.8	-7.3	-7.9

Exhibit 19-2c
Specimen Bank
399 Park Avenue Branch
Multiyear Income Statements ($ Thousands)

Years Ending December 31

Income Statements

	Initial	1991	1992	1993	1994	1995	1996	1997	1998	1999	2000
Interest on purchased loans		0	0	0	0	0	0	0	0	0	0
Interest on other earning assets		$1,767	$1,455	$1,477	$1,544	$1,636	$1,735	$1,839	$1,949	$2,066	$2,190
Total interest income		1,767	1,455	1,477	1,544	1,636	1,735	1,839	1,949	2,066	2,190
Interest on NOW and SuperNOW		92	76	77	81	86	91	96	102	108	114
Interest on MMDA		186	153	155	162	172	182	193	205	217	230
Interest on savings		187	154	156	163	173	183	194	206	218	231
Interest on time deposits		399	328	333	348	369	392	415	440	466	494
Total interest expense		864	711	722	754	800	848	899	953	1,010	1,070
Net interest income		$ 903	$ 744	$ 755	$ 789	$ 837	$ 887	$ 940	$ 997	$1,056	$1,120
Deposit service charges	$ 194	97	97	100	106	112	119	126	134	142	150
Overdraft and stop-payment fees	136	68	68	70	74	79	83	88	94	99	105
Other fee income	42	21	21	22	23	24	26	27	29	31	33
Total fee income		186	186	192	203	215	228	242	256	272	288
Personnel expense	334	334	347	361	383	406	430	456	483	512	543
Occupancy expense	17	17	18	18	19	21	22	23	25	26	28
Other operating expense	5	5	5	5	6	6	6	7	7	8	8
Building depreciation		18	18	18	18	18	18	18	18	18	18
Equipment depreciation		11	11	11	11	11	11	11	11	11	11
Amortization of deposit premiums		115	115	115	115	115	115	115	115	115	115
Total noninterest operating expense		500	514	529	552	576	602	630	659	690	723
Provision for loan loss/purchased loans		0	0	0	0	0	0	0	0	0	0
Provision for loan loss/other earning assets		65	46	46	47	50	53	56	60	63	67
Pretax income		524	370	372	393	426	460	496	534	575	618
Taxes		186	134	134	142	152	164	176	189	203	218
Net income		338	236	238	252	273	296	320	345	372	400
Dividends		453	351	353	367	388	410	434	460	487	515
Cash flow (Net income + Depreciation + Amortization)		$ 482	$ 380	$ 382	$ 395	$ 417	$ 439	$ 463	$ 489	$ 515	$ 544
Yield on earning assets (%)		9.53	9.54	9.54	9.53	9.53	9.53	9.53	9.53	9.53	9.52
Cost of earning assets (%)		4.66	4.66	4.66	4.66	4.66	4.66	4.66	4.66	4.65	4.65
Net yield on earning assets (%)		4.87	4.88	4.87	4.87	4.87	4.87	4.87	4.87	4.87	4.87
Cost of interest-bearing funds (%)		6.32	6.32	6.32	6.32	6.32	6.32	6.32	6.32	6.32	6.32
Net spread (%)		3.21	3.22	3.22	3.22	3.22	3.21	3.21	3.21	3.21	3.21
Fee income/average assets (%)		0.85	1.01	1.03	1.06	1.07	1.09	1.10	1.11	1.12	1.13
Noninterest operating expense/average assets (%)		2.28	2.79	2.86	2.88	2.87	2.87	2.86	2.85	2.84	2.82
Pretax return on average assets (%)		2.39	2.01	2.01	2.05	2.12	2.19	2.25	2.31	2.36	2.42
Return on average assets (%)		1.54	1.29	1.28	1.32	1.36	1.41	1.45	1.49	1.53	1.56
Return on average equity (%)		13.92	10.21	10.80	12.07	13.85	15.93	18.35	21.20	24.59	28.65

Exhibit 19-2d
Specimen Bank
399 Park Avenue Branch
Multiyear Projections ($ Thousands) Assumptions

	Initial						Years Ending December 31					
		1991	1992	1993	1994	1995	1996	1997	1998	1999	2000
Years to amortize/depreciate											
Building	20	Future capital expenditures on building and equipment are assumed to match									
Equipment	7	depreciation expense									
Core deposit premium	10										
Growth rates											
Demand deposits (%)		– 30.00	0.00	3.00	6.00	6.00	6.00	6.00	6.00	6.00	6.00
NOW and SuperNOW (%)		– 30.00	0.00	3.00	6.00	6.00	6.00	6.00	6.00	6.00	6.00
MMDA (%)		– 30.00	0.00	3.00	6.00	6.00	6.00	6.00	6.00	6.00	6.00
Savings (%)		– 30.00	0.00	3.00	6.00	6.00	6.00	6.00	6.00	6.00	6.00
Time deposits (%)		– 30.00	0.00	3.00	6.00	6.00	6.00	6.00	6.00	6.00	6.00
Reserve ration DDA/NOW	12%										
Dividend payout ratio	NI + AMRT	NI + AMRT	NI + AMRT	NI + AMRT	NI + AMRT	NI + AMRT	NI + AMRT	NI + AMRT	NI + AMRT	NI + AMRT	NI + AMRT
Interest yields/costs											
Purchased loans (%)		0.00	0.00	0.00	0.00	0.00	0.00	0.00	0.00	0.00	0.00
Other earning assets (%)		9.50	9.50	9.50	9.50	9.50	9.50	9.50	9.50	9.50	9.50
NOW and SuperNOW (%)		5.25	5.25	5.25	5.25	5.25	5.25	5.25	5.25	5.25	5.25
MMDA (%)		6.00	6.00	6.00	6.00	6.00	6.00	6.00	6.00	6.00	6.00
Savings (%)		5.50	5.50	5.50	5.50	5.50	5.50	5.50	5.50	5.50	5.50
Time deposits (%)		7.35	7.35	7.35	7.35	7.35	7.35	7.35	7.35	7.35	7.35
Fee income/operating-expense growth											
Deposit fee income (%)		– 50.00	0.00	3.00	6.00	6.00	6.00	6.00	6.00	6.00	6.00
Overdraft fees (%)		– 50.00	0.00	3.00	6.00	6.00	6.00	6.00	6.00	6.00	6.00
Other fee income (%)		– 50.00	0.00	3.00	6.00	6.00	6.00	6.00	6.00	6.00	6.00
Personnel expense (%)		0.00	4.00	4.00	6.00	6.00	6.00	6.00	6.00	6.00	6.00
Occupancy expense (%)		0.00	4.00	4.00	6.00	6.00	6.00	6.00	6.00	6.00	6.00
Other operating expense (%)		0.00	4.00	4.00	6.00	6.00	6.00	6.00	6.00	6.00	6.00
Provision for loan losses											
Purchased loans (%)		0.00	0.00	0.00	0.00	0.00	0.00	0.00	0.00	0.00	0.00
Other earning assets (%)		0.30	0.30	0.30	0.30	0.30	0.30	0.30	0.30	0.30	0.30
Income tax rate (%)		34.00	34.00	34.00	34.00	34.00	34.00	34.00	34.00	34.00	34.00

because, in this case, no specific loans or securities are being transferred with the branch.[3]

On the income statement, the yields on earning assets and deposit rates are projected to remain stable. Although highly sophisticated interest rate forecasts can be incorporated into a branch acquisition analysis, it is advisable to begin with a level-rate projection as a starting point; otherwise, the analysis may be distorted by a particular rate forecast that cannot be certain. Correctly estimating the long-term spread is much more important than correctly guessing the future level of interest rates. Nevertheless, it is important to look at a maturity breakdown of the branch's time deposits to determine if the current average cost of funds is a good predictor of the long-term trend.

If there are blocks of unusually high-cost or low-cost deposits whose maturities will significantly affect the average—that is, if deposit rates are not uniformly distributed with respect to remaining term—this situation needs to be factored into the interest rate forecast. For example, if a block of old, high-cost long-term CDs are due to mature within the next several months and their yields substantially increase the current branch average cost of funds, the postmaturity branch average cost of funds needs to be considered in the projection; otherwise, value will tend to be underestimated because the long-term cost of funds will be overestimated.

Overhead is expected to remain flat. In this case, the buyer was unable to identify any potential staff reductions or operating expense economies. Fee income was projected to decline 50 percent from the presale level, both as a conservative assumption and to reflect the assumption that deposits were lost.

The proper use of the model is to vary assumptions to see the impact of the changes on projected earnings and value. This process allows a prospective buyer to develop a feel for the potential risks and rewards from acquiring the branch. Such an analysis also enables a potential seller to develop a rational pricing expectation with regard to the branch: It is worth no more than the present value of the net benefits it can provide to an efficient purchaser (at the purchaser's required discount rate).

In summary, there are several key items to consider in valuing a branch, either in terms of how much a purchaser should expect to pay for it or how much a seller should expect to receive for it:

1. What is the branch's average cost of funds? What is the maturity and cost of funds distribution of its time deposits? How does its cost of funds compare to prevailing local market rates?
2. How volatile is the branch's deposit base? Is there a high dependency on jumbo CDs, competitively bid government or corporate deposits, or brokered accounts? What kind of runoff is likely if deposit rates are lowered?
3. Do transaction and savings accounts make up a large percentage of the total deposit balances domiciled in the branch? How do deposit

---

[3]If a portfolio of higher-yielding, good-quality loans is domiciled at the branch and offered in the sale, the value of the branch is enhanced by the resulting improvement in the average yield available on the pool of earning assets into which the acquired deposits are invested. Similarly, a branch with loan origination capability would be more attractive to a buyer because it would be able to make an ongoing contribution to the acquiring bank's earning asset base.

service charges compare with the local competition? What kind of runoff can be expected if fees are raised? What percentage of total fees collected are overdraft charges?

4. Are earning assets (loans or securities) to be included in the sale? What is their credit quality? What are their yields and maturity distribution? What is the fair market value of the earning assets? How liquid are they? Are the yields (adjusted for credit loss provisions) on the earning assets to be transferred high enough to improve the average yield on the reinvestment of the acquired deposits? Does the branch have a loan origination capacity that will allow it to contribute to ongoing earning asset growth and maintain above-average earning asset yields?

5. Is the branch understaffed, overstaffed, or adequately staffed? Is staff compensation in line with the bank peer group and the local labor market? Will the termination or reassignment of excess staff following the sale result in lost customers?

6. Are the branch's building and facilities adequate to support deposit growth? Is the equipment compatible with the purchaser's data processing system? Is there an adequate number of parking spaces? Is the branch conveniently located? Do the branch and its neighboring buildings have an attractive appearance? Do the demographics of the neighborhood indicate potential for sustained deposit growth over the foreseeable future?

All of these factors will have an effect on the key determinants of value for an acquired branch: deposit growth, customer turnover, overhead expense, fee income, net interest income, and the relative size of the investment in fixed assets. Appendix E provides an Information Checklist for Purchase or Sale of Bank or Thrift Branch for use in developing the information base necessary to analyze and value a bank or thrift branch.

Core Deposit Intangible Asset Appraisals

In this section of the chapter, we will discuss the conceptual approach to the valuation of core deposit intangible assets, as well as the tax and regulatory background relating to this specialized valuation activity. The next major section of the chapter will apply the conceptual framework in a hypothetical valuation situation.

Specimen Bank is negotiating to acquire the 555 California Street Branch of ABC Bank. The basic premium for the branch has been determined to be in the range of 6–7 percent of the deposits under $100,000, or in the range of $2.4–2.8 million. Management of Specimen Bank desires an estimate of the value of the core deposit intangible base in order to determine that portion of the purchase premium that would be tax deductible prior to completing negotiations for the branch. The last section of this chapter will place this hypothetical, but realistic, appraisal requirement in the context of the theoretical discussion of core deposits that follows.

Background on Core Deposits and the Related Intangible Asset

Core deposits are commonly defined as total deposits excluding jumbo CDs (time deposits with balances in excess of $100,000) and brokered deposits. Our definition of core deposits includes all consumer and business demand and savings accounts and "retail" certificates of deposit. Certificates of deposit over $100,000 are excluded from the core deposit base because they tend to be highly rate sensitive and do not typically have the stable retention characteristics associated with demand and savings accounts. Brokered deposits are also excluded, again because they are a high-cost source of funds where the interest rate paid tends to be the sole consideration when a consumer decides whether or not to place funds with a particular bank or thrift. Such deposits do not represent stable, long-term deposit relationships.

Core deposits at most banks and thrifts can be summarized as a mixture of demand deposits, interest-bearing transaction (NOW) accounts, passbook savings accounts, money market deposit accounts, and locally originated time deposits with balances under $100,000—all sometimes styled as *retail time deposits*. Retail time deposits (certificates of deposit) often make up the bulk of the aggregate dollar amount of the accounts.

The presence of core deposits in an acquired institution generates an *intangible asset* that must be distinguished from general *goodwill,* or *cost in excess of fair value of assets acquired.*

Definition of Goodwill

The U.S. Internal Revenue Service (IRS) views goodwill as all *unidentifiable* intangible assets that affect the earning capacity of a going concern. *Goodwill under this view is generated by the excess of earnings over and above a fair return on the value of net tangible assets.* Where the taxpayer can establish that an intangible asset has value separate and distinct from goodwill and has a life, the duration of which can be ascertained with reasonable accuracy, the intangible asset generally can be severed from goodwill and amortized. Various court case opinions have defined goodwill in the following ways:

1. "[Goodwill is] the probability that old customers will resort to the old place without contractual compulsion." (*Brooks* v. *C.I.R.,* 36 T.C. 1128, 1133, cited by *C.I.R.* v. *Seaboard Finance Company et al.,* 367 F.2d 646 [1966]).
2. "[Goodwill is] the habit of customers to return to the concern with which they have been previously dealing." (*Meeker* v. *Stuart,* D.C.D.C., 188 F.Supp. 272,275, aff'd 110 U.S.App.D.C. 161, 289 F.2d 902, cited by *Seaboard Finance Company et al.,* 367 F.2d 646 [1966]).
3. "[Goodwill is] the advantage or benefit, which is acquired by an establishment, beyond the mere value of the capital stock, funds, or property employed therein, in consequence of the general public patronage and encouragement which it receives from constant or habitual customers, on account of its local position, or common celebrity, or reputation for skill or affluence, or punctuality, or from other

accidental circumstances or necessity, or even from ancient par-
tialities or prejudices." (*Metropolitan National Bank of New York* v.
St. Louis Post Dispatch, 149 U.S. 436, 446 (1893), as cited in *Seaboard
Finance Company, et al.,* 64,253 P-H Memo T.C.).

4. "[The] essence of good will is the expectancy of continued patronage,
   for whatever reason." (*Richard M. Boe and Mary Lois Boe* v. *C.I.R.,*
   307 F.2d 339 [1962]).

The court cases focus on repetitive patronage as an essential element
of goodwill.

Definition of Deposit Base Intangible Asset

It is generally understood within the financial services industry that
premiums paid in acquisition situations generally represent premiums
for the acquisition of customer deposit relationships. It is, after all, these
relationships that give rise to a stable source of investable funds. It is
the earnings stream resulting from the investment of deposit funds over
time that is the source of economic value.

In the financial services industry, deposit relationships represent the
most favorable source of funds and are one of the most important factors
with respect to the profitability of a bank or thrift. While banking
organizations provide a variety of services to their customers, demand
deposits and savings deposits tend to be the focal point of other financial
service relationships. As a result, there is a great focus in the banking
business on keeping existing customers.

Account bases consist of individual accounts, each of which represents
a unique customer relationship. Each customer relationship has a unique
beginning date and is identifiable throughout its life on the books of a
banking institution. Each account also has a unique termination date.
Each account, therefore, is on the books for a finite period of time.

Attrition occurs within a block of deposit accounts for many reasons.
Individual customers get married, relocate, divorce, die, are lured away
by competitor institutions, or terminate relationships for many other
reasons. Businesses fail, are sometimes acquired, are lured away by competition, or terminate services for other reasons. In short, deposit relationships are a wasting asset.

Although it is not possible to predict the finite life of any particular
deposit relationship, it is possible, given a large block of deposits, to
predict the average life of the deposits within the group based upon
historical studies of the actual lives of customer relationships of an institution. While there are no definitive rules of thumb, about half of the
deposit relationships can be expected to terminate over a seven-to-nine-
year period, measured either in terms of the number of accounts or the
number of customer relationships. Some of the deposits can be expected
to be maintained over much longer periods. (This can be especially true
in small, rural banks where there are few banking alternatives.) These
longer-lasting deposit relationships tend to be associated with larger
average-deposit balances. The actual "half-life" of the deposit base will
vary from institution to institution based upon unique locational,
historical, and operating characteristics.

Two important points have been made in this section. First, deposit relationships are the major source of economic value in a banking or thrift organization in that they generate the primary stream of net income that is capitalized in any valuation. Second, deposit relationships are a wasting asset that have a measurable, finite life.

Because deposit relationships are wasting assets, the focus of banking institutions tends to be on keeping existing customers. The marketing of bank services to acquire customers from competitors is a slow process. Growth in deposit relationships usually comes more from new customers in the community, either persons moving in or new business formations, than from taking business from other competitors.

In our experience, the underlying rationale for most acquisitions of banking institutions, including an existing branch of another bank or thrift, is the assumption of the underlying deposit liabilities, rather than the purchase of other banking assets. Banking assets typically have much shorter lives than the underlying deposit relationships. As a result, an acquirer of deposit relationships has the ability to derive economic value from the intangible asset acquired for as long as the customer relationships are maintained. The purpose of an analysis of core deposit intangible values is therefore twofold: to determine that the intangible asset represented by core deposit relationships has specific economic value, separate and apart from goodwill; and to demonstrate that the core deposit intangible asset acquired is, in fact, a wasting asset with a limited useful life that can be reasonably estimated.

Recognition of Deposit Base Intangible Assets

Conceptually, intangible assets are those assets that, while not appearing on a balance sheet under most circumstances, nevertheless contribute significantly to the earnings capacity of an enterprise. Some assets, while physically intangible, lend themselves to financial definition and are called identifiable intangible assets. Core deposit intangible assets are one example of identifiable intangible assets. Other intangible assets, called *unidentified intangible assets,* have historically been lumped into the category called *goodwill.*

Internal Revenue Service

The Internal Revenue Service Code of 1954 (the Regulations) provides that, relative to the amortization of intangible assets,

> If an intangible asset is known from experience or other factors to be of use in the business or in the production of income for only a limited period, the length of which can be estimated with reasonable accuracy, such an intangible asset may be the subject of a depreciation allowance. Examples are patents and copyrights. An intangible asset, the useful life of which is not limited, is not subject to an allowance for depreciation. No allowance will be permitted merely because, in the unsupported opinion of the taxpayer, the intangible asset has a limited useful life. No deduction for depreciation is allowable with respect to goodwill (Regulations, Section 1.167[a]-3).

There is considerable other precedence for the utilization of core deposit intangible assets by banking institutions. Specifically, accounting regulations and bank regulatory edicts consolidate the evidence relative to the existence of core deposit intangible assets.

Regulatory Agencies

Until recently, bank regulatory authorities have required that goodwill recorded using the purchase method of accounting be written off immediately in bank financial statements. This requirement was not in conformity with generally accepted accounting principles (GAAP), and it obviously had a deterrent effect on bank acquisitions by other banks. Bank holding companies, on the other hand, have been able to use GAAP accounting since 1971 and have not been required to write off goodwill items at the time of acquisition, but they have been able to amortize them over a period of years.

Bank regulators have long been concerned about the "soft" capital that the recording of intangible assets would allow. However, given the increasing pace of mergers and combinations, the regulators could not continue to apply inconsistent regulations to different classes of banking institutions.

The two primary bank regulatory agencies, the Office of the Comptroller of the Currency (OCC) and the Federal Deposit Insurance Corporation (FDIC), took steps to deal with the issue of core deposit intangibles. The OCC issued Banking Circular 164 (December 29, 1981), its policy with respect to the accounting treatment for purchased core deposit intangibles. The FDIC issued BL-5-82 (March 5, 1982), its policy on the accounting treatment for purchased core deposit intangibles.

Since 1971, the Federal Reserve Board (Fed) has allowed bank holding companies under its supervision to use generally accepted accounting principles to record intangible assets. The Office of Thrift Supervision (OTS) also allows the utilization of GAAP accounting for core deposit intangible assets. In all likelihood, the Fed and the OTS will continue to condone the use of GAAP accounting for bank holding companies and thrifts, including the most recent pronouncements of the Financial Accounting Standards Board (FASB) relative to intangibles.

Generally Accepted Accounting Principles

GAAP accounting has long allowed the amortization of goodwill (unidentified intangibles) over a period not exceeding 40 years. In addition, purchased assets are valued at fair market value. The combination of the two rules led to abuses under "purchase accounting" by many thrift institutions and some banks.

In purchase situations, long-term, interest-bearing assets were marked-to-market. The resulting discount from original book prices was then scheduled into income over the remaining lives of the interest-bearing assets. Any goodwill recorded in the transaction was amortized into expense over much longer periods, usually 40 years.

The resulting mismatch in time between the booking of earnings from discounted assets and the expensing of goodwill often allowed earnings to increase for the combined institution, even though nothing else had changed. Thrifts and banks using the technique could, in effect, appear to make money simply by buying other institutions. At the very least, the dilutive effect of acquisition premiums was mitigated by purchase accounting techniques.

In February 1983, the FASB issued its Statement No. 72, "Accounting for Certain Acquisitions of Banking or Thrift Institutions." FAS 72 is an industry-specific rule that addresses several purchase accounting issues. Its basic conclusion is that banks and thrifts cannot report earnings simply by buying other institutions.

The new standard clearly recognizes the role of identified intangible assets in bank purchase situations. It requires that identified intangible assets, such as core deposit intangible assets, be recognized as separate and apart from goodwill. It further disallows any mismatching between the accrual of asset discounts into income and the expensing of goodwill items. The basic thrust of FAS 72 is that the income statement will have to bear the brunt of amortization of acquisition premiums over lives estimated by the extent of identified intangible assets.

United States Tax Court

In *Citizens and Southern Corporation and Subsidiaries* v. *Commissioner*, Docket 35465-86, 91TC No. 35, filed September 6, 1988, the United States Tax Court allowed a deduction for depreciation of deposit base intangible assets at nine banks acquired in 1981 and 1982. The deposit bases in this case represented core deposits that included deposit transaction accounts, regular savings accounts, and time deposit open accounts. The depreciation deduction allowed was the present value of the difference in costs between the acquired core deposits and market-alternative costs. The U.S. Tax Court made a similar decision in *Colorado National Bankshares, Inc., and Subsidiaries* v. *Commissioner*, Docket 3273-88, T.C. Memo. 1990-495, filed September 17, 1990.

Conclusion

The recognition of the intangible asset associated with core deposits as an identifiable intangible asset is now virtually complete within the thrift, banking, bank accounting, and bank regulatory agencies and the courts. Given the extent of their recognition, it would be difficult to argue that core deposit intangible assets do not exist. The FASB and regulators have agreed that core deposit intangible assets are identifiable intangible assets with limited lives that are reasonably determinable. In *Citizens and Southern Corporation* and *Colorado National Bankshares, Inc.*, the U.S. Tax Court has also agreed with this concept.

Alternative Methodologies to Fair Market Value

There are three basic valuation methodologies that could be utilized in the valuation of core deposit intangible assets: a market-based approach, a replacement cost-based approach, and an approach based upon the (discounted) present value of probable future earnings or cost savings.

Market Method

A market-based method implies an investigation of comparable transactions. This information is of limited usefulness in determining value in a particular situation, however, because little information is available about the particulars of possible comparable transactions.

Information on transactions of existing bank or thrift branches is also of limited usefulness in developing a market-based approach to the valuation of core deposit intangible assets. While purchase price information may be recorded publicly, details of transactions, which often involve fixed assets and other assets, make direct comparisons with acquired deposits impossible to interpret without details of the transactions.

Replacement Cost Method

A replacement cost–based method of valuing core deposit intangible assets is of limited usefulness. Given the lack of relevant data, estimating the cost of developing a comparable base of core deposits from scratch is not practical. Marketing and development costs are definable for specific institutions, but they are not generally made available for all banks and thrifts. In addition, many bank costs that properly should be allocated to marketing in a cost-based approach are not readily available.

Earnings Method

The last valuation method examines the present value of estimated future earnings attributable to the core deposit base. When entire institutions are acquired, analysts can examine current earnings streams and capitalize them based upon comparisons with price/earnings ratios of similar institutions trading in the public marketplace. Previous analysis has already shown that there are no acceptable market multiples available to capitalize deposit-generated earnings. Further, deposit bases are subject to attrition over time, so the earnings stream from acquired deposits is a declining earnings stream. The valuation of core deposit intangible assets, then, presents a classic case requiring the use of discounted future earnings.

There are two approaches to the earnings method whose key difference lies in the definition of the future earnings benefit attributable to the core deposit base. The first approach recognizes as the future earnings benefit the entire spread between the annual expense of maintaining the core deposit base (including interest and operating expenses) and the yield on a portfolio of earning assets funded by the deposit base. The second approach limits the future earnings benefit to the stream of cost savings represented by the expense of maintaining the core deposit base versus the cost of an alternative open-market funding source, for example, brokered jumbo certificates of deposit.

The market alternative approach is consistent with the methodology accepted by the U.S. Tax Court in the *Citizens and Southern* case (see above). The main weakness in the market-alternative approach to valuing core deposit intangibles is its failure to incorporate the benefits of the stability and predictability of core deposits as compared to wholesale money market alternatives such as negotiable jumbo CDs, Federal Funds purchased, and Eurodollar obligations.

Several large commercial bank failures in recent years, including Continental Illinois National Bank and Trust Company of Chicago, involved banks located in states that at the time had unitary banking laws.

The legal restriction on branch networks in several states prevented the banks from developing a large base of core deposits, which forced them to rely on wholesale funding from institutional investors. Institutional funds proved to be highly sensitive to market interest rates and general perceptions of the banks' credit quality, resulting in the banks suffering severe liquidity problems at the first indication of difficulties.

On the other hand, troubled financial institutions with large bases of core deposits have generally avoided substantial, rapid outflows of funds following the announcement of unfavorable information. The use of core deposits to fund the operations of a financial institution can therefore generally be said to involve not only a lower interest cost when compared to wholesale money market alternatives but also, clearly, a lower level of risk.

In our opinion, limiting the definition of economic benefits attributable to a base of core deposits to merely the savings in funding costs relative to an alternative open-market source is in many cases too restrictive. A gross earnings approach, rather than a market alternative cost savings approach, is frequently the more appropriate valuation methodology because it recognizes the entire future earnings stream supported by the core deposit base and thus implicitly includes the economic benefit of the lower-risk profile of a base of core deposits.

Summary Valuation of the Core Deposit Intangible Asset of 555 California Street Branch

Specimen Bank is negotiating to acquire approximately $40.3 million of core deposits at the 555 California Street Branch of ABC Bank. The deposits to be acquired are detailed in Exhibit 19-3. In this section, we will work through a "valuation" of the core deposits to be acquired. Although the presentation is not intended to represent the format of a completed valuation report, it will carry the reader through the steps necessary to reach and present a valuation conclusion related to core deposit intangible assets.

Other methodologies for the valuation of core deposit intangible assets have been developed by other appraisers. Several of these alternative approaches are mentioned in this section. We believe the methodology presented below is logical, rational, and reasonable for the valuation of core deposit intangible assets. We further believe it is consistent with current cases allowing the tax deductibility of core deposit intangible assets. However, any appraiser attempting to conduct a core deposit intangible asset valuation is responsible for developing his or her own background research, data collection and analysis, and valuation methodologies and techniques.

It should be noted that any appraiser's approach and presentation with respect to any particular type of assignment tends to change over time and with experience. The reader should not infer that the following exposition represents the final, definitive approach to valuing core deposits. Mercer Capital has approached core deposit appraisals differently in the past, and our methodology is likely to continue to evolve in the future. As with any appraisal assignment, the economic reality of the assumptions and the reasonableness of the results are key.

Applying the Earnings Method

Once the deposits under consideration have been defined, the methodology in the valuation of core deposits requires three distinct, but related, steps. First, an estimate of annual cost savings (differences in interest expense adjusted for float, operating expense, and fee income) attributable to the core deposit base relative to alternative funding sources must be made. Second, the history of customer retention at the acquired institution must be investigated to develop an estimate of the economic life of the core deposit base. And finally, the present value of the cost savings stream attributable to the core deposit base must be determined based upon cost savings spreads, customer retention rates, and estimated economic life.

The unique customer retention characteristics of the subject institution are superimposed on the core deposit base to determine the projected rates of customer attrition and the estimated deposit base lives. The projected streams of cost savings (or earnings on the investment of the deposits in a pool of earning assets) are then discounted to the present at an appropriate discount rate to determine the valuations of the core deposit intangible assets.

Exhibits 19-3 through 19-8 provide sample valuation tables showing the elements of a core deposit appraisal.

Determination of Cost Savings

The determination of cost savings for an acquired core deposit account base should consider the following factors:

1. The total interest and operating expenses associated with using a market-alternative funding source.
2. The amount of float inherent in the deposit base.
3. The operating expenses associated with maintaining the deposit base.
4. The service fees assessed on the deposit base.
5. The marginal tax rate for the acquiring banking institution.[4]

The sources for the statistics used in the estimation of expenses and earnings are typically as follows:

1. The number of accounts by type and corresponding balances and weighted average interest rates are derived from the trial balances and other management information systems of the acquired institution. It is up to the analyst to determine if the interest cost of funds based on the rates prevailing on the day the transfer closed or a cost of funds based on average rates for some longer period preceding the transfer is a more appropriate indication of ongoing deposit interest expense.

---

[4]Some analysts may prefer to value core deposits on a pretax basis. As long as an appropriate pretax discount rate is applied, such an approach would appear valid.

Exhibit 19-3
Specimen Bank
555 California Street Branch
Analysis of Core Deposit Base

Deposit Account Type	Gross $ Balance (1)	Number of Accounts (1)	Gross $ Balance Per Account	Available Funds % (2)	Available $ Balance	Available $ Balance Per Account
Non-interest-bearing demand	$ 8,774,474	1,653	$ 5,308	84.02%	$ 7,372,313	$ 4,460
Interest-bearing transaction	4,051,524	1,234	3,283	88.19%	3,573,039	2,895
Money market deposit	3,858,317	321	12,020	98.67%	3,807,001	11,860
Regular savings	3,453,143	1,300	2,656	98.70%	3,408,252	2,622
Certificates of deposit under $100,000	20,213,224	954	21,188	98.91%	19,992,900	20,957
Total core deposits	$40,350,682	5,462	$ 7,388	94.55%	$38,153,505	$ 6,985
Certificates of deposit over $100,000	4,480,686	21				
Total deposits	$44,831,368	5,483				

Deposit Account Type	Interest Cost of Funds % (1)	Operating Expense % (2)	Operating Income % (2)	Total Cost of Funds %	Available Funds % (2)	Effective Cost of Funds %
Non-interest-bearing demand	0.00	6.28	− 3.19	3.09	84.02	3.68
Interest-bearing transaction	4.50	1.33	− 0.28	5.55	88.19	6.29
Money market deposit	5.25	1.06	0.00	6.31	98.67	6.40
Regular savings	5.00	2.52	− 0.18	7.34	98.70	7.44
Certificates of deposit under $100,000	7.73	0.19	0.00	7.92	98.91	8.01
Total core deposits (weighted by gross balances)	5.25%	1.91%	− 0.74%	6.43%	94.55%	6.69%

SOURCES: (1) Summary deposit trial balance; (2) Federal Reserve functional cost analysis.

Exhibit 19-4
Specimen Bank
555 California Street Branch
Alternative Cost of Funds and Discount Rate

Derivation of Market Alternative Cost of Funds to Apply to Core Deposit Base

Average interest rate on large certificates of deposit in the secondary market (3)	8.37%
Plus operating expense (2)	0.19%
Less operating income (2)	0.00%
Plus estimated brokerage fees	0.25%
Total cost of funds	8.81%
Divided by available funds percentage (2)	98.91%
Effective cost of secondary market (CDs)	8.91%

Derivation of Discount Rate for Future Cost Savings Generated by Core Deposit Base

Average compound total return on small-company stocks, 1947–1990 (4)	13.30%
Less income taxes at the current 34% rate	− 4.52%
Nominal after-tax total return	8.78%
Less average compound inflation rate, 1947–1990 (4)	− 4.20%
Net real total return	4.58%

SOURCES: (1) Summary deposit trial balance; (2) Federal Reserve functional cost analysis; (3) Federal Reserve statistical release (H.15); (4) *Stocks, Bonds, Bills, and Inflation: 1991 Yearbook* (Chicago: Ibbotson Associates, 1991).

Exhibit 19-5
Specimen Bank
555 California Street Branch
Cost Spreads on Core Deposit Base

Deposit Account Type	Effective Cost of Funds %	Alternative Cost of Funds %	Pretax Cost Spread %	Income Taxes @ 34%	Net Cost Spread %
Non-interest-bearing demand	3.68	8.91	5.23	1.78	3.45
Interest-bearing transaction	6.29	8.91	2.62	0.89	1.73
Money market deposit	6.40	8.91	2.51	0.85	1.66
Regular savings	7.44	8.91	1.47	0.50	0.97
Certificates of deposit under $100,000	8.01	8.91	0.90	0.31	0.59
Total core deposits (weighted by available balances)	6.80%	8.91%	2.11%	0.72%	1.39%

Deposit Account Type	Net Net Cost Spread %	Available $ Balance Per Account	Annual Net Cost Savings $ Per Account
Non-interest-bearing demand	3.45	$4,460	$153.87
Interest-bearing transaction	1.73	2,895	50.09
Money market deposit	1.66	11,860	196.87
Regular savings	0.97	2,622	25.43
Certificates of deposit under $100,000	0.59	20,957	123.65
Total core deposits (weighted by available balances)	1.39%	$6,985	$ 97.10

Exhibit 19-6a
Specimen Bank
555 California Street Branch
Demand, Interest-Bearing Transaction and Money Market Deposit Accounts
Retention Analysis

Opened Before	Total Accounts	Accounts Remaining December 31					
		1985	1986	1987	1988	1989	1990
12-31-1984	5,542	4,008	3,060	2,372	2,074	1,758	1,552
1985	1,222	n.m.*	706	474	396	310	262
1986	978	n.m.	n.m.	486	342	268	177
1987	878	n.m.	n.m.	n.m.	570	430	324
1988	880	n.m.	n.m.	n.m.	n.m.	532	340
1989	1,004	n.m.	n.m.	n.m.	n.m.	n.m.	553

Year-to-Year Retention Rates December 31					
1985	1986	1987	1988	1989	1990
72.3%	76.3%	77.5%	87.4%	84.8%	88.3%
n.m.	57.8%	67.1%	83.5%	78.3%	84.5%
n.m.	n.m.	49.7%	70.4%	78.4%	66.0%
n.m.	n.m.	n.m.	64.9%	75.4%	75.3%
n.m.	n.m.	n.m.	n.m.	60.5%	63.9%
n.m.	n.m.	n.m.	n.m.	n.m.	55.1%

Average Annual Retention Rates
1-year-old accounts 60.0%
2-year-old accounts 70.6%
3-year-old accounts 78.7%
4-year-old accounts 77.3%
5-year-old accounts 84.6%
6-year-old accounts 88.3%

*n.m. = not meaningful.

Exhibit 19-6b
Specimen Bank
555 California Street Branch
Savings Accounts
Retention Analysis

Opened Before	Total Accounts	Accounts Remaining December 31					
		1985	1986	1987	1988	1989	1990
12-31-1984	3,710	1,922	1,224	844	662	552	412
1985	788	n.m.*	456	216	156	108	65
1986	670	n.m.	n.m.	326	212	150	107
1987	562	n.m.	n.m.	n.m.	374	222	136
1988	566	n.m.	n.m.	n.m.	n.m.	322	207
1989	690	n.m.	n.m.	n.m.	n.m.	n.m.	373

	Year-to-Year Retention Rates December 31					
1985	1986	1987	1988	1989	1990
51.8%	63.7%	69.0%	78.4%	78.9%	78.9%
n.m.	57.9%	47.4%	72.2%	69.2%	60.2%
n.m.	n.m.	48.7%	65.0%	70.8%	71.3%
n.m.	n.m.	n.m.	66.5%	59.4%	61.3%
n.m.	n.m.	n.m.	n.m.	56.9%	64.3%
n.m.	n.m.	n.m.	n.m.	n.m.	54.1%

Average Annual Retention Rates

1-year-old accounts	56.0%
2-year-old accounts	59.9%
3-year-old accounts	68.3%
4-year-old accounts	73.0%
5-year-old accounts	69.5%
6-year-old accounts	78.9%

*n.m. = not meaningful.

Exhibit 19-6c
Specimen Bank
555 California Street Branch
Time Deposit Accounts
Retention Analysis

Opened Before	Total Accounts	Accounts Remaining December 31				
		1986	1987	1988	1989	1990
12-31-1985	978	704	548	400	276	222
1986	308	n.m.*	206	110	74	60
1987	226	n.m.	n.m.	142	70	52
1988	156	n.m.	n.m.	n.m.	102	80
1989	318	n.m.	n.m.	n.m.	n.m.	222

Year-to-Year Retention Rates December 31				
1986	1987	1988	1989	1990
75.7%	74.1%	73.0%	69.0%	80.4%
n.m.	66.9%	53.4%	67.3%	81.1%
n.m.	n.m.	62.8%	49.3%	74.3%
n.m.	n.m.	n.m.	65.4%	78.4%
n.m.	n.m.	n.m.	n.m.	69.8%

Average Annual Retention Rates
1-year-old accounts	68.1%
2-year-old accounts	63.8%
3-year-old accounts	71.5%
4-year-old accounts	75.0%
5-year-old accounts	80.4%

*n.m. = not meaningful.

Exhibit 19-7a
Specimen Bank
555 California Street Branch
Core Deposit Valuation
Retention Rates and Net Present Value

Non-Interest-Bearing Demand Deposits

Year	Retention Rates*	Year-End Number of Open Accounts†	Average Number of Open Accounts	Total Savings at $153.87 Per Account‡	Discounted Present Value at 4.58%§	Percentage of Acquired Accounts Remaining (%)	Percentage of Value Remaining (%)
0		1,653				100.00	100.00
1	60.00%	992	1,323	$203,570	$199,063	60.01	73.39
2	70.60%	700	846	130,174	121,717	42.35	57.12
3	78.70%	551	626	96,323	86,121	33.33	45.61
4	77.30%	426	489	75,242	64,327	25.77	37.01
5	84.60%	360	393	60,471	49,434	21.78	30.41
6	88.30%	318	339	52,162	40,774	19.24	24.96
7	88.30%	281	300	46,161	34,503	17.00	20.34
8	88.30%	248	265	40,776	29,143	15.00	16.45
9	88.30%	219	234	36,006	24,607	13.25	13.16
10	88.30%	193	206	31,697	20,714	11.68	10.39
11	88.30%	170	182	28,004	17,499	10.28	8.05
12	88.30%	150	160	24,619	14,710	9.07	6.08
13	88.30%	132	141	21,696	12,396	7.99	4.43
14	88.30%	117	125	19,234	10,508	7.08	3.02
15	88.30%	103	110	16,926	8,842	6.23	1.84
16	88.30%	91	97	14,925	7,455	5.51	0.84
17	88.30%	80	86	13,233	6,321	4.84	0.00
Total				$911,219	$748,134		

*Retention rates per Exhibit 19-5a.
†Initial number of accounts per Exhibit 19-2.
‡Net cost savings per Exhibit 19-4.
§Discount rate per Exhibit 19-3.

Exhibit 19-7b
Specimen Bank
555 California Street Branch
Core Deposit Valuation
Retention Rates and Net Present Value

Interest-Bearing Transaction Accounts

Year	Retention Rates*	Year-End Number of Open Accounts†	Average Number of Open Accounts	Total Savings at $50.09 Per Account‡	Discounted Present Value at 4.58%§	Percentage of Acquired Accounts Remaining (%)	Percentage of Value Remaining (%)
0		1,234				100.00	100.00
1	60.00%	740	987	$ 49,439	$ 48,344	59.97	73.41
2	70.60%	522	631	31,607	29,554	42.30	57.16
3	78.70%	411	467	23,392	20,914	33.31	45.66
4	77.30%	318	365	18,283	15,631	25.77	37.06
5	84.60%	269	294	14,726	12,038	21.80	30.44
6	88.30%	238	254	12,723	9,945	19.29	24.97
7	88.30%	210	224	11,220	8,386	17.02	20.36
8	88.30%	185	198	9,918	7,089	14.99	16.46
9	88.30%	163	174	8,716	5,957	13.21	13.18
10	88.30%	144	154	7,714	5,041	11.67	10.41
11	88.30%	127	136	6,812	4,257	10.29	8.07
12	88.30%	112	120	6,011	3,592	9.08	6.09
13	88.30%	99	106	5,310	3,034	8.02	4.43
14	88.30%	87	93	4,658	2,545	7.05	3.03
15	88.30%	77	82	4,107	2,145	6.24	1.85
16	88.30%	68	73	3,657	1,827	5.51	0.84
17	88.30%	60	64	3,206	1,531	4.86	0.00
Total				$221,499	$181,830		

*Retention rates per Exhibit 19-5a.
†Initial number of accounts per Exhibit 19-2.
‡Net cost savings per Exhibit 19-4.
§Discount rate per Exhibit 19-3.

Exhibit 19-7c
Specimen Bank
555 California Street Branch
Core Deposit Valuation
Retention Rates and Net Present Value

Money Market Deposit Accounts

Year	Retention Rates*	Year-End Number of Open Accounts†	Average Number of Open Accounts	Total Savings at $196.87 Per Account‡	Discounted Present Value at 4.58%§	Percentage of Acquired Accounts Remaining (%)	Percentage of Value Remaining (%)
0		321				100.00	100.00
1	60.00%	193	257	$50,596	$49,476	60.12	73.55
2	70.60%	136	165	32,484	30,374	42.37	57.32
3	78.70%	107	122	24,018	21,474	33.33	45.84
4	77.30%	83	95	18,703	15,990	25.86	37.29
5	84.60%	70	77	15,159	12,392	21.81	30.67
6	88.30%	62	66	12,993	10,156	19.31	25.24
7	88.30%	55	59	11,615	8,682	17.13	20.60
8	88.30%	49	52	10,237	7,317	15.26	16.69
9	88.30%	43	46	9,056	6,189	13.40	13.38
10	88.30%	38	41	8,072	5,275	11.84	10.56
11	88.30%	34	36	7,087	4,428	10.59	8.20
12	88.30%	30	32	6,300	3,764	9.35	6.18
13	88.30%	26	28	5,512	3,149	8.10	4.50
14	88.30%	23	25	4,922	2,689	7.17	3.06
15	88.30%	20	22	4,331	2,262	6.23	1.85
16	88.30%	18	19	3,741	1,869	5.61	0.85
17	88.30%	16	17	3,347	1,599	4.98	0.00
Total				$228,173	$187,085		

*Retention rates per Exhibit 19-5a.
†Initial number of accounts per Exhibit 19-2.
‡Net cost savings per Exhibit 19-4.
§Discount rate per Exhibit 19-3.

Exhibit 19-7d
Specimen Bank
555 California Street Branch
Core Deposit Valuation
Retention Rates and Net Present Value

Regular Savings Accounts

Year	Retention Rates*	Year-End Number of Open Accounts†	Average Number of Open Accounts	Total Savings at $25.43 Per Account‡	Discounted Present Value at 4.58%§	Percentage of Acquired Accounts Remaining (%)	Percentage of Value Remaining (%)
0		1,300				100.00	100.00
1	56.00%	728	1,014	$25,786	$25,215	56.00	60.80
2	59.90%	436	582	14,800	13,838	33.54	39.28
3	68.30%	298	367	9,333	8,344	22.92	26.31
4	73.00%	218	258	6,561	5,609	16.77	17.59
5	69.50%	152	185	4,705	3,846	11.69	11.61
6	78.90%	120	136	3,458	2,703	9.23	7.41
7	78.90%	95	108	2,746	2,053	7.31	4.21
8	78.90%	75	85	2,162	1,545	5.77	1.81
9	78.90%	59	67	1,704	1,165	4.54	0.00
Total				$71,255	$64,318		

*Retention rates per Exhibit 19-5b.
†Initial number of accounts per Exhibit 19-2.
‡Net cost savings per Exhibit 19-4.
§Discount rate per Exhibit 19-3.

Exhibit 19-7e
Specimen Bank
555 California Street Branch
Core Deposit Valuation
Retention Rates and Net Present Value

Certificates of Deposit under $100,000

Year	Retention Rates*	Year-End Number of Open Accounts†	Average Number of Open Accounts	Total Savings at $123.65 Per Account‡	Discounted Present Value at 4.58%§	Percentage of Acquired Accounts Remaining (%)	Percentage of Value Remaining (%)
0		954				100.00	100.00
1	68.10%	650	802	$ 99,167	$ 96,971	68.13	67.97
2	63.80%	415	533	65,905	61,623	43.50	47.61
3	71.50%	297	356	44,019	39,357	31.13	34.61
4	75.00%	223	260	32,149	27,485	23.38	25.53
5	80.40%	179	201	24,854	20,318	18.76	18.82
6	80.40%	144	162	20,031	15,658	15.09	13.65
7	80.40%	116	130	16,075	12,015	12.16	9.68
8	80.40%	93	105	12,983	9,279	9.75	6.61
9	80.40%	75	84	10,387	7,099	7.86	4.27
10	80.40%	60	68	8,408	5,495	6.29	2.45
11	80.40%	48	54	6,677	4,172	5.03	1.07
12	80.40%	39	44	5,441	3,251	4.09	0.00
Total				$346,096	$302,723		

*Retention rates per Exhibit 19-5c.
†Initial number of accounts per Exhibit 19-2.
‡Net cost savings per Exhibit 19-4.
§Discount rate per Exhibit 19-3.

Exhibit 19-8
Specimen Bank
555 California Street Branch
Fair Market Value of Core Deposit Base

Deposit Account Type	Number of Accounts Acquired	Gross $ Balance	Fair Market $ Value	Fair Market Value as a % of Gross $ Balance	Estimated Life of Deposit Base (Years)*
Non-interest-bearing demand	1,653	$8,774,474	$ 748,134	8.53%	17.0
Interest-bearing transaction	1,234	4,051,524	181,830	4.49	17.0
Money market deposit	321	3,858,317	187,085	4.85	17.0
Regular savings	1,300	3,453,143	64,318	1.86	9.0
Certificates of deposit under $100,000	954	20,213,224	302,723	1.50	12.0
Total core deposit base	5,462	$40,350,682	$1,484,090	3.68%	15.6

*Estimated life of total acquired deposit base is the average of the estimated life of each account type weighted by its dollar fair market value.

2. *Functional Cost Analysis* (FCA), published annually by the Federal Reserve Board is based on surveys of banks throughout the United States. The FCA provides extensive detail on rationally allocated operating expenses and fee income by banking activity (i.e., deposit taking by type of deposit, lending by type of loan, trust activities, etc.), providing average ratios for commercial banks grouped by asset-size category. Use of average ratios from the FCA provides an important element of "arm's-lengthedness" to the appraisal. Overhead allocations, operating expense, and fee income allocations provided by the buyer or seller may be inaccurate or intentionally distorted or may represent short-term conditions. Because core deposit bases are relatively long lived (usually with economic lives of 5–15 years or more), it is most appropriate to base expense ratios on industry norms; otherwise, some aspects of value (i.e., goodwill) not directly attributable to the core deposit base itself might creep into the valuation.

3. The *Federal Reserve Statistical Release H.15* and *The Wall Street Journal* provide useful statistics on market interest rates for a variety of instruments.

Given assumptions relative to market interest rates, interest expenses, account operating expenses, and service and fee income, the methodology for estimating after-tax earnings is fairly straightforward. An example of this process is presented in Exhibit 19-3, 19-4, and 19-5. As is outlined in the three exhibits, the basic approach is to calculate a net cost savings spread and apply an appropriate tax rate in order to derive the after-tax cost savings spread for the deposit base relative to an alternative market funding source. The major assumptions and procedures represented in Exhibits 19-3, 19-4, and 19-5 are discussed below.

The first step is to calculate the effective cost of funds of the core deposit base:

1. *Core deposit balances.* Each category of core deposit is presented separately. The breakdown of core deposits into four major categories (transaction or NOW accounts, money market deposit accounts, reg-

ular savings accounts, and "retail" certificates of deposit under $100,000) is shown in Exhibit 19-3. Because of differing account retention, interest cost, float, and operating-expense characteristics, it is most appropriate to value each of the four categories separately. Both gross balances and available (i.e., investable) balances (net of float and reserves) are shown. Also shown are average gross and available balances per account in order to emphasize that it is really the acquired account relationships themselves, rather than the aggregate acquired deposit balances, that are being valued.

2. *Interest cost of funds.* The average interest rate on each deposit category is used to represent the unadjusted interest cost of funds from that category. It is up to the analyst to make sure that the rates used represent a reasonable estimate of ongoing interest expense. Adjustments and/or the use of a long-term average may be necessary to obtain an accurate estimate of the interest cost of funds.

3. *Operating expense and fee income.* Operating expense and fee income attributable to each deposit category are expressed as percentages of the dollar balance of each deposit category. The ratios are taken from the FCA and as such represent industry norms. These ratios reflect the average cost of administering deposit accounts and average service charges collected related to dollar balances for the banks surveyed by the Federal Reserve.

4. *Total cost of funds.* The total cost of funds for each category is its interest expense plus allocated overhead expense less any fee income, per the ratios given in the FCA.

5. *Available funds percent.* The percentage of the balance of each deposit category available for investment in earning assets was taken from the functional cost analysis. This figure takes into consideration that not all deposit funds are investable and eliminates nonearning funds tied up as required reserves, as well as items in the process of collection (float) and therefore not investable.

6. *Effective cost of funds.* Interest to be paid to depositors is assumed to be calculated by applying the stated interest rate to the gross balance of the account. Similarly, the overhead expense and fee income ratios given in the FCA are in relation to gross deposit balances. Since less than 100 percent of the account balances are investable, the effective cost is higher. The effective cost is derived by dividing the total cost of funds by the investable percentage for each deposit category. Basing the analysis on the effective cost and the investable amount of each category of acquired deposit ensures that costs and future economic benefits will be measured consistently and will be fully comparable between different funding sources.

The next step is to derive an effective cost of funds for an alternative source of funds. Exhibit 19-4 presents the derivation of a market-alternative cost of funds from which to derive the stream of anticipated cost savings provided by the core deposit base:

7. *Alternative funding instrument.* For most community and regional banks, the certificates of deposit over $100,000 with maturities of 90 days to one year, sold in the secondary market, would appear

to be the most appropriate alternative funding instrument. Shorter-term money market instruments such as Federal Funds are considered to be too volatile by regulators to be a primary funding source for all but the large money center banks. Debt and longer-term jumbo CDs are usually prohibitively difficult and expensive to place for community banks or even regional banks. Raising additional funds through an acquirer's existing retail branch network is usually cost prohibitive. Rate or service concessions used to capture incremental market share over any lengthy period ultimately have to be passed on to the entire customer base, resulting in an overall increase in the acquirer's cost of funds, which likely would offset any benefits derived from the funds acquired at the margin.

8. *Effective cost of alternative funding source.* As is shown in Exhibit 19-4, the prevailing secondary market rate for large CDs was adjusted by adding the operating expense ratio for CDs given in the Federal Reserve functional cost analysis and an estimated brokerage fee and then applying the available funds percentage. In most cases, it would be necessary to use brokers to obtain the incremental funds without affecting the cost of funds of the acquirer's existing deposit base. Fees to CD brokers typically run in the range of 0.25–1.00 percent per year. The effective cost of the alternative funding source is simply the stated yield on the market-alternative instrument adjusted for the operating costs and estimated brokerage fees and the available-funds percentage. The interest cost of the market-alternative instrument should be calculated over the same period as was used for the core deposit base. It is up to the analyst to make sure that the relationship, the spread, between the market alternative and the core deposit base is both reasonable and likely to be maintained over the expected life of the core deposit base.[5]

Having derived an effective cost of funds for the core deposit base and an effective cost of the market-alternative funding source, the next step is to calculate a net after-tax cost savings spread (see Exhibit 19-5):

9. *Pretax cost spread.* The pretax earnings spread for each deposit category is derived by subtracting the effective cost of the deposit category from the effective cost of funds of the alternative funding source.

10. *Tax rates.* The after-tax spread is determined by applying the current maximum marginal federal income tax rate (34 percent) to the stream of cost savings. An appropriate amount is subtracted from the pretax spread for each category to adjust for income taxes.

11. *Net cost savings spread.* The net cost savings spreads derived for the four core deposit categories result from deducting income taxes for the pretax cost savings spread.

---

[5]If the appraiser considers using the earnings spread approach rather than the cost savings spread approach, a reasonable estimate of the yield on earning assets into which the core deposit base can be reinvested must be made. A good candidate for a reinvestment rate is the current peer group average yield on earning assets given in the purchaser's Uniform Bank Performance Report. This rate should be adjusted for the peer average ratio of loan loss provisions to earning assets (derived by multiplying the peer ratio of loan loss provisions to average total assets by the peer ratio of average earning assets to average total assets, both given in the UBPR) and the expense ratios of the investment and lending functions given in the FCA.

12. *Annual net cost savings per account.* The economic benefit reflected in the net cost spread is converted to an annual dollar amount per account by multiplying the percentage spread for each category from Exhibit 19-5 by the investable dollar balance per account shown in Exhibit 19-3. This presentation emphasizes that we are valuing the core deposit intangible asset based on the expected future economic benefits conferred by the individual acquired accounts.

Rates paid on various categories of acquired funds by banks will change over time as interest rate levels change in the national economy. The important issue from a valuation standpoint is the overall reasonableness of the spread between rates paid on core deposits and the cost of open-market funding sources, adjusted for net noninterest expenses. The implicit assumption of the analysis is that the derived spreads can be maintained over the life of the deposit base.

Customer Retention Analysis

Prevalent Approaches

Numerous techniques have been developed to estimate historical customer retention rates. Some analysts take a cross-section of customer relationship ages as of a given date and use the proportion of customers of various ages to develop an estimate of retention. This technique would appear to produce a negative bias to retention statistics because new customers would be overrepresented in a single-date sample.

Other analysts use a technique of analyzing accounts that actually closed in a given sample period, using the age characteristics of the closed accounts to develop representative retention statistics by account type. This methodology suffers from two shortcomings. First, it is heavily dependent upon a single time period. Unusual occurrences relating to the particular organizational dynamics or to the local or national economy could bias the sample, plus or minus. Second, a single-time-period analysis overlooks the dynamics of retention over time.

The strongest analytical approach is to examine customer retention characteristics of the core deposit base over several successive time periods. This method seeks to develop year-by-year retention statistics over a multiyear period. The basic premise of the analysis is that a branch's (or a bank's) actual historical retention record is the best predictor of future retention prospects.

The determination of the deposit base life and customer retention rates for an acquired core deposit base is based upon the probability that an active customer will be retained for one annual period, given that the customer relationship was in force at the beginning of the period. The probability of retaining a customer relationship tends to increase with the age of the relationship. This analysis corresponds with common sense. Turnover in accounts is most apt to occur in the early years, as transient elements in a population move. As accounts mature, the individuals and businesses involved are more likely to be stable elements of the community. At some point, the age of the relationship makes little difference and all customer relationships of that age or older have essentially the same probability of retention. This terminal retention rate can be called the *optimal retention rate*.

The probability that a customer relationship will be retained for a given annual period is determined by analyzing the customer base at different times. These data are then used to determine the percentage of customers that were retained from period to period. The derived percentages represent sample estimates of the probabilities of relationship retention. The average of the retention rates is calculated and used as the statistical estimate of future customer relationship retention rates.

Although retention rates measure the retention of accounts, the objective is to value the acquired deposit base. Therefore, the retention of accounts or customers is used as a proxy for the retention of dollar-denominated deposit balances. The implicit assumption is that retention characteristics for each deposit type are uniform with respect to dollar amount and the dollar balances will thus exhibit the same attrition rates as the number of open accounts. It is up to the analyst to determine whether unusual conditions are present in the deposit base that would indicate the need for a more detailed retention study, with accounts stratified by dollar balance in each account type.

Because every certificate of deposit has a maturity date, a slight departure from the account-based methodology is required. Although all CDs mature, the customers who own them often roll them over at maturity or purchase new CDs. The customer relationship itself, rather than the individual certificate, is therefore the relevant factor in deposit base retention and is the subject of analysis. Consequently, our analytical focus is on tracking CD customer relationships rather than CDs themselves.

Historical Customer Retention Analysis

Exhibit 19-6 provides a sample retention analysis based on the multi-period approach described above. The particular analysis is based on a cross-tabulation of *all* open savings and transaction accounts per the seller's historical deposit trial balances at each of the indicated year-ends.[6] All open accounts listed in each year-end trial balance are matched against subsequent account lists to determine how many accounts remain open at the later date.

The resulting year-to-year retention rates are then grouped by the age of accounts, and an age-group average retention rate is calculated. For time deposits, Internal Revenue Service Form 1099 (Reports of Interest Paid) data are used to develop retention rates. Lists of Social Security and Tax Identification Numbers for each available year are edited to include only those accounts on which CD interest was paid. Each annual list is then cross-tabulated against subsequent lists to determine the number of remaining CD customers.

In Exhibit 19-6a, cross-comparisons of account lists as of December 31, 1984–1990, indicate that 5,542 accounts were opened before the end of 1984, 1,222 accounts were opened after year-end 1984 but before the end of 1985, 978 accounts were opened after year-end 1985 but before the end of 1986, and so on. Of the 5,542 accounts opened in 1984, 4,008

---

[6]Although we prefer to analyze complete account lists (100 percent samples) derived from trial balances and Forms 1099, it is also valid to use a sampling approach, provided the samples are of a statistically meaningful size, to develop retention rates.

were remaining in 1985, 3,060 were remaining in 1986, etc. The number of accounts opened in each base year and the number of those accounts remaining in each subsequent year are shown in the upper table in Exhibit 19-6a.

The numbers of accounts remaining open are used to derive the year-to-year retention rates shown in the lower table. These annual statistics are grouped by age, and the average rate for each age group is shown at the bottom of the exhibit. The age of the account group is a function of the number of years elapsed since the base year. For example, the 2,074 accounts remaining at the end of 1988 that were opened before year-end 1984 are classed as four-year-old accounts, as are the 310 accounts remaining at year-end 1989 that were opened during 1985. Retention observations for accounts of the same age, but with different base years, lie along the diagonals running from the upper left corner to the lower right corner in the "Accounts Remaining" and "Year-to-Year Retention Rate" grids of each table in the Exhibit 19-6a.

We typically make the conservative assumption that all accounts were new as of the first date for which information was available—December 31, 1984, in Exhibit 19-6a. The retention rate for the oldest deposit age group analyzed (six years old in the exhibit) is usually considered to be the optimal retention rate, and this rate is applied to all subsequent years. Normalizing adjustments may be appropriate whenever the actual averages for any given age group seem to contradict the apparent trend of retention rates to increase with account age or if it can be determined that the observed retention rates have been distorted by some identifiable factor that is unlikely to recur.

We normally make the conservative assumption that all acquired core deposits are new as of the valuation date. The assumption that all acquired accounts are new as of the valuation date addresses the *separability* issue in distinguishing a deductible intangible asset from general goodwill. Treating the accounts as if they were new by applying the lower retention rates observed historically for new accounts, in effect, simulates the impact of transferring the accounts to the purchasing entity without transferring the seller's building and personnel. The accounts are, in fact, new to the purchasing entity and are treated as such in the valuation through the assumption that account attrition will be higher in the initial years of the valuation.

It is worth noting at this point that having developed an estimate of the retention rate, one minus the retention rate is the attrition rate. Mortgage prepayment rates are in effect attrition rates for the remaining principal balances of mortgage-backed security pools. The use of retention rates in valuing core deposits can thus be seen as a close parallel of the widespread use of prepayment rates (single-month mortality rates, or SMM, and conditional-prepayment rates, or CPR) in valuing mortgage-backed securities, mortgage servicing rights, and excess service fees on mortgage pools.

Account Life Estimation

The economic life of a core account base is determined by estimating the time in years that it will take the acquired deposit base to reach a negligible percentage of the original number of accounts acquired. We consider the 5 percent level to represent the point at which the deposit base is effectively depleted for purposes of determining value.

The procedure for determining the number of years it takes to deplete the core deposit base is quite simple. First, the statistically determined retention rates are applied to the acquired accounts. Second, the average number of open accounts is determined during each future year by taking the average number of accounts remaining from the original group at the beginning and end of each year. Third, the account base is assumed to reach its maximum age when the number of remaining accounts falls below 5 percent of the original number of acquired accounts. This process is illustrated in Exhibit 19-7.

Economic life is defined under this methodology as the number of years necessary for the acquired account base to decline, based on statistical attrition, to a number less than or equal to 5.0 percent of the initial number of acquired accounts.

It should be noted that alternative retention estimation approaches work in the opposite direction. Samples of open and closed accounts are used to develop statistics on *account life* (lifing studies)—that is, the average number of years to account termination—rather than to determine year-to-year retention rates by age group. The account life statistics are then fit to "Iowa Curves" to estimate period-to-period retention rates.[7] Although we believe the retention rate methodology detailed in the preceding paragraphs is more straightforward and more easily grasped by appraisal report users who lack an extensive statistical background, the use of Iowa Curves is considered to be valid and is preferred by a number of intangible-asset appraisers.

Deriving a Discount Rate

The final step in the valuation process is to discount the projected stream of future cost savings from the core deposit base relative to the alternative funding source at an appropriate rate to derive their present values. All of the projections in this example have been made on a *constant-dollar basis*. No allowance has been made for inflationary trends, so the average dollar amount of the surviving accounts in each year is not assumed to increase with inflation and the compounding of interest paid the depositors. The required corollary assumption is that the discount rate should be a real rate, with no inflationary expectations built in. Further, since all projections in the example have been made on an after-tax basis, the discount rate should be a net after-tax rate.

Intangible assets are a hybrid of fixed-income investments (loans and bonds) and equity investments. They have limited lives like fixed-income investments but generally entail risks more related to those of equity securities. (Account attrition may prove more rapid than expected, expense and revenue relationships may change adversely over time, and so on.) In our opinion, it is more appropriate to develop the discount rate

---

[7]Iowa Curves are a family of curves that were empirically developed at Iowa State University. The studies were designed to determine if the useful life of an asset could be reasonably estimated from incomplete data. For a general discussion of Iowa Curves and their application to asset life measurement, see Marston, Winfrey, and Hempstead, *Engineering Valuation and Depreciation* (Ames: Iowa State University Press, 1953).

for core deposit intangible assets based upon a riskier, equity investment series. The risks involved in acquiring a bank deposit base more closely approximate those of investments in equity securities than in bonds.

We consider the Total Return Index of Small Company Stocks, as published in *Stocks, Bonds, Bills and Inflation: 1991 Yearbook* by Ibbotson Associates, to be the best basis for deriving a discount rate. We have selected 1947 as the base year of the series in order to develop long-term average rates of return on small-company common stocks during the era following the Great Depression and World War II.[8] To derive an after-tax, after-inflation discount rate for the branch under consideration, we took the average annual compound rate of total return from the Ibbotson series from 1947 through the full year prior to the valuation date (1990) and then adjusted for taxes and inflation. The derivation of an after-tax, after-inflation discount rate is presented in Exhibit 19-4.

Every appraiser will have individual preferences for developing discount rates. Although we consider the discount rate described in the preceding paragraphs to be both reasonable and appropriate for valuing core deposits, we do not claim it is the only method for developing a discount rate. The important factors in developing a discount rate in valuing intangibles are (1) to reflect market rates of return on alternative investments, (2) to consider the relative riskiness of the intangible assets, (3) to reflect the impact of inflation on the value of the intangibles, and (4) to reflect the impact of taxes on the value of the intangibles.

Final Determination of Value

The valuation of each category of core deposits is shown in Exhibit 19-7. The projected ending number of accounts for each year of the remaining economic life of the account type is calculated based on the original number of acquired accounts and the account-age-related retention rate. The average (midpoint) number of accounts remaining in each year and the net cost savings per account are multiplied to derive the projected dollar amount of cost savings in each year. The sum of the discounted annual cost savings is the value of the deposit category. It is interesting to note that the present value of the projected cost savings approaches a negligible amount at the time the remaining number of accounts in the deposit category falls below 5 percent, validating the use of this measure as the effective end of the asset's economic life. Values are summarized in Exhibit 19-8.

In this hypothetical situation, the core deposit intangible assets of the 555 California Street Branch were valued at $1.5 million, or 3.7 percent of the deposits to be acquired by Specimen Bank. As previously discussed, the negotiating range for the branch acquisition was in the range of 6–7 percent of the deposits to be acquired, so in this hypothetical valuation example, the core deposit intangible asset accounted for approximately one half of the expected branch premium.

---

[8]This is one example of how the Ibbotson Associates annual studies can be used by appraisers to develop discount or capitalization rates. As noted in Chapters 13 and 14, this source contains historical data such that returns can be estimated for any multiyear period covered in the annual studies (normally back to 1926).

Conclusion

In a time of consolidation in the banking industry, it is clear that transactions involving the purchase or sale of bank and thrift branches will continue to be a viable means of achieving the strategies of financial institutions as they continue to adapt to their changing economic and regulatory circumstances. The concepts and techniques regarding branch valuations and core deposit intangible asset appraisals should be helpful to banks, appraisers, and consultants during this period.

Chapter 20

Expert Witnesses and Expert Testimony

Lucy: "I've just come up with the perfect theory. It's my theory that Beethoven
would have written even better music if he had been married."
Schroeder: "What's so perfect about that theory?"
Lucy: "It can't be proved one way or the other!"

Charles Schultz
Peanuts (1976)

Introduction

Litigation involving business valuation issues has been on the rise for
a number of years. As a result, opinions of business valuation experts
are often required in litigated situations, including corporate or partnership dissolutions, dissenting minority shareholder cases, divorces involving significant closely-held business interests, and economic damages
cases involving disputes over lost earnings under contracts, wrongful acts
of officers or directors, antitrust violations and the like.

There are a number of books and articles dealing with expert testimony and litigation support, as well as chapters in books that deal with
various aspects of the subjects.[1] The purpose of this chapter is to provide
a brief discussion of expert witnesses and expert testimony as a short
reference for readers of this book. Hopefully, some of the following insights will be of benefit both to experienced valuation expert witnesses
and to those who may be facing their initial experiences as expert
witnesses.[2] This chapter is necessarily written from the viewpoint of the
appraiser as expert witness, flavored by my personal experiences as an
expert witness over the last dozen or so years.

Expert Witnesses

Expert witnesses are used by the courts when the opinions of lay persons on scientific, technical, or other specialized knowledge will help the
trier of fact (or a jury) in reaching appropriate decisions. Article VII of
the Federal Rules of Evidence suggests that expert testimony can be
helpful:

> If scientific, technical, or other specialized knowledge will assist the trier
> of fact to understand the evidence or to determine a fact in issue, a witness
> qualified as an expert by knowledge, skill, experience, training, or educa-
> tion, may testify thereto in the form of an opinion or otherwise.[3]

---

[1]See the Shannon Pratt books and the James Zukin book cited elsewhere and in the Bibliography for excellent
discussions of these subjects. The American Society of Appraisers has recently prepared a seminar for expert
witnesses. The AICPA has prepared notebooks and course work on the subject, as well.

[2]It is highly recommended that potential expert witnesses read a variety of sources for insights and instruc-
tion. While there is no substitute for experience in expert testimony, all of one's experiences need not be first-hand!

[3]*Federal Rules of Evidence: Article VII, Opinions and Expert Testimony, Rule 702, Testimony by Experts.*

The questions provided in Exhibit 16-1, as applied to individual valuation consultants in valuation firms, provide a good list to determine if an individual is, or could be, an expert witness regarding a bank or business valuation issue.

There are experts and there are experts. Essentially, a person is an expert if he or she is accepted by a court as an expert. In accepting an individual as an expert, however, courts retain the right to consider the overall credibility of the individual and his or her testimony in the weight ultimately accorded the testimony.

Expert Testimony

Most treatises on expert testimony consider primarily the situation where an expert is retained to provide a valuation opinion in a known litigation situation. This would suggest that only those business appraisers who are interested in developing litigation-related assignments might have an interest in the subject of expert testimony. However, as noted at several points in this book, valuation assignments and valuation reports sometimes have long lives. Valuation opinions rendered in the normal course of business—for example, for ESOPs, gift or estate taxes, buy-sell agreements or for many other purposes—may become the subject of litigation years after the actual report is rendered. So every business appraiser who prepares and signs valuation reports should be interested in the subject of expert testimony. Appraisers who never accept assignments specifically for litigation purposes will, in all probability, have to defend a small percentage of their appraisals over time due to factors that were not forseeable at the time of the original appraisal.

There are several potential stages of an expert's involvement in business valuation litigation, from the process of being retained, through preparations for trial, to actual testimony and cross-examination, to post-trial involvement.

Being Retained as an Expert Witness

In many cases, attorneys, upon realizing the need to have an expert testify relative to the valuation of a bank or company, will begin a process of seeking a qualified expert. Business appraisers should remember, however, that there is a fundamental difference between attorneys, who are hired as advocates for their clients' positions, and business appraisers, who are hired to provide expert testimony as noted in Rule 702 of the *Federal Rules of Procedure* quoted above.

An attorney-advocate may have reason to desire other than a totally objective valuation opinion from an expert. This distinction is highlighted by the authors of an interesting article on expert testimony:

> An important distinction must be drawn between "substantive" advocacy and "procedural" advocacy. Substantive advocacy is altering the objectivity of an appraisal conclusion to advance a client's interest. An ethical valuation expert will not be a party to substantive advocacy. Procedural advocacy is

an awareness of the tactics and strategies of litigation. If the valuation expert is to be effective, he must be able to advance his opinion successfully within the litigation context. Consequently, it is essential for the valuation expert to be aware of the tactics and strategies of litigation.[4]

It is also essential for the valuation expert to be on the lookout for potential problems in conversations with attorneys concerning litigation assignments. The fact is, in the process of advocating their clients' interests, some attorneys will "shop" for an opinion from an expert. In initial conversations, the valuation expert must be able to determine whether she or he will be allowed to develop an objective, independent valuation conclusion. It is far better to recognize the potential for conflict between desired and likely valuation results and to decline an assignment than it is to get in the middle of the assignment and be the subject of unreasonable pressure to change an opinion.

Developing a Valuation Opinion

Once retained for a litigation assignment, the business appraiser must develop his or her valuation conclusion. My personal preference is to provide to counsel a detailed, stand-alone valuation report that will be the basis for possible future testimony. (See the discussion in Chapter 15 regarding the preparation and presentation of valuation conclusions and the Sample Bank Valuation in Chapter 22.) Sometimes, however, counsel will prefer that an expert testify from a minimal set of schedules and a bullet-point summary of the key points of the analysis. There is obviously room between these two positions for varying degrees of documentation. The valuation opinion of the expert witness should nevertheless comply with the Uniform Standards of Professional Appraisal Practice and applicable standards of the American Society of Appraisers.

A valuation report prepared for litigation should be complete—or as complete as agreed upon between the appraiser and counsel. It should state explicitly, or show evidence of consideration, of all relevant information related to the subject opinion. The report should provide a detailed listing of documents reviewed in the appraisal process. It should also provide appropriate citations for external sources utilized in arriving at its conclusion(s). Because the report will be provided to the "other side" in the litigation, it is essential that it be error free and that a logical, internally consistent and compelling case be built for its conclusion(s). Finally, the appraiser should "own" the language, tables, exhibits, and appendixes so that he or she can readily respond to any questions that might be raised by opposing counsel or a judge.

Files and work papers should be organized and complete. Extraneous work papers should be eliminated from a file as soon as the conclusion is known. Such work papers can be a source of unnecessary confusion

---

[4]Brian P. Brinig, and Michael W. Prairie, "Expert Testimony: The Business Appraiser as a Valuation Expert Witness," *Business Valuation News* (now *Business Valuation Review*), Vol. 4, no. 1, March 1985, pp. 8–23.

at a later time.[5] I do not mean to suggest in any way that the valuation analyst should remove critical information or even potentially conflicting data that must be dealt with in reaching a valuation conclusion. Examples of extraneous work papers would include the draft reports noted in Footnote 5 as well as interim-stage spreadsheets used in the process of creating the actual model used in the opinion.

The Deposition

The article by Brinig and Prairie cited above provides "Ten Commandments for Effective Depositions," which make good reading for anyone preparing for a deposition. These commandments are reproduced as Exhibit 20-1. Personal experience leads to the following points for addition or emphasis:

1. Totally prepare for every deposition. Sometimes, experts overlook the importance of depositions in trial preparation and settlement negotiations and think that "the real thing" is what happens in court. Depositions are real and are an important step in trial preparations for both sides in litigated cases.
2. Answer only the questions asked. Answer the questions truthfully and fully, but only those that are asked. Opposing counsel may be on a fishing expedition in a deposition. If he or she "gets a bite" or finds a point of seeming weakness or inconsistency, he or she may decide to stay and "fish" in that hole for a long time.
3. Remember that anything you say in a deposition can be used later in court to impeach your testimony. So remember what you said, and obtain and review a copy of your deposition(s) immediately prior to trial.
4. Provide your valuation in draft form for a deposition, if possible. It is much easier to make a small change (based upon new information or a possible mistake) prior to court from a draft opinion than from a final report.
5. Remember that you are creating a written record in a deposition. Speak in complete sentences. Avoid sloppy speech mannerisms, such as "Uh-huh," "Yeah," "Nope," or "You know." Take your time in responding in order to avoid lapsing into mannerisms that detract from the credibility of the deposition.
6. "Yes," "No," and "I don't know" can be full and complete responses to a question. Avoid the temptation to tell everything you know. There is nothing wrong with the silence following a complete answer of "Yes" or "No" or "I don't know."

---

[5]Several years ago, a young analyst was assisting me in a litigation case. He was working on a draft document, and every time he worked on the file, he created a new "draft report." Further, every time he worked on the file, he tried his hand at valuing the business. In all, there were about a dozen drafts in the file. We were asked to produce our work papers for opposing counsel prior to my deposition in the matter. To my chagrin, we provided a dozen drafts, the first 10 or so of which had totally different conclusions, with seemingly no rationale for the changes between drafts. Opposing counsel started with the first draft and began to question me about each one. When I realized what had happened, I directed the attorney to the first draft on which my handwritten notes appeared (about the 10th one) and suggested that we refer to it as the "first draft." Fortunately, there was consistency and reason from that draft through to the final draft and final conclusion. The case eventually settled at very close to our conclusion; but I will never forget that deposition!

Exhibit 20-1
Ten Commandments for Effective Depositions

1. Tell the truth, but answer only the question that is asked. Do not volunteer information, and avoid long narrative answers. The more topics that you bring up in your answer, the more questions the examining lawyer may ask. The deposition is an opportunity for the opponent to obtain information; it is not the trial.

2. Think about the question before answering it. This will give you time to formulate an appropriate response. It will also give your party's lawyer time to analyze the question and interpose any objections. Remember that the examining lawyer may attempt to develop an informal, rapid conversation to elicit from you as much information as possible. Watch out for an examiner who attempts to catch you off guard with a casual, friendly manner or flattering questions.

3. Do not answer a question unless you understand it. If a question is unclear, ask the examining lawyer to repeat or rephrase the question or have the court reporter read back the question.

4. Do not guess or speculate. If you do not know the answer to a question, say so. If you are not sure, qualify your answer by saying ''approximately'' and the like. Beware of hypothetical questions. Before answering a hypothetical, make sure that all essential facts or assumptions are included. Remember that at trial, a portion of the deposition may be taken out of context and used to impeach you.

5. Do not bring notes, diagrams, books, or other written material to the deposition unless they are required by a subpoena or unless you have been instructed by your party's lawyer to bring them. If asked to testify regarding documents or other exhibits, take the time to review them carefully before answering questions about them.

6. Listen carefully to objections made by your party's lawyer. The objection may be intended to alert you to a trick question or some other problem with the question. If your party's lawyer instructs you not to answer a question, follow the instructions, even if the examining lawyer threatens you with court sanctions.

7. Do not argue or become angry or hostile with the examining lawyer. Such a reaction will communicate to the lawyer a lack of confidence that will be exploited at trial. It may also alert the examining lawyer to weaknesses in your theories or conclusions.

8. Even if the question calls for a yes or no answer, ask to explain your answer briefly if a qualification or explanation is necessary. However, do not be concerned if your answer does not apply all information that would be required for a complete understanding of the topic. Your party's lawyer will decide whether to obtain a more complete explanation during the deposition or at trial.

9. Watch out for questions that involve absolute terms, such as ''Have you identified *all* of the documents that you have relied upon?'' If possible, provide a qualified answer in the event that you inadvertently failed to identify a pertinent document or fact.

10. Do not memorize your answers in advance of the deposition. Provide a direct and factual response to the questions.

SOURCE: Brian P. Brinig, and Michael W. Prairie, ''Expert Testimony: The Business Appraiser as a Valuation Expert Witness,'' *Business Valuation News* (now *Business Valuation Review*), Vol. 4, no. 1, March 1985, pp. 11–12.

Trial Preparation

It is essential that an expert witness be prepared for trial. Preparation will involve having the agreed-upon documented completed, but it also involves several other steps. The expert should:

1. Review the total file. The objective is to be able to recall every piece of information that went into the preparation of an opinion. When the expert knows what is in the file, he or she also knows what is not in the file. The distinction can be critical for some lines of questioning.

2. Meet with counsel to organize direct testimony. Some attorneys are more thorough than others in the process of trial preparation. However, neither the expert nor the attorney should be surprised by either the questions or the responses in direct testimony. The only way to accomplish this objective is for both to discuss the components

of the testimony, the order of questioning, and the degree of independence expected of the expert in presenting an opinion.

3. Agree with counsel on the extent of a report to be presented in court. Some attorneys prefer their experts to testify from brief exhibits. Others prefer fully documented reports.

4. Agree with counsel on the use of visual aids to supplement testimony.

5. Prepare a list of foundational questions such as presented in Exhibit 20-2. These questions provide the foundation from which the expert's credentials and opinions are presented to the court. The objective is not to memorize questions and answers but to be familiar with the likely process by which direct testimony will be presented. Never forget, however, that things can change in the middle of a trial. Counsel may change strategy based upon what has occurred immediately preceding an expert's appearance. The key is to be prepared and to be flexible.

6. Anticipate the likely lines of questioning to expect from opposing counsel upon cross-examination. Every opinion has relative strengths and weaknesses. It is critical to know the points of likely attack and to prepare to respond in the context of the overall opinion.

7. Review the expert's role in analyzing, criticizing, or correcting written opinion materials or depositions by the expert(s) from the opposing side in the litigation.

8. Review the witness's deposition(s) in the present case in the context of the overall opinion. First, it is important to ensure that nothing was said that is inconsistent with the opinion to be rendered in court. If there are any actual or apparent inconsistencies, the expert should be able to reconcile the deposition to the testimony based upon the factor(s) that caused the inconsistencies. And second, it is critical to be sufficiently familiar with the deposition to know when quotes are being taken out of context by opposing counsel and to be able to direct the court to the appropriate sections of the deposition or the opinion for the appropriate context.

9. If the expert has testified previously in similar cases, it is important to review those cases in order to be able to respond to questions raised by actual or apparent inconsistencies with the present opinion. If the monetary stakes are sufficiently high, opposing counsel may search for those cases and review them with the idea of catching the expert in a real or apparent inconsistency.

It is clear from this discussion that trial preparations can be extensive, time consuming, and expensive. Counsel, the client, and the expert should have a good understanding of the preparation process as well as its potential expense in order to avoid misunderstandings.

Trial Testimony

Trial testimony consists of several phases, including direct testimony, cross-examination, rebuttal testimony, redirect testimony, and recross-examination.

Exhibit 20-2
Expert Witness Sample Foundational Questions
John Q. Appraiser, ASA, CFA

1. Please state your name and age for the court.
2. What is your current address?
3. What is your current occupation?
4. By what firm are you employed, and how long have you been employed there?
5. What is the nature of Bank Appraisers, Inc., and what are your responsibilities there?
6. Do you hold any professional credentials that qualify you to give your opinion of the value of ABC Bank?
7. What is the American Society of Appraisers, and how does one attain Accredited Senior Appraiser status with this organization?
8. Do you hold any positions of responsibility with the American Society of Appraisers? If so, please describe your duties in such positions.
9. What is the Association for Investment Management and Research? How does one attain the Chartered Financial Analyst designation from this organization?
10. Have you written any papers, books, or articles on the subject of banks and/or bank appraisal? Of business appraisal generally?
11. Have you presented any speeches or lectures on subjects related to banks or bank appraisal? To business appraisal generally?
12. What is your educational background?
13. Have you been accepted by this or other courts as an expert witness on business valuation issues?
14. What is your employment background prior to joining Bank Appraisers, Inc.?
15. Does your firm issue valuation opinions with respect to the purchase or sale of financial institutions? If so, please describe for the court the nature of a couple of transactions you have been involved with.
16. How many bank appraisals does your firm provide each year?
17. Over the course of your career, approximately how many bank valuations have you performed?
18. Do independent third parties customarily rely upon your firm's valuation opinions?
19. Would you describe some of the kinds of independent parties that rely upon your valuation opinions (accounting firms, governmental agencies, etc.)?
20. For what reasons does your firm provide independent valuation opinions for the parties you have just described?
21. Who retained you for this assignment, and when and how were you first contacted?
22. What is the basis of your compensation for this engagement?
23. Was there any suggestion during the course of your assignment as to what the results of your analysis should be?
24. Exactly what was the nature of your assignment in the matter before the court? (Refer to paragraph 1, page 1, if using a written report.)
25. Your assignment was to determine the fair market value (or other standard of value) of certain shares. Will you please define fair market value (or other standard of value)? (Define and refer to discussion in text.)
26. Generally, what factors did you consider in the formulation of your opinion of fair market value of ABC Bank's shares? (Refer to the general factors listed in report.)
27. What information did you rely upon in the formulation of your opinion of the fair market value of ABC Bank's shares? (Refer to list in report and mention that other sources are cited in the text.)
28. Were your due diligence efforts limited in any way? If so, what impact could these limitations have on your final conclusion in this matter?
29. Other than the limitation(s) you have just described, did you conduct such due diligence as is normal in valuations of the present nature, and did you utilize generally accepted valuation methods and/or techniques in the formulation of your opinion?
30. Are you familiar with the Uniform Standards of Professional Appraisal Practice? What is their applicability to the field of business appraisal?
31. Have you prepared your report in accordance with the Uniform Standards of Professional Appraisal Practice?
32. Are you familiar with the Business Valuation Standards of the American Society of Appraisers? What is their applicability to the field of business appraisal?
33. Did you prepare your report in accordance with the current Business Valuation Standards of the American Society of Appraisers? Please explain your reasons for any departures from these standards.
34. Did you arrive at an opinion of the fair market value of ABC Bank's shares? And if so, what is that opinion? (State the opinion, the block of shares to which it refers, and the as-of date and the purpose of the opinion.)

Exhibit 20-2 (*continued*)

35. Did you prepare a report summarizing your due diligence efforts, valuation methodologies, and conclusion of value? (If no, individual exhibits will need to be presented, identified, and discussed, as appropriate.)
36. Is this a copy of your report? Please identify it for the court.
37. Please describe briefly for the court the general contents of the report. (Refer to the signature page and the table of contents. Be sure to generally describe the exhibits.)
This is usually a good time to get the report into evidence.
38. What were the relevant local economic and competitive factors bearing on your analysis?
39. Your report considers several major categories of assets on the bank's balance sheet. Regarding the loan portfolio, what does your analysis indicate about the overall quality of the loan portfolio and of the adequacy of the loan loss reserve?
40. What is the general nature and condition of the bank's investment portfolio?
41. Does the bank own any real estate other than its premises? Please describe the nature of "real estate owned" and its impact on the bank's earnings? Does the bank have more real estate owned than comparable banks?
42. Are there any unusual factors about the bank's deposit liability base that could have a bearing on valuation?
43. Briefly, what is interest rate risk in a financial institution? What is the bank's gap position?
44. Is the bank adequately capitalized? What factors lead to this conclusion?
45. How would you describe the bank's earnings record over the last several years? Is the bank a good earner?
46. Would you describe briefly how banks generally make money, and then place this bank into perspective with your earnings model? (Cover spread, net interest income, other income, operating expenses, basic operating income, loan losses, etc.)
47. How would you characterize the returns offered by the bank to its shareholders (ROE, dividends)?
48. Will you please summarize the major strengths reflected in your analysis of ABC Bank? And the weaknesses?
49. Did you use a group of publicly traded banks or bank holding companies as part of your analysis? Which banks did you select, and how did you go about making the selections?
50. Is this group of publicly traded institutions of sufficient comparability with ABC Bank for purposes of drawing guidelines for the valuation of ABC Bank?
51. What is a guideline company? How are groups of guideline companies used to help derive valuation conclusions?
52. How would you characterize the "market" for the bank's shares? Compared to similar banks you have valued, would the market be more or less liquid?
53. Are you familiar with the concepts of control premiums, minority interest discounts, and marketability discounts? Please explain the meaning of each of these concepts. (Refer to an exhibit similar to Exhibit 12-1 in Chapter 12.)
54. Are minority interest discounts and marketability discounts the same? Please explain the difference.
55. Given your chart of valuation relationships, please explain where your conclusion of value for ABC Bank lies on the chart and explain why that is the case?
56. What specific valuation approaches and methodologies did you utilize in reaching your conclusion of value?
57. Will you please describe each of the valuation approaches you used and the specific methodologies within the approaches and explain why you thought its use was appropriate in your analysis? (Discuss market transactions, net assets, earnings capitalization, other.)
58. Will you please restate your conclusion of the fair market value of the common stock of ABC Bank, and explain in some detail how you reached the conclusion? (By reference to appropriate exhibits in the report, go through the valuation, explain how each method was used, derive each valuation observation, explain the weightings applied to each method, and reiterate the conclusion.)
59. Based upon your overall analysis of this bank and your experience in valuing many other banks, is your conclusion reasonable? Why?

Direct Testimony

Direct testimony should go smoothly if the expert and counsel have prepared as indicated above. The actual presentation of the opinion will be a function of the strategies outlined in the trial preparation phase with respect to the form of the valuation opinion and the use of supplementary visual aids to testimony.

The objective of direct testimony is to establish the expert's credentials for the case at hand, to indicate the depth of the research and analysis leading to the expert's conclusion, and to present the direct testimony in a clear, convincing, and interesting fashion.

The foundational questions in Exhibit 20-2 provide an example of one approach to direct testimony that focuses first on the expert's credentials, then moves to discuss the background of the research and analysis, and then to the opinion itself. The expert witness and counsel must decide upon the exact approach to be taken. The exhibit provides for considerable involvement on the part of counsel in direct testimony. Alternatively, counsel may prefer to focus on broader questions that allow the expert more freedom in presenting the opinion. In any event, the detailed question list provides something of a checklist for discussion between the expert and counsel regarding the extent and depth of direct testimony.

The challenge for the expert witness is to make the presentation of her or his opinion as interesting as possible to the trier of fact or the jury. This can be difficult with technical financial data. However, the expert witness should work to simplify the presentation as much as possible and try to discuss valuation concepts in terms that nonexperts can understand.

Simplifying exhibits using flip charts, overhead projectors, or other visual aids can be extremely helpful in presenting direct testimony. Figures 20-1 and 20-2 provide two illustrations of how one analyst used visuals to make important analytical and valuation points. Figure 20-1 allowed the expert to discuss, conceptually, in the first visual "how banks compete." In the second, the subject bank's performance is summarized in the general context of the model presented in the first visual. Finally, the third visual summarizes the important analytical points the analyst wanted to make.

Figure 20-2 provides a second example to show how another analyst used visuals to discuss the concept of capital shortfall (and above-normal leverage) for a jury trial. The analysts have used (hopefully) generally familiar concepts like price, service, and quality to explain one bank's performance (Figure 20-1) and assets and liabilities (Figure 20-2) to explain the concept of *book value* and then the meaning of a *capital shortfall* and the resulting condition of being excessively leveraged.

As noted earlier, every analytical argument has relatively stronger and weaker elements. I believe it is important to address actual or perceived weaknesses frontally in direct testimony. It is highly preferable to consider potentially damaging or conflicting information openly and then move on to other aspects of the analysis than to try to ignore it. Otherwise, if the issues are brought out in cross-examination, it can appear that the expert was trying to hide or overlook the weakness.

Figure 20-1
Sample Visual Aids for Testimony

The Concept

> **How Banks Compete**
> _____
>
> • Quality
>
> • Service
>
> • Price

As Developed

> **How Banks Compete**
> _____
>
> Price: Loans: near-peer yields
>   Deposits: paid higher rates
>   Service charges: charged
>   high fees
>
> Quality: Lower credit standards
>   (High loan losses)
>
> Service: High operating costs

The Implications

> **How Banks Compete**
> _____
>
> Low earning capacity
> Severe losses experienced in 1988-89

Figure 20-2
Sample Visual Aids for Testimony

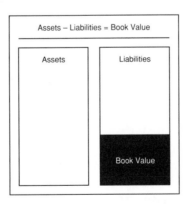

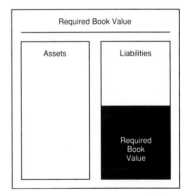

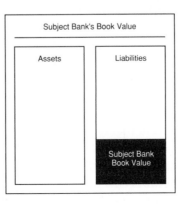

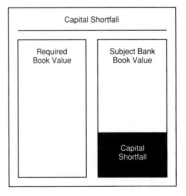

The end result of solid analysis and research and the necessary degree of pretrial preparations should be a clear, convincing, and credible presentation of an expert's opinion during direct testimony.

Qualification of the Expert Witness

This section is inserted between the discussion of direct testimony and cross-examination because it is possible that the expert will be cross-examined regarding his or her qualifications prior to being approved by the court as an expert or to being allowed to present the actual expert opinion.

It is important that the expert be prepared for cross-examination with respect to qualifications as an expert. Opposing counsel can raise questions about the *general qualifications* of an expert relating to education, credentials, training, experience, or other background. These questions are most common until a person has been qualified by a sufficient number of courts that opposing counsel will consider this line of questioning to be nonproductive. Alternatively, questions can be raised about *specific qualifications* to perform the present assignment at any time.

Questions relating to general qualifications can follow several lines. Examples include:

1. "So you did not take a single business appraisal course in college or graduate school?" Never mind that the expert may have majored in finance and had minors in economics and accounting or that courses in business appraisal did not exist when the person went to college.
2. "You have testified that the majority of the educational courses you have attended were given in conjunction with conventions of the American Society of Appraisers (or some other group), so most of your business valuation education was really obtained in conjunction with social events?"
3. An actual question I remember from several years ago: "Mr. Mercer, you only received your Chartered Financial Analyst designation last month, so what have you learned in the last month that makes you feel qualified to testify as an expert witness in this case?" Never mind that the CFA designation requires a minimum of three years of programmed study covering areas that are obviously relevant to business appraisal, as well as the passing of three rigorous examinations that are offered only once a year and that must be taken in three separate years, during which time the candidate's work experience must have been related to securities analysis in a fashion deemed appropriate by the Association of Investment Management and Research.
4. Or, "Ms. Appraiser, how many businesses have you either bought or sold personally in the last 10 years? Likely answer: "None." Likely follow-up question: "Then, Ms. Appraiser, you don't have any idea what businesses are *really worth,* do you?"

Needless to say, expert witnesses must be prepared to answer questions designed simultaneously to deprecate their experience and to fluster or frustrate otherwise highly qualified valuation analysts.

Questions can always be raised about an analyst's qualifications to serve as an expert in a specific situation. This line of questioning can be carried to extreme lengths and can be particularly frustrating for the inexperienced expert witness. Examples include the following:

1. "Ms. Appraiser, exactly how many banks (or transmission remanufacturing companies) have you personally valued in the last five years?" If an appraiser lacks proven *industry expertise,* he or she must be able to show that any shortcoming is more than overcome by *valuation expertise.* In point of fact, banking and a few other industries aside, there are no real industry experts for most industry niches. There simply are not enough companies in most industries to enable specialization by business appraisers.
2. "Ms. Appraiser, how many banks have you valued in the state of Ohio (or Tennessee, or Hawaii, or wherever the trial is being held) whose total assets are between $25 million and $26 million and were located in towns with populations of between 75,000 and 75,500, and which have had losses in two of the last four years, but are currently profitable?" The answer is very likely none. In other words, because Ms. Appraiser has not valued *this bank* before, by implication, she is not qualified to value *this bank!*
3. "Mr. Appraiser, what specifically did you learn in college (and then in graduate school, and then in the army, and then in your first job, and then in your second job, and so on) that relates, again specifically, to your qualifications to render an opinion as an expert in this case?" By taking small enough bites, opposing counsel can try to leave the impression that the appraiser has not learned anything at any time that qualifies him for the present case. While the approach probably will not work to disqualify anyone, I have seen it work to frustrate an expert beyond words, which reduced the effectiveness of his later testimony, which, of course, was precisely the purpose of that line of questioning in the first place.

The expert must be ready for almost any line of questioning that will serve to show limitations on qualifications. Above all, however, the successful expert witness will learn how to deal with ridiculous questions about qualifications in a positive vein and to turn them to advantage by showing, through explanatory answers, why his or her background, experience, training, education, and credentials are appropriate for the case at hand.

Cross-Examination

Cross-examination can be less friendly and is certainly less predictable than direct testimony. The expert should remember portions of the discussion above regarding depositions as well as the Ten Commandments for Depositions found in Exhibit 20-1. However, depositions and trial testimony have distinctly different objectives. The objective of a deposition is to answer, fully and truthfully, the questions asked by opposing counsel. The objective of trial testimony is to present and to defend a valuation opinion.

Cross-examination techniques vary widely among attorneys. A well-prepared expert, however, should be prepared for most approaches. *Opposing counsel's objective,* however, is generally the same: to call the expert's credibility into question and, therefore, the credibility of his or her valuation opinion. As a reminder of *my objectives,* at the beginning of cross-examination I place a writing pad with the following notes directly in front of me:

1. Look.
2. Listen and hear.
3. Wait and formulate.
4. Answer *the* question.
5. Stop and wait for the next question.
6. Do not anticipate!
7. Be calm!

It is important to look at counsel when questions are being addressed. It is helpful to see the questions being asked and to be able to observe his or her body language. Some attorneys try the "friendly" approach, attempting to take the expert into confidence, hoping to "lower his guard" a bit. Others take an intimidating approach. By looking at the counsel, the expert can observe what is going on and increase the probability of understanding the questions posed.

The "Listen and hear" reminder is a warning to listen carefully to the question as it is posed. Many attorneys like to ask hypothetical questions based upon explicit or implicit assumptions. The expert should be sure that he or she understands the assumptions underlying every question in order to be able to respond properly. For example:

> Suppose opposing counsel asked a question like: "Have you stopped beating your wife?" Proper courtroom response normally requires a yes or no answer to a question, followed by an opportunity to explain. A similar (and more likely) question is: "Mr. Appraiser, you did give your clients the answers they wanted, didn't you?" The expert who missed the underlying assumptions—that he is currently beating his wife or that he is an *advocate* for his client (rather than for his independent, expert opinion)—will have a real problem answering the questions. The hidden assumptions in cross-examination questions may not be so obvious as these, so a clear understanding of every question is required. The unwary expert will discredit himself or herself with careless answers.

If the expert does not understand a question, she or he should request that it be repeated. Many attorneys have a tendency to pose questions in the form of speeches with a variety of hidden assumptions. The actual question may be somewhat obscure as a result. If the expert does not understand a question, she should ask to have it repeated. The question will almost invariably be simplified if it is repeated. Further, opposing counsel may sometimes be frustrated that the "speech question" did not work and will withdraw it.

Another technique often used by attorneys in cross-examination is to ask multiple questions in the from of a single question. If the expert listens and hears the questions, she can ask for it to be repeated or can ask which question opposing counsel prefers her to answer.

Attorneys will sometimes mischaracterize the facts in prefatory comments leading to a question. It this has been done, the expert should feel free to either point out the mischaracterization, correct it, or do both before answering the question. At the very least, "friendly" counsel should be able to interject to ask that the court require that the question be asked in the form of a hypothetical question given the "hypothetical" (and mischaracterized) facts.

Still another technique used by some attorneys is to mischaracterize previous comments by an expert witness or take them out of context. Another form of this technique is to read statements from the expert's deposition into the record as background and then to pose a question. It is critical that the expert remember exactly what he or she has said, as well as the context in which the comments or answers were made, for the duration of a trial. Any mischaracterizations of previous comments can then be corrected before providing a response to the question.

The expert should also remember that anything he or she has said or written for the public record is fair game for questioning in cross-examination, particularly if opposing counsel can make some connection or find some inconsistency between previous statements (or valuation reports, articles, speeches, etc.) in the public record and the present testimony. Hopefully, the expert has been relatively consistent with positions on important issues over time or can make a clear distinction between the previous comments and the present case.

Finally, at least for this chapter, the expert should remember that any authoritative source normally consulted by valuation experts can be used to call testimony into question.[6] The expert witness must, therefore, have a well-grounded knowledge of current valuation theory and practice in order to be able to respond to such challenges with credibility.

The cross-examination techniques outlined above (from the receiving end) can fluster the unwary or unprepared expert witness. That is exactly what they are designed to do, because a flustered witness will often answer questions improperly, provide information not called for by the questions, or get defensive or angry in response. If any of these things happen, the expert "loses" and his or her credibility can be damaged.

Upon understanding a question, the expert should "Wait and formulate" a response. This may take only seconds, but it is a critical step in responding to cross-examination.[7] It is helpful to make a mental outline of a response prior to speaking. Sometimes it is helpful to jot a quick note or two to ensure that the points of the question are covered. Excessive waiting may try the patience of the court (as it certainly will try the patience of opposing counsel), but thoughtful consideration of questions is appropriate.

"Answer the question" means just that. Answer the question posed and not some other question. If the question is answered in the valua-

---

[6]For example, Shannon Pratt's books (and several others) have been placed on the list of authoritative references by the Business Valuation Committee of the American Society of Appraisers. His latest book contains over 700 pages of material. Opposing counsel (or the opposing expert witness) can probably find something in that book that apparently contradicts some portion of an expert's methodology or opinion. It is critical in such situations to obtain the reference from opposing counsel, to read carefully the quoted section, and to be able to place what was said into proper context given the particular facts and circumstances at hand. Chances are, the comments were made in a much more general context than the current valuation situation.

[7]In other words, the expert witness should remember and follow the old adage "Be sure the brain is in gear before putting the mouth into motion."

tion opinion, it is helpful to refer to the section of the report (always mentioning the page number and position of the response for the court) to indicate that the question is addressed in the report. It is sometimes appropriate to read the answer straight from the report. If a significant number of opposing counsel's questions are answered in the report, either directly or by direct inference, the report, the expert, and the conclusions will likely gain credibility.

Sometimes, questions cannot be answered with a simple yes or no. If that is the case, the expert should simply say so. It may be appropriate or necessary to offer the qualification(s) to the question or to the answer that will enable the expert to answer the question.

After answering the question, it is appropriate to "Stop and wait" for the next question. Too often, in the silent moments following an initial response to a question, an expert will be tempted to add further explanatory comments to an answer. Opposing counsel will often use the discomfort of silence to try to elicit just these additional responses, which can open up entirely new areas of questioning. It is the expert's job to answer each question honestly, completely, and convincingly, not to fill moments of silence in a courtroom.

"Do not anticipate!" is written with an exclamation point for emphasis. An expert witness who anticipates the questions of an opposing counsel in cross-examination will likely answer the question that the attorney did not know to ask or open up the cross-examination to entirely new and potentially damaging areas of questioning.

"Be calm!" is also emphasized. Grace under pressure comes naturally for some people. However, grace under the pressure of cross-examination, where the rules of the game are defined by lawyers (rather than appraisers), is a critical characteristic to be developed by an expert witness. It does not come naturally in an environment where "fight-or-flight" responses can be evoked. The expert should always remember: (1) There is no place to run until the opposing counsel finishes, and (2) It does no good to fight. The expert's objective is to present opinions clearly, convincingly, credibly, and calmly.

The expert witness should be prepared to answer questions regarding the critical assumptions of the analysis during cross-examination. Questions relating to the sensitivity of the conclusion to assumptions or judgments made are fair game. These questions provide an opportunity for the prepared expert to reiterate the logic of the valuation rationale and the reasonableness of the conclusion.

If the opposing side surfaces a material error in a valuation opinion or in an assumption leading to the opinion, the expert must be willing to consider the impact of the error on the conclusion and to adjust the conclusion for the error.

Occasionally, an attorney will engage in what was referred to earlier as a fishing expedition, asking a wide range of questions in the hope of finding an area of weakness to pursue. When this occurs, the expert may have numerous opportunities to reiterate and strengthen the basic arguments leading to the final opinion.

The objective of cross-examination, from the viewpoint of the expert witness, is to answer opposing counsel's questions calmly and convincingly and to reinforce, whenever possible, the overall reasonableness of the opinion or its underlying assumptions. A good summary and amplification of many of the points related to cross-examination are found in the Brinig and Prairie article. They are presented in Exhibit 20-3, "Techniques of Cross-Examination."

Exhibit 20-3
Techniques of Cross-Examination

1. In general, many of the Ten Commandments of effective depositions apply to cross-examination.
2. The best preparation for cross-examination is a thorough, professional job on the valuation assignment. Nothing is easier than defending a sound economic position.
3. Each assumption in the valuation expert's analysis is subject to question on cross-examination. During the appraisal process, the expert should have questioned each assumption and weighed alternative positions.
4. The expert should be thoroughly versed in any opposing expert's valuation analysis because that analysis will certainly be one of the foundations of the cross-examining lawyer's questions.
5. A valuation (or an appraisal) should not be approached like an accounting problem. There is no exact answer that can be *calculated.* It should be noted that numbers, per se, are very easy to cross-examine because there is only one right answer and any other conclusion is therefore wrong.
6. Frequently, a series of facts or premises will be compounded into a question or a series of questions. A simple yes or no will then be asked for. If the question cannot be fairly answered with yes or no, do not hesitate to state that the question cannot be so simply answered. Shift the burden back to the lawyer to frame a proper question or require that a more general question—permitting fair explanation—be asked.
7. Answer only the questions asked. Many times, additional qualifying information given by the expert will be turned around by the cross-examining lawyer and used against the expert.
8. To the extent possible, the expert should be familiar with the background and litigation skills of the cross-examining lawyer.
9. Do not try to vary your personal style, but be aware of negative habits that may be distracting from the quality or credibility of your testimony.
10. Be polite. It is generally more effective to answer questions in a pondering or reflective manner, rather than in a defensive manner.
11. Avoid the appearance of bias or untrustworthiness. Certain facts or arguments will go against any economic position. Do not hesitate to acknowledge these things if you are challenged.
12. Do not hesitate to concede an error. However, do not accept the opponent lawyer's characterization of the facts of your testimony. Examples:
    a. "So, you just *picked* a number?"
    b. "Your study *isn't accurate,* then, is it?"
    c. "So, after this *brief, informal interview,* you decided to . . ."
13. Do not overstate your opinion. Any extreme or absolute position is very easy to cross-examine.

SOURCE: Brian P. Brinig, and Michael W. Prairie, "Expert Testimony: The Business Appraiser as a Valuation Expert Witness," *Business Valuation News* (now *Business Valuation Review*), Vol. 4, no. 1, March 1985, pp. 11–12.

Redirect and Recross Testimony

Upon the completion of cross-examination by opposing counsel, "friendly" counsel often has the opportunity to ask questions or to clarify issues that may have developed as result of cross-examination. If opposing counsel has "damaged" the expert's opinion, friendly counsel has an opportunity to ask questions geared to "rehabilitate" either the witness, the opinion, or both. If friendly counsel is not careful, however, he or she can open a Pandora's box of problems for the expert witness by asking the wrong questions. It is an area that the expert and counsel can discuss during trial preparations.

The scope of redirect is normally limited to issues covered in cross-examination, and the scope of recross is normally limited to issues covered in redirect. There is, in effect, a winding down of the process until the expert's testimony is completed and excused. As Casey Stengel once said, "It ain't over until its over!"

Rebuttal Testimony

An expert witness is often called upon to examine the valuation opinion of the opposing expert witness and to be prepared to discuss that opinion in court. Sometimes the experts are allowed to be present in court when the other expert(s) are testifying. In other cases, experts are not allowed to enter the courtroom until they are to testify. Normally, experts can remain in the courtroom following their testimony.

When reviewing the opinion of opposing experts, it is helpful to use a review checklist similar to that found in the Summary Review Checklist in Exhibit 15-2. The expert can then examine the various elements of the opponent's opinion in a systematic and objective manner and can note problems that are found in this context.

Occasionally, an expert is asked to prepare schedules or comments that analyze an opponent's opinion and then to present that rebuttal testimony to the court. It is important that rebuttal testimony be presented in the same calm, objective fashion as recommended for direct testimony. Experts can hurt their credibility with the court by becoming overly zealous in the presentation of rebuttal testimony. Errors of fact, assumption, emphasis, calculation, or judgment should be noted objectively, and the impact of the errors should be summarized carefully.

One technique of rebuttal that is sometimes effective is to compare the elements of an opponent's valuation with those of her or his own and to note the differences. Then, in another column, the expert can correct the opposing expert's errors (which may be errors of emphasis, assumption, fact, or judgment, as well as numerical or other mistakes) and reconcile the two opinions. It is often the case that widely different valuation conclusions have many similarities and differ only in one or two key assumptions.

Assisting with Cross-Examination of the Opposing Expert Witness

Expert witnesses are often called upon to assist friendly counsel in the preparation of questions to cross-examine the opposing expert witness. Preparations for rebuttal testimony, if it is being used, will help in this process. The answers to the questions from the review checklist become a first pass at a question list for cross-examination. In addition, the expert can normally prepare a more detailed list of questions based upon a review that will help prepare counsel for cross-examination.

Conclusion

Bank analysts and other valuation analysts can look forward to their first (or next) experience as an expert witness. Any analyst in a sufficiently responsible position with a valuation firm to sign valuation reports is a potential expert witness over time. And some analysts will find that their next assignment will be one that is part of current litigation and will require that they prepare to be an expert witness. It is therefore important for all valuation analysts to become sensitive to the requirements of valuation litigation and of the supporting role that they play in litigated cases.

Part V

Conclusion

Chapter 21

Outlook for the Future of Banking and Business Appraisal

. . . The strategic aim of a business [is] to earn a return on capital, and if in any particular case the return in the long run is not satisfactory, then the deficiency should be corrected or the activity abandoned for a more favorable one.

Alfred P. Sloan, Jr.

How to have your cake and eat it too: Lend it out at interest.

Unknown

The cost of capital is like that Great Dark Room: many go in, but few return.

The Age of Chivalry is gone; that of sophisters, economists, and calculators has succeeded.

Edmund Burke

Introduction

Chapter 21 is the concluding chapter of *Valuing Financial Institutions.* Chapter 22 provides the sample appraisal of Sample Bancshares, Inc., which has been referred to at numerous places in the preceding text. In this concluding chapter, we will:

1. Discuss current trends and the outlook for the banking industry in the context of the industry's historical performance.
2. Discuss several emerging trends in the business appraisal field that are significant to business and bank appraisers, as well as to users of appraisal reports.
3. Provide some brief introductory and explanatory comments about the Sample Bank Appraisal in Chapter 22.

Banking Industry Trends and Outlook

The banking industry is in the midst of a structural transition that is creating massive changes, both in a macro (industry) sense and in a micro (bank-specific) sense. Bankers will have to respond as never before in order to provide needed customer and business banking services in a cost-effective manner and to achieve competitive returns on the capital invested in the industry.

Exhibits 21-1 through 21-4 provide several perspectives on the overall commercial banking industry for the decade from 1981 to 1990. The figures provided are for all FDIC-insured commercial banks in existence at each year-end. They provide an overview of industry performance on a consolidated basis. As such, the figures are necessarily influenced by the performance of the larger banking institutions that dominate this fairly concentrated industry. Nevertheless, they do provide the ability to analyze trends in performance over the last decade.

Exhibit 21-1
FDIC-Insured Commercial Banks Income Statements ($ Thousands)*

	1981	1982	1983	1984	1985	1986	1987	1988	1989	1990
Interest income	$ 217,226	$ 238,345	$217,226	$250,311	$248,210	$237,809	$244,849	$272,290	$317,282	$ 320,390
Interest expense	143,887	169,373	143,887	169,061	157,300	142,823	144,954	165,033	205,047	204,853
Net interest income	73,339	68,972	73,339	81,250	90,910	94,986	99,895	107,257	112,234	115,537
Noninterest income	23,270	20,184	23,270	26,512	31,037	35,898	41,458	44,941	51,439	55,067
Adjusted gross income	96,609	89,156	96,609	107,762	121,947	130,884	141,353	152,198	163,674	170,603
Personnel expense	33,877	31,442	33,877	36,876	39,986	42,920	45,189	46,567	49,333	51,734
Occupancy expense	11,181	10,037	11,181	11,883	13,290	14,492	15,239	15,785	16,641	17,414
Other expense	21,852	20,137	21,852	25,042	29,045	32,824	36,818	38,956	42,369	46,363
Total noninterest operating expense	66,910	61,616	66,910	73,801	82,321	90,236	97,246	101,308	108,343	115,511
Basic operating income	29,699	27,540	29,699	33,961	39,626	40,648	44,107	50,890	55,330	55,092
Loan loss allowance	10,802	8,507	10,802	13,813	17,717	22,027	37,541	17,071	30,377	31,731
Net securities	– 20	– 1,275	– 20	– 138	1,567	3,927	1,430	280	798	473
Pretax income	18,877	17,758	18,877	20,010	23,476	22,548	7,996	34,099	25,751	23,835
Taxes	4,017	2,980	4,017	4,721	5,643	5,304	5,407	9,991	9,829	7,853
Net before extraordinary items	14,860	14,778	14,860	15,289	17,833	17,244	2,589	24,108	15,922	15,982
Net income	$ 14,933	$ 14,843	$ 14,933	$ 15,506	$ 18,057	$ 17,514	$ 2,814	$ 24,939	$ 16,225	$ 16,607
Total dividends	5,840	6,543	7,366	8,625	8,529	9,227	10,667	13,218	13,218	13,866
Dividend payout	39.1 %	44.1 %	49.6 %	56.4 %	47.8 %	53.5 %	412.0 %	54.8 %	83.0 %	86.8 %
BE + NI – DIV	$ 118,135	$ 126,435	135,948	146,676	162,777	176,494	172,986	191,491	197,787	$ 208,671
Ending equity	$ 118,135	128,381	139,795	153,249	168,207	180,839	179,770	194,780	205,930	$ 218,945
Implied new capital	n.a.†	1,946	3,847	6,573	5,430	4,345	6,784	3,289	8,143	$ 10,274
Number employees (M)	1,506	1,498	1,509	1,526	1,562	1,563	1,545	1,527	1,537	1,517
Average number employees (M)	1,496	1,502	1,504	1,518	1,544	1,562	1,554	1,536	1,532	1,527
Number banks	14,415	14,462	14,460	14,477	14,404	14,200	13,699	13,139	12,729	12,342
Total assets	$2,029,148	2,193,867	2,341,952	2,508,407	2,730,498	2,941,082	3,000,914	3,130,945	3,303,595	$3,388,461
Average assets	$1,930,681	2,111,508	2,267,910	2,425,180	2,619,453	2,835,790	2,970,998	3,065,930	3,217,270	$3,346,028
Total equity	$ 118,135	128,381	139,795	153,249	168,207	180,839	179,770	194,780	205,930	$ 218,945
Average equity	113,405	123,258	134,088	146,522	160,728	174,523	180,305	187,275	200,355	212,438
ROAA	0.74%	0.70%	0.66%	0.63%	0.68%	0.61%	0.09%	0.79%	0.49%	0.48%
ROAE	13.17%	11.99%	11.08%	10.43%	11.10%	9.88%	1.44%	12.87%	7.95%	7.52%
Assets/employee	$ 1,347	1,464	1,552	1,643	1,748	1,882	1,942	2,050	2,150	$ 2,233
Average AGI/employee	$64.6	$59.4	$64.2	$71.0	$79.0	$83.8	$91.0	$99.1	$106.8	$111.7
Operating income/employee	$19.9	$18.3	$19.8	$22.4	$25.7	$26.0	$28.4	$33.1	$36.1	$36.1
Ending equity/assets	5.82%	5.85%	5.97%	6.11%	6.16%	6.15%	5.99%	6.22%	6.23%	6.46%
Personnel expense/employee	$22.6	$20.9	$22.5	$24.3	$25.9	$27.5	$29.1	$30.3	$32.2	$33.9
% delta personal expense/employee	n.a.	– 7.6 %	7.6 %	7.8 %	6.6 %	6.1 %	5.9 %	4.3 %	6.2 %	5.2 %
Tax rates	21.28%	16.78%	21.28%	23.59%	24.04%	23.52%	67.62%	29.30%	38.17%	32.95%

*Data for 1981–88 were obtained from *Annual Reports of the FDIC*; data for 1988–90 are FDIC data as compiled by W. C. Ferguson and Company.
†n.a. = not available.

Exhibit 21-2
FDIC-Insured Commercial Banks

Income Statements as a Percentage of Average Assets

	1981	1982	1983	1984	1985	1986	1987	1988	1989	1990
Interest income	11.25%	11.29%	9.58%	10.32%	9.48%	8.39%	8.24%	8.88%	9.86%	9.58%
Interest expense	7.45	8.02	6.34	6.97	6.01	5.04	4.88	5.38	6.37	6.12
Net interest income	3.80	3.27	3.23	3.35	3.47	3.35	3.36	3.50	3.49	3.45
Noninterest income	0.70	0.60	0.70	0.79	0.93	1.07	1.24	1.34	1.54	1.65
Adjusted gross income	5.00	4.22	4.26	4.44	4.66	4.62	4.76	4.96	5.09	5.10
Personnel expense	1.75	1.49	1.49	1.52	1.53	1.51	1.52	1.52	1.53	1.55
Occupancy expense	0.58	0.48	0.49	0.49	0.51	0.51	0.51	0.51	0.52	0.52
Other expense	1.13	0.95	0.96	1.03	1.11	1.16	1.24	1.27	1.32	1.39
Total NIOE	3.47	2.92	2.95	3.04	3.14	3.18	3.27	3.30	3.37	3.45
Basic operating income	1.54	1.30	1.31	1.40	1.51	1.43	1.48	1.66	1.72	1.65
Loan loss allowance	0.56	0.40	0.48	0.57	0.68	0.78	1.26	0.56	0.94	0.95
Net securities	−0.00	−0.06	−0.00	−0.01	0.06	0.14	0.05	0.01	0.02	0.01
Pretax income	0.98	0.84	0.83	0.83	0.90	0.80	0.27	1.11	0.80	0.71
Taxes	0.21	0.14	0.18	0.19	0.22	0.19	0.18	0.33	0.31	0.23
Net before extraordinary	0.77%	0.70%	0.66%	0.63%	0.68%	0.61%	0.09%	0.79%	0.49%	0.48%

Income Statement as % of Adjusted Gross Income

	1981	1982	1983	1984	1985	1986	1987	1988	1989	1990
Interest income	224.9%	267.3%	224.9%	232.3%	203.5%	181.7%	173.2%	178.9%	193.9%	187.8%
Interest exense	148.9	190.0	148.9	156.9	129.0	109.1	102.5	108.4	125.3	120.1
Net interest income	75.9	77.4	75.9	75.4	74.5	72.6	70.7	70.5	68.6	67.7
Noninterest income	24.1	22.6	24.1	24.6	25.5	27.4	29.3	29.5	31.4	32.3
Adjusted gross income	100.0	100.0	100.0	100.0	100.0	100.0	100.0	100.0	100.0	100.0
Personnel expense	35.1	35.3	35.1	34.2	32.8	32.8	32.0	30.6	30.1	30.3
Occupancy expense	11.6	11.3	11.6	11.0	10.9	11.1	10.8	10.4	10.2	10.2
Other expense	22.6	22.6	22.6	23.2	23.8	25.1	26.0	25.6	25.9	27.2
Total NIOE	69.3	69.1	69.3	68.5	67.5	68.9	68.8	66.6	66.2	67.7
Basic operating income	30.7	30.9	30.7	31.5	32.5	31.1	31.2	33.4	33.8	32.3
Loan loss allowance	11.2	9.5	11.2	12.8	14.5	16.8	26.6	11.2	18.6	18.6
Net securities	−0.0	−1.4	−0.0	−0.1	1.3	3.0	1.0	0.2	0.5	0.3
Pretax income	19.5	19.9	19.5	18.6	19.3	17.2	5.7	22.4	15.7	14.0
Taxes	4.2	3.3	4.2	4.4	4.6	4.1	3.8	6.6	6.0	4.6
Net before extraordinary	15.4%	16.6%	15.4%	14.2%	14.6%	13.2%	1.8%	15.8%	9.7%	9.4%

Exhibit 21-3
FDIC-Insured Commercial Banks Income Statement Growth Analysis (Compound Growth Rate = CGR)

	1 YR CGR 1989–90	2 YR CGR 1988–90	3 YR CGR 1987–90	4 YR CGR 1986–90	5 YR CGR 1985–90	6 YR CGR 1984–90	7 YR CGR 1983–90	8 YR CGR 1982–90	9 YR CGR 1981–90
Interest income	1.0%	8.5%	9.4%	7.7%	5.2%	4.2%	5.7%	3.8%	4.4%
Interest expense	– 0.1	11.4	12.2	9.4	5.4	3.3	5.2	2.4	4.0
Net interest income	2.9	3.8	5.0	5.0	4.9	6.0	6.7	6.7	5.2
Noninterest income	7.1	10.7	9.9	11.3	12.2	13.0	13.1	13.4	10.0
Adjusted gross income	4.2	5.9	6.5	6.9	6.9	8.0	8.5	8.5	6.5
Personnel expense	4.9	5.4	4.6	4.8	5.3	5.8	6.2	6.4	4.8
Occupancy expense	4.6	5.0	4.5	4.7	5.6	6.6	6.5	7.1	5.0
Other expense	9.4	9.1	8.0	9.0	9.8	10.8	11.3	11.0	8.7
Total NIOE	6.6	6.8	5.9	6.4	7.0	7.8	8.1	8.2	6.3
Basic operating income	– 0.4	4.0	7.7	7.9	6.8	8.4	9.2	9.1	7.1
Loan loss allowance	– 4.5	36.3	– 5.5	9.6	12.4	14.9	16.6	17.9	12.7
Net securities	– 40.7	30.0	– 30.8	– 41.1	– 21.3	n.m.	n.m.	n.m.	n.m.*
Pretax income	– 7.4	– 16.4	43.9	1.4	0.3	3.0	3.4	3.7	2.6
Taxes	– 20.1	– 11.3	13.2	10.3	6.8	8.9	10.0	12.9	7.7
Net before extraordinary	0.4	– 18.6	83.4	– 1.9	– 2.2	0.7	1.0	1.0	0.8
Net income	2.4%	– 18.4%	80.7%	– 1.3%	– 1.7%	1.1%	1.5%	1.4%	1.2%
Total dividends	4.9%	2.4%	9.1%	10.7%	10.2%	8.2%	9.5%	9.8%	10.1%
Dividend payout percentage	4.5	25.8	– 40.5	12.8	12.6	7.4	8.3	8.8	9.3
BE + NI – DIV	5.5	4.4	6.5	4.3	5.1	6.1	6.3	6.5	6.5
Ending equity	6.3	6.0	6.8	4.9	5.4	6.1	6.6	6.9	7.1
Implied new capital	26.2%	76.7%	14.8%	24.0%	13.6%	7.7%	15.1%	23.1%	n.a.†
Number employees	– 1.2	– 0.3	– 0.6	– 0.7	– 0.6	– 0.1	0.1	0.2	0.1
Average number employees	– 0.3	– 0.3	– 0.6	– 0.6	– 0.2	0.1	0.2	0.2	0.2
Number banks	– 3.0	– 3.1	– 3.4	– 3.4	– 3.0	– 2.6	– 2.2	– 2.0	– 1.7
Total assets	2.6	4.0	4.1	3.6	4.4	5.1	5.4	5.6	5.9
Average assets	4.0	4.5	4.0	4.2	5.0	5.5	5.7	5.9	6.3
Total equity	6.3	6.0	6.8	4.9	5.4	6.1	6.6	6.9	7.1
Average equity	6.0%	6.5%	5.6%	5.0%	5.7%	6.4%	6.8%	7.0%	7.2%
ROAA	– 3.5	– 22.1	76.3	– 5.9	– 6.8	– 4.5	– 4.4	– 4.7	n.a.
ROAE	– 5.3	– 23.6	73.7	– 6.6	– 7.5	– 5.3	– 5.4	– 5.7	n.a.
Average assets/employee	3.9	4.4	4.8	4.4	5.0	5.2	5.3	5.4	n.a.
Average AGI/employee	4.6	6.2	7.1	7.5	7.2	7.8	8.2	8.2	6.3
Operating income/employee	– 0.1%	4.4%	8.3%	8.5%	7.0%	8.3%	9.0%	8.8%	6.9%

*n.m. = not meaningful.
†n.a. = not available.

485

Exhibit 21-4
FDIC-Insured Commercial Banks Income Statement Growth Rate Analysis (Year-to-Year Growth)

	1981–82	1982–83	1983–84	1984–85	1985–86	1986–87	1987–88	1988–89	1989–90
Interest income	9.7%	− 8.9%	15.2%	− 0.8%	− 4.2%	3.0%	11.2%	16.5%	1.0%
Interest expense	17.7	− 15.0	17.5	− 7.0	− 9.2	1.5	13.9	24.2	− 0.1
Net interest income	− 6.0	6.3	10.8	11.9	4.5	5.2	7.4	4.6	2.9
Noninterest income	− 13.3	15.3	13.9	17.1	15.7	15.5	8.4	14.5	7.1
Adjusted gross income	− 7.7	8.4	11.5	13.2	7.3	8.0	7.7	7.5	4.2
Personnel expense	− 7.2	7.7	8.9	8.4	7.3	5.3	3.0	5.9	4.9
Occupancy expense	− 10.2	11.4	6.3	11.8	9.0	5.2	3.6	5.4	4.6
Other expense	− 7.8	8.5	14.6	16.0	13.0	12.2	5.8	8.8	9.4
Total NIOE	− 7.9	8.6	10.3	11.5	9.6	7.8	4.2	6.9	6.6
Basic operating income	− 7.3	7.8	14.4	16.7	2.6	8.5	15.4	8.7	− 0.4
Loan loss allowance	− 21.2	27.0	27.9	28.3	24.3	70.4	− 54.5	77.9	4.5
Net securities	n.m.*	− 98.4	590.0	n.m.	150.6	− 63.6	− 80.4	185.0	− 40.7
Pretax income	− 5.9	6.3	6.0	17.3	− 4.0	− 64.5	326.5	− 24.5	− 7.4
Taxes	− 25.8	34.8	17.5	19.5	− 6.0	1.9	84.8	− 1.6	− 20.1
Net before extraordinary	− 0.6	0.6	2.9	16.6	− 3.3	− 85.0	831.2	− 34.0	0.4
Net income	− 0.6%	0.6%	3.8%	16.5%	− 3.0%	− 83.9%	786.2%	− 34.9%	2.4%
Total dividends	12.0%	12.6%	17.1%	− 1.1%	8.2%	15.6%	23.9%	0.0%	4.9%
Dividend payout percentage	12.7	12.4	13.8	− 15.2	11.9	670.0	− 86.7	51.4	4.5
BE + NI − DIV	7.0	7.5	n.m.	11.0	8.4	− 2.0	10.7	3.3	5.5
Ending equity	8.7	8.9	9.6	9.8	7.5	− 0.6	8.3	5.7	6.3
Implied new capital	n.a.†	97.7%	70.9%	− 17.4%	− 20.0%	56.1%	− 51.5%	147.6%	26.2%
Number employees	− 0.5	0.7	1.1	2.3	0.1	− 1.2	− 1.2	0.6	− 1.2
Average number employees	0.4	0.1	0.9	1.7	1.2	− 0.5	− 1.2	− 0.3	− 0.3
Number banks	0.3	− 0.0	0.1	− 0.5	− 1.4	− 3.5	− 4.1	− 3.1	− 3.0
Total assets	8.1	6.7	7.1	8.9	7.7	2.0	4.3	5.5	2.6
Average assets	9.4	7.4	6.9	8.0	8.3	4.8	3.2	4.9	4.0
Total equity	8.7	8.9	9.6	9.8	7.5	− 0.6	8.3	5.7	6.3
Average equity	8.7%	8.8%	9.3%	9.7%	8.6%	3.3%	3.9%	7.0%	6.0%
ROAA	− 4.9	− 6.4	− 3.8	8.0	− 10.7	− 85.7	802.3	− 37.1	− 3.5
ROAE	8.9	− 7.6	− 5.8	6.3	− 10.9	− 85.5	796.5	− 38.3	− 5.3
Average assets/employee	5.9	6.0	5.9	6.4	7.6	3.2	5.6	4.9	3.9
Average AGI/employee	− 8.1	8.2	10.5	11.2	6.1	8.6	8.9	7.8	4.6
Operating income/employee	− 7.7%	7.7%	13.3%	14.7%	1.4%	9.1%	16.7%	9.0%	− 0.1%

*n.m. = not meaningful.
†n.a. = not available.

Earnings and Returns

The trend in earnings and returns, based on the traditional measures of return on assets and return on equity found in Exhibit 21-1, is clearly downward.

Income Related to the Balance Sheet

The industry has earned a return on equity in excess of 10 percent in only one of the last five years (1987, when ROAE was 12.9 percent), and that year's performance, in retrospect, appears to have reflected a misjudgment by bankers collectively that international, real estate, and other credit problems recognized beginning in the mid-1980s would be resolved sooner than in reality.

The industry's basic operating income, however, has generally improved. Efforts to overcome the massive spread pressure experienced in the high rate environment of the early 1980s, combined with a more favorable operating environment (from the perspective of interest rates), have resulted in banks that are clearly more focused on maintaining spreads (see particularly the margin analysis in Exhibit 21-2). Net interest income as a percentage of assets has risen from a trough of 3.27 percent in 1983 (down from 3.80 percent in 1981) to the range of 3.40–3.50 percent in the late 1980s and 1990.

Fee income growth has experienced high priority in the industry, particularly among large banks. Fee income has risen from the range of 0.60–0.70 percent of average assets in the early 1980s to 1.65 percent of average assets in 1990.

Growth in noninterest operating expenses (as a percentage of average assets), however, has offset much of the improvement in interest spreads and fee income. Noninterest expenses were under 3.0 percent of average assets in the early 1980s and have risen to more than 3.4 percent of average assets because expenses have been growing faster than the asset base over the period (see Exhibits 21-3 and 21-4).

Income Statement Related to Sales

The most telling analysis of the banking industry income statement over the 1980s may be in Exhibit 21-2, where income items are related to sales (adjusted gross income). As noted above, the mix of sales (i.e., total revenues net of interest expense) has been changing aggressively toward fee income.

Personnel expenses as a percentage of AGI have been reduced from a peak of 35.3 percent in 1982 to 30.3 percent in 1990. This trend clearly indicates that banks have been focusing on personnel expenses. However, the basic strategy followed by most banks has clearly been to attempt to manage personnel expenses by holding headcount constant and lowering relative expenses by raising the asset base. Industry employment stood at 1.5 million at year-end 1980 and remained virtually unchanged 10 years later at year-end 1990 (see Exhibit 21-1).

Occupancy expenses per dollar of sales have been reduced from 11.6 percent to 10.2 percent over the decade. Unfortunately, much of the improvement experienced in personnel and occupancy expenses was offset because all other expenses rose fairly sharply (from 22.6 percent to 27.2 percent of sales). The growth in other expenses has likely been driven by the expenses of real estate owned and other nonearning assets, which have risen dramatically over the decade, as well as by expenses associated with the rise in noninterest income noted earlier.

The result of the above income and expense trends has enabled basic operating income to rise moderately, from around 31 percent to the range of 32–33 percent of AGI over the decade under consideration. For all the focus on improving bank productivity in recent years, there has been only a modest improvement in the basic operating income margin and, therefore, in the percentage of every dollar of net revenue (AGI) available to cover loan losses, taxes, and shareholder dividends.

The increase in basic operating income in the banking system has been more than offset by rising levels of loan losses, which are reflected in higher provisions for loan losses. The loan loss provision as a percentage of AGI averaged 11.2 percent during the period from 1981–1984, a high level by historical standards, and included provisions associated with the 1981–1982 recession and the historically high interest rates of that period.

Since 1985, the loan loss provision for the commercial banking industry has averaged 17.7 percent, indicating that nearly 18 cents of every dollar of net sales has been devoted to providing for current credit losses or to building loan loss reserves against possible future losses. The banking system is too leveraged and fragile to sustain losses of this magnitude over the long term.

The pretax margin for the banking industry has dropped from the 19–20 percent range during the early 1980s to the 14–15 percent range currently as a direct result of the trends noted above and shown in Exhibit 21-2.

Recent Growth Trends

Historically, the banking industry achieved a return on equity on the order of 12–13 percent. We saw in the analytical chapters that there is a correlation between a bank's return on equity and its ability to grow. With lower returns in recent years has come a slowdown in asset and revenue growth (see Exhibit 21-3). Industry assets were growing in the range of 5–6 percent per year in the early 1980s. In recent years, however, asset growth has slowed to 4 percent or lower. Slowing asset growth has contributed to a corresponding reduction in the growth of banking industry AGI (sales).

Slowing growth in an inflationary environment has placed increasing pressures on operating income for the industry. That pressure can be seen in the relationship between the growth in noninterest operating expenses and average assets. For much of the last decade, the growth rates of noninterest expenses have exceeded those of assets and revenues.

The Banking Industry Is Overbanked

One of the factors contributing to the earnings pressures for the banking industry relates to the existing physical delivery structure of the industry.

The banking industry is clearly "overbanked."[1] There is massive overcapacity in many banking markets. There are too many banks and banking offices. By and large, delivery systems are inefficient in relationship to overhead levels that will allow a reasonable return on investment going forward.

A Look at One Market

The purpose of this section is not to discuss the particulars of the Memphis banking market, which might be of little interest to readers elsewhere. I have used Memphis because of my familiarity with the market (and the fact that a copy of the Yellow Pages is handy). The example is illustrative, however, of conditions in many markets.

There were 43 banking institutions (defined as banks or thrifts) listed in the Yellow Pages in Memphis as of December 1990 and 222 full-service banking locations under the category "Banks." The metropolitan area's population is approximately 1.0 million, which means that there is approximately one full-service banking location for every 4,500 persons.[2]

Consumer Banking

The top three financial institutions have 89 full-service branches and a host of stand-alone, 24-hour teller locations. The top six banks and thrifts have 137 branches. Casual observation indicates two things: (1) most bank branches do not operate "at capacity" most of the time (although many do experience peak-hour loads), and (2) the big banks are like fast-food operations in that they tend to locate near each other. The implication is that other than perhaps sharing in peak-hour traffic, little incremental locational benefit is derived from many adjacent branches, from the viewpoint of the banking industry (although not necessarily from the vantage point of consumer preference or convenience).

Commercial Lending

With 43 bank "players" in the market area, there is a plethora of loan officers capable of making commercial loans. Even the relatively small banks can make loans to the majority of businesses in town, so there is increasing competitive pressure on loan rates. Bankers at the larger

---

[1]This should not be construed as an anticompetitive statement. The concept of overbanking here relates to the number of physical branches and their costs in relationship to the ability of existing institutions to earn a competitive rate of return based on invested capital (see the discussion on returns that follows).

[2]Under the heading "Credit Unions," there were an additional 28 offices in the Memphis area. Those credit unions listed a total of 12 additional branch locations in the area, for a total of 40 credit union offices. In addition, one statewide credit union listed an 800 telephone number for its main office in Nashville. The factor of credit unions exacerbates the problem of overbanking.

banks frequently complain that every time they consider a sizable deal, there are half a dozen or more other bankers looking at it. This kind of competitive pressure can lead to the lowering of credit standards (to get "higher-rate" loan business) or extreme competitive pressure on price for commercial loan business.

Mortgage Banking

There were 127 companies in the Memphis Yellow Pages under the category "Mortgages" as of December 1990, many of which provided this service from multiple branch locations around the city. About half of the banks counted above provided a separate listing for mortgage lending, which suggests there are more than 100 other companies offering this basic banking service within the metropolitan area.[3] Needless to say, competitive pressures are intense in the mortgage lending area.

Liability Gathering

With so many banks competing for deposit business in a relatively small area, there is continual competitive pressure to offer higher consumer deposit rates, particularly for the smaller and newer entrants into the market (of which there have been a large number in the last five years). The larger banks, with their dispersed branch networks, do offer convenience to consumers in the immediate areas of their branches, as well as anywhere else in town those customers may desire to bank. New entrants typically have only a single location and cannot offer area-wide convenience, other than through hooking up with CIRRUS, MOST, or another multi-institution network of 24-hour banking locations.

Some Implications for the Future in Memphis

There will be a continuing consolidation of banking assets in the Memphis area. Few of the bank start-ups of recent years will realize the growth and earnings objectives originally hoped for, and the new entrants will find that growing to significant size in the Memphis market will be a function of market area growth rates (fairly slow) over periods of many years. The near-term market share goals for acceptable-quality business of many of the smaller competitors will simply not be met over the next few years.

The returns realized by investors in recent bank start-ups will therefore not be as exciting as hoped for. Growth and reasonable profitability levels will be longer in coming than anticipated. While this ought to dampen the enthusiasm of new bank organizers, hope does spring eternal, so there will still be an occasional new entrant in the market, which will only exacerbate the already intense competitive pressures.

The only realistic alternatives for profitable growth for the newer market entrants are to establish themselves as niche specialists who are somehow able to draw customers to their single locations from across town or to have the good fortune of locating in a *new growth area* of town. (If it is a known growth area, chances are that one or more competitors will already be there!)

---

[3]The credit unions did not list themselves under this category, so to the extent they offer mortgage loans, home equity lines, or other loans secured by equity in their members' homes, the market is even more competitive.

Some of the newer banks (and perhaps a few of the larger institutions as well) will try to defy the economic realities of the marketplace and achieve short-term market share and profitability goals by lowering credit standards. These efforts *always* (if ever there is an "always") result in future problems, and "the future" is the present for more than one area institution already experiencing earnings problems. Successful niche banking is easier said than achieved.

The combination of these factors will force consideration of mergers between some of the smaller banks in town. Others will hope to be acquired by the larger institutions, or they will hope that entrants from outside the area will acquire them as they try to establish "beachheads" in the Memphis market.

However, the days of a bank automatically being worth a multiple of book value shortly after turning profitable are over, at least for the present time. Several of the mergers between the smaller banks will likely occur on nonpremium terms for either bank, and those selling to larger institutions will probably be disappointed in the prices offered.

Some Broader Implications

The point of this brief analysis is not to focus on Memphis, where I happen to live, but to provide a concrete example of the kinds of competitive pressures facing bankers in metropolitan areas around the nation. Readers can substitute Atlanta, New York, Seattle, Los Angeles, or another city for Memphis, and the basics of the discussion will probably be reasonably accurate.

Many smaller banking markets are no less overbanked. Other areas that may have fewer banking locations (relative to population) may lack the wealth often created by larger businesses in the metropolitan areas. The result may still be very stiff levels of competition.

Expectations for Banking Industry Earnings and Returns

Over the long run, the stock markets expect total returns on the order of 12 percent or more from investments in larger capitalization common stocks. For example, the arithmetic mean of annual returns for the period 1926–1990, as calculated by Ibbotson Associates, was 12.1 percent.[4] Over the longer run, returns, which come in the form of dividend yields and price appreciation, tend to correlate with the returns on equity of the underlying companies.

Industry Returns Are Lacking

It is clear from the return figures in Exhibit 21-1 that the banking industry return on average equity has fallen considerably below the 12–13 percent range that would yield total returns, over the longer run, comparable to those of the overall market. While some segments of the banking industry are performing at these levels or better (e.g., selected bank holding companies in economically advantaged regions), other major

---

[4]*Stocks, Bonds, Bills, and Inflation 1991 Yearbook* (Chicago: Ibbotson Associates, 1991), p. 32.

segments (such as the money center banks) are performing below historical levels.

A simple analysis from Exhibit 21-1 will "prove" that the industry will be under increasing pressure to raise shareholder returns back to the historical 12–13 percent range. During the last five years (1986–1990), we note that, for the banking industry:

	$ Millions	
Total net income	$ 78,099	
Less total dividends paid	60,196	(payout = 77.1%)
Equals system generated equity	$ 17,903	
Beginning equity (12/31/85)	$168,207	
Plus system generated equity	17,903	
Equals implied ending equity	$186,110	
Actual ending equity (12/31/90)	$218,945	
Less implied ending equity	186,110	
Equals net new investment in industry	$ 32,835	

During the last five years, the industry ratio of equity to total assets has improved from 6.16 percent (year-end 1985) to 6.46 percent (year-end 1990). Had the banking system been limited to internally generated capital during the last five years, total banking equity would have been $186.1 billion and the ratio of equity to total assets would have fallen to 5.49 percent. Effectively, then, the banking industry has obtained $32.8 billion of net new capital from all sources during the last five years.[5]

It is clear that regulatory pressure will only intensify for banks to continue to improve their capital ratios. It is also clear that internally generated capital, based upon earnings at levels similar to the last five years, will not be sufficient to continue to improve capital ratios, to maintain dividends at their historical dollar levels, and to provide an adequate return on the *new capital* recently placed into the system, much less the previously existing capital.

Because additional external capital appears to be essential to achieve banking industry regulatory guidelines, it will be necessary to improve industry returns in order to attract that capital. The basic conclusion to be derived from this brief historical analysis is that bankers must work exceedingly hard to raise their earnings and returns in order to finance growth over the next decade (either through retained earnings or by attracting new capital) while building capital to regulatory minimums in the process.

Summary of Industry Modeling for 1991–2000

We have developed a model to help to anticipate some of the changes to be expected in the banking industry over the next decade. The purpose of the model is not to provide a specific forecast for the industry, but rather to draw fairly specific conclusions regarding what has to hap-

---

[5]This brief analysis, derived from Exhibit 21-1, is based upon consolidated results of the banking industry at the level of individual banks reporting to the FDIC, not at the bank holding company level. Indeed, much of the net new capital reflected above was raised by bank holding companies, either through borrowing or the sale of shares, and injected into their subsidiary banks. The implications of the analysis, however, remain the same despite this intermediate step in raising capital for the banking industry.

pen in the banking industry over the next decade in order to achieve a competitive level of returns. Basic assumptions of the model include:

1. Spreads will be under continuing pressure, although bankers will maintain the net interest margin (net interest income divided by average assets) at the 1990 level of 3.45 percent over the period. Spreads will vary over time, of course, but the prospects for a general improvement from current levels seem modest.
2. Noninterest income will continue to improve, both in relationship to average assets and to adjusted gross income. In addition, fee income per employee will rise substantially.
3. Bankers will realize that their greatest leverage for improving earnings is through continued improvements in productivity. However, the growth rate of personnel expense *per employee* is assumed to be at the level of 1.0 percent per year in excess of the growth rate of total assets, which are assumed to grow at 5.0 percent per year over the coming decade. This assumption is necessary because of the continuing improvement projected for fee income per employee.
4. In the "optimistic" version of the model (Exhibit 21-5), the loan loss provision is reduced over the next five years to approximately 0.60 percent of average assets. Few observers hope for a lower level of losses over the period. In the "pessimistic" version of the model (Exhibit 21-6), the loan loss provision is reduced to 0.80 percent of average assets and then maintained at that level.
5. The ratio of equity to total assets improves to 7.0 percent by 1995 and is then maintained at that level.

Importantly, the model assumes that the industry will achieve a return on average equity of approximately 13 percent by 1995 and then maintain or moderately improve from that level until 2000. Because specific assumptions are made about interest spreads, fee income, and return on equity (which determines dollar earnings), the model then "solves" for the operating performance in the area of noninterest operating expenses and fee income necessary to allow the capital and return objectives to be met.

The optimistic and pessimistic models were run under the assumptions outlined above. The results of the runs are summarized in Exhibits 21-5 and 21-6.

A key line in both forecasts refers to the implied number of employees. Under both the optimistic and pessimistic scenarios, banking industry employment must decline sharply over the next decade if the industry is to achieve a return on equity in the approximate range of 12–13 percent. Under the optimistic scenario, industry employment will fall from the current level of 1.5 million to 1.3 million by 1995, after which employment will decline slightly but remain near 1.3 million. Under the pessimistic scenario, employment will fall to about 1.2 million by 1995 and remain there for the next five years.

In either case, the key to reachieving competitive returns for the banking industry over the next several years is fairly simple: Productivity, as measured by adjusted gross income per employee, must grow at a rate significantly in excess of the underlying asset growth of the industry. And this must be accomplished while spending less per dollar

Exhibit 21-5
FDIC-Insured Commercial Banks Optimistic Projection Model

	1990 Actual	1991	1992	1993	1994	1995	1996	1997	1998	1999	2000
($ Millions)											
Total assets	$3,388,461	$3,557,884	$3,735,778	$3,922,567	$4,118,696	$4,324,630	$4,540,862	$4,767,905	$5,006,300	$5,256,615	$5,519,446
Total equity	$ 218,945	$ 233,806	$ 249,606	$ 266,401	$ 284,251	$ 303,221	$ 318,382	$ 334,301	$ 351,016	$ 368,567	$ 386,995
Net income	$ 15,982	$ 19,427	$ 23,534	$ 28,012	$ 32,887	$ 38,188	$ 40,264	$ 42,453	$ 44,760	$ 47,191	$ 49,754
ROAA		0.56%	0.65%	0.73%	0.82%	0.90%	0.91%	0.91%	0.92%	0.92%	0.92%
ROAE		8.58%	9.74%	10.86%	11.94%	13.00%	12.96%	13.01%	13.06%	13.12%	13.17%
Equity/total assets	6.46%	6.57%	6.68%	6.79%	6.90%	7.01%	7.01%	7.01%	7.01%	7.01%	7.01%
(Thousands)											
Implied number employees	1,527	1,470	1,431	1,392	1,354	1,316	1,308	1,299	1,291	1,282	1,274
% change	n.a. *	- 3.7 %	- 2.7 %	- 2.7 %	- 2.7 %	- 2.8 %	- 0.7 %	- 0.7 %	- 0.7 %	- 0.7 %	- 0.7 %
Assets per employee	2.233	2,420	2,610	2,817	3,041	3,285	3,472	3,670	3,879	4,100	4,333
AGI (sales)/employee	$111.7	$120.8	$130.7	$141.5	$153.2	$166.0	$175.9	$186.5	$197.6	$209.5	$222.1
Growth rate	n.a.	8.15%	8.18%	8.23%	8.28%	8.33%	6.00%	6.00%	6.00%	6.00%	6.00%
Growth rate of AGI	n.a.	4.1 %	5.3 %	5.3 %	5.3 %	5.3 %	5.3 %	5.3 %	5.3 %	5.3 %	5.3 %
Fee income/AGI (sales)	32.3 %	32.6 %	32.7 %	32.9 %	33.1 %	33.3 %	33.5 %	33.7 %	33.9 %	34.1 %	34.3 %
Personnel expense/assets	1.55%	1.52%	1.49%	1.47%	1.44%	1.41%	1.42%	1.42%	1.43%	1.43%	1.43%
NIOE/assets	3.45%	3.41%	3.37%	3.32%	3.28%	3.23%	3.24%	3.25%	3.26%	3.27%	3.28%

*n.a. = not available.

SOURCE: 1990 Actual is from Figure 21-1. Projections are by Mercer Capital.

Exhibit 21-6
FDIC-Insured Commercial Banks Pessimistic Projection Model

	1990 Actual	1991	1992	1993	1994	1995	1996	1997	1998	1999	2000
($ Millions)											
Total assets	$3,388,461	$3,557,884	$3,735,778	$3,922,567	$4,118,696	$4,324,630	$4,540,862	$4,767,905	$5,006,300	$5,256,615	$5,519,446
Total equity	$ 218,945	$ 233,806	$ 249,606	$ 266,401	$ 284,251	$ 303,221	$ 318,382	$ 334,301	$ 351,016	$ 368,567	$ 386,995
Net income	$ 15,982	$ 19,408	$ 23,509	$ 27,994	$ 32,892	$ 38,234	$ 40,450	$ 42,792	$ 45,267	$ 47,883	$ 50,647
ROAA		0.56%	0.64%	0.73%	0.82%	0.91%	0.91%	0.92%	0.93%	0.93%	0.94%
ROAE		8.57%	9.73%	10.85%	11.95%	13.02%	13.01%	13.11%	13.21%	13.31%	13.41%
Equity/total assets	6.46%	6.57%	6.68%	6.79%	6.90%	7.01%	7.01%	7.01%	7.01%	7.01%	7.01%
(Thousands)											
Implied number employees	1,527	1,448	1,387	1,327	1,267	1,208	1,202	1,196	1,191	1,185	1,179
% change	n.a.*	− 5.2 %	− 4.2 %	− 4.4 %	− 4.5 %	− 4.7 %	− 0.5 %	− 0.5 %	− 0.5 %	− 0.5 %	− 0.5 %
Assets per employee	2,233	2,457	2,693	2,956	3,251	3,581	3,778	3,986	4,205	4,436	4,681
AGI (sales)/employee	$111.7	$122.9	$135.4	$149.3	$165.0	$182.7	$193.6	$205.2	$217.6	$230.6	$244.4
Growth rate	n.a.	10.01%	10.15%	10.32%	10.50%	10.70%	6.00%	6.00%	6.00%	6.00%	6.00%
Growth rate of AGI	n.a.	4.3 %	5.5 %	5.5 %	5.5 %	5.5 %	5.5 %	5.5 %	5.5 %	5.5 %	5.5 %
Fee income/AGI (sales)	32.3 %	32.7 %	33.0 %	33.3 %	33.7 %	34.0 %	34.3 %	34.6 %	34.9 %	35.2 %	35.5 %
Personnel expense/assets	1.55%	1.50%	1.45%	1.40%	1.35%	1.30%	1.30%	1.31%	1.32%	1.32%	1.33%
NIOE/assets	3.45%	3.38%	3.31%	3.23%	3.16%	3.08%	3.10%	3.11%	3.13%	3.14%	3.16%

*n.a. = not available.

SOURCE: 1990 Actual is from Figure 21-1. Projections are by Mercer Capital.

495

of assets or adjusted gross income each year for at least the next five years. The decade of the 1990s, then, will need to become the "Management Decade."

Implications for Bank Values

The workout from the loan problems of the 1980s will be slow and tortuous for many banks. Those who focus quickly and consistently on enhancing productivity (while continuing to serve their customers) and who can successfully reduce the risk in their loan portfolios will come closest to the mark in terms of achieving returns for their investors.

Many banks will attempt to achieve increased returns through mergers and acquisitions. We should point out, however, that merger economies are by no means automatic. Banks that merge must be willing to work hard to achieve economies. Because of their enhanced potential for economies, emphasis on intramarket mergers will increase. The necessary employment reductions will be exceedingly difficult to achieve without opportunities to consolidate branches and back-office operations offered by the merger of banks in the same or overlapping markets. Again, however, the pressure will be on bank management to turn potential economies into actual shareholder returns.

The implications of the bank modeling exercise in Exhibits 21-5 and 21-6 suggest that bank values will continue to be under pressure for the foreseeable future. That is not to say that the stock markets will not, even for periods of time, overpay for bank stocks in anticipation of mergers or takeovers. But not every bank can be acquired. Further, we believe that many of the mergers over the next few years will be at nonpremium (or low premium) prices, which will force the markets to become more discerning over time. If the markets are basically rational (even with pockets of irrationality), as we believe they are, bank stock prices will come to distinguish more clearly between banks, based upon their proven records of and outlooks for performance. Similarly, the relative values of community banks will tend to vary more in relationship to performance than they have in the recent past.

Trends in Business Appraisal

The basic trend in evidence in the business appraisal profession today is a growing focus on standards and professionalism. A portion of the emphasis is being provided externally, in reaction to FIRREA's response to the real estate appraisal crisis that was both a part of and precipitated by the thrift crisis of the 1980s. The same pressures that are requiring increased regulation of the real estate profession are increasing the focus on and regulation of the business appraisal profession by state and federal legislative and regulatory bodies.

The remainder of the trend, however, is toward increasing self-regulation by the business appraisal profession. The American Society of Appraisers, through its Business Valuation Committee, is developing standards applicable to the business appraisal profession. In Chapter 3, we briefly discussed Business Valuation Standards 1 and 2, which are reproduced as Appendix A.

Business appraisers, at least those active in the American Society of Appraisers, have also embraced the more general appraisal standards known as the Uniform Standards of Professional Appraisal Practice, which are promulgated by the Appraisal Foundation (see the discussion in Chapter 3 and in Appendix B).

The Business Valuation Committee of the American Society of Appraisers is actively pursuing the development of additional business valuation standards. Three such standards have been passed by the Business Valuation Committee and are expected to be approved by the American Society of Appraisers Board of Governors in 1992.[6] The Business Valuation Committee is currently working on additional standards for future approval and use by the profession.

Introduction to the Sample Bank Appraisal in Chapter 22

The overall purpose of the Sample Appraisal in the context of this book is to provide an example of the use of some of the techniques of analysis and the impact of some of the valuation issues discussed in the book. Its purpose is also to promote the cross-fertilization of ideas, formats, procedures, and methodologies within the appraisal profession.

The Sample Bank Appraisal is a full, written valuation report that conforms to the prevailing standards of business appraisal (see the discussion above and in Chapter 3). It is relevant to business and bank appraisers, other professionals, bankers, and other users of bank valuation reports both as an example and as a basis for comparison.

Sample Bank is not a real bank, and Sample Bancshares, Inc., is not a real holding company. We intentionally created a mid-sized bank— that is, neither a small community bank nor a regional institution—to show the general applicability of the analytical and valuation techniques discussed in the book. This bank, while not a problem bank, does provide more issues for the appraisers to address than are found in the usual appraisal situation (if, indeed, there is ever a usual situation!). These issues provide the basis for dealing with a fairly wide range of topics in the context of a single sample appraisal.

---

[6]The pending standards, which were adopted by the Business Valuation Committee of the American Society of Appraisers in June 1991, are: (1) Business Valuation Standard BVS-III, "General Performance Requirements for Business Valuation," (2) BVS-IV, "Asset Based Approach to Business Valuation," and (3) BVS-V, "The Guideline Company Valuation Method." Copies of the pending standards have been distributed to members of the American Society of Appraisers and are available from the Business Valuation Committee. For copies, write *Business Valuation Review*, 2777 South Colorado Blvd., Suite 200, Denver, CO 80222.

Chapter 22

Sample Bank Valuation

Valuation
of the
Common Stock
of
Sample Bancshares, Inc.

Anytown, Tennessee

As of
December 31, 1990

Report dated
June 30, 1991

June 30, 1991

Ms. Marie McKnight
Trustee, Sample Bancshares, Inc.
Employee Stock Ownership Plan
Sample Bank
P.O. Box 120
Anytown, Tennessee   38000

Dear Ms. McKnight:

The enclosed valuation report has been developed for your exclusive and confidential use as the Trustee of the Sample Bancshares, Inc., Employee Stock Ownership Plan, Anytown, Tennessee. The report has been prepared by Mercer Capital Management, Inc., and was made by and/or under the direct supervision of the undersigned.

The report has been prepared in accordance with the Uniform Standards of Professional Appraisal Practice and the Business Valuation Standard II (BVS-II), Full Written Business Valuation Report, of the American Society of Appraisers. In addition, the report is prepared in accordance with the proposed guidelines related to ESOPs recently published by the Department of Labor (29 CFR Part 2510, "Regulation Relating to the Definition of Adequate Consideration; Notice of Proposed Rulemaking," *Federal Register,* May 17, 1988).

Based upon the analysis of this report, it is our opinion that the fair market value of a minority interest of the common stock of Sample Bancshares, Inc., for purposes of ESOP transactions was $48.00 per share as of December 31, 1990. This valuation is valid only for the stated valuation date and for the stated purpose.

I certify that, to the best of my knowledge and belief:

1. The statements of fact contained in this report are true and correct.
2. The reported analyses, opinions, and conclusions are limited only by the reported assumptions and limiting conditions and are my personal, unbiased professional analyses, opinions, and conclusions.
3. I have no present or prospective interest in the property that is the subject of this report, and I have no personal interest or bias with respect to the parties involved.
4. My compensation is not contingent on an action or event resulting from the analyses, opinions, or conclusions in, or the use of, this report.

Thank you for this opportunity to provide valuation services on behalf of the Sample Bancshares, Inc., Employee Stock Ownership Plan.

Sincerely yours,

Mercer Capital Management, Inc.

J. Michael Julius, ASA, CFA
Vice President

Terry S. Brown, AM
Vice President

Eva M. Lang, CPA
Director of Research

JMJ/lam

Enclosure

CONTENTS

I. Introduction

Mercer Capital Management, Inc. (Mercer Capital), has been retained by the Trustee of the Employee Stock Ownership Plan (the Trustee) (the ESOP) of Sample Bancshares, Inc., (the Company or Sample Bancshares), Anytown, Tennessee, to determine the fair market value of a minority equity interest in the Company's 507,918 shares of common stock issued and outstanding as of December 31, 1990. It is our understanding that this report will be used by the Trustee for purposes of determining the price at which ESOP transactions in Company stock will occur. Mercer Capital provided an independent valuation of Sample Bancshares as of December 31, 1989, for purposes of the ESOP.

The Company's primary asset is its 100 percent ownership interest in Sample Bank (the Bank), Anytown, Tennessee. Our analysis will focus initially upon the condition and financial performance of the Bank. Factors related solely to the Company will be discussed in the Parent Company section of the report.

II. Summary Conclusion of Fair Market Value

Based upon the analysis of this report, it is our opinion that the fair market value of a minority interest of the common stock of Sample Bancshares, Inc., for purposes of ESOP transactions was $48.00 per share as of December 31, 1990. This valuation is valid only for the stated valuation date and for the stated purpose and is contingent upon the certifications in the accompanying cover letter, as well as to the statement of contingent and limiting conditions provided as Appendix A to this report.

III. Sources of Information

Historical financial information used in the preparation of this valuation report has been obtained from the Company's annual reports, which contain consolidated audited financial statements issued by Sample Bancshares for the fiscal years ending December 31, 1985–1990. During this period, the Company's financial statements were audited by the firm of Peat and Price Associates, Nashville, Tennessee (1985–1987) and Coopers and Touche Company, Chattanooga, Tennessee (1988–1990). All audits have resulted in unqualified opinions. In addition, we have reviewed:

1. Consolidated U.S. Corporation Income Tax Returns for the years ending December 31, 1986–1990.
2. Call Reports filed by the Bank with the Federal Deposit Insurance Corporation for the years ending December 31, 1984–1990, and the forms FR Y-9C and FR Y-9 LP filed by the Company with the Federal Reserve System as of December 31, 1990.
3. Uniform Bank Performance Reports, December 1987–1989 and September 30, 1990.
4. Bank Holding Company Performance Reports, December 31, 1987–1989, and September 30, 1990.
5. Written loan and investment policies for the Bank as updated in August 1990.
6. Sample Bank Capital Plan and Strategic Plan as updated in December 1988.
7. Sample Bank Employee Stock Ownership Plan document.
8. Valuation of the common stock of Sample Bancshares, Inc., as of December 31, 1989, prepared by Mercer Capital Management, Inc.; and Valuations of

the Common Stock of the Company as of December 31, 1986–1988, prepared by Other Appraisal Company, Inc.

9. Other pertinent information deemed necessary to render this valuation opinion.

In all cases, we have relied upon the referenced information without independent verification. In conjunction with the preparation of the Company's valuation, Mr. John Michael Julius, ASA, CFA, and Ms. Terry S. Brown, AM, both Vice Presidents of Mercer Capital, visited with management in Anytown, Tennessee. This visit, together with other conversations with management, provided an important perspective to our understanding of the information reviewed and analyzed in the preparation of this valuation opinion.

Market and industry data were obtained from publications of Standard and Poor's Corporation, the *SNL Bank Securities Monthly,* annual reports and other shareholder disclosure documents filed by referenced public banking companies, and press releases. Economic information and industry analyses were obtained from reviews of current publications and forecasts from a variety of sources without independent verification.

In the remainder of this report, exhibits, schedules, and text refer to comparisons made with "peer group" statistics. The peer group used for analytical purposes consists of all insured commercial banks having assets between $300 million and $500 million with three or more banking offices. The peer group data are prepared by the Federal Financial Institutions Examination Council and are provided in the Uniform Bank Performance Reports referenced throughout this appraisal.

IV. Loan Portfolio Disclaimer

We have not examined the loan portfolio of the Company or of the Bank. Direct examination would have been beyond the scope of this valuation assignment. We have discussed the general condition of the loan portfolio and several larger credits with management, focusing on such aspects as delinquencies, nonaccrual loans, geographic concentrations, industry concentrations, credit to related parties, known problem loans, and potential losses in the portfolio. Management represented that the valuation reserve for loan losses was adequate as of December 31, 1990. The valuation conclusion of this report is rendered in direct reliance upon the representations by management.

V. Definition of Fair Market Value

Fair market value is the logical framework through which an effort is made to determine the price at which the Company's common shares would trade under the presumption that a market exists. Fair market value is considered to represent a value at which a willing buyer and a willing seller, both being informed of the relevant facts about the business, could reasonably conduct a transaction, neither party acting under compulsion to do so.

Among other factors, this valuation takes into consideration the elements listed in the Internal Revenue Service's Revenue Ruling 59–60, which provides guidelines for valuation of closely-held companies, and the Department of Labor's "Proposed Regulation Relating to the Definition of Adequate Consideration," published May 17, 1988, in 53 FR 17632. These pronouncements state that a sound valuation will be based upon the relevant facts, but the elements of common sense, informed judgment, and reasonableness must enter the process of weighing those facts and determining their aggregate significance. Among the relevant factors to be considered are the following:

1. The nature of the business and the history of the enterprise since its inception.
2. The economic outlook in general and the condition of the specific industry in particular.
3. The book value of the stock and the financial condition of the business.
4. The earnings capacity of the company.
5. The dividend-paying capacity of the company and the company's history of and prospects for paying dividends.
6. Whether the enterprise has goodwill or other intangible value.
7. Sales of stock and the size of the block of stock to be valued.
8. The market price of stocks of corporations engaged in the same or similar lines of business having their stocks actively traded in a free and open market, either in an exchange or over the counter.
9. The marketability, or lack thereof, of the securities.
10. Whether the seller would be able to obtain a control premium from an unrelated third party with regard to the block of securities being valued.

VI. Historical Development of the Company

Sample Bank was formed in 1919 by a group of businesspersons from Anytown, Tennessee. The Bank is a state-chartered bank, regulated by the Tennessee Department of Financial Institutions. The Bank grew steadily up to and through the Great Depression.

Sample Bank grew unspectacularly, but steadily, through the 1940s, 1950s, and 1960s. In 1973, the Bank merged with First National Bank of Nearby, Tennessee, following rather severe problems experienced by First National. As a result, Sample Bank grew about one third in size, and assets reached approximately $150 million.

The Bank has continued to grow consistently since the merger with First National. Total assets at year-end 1990 reached $441 million.

The Bank has four offices: its main office, co-located with the Company's headquarters, the uptown branch, and the suburban drive-in branch, located across from the regional shopping mall. The fourth branch, located in Nearby, is the old main office of First National Bank.

A holding company, Sample Bancshares, Inc., was formed in 1975 as a Tennessee corporation. One share of Sample Bancshares was issued for each share of common stock then outstanding of Sample Bank. The holding company remained unleveraged until 1985. At that time, the holding company borrowed approximately $3.5 million to acquire a group of problem loans from the Bank. Those loans were collateralized by real estate, and in 1988 the underlying real estate assets were acquired in a foreclosure proceeding. During 1990, the properties were sold, and the remaining holding company debt was liquidated.

VII. Economic Conditions

National Economy

In conjunction with the preparation of this valuation opinion, we have reviewed and analyzed current economic conditions and have assessed the banking industry's outlook and how the Bank might be impacted. Our summary economic and banking industry review is contained in Appendix C.

Bank's Marketplace: The Local Economy

The principal operations of the Bank are in Anytown, Mythical County, Tennessee. The following discussion of the area economy is derived from information obtained from the Anytown Chamber of Commerce, as well as *The Complete Economic and Demographic Datasource,* published by Wilson and Poole, Inc., and the Tennessee Commission on Employment Security.

Anytown and Mythical County had estimated populations in 1989 of 49,000 and 103,000, respectively. According to data provided by the Anytown Chamber of Commerce, Mythical County population was projected to grow to approximately 108,000 by 1990. The county has a diversified economic base that includes retail and wholesale distribution, manufacturing, and agricultural concerns.

Agriculture continues to play a significant role in the county's economy. Mythical County leads the state in row-crop production of soybeans, milo, and wheat. The latest agricultural census indicates the largest crop produced is soybeans, with approximately 126,000 acres farmed in 1989.

Mythical County markets itself as a major transportation corridor and as a result has become a choice location of various manufacturers and distributors. In 1988, 95 manufacturing firms employed 14,000 people, or approximately 25 percent of the average annual labor force. Average annual wages for manufacturing employment are higher than the state average due to the types of manufacturers that have located in Mythical County. Some of the products and services manufactured and distributed include rubber-roll roofing, knitted textile fabrics, commercial printing, dairy products, and steel door frames and accessories.

Mythical County is considered to be economically stable and an area with recognized growth potential, particularly in industrial jobs. New plants and expansions in the first six months of 1990 created 2,100 new jobs, compared to 2,043 new jobs created for all of fiscal 1989.

VIII. Overview of the Bank

Bank's Marketplace: The Competition

The Bank's marketplace can be described as highly competitive for both loans and deposits. Management considers the customer base to be fairly sophisticated. According to a market share analysis prepared for management by Specialized Marketing Services, Inc., the Bank holds approximately 60 percent of the deposits domiciled in Mythical County, compared with Regional Subsidiary Bank (approximately 23 percent of total County deposits), Mega-Regional Subsidiary Bank (approximately 12 percent market share), and Farmers Bank (approximately 4 percent market share).

Although the Bank has a dominant share of its marketplace, its two major competitors are subsidiaries of much larger banking organizations that are aggressively attempting to increase their shares of the market. Nevertheless, management believes it is well positioned to take advantage of the customer loyalty and account patronage in its customer base and that market share will be maintained through the ability to remain competitive with larger institutions in the Bank's marketplace.

Management

Table 1 presents a summary of the senior officers of the Bank:

Table 1

Sample Bank Summary of Key Officers

Name	Position	Years of Service	Age
James S. Jacoby	President and Chairman	29	62
Mark R. McKnight	Executive Vice President	19	55
Larry W. Cooper	Senior Vice President and Senior Lending Officer	15	56
Robert D. Mitchell	Senior Vice President and Loan Administrator	10	47
Marie R. McKnight	Senior Vice President and Personnel Officer	23	51

Virtually all of the Bank's key officers have had long-standing relationships with the Bank. Length of service ranges from 10 years for Robert D. Mitchell, the Senior Vice President and Loan Administrator, to 29 years for James S. Jacoby, the Bank's President and Chairman of the Board. Mr. Jacoby is expected to retire in three years at the Company's mandatory retirement age of 65. By that time, it is expected that at least one senior executive will need to be hired from outside the Bank to round out the management team. No specific successor to Mr. Jacoby has yet been announced.

IX. Review of the Bank's Financial Position and Performance

We have reviewed the financial position and performance of the Bank over the relevant period of analysis. This review entailed an analysis of the Bank's current financial statements in comparison with prior years and in comparison with the peer group. Our analysis was supplemented by detailed discussions with management that enhanced our understanding of the business reasons for changes in the financial statements. Results of this review that have specific valuation implications are noted below or at the appropriate point in the valuation section of this report.

Overview

The Bank's asset growth has been moderate since the mid-1980s. Management has made a conscious effort to control growth in order to absorb losses associated with problem loans and to remain within desired capital ratios. Asset growth over the period has been driven by loan growth. Assets grew from $316 million at year-end 1985 to $442 million at year-end 1990, a compound annual growth rate of 7.0 percent. Assets grew 6.3 percent during the year just ended. Growth can be attributed in part to a healthy local economy and to the Bank's aggressive position in the marketplace.

The Bank was profitable over the period analyzed (1985–1990), although earnings have been affected in some years by higher than normal loan loss provisions, securities gains and losses, and extraordinary items. Reported net income ranged from a low of $1.3 million in 1986 to a high of $3.3 million in 1989. Earnings before extraordinary charges remained at the $3.3 million level during 1990.

Balance Sheets

Historical balance sheets, derived from the Bank's Call Reports as of December 31, 1985–1990, are provided in Exhibit 1. Percentage balance sheets, relating the components of each year's balance sheet to the corresponding level of total assets, are shown in Exhibit 2. Schedules 1 through 7 provide additional detail regarding the components of the balance sheet.

Earning Assets

Asset utilization, as measured by the ratio of average earning assets to average total assets, has fluctuated in the range of 91–92 percent. Asset utilization has eased downward since 1988 as a result of increases in nonearning assets relative to overall asset growth. Average earning assets as a percentage of average assets was 91.3 percent in 1990, which was slightly less than the peer ratio of 92.0 percent.

The mix of earning assets differs somewhat from that of the peer group. Total securities as a percentage of total assets at each year-end until 1989 were in the range of 34–36 percent, but this ratio decreased to 30.4 percent at year-end 1990, primarily as a result of growth of the loan portfolio. The peer group average was a less liquid 23.8 percent of assets. Net loans have grown (as a percentage of assets) from 47.6 percent at year-end 1987 to 55.3 percent at year-end 1990. Nevertheless, the Bank's balance sheet is considerably less "loaned up" than the peer group median level of 61.9 percent of assets. Fed Funds sold and certificates of deposit of other banks stood at 5.0 percent of total assets, or close to the peer group level of 4.6 percent of total assets.

As just noted, a shift in the mix of earning assets toward more loans has taken place since 1987. This shift occurred as the Bank began to recover from significant loan portfolio losses in the early 1980s, which continued through 1987. In addition, the securities portfolio underwent a restructuring process in 1988 that was designed to increase the portfolio's holdings of more-traditional securities.

Loan Portfolio

The composition of the loan portfolio by loan type is summarized in dollar amounts in Schedule 1 and as percentages of gross loans in Schedule 2. Total and net loans as a percentage of total assets are shown in the percentage balance sheets in Exhibit 2.

Loans, net of unearned income, grew at a compound annual rate of 9.4 percent from 1985 to 1990, which figure is somewhat higher than the rate of asset growth of 7.0 percent; and it grew 11.0 percent in 1990, which was significantly higher than the rate of asset growth. Loan volume (net of unearned income) has increased from $158 million at year-end 1985 to $247 million at year-end 1990. Growth is a function of increased loan demand and the careful balancing of the desire for a larger loan portfolio against regulatory capital constraints.

The Bank's current loan volume and policies are in part a response to a healthy local economy and an aggressive posture in the marketplace. The Bank's primary lending market is Mythical County and the southern portion of Nearby County. Management's loan portfolio strategy is to meet the lending needs of local and surrounding communities, while striving to maintain credit quality and profitability.

Real estate loans have grown rapidly in dollar terms since 1985 (18.1 percent per year) and have increased as a percentage of gross loans each year (except 1988), from 41.0 percent of loans in 1985 to a high of 60.8 percent of loans in 1990. This level of real estate loans is significantly higher than the peer median ratio of 47.2 percent of gross loans. Real estate loans are comprised almost totally of loans secured by 1–4-family residential and commercial properties, many of which are nonconforming to national secondary market standards and therefore not readily marketable. Management indicated most of the loan portfolio is priced at variable rates. Residential mortgage loans generally have fixed rates, but the portfolio is structured so that a large portion of the loans have relatively short (out to three-year) maturities or repricing opportunities.

Agricultural lending has decreased from its historical position of prominence at the Bank. Agricultural loans as a percentage of gross loans have ranged in the 4–5 percent range in recent years, considerably higher than its generally more metropolitan peer group.

The shift to real estate lending over the 1985–1990 period was offset by a relative decrease in commercial and industrial and consumer lending. Commercial and industrial loans decreased from 21.2 percent of gross loans at year-end 1985 to 16.0 percent at year-end 1990. This level of commercial and industrial loans is considerably less than the peer group ratio of 24.0 percent of loans. Consumer loans as a percentage of gross loans decreased from 22.8 percent at year-end 1985 to 16.3 percent at year-end 1990, compared to 21.7 percent for the peer group.

Quality of the Loan Portfolio

Schedule 3 presents a historical reconciliation of the loan loss reserve along with a summary of various measures of loan portfolio quality.

The Bank suffered significant loan losses, in the range of 1.2–1.5 percent of average loans, over the 1985–1987 period, compared to median losses in the range of 0.5–0.6 percent of average loans for the peer group over the same period. Net losses as a percentage of average loans have decreased each year since 1987 and fell substantially below peer averages in 1989 and 1990. Efforts by management to improve the condition of the loan portfolio reduced net losses to 0.2 percent of average loans in 1989 and 1990. Dollar volume of net loan losses decreased from $2.6 million in 1987 to $456,000 in 1990.

The ending reserve as a percentage of loans (net of unearned income) has fluctuated based on increasing loan volume and provisions required to absorb losses related to a particular year. Ending reserves as a percentage of loans decreased from an above-peer-level of 2.0 percent in 1986 to a low of 1.1 percent in 1990. Since 1988, this ratio has been somewhat below the peer group. Reserve policy is to maintain a loan loss allowance (reserve) of a minimum of 1.0 percent of the net loan portfolio. Management believes the reserve is adequate to cover known and reasonably foreseeable losses.

The decrease in the reserve parallels a substantial decrease in nonaccrual loans over the period 1986–1990, caused primarily by the reclassification of a shopping center loan to other real estate. The ratio of ending reserves to nonaccrual loans improved significantly, from 1.2x in 1987 to 3.1x in 1990.

The provision as a percentage of average loans (net of unearned income) was higher than the peer group median each year until 1987, when it decreased to below peer levels. The provision has decreased from 1.0 percent of average loans in 1987 to 0.2 percent in 1990. The current provision as a percentage of average loans is considerably less than the peer ratio of 0.6 percent.

Management attributes past problems in the loan portfolio primarily to inadequate administration. Efforts to improve credit quality include stronger documentation, increased supervision, and a more conservative lending approach.

Investment Portfolio and Other Liquid Assets

A historical analysis of investment securities and other liquid assets is presented in Schedules 4 and 5. A summary of year-end market appreciation and depreciation relative to the amortized cost basis of the securities portfolios is shown below Schedule 4.

During the period 1985–1989, the securities portfolio grew steadily from $112 million to $146 million. In 1990, however, the securities portfolio decreased 7.9 percent (to $134 million at year-end) as maturing securities were used to fund loan growth. Investment decisions are made based on the recommendations of a Board committee and are a function of the lending and liquidity needs of the Bank. The portfolio contains an assortment of short- and intermediate-term securities that are selected based on maximizing yield.

The securities portfolio has historically consisted, for the most part, of U.S. Treasury and agency securities. U.S. Treasury and agency securities comprised 24.5 percent of total assets at year-end 1990, compared to 15.6 percent of assets for the peer group median. The mix of taxable versus tax-free investments has changed as a result of efforts begun in 1987 to reduce tax-free investments. Tax-free securities decreased from 10.5 percent of total assets at year-end 1986 to 3.4 percent of assets at year-end 1990, compared with a level of 5.3 percent of assets for the typical peer group bank.

The Bank utilizes Fed Funds and interest-bearing deposits placed with other banks to meet seasonal liquidity needs. Fed Funds sold and CDs fluctuated somewhat over the 1985–1990 period and were 5.0 percent of total assets at year-end 1990. The increase (from 2.1 percent of assets in 1989) can be specifically attributed to preparation to handle a dissemination of funds by one of the Bank's larger customers; however, this portion of the liquidity portfolio is well within the normal range.

Efforts began in 1987 to reduce nontraditional holdings in the investment portfolio and to shorten maturities. Management's future policy is to focus on investments with maturities of three years or less, with no maturity exceeding five years, and to utilize the investment portfolio as a source of liquidity and secondary income.

The market value of the Bank's investment portfolio has been below its cost basis at each of the last six year-ends. The market value of the securities portfolio at December 31, 1990, was $908,000 less than amortized book value (0.7 percent). This is a considerable improvement from year-end 1989, when market depreciation totaled $4.1 million, or 2.8 percent of the total cost basis value of the portfolio. The large swing during 1990, although positive, provides evidence that historical investment decisions focused on more volatile, longer-term investments than called for by current policy. It will take several years to shorten the average maturity of the portfolio to target levels.

Fixed Assets

The Bank owns and operates a four-story building in Anytown that contains approximately 150,000 square feet. In an effort to combine lending and loan-related functions, an expansion program in 1988 doubled the existing floor space. The Bank also owns an operations building containing approximately 50,000 square feet.

The land and building occupied by the suburban drive-in branch are also owned by the Bank. The building contains approximately 5,000 square feet. Also at this location is a separate ATM facility.

The uptown branch is housed in a facility that is also owned by the Bank and contains approximately 6,000 square feet. This branch was purchased during 1988. In addition, a motor bank is located adjoining the uptown branch, and it contains a servicing facility and six remote-teller stations.

The Nearby Branch, located in Nearby, Tennessee, and a separate facility housing an ATM are also owned by the Bank.

Fixed assets stood at 3.3 percent of total assets at year-end 1990, which is more than double the peer median of 1.6 percent of assets. Increases since 1987 have been the result of remodeling and renovation of the various facilities, as well as the building of the operations building. Management believes its facilities are adequate for future anticipated growth. However, in relationship to its peer group, the Bank's earnings will be penalized for some time (because of the higher level nonearning assets and depreciation charges), until normal asset growth brings this ratio into line.

Other Real Estate Owned

Other real estate owned increased from 0.4 percent of total assets at year-end 1989 to 0.7 percent at year-end 1990, which was higher than the peer median ratio of 0.2 percent of assets. The Bank foreclosed on an apartment building in 1990, but management has several potential buyers and anticipates an orderly sale at no loss from current book value.

Deposits

The composition of the deposit base by deposit category is summarized in dollar amounts in Schedule 6 and as percentages of total deposits in Schedule 7. Demand deposits, time and savings deposits, and total deposits as percentages of total assets are shown in the percentage balance sheets in Exhibit 2.

Over the period 1985–1990, total deposits grew from $279 million to $384 million, or at a compound annual rate of 6.6 percent. Historically, the deposit base has remained stable, with concentrations in time and savings deposits. Demand deposits as a percentage of total deposits remained relatively unchanged over the period analyzed and were 12.1 percent at year-end 1990, compared to 16.8 percent for the peer group median. The explanation for this significant deviation from the peer group may lie in the greater portion of business loans in the peer group with their typical compensating balances. The Bank's deposit base appears more "retail" in nature than its peer group.

Savings deposits ranged from 20 to 25 percent of total deposits over the 1985–1990 period and were 21.3 percent of total deposits at year-end 1990. Fluctuations between the level of time deposits and money market deposits are a result of prevailing interest rates. The Bank has a loyal deposit base, but the marketplace is very competitive. Time deposits under $100,000 fluctuated in the range of 40 to 50 percent of total deposits over the period analyzed and stood at 46.4 percent of deposits at year-end 1990, compared to a much lower ratio of 32.9 percent of deposits for the typical peer bank. Again, the Bank's deposit base seems more "retail" than that of the peer group. Money market deposits decreased from 14.7 percent of total deposits at year-end 1987 to 7.0 percent of deposits at year-end 1990, which was significantly less than the peer group median ratio of 14.7 percent. Time deposits over $100,000 began an upward trend in 1986 and increased to 13.3 percent of deposits at year-end 1990, or just below the peer group average of 14.0 percent of deposits.

The Bank has a solid core deposit base with short maturities. Pricing is based on the local market and Treasury Bill rates and generally follows the competition. Management recognizes it is competing with larger financial institutions and understands that its future competitive response will have to be aggressive to attract new customers and retain its existing deposit base.

The deposit base does not contain any significant amounts of brokered deposits and government deposits are confined to the funds of area governmental bodies.

Borrowed Funds

The Bank and the peer group have similar levels of other borrowed funds and Fed Funds purchased to total assets. Funds categorized as other borrowed funds consist of the Treasury, Tax, and Loan account, and funds recorded as Fed Funds purchased are repurchase agreements. To meet the needs of corporate customers, the Bank has a "Max Account" designed to maximize the net invested positions in corporate accounts. The account provides for funds in excess of a predetermined level of collected balances to be transferred daily into a repurchase agreement. This account reduces deposit totals to some degree and distorts comparisons of deposit growth in the area. Fed Funds purchased and borrowed funds totaled 5.3 percent of assets, compared to 4.6 percent of assets for the peer group median. The Fed Funds purchased account was higher than normal at year-end 1990 because of funds in the Max Account.

Leverage and Capital Adequacy

Leverage, as measured by the ratio of equity to total assets, stood at 6.5 percent at year-end 1990, fairly close to its average level over the period of analysis and somewhat below the peer group average of 7.1 percent. Depressed earnings combined with asset growth have placed some pressure on the Bank's equity, but recent increases in retained earnings and the issuance of new stock through a purchase of shares by the parent company (see "Review of the Parent Company," below) have helped to maintain this ratio.

Capital adequacy, as measured by primary capital to total assets, has been maintained in the range of 6.9–7.4 percent for the last six years. The capital ratio is currently within management's minimum target ratio of 7.0 percent, although somewhat below the peer group average ratio of 8.1 percent.

Historical Income Statements

Historical income statements derived from the Bank's Call Reports for the years ending December 31, 1985–1990, are provided in Exhibit 3. Percentage income statements shown in Exhibit 4 relate the components of each year's income statement to the corresponding level of average total assets. Schedules 8 through 11 provide further detail from these statements. The following discussion focuses on the components of basic operating income, including net interest income, noninterest income, and noninterest expense.

Net Interest Income

Net interest income (tax equivalent) grew at a compound annual rate of 6.8 percent over the 1985–1990 period, which is just slightly less than the rate of asset growth of 7.0 percent over the same period. Net interest income (tax equivalent) increased 5.1 percent from 1989 to 1990 and totaled $17.5 million for the year ending December 31, 1990. Net interest income as a percentage of average assets reached a high of 4.47 percent in 1986, but then began a downward trend, decreasing to a low of 4.09 percent in 1990, a level somewhat below the median ratio of 4.28 percent for the peer group.

An analysis of spread relationships can be found in Schedule 8. The net spread, defined as the yield on average earning assets less the cost of interest-bearing funds, rose to a high of 4.07 percent in 1988, but has declined since then to 3.82 percent in 1990. The net spread for the peer group has also followed a downward trend since 1986. During 1988 and 1989, the Bank's cost of funds was lower than peer, but its cost of funds rose sharply during 1990 to 7.22 percent, or almost identical to the peer group median. The increased cost during 1990 was the result of a shift of funds from savings and money market deposit accounts to time deposits. Efforts to improve the net interest spread include improving asset yields through emphasis on loan growth.

The Bank has also experienced a decrease in its net yield on earning assets since 1986. The net yield on earning assets decreased from a high of 4.83 percent in 1986 to a low of 4.48 percent in 1990, which was somewhat less than the peer ratio of 4.65 percent.

In summary, the Bank's higher than peer group level asset yields are more than offset by its lower utilization ratio (see discussion above) and its lower equity and demand deposit levels, which require that a much higher portion of assets be funded by interest-bearing liabilities (82.9 percent for the Bank versus 77.7 percent for the peer group, as shown at the bottom of Exhibit 1). This discrepancy places the basic earnings stream of the Bank at some disadvantage compared to similar banks.

Noninterest Income

Excluding a nonrecurring spike in 1987, the ratio of noninterest income to average assets has risen each year since 1985, reaching 0.97 percent in 1990, a level somewhat above the peer group ratio of 0.88 percent. The 1987 rise was accounted for by a nonrecurring fee in the Trust Department. The Bank's Product and Pricing Committee, organized during 1985, monitors service charges and methods to generate additional fee income. Service fees, loan fees, and deposit account charges were increased in 1986, and then again in 1989.

Noninterest Operating Expenses

An analysis of noninterest operating expenses and employee productivity is found in Schedule 9. Other details of operating expenses in relationship to the income statement are found in Exhibits 3 and 4.

The dollar volume of noninterest operating expenses increased at a compound rate of 11.4 percent from 1985–1990, but growth in expenses slowed to 8.7 percent in 1990. Operating expenses have grown more rapidly than the Bank's underlying asset base, which, together with the spread pressure noted above, is placing pressure on operating earnings. Management is making conscious efforts to control noninterest operating expenses through zero-based budgeting, increased awareness of potential areas for staffing reductions, and bonus incentives for supervisors who meet or exceed budgeted expectations for operating income in their departments.

The Bank experienced an increase in the level of noninterest expenses as a percentage of average assets from 1985 to 1987. Noninterest operating expenses peaked at 4.11 percent of average assets in 1987. This ratio decreased in 1988 and 1989, but it rose slightly in 1990 to 3.79 percent of average assets.

Employment rose sharply until 1987, reaching 330 full-time-equivalent employees that year and peaking at 334 in 1988. Personnel expense in dollar terms escalated in 1986 (12.7 percent) and 1987 (36.0 percent). Since 1987, employment has been reduced to 314, and personnel expenses have been much more tightly controlled.

Personnel expenses have declined from 2.12 percent of average assets in 1987 to 1.84 percent in 1990. Although improving, the ratio is considerably higher than the peer group level of 1.54 percent of assets. This translates to a dollar level of personnel expenses $1.3 million above the peer group median level (assuming a peer bank at the Bank's current asset size).

All other noninterest operating expenses totaled 1.94 percent of average assets, considerably above the peer group level of 1.77 percent. Occupancy expenses increased sharply in 1989, largely as result of the completion of the new operations building and the acquisition of a new computer system. While the short-run impact of these additions reduces earnings, management believes that other expenses can be better managed with the new systems and that the Bank's ability to compete with its "big bank" local competition will be enhanced. In total, dollar operating expenses are about $2.1 million above the median level for the Bank's peer group.

As shown in Schedule 9, the Bank had 314 full-time equivalent employees at year-end 1990. The average employee supported approximately $1.4 million of banking assets. By way of comparison, the average peer bank had about 229 employees and the average level of banking assets per employee for the peer group was $1.9 million. Both the bank and the peer group have improved this measure of productivity over the period of analysis, but the improvement has been much greater for the peer group.

The cumulative impact of rapidly rising employment levels through the 1987–1988 period and the fixed asset expansion program described above leaves the Bank's level of noninterest expenses (at 3.79 percent of average assets at year-end 1990) at a significantly higher level than the peer median level of 3.31 percent of average assets. The Bank is therefore a relatively "high expense" institution. As noted earlier, management is working to bring expenses back into line with the peer group, but this process will likely take several years.

Relative "Sales" Analysis

Schedule 10 provides historical summary income statements for the analysis period as a percentage of adjusted gross income. We define *adjusted gross income* as *total taxable equivalent income less interest expense.* In effect, adjusted gross income is "net sales" for a banking institution.

The Bank's net interest income comprised 80.8 percent of adjusted gross income during 1990, and fee income provided the remaining 19.2 percent. The fee income portion of adjusted gross income has improved from 16.1 percent in 1985 to the current level in 1990, largely as result of the Bank's focus on fee income and its larger-than-normal (for a bank of its size) Trust Department. The comparable ratios for the peer group are currently 83.0 percent and 17.0 percent for net interest income and fee income, respectively. The Bank produces a relatively high portion of income in the form of fees.

The same differentials noted in the discussion of expenses in relation to average assets exist when compared to adjusted gross income. While the average peer bank spends about 64 cents to generate a dollar of "sales," the Bank is currently spending about 75 cents per dollar of sales.

Therefore, when looking at sales per employee and fee income per employee (see Schedule 9 for calculations), the Bank is significantly underperforming a bank of equivalent size operating at the peer group median level of performance.

Basic Operating Income

Basic operating income consists of net interest income plus fee income less noninterest operating expense. The Bank's basic operating income since 1985 has been affected by a number of factors, primarily rising overhead expense. After peaking in 1986 at 1.93 percent of average assets and a dollar level of $6.4 million, basic operating income has declined in both relative and absolute terms. Basic operating income totaled $5.5 million in 1990, or 1.28 percent of average assets. The peer group median ratio for basic operating income was 1.85 percent of assets.

Loan Loss Provision

The Bank experienced very high levels of loan losses during 1985–1987, resulting in high loan loss provisions in those years. The loan loss provision as a percentage of average assets has been on a downward trend since a high provision of 1.07 percent of average assets was recorded in 1986. The loss provision decreased to 0.09 percent of average assets in 1990, which is considerably less than the peer median ratio of 0.39 percent of average assets. A provision for loan losses of $400,000 is budgeted for 1991. Given the Bank's below-peer allowance for loan losses and its overall portfolio composition, the loan loss provision can likely be expected to move back toward peer levels over the coming years, placing another source of pressure on earnings.

Securities Transactions

During 1986 and 1987, earnings were supported by significant gains taken on sales of investment securities. During 1988, the Bank took advantage of an extraordinary gain (see below) to restructure a portion of the investment portfolio. Pretax losses of $702,000 were taken. Since then, gains have been taken when opportunities have presented themselves to continue the restructuring by liquidating long-term securities. Management is now attempting to minimize fluctuations in earnings resulting from securities gains or losses and does not anticipate any significant securities gains or losses in the forseeable future.

Taxes

Income tax benefits created by refunds resulting from carryforward of tax losses and unused credits in prior years have been exhausted.

Extraordinary Items

A transfer of overfunding ($890,000) from the Bank's terminated pension plan was reflected as extraordinary income in 1988. The Bank experienced a net loss of $656,000 during 1990 as a result of a lender liability lawsuit. The case is on appeal, and counsel believes there is a reasonable chance that the verdict will be overturned. Nevertheless, the loss was booked during 1990.

Return on Average Assets (ROA)

A historical analysis of ROA and a comparison with the peer group are presented in Schedule 11.

For the reasons discussed at length above, return on assets has been significantly below peer group levels (currently at 1.04 percent ROA) for the period of analysis. Exclusive of securities gains and extraordinary items, the Bank has experienced an ROA in the range of 0.75–0.80 percent during 1989 and 1990. However, the current year's results were relatively weaker than 1989 because of lower basic operating income and an unsustainably low loan loss provision.

Management is budgeting a 1.0 percent ROA for 1991. The budgeted performance would reflect a substantial improvement over recent years. However, our analysis suggests it may take two or more years to reach peer group performance in the absence of more aggressive cost reducing measures than indicated by either recent history or the 1991 budget.

Return on Average Equity (ROE)

Return on (average) shareholders' equity (ROE) is a critical determinant of the value of a banking institution. It is a driving factor in the valuation of public or private companies. Return on equity for a bank is a function of two variables: return on assets and leverage. Schedule 11 provides the historical components of return on average equity and a comparison with the peer group. In essence, it summarizes the detailed discussion above and focuses on the historical composition of ROE.

Analysis of Schedule 11 indicates that ROE has been below peer level since 1985. ROE reached a high of 12.9 percent in 1989, which was slightly less than the peer group ROE of 14.2 percent. ROE decreased to 9.3 percent in 1990 because of declines in both ROA and leverage. Adjusted for the extraordinary loss in 1990, ROE would have been 11.5 percent, still considerably below the current peer group average ratio of 14.2 percent.

Dividends at the Bank Level

The Bank paid the Company $1.3 million in dividends in 1990, or 49.3 percent of net income. On average, the Bank paid 55.9 percent of its earnings as dividends over the 1985–1990 period.

Dividend policy is a function of the cash requirements of the Company and the capital requirements of the Bank. Elimination of the holding company debt in 1990 should result in a reduction of bank dividends. Dividends of $1.1 million are projected for 1991.

X. Review of the Parent Company

Financial statements for the Parent Company Only are presented in Exhibits 5–7.

Parent Company Only total assets of the Company were $31.5 million at December 31, 1990. Assets consisted of 100 percent ownership of Sample Bank, $59,000 in cash, $2.3 million in other real estate owned, $10,000 in tax benefits receivable, $140,000 in deferred taxes, and an investment in a credit life insurance company totaling $100,000.

Proceeds from the sale of real estate owned at the parent level in 1990 were utilized to retire the Company's debt, so the Company had no outstanding liabilities at December 31, 1990, other than the ESOP debt (of $697,000), and stockholders equity totaled $30.8 million.

The Company received $1.3 million in dividends from the Bank for the fiscal year ending December 31, 1990, and earned $36,000 in other income. Equity in the undistributed earnings of the Bank was $1.3 million. Interest expense was $162,000, other expenses were $95,000, and the tax benefit of filing a consolidated federal income tax return was $143,000. Net income for 1990 was therefore $2.5 million for the Company, compared with net income of $3.2 million recorded in 1989.

Consolidated total equity exceeds the investment in Sample Bank (at equity) by $1.9 million. The excess equity at the parent company is invested primarily in other real estate. If these properties are liquidated over the next two years, as management anticipates, the holding company will have liquid assets available for reinvestment in Sample Bank to finance future growth or for investment in other opportunities. In the meantime, the real estate assets are leverageable, so the parent company is a viable source of capital for Sample Bank.

XI. Characteristics of Common Stock

Employee Stock Ownership Plan (ESOP)

The Company established the Sample Bancshares, Inc., Employee Stock Ownership Plan in August 1984, and 40,235 shares of the Company's stock and $500,000 in liquid assets were transferred to the ESOP from a previously existing profit sharing plan, which was terminated with the implementation of the ESOP. The Bank also continued to maintain a pension plan that had been in existence for about 25 years.

In late 1985, the ESOP acquired 30,000 shares from the estate of a deceased shareholder at a price of $38.00 per share. The ESOP borrowed $1.14 million from a regional bank to fund the transaction. The note had an original maturity of 10 years and a fixed interest rate of 9.5 percent. The loan was guaranteed by the Company. Contributions by the Bank have been used to amortize the loan since the purchase. At December 31, 1990, the remaining principal balance of the ESOP loan was $697,000, which is now being amortized (principal and interest) at the rate of $182,000 per year.

In August 1987, the Board adopted a resolution to terminate the Bank's pension plan. Termination of the pension plan resulted in excess assets, which were recovered by the Bank in 1988 (see the discussion of extraordinary items above).

The ESOP's assets now consist of 70,235 shares of the Company's stock, representing 13.8 percent of the total shares outstanding. At the current appraised value of $48.00 per share (see below), the ESOP's share position is worth $3.4 million. In addition to the Company's stock, the ESOP has $769,000 in cash and marketable securities.

The ESOP document contains a right of first refusal whereby shares of stock distributed to a participant may be sold to another party only after they are first offered to the Company at the price offered by the third party. A put option allows participants who receive vested shares to sell them back to the ESOP at fair market value. If the ESOP chooses not to purchase the shares, the put option passes to the Company, which is also required to repurchase the stock at its fair market value as determined by the most recent independent appraisal.

Contributions to the ESOP totaled $275,000 in 1989 and $300,000 in 1990, or at a level somewhat in excess of the debt service requirement. However, redemptions of shares of departing or retiring employees have been increasing in recent years, to $150,000 in 1989 and $175,000 in 1990. There has been no formal repurchase liability study performed on behalf of the ESOP. Nevertheless, it is clear from a cursory analysis of the age structure of the employee group that several key employees (and beneficiaries of the ESOP) will be retiring within the next few years. This will very likely create pressure to increase the annual ESOP contribution, which will place additional pressure on the Company's earnings stream. It is possible, however, that the existing debt can be restructured to smooth out the expected bulge in repurchase requirements, which could hold the annual ESOP contribution steady.

We have recommended to management that a study of the ESOP's emerging repurchase liability be performed over the next year to facilitate a clearer understanding of repurchase requirements and financing options.

Book Value

The book value (shareholders' equity, or net worth) of a company is not definitive of value for that company. Many analysts, however, use book value as a benchmark for comparison over time, and in comparison with other companies currently.

Reported book value as of December 31, 1990, was $30,781,000 or $60.60 per share for the 507,918 outstanding shares of common stock.

Asset valuation adjustments considered necessary for purposes of this analysis are presented in the valuation section of this report.

Recent Transactions

There have been numerous transactions in the Company's stock over the 1985–1990 period. When trades do occur, management is generally consulted about the fair market value of the stock at the time. Trades during the last two years have generally taken place at values at or near the then most recent appraisal.

The Company has raised approximately $2.1 million in equity through the sale of common stock in 1988, 1989, and 1990. A significant portion of the equity was the result of a dividend reinvestment plan under which shares were sold to holders making the election at a discount from the annual ESOP appraisal valuation. Additional shares were sold (at then appraised values) to certain qualified investors. The proceeds of these stock sales were downstreamed to Sample Bank to shore up its capital position.

A 5 percent stock dividend was issued in December 1990. A 10 percent stock dividend was issued in 1989. All per share figures in the text and accompanying exhibits have been restated to give effect for these stock dividends.

Current Ownership

Milton R. Tabor directly or beneficially owns 37,478 (7.4 percent) of the 507,918 outstanding shares, and Elizabeth Patton owns 15,168 (3.0 percent) of the total outstanding shares. Mr. Tabor and Mrs. Patton, who are brother and sister, own 26,070 shares in which they both hold a voting interest. These shares are included in Mr. Tabor's total number of shares. Officers and directors of the Company directly or beneficially own 39,922, or 7.9 percent, of the total shares of outstanding Company stock. The ESOP is the Company's largest shareholder, with 70,235 shares, or a 13.8 percent ownership position. Approximately 400 shareholders, none of whom own more than 5 percent of the outstanding shares, own the remaining 345,115 shares outstanding.

Dividends

Sample Bancshares has paid out 39.9 percent of its earnings as dividends, on average, over the 1985–1990 period. Management plans to increase the dividend in 1991 from $2.00 per share to $2.10 per share.

Recent Purchase Offers

Management has not received any recent offers to purchase Sample Bancshares. Occasionally, management is approached by parties interested in the Company, but no prices have ever been formally discussed. In any event, the board of directors has publicly expressed its desire that the Company remain independent for the foreseeable future.

Other Considerations

At December 31, 1990, the Company was a defendant in a lawsuit along with three other defendants, brought as a result of the sale of certain property by the Company. Counsel for the Company has provided its opinion that there will be no material loss from the litigation, other than the ongoing cost of its defense.

The Company is currently in the process of attempting to sell its other real estate owned, which is located in Nearby County. Negotiations on an option contract are underway, and management has had other inquiries regarding the sale of the property. No loss is expected on disposition, which is expected to be finalized by year-end 1992.

XII. Determination of Fair Market Value

General Approach to Valuation

The performance of Sample Bank, which has been discussed at length above, dominates the operating results of the Company. Further, there are no nonbanking operations of significance that might require individual subsidiary valuation. Consequently, we have determined that it is appropriate to develop the valuation conclusion of this analysis based upon the consolidated earning power of Sample Bancshares, Inc.

Valuation is ultimately a matter of informed judgment, based upon a full consideration of all relevant data, as well as the purposes of the valuation. Based upon our overall review, we have considered several valuation methods in the determination of value for the Company. The valuation methods actually used are discussed in the following sections.

Specific Approaches to Valuation

According to BVS-I regarding terminology, an *appraisal approach* is "a general way of determining value using one or more specific appraisal methods." An *appraisal method* is defined as: "within approaches, a specific way to determine value." Finally, an *appraisal procedure* is defined as: "the act, manner and technique of performing the steps of an appraisal method."[1]

BVS-I also defines three basic approaches to valuation for business appraisal:

1. Asset Based Approach. A general way of determining a value indication of a business's assets and/or equity interest using one or more methods based directly on the value of the assets of the business less liabilities.
2. Income Approach. A general way of determining a value indication of a business or equity interest using one or more methods wherein a value is determined by converting anticipated benefits.
3. Market Approach. A general way of determining a value indication of a business or equity interest using one or more methods that compare the subject to similar investments that have been sold.

For purposes of this appraisal of Sample Bancshares, we are using two of the basic approaches noted above to develop valuation indications for the Company. The first broad approach is the Asset Based Approach. Within this approach, we utilize the Asset Value Method, as described below.

The other broad approach is the Market Approach. Within this broad approach, we utilize two specific methods. The first method considered under the Market Approach is the Transaction Method, which involves a historical analysis of transactions in a subject company's own shares. The second method considered under the Market Approach is defined below as the Earnings (Investment) Value Method, which is based upon comparisons with a selected group of guideline public companies.

The Income Approach, which might consider methods as the Discounted Cash Flow Method or the Discounted Future Earnings Method, is not considered specifically in this appraisal. In our opinion, given the existence of the group of comparable (guideline) companies described below and in Exhibit 9, the capitalization of earning power as developed in the Earnings (Investment) Value Method below is an appropriate and sufficient earnings-based methodology for the current appraisal, taken in combination with the other valuation methods considered.

Transaction Method

When a stock is not listed on an exchange and no active market exists for it, but some transactions have occurred, a market value can sometimes be derived and used as an element in the determination of fair market value. Even if limited transactions have occurred at arm's length, inferences can be drawn about fair market value based on the limited transaction volume.

There have been numerous transactions in the Company's stock over the 1985–1990 period, and the majority of transactions have occurred at or near the annual appraised share prices. Given that transactions are made based upon the appraisal, it would be circular to base the appraisal upon the transactions.

---

[1]Business Valuation Standard "BVS-I Terminology," adopted by the ASA Business Valuation Committee, June 1988, approved by the ASA Board of Governors, January 1989 (see Appendix A of the book).

Given these facts, we have concluded that a limited market exists for the shares; but in our opinion, the transaction method is not appropriate for use in the determination of fair market value at this time because of the influence of independent appraisals upon the recent transactions prices.

Asset Value Method

The determination of asset value begins with the corporation's reported financial statements. In our opinion, strict valuation based upon stated book value is inappropriate for most banking organizations. Adjustments are made, as necessary or appropriate, to reflect the market values of the corporation's assets and liabilities, as opposed to their book values. The objective is to arrive at a net asset value, which is defined as the difference between the adjusted valuation of all assets and liabilities. Net asset value should reflect the valuation of assets and liabilities in the context of a going concern. Net asset value is not liquidation value, although it could be considered a quasi-liquidation value, where assets are sold or realized in the context of a going concern.

In our opinion, the asset value of the Company is not completely reflected in the balance sheet provided in Exhibit 5. One adjustment to audited book value of $30,781,080 is necessary to derive asset value, which is shown in Exhibit 8a under the heading "Asset Value Method." The investment in the Company was decreased by the amount of the depreciation in the securities portfolio, net of taxes at an estimated marginal effective tax rate of 38 percent, or $563,499.

Cash, other investments, notes receivable, and all liabilities were valued without discount. No adjustment was made based upon appreciated banking properties held by the Company, primarily because of their essential roles in the operations of the Company. No adjustment was made regarding the other real estate owned by the Company based upon management's representation that it is on the books at net realizable value in an orderly selling process that is currently underway.

The derivation of asset value, as shown in Exhibit 8a, is $30,217,501 as of December 31, 1990. The derivation of asset value is considered in the "Initial Determination of Value" section below.

Earnings (Investment) Value Method

The determination of value using the earnings method is a two-step process. First a determination of ongoing earning power must be made. Second, a rate must be identified with which to capitalize those earnings. It should be noted that, in our opinion, the dividend-paying capacity of the corporation is considered in the investment value method.

Determination of Ongoing Earning Power

In our opinion, the ongoing earning power of Sample Bancshares is not completely reflected in the income statements in Exhibit 7. The following adjustments to reported net income are necessary, in our opinion, to develop our estimate of ongoing earning power. The numbers below correspond to the numbered adjustments in Exhibit 8b:

1. The extraordinary loss related to the lender liability lawsuit is *added back* to reported earnings for 1990. This amount, presented net of the related income tax effect in the audited financial statements, is $655,328.
2. The net (after-tax) gain on the termination of the pension plan of $890,000 is *subtracted from* reported net income for 1988.
3. Pretax securities gains of $116,000 and $284,000 are *subtracted from* reported net income for 1990 and 1989, respectively. Pretax securities losses of $702,000 are *added back* to reported net income for 1988.

4. Interest expense is added back because the debt has been paid from the sale of assets and is not expected to be recurring.
5. The related tax effects are taken into account for the securities transactions and interest expense add-back noted in 3 and 4 above on this line. The tax effects are calculated at an effective marginal rate of 38 percent.

On an adjusted basis, ongoing earning power improved moderately from $3.17 million in 1989 to $3.23 million in 1990. The Company's debt was retired in 1990, and management does not anticipate any additional drain on earnings as a result of the renovation and remodeling of the subsidiary's facilities. In addition, major litigation in the Bank subsidiary has been resolved.

Based on the Company's improved earnings since 1988 and relatively flat earnings from 1989 to 1990, we have elected to use 1990 adjusted net income of $3.2 million as our estimate of ongoing earning power.

The determination of ongoing earning power as presented in Exhibit 8b is therefore $3,225,000. We believe this methodology reasonably estimates the Company's current level of ongoing earning power. The determination of ongoing earning power is capitalized in the "'Derivation of Earnings Value" section that follows.

Comparative Analysis to Derive a Base Capitalization Factor

One of the generally accepted methods of determining a capitalization factor is through the use of comparisons with similar companies whose stocks are publicly traded.[2] The comparative method is used below. We should mention, however, three major limitations of this approach. First, it is virtually impossible to find perfectly comparable companies. All of the companies listed in Exhibit 9 are bank holding companies, with operations centered in the Mid-South and Southeast. The comparable group is used either to provide an indication of how the public markets would treat Sample Bancshares if the market for its stock were active and public or to provide guidelines for developing appropriate capitalization rates.

Second, required disclosure for public companies notwithstanding, we are not privy to "inside" information for any of the comparable companies. Consequently, we use reported financial information without any adjustments. We believe this is proper because the impersonal market makes all necessary adjustments and reflects them in the market prices of each stock. Abnormal valuation indications from the marketplace are eliminated based upon the analysis of the comparable group below.

The third limitation results from the first two: It is left to the analyst to derive an appropriate capitalization rate for the Company based upon a review of the Company and the comparable group.

By convention, analysts express the relationship between the price of a stock and its historical earnings in the form of the ratio of current market price to the reported earnings for the most recent 12 months (i.e., the price/earnings ratio). If the industry comparable group is sufficiently homogeneous with respect to the companies selected, their recent performances, and the public market's reaction to their performance, analysts typically calculate some form of average price/earnings ratio as representative of the group.

We have chosen a group of states loosely defined as the Mid-South as the geographical area from which to develop a comparable group of regional bank holding companies. The seven states include Alabama, Arkansas, Kentucky,

---

[2]In June, 1991, the Business Valuation Committee of the American Society of Appraisers adopted Business Valuation Standard BVS-V, The Guideline Company Valuation Method. This standard is expected to receive approval from the Board of Governors of the American Society of Appraisers during 1992. The Earnings (Investment) Method as presented in this sample appraisal is in conformity with the Guideline Company Method of BVS-V. It will take some time for appraisers to fully adapt to the new terminology. As a result, the sample valuation often refers to "comparable companies" rather than "guideline companies," although the terms are considered to be equivalent by the authors of the sample appraisal and the author of this book.

Louisiana, Mississippi, Missouri, and Tennessee. The first screen for selection included all bank holding companies with total assets exceeding $1.0 billion, as identified in the *SNL Quarterly Bank Digest,* December 1990. There were 33 bank holding companies in this initial group, a number of which have only recently grown to the $1.0 billion asset size. Of the 33 banks, 23 were included in the Mid-South group found in Exhibit 9, and each state in the region was given representation.

Several of the initial banks were excluded because of recent losses or the lack of available data in the *SNL Quarterly Bank Digest,* and a few were excluded to avoid overrepresentation in any one state. In addition, because we have followed the company for several years and because data are available, First United Bancshares, Inc., of El Dorado, Arkansas, was included in the group, even though its total assets are somewhat below $1.0 billion.

Based upon the 24-bank group selected, as well as our experience in following financial institutions in the Mid-South for more than 15 years, we believe the group of 24 regional bank holding companies presented in Exhibit 9 is sufficiently representative of the region's financial institutions for use in developing market-based capitalization factors (earnings multiples) in the present valuation of Sample Bancshares, Inc. The objective is to determine the multiple at which the Company's shares would trade *if there were an active public market for the stock.*

It would be preferable from a theoretical standpoint to utilize a group of banks more nearly like the Company in size and structure. However, based upon our research and observation of financial institutions for more than two decades, no such group exists where the individual institutions have *active public markets for their shares.*

Based upon our analysis of the individual institutions and the overall market, the shares of five institutions in the group were excluded from consideration in the development of capitalization factors in the present valuation. Institutions with current price/earnings multiples that were positive, but less than 5.0x or more than 10.0x, were excluded. These screens caused the elimination of Colonial Banc-Group (Ala.), First Security (Ky.), and Mid-America Bancorp (Ky.). In addition, the two institutions reporting losses during 1990, Hibernia Corp. (La.) and First American Corporation (Tenn.), were also excluded.

We should note that only three of the considered institutions had market prices exceeding book value as of December 31, 1990, and a fourth company's shares were trading at exactly book value. The average price/book ratio for the group was 87 percent of book value, and the median was virtually identical. By way of comparison, only 5 of the 18 institutions in the considered group in 1989 had share prices under their book values at December 31, 1989, when the average price/book value ratio was 114 percent.

Clearly, the market's pricing of financial institutions' stocks deteriorated during 1990. See Appendix C for a more detailed discussion of the banking industry and for greater insight into the reasons for the decline in bank share prices. Share prices for only 2 of the 19 considered banks in the 1990 comparable group rose over the course of the year. The present ESOP appraisal must be considered in the context of the current market.

The median price/earnings ratio for the remaining 19 institutions was 7.04x related to 1990 earnings. The average price/earnings ratio was virtually identical. Based upon our overall analysis, we have considered the median price/earnings multiple of the group of 7.04x as our base capitalization factor in the present valuation. This compares with a base capitalization factor of 8.88x related to 1989 earnings for the same group one year ago, at which time the base multiple was derived similarly.

Numerous comparisons of the current and historical operating performance of Sample Bancshares, Inc., with the group of selected comparable bank holding companies are found in Exhibit 9. On balance, return measures related to average assets or average equity are considerably lower for the Company than for the comparable group, although the Company's performance is well within the range of observations for the group. As adjusted, the Company's earnings per share have grown more rapidly than the reported earnings of the comparable group since 1986, albeit from a lower performance base in 1986.

The analysis of the Company's financial performance in preceding sections indicated several sources of pressure on future earnings. Nevertheless, management is involved in several initiatives that, we believe, will overcome these pressures and allow earnings to rise over the next several years. We do not disagree with management over the direction of earnings, although we do believe that gains will come more slowly than indicated by the current budget and plans. Nevertheless, we believe that the Company's earnings will experience above-average growth over the next several years, albeit from a below-average base.

Based upon our overall analysis, we believe that the Company's earnings growth will exceed the current level of expected growth for the comparable group (which we believe to be on the order of 8 percent) for the next several years. Sample Bancshares is in an area of moderately above average growth potential. In addition, we expect management's pricing and productivity programs to push the Company's ROA to 0.80–0.90 percent over the next several years, yielding reasonably achievable growth in earnings per share on the order of 10–11 percent or a bit higher for this period.

Taking all factors of the analysis into consideration, we are using the median price/earnings multiple of the comparable group of 7.04x as the appropriate multiple for the present valuation.

Derivation of Earnings Value

Exhibit 8b presents the derivation of earnings value of Sample Bancshares for the ESOP based on the estimate of earning power and the base capitalization factor. Specifically, the ongoing earning power of $3,225,000 is multiplied by the base capitalization factor of 7.04x.

The derivation of earnings value of Sample Bancshares, as shown in Exhibit 8b, is $22,704,000 as of December 31, 1990. The derivation of earnings value is considered in the "Initial Determination of Fair Market Value" section below.

Initial Determination of Fair Market Value

Based upon the entire analysis, it is our opinion that the fair market value of Sample Bancshares should be determined by assigning appropriate weights to the values previously derived. While the weighting process may appear somewhat subjective, we believe that the collective decisions of various market participants effectively accomplish the same weighting process for individual publicly traded securities. The weights discussed below provide, in our judgment, the approximate weightings of the various indicators of value that "the market" would place on the Company if its shares were actively and publicly traded.

Exhibit 8c shows the initial determination of value of the Company as of December 31, 1990. The weights assigned to the various methods of valuation properly reflect, in our opinion, the relative importance of each particular indicator of value.

In our opinion, the earnings of a bank (or the prospects for future earnings) are of critical importance in determining value. The weighting of 60 percent placed on the earnings value method reflects our emphasis (and that of the public markets) on earnings as one of the primary determinants of value.

Asset values are also normally of significant importance in the valuation of banking institutions. When there is some uncertainty as to the future earnings of an institution or when earnings are below normal, more weight may be attached to asset values. The lower weight of 40 percent on the asset value method reflects the importance of assets in the present appraisal. This significant weighting on the higher asset value places an upward bias to the valuation indicator derived from earnings alone and effectively captures a portion of the expected earnings improvement into the current appraisal. No weight was assigned to the market value method.

Our initial determination of value for Sample Bancshares is $24,423,930 (see Exhibit 8c under the heading "Initial Determination of Value").

Although the valuation methods used and the weightings assigned are reasonable for the present valuation, in our opinion, they should not be applied rigidly from year to year. Therefore, they must be carefully reviewed for purposes of future valuations of the Company to reflect changing conditions.

Adjustment for Lack of Marketability

The valuation of shares of stock in closely-held corporations typically warrants large discounts (50 percent or more) for lack of marketability. An interest in a public company can readily be sold at or near its quoted price. Shares in closely-held corporations are not easily sold due to the lack of a public market. The marketability discount for a minority block in Sample Bancshares must reflect the lack of any established market for the closely-held shares being valued.

The ability of the ESOP and the Company to create a market for the shares mitigates the marketability discount for holders of ESOP shares. In addition, the put option provision discussed earlier affords the recipients of shares from the ESOP an additional element of marketability. In last year's report, a marketability discount of 5 percent was used based upon our overall analysis of the ESOP, the Company, and their joint ability to handle the ESOP's repurchase liabilities over the foreseeable future. A similar discount is used in the present appraisal. We will review this position next year with the benefit of a formal repurchase liability study.

Marketability is considered in Exhibit 8c under the heading "Conclusion of Total Value," and the 5 percent marketability discount is deducted from the initial determination of value.

XIII. Conclusion

Our final conclusion of the fair market value of the common stock of Sample Bancshares, Inc., is $24.4 million, or $48.00 per share as of December 31, 1990. This valuation is prepared on a minority interest basis for purposes of the Company's ESOP. The conclusion is presented in Exhibit 8c under the heading "Conclusion of Fair Market Value per Share."

The conclusion is rounded to reflect the imprecision inherent in the many valuation decisions made in its development. The conclusion represents 79 percent of the Company's book value of $60.60 per share as of December 31, 1990. The range for the companies in the comparable group is from a low of 51 percent to a high of 135 percent, with a median of 89 percent.

The Company's current dividend of $2.10 per share provides a yield of 4.4 percent based upon our conclusion of fair market value. The median dividend yield for the Mid-South (comparable group) regional bank holding companies is 5.6 percent.

XIV. Reconciliation of Value

Exhibit 8d presents a reconciliation of the current-valuation conclusion with our conclusion of one year ago, which was prepared on the same basis and for the same purpose. It was our opinion that the fair market value of the Company's shares was $50.25 per share as of December 31, 1989. The current conclusion of $48.00 per share represents a 4.5 percent decrease from the valuation as of December 31, 1989.

The major reason for the decline in value was the nearly 21 percent decrease in the base capitalization factor (from 8.88x at year-end 1989 to 7.04x at year-end 1990). A 7.5 percent increase in our earning power estimate and a 10 percent increase in asset value mitigated the decline of the base capitalization somewhat. In addition, the weighting of the asset value method was increased from 25 percent in 1989 to 40 percent in 1990. Given the substantial decline in the earnings value method (in spite of the modest *increase* in earning power), in our opinion, a higher weighting on the asset value method is now appropriate.

While the individual assumptions may not be precise, taken as a whole, the conclusion of value is reasonable, in our opinion, and meets the standards set out in the section on fair market value. The valuation has considered all of the relevant factors reviewed during our due diligence process, whether referenced in this report or not.

XV. Sample Bank Exhibits and Schedules

Exhibit 1
Sample Bank
Historical Balance Sheets ($ Thousands)
As of December 31

Assets	1990	1989	1988	1987	1986	1985	Growth Rates 1985–90	Growth Rates 1989–90
U.S. Treasury and agency securities	$108,294	$114,416	$ 87,622	$ 86,424	$ 71,560	$ 83,774	5.27%	−5.35%
State/municipal securities	15,044	16,664	25,624	18,314	36,674	23,772	−8.74	−9.72
All other securities	10,878	14,588	18,996	24,318	12,614	4,774	17.91	−25.43
Total securities	134,216	145,668	132,242	129,056	120,848	112,320	3.63	−7.86
Fed Funds sold and CDs	22,298	8,660	16,500	23,156	17,000	17,550	4.91	157.48
Loans net of unearned income	246,998	222,600	202,542	171,814	180,574	157,970	9.35	10.96
Loan loss allowance	2,742	2,822	2,538	2,752	3,580	2,034	6.16	−2.83
Net loans	244,256	219,778	200,004	169,062	176,994	155,936	9.39	11.14
Total earning assets	400,770	374,106	348,746	321,274	314,842	285,806	7.00	7.13
Cash and due from banks	14,482	21,684	22,290	17,688	19,030	14,876	−0.54	−33.21
Bank premises	14,438	11,468	7,208	4,268	3,846	4,258	27.66	25.90
Other real estate owned	3,194	1,718	2,222	3,048	4,122	2,720	3.27	85.91
Investment in unconsolidated subsidiary	0	0	0	0	0	0	0.00	0.00
Other assets	9,072	6,890	6,586	8,674	7,850	8,124	2.23	31.67
Total assets	$441,956	$415,866	$387,052	$354,952	$349,690	$315,784	6.95%	6.27%
Liabilities and Equity								
Demand deposits	$ 46,300	$ 44,136	$ 42,548	$ 39,812	$ 35,578	$ 31,854	7.7%	4.90%
Time and savings deposits	337,824	322,128	299,072	278,552	275,826	247,630	6.41	4.87
Total deposits	384,124	366,264	341,620	318,364	311,404	279,484	6.57	4.88
Fed Funds purchased	21,102	16,142	14,564	9,596	10,890	8,498	19.95	30.73
Other borrowings	2,000	2,042	3,038	1,284	2,140	2,238	−2.22	−2.06
Subordinated debt	0	0	0	0	0	0	0.00	0.00
Total acquired funds	407,226	384,448	359,222	329,244	324,434	290,220	7.01	5.92
Other liabilities	5,880	3,896	3,648	3,180	3,698	4,302	6.45	50.92
Equity	28,850	27,522	24,182	22,528	21,558	21,262	6.29	4.83
Total liabilities and equity	$441,956	$415,866	$387,052	$354,952	$349,690	$315,784	6.95%	6.27%
Average earning assets	$390,376	$367,639	$349,152	$318,851	$304,960	$277,374	7.07%	6.18%
Average total assets	427,519	399,912	377,748	346,652	329,402	303,672	7.08	6.90
Average interest-bearing funds	354,533	332,687	314,286	288,588	272,415	247,128	7.48	6.57
Average total equity	$ 28,186	$ 25,852	$ 23,355	$ 22,043	$ 21,410	$ 20,836	6.23	9.03
Average earning assets/average assets	91.31%	91.93%	92.43%	91.98%	92.58%	91.34%		
Peer group 9/90	92.04	92.04	91.71	91.34	90.90	90.82		
Average interest-bearing funds/average assets	82.93	83.19	83.20	83.25	82.70	81.38		
Peer group 9/90	77.72	77.72	76.80	76.09	75.38	74.61		
Sample Bancshares Consolidated Assets	$444,592	$420,885	$391,643	$359,332	$353,925	$319,902		

SOURCE: Call Reports and Uniform Bank Performance Reports.

Exhibit 2
Sample Bank
Historical Percentage Balance Sheets
As of December 31

Assets	1990	1989	1988	1987	1986	1985	Peer Group 9/90
U.S. Treasury and agency securities	24.5%	27.5%	22.6%	24.3%	20.5%	26.5%	15.6%
State/municipal securities	3.4	4.0	6.6	5.2	10.5	7.5	5.3
All other securities	2.5	3.5	4.9	6.9	3.6	1.5	2.9
Total securities	30.4	35.0	34.2	36.4	34.6	35.6	23.8
Fed Funds sold and CDs	5.0	2.1	4.3	6.5	4.9	5.6	4.6
Loans net of unearned income	55.9	53.5	52.3	48.4	51.6	50.0	62.7
Loan loss allowance	0.6	0.7	0.7	0.8	1.0	0.6	0.8
Net loans	55.3	52.8	51.7	47.6	50.6	49.4	61.9
Total earning assets	90.7	90.0	90.1	90.5	90.0	90.5	90.4
Cash and due from banks	3.3	5.2	5.8	5.0	5.4	4.7	5.7
Bank premises	3.3	2.8	1.9	1.2	1.1	1.3	1.6
Other real estate owned	0.7	0.4	0.6	0.9	1.2	0.9	0.2
Investment in unconsolidated subsidiary	0.0	0.0	0.0	0.0	0.0	0.0	0.0
Other assets	2.1	1.7	1.7	2.4	2.2	2.6	2.1
Total assets	100.0%	100.0%	100.0%	100.0%	100.0%	100.0%	100.0%
Liabilities and equity							
Demand deposits	10.5%	10.6%	11.0%	11.2%	10.2%	10.1%	14.5%
Time and savings deposits	76.4	77.5	77.3	78.5	78.9	78.4	72.1
Total deposits	86.9	88.1	88.3	89.7	89.1	88.5	86.6
Fed Funds purchased	4.8	3.9	3.8	2.7	3.1	2.7	4.0
Other borrowings	0.5	0.5	0.8	0.4	0.6	0.7	0.6
Subordinated debt	0.0	0.0	0.0	0.0	0.0	0.0	0.0
Total acquired funds	92.1	92.4	92.8	92.8	92.8	91.9	91.2
Other liabilities	1.3	0.9	0.9	0.9	1.1	1.4	1.7
Equity	6.5	6.6	6.2	6.3	6.2	6.7	7.1
Total liabilities and equity	100.0%	100.0%	100.0%	100.0%	100.0%	100.0%	100.0%
Earnings assets/interest-bearing funds	110.11%	110.51%	111.09%	110.49%	111.95%	112.24%	
Average assets/average equity	15.17%	15.47%	16.17%	15.73%	15.39	14.28%	
Equity capital/total assets	6.53%	6.62%	6.25%	6.35%	6.16%	6.73%	
Peer group 9/90	7.13%	7.13%	7.11%	7.13%	6.64%	6.81%	
Primary capital/total assets	7.15%	7.30%	6.90%	7.12%	7.19%	7.38%	
Peer Group 9/90	8.07%	8.07%	7.98%	8.04%	7.66%	7.67%	

SOURCE: Call Reports and Uniform Bank Performance Reports.

Exhibit 3
Sample Bank
Historical Income Statements ($ Thousands)
For the Fiscal Years Ending December 31

	1990	1989	1988	1987	1986	1985	Growth Rates 1985–90	Growth Rates 1989–90
Interest Income								
Taxable loans	$29,754	$24,080	$20,664	$20,798	$21,194	$20,804	7.42%	23.56%
Tax-free loans	396	552	390	274	324	388	0.41	−28.26
Fed Funds sold and CDs	948	1,400	1,532	1,174	1,572	1,458	−8.25	−32.29
Taxable securities	10,212	9,598	9,792	9,354	9,438	9,110	2.31	6.40
Tax-free securities	1,028	1,158	1,598	1,594	1,736	1,434	−6.44	−11.23
Estimated tax benefit	734	881	1,024	1,245	1,755	1,552	−13.92	−16.73
Other interest income	0	0	0	0	0	0	0.00	0.00
Total interest income (FTE)	$43,072	$37,669	$35,000	$34,439	$36,019	$34,746	4.39	14.34
Interest Expense								
Large CDs	$ 3,892	$ 2,546	$ 1,984	$1,986	$ 1,686	$ 2,136	12.75%	52.87%
Other deposits	20,352	17,536	15,796	16,740	18,758	19,298	1.07	16.06
Fed Funds purchased	1,190	808	802	612	740	608	14.37	47.28
Other interest expense	156	138	126	112	112	144	1.61	13.04
Total interest expense	$25,590	$21,028	$18,708	$19,450	$21,296	$22,186	2.90	21.69
Net interest income (FTE)	17,482	16,641	16,292	14,989	14,723	12,560	6.84	5.05
Other Income								
Service charges deposit accounts	$ 1,886	$ 1,606	$ 1,278	$ 1,160	$ 1,262	$ 988	13.80%	17.43%
Other operating income	2,274	2,232	2,162	2,824	1,594	1,420	9.88	1.88
Total other income	$ 4,160	$ 3,838	$ 3,440	$ 3,984	$ 2,856	$ 2,408	11.55	8.39
Adjusted gross income (FTE)	21,642	20,479	19,732	18,973	17,579	14,968	7.65	5.68
Noninterest Operating Expense								
Salaries and benefits	$ 7,858	$ 7,404	$ 7,660	$ 7,336	$ 5,394	$ 4,788	10.42%	6.13%
Net occupancy	4,124	3,674	2,554	2,384	2,278	1,800	18.03	12.25
Other operating expense	4,200	3,816	4,836	4,516	3,540	2,856	8.02	10.06
Total noninterest operating expense	$16,182	$14,894	$15,050	$14,236	$11,212	$9,444	11.37	8.65
Basic operating income (FTE)	5,460	5,585	4,682	4,737	6,367	5,524	−0.23	−2.24
Security transactions	$ 116	$ 284	− 702	$ 890	$ 302	$ 44	21.40%	−59.15%
Loan loss provision	376	714	676	1,776	3,532	1,902	−27.69	−47.34
Pretax income (FTE)	5,200	5,155	3,304	3,851	3,137	3,666	7.24	0.87
FTE adjustment	734	881	1,024	1,245	1,755	1,552	−13.92	−16.73
Pretax income	4,466	4,274	2,280	2,606	1,382	2,114	16.13	4.49
Taxes	1,192	948	274	206	102	182	45.63	25.74
Income before extra items	3,274	3,326	2,006	2,400	1,280	1,932	11.13	−1.56
Net extraordinary items	−656	0	890	0	0	0	n.m.*	n.m.
Net income	$ 2,618	$ 3,326	$ 2,896	$ 2,400	$ 1,280	$ 1,932	6.27%	−21.29%
Total dividends	1,290	1,586	1,750	1,430	984	800	10.03%	−18.66%
Dividend payout rate	49.27%	47.68%	60.43%	59.58%	76.87%	41.41%	n.m.	n.m.
Peer group dividend payout	n.a.†	50.28%	40.11%	37.21%	38.47%	34.96%	n.m.	n.m.

*n.m. = not meaningful.
†n.a. = not applicable.

SOURCE: Call Reports and Uniform Bank Performance Reports.

Exhibit 4
Sample Bank
Historical Income Statements as a Percentage of Average Assets
For the Fiscal Years Ending December 31

	1990	1989	1988	1987	1986	1985	Peer Group 9/90
Interest Income							
Taxable loans	6.96%	6.02%	5.47%	6.00%	6.43%	6.85%	—
Tax-free loans	0.09	0.14	0.10	0.08	0.10	0.13	—
Fed Funds sold and CDs	0.22	0.35	0.41	0.34	0.48	0.48	—
Taxable securities	2.39	2.40	2.59	2.70	2.87	3.00	—
Tax-free securities	0.24	0.29	0.42	0.46	0.53	0.47	—
Estimated tax benefit	0.17	0.22	0.27	0.36	0.53	0.51	—
Other interest income	0.00	0.00	0.00	0.00	0.00	0.00	—
Total interest income (FTE)	10.07	9.42	9.27	9.93	10.93	11.44	9.90%
Interest Expense							
Large CDs	0.91%	0.64%	0.53%	0.57%	0.51%	0.70%	—
Other deposits	4.76	4.38	4.18	4.83	5.69	6.35	—
Fed Funds purchased	0.28	0.20	0.21	0.18	0.22	0.20	—
Other interest expense	0.04	0.03	0.03	0.03	0.03	0.05	—
Total interest expense	5.99	5.26	4.95	5.61	6.47	7.31	5.62
Net interest income (FTE)	4.09	4.16	4.31	4.32	4.47	4.14	4.28
Other Income							
Service charges deposit accounts	0.44%	0.40%	0.34%	0.33%	0.38%	0.33%	—
Other operating income	0.53	0.56	0.57	0.81	0.48	0.47	—
Total other income	0.97	0.96	0.91	1.15	0.87	0.79	0.88
Adjusted gross income (FTE)	5.06	5.12	5.22	5.47	5.34	4.93	5.16
Noninterest Operating Expense							
Salaries and benefits	1.84%	1.85%	2.03%	2.12%	1.64%	1.58%	1.54%
Net occupancy	0.96	0.92	0.68	0.69	0.69	0.59	0.49
Other operating expense	0.98	0.95	1.28	1.30	1.07	0.94	1.28
Total noninterest operating expense	3.79	3.72	3.98	4.11	3.40	3.11	3.31
Basic operating income (FTE)	1.28	1.40	1.24	1.37	1.93	1.82	1.85
Security transactions	0.03%	0.07%	-0.19%	0.26%	0.09%	0.01%	0.01%
Loan loss provision	0.09	0.18	0.18	0.51	1.07	0.63	0.39
Pretax income (FTE)	1.22	1.29	0.87	1.11	0.95	1.21	1.47
FTE adjustment	0.17	0.22	0.27	0.36	0.53	0.51	n.a.*
Pretax income	1.04	1.07	0.60	0.75	0.42	0.70	1.47
Taxes	0.28	0.24	0.07	0.06	0.03	0.06	0.44
Income before extra items	0.77	0.83	0.53	0.69	0.39	0.64	1.03
Net extraordinary items	-0.15	0.00	0.24	0.00	0.00	0.00	0.01
Net income (ROAA)	0.61%	0.83%	0.77%	0.69%	0.39%	0.64%	1.04%
Peer group ROAA 9/90	1.04%	1.04%	1.04%	1.04%	1.05%	1.03%	
Return on average equity	9.29	12.87	12.40	10.89	5.98	9.27	
Peer group ROAE 9/90	14.21	14.21	14.38	14.41	15.05	14.89	

*n.a. = not applicable.

SOURCE: Call Reports and Uniform Bank Performance Reports.

Schedule 1
Sample Bank
Loan Portfolio Composition ($ Thousands)
As of December 31

Loan Category	1990	1989	1988	1987	1986	1985	Growth Rates 1985-90	1989-90
Construction and development	$ 12,192	$ 7,016	$ 7,878	$ 6,038	$ 4,818	$ 3,754	26.57%	73.77%
1-4-family residential	71,000	57,821	42,861	38,594	33,690	24,901	23.31	22.79
Other real estate	67,894	69,521	64,487	56,258	54,514	36,995	12.91	-2.34
Total real estate	151,086	134,357	115,225	100,889	93,021	65,650	18.14	12.45
Financial institution and BAs	1,556	1,894	8,586	0	0	5,188	-21.40	-17.85
Agricultural	10,970	8,030	9,626	7,362	9,544	8,848	4.39	36.61
Commercial/industrial	39,710	30,382	22,538	19,258	33,262	33,954	3.18	30.70
Consumer	40,500	37,462	34,274	34,872	40,530	36,540	2.08	8.11
All other	4,856	12,048	13,722	10,940	6,408	10,028	-13.50	-59.69
Gross loans	248,678	224,173	203,971	173,321	182,765	160,208	9.19	10.93
Unearned income (−)	-1,680	-1,573	-1,429	-1,707	-2,191	-2,238	n.m.*	n.m.
Loans net of unearned income	$246,998	$222,600	$202,542	$171,614	$180,574	$157,970	9.35%	10.96%
Total loans net of unearned income/total assets	55.89%	53.53%	52.33%	48.40%	51.64%	50.02%		
Peer group 9/90	62.72%	62.72%	62.37%	60.64%	59.51%	58.38%		
Loan/deposit ratio	64.30%	60.78%	59.29%	53.97%	57.99%	56.52%		

*n.m. = not meaningful.

SOURCE: Call Reports and Uniform Bank Performance Reports.

Schedule 2
Sample Bank
Loan Portfolio Composition as a Percentage of Gross Loans
As of December 31

Loan Category	1990	1989	1988	1987	1986	1985	Peer Group 9/90
Construction and development	4.9%	3.1%	3.9%	3.5%	2.6%	2.3%	4.4%
1-4-family residential	28.6	25.8	21.0	22.3	18.4	15.5	24.1
Other real estate	27.3	31.0	31.6	32.5	29.8	23.1	18.6
Total real estate	60.8	59.9	56.5	58.2	50.9	41.0	47.2
Financial institution and BAs	0.6	0.8	4.2	0.0	0.0	3.2	0.1
Agricultural	4.4	3.6	4.7	4.2	5.2	5.5	0.5
Commercial/industrial	16.0	13.6	11.0	11.1	18.2	21.2	24.0
Consumer	16.3	16.7	16.8	20.1	22.2	22.8	21.7
All other	2.0	5.4	6.7	6.3	3.5	6.3	6.5
Gross loans	100.0%	100.0%	100.0%	100.0%	100.0%	100.0%	100.0%

SOURCE: Call Reports and Uniform Bank Performance Reports.

533

Schedule 3
Sample Bank
Loan Portfolio Quality ($ Thousands)
As of December 31

Loan Loss Reserve Reconciliation	1990	1989	1988	1987	1986	1985
Beginning balance	$2,822	$2,538	$2,752	$3,580	$2,034	$2,004
Net charge-offs						
Gross loan losses	816	1,088	1,228	3,568	2,446	2,418
Recoveries	360	658	338	966	460	546
Other adjustments	0	0	0	0	0	0
Net charge-offs	456	430	890	2,602	1,986	1,872
Provision	376	714	676	1,776	3,532	1,902
Ending reserve	2,742	2,822	2,538	2,754	3,580	2,034
Nonaccrual loans	888	1,428	1,074	2,364	2,468	1,376
Ending other real estate owned	$3,194	$1,718	$2,222	$3,048	$4,122	$2,720
Ending reserve/loans (%)*						
Bank	1.11%	1.27%	1.25%	1.60%	1.98%	1.29%
Peer group 9/90	1.30%	1.30%	1.31%	1.25%	1.20%	1.17%
Net losses/average loans (%)*						
Bank	0.19%	0.20%	0.48%	1.48%	1.17%	1.24%
Peer group 9/90	0.51%	0.51%	0.43%	0.49%	0.59%	0.56%
Nonaccrual loans/total loans (%)						
Bank	0.36%	0.64%	0.53%	1.37%	1.37%	0.87%
Peer group 9/90	0.58%	0.58%	0.50%	0.47%	0.47%	0.64%
Provision/average loans (×)*						
Bank	0.16	0.34	0.36	1.01	2.09	1.26
Peer group 9/90	0.60	0.60	0.51	0.63	0.75	0.71
Ending reserve/nonaccrual loans (×)						
Bank	3.09	1.98	2.36	1.16	1.45	1.48
Peer group 9/90	2.24	2.24	2.61	2.68	2.57	1.84
Ending reserve/ORE (×)						
Bank	0.86	1.64	1.14	0.90	0.87	0.75
Peer group 9/90	5.06	5.06	5.27	5.00	3.65	3.00

*Net of unearned income.

SOURCE: Call Reports and Uniform Bank Performance Reports.

Schedule 4
Sample Bank
Liquid Assets ($ Thousands)
As of December 31

Liquid Assets	1990	1989	1988	1987	1986	1985	Growth Rates 1985-90	Growth Rates 1989-90
U.S. Treasury and agencies	$108,294	$114,416	$87,622	$86,424	$71,560	$83,774	5.27%	-5.35%
Tax-free securities	15,044	16,664	25,624	18,314	36,674	23,772	-8.74	-9.72
Other	10,878	14,588	18,996	24,318	12,614	4,774	17.91	-25.43
Total securities	134,216	145,668	132,242	129,056	120,848	112,320	3.63	-7.86
Fed Funds sold and CDs	22,298	8,660	16,500	23,156	17,000	17,550	4.91	157.48
Total liquid earning assets	156,514	154,328	148,742	152,212	137,848	129,870	3.80	1.42
Cash and due from banks	14,482	21,684	22,290	17,688	19,030	14,876	-0.54	-33.21
Total liquid assets	$170,996	176,012	$171,032	$169,900	$156,878	$144,746	-3.39%	-2.85%
Market appreciation/-depreciation in securities portfolio ($000)								
Bank (%)	$ -908 / -0.68%	$ -4,096 / -2.81%	$ -3,436 / -2.60%	$ 1,696 / 1.31%	$ -1,036 / -0.86%	$ -4,684 / -4.17%		
Peer group 9/90 (%)	-1.00%	0.70%	-1.29%	-0.44%	2.89%	0.87%		

Schedule 5
Sample Bank
Liquid Assets as a Percentage of Total Assets
As of December 31

Percent of Average Total Assets

Liquid Assets	1990	1989	1988	1987	1986	1985	Peer Group 9/90
U.S. Treasury and agencies	24.5%	27.5%	22.6%	24.3%	20.5%	26.5%	15.6%
Tax-free securities	3.4	4.0	6.6	5.2	10.5	7.5	5.3
Other	2.5	3.5	4.9	6.9	3.6	1.5	2.9
Total securities	30.4	35.0	34.2	36.4	34.6	35.6	23.8
Fed Funds sold and CDs	5.0	2.1	4.3	6.5	4.9	5.6	4.6
Total liquid earning assets	35.4	37.1	38.4	42.9	39.4	41.1	28.4
Cash and due from banks	3.3	5.2	5.8	5.0	5.4	4.7	5.7
Total liquid assets	38.7%	42.3%	44.2%	47.9%	44.9%	45.8%	34.2%

SOURCE: Call Reports and Uniform Bank Performance Reports.

Schedule 6
Sample Bank
Deposit Base Composition ($ Thousands)
As of December 31

Deposit Category	1990	1989	1988	1987	1986	1985	Growth Rates 1985–90	1989–90
Demand deposits	$ 46,300	$ 44,136	$ 42,548	$ 39,812	$ 35,578	$ 31,854	7.77%	4.90%
Regular savings and NOW	81,942	87,730	83,822	70,376	62,740	70,954	2.92	–6.60
Time deposits under $100,000	178,126	156,646	143,226	129,992	161,486	123,326	7.63	13.71
MMDA and SuperNOW	26,804	33,708	36,302	46,702	39,120	36,632	–6.06	–20.48
Time deposits over $100,000	50,952	44,044	35,722	31,482	12,480	16,718	24.97	15.68
Total deposits	$384,124	$366,264	341,620	$318,364	$311,404	$279,484	6.57%	4.88%

Schedule 7
Sample Bank
Deposit Base Composition as a Percentage of Total Deposits
As of December 31

Deposit Category	1990	1989	1988	1987	1986	1985	Peer Group 9/90
Demand deposits	12.1%	12.1%	12.5%	12.5%	11.4%	11.4%	16.8%
Regular savings and NOW	21.3	24.0	24.5	22.1	20.1	25.4	21.6
Time deposits under $100,000	46.4	42.8	41.9	40.8	51.9	44.1	32.9
MMDA and SuperNOW	7.0	9.2	10.6	14.7	12.6	13.1	14.7
Time deposits over $100,000	13.3	12.0	10.5	9.9	4.0	6.0	14.0
Total deposits	100.0%	100.0%	100.0%	100.0%	100.0%	100.0%	100.0%

SOURCE: Call Reports and Uniform Bank Performance Reports.

Schedule 8
Sample Bank
Spread Relationships
For the Years Ending December 31

	1990	1989	1988	1987	1986	1985
Bank						
Interest income (FTE)/average assets	10.07%	9.42%	9.27%	9.93%	10.93%	11.44%
Interest expense/average assets	5.99	5.26	4.95	5.61	6.47	7.31
Net interest income (FTE)/average assets	4.09%	4.16%	4.31%	4.32%	4.47%	4.14%
Peer group 9/90						
Interest income (FTE)/average assets	9.90	9.90	9.13	9.01	9.71	10.56
Interest expense/average assets	5.62	5.62	4.89	4.60	5.04	5.79
Net interest income (FTE)/average assets	4.28%	4.28%	4.24%	4.41%	4.67%	4.77%
Bank						
Yield on average earning assets (FTE)	11.03	10.25	10.02	10.80	11.81	12.53
Cost of interest-bearing funds	7.22	6.32	5.95	6.74	7.82	8.98
Net spread (FTE)	3.82%	3.93%	4.07%	4.06%	3.99%	3.55%
Peer group 9/90						
Yield on average earning assets (FTE)	10.76	10.76	9.97	9.90	10.71	11.64
Cost of interest-bearing funds	7.23	7.23	6.36	6.00	6.66	7.76
Net spread (FTE)	3.53%	3.53%	3.61%	3.90%	4.05%	3.88%
Bank						
Yield on average earning assets (FTE)	11.03	10.25	10.02	10.80	11.81	12.53
Cost of average earning assets	6.56	5.72	5.36	6.10	6.98	8.00
Net yield on earning assets (FTE)	4.48%	4.53%	4.67%	4.70%	4.83%	4.53%
Peer group 9/90						
Yield on average earning assets (FTE)	10.76	10.76	9.97	9.90	10.71	11.64
Cost of average earning assets	6.11	6.11	5.33	5.02	5.55	6.40
Net yield on earning assets (FTE)	4.65%	4.65%	4.64%	4.88%	5.16%	5.24%
Average earning assets/average assets	91.31%	91.93%	92.43%	91.98%	92.58%	91.34%
Peer group 9/90	92.04	92.04	91.71	91.34	90.90	90.82
Average interest-bearing funds/average assets	82.93%	83.19%	83.20%	83.25%	82.70%	81.38%
Peer group 9/90	77.72	77.72	76.80	76.09	75.38	74.61

SOURCE: Call Reports and Uniform Bank Performance Reports.

Schedule 9
Sample Bank
Noninterest Expenses and Bank Productivity
For the Years Ending December 31

Noninterest Expenses	1990 ($ 000)	Percent of Average Total Assets						Peer Group 9/90
		1990	1989	1988	1987	1986	1985	
Personnel	$ 7,858	1.84%	1.85%	2.03%	2.12%	1.64%	1.58%	1.54%
Occupancy	4,124	0.96	0.92	0.68	0.69	0.69	0.59	0.49
Other	4,200	0.98	0.95	1.28	1.30	1.07	0.94	1.28
Noninterest operating expenses	16,182	3.79	3.72	3.98	4.11	3.40	3.11	3.31
Loan loss provision	376	0.09	0.18	0.18	0.51	1.07	0.63	0.39
Noninterest expenses	$16,558	3.87%	3.90%	4.16%	4.62%	4.48%	3.74%	3.70%
Average assets ($ 000)		$427,519	$399,912	$377,748	$346,652	$329,402	$303,672	
Noninterest operating expenses		$ 16,182	$ 14,894	$ 15,050	$ 14,236	$ 11,212	$ 9,444	
Number of employees		314	306	334	330	284	266	
Peer group†		229	214	211	206	201	207	
Personnel expense/employee ($ 000)								
Bank		$ 25.03	$ 24.20	$ 22.93	$ 22.23	$ 18.99	$ 18.00	
Peer group 9/90		$ 26.30	$ 26.30	$ 25.26	$ 24.45	$ 23.02	$ 22.47	
Average assets/employee ($ 000)								
Bank		$ 1,362	$ 1,307	$ 1,131	$ 1,050	$ 1,160	$ 1,142	
Peer group 9/90		$ 1,870	$ 1,870	$ 1,790	$ 1,680	$ 1,640	$ 1,470	
Fee income/employee ($ 000)								
Bank		$ 13,248	$ 12,542	$ 10,299	$ 12,073	$ 10,056	$ 9,053	
Peer group 9/90		$ 16,429	n.a. *	n.a.	n.a.	n.a.	n.a.	
Adjusted gross income/employee ($ 000)								
Bank		$ 68,922	$ 66,925	$ 59,078	$ 57,495	$ 61,897	$ 56,271	
Peer group 9/90		$ 96,332	n.a.	n.a.	n.a.	n.a.	n.a.	
Noninterest operating expense/employee ($ 000)								
Bank		$ 51,535	$ 48,673	$ 45,060	$ 43,139	$ 39,479	$ 35,504	
Peer group 9/90		$ 61,794	n.a.	n.a.	n.a.	n.a.	n.a.	
Effective tax rate (taxes/pretax income)		26.69%	22.18%	12.02%	7.90%	7.38%	8.61%	

*n.a. = not applicable.
†Equivalent peer bank size based on the bank's average total assets: $427,519 $399,912 $377,748 $346,652 $329,402 $303,672

SOURCE: Call Reports and Uniform Bank Performance Reports.

Schedule 10
Sample Bank
Summary Income Statement as a Percentage of Adjusted Gross Income for the Years Ending December 31

	1990	1989	1988	1987	1986	1985	Peer Group 9/90
Net interest income	80.78%	81.26%	82.57%	79.00%	83.75%	83.91%	82.95%
Fee income	19.22	18.74	17.43	21.00	16.25	16.09	17.05
Adjusted gross income (sales)	100.00%	100.00%	100.00%	100.00%	100.00%	100.00%	100.00%
Noninterest expenses							
Personnel	36.31	36.15	38.82	38.66	30.68	31.99	29.84
Occupancy	19.06	17.94	12.94	12.57	12.96	12.03	9.50
Other	19.41	18.63	24.51	23.80	20.14	19.08	24.81
Noninterest operating expense	74.77%	72.73%	76.27%	75.03%	63.78%	63.09%	64.15%
Basic operating income	25.23	27.27	23.73	24.97	36.22	36.91	35.85
Securities transactions	0.54	1.39	−3.56	4.69	1.72	0.29	0.19
Loan loss provision	1.74	3.49	3.43	9.36	20.09	12.71	7.56
Pretax income	24.03%	25.17%	16.74%	20.30%	17.84%	24.49%	28.49%

SOURCE: Call Reports and Uniform Bank Performance Reports.

Schedule 11
Sample Bank
Historical Return on Average Equity for the Years Ending December 31

Components of ROAE	Percent of Average Total Assets						Peer Group 9/90
	1990	1989	1988	1987	1986	1985	
Basic operating income (FTE)	1.28%	1.40%	1.24%	1.37%	1.93%	1.82%	1.85%
+ Securities transactions	0.03	0.07	−0.19	0.26	0.09	0.01	0.01
− Loan loss provision	−0.09	−0.18	−0.18	−0.51	−1.07	−0.63	−0.39
− FTE adjustment	−0.17	−0.22	−0.27	−0.36	−0.53	−0.51	n.a.
− Taxes	−0.28	−0.24	−0.07	−0.06	−0.03	−0.06	−0.44
+ Net extraordinary items	−0.15	0.00	0.24	0.00	0.00	0.00	0.01
= Return on average assets	0.61	0.83	0.77	0.69	0.39	0.64	1.04
× Average assets/average equity	15.17	15.47	16.17	15.73	15.39	14.28	14.03
= Return on average equity	9.29%	12.87%	12.40%	10.89%	5.98%	9.09%	14.21%
Peer group ROAE	14.21%	14.21%	14.38%	14.41%	15.05%	14.89%	
Peer group ROAA	1.04%	1.04%	1.04%	1.05%	1.03%		

SOURCE: Call Reports and Uniform Bank Performance Reports.

Schedule 12
Sample Bank
Changes in Equity Capital ($ Thousands) for the Years Ending December 31

	1990	1989	1988	1987	1986	1985
Beginning equity capital	$27,522	$24,182	$22,528	$21,558	$21,262	$20,410
Net income (loss)	2,618	3,326	2,896	2,400	1,280	1,932
Net sale, conversion, acquisition, retirement of stock						
Preferred stock	0	0	0	0	0	0
Common stock	0	1,600	400	0	0	0
Cash dividends, preferred stock	0	0	0	0	0	0
Cash dividends, common stock	−1,290	−1,586	−1,750	−1,430	−984	−800
Cumulative effect of change in accounting principles	0	0	0	0	0	0
Change in net unrealized loss on marketable equity securities	0	0	0	0	0	0
Other adjustments	0	0	108	0	0	−280
Ending equity capital	$28,850	$27,522	$24,182	$22,528	$21,558	$21,262
Dividend payout ratio	49.27%	47.68%	60.43%	59.58%	76.87%	41.41%

SOURCE: Audited financial statements, Call Reports and Uniform Bank Performance Reports.

XVI. Sample Bancshares, Inc., Exhibits and Valuation

Exhibit 5
Sample Bancshares, Inc.
Parent Company Only Historical Balance Sheet ($ Thousands)
As of December 31

Assets	1990	1989	1988	1987	1986	1985	Growth Rates	
							1985–90	1989–90
Cash	$ 59	$ 18	$ 16	$ 59	$ 90	$ 4	73.14%	237.85%
Investment in subsidiary†	28,846	27,518	24,180	22,527	21,559	21,263	6.29	4.83
Real estate owned	2,323	4,512	4,471	0	0	0	n.m.*	−48.51
Loans receivable	0	0	0	3,559	3,559	3,559	n.m.	0.00
Accrued interest receivable	0	0	0	604	604	483	n.m.	0.00
Other assets	250	234	263	324	195	184	6.28	6.68
Total assets	$ 31,478	$ 32,281	$ 28,930	$ 27,072	$ 26,007	$ 25,493	4.31%	− 2.49%
Liabilities and Equity								
ESOP debt	$ 697	$ 802	$ 899	$ 987	$ 1,067	$ 1,140	38.43%	13.09%
Long-term debt	0	2,284	2,801	3,315	3,572	3,572	n.m.	−100.00
Accrued interest payable	0	22	23	22	72	89	n.m.	−100.00
Other liabilities	0	48	79	31	34	16	n.m.	−100.00
Total liabilities	$ 697	$ 3,156	$ 3,801	$ 4,355	$ 4,744	$ 4,816	−32.06%	−77.91%
Stockholders' Equity								
Common stock	$ 5,079	$ 4,832	$ 4,078	$4,000	$ 4,000	$ 4,000	4.89%	5.11%
Surplus	10,637	7,636	6,322	6,000	6,000	6,000	12.13	39.31
Retained earnings	15,762	17,459	15,633	13,703	12,358	11,845	5.88	−9.72
Less treasury stock at cost	0	0	(6)	0	(29)	(29)	n.m.	0.00
ESOP debt	(697)	(802)	(899)	(987)	(1,067)	(1,140)	n.m.	n.m.
Total equity	$ 30,781	$ 29,125	$ 25,128	$ 22,716	$ 21,263	$ 20,677	8.28%	5.69%
Total liabilities and equity	$ 31,478	$ 32,281	$ 28,930	$ 27,072	$ 26,007	$ 25,493	4.31%	− 2.49%
Shares outstanding‡	507,918	507,393	470,922	462,000	462,000	462,000	1.91%	0.10%
Book value per share	$ 60.60	$ 57.40	$ 53.36	$ 49.17	$ 46.02	$ 44.76	6.25%	5.58%
Consolidated assets ($000)	$444,592	$ 420,885	$391,643	$359,332	$353,925	$319,902	—	—

*n.m. = not meaningful.
†Slight differences in the investment in the subsidiary and bank equity are due to rounding of Call Report data.
‡Restated to reflect a 5% stock dividend at December 31, 1990, and a 10% stock dividend at December 31, 1989.

SOURCE: Audited financial statements.

Exhibit 6
Sample Bancshares, Inc.
Consolidated Historical Changes in Stockholders' Equity ($ Thousands)
For the Years Ending December 31

	1990	1989	1988	1987	1986	1985
Beginning equity	$29,125	$25,128	$22,716	$21,263	$20,677	$20,617
Net income	2,539	3,194	2,770	2,183	1,353	1,999
Cash dividends paid	(1,016)	(906)	(840)	(839)	(839)	(799)
Cash paid in lieu of fractional shares on stock dividend*	(32)	(28)				
Sale of common stock	59	1,633	400	29		
Treasury stock transactions, net		6	(6)			
Prior period adjustments						
ESOP debt	105	97	88	80	73	(1,140)
Other adjustments				1	(1)	
Ending equity	$30,781	$29,125	$25,128	$22,716	$21,263	$20,677

*In December 1990 and December 1989, Sample Bancshares, Inc., declared 5% and 10% stock dividends, respectively.

Holding Company Ratio Analysis

	1990	1989	1988	1987	1986	1985
Double leverage	0.94	0.94	0.96	0.99	1.01	1.03
Double leverage at cost	0.94	0.94	0.96	0.99	1.01	1.03
Tangible double leverage	0.94	0.94	0.96	0.99	1.01	1.03
Double-leverage payback (years)	0.00	0.00	0.00	0.00	0.22	0.29
Debt/equity	0.00	0.08	0.11	0.15	0.17	0.17
Liabilities/equity	0.02	0.11	0.15	0.19	0.22	0.23
Interest coverage (×)	7.58	6.30	6.63	4.55	4.01	3.73
Equity/consolidated total assets	6.92%	6.92%	6.42%	6.32%	6.01%	6.46%

Exhibit 7
Sample Bancshares, Inc.
Parent Company Only Historical Income Statements ($ Thousands)
For the Years Ending December 31

	1990	1989	1988	1987	1986	1985	Growth Rates	
							1985–90	1989–90
Dividends from bank subsidiary	$ 1,289	$ 1,588	$ 1,749	$ 1,432	$ 983	$ 1,080	3.60%	−18.81%
Interest and fees on loans	0	0	0	0	461	499	n.m.*	0.00
Other income	36	63	39	26	20	28	5.10	−43.13
Total income	$ 1,325	$ 1,651	$ 1,788	$ 1,458	$ 1,464	$ 1,607	−3.78%	−19.74%
Interest on long-term debt	$ 162	$ 251	$ 263	$ 312	$ 359	$ 421	−17.37%	−35.35
Amortization	0	17	22	22	22	22	n.m.	−100.00
Other expenses	95	52	22	15	2	13	49.44	81.11
Total expenses	$ 257	$ 320	$ 307	$ 350	$ 384	$ 456	−10.84%	−19.68%
Income before taxes and equity in undistributed earnings of subsidiary	$ 1,068	$ 1,331	$ 1,481	$ 1,109	$ 1,081	$ 1,150	−1.48%	−19.76%
Income tax expense (benefit)	(143)	(125)	(36)	(107)	25	4	n.m.	n.m.
Equity in undistributed earnings of bank subsidiary	1,328	1,738	1,253	967	297	853	9.26	−23.58
Net income	$ 2,539	$ 3,194	$ 2,770	$ 2,183	$ 1,353	$ 1,999	4.90%	−20.50%
Dividends	$ 1,106	$ 906	$ 840	$ 839	$ 839	$ 799	4.92%	12.13%
Dividend payout	40.0%	28.4%	30.3%	38.4%	62.0%	40.0%		
Weighted average shares outstanding†	507,656	489,158	466,461	462,000	462,000	430,682	3.34%	3.78%
Earnings per share†	$5.00	$6.53	$5.94	$4.72	$2.93	$4.64	1.51%	−23.40%
Dividends per share†	$2.00	$1.85	$1.80	$1.80	$1.80	$1.80	2.14%	8.16%

*n.m. = not meaningful.
†Restated to reflect a 5% stock dividend at December 31, 1990, and a 10% stock dividend at December 31, 1989.

Exhibit 8a
Sample Bancshares, Inc.
Determination of Fair Market Value
Transaction and Asset Value Methods

Transaction Method

Transaction price per share	n.a.	Per text
Total shares outstanding	507,918	
Derivation of market value	none	

Asset Value Method

Reported book value at December 31, 1990	$30,781,000
Adjustment: Market depreciation in securities portfolio net of tax impact (see calculation below)	(563,499)
Derived asset value	$30,217,501
Market value of securities per audit	$133,306,612
Less book value of securities per audit	134,215,482
Total depreciation in securities portfolio	(908,870)
Less tax effect at estimated effective rate (38%)	345,371
Securities depreciation net of tax impact	($563,499)

Exhibit 8b
Sample Bancshares, Inc.
Determination of Fair Market Value
Earnings (Investment) Value Method

Determination of Ongoing Earning Power	1990	1989	1988
Reported net income	$2,539,206	$3,194,064	$2,770,020
Adjustments			
(1) Eliminate extraordinary loss related to lender liability lawsuit*	655,328	0	0
(2) Eliminate gain on pension termination*	0	0	(890,000)
(3) Eliminate gains and losses on securities transactions	(116,000)	(284,000)	702,000
(4) Eliminate interest expense on paid-off parent-company debt	162,000	251,000	263,000
(5) Tax effect of (3) and (4) at 38%	(17,480)	12,540	(366,700)
Adjusted net income	$3,223,054	$3,173,604	$2,478,320
Consolidated average assets ($ 000)	$430,151	$404,675	$382,498
Consolidated average equity ($ 000)	$29,953	$27,127	$23,922
Return on average assets	0.75%	0.78%	0.65%
Return on average equity	10.76%	11.70%	10.36%
Weight	1	0	0
Estimated ongoing net income	$3,223,054		
Estimated ongoing earning power (rounded)	$3,225,000		

*Net of tax impact per audited financial statements.

Capitalization Factor	Capitalization of Earnings	
Base capitalization factor	7.04	Per text and Exhibit 9
Fundamental discount	0.00%	
Adjusted capitalization factor	7.04	

Derivation of Earnings (Investment) Value

Estimated ongoing earning power	$3,225,000
Adjusted capitalization factor	× 7.04
Derived earnings (investment) value	$22,704,000

Exhibit 8c
Sample Bancshares, Inc.
Valuation Conclusion as of December 31, 1990

Initial Determination of Value

Valuation Methods	Valuation	Weight	Product
Transaction method	none	0%	0
Asset value method	$30,217,501	40%	$12,087,000
Earnings (investment) value method	$22,704,000	60%	$13,622,400
Initial determination of value			$25,709,400

Conclusion of Total Value

Initial determination of value			$25,709,400
Marketability discount		5.0%	$ 1,285,470
Conclusion of total value			$24,423,930

Conclusion of Fair Market Value per Share

Conclusion of total value			$24,423,930
Existing number of shares outstanding			$ 507,918
Value per share			$48.09 per share
Conclusion of fair market value per share (rounded, nearest $0.25)			$48.00 per share

(As of December 31, 1990; minority-interest basis; for purposes of the ESOP)

Exhibit 8d
Sample Bancshares, Inc.
Reconciliation of Value

	For the Years Ending		% Change
Valuation Components	December 31 1990	December 31 1989	
Base capitalization rate	7.04	8.88	− 20.7%
Fundamental discount (%)	0%	0%	
Adjusted capitalization rate	7.04	8.88	− 20.7%
Estimate of ongoing earning power	$3,225,000	$3,000,000	7.5%
Derivation of earnings value	$22,704,000	$26,640,000	− 14.8%
Weight	60%	75%	− 20.0%
Derivation of asset value	$30,217,501	$27,386,581	10.3%
Weight	40%	25%	60.0%
Derivation of transaction value	none	none	n.m.[a]
Weight	0%	0%	n.m.
Initial determination of value	$25,709,400	$26,826,645	− 4.2%
Marketability discount	5.0%	5%	0.0%
Conclusion of total value	$24,423,930	$25,485,313	− 4.2%
Total shares outstanding[b]	507,918	507,393	0.1%
Initial conclusion per share	$48.09	$50.23	− 4.3%
Conclusion per share (rounded)	$48.00	$50.25	− 4.5%
Total book value	$30,781,000	$29,125,000	5.7%
Net asset value	30,217,501	29,572,306	2.2%
Final value % of book value	79%	88%	− 9.5%
Value % of asset value	81%	86%	− 6.4%
Implied price/earnings ratio[c]	7.57	8.50	
Implied dividend yield[d]	4.2%	3.6%	
Implied return on equity[e]	13.2%	11.8%	

[a]n.m. = not meaningful.
[b]Restated to reflect 5% stock dividend December 1989.
[c]Conclusion of value/estimate of ongoing earning power.
[d]Dividends/conclusion of value.
[e]Estimate of ongoing earning power/conclusion of total value.

Exhibit 9

Mid-South Regional Bank Holding Companies
Comparable Company Data as of December 31, 1990

Southeast Region	Price 12/31/90	Earnings 1990	Book Value Per Share	Indicated Dividends Per Share	Total Assets ($000s)	No. of Shares ($000s)	Price/ Earnings	Price/ Book	Price/ Assets	Dividend Yield	Current Return on Equity	Indicated Dividend Payout
Alabama												
AmSouth BanCorp	$19.50	$3.26	$25.13	$1.40	$ 8,706,106	23,420	5.98	0.78	5.25%	7.18%	13.49%	42.94%
Central Bancshares South	$14.25	$2.34	$15.98	$0.80	$ 4,914,837	20,753	6.09	0.89	6.02%	5.61%	15.41%	34.19%
First Alabama Bancshares	$17.25	$2.10	$15.99	$0.92	$ 6,344,406	32,771	8.45	1.11	9.17%	5.18%	13.64%	43.81%
Arkansas												
First Commercial Corp.	$15.50	$2.35	$15.87	$0.62	$ 2,121,956	9,445	6.60	0.98	6.90%	4.00%	14.80%	26.38%
First United Bancshares	$24.50	$3.48	$31.05	$1.00	$ 797,242	2,136	7.04	0.79	6.56%	4.08%	11.68%	28.74%
Worthen Banking Corp.	$11.50	$1.76	$10.15	$0.00	$ 2,143,669	10,931	6.53	1.13	5.86%	0.00%	17.39%	0.00%
Kentucky												
Liberty National Bancorp	$21.50	$2.85	$23.82	$0.94	$ 3,713,467	11,558	7.54	0.90	6.69%	4.37%	12.50%	32.98%
Louisiana												
First Commerce Corp.	$14.00	$1.77	$19.58	$1.20	$ 4,467,535	11,506	7.91	0.72	3.61%	8.57%	9.22%	67.80%
Mississippi												
Bancorp of Mississippi	$20.00	$3.02	$22.30	$0.92	$ 1,513,706	4,661	6.62	0.90	6.16%	4.60%	14.66%	30.46%
Deposit Guaranty	$19.75	$3.10	$33.63	$1.56	$ 4,923,048	7,900	6.37	0.59	3.17%	7.90%	9.45%	50.32%
Grenada Sunburst	$ 8.25	$1.17	$13.68	$0.60	$ 1,863,484	9,012	7.05	0.60	3.99%	7.27%	8.78%	51.28%
Trustmark Corp.	$17.50	$2.96	$25.48	$1.00	$ 3,700,022	9,825	5.91	0.69	4.65%	5.71%	12.05%	33.78%
Missouri												
Boatman's Bancshares	$31.75	$3.90	$33.06	$2.12	$17,468,547	34,691	8.14	0.96	6.31%	6.68%	12.11%	54.36%
Commerce Bancshares	$23.13	$3.12	$24.61	$0.72	$ 6,709,148	18,602	7.41	0.94	6.41%	3.11%	13.46%	23.08%
Mercantile Bancorp	$21.00	$3.50	$27.07	$1.40	$ 7,617,155	16,257	6.00	0.78	4.48%	6.67%	13.40%	40.00%
United Missouri	$27.00	$2.97	$27.39	$0.80	$ 4,271,606	12,527	9.09	0.99	7.92%	2.96%	11.31%	26.94%
Tennessee												
National Commerce Bancorp	$19.38	$2.45	$14.31	$0.86	$ 1,977,175	10,275	7.91	1.35	10.07%	4.44%	18.71%	35.10%
First Tennessee	$22.63	$3.01	$25.32	$1.68	$ 6,707,672	15,710	7.52	0.89	5.30%	7.43%	12.33%	55.81%
Union Planters	$ 6.88	$1.20	$13.61	$0.48	$ 4,004,710	17,091	5.73	0.51	2.93%	6.98%	9.32%	40.00%
Averages							7.05	0.87	5.87%	5.41%	12.83%	37.79%
Medians							7.04	0.89	6.02%	5.61%	12.50%	35.10%
Sample Bancshares, Inc. (as adjusted)	$48.00	$6.35	$60.60	$2.10	$ 444,592	508	7.57	0.79	5.48%	4.17%	10.48%	33.10%
Also Considered												
Colonial BancGroup AL	$ 6.88	$1.40	$11.97	$0.60	$ 1,531,202	5,856	4.91	0.57	2.63%	8.73%	11.70%	42.86%
First Security KY	$11.50	$0.71	$13.19	$0.52	$ 1,800,642	8,721	16.20	0.87	5.57%	4.52%	5.38%	73.24%
Mid-America Bancorp KY	$12.75	$0.95	$15.64	$0.60	$ 982,764	6,555	13.42	0.82	8.50%	4.71%	6.08%	63.16%
Hibernia Corp. LA	$ 6.63	($0.40)	$13.16	$0.90	$ 7,357,850	27,847	-16.56	0.50	2.51%	13.58%	-3.04%	-225.00%
First American TN	$ 6.38	($2.69)	$15.79	$0.00	$ 6,480,262	23,311	-2.37	0.40	2.29%	0.00%	-17.04%	0.00%

SOURCE: Standard and Poor's *Corporation Stock Guide*, *SNL Bank Securities Monthly*, and corporate press releases.

Exhibit 9 (continued)
Mid-South Regional Bank Holding Companies
Comparable Company Data as of December 31, 1990

Southeast Region	Equity/ Assets 1990	Return on Equity					Return on Assets				
		1990	1989	1988	1987	1986	1990	1989	1988	1987	1986
Alabama											
AmSouth BanCorp	6.76%	13.49%	11.49%	15.70%	13.32%	16.39%	0.90%	0.76%	1.00%	0.90%	1.18%
Central Bancshares South	6.75	15.41	14.13	15.12	12.57	16.20	1.04	0.98	1.05	0.86	1.03
First Alabama Bancshares	8.26	13.64	13.25	13.29	13.81	14.63	1.09	1.20	1.24	1.31	1.36
Arkansas											
First Commercial	7.06	14.80	14.39	13.83	12.59	8.98	1.05	1.02	0.91	0.83	0.56
First United Bancshares	8.32	11.68	10.50	12.55	13.92	16.17	0.95	0.82	1.15	1.39	1.49
Worthen Banking Corp.	5.18	17.39	11.70	10.93	-9.10	-32.62	1.04	0.64	0.54	n.m.*	n.m.
Kentucky											
Liberty National Bancorp	7.41	12.50	14.51	14.34	14.31	14.50	0.92	1.03	1.00	1.02	0.95
Louisiana											
First Commerce Corp.	5.04	9.22	12.20	10.92	9.16	1.84	0.49	0.67	0.62	0.56	0.11
Mississippi											
Bancorp of Mississippi	6.87	14.66	14.87	16.09	15.60	18.76	0.97	0.97	1.02	0.98	1.36
Deposit Guaranty	5.40	9.45	12.82	13.70	11.72	17.07	0.54	0.89	0.92	0.79	1.07
Grenada Sunburst	6.62	8.78	4.68	10.49	10.33	12.60	0.58	0.32	0.77	0.85	0.98
Trustmark Corp.	6.77	12.05	12.60	13.51	14.16	15.17	0.86	0.93	0.98	0.99	1.01
Missouri											
Boatman's Bancshares	6.57	12.11	12.08	6.72	9.76	11.66	0.92	0.91	0.49	0.66	0.78
Commerce Bancshares	6.82	13.46	15.14	13.24	11.56	11.72	1.00	1.09	0.97	0.79	0.80
Mercantile Bancorp	5.78	13.40	0.12	6.69	-5.39	12.31	0.81	0.01	0.44	n.m.	0.85
United Missouri	8.03	11.31	12.74	11.64	11.93	12.50	0.94	1.09	1.00	1.01	1.08
Tennessee											
National Commerce Bancorp	7.44	18.71	19.28	19.45	19.08	17.49	1.37	1.38	1.40	1.35	1.15
First Tennessee	5.93	12.33	7.68	14.84	10.40	15.59	0.74	0.47	0.90	0.59	0.88
Union Planters	5.81	9.32	-8.40	8.59	3.95	4.88	0.56	n.m.	0.63	0.32	0.33
Averages	6.67%	12.83%	11.90%	12.72%	11.39%	11.43%	0.93%	0.84%	0.90%	0.89%	0.94%
Medians	6.76%	12.50%	12.60%	13.29%	11.93%	14.50%	0.92%	0.91%	0.97%	0.85%	0.98%
Sample Bancshares, Inc. (as adjusted)	6.92%	10.43%	11.13%	9.68%	9.61%	6.37%	0.73%	0.75%	0.61%	0.61%	0.38%
Also Considered											
Colonial BancGroup — AL	4.58%	10.34%	-32.91%	6.33%	1.43%	14.13%	0.52%	-2.55%	0.51%	0.12%	1.10%
First Security — KY	6.39%	5.33%	15.05%	15.14%	11.29%	15.07%	0.38%	1.07%	1.00%	0.79%	1.02%
Mid-America Bancorp — KY	10.43%	6.49%	10.99%	10.59%	9.11%	7.63%	0.78%	1.40%	1.39%	1.23%	1.06%
Hibernia Corp. — LA	4.98%	-2.89%	16.95%	17.13%	17.02%	17.07%	-0.15%	0.99%	1.00%	1.02%	1.02%
First American — TN	5.68%	-15.71%	0.91%	6.53%	11.67%	15.22%	-0.93%	0.06%	0.43%	0.79%	1.01%

*n.m. = not meaningful.

SOURCE: The *SNL Bank Digest*, corporate annual reports, and Standard and Poor's *Corporation Stock Guide*.

Exhibit 9 (continued)
Mid-South Regional Bank Holding Companies
Comparable Company Data as of December 31, 1990

Southeast Region	($M) Market Capitalization	Earnings Per Share					P/E Ratio				
		1990	1989	1988	1987	1986	1990	1989	1988	1987	1986
Alabama											
AmSouth BanCorp	$ 456,686	$3.26	$2.60	$3.30	$2.57	$2.89	5.98	9.13	6.89	9.00	10.90
Central Bancshares South	295,734	$2.34	$1.95	$1.91	$1.47	$1.71	6.09	6.67	7.66	7.99	10.67
First Alabama Bancshares	581,687	$2.10	$1.90	$1.77	$1.71	$1.67	8.45	9.14	8.69	8.04	12.95
Arkansas											
First Commercial	146,392	$2.35	$2.04	$1.74	$1.42	$0.92	6.60	8.96	8.70	7.79	12.02
First United Bancshares	52,335	$3.48	$2.90	$3.21	$3.19	$3.41	7.04	9.40	7.63	7.05	n.m.
Worthen Banking Corp.	125,711	$1.76	$1.01	$0.88	($0.67)	($3.49)	6.53	11.88	9.23	n.m.	n.m.
Kentucky											
Liberty National Bancorp	248,501	$2.85	$3.07	$2.76	$2.48	$2.25	7.54	8.88	8.88	8.77	9.67
Louisiana											
First Commerce Corp.	161,079	$1.77	$2.26	$1.91	$1.52	$0.10	7.91	10.29	9.55	9.87	n.m.
Mississippi											
Bancorp of Mississippi	93,211	$3.02	$2.76	$2.67	$2.33	$2.42	6.62	7.43	8.15	8.69	8.68
Deposit Guaranty	156,025	$3.10	$3.98	$3.94	$3.17	$4.15	6.37	6.78	7.99	10.17	8.43
Grenada Sunburst	74,348	$1.17	$0.62	$1.32	$1.23	$0.20	7.05	n.m.	10.20	11.79	73.75
Trustmark Corp.	171,938	$2.96	$2.86	$2.80	$2.67	$2.58	5.91	7.17	8.35	8.61	10.27
Missouri											
Boatman's Bancshares	1,101,444	$3.90	$3.72	$2.01	$2.83	$3.20	8.14	8.60	15.42	11.04	10.98
Commerce Bancshares	430,176	$3.12	$3.12	$2.46	$1.94	$1.88	7.41	8.53	8.49	7.67	9.18
Mercantile Bancorp	341,397	$3.50	$0.03	$1.79	($1.53)	$3.49	6.00	n.m.	14.25	n.m.	8.02
United Missouri	338,242	$2.97	$3.08	$2.59	$2.43	$2.33	9.09	9.82	10.14	11.11	10.12
Tennessee											
National Commerce Bancorp	199,072	$2.45	$2.21	$1.96	$1.70	$1.38	7.91	10.18	12.15	13.75	10.12
First Tennessee	355,429	$3.01	$1.82	$3.34	$2.20	$3.03	7.52	13.67	7.34	10.11	10.15
Union Planters	117,502	$1.20	($1.19)	$1.20	$0.54	$0.60	5.73	n.m.	10.52	n.m.	n.m.
Averages							7.05	9.16	9.49	9.47	14.39
Medians							7.04	8.88	8.70	8.69	10.12
Sample Bancshares, Inc. (as adjusted)	24,380	$6.35	$6.48	$5.36	$4.72	$2.93	7.57	7.75	n.a.†	n.a.	n.a.
Also Considered											
Colonial BancGroup AL	40,261	$1.40	($5.81)	$1.09	$0.25	$2.20	4.91	-1.53	10.09	44.00	10.57
First Security KY	100,292	$0.71	$1.87	$1.68	$1.15	$1.39	16.20	9.89	9.08	11.30	12.41
Mid-America Bancorp KY	83,580	$0.95	$1.53	$1.38	$1.10	$0.88	13.42	10.84	10.10	10.94	17.37
Hibernia Corp. LA	184,489	($0.40)	$2.30	$2.08	$1.87	$1.63	-16.56	9.57	8.37	8.15	9.03
First American TN	148,610	($2.69)	$0.18	$1.32	$2.25	$2.63	-2.37	115.28	16.76	9.39	9.79

†n.a. = not applicable.

SOURCE: The SNL Bank Digest, corporate annual reports, and Standard and Poor's Corporation Stock Guide.

Exhibit 9 *(continued)*
Mid-South Regional Bank Holding Companies
Comparable Company Data as of December 31, 1990

Southeast Region	Book Value Per Share					Price/Book Value Ratio				
	1990	1989	1988	1987	1986	1990	1989	1988	1987	1986
Alabama										
AmSouth BanCorp	$25.13	$23.25	$22.03	$20.65	$18.51	0.78	1.02	1.03	1.12	1.70
Central Bancshares South	$15.98	$14.43	$13.21	$12.07	$11.17	0.89	0.90	1.11	0.97	1.63
First Alabama Bancshares	$15.99	$14.83	$13.80	$12.80	$11.91	1.11	1.17	1.11	1.07	1.82
Arkansas										
First Commercial	$15.87	$14.18	$12.58	$11.28	$10.25	0.98	1.29	1.20	0.98	1.08
First United Bancshares	$31.05	$28.57	$26.66	$24.45	$22.26	0.79	0.95	0.92	0.92	n.m.
Worthen Banking Corp.	$10.15	$ 8.67	$ 8.01	$ 7.32	$10.70	1.13	1.38	1.01	0.87	1.03
Kentucky										
Liberty National Bancorp	$23.82	$22.17	$20.29	$18.47	$13.95	0.90	1.23	1.21	1.18	1.56
Louisiana										
First Commerce Corp.	$19.58	$19.00	$17.90	$17.17	$16.93	0.72	1.22	1.02	0.87	0.87
Mississippi										
Bancorp of Mississippi	$22.30	$20.14	$18.15	$16.21	$14.62	0.90	1.02	1.20	1.25	1.44
Deposit Guaranty	$33.63	$32.09	$28.76	$27.05	$24.30	0.59	0.84	1.10	1.19	1.44
Grenada Sunburst	$13.68	$13.16	$13.10	$12.42	$11.17	0.60	0.93	1.03	1.17	1.32
Trustmark Corp.	$25.48	$23.53	$21.63	$19.72	$17.84	0.69	0.87	1.08	1.17	1.49
Missouri										
Boatman's Bancshares	$33.06	$31.33	$29.72	$29.31	$28.01	0.96	1.02	1.04	1.07	1.25
Commerce Bancshares	$24.61	$21.91	$19.55	$17.61	$16.67	0.94	1.22	1.07	0.84	1.03
Mercantile Bancorp	$27.07	$25.14	$26.68	$26.41	$29.43	0.78	1.03	0.96	0.73	0.95
United Missouri	$27.39	$25.22	$23.25	$21.31	$19.52	0.99	1.20	1.13	1.27	1.21
Tennessee										
National Commerce Bancorp	$14.31	$12.67	$11.16	$ 9.77	$ 8.49	1.35	1.78	2.13	2.39	1.65
First Tennessee	$25.32	$23.89	$23.56	$21.57	$20.46	0.89	1.04	1.04	1.03	1.50
Union Planters	$13.61	$12.46	$14.14	$13.49	$13.15	0.51	0.90	0.89	0.81	1.41
Averages						0.87	1.11	1.12	1.10	1.35
Medians						0.89	1.03	1.07	1.07	1.41
Sample Bancshares, Inc.	$60.60	$57.40	$53.36	$49.17	$46.02	0.79	0.88	n.a.	n.a.	n.a.
Also Considered										
Colonial BancGroup AL	$11.97	$11.19	$17.51	$16.87	$16.43	0.57	0.79	0.63	0.65	1.42
First Security KY	$13.19	$13.17	$11.80	$10.60	$ 9.82	0.87	1.40	1.29	1.23	1.76
Mid-America Bancorp KY	$15.64	$16.77	$18.04	$16.64	$17.64	0.82	0.99	0.77	0.72	0.87
Hibernia Corp. LA	$13.16	$14.45	$13.40	$11.56	$11.86	0.50	1.52	1.30	1.32	1.24
First American TN	$15.79	$18.82	$19.91	$19.82	$18.55	0.40	1.10	1.11	1.07	1.39

SOURCE: The *SNL Bank Digest*, corporate annual reports, and Standard and Poor's *Corporation Stock Guide.*

Exhibit 9 (*concluded*)
Mid-South Regional Bank Holding Companies
Comparable Company Data as of December 31, 1990

Southeast Region	Actual Dividends Paid Per Share					Dividend Yield				
	1990	1989	1988	1987	1986	1990	1989	1988	1987	1986
Alabama										
AmSouth BanCorp	$1.41	$1.34	$1.26	$1.18	$1.07	7.23%	5.64%	5.54%	5.10%	3.40%
Central Bancshares South	$0.80	$0.77	$0.70	$0.66	$0.59	5.61	5.92	4.79	5.62	3.23
First Alabama Bancshares	$0.92	$0.84	$0.80	$0.76	$0.64	5.18	4.83	5.20	5.53	2.96
Arkansas										
First Commercial	$0.62	$0.49	$0.40	$0.37	$0.32	4.00	2.68	2.64	3.35	2.89
First United Bancshares	$1.00	$1.00	$1.00	$1.00	$0.85	4.08	3.67	4.08	4.44	n.m.
Worthen Banking Corp.	$0.00	$0.00	$0.00	$0.00	$0.00	0.00	0.00	0.00	0.00	0.00
Kentucky										
Liberty National Bancorp	$0.94	$0.82	$0.72	$0.64	$0.57	4.37	3.01	2.94	2.92	2.62
Louisiana										
First Commerce Corp.	$1.20	$1.20	$1.20	$1.20	$1.20	8.57	5.16	6.58	8.00	8.14
Mississippi										
Bancorp of Mississippi	$0.86	$0.78	$0.70	$0.66	$0.58	4.30	3.80	3.22	3.26	2.74
Deposit Guaranty	$1.56	$1.53	$1.46	$1.38	$1.19	7.90	5.67	4.63	4.28	3.40
Grenada Sunburst	$0.60	$0.60	$0.60	$0.60	$0.50	7.27	4.90	4.44	4.14	3.39
Trustmark Corp.	$1.01	$0.96	$0.90	$0.79	$0.74	5.77	4.68	3.85	3.43	2.79
Missouri										
Boatman's Bancshares	$2.12	$2.03	$2.00	$1.84	$1.65	6.68	6.34	6.45	5.89	4.70
Commerce Bancshares	$0.70	$0.63	$0.59	$0.56	$0.54	3.03	2.37	2.83	3.76	3.13
Mercantile Bancorp	$1.40	$1.40	$1.40	$1.40	$1.40	6.67	5.38	5.49	7.27	5.00
United Missouri	$0.80	$0.87	$0.65	$0.62	$0.61	2.96	2.88	2.48	2.30	2.59
Tennessee										
National Commerce Bancorp	$0.86	$0.75	$0.61	$0.45	$0.34	4.44	3.33	2.56	1.93	2.43
First Tennessee	$1.62	$1.45	$1.28	$1.18	$1.13	7.16	5.83	5.22	5.30	3.67
Union Planters	$0.48	$0.48	$0.35	$0.25	$0.00	6.98	4.27	2.77	2.29	0.00
Averages						5.38%	4.23%	3.99%	4.15%	3.17%
						5.61%	4.68%	4.08%	4.14%	2.96%
Medians						4.17%	3.68%	n.a.	n.a.	n.a.
Sample Bancshares, Inc.	$2.00	$1.85	$1.80	$1.80	$1.80					
Also Considered										
Colonial BancGroup AL	$0.60	$0.60	$0.60	$0.60	$0.60	8.73%	6.76%	5.45%	5.45%	2.58%
First Security KY	$0.48	$0.44	$0.41	$0.40	$0.38	4.17%	2.38%	2.69%	3.08%	2.17%
Mid-America Bancorp KY	$0.61	$0.59	$0.43	$0.39	$0.37	4.78%	3.56%	3.09%	3.24%	2.42%
Hibernia Corp. LA	$0.90	$0.91	$0.85	$0.77	$0.64	13.58%	4.14%	4.87%	5.04%	4.35%
First American TN	$0.31	$1.25	$1.25	$1.08	$0.99	4.86%	6.02%	5.65%	5.09%	3.84%

SOURCE: The *SNL Bank Digest*, corporate annual reports, and Standard and Poor's *Corporation Stock Guide*.

Appendix A

Sample Appraisal Report

Contingent and Limiting Conditions

This report has considered all the information referenced in it, whether specifically mentioned in the report or not. The various estimates and conclusions presented apply to this report only, and may not be used out of the context presented herein. This appraisal has been prepared in accordance with the Uniform Standards of Professional Appraisal Practice.

As stated earlier in this report, we have not examined the loan portfolio of the Company. Direct examination would have been beyond the scope of this valuation assignment. We have discussed the general condition of the loan portfolio with management, focussing on such aspects as delinquencies, non-accruing loans, geographic and industry concentrations, problem loans, potential losses in the portfolio and the loan administration/review program. Management has represented to Mercer Capital that the valuation allowance at the valuation date is believed to be adequate. The valuation conclusion of this report is rendered in direct reliance upon the representations by management.

Possession of the original or copies of this report do not carry with it the right of publication of all or part of it. It was prepared for the exclusive use of the client, and may not be used without the previous written consent of Mercer Capital Management, Inc., or the client, and in any event, only with proper attribution. No copies of this report will be furnished to persons other than the client without the client's specific permission or direction unless ordered by a court of competent jurisdiction.

No officer or employee of Mercer Capital Management, Inc., is required to give testimony in court, or be in attendance during any hearings or depositions with reference to the Company. In any event, professional fees for such services are independent of this review and are subject to arrangements made satisfactory to the client and Mercer Capital Management, Inc.

Mercer Capital Management, Inc., its officers, and its staff have no present business interest in the Company. No benefits will accrue to Mercer Capital, as the result of this review, other than the professional fees previously agreed to by the Company. Fees paid to Mercer Capital for the preparation of this review are neither dependent or contingent upon any transaction nor upon the results of the review.

Appendix B

Sample Appraisal Report

Qualifications of Appraiser

Since founding in 1982, Mercer Capital has become one of the larger independent business valuation firms in the nation, as well as one of the larger appraisers of Employee Stock Ownership Plans. Through our offices in Memphis, Tennessee, Tampa, Florida, and Los Angeles, California, we handle hundreds of valuation assignments yearly for clients throughout the United States. Valuation opinions have been rendered for a wide variety of purposes, and have been used to facilitate many public and private transactions.

Our clients include legal and accounting professionals, individuals, closely-held companies representing over two hundred different industry categories, banks, thrifts, public companies and governmental agencies.

Mercer Capital's professionals adhere to the standards of the American Society of Appraisers and the Association for Investment Management and Research. Our reports are prepared and presented in conformity with the Uniform Standards of Professional Appraisal Practice promulgated by the Appraisal Foundation, and the Business Valuation Standards established by the American Society of Appraisers.

Mercer Capital's work has been reviewed and accepted by Federal and State courts, as well as numerous governmental agencies such as the Internal Revenue Service, the Federal Deposit Insurance Corporation, the Resolution Trust Corporation, the Small Business Administration, the Office of Thrift Supervision, the Department of Labor, and many of the premier legal and accounting firms in the country.

Mercer Capital's professionals have earned or are pursuing Senior Member (the ASA designation) or Accredited Member (AM designation) status with the American Society of Appraisers. Several have earned the Chartered Financial Analyst (CFA) designation from the Association for Investment Management and Research, and others are certified public accountants. Most of our professionals have advanced degrees as well as strong backgrounds in finance and banking. We have qualified as expert witnesses in numerous federal, state and local courts. Biographical and qualifications information on our individual professionals is available upon request.

Appendix C

Sample Appraisal Report

Economic and Banking Industry Outlook

The National Economic Outlook

The following analysis of the economic outlook for the fourth quarter of 1990 and early 1991 is based upon a review of current economic statistics, articles in the financial press and economic reviews found in current business periodicals. Based upon our review, we have attempted to state what we believe is representative of the "consensus" outlook for the national economy as of the fourth quarter of 1990.

According to several notable publications, the economic expansion that began in the early 1980s and continued into 1990, has begun to slow. While the Bureau of Economic Research, the independent, non-profit organization that dates when a recession begins and ends, has not made an official announcement that the country is in recession, several of the major economic indicators are pointing in that direction.

The Conference Board's index of consumer confidence fell to an eight year low in October, 1990, posting the largest one month drop in its history. Real disposable income stopped growing in the third quarter of 1990 and given the weakness in the labor markets, incomes are expected to remain depressed in the fourth quarter. Savings, as a percentage of disposable income fell to 4% in October, the lowest rate in three years.

Consumer spending is expected to remain weak. This will have a significant impact on the economy because consumer spending makes up two thirds of the gross national product. In the fourth quarter of 1990, spending by war-sensitive consumers fell 21 percent. The sharpest drop came in purchases of autos, but demand for furniture, food, and clothing was also down.

Inflation slowed to 4.1 percent in the fourth quarter of 1990. Inflation could increase in 1991 if oil prices climb as a result of the Persian Gulf War. After an initial increase at the onset of hostilities, oil prices have moderated. But many analysts expect oil prices to increase as a result of war damage to production facilities in the Gulf region.

The Federal Reserve Bank has also moved to lower short-term interest rates. According to Federal Reserve Chairman Alan Greenspan, weak monetary growth triggered the Federal Reserve to supply credit to the economy. However, banks have been slow to pass the lower rates to their customers. The Federal Funds rate was 5.53 percent on December 31, 1990, compared with 7.97 percent at year-end 1989. Over the same period, the prime rate only declined from 10.5 percent to 10.0 percent and the one-year Treasury bill rate declined from 7.83 percent to 6.82 percent, leaving the real cost of borrowing higher than suggested by nominal rates.

In 1990, U.S. companies defaulted on over $13 billion of publicly issued debt, more than in any other year and more than three times the 1989 total. Retailing and service industries are the most overextended.

Unemployment increased in 1990. The national unemployment rate at December 31, 1990, was 6.1 percent, compared with 5.1 percent at year-end 1989. Many economists are predicting that the unemployment rate will exceed 7 percent by mid-1991. Unemployment has increased faster since June 1990, when the rate was a relatively low 5.3 percent, than at any time since 1982. In the second half of 1990, 1.2 million people became unemployed and more than 1 million jobs were eliminated according to a Labor Department survey.

In July 1990, the Dow Jones industrial average approached the 3000 level, but by year-end the slowing economy made for a bearish market. The Dow closed at 2633.66, down 4.34 percent for the year. Other market indicators were also down, including a 6.56 percent decline in the Standard and Poor's 500 and a 17.8 percent decline in the NASDAQ composite index. Stock mutual funds declined 6.9 percent, making 1990 the worst year for stock funds since 1974.

The bond market was volatile in 1990, and many analysts believe that 1991 will be another tumultuous year for bonds. The Federal Reserve's efforts to stimulate the economy by lowering interest rates triggered a powerful fourth-quarter rally in the bond market. But these year-end gains were not enough to offset the market slide that pushed bond prices down earlier in the year. Many analysts believe that the weakening economy will cause the Federal Reserve to continue reducing short-term interest rates. This should result in gains for holders of short-term notes and bills. Long-term bond rates may move somewhat in sympathy, but long-term rates should remain reasonably stable pending clarification of the recession's impact on the rate of inflation.

Housing starts in 1990 totaled 1.19 million, down from nearly 1.38 million in 1989, the lowest level since 1982. The Dodge Construction Index was down 26 percent in 1990, the steepest year-to-year decline since the early 1970s. Total construction value for 1990 fell 11 percent to $239.9 billion, from $270.6 billion in 1989. The tight credit situation, high real borrowing costs, and prospects of war discouraged new construction.

Most of the decline in housing starts can be attributed to the decrease in multifamily home construction. In December 1990, while single-family home starts fell only slightly, multifamily housing starts fell 32 percent. Building permits were also down in 1990. Since peaking in January 1990, housing permits continually declined and ended the year down 18 percent.

The economic outlook for 1991 is clouded by the war in the Middle East. No one can know what its effect will be on the depth and length of the expected recession. Many economists and government officials believe that if the war ends with a quick Allied victory, consumer confidence could rebound and soften the economic downturn.

The Banking Industry Outlook

The following analysis of the banking industry is based upon a review of current banking statistics, articles in the financial press, and industry surveys found in current business periodicals. Based upon our review, we have attempted to identify what we believe is representative of the "consensus" outlook for the industry for 1991.

The primary issues and concerns affecting the banking industry during 1990 were tied closely to general economic issues. The slowdown in U.S. economic growth in 1990 was reflected in a decline in loan demand as corporations limited expansion and consumers delayed major purchases. Net interest margins narrowed as interest rates declined and funds originally earmarked for commercial loans were diverted to lower yielding Treasury securities.

In 1990, the value of publicly traded banking stocks plummeted. Bank stocks were one of the worst performing groups in the market. The Dow Jones industry indexes of money-center and regional bank stocks both declined more than 30%, compared with a 6.56% decline in the overall market, as measured by the Standard and Poor's 500 stock index. Salomon Brothers' stock index of 35 major banks was down 50% compared to 1989.

Among the 24 southeastern bank stocks tracked by Mercer Capital, 22 declined in value during 1990. As a group, these stocks declined 41%. Increased loan loss provisions hurt the earnings of many banks, but prices were down even among banks showing increased earnings. Investors' apprehensions about the industry are extending to healthy banks as well as troubled ones.

Bank failures continued in 1990 and the Federal Deposit Insurance Corporation is estimating that 200 banks could fail in 1991 compared with 180 that closed in 1990. According to Congressional Budget Office projections, more than 600 banks will fail between 1990 and 1993.

The bank failures have severely burdened the Federal Deposit Insurance program. The Office of Management and Budget has projected a $4 billion deficit at the FDIC in 1992. At December 30, 1990, the Bank Insurance Fund had $9 billion in reserves, but FDIC Chairman William Seidman has said that the level will fall to $4 billion by the end of 1991. The FDIC continues to raise the premiums paid by the banks with an increase of from $0.125 to $0.195 per $100 of deposits in 1990 and a planned increase in 1991 to $0.23 per $100 of deposits.

Rating agencies have rushed to downgrade debt ratings for banks. Banks and thrifts accounted for nearly a third of the U.S. corporate debt that Moody's Investors Service downgraded in 1990. Moody's downgraded 114 bank and thrift issues for a total of $108.9 billion in debt. The downgrading makes it more difficult for banks to access the capital markets. Senior economists at Moody's do not expect to see improvements in the commercial real estate market that could help bank ratings.

Mergers and acquisitions in the banking industry slowed considerably during 1990 and government assisted acquisitions dominated the market. The Resolution Trust Corporation handled 267 resolutions in 1990. The Federal Deposit Insurance Corporation assisted in another 150 deals. In the private sector, activity was limited and buyers purchased only $45 billion in assets. Depressed prices, such as the Magna Group's acquisition of Landmark Bancshares at 51% of book value, had an impact on merger activity. The average price to book ratio transactions announced in the fourth quarter of 1990 was lower than at any point in the last five years.

The decline in bank share prices has been one factor in the slowdown in takeovers. Another factor is the increased due diligence being performed by cautious banks anxious to uncover asset quality problems. Often these more thorough examinations discover problems that will terminate the acquisition. According to industry analysts, approximately 30% of mergers announced in 1990, will not be completed. Bank mergers in 1991 will be charged with uncertainty and increasingly reflect the concerns of buyers, sellers, and regulators. With participants acting with greater caution, deal structures have become more elaborate, negotiations more difficult and the chance of success lower.

On balance, 1991 is expected to be another difficult year in the industry. The slowing of national economic growth, declining loan activity and concerns about the financing and availability of deposit insurance will all impact on the banking industry.

SOURCES: *Business Week*, Jan. 14, 1991; *Forbes*, Jan. 7, 1991; *The Wall Street Journal*, "Year End Review," Jan. 2, 1991; Federal Reserve Statistical Releases; Department of Labor Statistical Releases; *American Banker*, selected issues from January 1991; *National Mortgage News*, Jan. 21, 1991; *S&P Industry Survey*, Oct. 18, 1990.

Appendix A

Business Valuation
Standards (BVS)
Adopted by the
American Society of Appraisers

BVS-I Definition of Terms
BVS-II Full Written Business
Valuation Report

AMERICAN SOCIETY OF APPRAISERS

— BUSINESS VALUATION STANDARDS —

The "Uniform Standards of Professional Appraisal Practice" as promulgated by The Appraisal Foundation and adopted by the eight constituent appraisal societies which are a part of it, states in its preamble:

It is essential that a professional appraiser arrive at and communicate his or her analyses, opinions, and advice in a manner that will be meaningful to the client and will not be misleading in the marketplace.

The Preamble further states:

These standards are for appraisers and the users of appraisal services. To maintain the highest level of professional practice, appraisers must observe these standards. The users of appraisal services should demand work performed in conformance with these standards.

While the above preamble does not specifically apply to the Business Valuation Standards of the American Society of Appraisers, its language certainly sets the stage for the publication of the business valuation standards.

*   *   *   *   *

The following Business Valuation Standards have been adopted by the Business Valuation Committee of the American Society of Appraisers and approved by ASA's International Board of Governors.

> BVS-I   Terminology
> BVS-II   Full Written Business Valuation Report

The Business Valuation Standards listed below have been adopted by the Business Valuation Committee of theAmerican Society of Appraisers and are currently awaiting approval of ASA's International Board of Governors. This action is expected not later than January 1992.

> BVS-III   General Performance Requirements for Business Valuation
> BVS-IV   Asset Based Approach to Business Valuation
> BVS-V   The Guideline Company Valuation Method

*   *   *   *   *

These standards are required to be followed for the valuation of businesses, business ownership interests or securities by ALL members of the American Society of Appraisers, be they Candidates, Accredited members (AM), Accredited Senior Appraisers (ASA), or Fellows (FASA), regardless of their discipline affiliation.

AMERICAN SOCIETY OF APPRAISERS
Business Valuation Standard

BVS-I   Terminology

Adopted by the ASA Business Valuation Committee, June 1988
Approved by the ASA Board of Governors, January 1989

ADJUSTED BOOK VALUE — The book value which results after one or more asset or liability amounts are added, deleted or changed from the respective book amounts.

APPRAISAL — The act or process of determining value. It is synonymous with valuation.

APPRAISAL APPROACH — A general way of determining value using one or more specific appraisal methods. (See Asset Based Approach, Market Approach and Income Approach definitions.)

APPRAISAL DATE — The date as of which the appraiser's opinion of value applies.

APPRAISAL METHOD — Within approaches, a specific way to determine value.

APPRAISAL PROCEDURE — The act, manner and technique of performing the steps of an appraisal method.

APPRAISED VALUE — The appraiser's opinion or determination of value.

ASSET BASED APPROACH — A general way of determining a value indication of a business's assets and/or equity interest using one or more methods based directly on the value of the assets of the business less liabilities.

BOOK VALUE — 1. With respect to assets, the capitalized cost of an asset less accumulated depreciation, depletion or amortization as it appears on the books of account of the enterprise.

2. With respect to a business enterprise, the difference between total assets (net of depreciation, depletion and amortization) and total liabilities of an enterprise as they appear on the balance sheet. It is synonymous with net book value, net worth and shareholders' equity.

BUSINESS APPRAISER — A person who by education, training and experience is qualified to make an appraisal of a business enterprise and/or its intangible assets.

BUSINESS ENTERPRISE — A commercial, industrial or service organization pursuing an economic activity.

BUSINESS VALUATION	— The act or process of arriving at an opinion or determination of the value of a business enterprise or an interest therein.
CAPITALIZATION	— 1. The conversion of income into value 2. The capital structure of a business enterprise. 3. The recognition of an expenditure as a capital asset rather than a period expense.
CAPITALIZATION FACTOR	— Any multiple or divisor used to convert income into value.
CAPITALIZATION RATE	— Any divisor (usually expressed as a percentage) that is used to convert income into value.
CAPITAL STRUCTURE	— The composition of the invested capital.
CASH FLOW	— Net income plus depreciation and other non-cash charges.
CONTROL	— The power to direct the management and policies of an enterprise.
CONTROL PREMIUM	— The additional value inherent in the control interest, as contrasted to a minority interest, that reflects it's power of control.
DISCOUNT RATE	— A rate of return used to convert a monetary sum, payable or receivable in the future, into present value.
ECONOMIC LIFE	— The period over which property may be profitably used.
ENTERPRISE	— See BUSINESS ENTERPRISE.
EQUITY	— The owners' interest in property after deduction of all liabilities.
FAIR MARKET VALUE	— The amount at which property would change hands between a willing seller and a willing buyer when neither is acting under compulsion and when both have reasonable knowledge of the relevant facts.
GOING CONCERN	— An operating business enterprise.
GOING CONCERN VALUE	— 1. The value of an enterprise, or an interest therein, as a going concern. 2. Intangible elements of value in a business enterprise resulting from factors such as having a trained workforce, an operational plant, and the necessary licenses, systems and procedures in place.
GOODWILL	— That intangible asset which arises as a result of name, reputation, customer patronage, location, products and similar factors that have not been separately identified and/or valued but which generate economic benefits.

INCOME APPROACH	— A general way of determining a value indication of a business or equity interest using one or more methods wherein a value is determined by converting anticipated benefits.
INVESTED CAPITAL	— The sum of the debt and equity in an enterprise on a long term basis.
MAJORITY	— Ownership position greater than 50% of the voting interest in an enterprise.
MAJORITY CONTROL	— The degree of control provided by a majority position.
MARKET APPROACH	— A general way of determining a value indication of a business or equity interest using one or more methods that compare the subject to similar investments that have been sold.
MARKETABILITY DISCOUNT	— An amount or percentage deducted from an equity interest to reflect lack of marketability.
MINORITY INTEREST	— Ownership position less than 50% of the voting interest in an enterprise.
MINORITY DISCOUNT	— The reduction, from the pro rata share of the value of the entire business, which reflects the absence of the power of control.
NET ASSETS	— Total assets less total liabilities.
NET INCOME	— Revenues less expenses, including taxes.
RATE OF RETURN	— An amount of income realized or expected on an investment, expressed as a percentage of that investment.
REPLACEMENT COST NEW	— The current cost of a similar new item having the nearest equivalent utility as the item being appraised.
REPORT DATE	— The date of the report. May be the same or different than the APPRAISAL DATE.
REPRODUCTION COST NEW	— The current cost of an identical new item.
VALUATION	— See APPRAISAL.
WORKING CAPITAL	— The amount by which current assets exceed current liabilities.

AMERICAN SOCIETY OF APPRAISERS
Business Valuation Standard

BVS-II   Full Written Business Valuation Report

Adopted by the Business Valuation Committee, June 1990
Approved by the ASA Board of Governors, June 1991

I. Preamble

A. To enhance and maintain the quality of business valuation reports, for the benefit of the business valuation profession and users of business valuation reports, the American Society of Appraisers, through its Business Valuation Committee, has adopted this standard. This standard is required to be followed in the preparation of full, written business valuation reports by all members of the American Society of Appraisers, be they candidate, accredited or senior members.

B. The purpose of this standard is to define and describe the requirements for the written communication of the results of a business valuation, analysis or opinion, but not the conduct thereof.

C. The American Society of Appraisers, in Sections 7.4 and 8 of its Principles of Appraisal Practice and Code of Ethics, includes requirements with respect to written appraisal reports, as does The Appraisal Foundation, in Section 10 of its Uniform Standards of Professional Appraisal Practice. The present standard includes these requirements, either explicitly or by reference,and is designed to provide additional requirements specifically applicable to full, written business valuation reports.

D. The American Society of Appraisers, through its Business Valuation Committee, has adopted, in Business Valuation Standard BVS-I (1/88), a set of defined terms used in business valuation. In the preparation of reports in accordance with the present standard, BVS-I (1/88) should be followed.

E. The present standard provides minimum criteria to be followed by business appraisers in the preparation of full, written reports.

F. Written reports must meet the requirements of the present standard unless, in the opinion of the appraiser, circumstances dictate a departure from the standard; if so, such a departure must be disclosed in the report.

G. For the purpose of this standard, the appraiser is the individual or entity undertaking the appraisal assignment under a contract with the client.

II. Signature and Certification

A. An appraiser assumes responsibility for the statements made in the full, written report and indicates the acceptance of that responsibility by signing the report. To comply with this standard, a full, written report must be signed by the appraiser.

B. Clearly, at least one individual is responsible for the valuation conclusion(s) expressed in the report. A report must contain a certification, as required by Standard 10 of the

<u>Uniform Standards of Professional Appraisal Practice</u> of The Appraisal Foundation, in which the individuals responsible for the valuation conclusion(s) must be identified.

III. Assumptions and Limiting Conditions

The following assumptions and/or limiting conditions must be stated:

1. Pertaining to bias — a report must contain a statement that the appraiser has no interest in the asset appraised, or other conflict, which could cause a question as to the appraiser's independence or objectivity or if such an interest or conflict exists, it must be disclosed.

2. Pertaining to data used — where appropriate, a report must indicate that an appraiser relied on data supplied by others, without further verification by the appraiser, as well as the sources which were relied on.

3. Pertaining to validity of the valuation — a report must contain a statement that a valuation is valid only for the valuation date indicated and for the purpose stated.

IV. Definition of the Valuation Assignment

The precise definition of the valuation assignment is a key aspect of communication with users of the report. The following are key components of such a definition and must be included in the report:

1. The business interest valued must be clearly defined, such as 100 shares of the Class A common stock of the XYZ Corporation or a 20% limited partnership interest in the ABC Limited Partnership. The existence, rights and/or restrictions of other classes of ownership in the business appraised must also be adequately described if they are relevant to the conclusion of value.

2. The purpose and use of the valuation must be clearly stated, such as the determination of fair market value for ESOP purposes or a determination of fair value for dissenters' rights purposes. If a valuation is being done pursuant to a particular statute, the particular statute must be referenced.

3. The standard of value used in the valuation must be stated and defined. The premise of value, such as a valuation on a minority interest basis or an enterprise basis, must be stated.

4. The appraisal date must be clearly identified. The date of the preparation of the report must be indicated.

V. Business Description

As evidence of the appraiser's due diligence in obtaining the pertinent facts about the business appraised, and to aid the user's comprehension of the valuation conclusion, a full, written business valuation report must include a business description which covers all relevant factual areas, such as:

1. Form of organization (corporation, partnership, etc.)

2. History

3. Products and/or services and markets and customers

4. Management

5. Major assets, both tangible and intangible

6. Outlook for the economy, industry and company

7. Past transactional evidence of value

8. Sensitivity to seasonal or cyclical factors

9. Competition

10. Sources of information used.

VI. Financial Analysis

A. An analysis and discussion of a firm's financial statements is an integral part of a business valuation and must be included. Exhibits summarizing balance sheets and income statements for a period of years sufficient to the purpose of the valuation and the nature of the subject company must be included in the valuation report.

B. Any adjustments made to the reported financial data must be fully explained.

C. If projections of balance sheets or income statements were utilized in the valuation, key assumptions underlying the projections must be included and discussed.

D. If appropriate, the company's financial results relative to those of its industry must be discussed.

VII. Valuation Methodology

A. The valuation method or methods selected, and the reasons for their selection, must be discussed. The steps followed in the application of the method or methods selected must be described and must lead to the valuation conclusion.

B. The report must include an explanation of how any variables such as discount rates, capitalization rates or valuation multiples were determined and used. The rationale and/or supporting data for any premiums or discounts must be clearly presented.

VIII. Full, Written Report Format

The full, written report format must provide a logical progression for clear communication of pertinent information, valuation methods and conclusions and must incorporate the other specific requirements of this standard, including the signature and certification provisions.

IX. Confidentiality of Report

No copies of the report will be furnished to persons other than the client without the client's specific permission or direction unless ordered by a court of competent jurisdiction.

X. Address

Copies of this standard and BVS-I (1/88) may be obtained from the American Society of Appraisers, P.O. Box 17265, Washington, DC 20041.

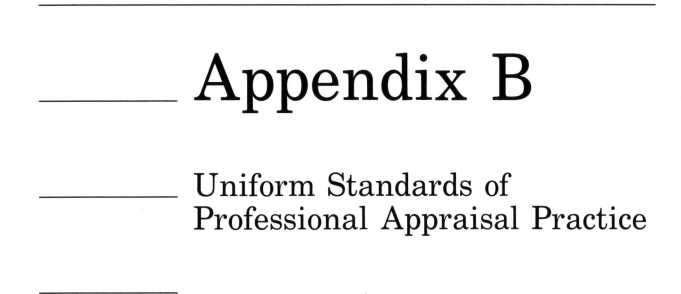

Appendix B

Uniform Standards of Professional Appraisal Practice

TABLE OF CONTENTS

UNIFORM STANDARDS OF PROFESSIONAL APPRAISAL PRACTICE

**as promulgated by the
Appraisal Standards Board of
The Appraisal Foundation**

UNIFORM STANDARDS OF
PROFESSIONAL APPRAISAL PRACTICE

as promulgated by the
Appraisal Standards Board of
The Appraisal Foundation

PREAMBLE

It is essential that a professional appraiser arrive at and communicate his or her analyses, opinions, and advice in a manner that will be meaningful to the client and will not be misleading in the marketplace. These Uniform Standards of Professional Appraisal Practice reflect the current standards of the appraisal profession.

The importance of the role of the appraiser places ethical obligations on those who serve in this capacity. These standards include explanatory comments and begin with an Ethics Provision setting forth the requirements for integrity, objectivity, independent judgment, and ethical conduct. In addition, these standards include a Competency Provision which places an immediate responsibility on the appraiser prior to acceptance of an assignment. The standards contain binding requirements, as well as specific guidelines to which a Departure Provision may apply under certain limited conditions. Definitions applicable to these standards are also included.

These standards deal with the procedures to be followed in performing an appraisal, review or consulting service and the manner in which an appraisal, review or consulting service is communicated. Standards 1 and 2 relate to the development and communication of a real property appraisal. Standard 3 establishes guidelines for reviewing an appraisal and reporting on that review. Standards 4 and 5 address the development and communication of various real estate or real property consulting functions by an appraiser. Standard 6 sets forth criteria for the development and reporting of mass appraisals for ad valorem tax purposes. Standards 7 and 8 establish guidelines for developing and communicating personal property appraisals. Standards 9 and 10 establish guidelines for developing and communicating business appraisals.

These standards are for appraisers and the users of appraisal services. To maintain the highest level of professional practice, appraisers must observe these standards. The users of appraisal services should demand work performed in conformance with these standards.

> Comment: Explanatory comments are an integral part of the Uniform Standards and should be viewed as extensions of the provisions, definitions, and standards rules. Comments provide interpretation from the Appraisal Standards Board concerning the background or application of certain provisions, definitions, or standards rules. There are no comments for provisions, definitions, and standards rules that are axiomatic or have not yet required further explanation; however, additional comments will be developed and others supplemented or revised as the need arises.

ETHICS PROVISION

Because of the fiduciary responsibilities inherent in professional appraisal practice, the appraiser must observe the highest standards of professional ethics. This Ethics Provision is divided into four sections: conduct, management, confidentiality, and record keeping.

> Comment: This provision emphasizes the personal obligations and responsibilities of the individual appraiser. However, it should also be emphasized that groups and organizations engaged in appraisal practice share the same ethical obligations.

Conduct

An appraiser must perform ethically and competently in accordance with these standards and not engage in conduct that is unlawful, unethical, or improper. An appraiser who could reasonably be perceived to act as a disinterested third party in rendering an unbiased appraisal, review, or consulting service must perform assignments with impartiality, objectivity, and independence and without accommodation of personal interests.

> Comment: An appraiser is required to avoid any action that could be considered misleading or fraudulent. In particular, it is unethical for an appraiser to use or communicate a misleading or fraudulent report or to knowingly permit an employee or other person to communicate a misleading or fraudulent report.
>
> The development of an appraisal, review, or consulting service based on a hypothetical condition is unethical unless: 1) the use of the hypothesis is clearly disclosed; 2) the assumption of the hypothetical condition is clearly required for legal purposes, for purposes of reasonable analysis, or for purposes of comparison and would not be misleading; and 3) the report clearly describes the rationale for this assumption, the nature of the hypothetical condition, and its effect on the result of the appraisal, review, or consulting service.
>
> An individual appraiser employed by a group or organization which conducts itself in a manner that does not conform to these standards should take steps that are appropriate under the circumstances to ensure compliance with the standards.

Management

The acceptance of compensation that is contingent upon the reporting of a predetermined value or a direction in value that favors the cause of the client, the amount of the value estimate, the attainment of a stipulated result, or the occurrence of a subsequent event is unethical.

The payment of undisclosed fees, commissions, or things of value in connection with the procurement of appraisal, review, or consulting assignments is unethical.

> Comment: Disclosure of fees, commissions, or things of value connected to the procurement of an assignment should appear in the certification of a written report and in any transmittal letter in which conclusions are stated. In groups or organizations engaged in appraisal practice, intra-company payments to employees for business development are not considered to be unethical. Competency, rather than financial incentives, should be the primary basis for awarding an assignment.

ETHICS PROVISION (continued)

Management (continued)

Advertising for or soliciting appraisal assignments in a manner which is false, misleading or exaggerated is unethical.

> Comment: In groups or organizations engaged in appraisal practice, decisions concerning finder or referral fees, contingent compensation, and advertising may not be the responsibility of an individual appraiser, but for a particular assignment, it is the responsibility of the individual appraiser to ascertain that there has been no breach of ethics, that the appraisal is prepared in accordance with these standards, and that the report can be properly certified as required by Standards Rules 2-3, 3-2, 5-3, 8-3 or 10-3.

The restriction on contingent compensation in the first paragraph of this section does not apply to consulting assignments where the appraiser is not acting in a disinterested manner and would not reasonably be perceived as performing a service that requires impartiality. This permitted contingent compensation must be properly disclosed in the report.

> Comment: Assignments where the appraiser is not acting in a disinterested manner are further discussed in the General Comment to Standard 4. The preparer of the written report of such an assignment must certify that the compensation is contingent and must explain the basis for the contingency in the report (See Standards Rule 5-3) and in any transmittal letter in which conclusions are stated.

Confidentiality

An appraiser must protect the confidential nature of the appraiser-client relationship.

> Comment: An appraiser must not disclose confidential factual data obtained from a client or the results of an assignment prepared for a client to anyone other than: 1) the client and persons specifically authorized by the client; 2) such third parties as may be authorized by due process of law; and 3) a duly authorized professional peer review committee. As a corollary, it is unethical for a member of a duly authorized professional peer review committee to disclose confidential information or factual data presented to the committee.

Record Keeping

An appraiser must prepare written records of appraisal, review, and consulting assignments — including oral testimony and reports — and retain such records for a period of at least five (5) years after preparation or at least two (2) years after final disposition of any judicial proceeding in which testimony was given, whichever period expires last.

> Comment: Written records of assignments include true copies of written reports, written summaries of oral testimony and reports (or a transcript of testimony), all data and statements required by these standards, and other information as may be required to support the findings and conclusions of the appraiser. The term written records also includes information stored on electronic, magnetic, or other media. Such records must be made available by the appraiser when required by due process of law or by a duly authorized professional peer review committee.

COMPETENCY PROVISION

Prior to accepting an assignment or entering into an agreement to perform any assignment, an appraiser must properly identify the problem to be addressed and have the knowledge and experience to complete the assignment competently; or alternatively:

1. disclose the lack of knowledge and/or experience to the client before accepting the assignment; and

2. take all steps necessary or appropriate to complete the assignment competently; and

3. describe the lack of knowledge and/or experience and the steps taken to complete the assignment competently in the report.

Comment: The background and experience of appraisers varies widely and a lack of knowledge or experience can lead to inaccurate or inappropriate appraisal practice. The competency provision requires an appraiser to have both the knowledge and the experience required to perform a specific appraisal service competently. If an appraiser is offered the opportunity to perform an appraisal service but lacks the necessary knowledge or experience to complete it competently, the appraiser must disclose his or her lack of knowledge or experience to the client before accepting the assignment and then take the necessary or appropriate steps to complete the appraisal service competently. This may be accomplished in various ways including, but not limited to, personal study by the appraiser; association with an appraiser reasonably believed to have the necessary knowledge or experience; or retention of others who possess the required knowledge or experience.

Although this provision requires an appraiser to identify the problem and disclose any deficiency in competence prior to accepting an assignment, facts or conditions uncovered during the course of an assignment could cause an appraiser to discover that he or she lacks the required knowledge or experience to complete the assignment competently. At the point of such discovery, the appraiser is obligated to notify the client and comply with items 2 and 3 of the provision.

The concept of competency also extends to appraisers who are requested or required to travel to geographic areas wherein they have no recent appraisal experience. An appraiser preparing an appraisal in an unfamiliar location must spend sufficient time to understand the nuances of the local market and the supply and demand factors relating to the specific property type and the location involved. Such understanding will not be imparted solely from a consideration of specific data such as demographics, costs, sales and rentals. The necessary understanding of local market conditions provides the bridge between a sale and a comparable sale or a rental and a comparable rental. If an appraiser is not in a position to spend the necessary amount of time in a market area to obtain this understanding, affiliation with a qualified local appraiser may be the appropriate response to ensure the development of a competent appraisal.

With regard to mass appraisal as defined herein, an appraiser must immediately take all necessary steps to ensure the mass appraisal is developed under the supervision of an appraiser who has the qualifications referred to in Standard 6.

DEPARTURE PROVISION

This provision permits limited exceptions to sections of the Uniform Standards that are classified as specific guidelines rather than binding requirements. The burden of proof is on the appraiser to decide before accepting a limited assignment that the result will not confuse or mislead. The burden of disclosure is also on the appraiser to report any limitations.

An appraiser may enter into an agreement to perform an assignment that calls for something less than, or different from, the work that would otherwise be required by the specific guidelines, provided that prior to entering into such an agreement:

1.   the appraiser has determined that the assignment to be performed is not so limited in scope that the resulting appraisal, review, or consulting service would tend to mislead or confuse the client, the users of the report, or the public; and

2.   the appraiser has advised the client that the assignment calls for something less than, or different from, the work required by the specific guidelines and that the report will state the limited or differing scope of the appraisal, review, or consulting service.

Exceptions to the following requirements are not permitted: Standards Rules 1-1, 1-5, 2-1, 2-2, 2-3, 2-5, 3-1, 3-2, 4-1, 5-1, 5-3, 6-1, 6-5, 6-6, 7-1, 8-1, 8-3, 9-1, 9-3, 9-5, 10-1, 10-3 and 10-5. This restriction on departure is reiterated throughout the document with the reminder comment: Departure from this binding requirement is not permitted.

> Comment: Before making a decision to enter into an agreement for appraisal services calling for a departure from a specific appraisal guideline, an appraiser must use extreme care to determine whether the scope of the appraisal service to be performed is so limited that the resulting analysis, opinion, or conclusion would tend to mislead or confuse the client, the users of the report, or the public. For the purpose of this provision, users of the report might include parties such as lenders, employees of government agencies, limited partners of a client, and a client's attorney and accountant. In this context the purpose of the appraisal and the anticipated or possible use of the report are critical.
>
> If an appraiser enters into an agreement to perform an appraisal service that calls for something less than, or different from, the work that would otherwise be required by the specific appraisal guidelines, Standards Rules 2-2(k), 5-2(i), 8-2(h), and 10-2(h) require that this fact be clearly and accurately set forth in the report.
>
> The requirements of the departure provision may be satisfied by the technique of incorporating by reference.
>
> For example, if an appraiser's complete file was introduced into evidence at a public hearing or public trial and the appraiser subsequently prepared a one-page report that 1) identified the property, 2) stated the value, and 3) stated that the value conclusion could not be properly understood without reference to his or her complete file and directed the reader to the complete file, the requirements of the departure provision would be satisfied if the appraiser's complete file contained, in coherent form, all the data and statements that are required by the Uniform Standards.
>
> Another example would be an update report that expressly incorporated by reference all the background data, market conditions, assumptions, and limiting conditions that were contained in the original report prepared for the same client.

JURISDICTIONAL EXCEPTION

If any part of these standards is contrary to the law or public policy of any jurisdiction, only that part shall be void and of no force or effect in that jurisdiction.

SUPPLEMENTAL STANDARDS

These Uniform Standards provide the common basis for all appraisal practice. Supplemental standards applicable to appraisals prepared for specific purposes or property types may be issued by public agencies and certain client groups, e.g. regulatory agencies, eminent domain authorities, asset managers, and financial institutions. Appraisers and clients must ascertain whether any supplemental standards in addition to these Uniform Standards apply to the assignment being considered.

DEFINITIONS

For the purpose of these standards, the following definitions apply:

APPRAISAL: (noun) the act or process of estimating value; an estimate of value.
(adjective) of or pertaining to appraising and related functions, e.g. appraisal practice, appraisal services.

APPRAISAL PRACTICE: the work or services performed by appraisers, defined by three terms in these standards: appraisal, review, and consulting.

> Comment: These three terms are intentionally generic, and not mutually exclusive. For example, an estimate of value may be required as part of a review or consulting service. The use of other nomenclature by an appraiser (e.g. analysis, counseling, evaluation, study, submission, valuation) does not exempt an appraiser from adherence to these standards.

CASH FLOW ANALYSIS: a study of the anticipated movement of cash into or out of an investment.

CLIENT: any party for whom an appraiser performs a service.

CONSULTING: the act or process of providing information, analysis of real estate data, and recommendations or conclusions on diversified problems in real estate, other than estimating value.

FEASIBILITY ANALYSIS: a study of the cost-benefit relationship of an economic endeavor.

INVESTMENT ANALYSIS: a study that reflects the relationship between acquisition price and anticipated future benefits of a real estate investment.

MARKET ANALYSIS: a study of real estate market conditions for a specific type of property.

MARKET VALUE: Market value is the major focus of most real property appraisal assignments. Both economic and legal definitions of market value have been developed and refined. A current economic definition agreed upon by federal financial institutions in the United States of America is:

> The most probable price which a property should bring in a competitive and open market under all conditions requisite to a fair sale, the buyer and seller each acting prudently and knowledgeably, and assuming the price is not affected by undue stimulus. Implicit in this definition is the consummation of a sale as of a specified date and the passing of title from seller to buyer under conditions whereby:

> 1.   buyer and seller are typically motivated;

> 2.   both parties are well informed or well advised, and acting in what they consider their best interests;

> 3.   a reasonable time is allowed for exposure in the open market;

> 4.   payment is made in terms of cash in United States dollars or in terms of financial arrangements comparable thereto; and

> 5.   the price represents the normal consideration for the property sold unaffected by special or creative financing or sales concessions granted by anyone associated with the sale.

Substitution of another currency for United States dollars in the fourth condition is appropriate in other countries or in reports addressed to clients from other countries.

DEFINITIONS (continued)

MARKET VALUE (continued)

Persons performing appraisal services that may be subject to litigation are cautioned to seek the exact legal definition of market value in the jurisdiction in which the services are being performed.

MASS APPRAISAL: the process of valuing a universe of properties as of a given date utilizing standard methodology, employing common data, and allowing for statistical testing.

MASS APPRAISAL MODEL: a mathematical expression of how supply and demand factors interact in a market.

PERSONAL PROPERTY: identifiable portable and tangible objects which are considered by the general public as being "personal," e.g. furnishings, artwork, antiques, gems and jewelry, collectibles, machinery and equipment; all property that is not classified as real estate.

REAL ESTATE: an identified parcel or tract of land, including improvements, if any.

REAL PROPERTY: the interests, benefits, and rights inherent in the ownership of real estate.

> Comment: In some jurisdictions, the terms real estate and real property have the same legal meaning. The separate definitions recognize the traditional distinction between the two concepts in appraisal theory.

REPORT: any communication, written or oral, of an appraisal, review, or analysis; the document that is transmitted to the client upon completion of an assignment.

> Comment: Most reports are written and most clients mandate written reports. Oral report guidelines (See Standards Rule 2-4) and restrictions (See Ethics Provision: Record Keeping) are included to cover court testimony and other oral communications of an appraisal, review or consulting service.

REVIEW: the act or process of critically studying a report prepared by another.

ADDITIONAL DEFINITIONS APPLICABLE TO STANDARDS 9 AND 10

BUSINESS ASSETS: Tangible and intangible resources other than personal property and real estate that are employed by a business enterprise in its operations.

BUSINESS ENTERPRISE: A commercial, industrial or service organization pursuing an economic activity.

BUSINESS EQUITY: The interests, benefits, and rights inherent in the ownership of a business enterprise or a part thereof.

> Comment: To the extent that several of the definitions cited on Pages I-7 and I-8 of these Standards apply to business appraisal and include a direct reference to real estate, they are modified for the purpose of Standards 9 and 10.

STANDARD 9

In developing a business appraisal, an appraiser must be aware of, understand, and correctly employ those recognized methods and techniques that are necessary to produce a credible appraisal.

> Comment: Standard 9 is directed toward the same substantive aspects set forth in Standard 1, but addresses business appraisal.

Standards Rule 9-1

In developing a business appraisal, an appraiser must:

(a)   be aware of, understand, and correctly employ those recognized methods and techniques that are necessary to produce a credible appraisal;

> Comment: S.R. 9-1(a) is identical in scope and purpose to S.R. 1-1(a). Changes and developments in the economy and in investment theory have a substantial impact on the business appraisal profession. Important changes in the financial arena, securities regulation, tax law and major new court decisions may result in corresponding changes in business appraisal theory and practice.

(b)   not commit a substantial error of omission or commission that significantly affects an appraisal;

> Comment: S.R. 9-1(b) is identical in scope and purpose to S.R. 1-1(b).

(c)   not render appraisal services in a careless or negligent manner, such as a series of errors that, considered individually, may not significantly affect the results of an appraisal, but which, when considered in the aggregate, would be misleading.

> Comment: S.R. 9-1(c) is identical in scope and purpose to S.R. 1-1(c).

Standards Rule 9-2

In developing a business appraisal, an appraiser must observe the following specific appraisal guidelines:

(a)   adequately identify the business enterprise, assets, or equity under consideration, define the purpose and the intended use of the appraisal, consider the scope of the appraisal, describe any special limiting conditions, and identify the effective date of the appraisal;

(b)   define the value being considered.

> Comment: S.R. 9-2(b) is identical in scope and purpose to S.R. 1-2(b).

STANDARD 9 (continued)

Standards Rule 9-2 (continued)

(i) if the appraisal concerns a business enterprise or equity interests, consider any buy-sell agreements, investment letter stock restrictions, restrictive corporate charter or partnership agreement clauses, and any similar features or factors that may have an influence on value.

(ii) if the appraisal concerns assets, the appraiser must consider whether the assets are:
(1) appraised independently; or
(2) appraised as parts of a going concern.

Comment: The value of assets held by a business enterprise may change significantly depending on whether the basis of valuation is acquisition or replacement, continued use in place, or liquidation.

(iii) if the appraisal concerns equity interests in a business enterprise, consider whether the interests are appraised on a majority or minority basis.

Comment: S.R. 9-2(b)(iii) is identical in scope and purpose to S.R. 1-2(d).

Standards Rule 9-3

In developing a business appraisal relating to a majority interest in a business enterprise, an appraiser must investigate the possibility that the business enterprise may have a higher value in liquidation than for continued operation as a going concern. If liquidation is the indicated basis of valuation, any real estate or personal property to be liquidated must be valued under the appropriate standard.

Comment: This rule requires the appraiser to recognize that continued operation of a marginally profitable business is not always the best approach as liquidation may result in a higher value. It should be noted, however, that this should be considered only when the business equity being appraised is in a position to cause liquidation. If liquidation is the appropriate basis of value, then assets such as real estate and personal property must be appraised under Standard 1 and Standard 7, respectively.

Standards Rule 9-4

In developing a business appraisal, an appraiser must observe the following specific appraisal guidelines when applicable:

(a) value the business enterprise, assets or equity by an appropriate method or technique.

(b) collect and analyze relevant data regarding:

(i) the nature and history of the business;
(ii) financial and economic conditions affecting the business enterprise, its industry, and the general economy;
(iii) past results, current operations, and future prospects of the business enterprise;
(iv) past sales of capital stock or partnership interests in the business enterprise being appraised;
(v) sales of similar businesses or capital stock of publicly held similar businesses;
(vi) prices, terms, and conditions affecting past sales of similar business assets;
(vii) physical condition, remaining life expectancy, and functional and economic utility or obsolescence.

No pertinent information shall be withheld.

STANDARD 9 (continued)

Standards Rule 9-4 (continued)

> Comment: This guideline directs the appraiser to study the prospective and retrospective aspects of the business enterprise and to study it in terms of the economic and industrial environment within which it operates. Further, sales of securities of the business itself or similar businesses for which sufficient information is available should also be considered.
>
> This guideline also requires the appraiser to investigate and take into account not only that loss of value that results from deterioration due to age but also loss of value due to functional and economic obsolescence. Economic obsolescence is a major consideration when assets are considered as parts of a going concern. It is also the criterion in deciding that liquidation is the appropriate basis for valuation.

Standards Rule 9-5

In developing a business appraisal, an appraiser must:

(a)   **select one or more approaches that apply to the specific appraisal assignments**

(b)   **consider and reconcile the quality and quantity of data available for analysis within the approaches that are applicable.**

> Comment: This rule requires the appraiser to use all approaches for which sufficient reliable data are available. However, it does not mean that the appraiser must use all approaches in order to comply with the rule if certain approaches are not applicable.

STANDARD 10

In reporting the results of a business appraisal an appraiser must communicate each analysis, opinion, and conclusion in a manner that is not misleading.

> Comment: Standard 10 is identical in scope and purpose to the appraisal reporting requirements in Standard 2.

Standards Rule 10-1

Each written or oral business appraisal report must:

(a)   **clearly and accurately set forth the appraisal in a manner that will not be misleading.**

> Comment: S.R. 10-1(a) is identical in scope and purpose to S.R. 2-1(a).

(b)   **contain sufficient information to enable the person(s) who receive or rely on the report to understand it properly.**

> Comment: S.R. 10-1(b) is identical in scope and purpose to S.R. 2-1(b).

(c)   **clearly and accurately disclose any extraordinary assumption or limiting condition that directly affects the appraisal and indicate its impact on value.**

> Comment: This rule requires a clear and accurate disclosure of any extraordinary assumptions or conditions that directly affect an analysis, opinion, or conclusion. Examples of such extraordinary assumptions or conditions might include items such as the execution of a pending lease agreement, atypical financing, infusion of additional working capital or making other capital additions, or compliance with regulatory authority rules.

Standards Rule 10-2

Each written business appraisal report must comply with the following specific reporting guidelines:

(a)   **identify and describe the business enterprise, assets or equity being appraised.**

(b)   **state the purpose of the appraisal.**

(c)   **define the value to be estimated.**

(d)   **set forth the effective date of the appraisal and the date of the report.**

> Comment: Every business appraisal report must include information sufficient to identify what is being appraised, for what purpose, what type of value is being sought and the date as of which that value applies. If the appraisal concerns equity, it is not enough to identify the entity in which the equity is being appraised but also the nature of the equity, for example: how many shares of common or preferred stock. The purpose may be to express an opinion of value but the intended use of the appraisal must also be stated.
>
> Not only the type of value being sought—fair market value, value in use, etc.—must be stated but it must also be defined clearly. The report date is when the report is submitted; the appraisal date or date of value is the effective date of the value conclusion. This date cannot be later than the report date.

(e)   **describe the scope of the appraisal.**

STANDARD 10 (continued)

Standards Rule 10-2 (continued)

(f)   set forth all assumptions and limiting conditions that affect the analyses, opinions, and conclusions.

(g)   set forth the information considered, the appraisal procedures followed, and the reasoning that supports the analyses, opinions and conclusions.

(h)   set forth any additional information that may be appropriate to show compliance with, or clearly identify and explain permitted departures from, the requirements of Standard 9.

Comment: S.R. 10-2(e), (f), (g), and (h) are identical in scope and purpose to S.R. 2-2(f), (g), (h), and (i).

(i)   include a certification in accordance with S.R. 10-3.

(j)   include a letter of transmittal signed by the person assuming technical responsibility for the appraisal.

Comment: An appraisal report cannot be anonymous. The appraiser or the person assuming technical responsibility for the appraisal must sign the report. The person assuming technical responsibility for the appraisal must be the person under whose direct supervision the appraisal investigation was conducted and who had final responsibility for the conclusions and opinions of value in the appraisal report. Reports issued by a firm may be signed by the person authorized to sign on behalf of the firm, only if the person assuming technical responsibility for the appraisal also signs.

Standards Rule 10-3

Each written business appraisal report must contain a certification that is similar in content to the following:

I certify that, to the best of my knowledge and belief:

—   the statements of fact contained in this report are true and correct.
—   the reported analyses, opinions, and conclusions are limited only by the reported assumptions and limiting conditions, and are my personal, unbiased professional analyses, opinions, and conclusions.
—   I have no (or the specified) present or prospective interest in the property that is the subject of this report, and I have no (or the specified) personal interest or bias with respect to the parties involved.
—   my compensation is not contingent on an action or event resulting from the analyses, opinions, or conclusions in, or the use of, this report.
—   my analyses, opinions, and conclusions were developed, and this report has been prepared, in conformity with the Uniform Standards of Professional Appraisal Practice.
—   no one provided significant professional assistance to the person signing this report. (If there are exceptions, the name of each individual providing significant professional assistance must be stated.)

STANDARD 10 (continued)

Standards Rule 10-4

To the extent that it is both possible and appropriate, each oral business appraisal report (including expert testimony) must address the substantive matters set forth in S.R. 10-2.

Comment: S.R. 10-4 is identical in scope and purpose to S.R. 2-4.

Standards Rule 10-5

An appraiser who signs a business appraisal report prepared by another, even under the label "review appraiser", must accept full responsibility for the contents of this report.

Comment: S.R. 10-5 is identical in scope and purpose to S.R. 2-5.

Appendix C

Revenue Ruling 59-60

Revenue Ruling 59-60

In valuing the stock of closely held corporations, or the stock of corporations where market quotations are not available, all other available financial data, as well as all relevant factors affecting the fair market value must be considered for estate tax and gift purposes. No general formula may be given that is applicable to the many different valuation situations arising in the valuation of such stock. However, the general approach, methods, and factors which must be considered in valuing such securities are outlined.

Section 1. Purpose.

The purpose of this Revenue Ruling is to outline and review in general the approach, methods and factors to be considered in valuing shares of the capital stock of closely held corporations for estate tax and gift tax purposes. The methods discussed herein will apply likewise to the valuation of corporate stocks on which market quotations are either unavailable or are of such scarcity that they do not reflect the fair market value.

Section 2. Background and Definitions.

.01 All valuations must be made in accordance with the applicable provisions of the Internal Revenue Code of 1954 and the Federal Estate Tax and Gift Tax Regulations. Sections 2031(a), 2032 and 2512(a) of the 1954 Code (sections 811 and 1005 of the 1939 Code) require that the property to be included in the gross estate, or made the subject of a gift, shall be taxed on the basis of the value of the property at the time of death of the decedent, the alternate date if so elected, or the date of gift.

.02 Section 20.2031-1(b) of the Estate Tax Regulations (section 81.10 of the Estate Tax Regulations 105) and section 25.2512-1 of the Gift Tax Regulations (section 86.19 of Gift Tax Regulations 108) define fair market value, in effect, as the price at which the property would change hands between a willing buyer and a willing seller when the former is not under any compulsion to buy and the latter is not under any compulsion to sell, both parties having reasonable knowledge of relevant facts. Court decisions frequently state in addition that the hypothetical buyer and seller are assumed to be able, as well as willing, to trade and to be well informed about the property and concerning the market for such property.

.03 Closely held corporations are those corporations the shares of which are owned by a relatively limited number of stockholders. Often the entire stock issue is held by one family. The result of this situation is that little, if any, trading in the shares takes place. There is, therefore, no established market for the stock and such sales as occur at irregular intervals seldom reflect all of the elements of a representative transaction as defined by the term "fair market value."

Section 3. Approach to Valuation.

.01 A determination of fair market value, being a question of fact, will depend upon the circumstances in each case. No formula can be devised that will be generally applicable to the multitude of different valuation issues arising in estate and gift tax cases. Often, an appraiser will find wide difference of opinion as to the fair market value of a particular stock. In resolving such differences, he should maintain a reasonable attitude in recognition of the fact that valuation is not an exact science. A sound valuation will be based upon all the relevant facts, but the elements of common sense, informed judgment and reasonableness must enter into the process of weighing those facts and determining their aggregate significance.

.02 The fair market value of specific shares of stock will vary as general economic conditions change from "normal" to "boom" or "depression," that is, according to the degree of optimism or pessimism with which the investing public regards the future at the required date of appraisal. Uncertainty as to the stability or continuity of the future income from a property decreases its value by increasing the risk of loss of earnings and value in the future. The value of shares of stock of a company with very uncertain future prospects is highly speculative. The appraiser must exercise his judgment as to the degree of risk attaching to the business of the corporation which issued the stock, but that judgment must be related to all of the other factors affecting value.

.03 Valuation of securities is, in essence, a prophesy as to the future and must be based on facts available at the required date of appraisal. As a generalization, the prices of stocks which are traded in volume in a free and active market by informed persons best reflect the consensus of the investing public as to what the future holds for the corporations and industries represented. When a stock is closely held, is traded infrequently, or is traded in an erratic market, some other measure of value must be used. In many instances, the next best measure may be found in the prices at which the stocks of companies engaged in the same or a similar line of business are selling in a free and open market.

Section 4. Factors to Consider.

.01 It is advisable to emphasize that in the valuation of the stock of closely held corporations where market quotations are either lacking or too scarce to be recognized, all available financial data, as well as all relevant factors affecting the fair market value, should be considered. The following factors, although not all-inclusive are fundamental and require careful analysis in each case:

(a) The nature of the business and the history of the enterprise from its inception.

(b) The economic outlook in general and the condition and outlook of the specific industry in particular.

(c)   The book value of the stock and the financial condition of the business.

(d)   The earning capacity of the company.

(e)   The dividend-paying capacity.

(f)   Whether or not the enterprise has goodwill or other intangible value.

(g)   Sales of the stock and the size of the block of stock to be valued.

(h)   The market price of stocks of corporations engaged in the same or a similar line of business having their stocks actively traded in a free and open market, either on an exchange or over-the-counter.

.02 The following is a brief discussion of each of the foregoing factors:

(a) The history of a corporate enterprise will show its past stability or instability, its growth or lack of growth, the diversity or lack of diversity of its operations, and other facts needed to form an opinion of the degree of risk involved in the business. For an enterprise which changed its form of organization but carried on the same or closely similar operations of its predecessor, the history of the former enterprise should be considered. The detail to be considered should increase with approach to the required date of appraisal, since recent events are of greatest help in predicting the future; but a study of gross and net income, and of dividends covering a long prior period, is highly desirable. The history to be studied should include, but need not be limited to, the nature of the business, its products or services, its operation and investment assets, capital structure, plan facilities, sales records and management, all of which should be considered as of the date of the appraisal, with due regard for recent significant changes. Events of the past that are unlikely to recur in the future should be discounted, since value has a close relation to future expectancy.

(b) A sound appraisal of a closely held stock must consider current and prospective economic conditions as of the date of appraisal, both in the national economy and in the industry or industries with which the corporation is allied. It is important to know that the company is more or less successful than its competitors in the same industry, or that it is maintaining a stable position with respect to competitors. Equal or even greater significance may attach to the ability of the industry with which the company is allied to compete with other industries. Prospective competition which has not been a factor in prior years should be given careful attention. For example, high profits due to the novelty of its product and the lack of competition often lead to increasing competition. The public's appraisal of the future prospects of competitive industries or of competitors within an industry may be indicated by price trends in the markets for commodities and for securities. The loss of the manager of a so-called "one-man" business may have a depressing effect upon the value of the stock of such business, particularly if there is a lack of trained personnel capable of succeeding to the management of the enterprise. In valuing the stock of this type of business, therefore, the effect of the loss of the manager on the future expectancy of the business, and the absence of management-succession potentialities are pertinent factors to be taken into consideration. On the other hand, there may be factors which offset, in whole or in part, the loss of the manager's services. For instance, the nature of the business and of its assets may be such that they will not be impaired by the loss of the manager. Furthermore, the loss may be adequately covered by life insurance, or competent management might be employed on the basis of the consideration paid for the former manager's services. These, or other offsetting factors, if found to exist should be carefully weighed against the loss of the manager's services in valuing the stock of the enterprise.

(c) Balance sheets should be obtained, preferably in the form of comparative annual statements for two or more years immediately preceding the date of appraisal, together with a balance sheet at the end of the month preceding that date, if corporate accounting will permit. Any balance sheet descriptions that are not self-explanatory, and balance sheet items comprehending diverse assets or liabilities, should be clarified in essential detail by supporting supplemental schedules. These statements usually will disclose to the appraiser (1) liquid position (ratio of current assets to current liabilities); (2) gross and net book value of principal classes of fixed assets; (3) working capital; (4) long-term indebtedness; (5) capital structure; and (6) net worth. Consideration also should be given to any assets not essential to the operation of the business, such as investments in securities, real estate, etc. In general, such nonoperating assets will command a lower rate of return than do the operating assets, although in exceptional cases the reverse may be true. In computing the book value per share of stock, assets of the investment type should be revalued on the basis of their market price and the book value adjusted accordingly. Comparison of the company's balance sheets over several years may reveal, among other facts, such developments as the acquisition of additional production facilities or subsidiary companies, improvement in financial position, and details as to recapitalizations and other changes in the capital structure of the corporation. If the corporation has more than one class of stock outstanding, the charter or certificate of incorporation should be examined to ascertain the explicit rights and privileges of the various stock issues including: (1) voting powers, (2) preference as to dividends, and (3) preference as to assets in the event of liquidation.

(d) Detailed profit-and-loss statements should be obtained and considered for a representative period immediately prior to the required date of appraisal, preferably five or more years. Such statements should show (1) gross income by principal items; (2) principal deductions from gross income including major prior items of operating expenses, interest and other expense on each item of long-term debt, depreciation and depletion if such deductions are made, officers' salaries, in total if they appear to be reasonable or in detail if they seem to be excessive, contributions (whether or not deductible for tax purposes) that the nature of its business and its community position require the corporation to make, and taxes by principal items, including income and excess profit taxes; (3) net income available for dividends; (4) rates and amounts of dividends paid on each class of stock; (5) remaining amount carried to surplus; and (6) adjustments to, and reconciliation with, surplus as stated on the balance sheet. With profit and loss statements of this character available, the appraiser should be able to separate recurrent from nonrecurrent items of income and expense, to distinguish between operating income and investment income, and to ascertain whether or not any line of business in which the company is engaged is operated consistently at a loss and might be abandoned with benefit to the company. The percentage of earnings retained for business expansion should be noted when dividend-paying capacity is considered. Potential future income is a major factor in many valuations of closely held stocks and all information concerning past income which will be helpful in predicting the future should be secured. Prior earnings records usually are the most reliable guide as to the future expectancy, but resort to arbitrary five-or-ten year averages without regard to current trends or future prospects will not produce a realistic valuation. If, for instance, a record of progressively increasing or decreasing net income is found, then greater weight may be accorded the most recent years' profits in estimating earning power. It will be helpful, in judging risk and the extent to which a business is a marginal operator, to consider deductions from income and net income in terms of percentage of sales. Major categories of cost and expense to be so analyzed include the consumption of raw materials and supplied in the case of manufacturers, processors and fabricators; the cost of purchased merchandise in the case of merchants; utility services; insurance; taxes; depletion or depreciation; and interest.

(e) Primary consideration should be given to the dividend-paying capacity of the company rather than to dividends actually paid in the past. Recognition must be given to the necessity of retaining a reasonable portion of profits in a company to meet competition. Dividend-paying capacity is a factor that must be considered in an appraisal, but dividends actually paid in the past may not have any relation to dividend-paying capacity. Specifically, the dividends paid by a closely held family company may be measured by the income needs of the stockholders or by their desire to avoid taxes on dividend receipts, instead of by the ability of the company to pay dividends. Where an actual or effective controlling interest in a corporation is to be valued, the dividend factor is not a material element, since the payment of such dividends is discretionary with the controlling stockholders. The individual or group in control can substitute salaries and bonuses for dividends, thus reducing net income and understating the dividend-paying capacity of the company. It follows, therefore, that dividends are less reliable criteria of fair market value than other applicable factors.

(f) In the final analysis, goodwill is based upon earning capacity. The presence of goodwill and its value, therefore, rests upon the excess of net earnings over and above a fair return on the net tangible assets. While the element of goodwill may be based primarily on earnings, such factors as the prestige and renown of the business, the ownership of a trade or brand name, and a record of successful operation over a prolonged period in a particular locality, also may furnish support for the inclusion of intangible value. In some instances it may not be possible to make a separate appraisal of the tangible and intangible assets of the business.

The enterprise has a value as an entity. Whatever intangible value there is, which is supportable by the facts, may be measured by the amount by which the appraised value of the tangible assets exceeds the net book value of such assets.

(g) Sales of stock of a closely held corporation should be carefully investigated to determine whether they represent transactions at arm's length. Forced or distress sales do not ordinarily reflect fair market value nor do isolated sales in small amounts necessarily control as the measure of value. This is especially true in the valuation of a controlling interest in a corporation. Since, in the case of closely held stocks, no prevailing market prices are available, there is no basis for making an adjustment for blockage. It follows, therefore, that such stocks should be valued upon a consideration of all the evidence affecting the fair market value. The size of the block of stock itself is a relevant factor to be considered. Although it is true that a minority interest in an unlisted corporation's stock is more difficult to sell than a similar block of listed stock, it is equally true that control of a corporation, either actual or in effect, representing as it does an added element of value, may justify a higher value for a specific block of stock.

(h) Section 2031(b) of the Code states, in effect, that in valuing unlisted securities the value of stock or securities of corporations engaged in the same or similar line of business which are listed on an exchange should be taken into consideration along with all other factors. An important consideration is that the corporations to be used for comparisons have capital stocks which are actively traded by the public. In accordance with section 2031(b) of the Code, stocks listed on an exchange are to be considered first. However, if sufficient comparable companies whose stocks are listed on an exchange cannot be found, other comparable companies which have stocks actively traded in on the over-the-counter market also may be used. The essential factor is that whether the stocks are sold on an exchange or over-the-counter there is evidence of an active, free public market for the stock as of the valuation date. In selecting corporations for comparative purposes, care should be taken to use only comparable companies. Although the only restrictive requirement as to comparable corporations specified in the statute is that their lines of business be the same or similar, yet it is obvious that consideration must be given to other relevant factors in order that the most valid comparison possible will be obtained. For illustration, a corporation having one or more issues of preferred stock, bonds or debentures in addition to its common stock should not be considered to be directly comparable to one having only common stock outstanding. In like manner, a company with a declining business and decreasing markets is not comparable to one with a record of current progress and market expansion.

Section 5. Weight to Be Accorded Various Factors.

The valuation of closely held corporate stock entails the consideration of all relevant factors as stated in section 4. Depending upon the circumstances in each case, certain factors may carry more weight than others because of the nature of the company's business. To illustrate:

(a) Earnings may be the most important criterion of value in some cases whereas asset value will receive primary consideration in others. In general, the appraiser will accord primary consideration to earnings when valuing stocks of companies which sell products or services to the public; conversely, in the investment or holding type of company, the appraiser may accord the greatest weight to the assets underlying the security to be valued.

(b) The value of the stock of a closely held investment or real estate holding company, whether or not family owned, is closely related to the value of the assets underlying the stock. For companies of this type the appraiser should determine the fair market values of the assets of the company. Operating expenses of such a company and the cost of liquidating it, if any, merit consideration when appraising the relative values of the stock and the underlying assets. The market values of the underlying assets give due weight to potential earnings and dividends of the particular items of property underlying the stock, capitalized at rates deemed proper by the investing public should be superior to the retrospective opinion of an individual. For these reasons, adjusted net worth should be accorded greater weight in valuing the stock of a closely held investment or real estate holding company, whether or not family owned, than any of the other customary yardsticks of appraisal, such as earnings and dividend paying capacity.

Section 6. Capitalization Rates.

In the application of certain fundamental valuation factors, such as earnings and dividends, it is necessary to capitalize the average or current results at some appropriate rate. A determination of the proper capitalization rate presents one of the most difficult problems in valuation. That there is no ready or simple solution will become apparent by a cursory check of the rates of return and dividend yields in terms of the selling prices of corporation shares listed on the major exchanges of the country. Wide variations will be found even for companies in the same industry. Moreover, the ratio will fluctuate from year to year depending upon economic conditions. Thus, no standard tables of capitalization rates applicable to closely held corporations can be formulated. Among the more important factors to be taken into consideration in deciding upon a capitalization rate in a particular case are: (1) the nature of the business; (2) the risk involved; and (3) the stability or irregularity of earnings.

Section 7. Average of Factors.

Because valuations cannot be made on the basis of a prescribed formula, there is no means whereby the various applicable factors in a particular case can be assigned mathematical weights in deriving the fair market value. For this reason, no useful purpose is served by taking an average of several factors (for example, book value, capitalized earnings and capitalized dividends) and basing the valuation on the result. Such a process excludes active consideration of other pertinent factors, and the end result cannot be supported by a realistic application of the significant facts in the case except by mere chance.

Section 8. Restrictive Agreements.

Frequently, in the valuation of closely held stock for estate and gift tax purposes, it will be found that the stock is subject to an agreement restricting its sale or transfer. Where shares of stock were acquired by a decedent subject to an option reserved by the issuing corporation to repurchase at a certain price, the option price is usually accepted as the fair market value for estate tax purposes. See Rev. Rul. 54-76, C.B. 1954-1, 194. However, in such case the option price is not determinative of fair market value for gift tax purposes where the option, or buy and sell agreement, is the result of voluntary action by the stockholders, such agreement may or may not, depending upon the circumstances of each case, fix the value for estate tax purposes. However, such agreement is a factor to be considered, with other relevant factors, in determining fair market value. Where the stockholder is free to dispose of his shares during life and the option is to become effective only upon his death, the fair market value is not limited to the option price. It is always necessary to consider the relationship of the parties, the relative number of shares held by the decedent, and other material facts, to determine whether the agreement represents a bonafide business arrangement or is a device to pass the decedent's shares to the natural objects of his bounty for less than an adequate and full consideration in money or money's worth. In this connection see Rev. Rul. 157 C.B. 1953-2, 255, and Rev. Rul. 189, C.B. 1953-2, 294.

Section 9. Effect on Other Documents.

Revenue Ruling 54-77, C.B. 1954-1, 187, is hereby superseded.

Appendix D

Financial Institution Valuation Information Request List

FINANCIAL INSTITUTION
VALUATION INFORMATION REQUEST LIST

BANK NAME _____

DATE OF VISIT _____

MERCER CAPITAL CONTACT (1) _____

MERCER CAPITAL CONTACT (2) _____

MERCER CAPITAL
5860 Ridgeway Center Parkway, Suite 410
Memphis, Tennessee 38120

Telephone: (901) 685-2120
Facsimile: (901) 685-2199

This is a generalized information request. Some items may not pertain to your institution, and some items may not be readily available to you. In such cases, please notify Mercer Capital so that other arrangements can be made to obtain or estimate the information. Please ignore any items already furnished to Mercer Capital.

- -

1. FINANCIAL STATEMENTS

A. Bank(s) Only

	AUDITS (1)	FEDERAL TAX (IF NOT CONSOLIDATED)	CALL REPORTS (2)	UBPR	INTERNAL	SHAREHOLDER COMM (3)
12/31/90	_____	_____	_____	_____	_____	_____
12/31/89	_____	_____	_____	_____		_____
12/31/88	_____	_____	_____			_____
12/31/87	_____		_____			_____
12/31/86	_____		_____			_____
12/31/85	_____		_____			_____

INTERIM	CALL REPORTS (2) Current	Prior Year			
Q1	_____	_____	_____	_____	_____
Q2	_____	_____	_____	_____	_____
Q3	_____	_____	_____	_____	_____

(1) Audits are sometimes presented in abbreviated form and with supplementary schedules. Please provide copies with supplementary schedules. Send annual audit for each year even if each audit presents comparative (i.e., two years') data. Also, please provide copies of auditors' management letters for most recent two years.

(2) If Call Reports have been amended, please send copies of reports as most recently amended.

(3) Shareholder Communications include: a) Annual Reports; and, b) Proxy Statements; other shareholder solicitations during the relevant years. If 10-K's or 10-Q's are prepared, please include.

FINANCIAL INSTITUTION
VALUATION INFORMATION
REQUEST LIST
Page 2

B. Bank Holding Company

	AUDITS (1)	FEDERAL TAX	FORM[2][3] Y-9's	HOLDING COMPANY PERF. REPORTS	INTERNAL	SHAREHOLDER COMM (4)
12/31/90	_____	_____	_____	_____	_____	_____
12/31/89	_____	_____	_____	_____		_____
12/31/88	_____	_____	_____			_____
12/31/87	_____		_____			_____
12/31/86	_____		_____			_____
12/31/85	_____		_____			_____

INTERIM

	FORM Y-9's[2][3] Current	Prior Year		INTERNAL	SHAREHOLDER
Q1	_____	_____			
Q2	_____	_____		_____	_____
Q3	_____	_____		_____	_____

(1) Audits are sometimes presented in abbreviated form and with supplementary schedules. Please provide copies with supplementary schedules. Send annual audit for each year even if each audit presents comparative (i.e., two years') data. Also, please provide copies of auditors' management letters for most recent two years.

(2) Parent Company Only and Consolidated.

(3) If Y-9's have been amended, please send copies of reports as most recently amended.

(4) Shareholder Communications include: a) Annual Reports; and, b) Proxy Statements; other shareholder solicitations during the relevant years. If 10-K's or 10-Q's are prepared, please include.

FINANCIAL INSTITUTION
VALUATION INFORMATION
REQUEST LIST
Page 3

C. Thrift(s) Only[1]

	AUDITS OR DIRECTORS' AUDITS [2]	FEDERAL TAX RETURNS	OTS & FHLB THRIFT FINANCIAL REPORTS[3,4]	ANY AVAILABLE PEER GROUP DATA REPORTS	INTERNAL FINANCIAL STATEMENTS	SHAREHOLDER COMMUNICATION[4]
12/31/91	_____	_____	_____	_____	_____	_____
12/31/90	_____	_____	_____	_____	_____	_____
12/31/89	_____	_____	_____	_____	_____	_____
12/31/88	_____	_____	_____	_____	_____	_____
12/31/87	_____		_____	_____	_____	_____
12/31/86	_____		_____	_____	_____	_____
12/31/85	_____		_____	_____	_____	_____

INTERIM

	REGULATORY REPORTS Current	Prior Year		
Q1	_____	_____	_____	_____
Q2	_____	_____	_____	_____
Q3	_____	_____	_____	_____

(1) Supply requested information for consolidated thrift holding company as well, if applicable.

(2) Audits are sometimes presented in abbreviated form and with supplementary schedules. Please provide copies with supplementary schedules. Also, please provide copies of auditors' management letters for most recent two years.

(3) If regulatory reports have been amended, please send copies of reports as most recently amended.

(4) Include all schedules.

(5) Shareholder Communications include: a) Annual Reports; and b) Proxy Statements; other shareholder solicitations during the relevant years. If 10-K's or 10-Q's are prepared, please include.

2. OTHER FINANCIAL DOCUMENTS

A. Employee Stock Ownership Plan/Trust (if applicable)

____ 12/31/90 Financial Statement (unaudited) or most recent if 12/31/90 audited statement not yet prepared
____ 12/31//89 Accountant's Report
____ If ESOP is leveraged, name lender, amount and terms of debt

FINANCIAL INSTITUTION
VALUATION INFORMATION
REQUEST LIST
Page 4

B. Other Financial Documents

____ Bank budget for 1991
____ Holding company budget for 1991
____ Detailed breakdown of Non-Interest Operating Expense and Non-Interest Operating Income for 1988, 1989, and 1990
____ Identify any major non-recurring income or expense item classified as non-interest operating income or non-interest operating expense in the last five years
____ Any multi-year projection or business plan available for the bank and/or the holding company
____ If you are a "public reporting company" with the SEC or the FDIC, copies of all documents filed with the SEC or FDIC during 1990
____ Copies of any offering materials prepared in conjunction with any offering of equity or debt securities during the last three years
____ Directors' examination reports
____ Management letters from outside auditors for last two years

3. CORPORATE DOCUMENTS AND RECORDS

A. Summary shareholder list (for the entity being valued) showing names and number of shares owned and detailing:

____ Directors and officers
____ Employee Stock Ownership Plan (if applicable)
____ All other 5% (or more) shareholders by name. If a family controls more than 5% even though no individual does, please note this

B. If there is a controlling group of shareholders, please provide:

____ The complete list of shareholders with their holdings
____ Copy of any Voting Trust Agreement between the controlling parties

C. Copy of any restrictive legends or agreements applicable to the institution's shares

D. Copy of documentation regarding any hybrid equity securities at either the bank or holding company level:

____ Stock options
____ Warrants (to purchase shares)
____ Other convertible securities (convertible debentures, convertible preferred stock, etc.)

FINANCIAL INSTITUTION
VALUATION INFORMATION
REQUEST LIST
Page 5

E. Board of Directors Minutes: Please provide copies of bank and/or holding company minutes during 1989 and 1990, or excerpts pertaining to discussions of the following topics:

____ Merger with or acquisition by another banking institution
____ Purchase or sale of branch facilities
____ Purchase, sale or creation of non-bank subsidiaries
____ Response to report of regulatory examination
____ Declaration or payment of dividends or establishment of dividend policy
____ Plans to raise capital in any form, including the refinancing of capital notes or HC debt
____ Plans to renovate existing facilities or to build new facilities
____ Discussions of or approval of any off-balance sheet hedging activities
____ Discussions of non-routine charges to the allowance for loan losses or provisions to the allowance for loan losses
____ Business planning or financial projections for 1990 and beyond

F. ESOP Documentation

____ Copy of ESOP document provisions related to repurchase of employee shares specifying obligation to repurchase, terms or repurchase, and other material factors
____ Specify ESOP's repurchase obligation and terms of repurchase
____ If the holding company has a repurchase option or obligation related to ESOP shares, please specify
____ Copy of any study of the ESOP's repurchase liability. If there is no study, please list known liquidity requirements for next three years from anticipated retirements or other commitments to repurchase shares
____ Current ESOP contribution policy or basis for determining annual contributions
____ Provide estimated ESOP contribution for 1991, 1992 and 1993
____ Accounting treatment of leveraged ESOP if not noted in financial statements

G. Please provide documentation of transactions during the last ____ year(s) on known stock transactions in the following form:

Date	Purchaser	Seller	# Shares	Price/ Share	Director/ Officer?	Explanatory Comments

FINANCIAL INSTITUTION
VALUATION INFORMATION
REQUEST LIST
Page 6

4. BANKING FACILITIES AND OTHER ASSETS

A. Fixed assets and banking facilities

_____ Provide a list of all banking branch facilities, indicating for each:

  [ ] Branch name/location
  [ ] Actual (or approximate) deposit and loan volumes
  [ ] Whether full service or specific limited services
  [ ] Number of Full Time Equivalent (FTE) employees at branch
  [ ] Whether facility owned or leased (if lease, from whom on what terms?)
  [ ] Approximate square footage of the facility
  [ ] Book value of facility on institution's books
  [ ] Approximate fair market value of the facility

_____ If the bank is holding improved or unimproved real estate for future expansion (or which is otherwise not presently occupied), please provide:

  [ ] Description
  [ ] Date acquired and acquisition cost
  [ ] Estimated (or appraised) current fair market value

B. Other Assets

_____ Provide a current list of equity securities (including convertible and preferred stocks) owned by the bank or holding company as of the date of the valuation, including:

  [ ] Name of security
  [ ] Original (or current carrying) cost
  [ ] Current market value

_____ Provide a list of all mutual fund investments owned, including:

  [ ] Name of fund(s)
  [ ] Original cost(s)
  [ ] Current carrying cost and the amount of any equity allowance related to the mutual funds

_____ Please provide bond portfolio printout summary page(s) detailing book value, market value, weighted average rate, and weighted average maturity by each major category of the bond portfolio:

  [ ] U.S. Government and Agencies
  [ ] Tax-exempt securities
  [ ] Other securities

_____ Please summarize the bank's present investment portfolio positioning strategy in a paragraph or so
_____ Any additional assets which may be considered temporary (debt repossessions) or not directly related to the bank's normal course of business

FINANCIAL INSTITUTION
VALUATION INFORMATION
REQUEST LIST
Page 7

C. Data processing facilities

_____ Please describe the current data processing system in use by the bank and discuss its adequacy for the current level of operations

_____ If the system is an in-house system, when did the bank go on it?

_____ If you are using a data center, who are you using and when did you begin?

_____ Do you currently have any plans for changing data centers or purchasing an in-house system? If so, please discuss briefly

D. Non-bank subsidiaries of the bank or bank holding company, whether controlled or not

_____ Name and describe the business of any operating non-bank subsidiaries

_____ Provide year-end financials for the subsidiaries if not in audited statements or in consolidating financial statements

E. Trust Department Activities

_____ Please provide brief description of trust activities, including services rendered, number of employees, assets under management, revenues for last three years, and, any internal profitability analysis for the Trust Department

_____ Summarize future plans for this department

5. LIQUIDITY AND ASSET/LIABILITY MANAGEMENT

A. Please state the bank's Liquidity Policy (or operating practice) in a paragraph or so in terms of objectives, target ratios, or other terms you use to track and monitor liquidity. If there is a written policy, please send a copy

B. GAP (Asset/Liability Management) Policy

_____ Send a copy of this policy

_____ Please state the bank's GAP policy in an overview paragraph or so

_____ Who are the management and board members of your ALCO Committee (or equivalent)

_____ If available, please provide a recent printout from your asset/liability system or planning model providing:

[ ] Projected balance sheets and income statements over projection horizon

[ ] GAP reports

[ ] A brief statement of the bank's positioning relative to its objectives

6. LOAN PORTFOLIO INFORMATION

A. Determining the adequacy of the allowance for loan losses (i.e., the loan loss reserve)

_____ Describe the method used and the frequency of the determination

_____ If a written report is developed, please provide a copy (or a summary of results) for the most recent determination

FINANCIAL INSTITUTION
VALUATION INFORMATION
REQUEST LIST
Page 8

B. Describe the system or process of loan review in use at the bank

C. Lending Policy and Practice

____ List the major types of loans routinely made by type and describe typical pricing and maturities for each type
____ Summarize (or provide a copy of the Loan Policy) the bank's:

[ ] Stated lending limit authorities
[ ] Effective lending limits in practice
[ ] Policy for out-of-territory loans
[ ] Number and dollar volume of loans by type
[ ] Number and dollar volume of loans outside your CRA (Community Reinvestment Act) territory, including any loan participations purchased

____ What is the bank's legal lending limit? What is the in-house lending limit?

D. Lending concentrations

____ Please list all loans of ____% of your lending limit or above. If credits to related borrowers constitute a concentration of 50% of the lending limit or more, please include the relationship totals
____ Does the bank have any known industry concentrations or exposures in its loan portfolio? If so, please discuss briefly

7. REGULATION AND REGULATORY COMPLIANCE

A. Please provide the dates of the two most recent regulatory examinations by appropriate category.

	BY STATE AGENCY	BANK BY FDIC NAT'L BANK OCC THRIFT BY OTS	HOLDING COMPANY BY FEDERAL RESERVE
Most Recent	_____	_____	_____
Next Most Recent	_____	_____	_____
Next Most Recent	_____	_____	_____

B. Is the bank and/or the holding company operating under a formal, written agreement with any regulatory body? If so, please provide:

____ Agency
____ Date and Type of Agreement (Memorandum of Understanding, Cease and Desist, Other)
____ Basic reasons for its issuance
____ General description of its requirements
____ Status of the institution's compliance with the order

**FINANCIAL INSTITUTION
VALUATION INFORMATION
REQUEST LIST
Page 9**

8. MANAGEMENT AND THE DIRECTORATE

A. Management compensation: For the top five officers of the bank and holding company, please provide:

____ Name/title
____ Annual compensation, including bonuses, for 1988, 1989 and 1990, and base salary and expect total compensation for 1991
____ Beneficial stock ownership in bank or bank holding company

B. Senior management: (key officers of the bank or holding company)

____ Name/title/age/years of service with bank
____ Current operating responsibilities
____ Prior jobs with bank
____ Prior banking experience
____ Other relevant experience
____ If bank carries life insurance on key executives, provide coverage amounts and annual premiums
____ If executive is working under an employment agreement, please summarize its terms

C. Board of Directors: Please summarize the following information for the bank and the holding company:

____ For Bank: Name/Board Title/Age/Board Tenure in Years/Occupation
____ For HC: Name/Board Title/Age/Board Tenure in Years/Occupation (for significant overlaps between bank and holding company, just provide entire list and indicate for each individual whether for bank, holding company, or both)
____ Please name and describe membership and functions of major board committees
____ How are outside board members compensated?

9. BACKGROUND AND HISTORY

A. For the bank, please provide:

____ Date of formation and name(s) of principal founder(s)
____ Type of charter
____ If applicable, approximate dates of acquisitions of other banks or branches since formation
____ Name changes, if any, since formation
____ If there is a current control group, the date this group obtained control
____ Other significant historical events
____ If a written history exists please provide a copy

B. For the holding company, please provide:

____ Date of formation and name(s) of principal founder(s)
____ Description of process of gaining control of the bank
____ Date control acquired

FINANCIAL INSTITUTION
VALUATION INFORMATION
REQUEST LIST
Page 10

10. COMPETITION AND THE LOCAL ECONOMY

A. Please list your major competitors (bank, thrift or credit union). If a market share study exists, please provide a copy of the most recent study

B. Please provide any background information you have readily available on the economy of your city/county/region (from Chamber of Commerce and local university economics departments, for example)

Appendix E

Information Checklist for
Purchase or Sale of
Bank or Thrift Branch

BANK OR THRIFT BRANCH
INFORMATION CHECKLIST FOR
PURCHASE OR SALE

SELLING BANK   _____

SELLING HOLDING COMPANY   _____

MAIN OFFICE ADDRESS   _____
_____
TELEPHONE   _____
FACSIMILE   _____

BRANCH TO BE SOLD   _____

ADDRESS   _____
_____
TELEPHONE   _____
FACSIMILE   _____

BRANCH MANAGER   _____

MERCER CAPITAL CONTACT (1)

_____

MERCER CAPITAL CONTACT (2)

_____

PLEASE SEND INFORMATION TO:

MERCER CAPITAL
5860 Ridgeway Center Parkway, Suite 410
Memphis, Tennessee 38120

Telephone: (901) 685-2120
Facsimile: (901) 685-2199

The following list requests exhaustive and specially formatted data. If you are unable to provide any of the requested items, please contact Mercer Capital so that we may discuss alternatives to the requested items

- -

I.   FINANCIAL DATA

A. General

_____   1.   Most recent Uniform Bank Performance Report (or thrift comparative report) for the parent bank

_____   2.   Last year-end Call Report and all subsequent quarterly Call Reports. (Comparable regulatory reports for thrifts)

_____   3.   Audited Bank and/or Parent Company and Consolidated Financial Statements for the last six (6) years

B. Branch Only

_____   1.   Current quarter/month-end and year-to-date Branch balance sheet and income statement

_____   2.   Year-end Branch Balance Sheets and Income Statements for the last six (6) years

_____   3.   Current budget for non-interest expense and fee income

_____   4.   Current summary of deposits and summaries as the last six (6) year-ends showing <u>by type</u> (from branch deposit trial balance reports):

     a. Number of accounts
     b. Total balance
     c. Weighted average interest rate
     d. Account opening dates for <u>currently</u> existing accounts

BANK OR THRIFT BRANCH
INFORMATION CHECKLIST FOR
PURCHASE OR SALE
Page 2

_____   5.   Current Certificate of deposit summary showing <u>by month of maturity</u> and <u>by type</u>:

a. Number of accounts
b. Total balance
c. Weighted average interest rate
d. Weighted average maturity

(Please separate Jumbo CDs from CDs under $100,000)

_____   6.   Current zip code listing <u>by department account type</u> and <u>account balances</u>

a. Account numbers
b. Customer name & address
c. City/State
d. Zip code
e. Balance

_____   7.   Deposit accounts greater than $10,000 <u>by type</u>

a. Name
b. Account numbers
c. City/State
d. Balance

_____   8.   Annual summary of the number accounts opened and closed in each of the last five (5) years and for the current year-to-date <u>by type</u>

_____   9.   Current detailed deposit trial balance

_____   10. Current loan summary and summaries as of the last five (5) year-ends showing <u>by type</u>:

a. Number of loans
b. Total balance
c. Balance of largest loan in each type
d. Weighted average interest rate
e. Weighted average maturity

_____   11. Current loan summary showing <u>by month of maturity or repricing</u> and <u>by type</u>:

a. Number of loans
b. Total balance
c. Weighted average interest rate

_____   12. Annual summaries of loans originated (by dollar amount) in each of the last six (6) years and year-to-date <u>by type</u>

_____   13. Current detailed loan trial balance

_____   14. 1099 reports for branch deposit customers for last six (6) years

**BANK OR THRIFT BRANCH
INFORMATION CHECKLIST FOR
PURCHASE OR SALE
Page 3**

II. OPERATIONS

A. Deposits

_____   1.   Description and explanations of account types

_____   2.   Key to interest accrual method <u>by type</u>

_____   3.   Fee schedule by type

B. Loans

_____   1.   Description and explanations of account types

_____   2.   Key to interest accrual and rate changes by type

C. Staff

_____   1.   Listing of all current branch employees showing:

      a.   Title
      b.   Function
      c.   Age
      d.   Number of years with the bank
      e.   Salary

_____   2.   Brief job descriptions for each branch employee

D. Computers

_____   1.   Name of processing system software

_____   2.   Name of service bureau or type of mainframe used by the Bank

_____   3.   Explanation of how loans and deposit account numbers have been assigned

_____   4.   Call your valuation consultant to discuss your system's capabilities to provide requested data via automated means

E. Branch profitability analysis reports (or income statements) for as many years back as are available

F. Current estimate of reasonable annual operating expenses for branch (as much detail as possible)

**BANK OR THRIFT BRANCH
INFORMATION CHECKLIST FOR
PURCHASE OR SALE
Page 4**

III. PHYSICAL FACILITIES

A. Description of Building

_____   1.   Size of lot

_____   2.   Number of parking spaces

_____   3.   Size of building

_____   4.   Description of building exterior (architecture)

_____   5.   Description of automobile access to the Branch

_____   6.   Building and land owned or leased? (If leased, provide a copy of the lease document.)

_____   7.   Map showing location of the branch and any other banking offices within a 15-mile radius (3 miles within metropolitan areas)

_____   8.   Interior layout of branch building (scale drawing)

_____   9.   Photographs of branch exterior (front--close-up and long-shot, back, sides, drive-up window and interior, including all major rooms, operating areas and the inside and outside of vault

_____   10.   Copy of any appraisals of the branch facility prepared during last three years

_____   11.   Insurance coverage on branch

B. Contents

_____   1.   Inventory listing of fixtures and equipment showing original cost and depreciated book value as of most recent date available

_____   2.   Description of attached features (number of teller stations, drive-thru windows, automated teller machines, etc.)

_____   3.   Type of vault (provide interior dimensions)

_____   4.   Number, size and fee schedule for safe deposit boxes; provide number rented and number available by size

_____   5.   Copy of any appraisals of the branch contents and fixtures prepared during the last three years

IV. HISTORY

_____   **A. Date opened**

_____   **B. Chronology of significant events affecting the community or the bank over the last five years**

_____   **C. Recent role of the Branch in the Bank's overall business strategy**

_____   **D. Please note specifically any changes of the Branch managers during the last five years**

Appendix F

Financial Institution Valuation Interview (Due Diligence) Questionnaire

FINANCIAL INSTITUTION
VALUATION INTERVIEW
QUESTIONNAIRE

BANK NAME _____

DATE OF VISIT _____

FOR MERCER CAPITAL _____

FOR MERCER CAPITAL _____

MERCER CAPITAL
5860 Ridgeway Center Parkway, Suite 410
Memphis, Tennessee 38120

Telephone: (901) 685-2120
Facsimile: (901) 685-2199

- -

PERSON(S) INTERVIEWED:

NAME	TITLE	POSITION
1.		
2.		
3.		
4.		
5.		

I.   REVIEW OF INFORMATION REQUEST STATUS: **Obtained**   **Needed**

Call Reports: _____   _____

Uniform Bank Performance Reports: _____   _____

Bank HC Performance Report: _____   _____

Corporate Tax Returns: _____   _____

Parent Company Only Statements: _____   _____

Written Policies:
(Loan, Investment, Dividend, ESOP, etc...)   _____   _____

Audits: _____   _____

History: _____   _____

Chamber of Commerce: _____   _____

Organizational Chart: _____   _____

ESOP Financials: _____   _____

FINANCIAL INSTITUTION
VALUATION INTERVIEW
QUESTIONNAIRE
Page 2

	Obtained	Needed
I. REVIEW OF INFORMATION REQUEST STATUS: *(Continued)*		

Insurance Coverage: _____ _____

Fixed Asset Appraisals: _____ _____

Compensation Schedule: _____ _____

Shareholder Distribution:
Parent Company
Bank _____ _____
(Identify 5% holders, officers, ESOP) _____ _____

Stock Transactions:
Parent Company
Bank _____ _____
(Including prices) _____ _____

Other: _____ _____ _____

_____ _____ _____

_____ _____ _____

BANK QUESTIONNAIRE

1.   Verify the purpose of the valuation and the specific entity or entities being valued. Review the engagement letter with management.

2.   Confirm the "as of" date of the valuation. Discuss the due date(s) for delivery of draft and final reports.

3.   Discuss the general background of the Institution. When was it founded; location of branches; name changes:

FINANCIAL INSTITUTION
VALUATION INTERVIEW
QUESTIONNAIRE
Page 3

4.   Organizational Structure & Management:

o   Review the management list and discuss responsibilities, titles, length of experience in the institution/banking in general of key officers.

o   Review organizational chart with management and discuss the management process in place at the Bank.

o   Are there obvious gaps in management coverage?

o   Do the individual key managers hold a significant equity stake in the bank (either directly or through option arrangements or other incentive plans)?

o   Is management's compensation in line with similar institutions?

o   Discuss management's assessment of overall quality of management and ability to manage the institution over the next five or more years.

5.   Local Economic Conditions:

o   Discuss the general economic outlook.

o   Discuss the major components of the economic base of the local economy.

o   How does the local/area economy compare with the state or region? (Discuss population growth, income levels, major industries, major attractions.)

o   What recent events (+ or -) have occurred?

6.   Area Competitive Situation - Who are they?

o   Discuss banks S&L's, credit unions and other competitors. Which ones are considered the most competitive? Why? Basis for competition?

o   Review the list of local competitors with management.

o   Discuss the Bank's market position in some detail.

o   On what basis does the Bank compete in the key areas (price, service, quality)?

FINANCIAL INSTITUTION
VALUATION INTERVIEW
QUESTIONNAIRE
Page 4

7.   **Review Regulatory Examinations and recent board minutes and discuss with management (attach notes to this questionnaire):**

Exam Date: _____   Examined by: _____

_____   _____

_____   _____

_____   _____

Board Minutes Reviewed:

From: _____   To: _____

Key issues noted in review:

8.   **What is the overall strategy for managing the balance sheet? What are the asset growth objectives? Are these consistent with capital constraints?**

9.   **What is the strategy for managing the investment and liquidity portfolio? Discuss the following issues and circumstances related to the portfolio:**

o   Types of securities purchased:

o   Number and size of transactions. Does the bank routinely take gains on sale of securities?

o   What is the current maturity structure? What maturities are being purchased?

o   Describe the current composition of the portfolio and the types of securities being purchased? Does the bank own any mutual funds or other equity securities? Does it own mortgage backed securities? Discuss in detail any "exotic" securities in the portfolio (Zero Coupons, IO or PO strips, etc.).

o   Does the Bank utilize CD's of other financial institutions?

o   Where does the bank sell Federal funds? Is there a policy to avoid undue credit exposure?

o   How are investment decisions made? What role does the Board of Directors play? The ALCO Committee?

FINANCIAL INSTITUTION
VALUATION INTERVIEW
QUESTIONNAIRE
Page 5

10.   Discuss the loan portfolio with emphasis on the following topics:

o   Describe the bank's lending market and philosophy.

o   What types of loans are considered most desirable?

o   Does the bank have concentrations of credit based on industry or borrowers?

o   What is the bank's lending limit? How many borrowing relationships does it have that are at least 80% of the lending limit?

o   How are loans approved? Does the bank have individual loan limits and loan committees?

o   How are loans priced and how are maturities or repricing opportunities structured?

o   Does the bank purchase or sell loan participations? If so, from whom or to whom?

o   Does the bank purchase indirect consumer paper? Discuss.

11.   Discuss loan quality with emphasis on the following topics:

o   Describe the bank's loan review procedures.

o   Review procedures for determining the adequacy of the loan loss reserve.

o   Ask management for their overall assessment of:

    - Quality of the loan portfolio

    - Adequacy of the allowance for possible loan losses

o   What are the trends in the level of the allowance for loan losses and the provision for loan losses? How do they compare with the peer group?

o   What has been the historical experience for loan losses? What are the prospects for future recoveries?

o   To what reasons does management attribute past loan problems?

o   What changes have been made in lending policies, personnel and procedures in recent years to improve loan quality?

o   What are the budgeted or forecasted additions to the loan loss reserve?

FINANCIAL INSTITUTION
VALUATION INTERVIEW
QUESTIONNAIRE
Page 6

11.   Discuss loan quality with emphasis on the following topics: *(Continued)*

o   Summarize the examiners' comments about the loan loss reserve if not included elsewhere in the notes. Does management agree with the assessment of the regulators?

o   Discuss the trends and volume of non-accrual loans. Are any large loans expected to go into non-accrual status?

o   Obtain a copy of the Bank's "watch list" for known or potential problem loans. Go over this list to gain understanding of management's grasp of detail or possible problems.

o   Obtain a copy of the Bank's loan concentration report if available. Discuss lending concentrations to single borrowers or related entities, to particular industries, or specific geographical concentrations.

o   Obtain loan files on two amortized loans and discuss briefly with management (optional).

o   Obtain loan files on two "healthy" loans and discuss with management.

o   Obtain two loan review write-ups and discuss with management.

12.   Discuss the Bank's fixed assets and other non-earning assets investment position, including:

o   Description (number & location of branches, data processing centers, etc.)

o   If the Bank does not own its major facilities, discuss the details of sale and related lease agreements in detail.

o   Management's assessment of the adequacy of existing facilities.

o   Any recent fixed asset additions or anticipated additions (and associated costs).

o   Status of Other Real Estate Owned Account and prospects for liquidation without loss.

FINANCIAL INSTITUTION
VALUATION INTERVIEW
QUESTIONNAIRE
Page 7

13. **Computer System: Describe existing computer system. How effective is it? When installed? What plans, if any, exist for a change of hardware or software. Does the system place any significant limitations on the Bank's ability to compete?**

14. **Deposits**

o   General Emphasis/Composition (review exhibits).

o   What is the Bank's basic deposit pricing strategy; how are prices set? Where is the Bank's pricing schedule in relationship with local competitors?

o   Discuss any particular variations in deposit composition from peer group average. Why?

o   Discuss the level of Jumbo CD's and the Bank's Strategy with jumbos.

o   Discuss the maturity structure of the deposit base.

15. **Mortgage agreements: Discuss type(s), terms and amount(s) outstanding.**

16. **Other bank borrowings. Focus in particular:**

o   Does the Bank borrow in the Federal funds market (Note: seasonal borrowings may not show up on annual or period ending statements). If so, discuss the nature and stability of borrowing relationships. Do back-up lines of credit exist?

o   Discuss any debentures or other debt arrangements with management and obtain details, if not already provided.

17. **Capital Position:**

o   Discuss Bank's Position Relative to Peer Banks.

o   Trends in Capital.

o   Recent Changes - Stock sales, Capital Injections, Prior Period Adjustments, Dividends declared.

o   Review stock options or warrants; determine the terms and conditions.

o   General assessment of adequacy at Report Date.

FINANCIAL INSTITUTION
VALUATION INTERVIEW
QUESTIONNAIRE
Page 8

18. **Is the Bank operating under any agreement(s) with its regulators? Review documents on location. Discuss the status of compliance with management.**

19. **Income Statement Analysis should cover at least:**

o   Gross yields: What has happened to yields over the last five years? How does this compare to the peer group? Are yield changes due to rate, volume or mix of earning assets?

o   Cost of Funds: Discuss the trend in the cost of funds. Is it due to rate or changes in composition of the liability base? If equity is below the peer group, this may account for the rising COF.

o   Net Interest Income: Discuss the reasons for changes in net interest income. Does the GAP position pose a threat to net interest income?

o   Other Income: Discuss the sources of other income. Are any unusual or non-recurring? How are fees in relationship to local area competitors? Ask if they obtain financials on their local competitors to check?

    a.   Service charges

    b.   Other income (such as credit life, mortgage originations, etc)

    c.   Other income items of a non-recurring nature

o   Non-interest expenses: What is management's philosophy toward managing expenses? Discuss in detail the trends in non-interest expenses. Note any unusual or non-recurring items of size.

    a.   Salaries, benefits and number and utilization of employees

    b.   Occupancy expenses

    c.   Other expenses

    d.   General assessment of "productivity"

    e.   Are there any significant non-recurring expense items during any of the last five years?

o   Securities gains/losses: Discuss the volume of transactions. What is the probability of future transactions? What is the impact of the securities portfolio positioning on the current income statement?

o   Tax position: Determine volume of carry-forwards and remaining investment tax credits. What is the Bank's position with respect to the alternative minimum tax?

o   Discuss any extraordinary or unusual items in the income statement in recent years.

FINANCIAL INSTITUTION
VALUATION INTERVIEW
QUESTIONNAIRE
Page 9

20. **Obtain a copy of the coming year budget. Review briefly with management to assess probability of achievement. Calculate implied balance sheet growth, ROA, ROE, loan loss provision and implied charge-offs, and ending leverage. Are the projections reasonable in light of history?**

21. **Discuss the Bank's dividend policy:**

    o   What is the historical payout record?

    o   What is the current (written or informal) dividend policy?

    o   What are prospects for future payments?

    o   Do holding company debt service requirements place unreasonable pressure on the Bank's dividend payout?

22. **Ownership Distribution of Entity Being Valued (Bank or Holding Company).**

    o   Determine ownership position of officers and directors.

    o   Number and percentage of shares owned by the ESOP or profit sharing plan.

    o   5% shareholders.

    o   Control group discussion (if applicable).

23. **Stock transactions:**

    o   Review any recent stock offering including the prospectus.

    o   Discuss the specific pricing in the local market and what management knows about how prices are set.

    o   Obtain a list of all stock transactions for the last two years. Review this list with management to understand the dynamics of transactions.

FINANCIAL INSTITUTION
VALUATION INTERVIEW
QUESTIONNAIRE
Page 10

24.   **ESOP documentation (if applicable):**

o   Obtain a copy of the ESOP plan.

o   Discuss historical contributions, the basis for them and the outlook for future contributions.

o   Review the ESOP stock liquidity features with management.

o   What provision has been made for emerging liability?

25.   **Other matters:**

o   Is there a multi-year business plan, capital plan or strategic plan? If so, obtain copy and review with management.

o   Identify any pending litigation.

o   Review any discussions of mergers and acquisitions. Make specific notes.

o   Other strengths and weaknesses. Ask management to specifically list 3-5 of bank's greatest strengths and 3-5 of its greatest weaknesses. Use these strengths and weaknesses to corroborate earlier discussions or to ask additional questions.

**FINANCIAL INSTITUTION
VALUATION INTERVIEW
QUESTIONNAIRE
Page 11**

PARENT COMPANY DISCUSSION

1.   **What percentage of the bank does the parent company own? (Verify actual numbers of shares owned and shares outstanding.)**

2.   **Review each asset and liability noted on the parent company only financial statement.**

   o   Discuss any non-bank investments.

   o   Does the investment in the bank agree with the bank's capital (as adjusted for the percentage of ownership)? Is the equity method of accounting being used? Explain any real or apparent discrepancies.

   o   Discuss any holding company debt, including lender, amount, terms, and collateral and status.

   o   Is the company in compliance with all loan agreements?

   o   Discuss the probability of a timely debt servicing of holding company debt based upon likely Bank dividend capacity.

   o   Is there a holding capital plan? Obtain copy and discuss.

   o   List any intangible assets. How did they arise and how are they being amortized?

3.   **Discuss any non-bank operations in detail.**

4.   **Review the budget for the coming year. Is there a longer-term business plan? Obtain and discuss.**

5.   **List major shareholders and stock transactions and basis for prices if not already provided.**

6.   **Review latest HC examination with management.**

FINANCIAL INSTITUTION
VALUATION INTERVIEW
QUESTIONNAIRE
Page 12

7.   Review trends in key parent company ratios, including leverage, capital adequacy, profitability and returns.

8.   What is the company's dividend history and prospects for future payment?

CATCH-ALL QUESTIONS

1.   Based upon the discussion thus far, does management have anything in particular that should be highlighted or focussed upon in more detail?

2.   Ask specifically: Is there anything of significance we have <u>not</u> discussed which (you believe) would have bearing on our discussion of valuation?

Bibliography

Auerbach, Ronald P. *Historical Overview of Financial Institutions.* Washington, D.C.: Federal Deposit Insurance Corporation, date unknown.

Austin, Douglas V. *Capital Planning for the Community Bank.* Rolling Meadows, Ill.: 1989.

Babcock, Henry A. *Appraisal Principles and Procedures.* Washington, D.C.: American Society of Appraisers, 1980.

Baughn, William H., and Charles E. Walker. *The Bankers' Handbook.* Homewood, Ill.: Dow Jones-Irwin, 1978.

Bernstein, Leopold A. *Financial Statement Analysis: Theory, Application and Interpretation,* 4th ed. Homewood, Ill.: Richard D. Irwin, 1989.

Blasi, Joseph R. *Employee Ownership: Revolution or Ripoff?* Cambridge, Mass.: Ballinger, 1988.

Brealey, Richard, and Steward Myers. *Principles of Corporate Finance.* New York,: McGraw-Hill, 1984.

Campbell, Ian R.; Robert B. Low; and Nora V. Murrant. *The Valuation and Pricing of Privately-Held Business Interests.* Toronto: Canadian Institute of Chartered Accountants, 1990.

Comptroller's Handbook for National Bank Examiners. Washington, D.C.: Office of the Comptroller of the Currency, 1990.

Copeland, Tom; Tim Koller; and Jack Murrin. *Valuation: Measuring and Managing the Value of Companies.* New York: John Wiley & Sons, 1990.

Copeland, Thomas E., and J. Fred Weston. *Financial Theory and Corporate Policy.* Reading, Mass.: Addison-Wesley Publishing, 1983.

Corporate Earning Estimator. Chicago: Zacks Investment Research, biweekly.

Cottle, Sidney, Roger F. Murray, and Frank E. Block. *Graham and Dodd's Security Analysis,* 5th ed. New York: McGraw-Hill, 1988.

Cox, Edwin B. *Bank Performance Annual.* Boston: Warren, Gorham & Lamont, 1987.

Directory of Companies Required to File Reports with the Securities and Exchange Commission. Washington, D.C.: U.S. Government Printing Office, annual.

Employee Ownership Resource Guide. Oakland, Calif.: The National Center for Employee Ownership, 1990.

Fabozzi, Frank J., and Irving M. Pollack. *The Handbook of Fixed Income Securities.* Homewood, Ill.: Dow Jones-Irwin, 1987.

Federal Deposit Insurance Corporation. *Statistics on Banking.* Washington, D.C.: Federal Deposit Insurance Corporation, annual.

Federal Deposit Insurance Corporation. *Annual Report.* Washington, D.C.: Federal Deposit Insurance Corporation, annual.

Federal Reserve Bulletin. Washington, D.C.: Board of Governors of the Federal Reserve System, monthly.

Federal Financial Institutions Examination Council. *Annual Report.* Washington, D.C.: Federal Financial Institutions Examination Council, annual.

Fishman, Jay E.; Shannon P. Pratt; and J. Clifford Griffith. *Guide to Business Valuations.* Fort Worth, Texas: Practitioners Publishing Company, 1991.

Frish, Robert A. *The Magic of ESOP's and LBO's.* Rockville Centre, N.Y.: Farnsworth, 1985.

Graham, Benjamin; David L. Dodd; and Sidney Cottle. *Security Analysis: Principles and Techniques, 4th ed.* New York: McGraw-Hill Book Company, 1962.

Guidelines for Appraisal Reports for the Valuation of Savings and Loan Associations and Savings Banks Converting from Mutual to Stock Form of Organization. Washington D.C.: Federal Home Loan Bank Board Office of Policy and Economic Research, 1983.

Handbook of Basic Economic Statistics. Washington, D.C.: Economics Statistics Bureau of Washington, annual.

Harrington, Diana R. *Modern Portfolio Theory, The Capital Asset Pricing Model & Arbitrage Pricing Theory: A User's Guide,* 2nd ed. Englewood Cliffs, N.J.: Prentice-Hall, 1987.

HLHZ Control Premium Study. Los Angeles: Houlihan, Lokey, Howard & Zukin, Inc., quarterly.

Ibbotson Associates. *Stocks, Bonds, Bills, and Inflation Yearbook.* Chicago: Ibbotson Associates, annual.

Institutional Brokers Estimate System (I/B/E/S). New York: Lynch, Jones & Ryan, weekly.

Jaffee, Dwight. *Money, Banking and Credit.* New York: Worth Publishers, 1989.

Johnson, Ivan, and William Roberts. *Money and Banking,* 3rd ed. Hinsdale, Ill.: Dryden Press, 1988.

Knecht, Luke D., and Michael L. McCowin. *Valuing Convertible Securities.* Chicago: Harris Trust & Savings Bank, 1986.

Kramer, Yale. *Valuing a Closely Held Business, Accountant's Workbook Series.* New York: Matthew Bender, 1987.

Levine, Sumner N., ed. *The Financial Analyst's Handbook,* 2nd ed. Homewood, Ill.: Dow Jones-Irwin, 1988.

Levine, Sumner N. *The Dow Jones-Irwin Business and Investment Almanac.* Homewood, Ill.: Dow Jones-Irwin, annual.

Marston, Winfrey, and Hempstead. *Engineering Valuation and Depreciation.* Ames, Iowa: Iowa State University Press, 1953.

McCarthy, George D., and Robert E. Healy. *Valuing a Company: Practices and Procedures.* New York: The Ronald Press Company, 1971.

Meek, Paul. *Open Market Operations.* New York: Federal Reserve Bank of New York, 1985.

Mergers and Acquisitions. Philadelphia: MLR Publishing Company, bimonthly.

Mergerstat Review. Schaumburg, Ill.: Merrill Lynch Business Brokerage & Valuation, 1990.

Miller, William D. *Valuing Banks and Thrifts.* New York: Executive Enterprises Publications, 1990.

Miller, Roger L., and Robert Pulvinelli. *Modern Money and Banking,* 2nd ed. New York: McGraw-Hill, 1989.

Moody's Bank and Finance Manual. New York: Moody's Investors Service, annual.

National Trade and Professional Associations of the United States. Washington, D.C.: Columbia Books, annual.

Office of Thrift Supervision. *Combined Financial Statements of Insured Institutions.* Washington, D.C.: Office of Thrift Supervision, annual.

Poynter, Daniel F. *The Expert Witness Handbook: Tips and Techniques for the Litigation Consultant.* Santa Barbara, Calif.: Para Publishing, 1987.

Pratt, Shannon P. *Valuing a Business: The Analysis and Appraisal of Closely Held Companies,* 2nd ed. Homewood, Ill.: Dow Jones-Irwin, 1989.

Pratt, Shannon P. *Reviewing a Business Appraisal Report.* Scottsdale, Ariz.: National Association of Review Appraisers & Mortgage Underwriters, 1989.

Proceedings of the ESOP Association Convention. Washington, D.C.: The ESOP Association, annual.

Sheshunoff Information Services. *Buying, Selling and Merging Banks.* Austin, Texas: Sheshunoff Information Services, 1990.

Smiley, Robert W., and Ronald J. Gilbert. *Employee Stock Ownership Plans.* Larchmont, N.Y.: Prentice-Hall, 1989.

Standard & Poor's *Bond Guide.* New York: Standard & Poor's Corporation, monthly.

Standard & Poor's *Earnings Forecaster.* New York: Standard & Poor's Corporation, weekly.

Standard & Poor's *Statistical Service.* New York: Standard & Poor's Corporation.

Standard & Poor's *Industry Surveys.* New York: Standard & Poor's Corporation, quarterly and annual.

Standard & Poor's *Outlook.* New York: Standard & Poor's Corporation, monthly.

Statistical Reference Index. Washington, D.C.: Congressional Information Service, monthly.

U.S. Council of Economic Advisors. *Economic Report of the President.* Washington, D.C.: U.S. Government Printing Office, annual.

U.S. Bureau of the Census, Department of Commerce. *State and Metropolitan Area Data Book.* Washington, D.C.: U.S. Government Printing Office, 1986.

U.S. Bureau of Economic Analysis, Department of Commerce. *Survey of Current Business.* Washington, D.C.: U.S. Government Printing Office, monthly.

U.S. Bureau of Industrial Economics, Department of Commerce. *U.S. Industrial Outlook.* Washington, D.C.: U.S. Government Printing Office, annual.

U.S. Bureau of the Census, Department of Commerce. *Statistical Abstract of the United States.* Washington, D.C.: U.S. Government Printing Office, annual.

U.S. Council of Economic Advisors. *Economic Indicators.* Washington, D.C.: U.S. Government Printing Office, annual.

U.S. Bureau of Economic Analysis, Department of Commerce. *Business Conditions Digest.* Washington, D.C.: U.S. Government Printing Office, monthly.

U.S. Bureau of Economic Analysis, Department of Commerce. *Business Statistics.* Washington, D.C.: U.S. Government Printing Office, biennial.

United States League of Savings Institutions. *Savings Institutions Sourcebook.* Washington, D.C.: United States League of Savings Institutions, annual.

Value Line Investment Survey. New York: Value Line, Inc., weekly.

Valuing ESOP Shares. Washington, D.C.: The ESOP Association, 1989.

Vinso, Joseph D. *Valuation of Closely Held Business Interests.* Redwood City, Calif.: California Society of Certified Public Accountants, 1990.

Woy, James, ed. *Encyclopedia of Business Information Sources,* 6th ed. Detroit: Gale Research, 1986.

Zukin, James H. *Financial Valuation: Businesses and Business Interests.* New York: Maxwell MacMillan, 1990.

Article Bibliography

Ackerman, David. "Innovative Uses of Employee Stock Ownership Plans for Private Companies." *DePaul Business Law Journal* (Spring 1990), pp. 227–254.

Barenbaum, Lester. "Utilizing the Gordon Model: Discounting Net Income vs. Available Cash Flow." *Journal of Business Valuation* (1987), pp. 119–127.

Blum, Robert. "Common Valuation Errors in Buy-Sell Agreements: How to Avoid Them." *Practical Accountant* (March 1986), pp. 27–37.

Bolton, Steven E.; James W. Brockardt; and Michael J. Mard. "Risk Components of Capitalization Rates." *ASA Valuation* (February 1988).

Bouchey, Keith E. "How to Purchase a Savings Association from the Resolution Trust Corp." *Bank News* (January 1991), pp. 9–14.

Brinig, Brian P., and Michael W. Prairie. "Expert Testimony: The Business Appraiser as a Valuation Expert Witness." *Business Valuation News* (March 1985), p. 8.

Brock, Thomas. "More on Capitalization Rates." *Business Valuation News* (December 1985), pp. 5–8.

Carn, Neil; Joseph Rabianski; and James D. Vernor. "Trial Techniques of Expert Witnesses." *Real Estate Review* (Spring 1986), pp. 66–74.

Czumak, Michael. "The Appraiser Goes to Court." *ASA Valuation* (June 1988), pp. 34–40.

Dietrich, William C. "A Risk Premium/Growth Model to Determine the Earnings Multiple." *Business Valuation News* (March 1986), pp. 10–17.

Emory, John D. "The Value of Marketability as Illustrated in Initial Public Offerings of Common Stock: January 1980 through June 1981." *Business Valuation Review* (September 1985), pp. 21–24.

Emory, John D. "The Value of Marketability as Illustrated in Initial Public Offerings of Common Stock: January 1985 through June 1986." *Business Valuation Review* (December 1986), pp. 12–14.

Emory, John D. "The Value of Marketability as Illustrated in Initial Public Offerings of Common Stock: February 1989 through July 1990." *Business Valuation Review* (December 1990), pp. 114–116.

ESOP Association. "ESOP's: Building Equity and Growth for America's Future." *Proceedings of 13th Annual Convention of ESOP Association* (1990), pp. 495–500.

Fishman, Jay E. "The Problem with Rules of Thumb in the Valuation of Closely Held Entities." *FAIR$HARE* (December 1984), pp. 13–15.

Gilbert, Gregory A. "Discount Rates and Capitalization Rates—Where Are We?" *Business Valuation Review* (December 1990), pp. 108–113.

Goodman, Barry R. "A Long Look at the Leveraged ESOP Transaction and Valuation Issues That It Brings Up." *Business Valuation News* (June 1986), pp. 20–32.

Handorf, William C. "Shaping Dividend Theory and Policy." *Bank Portfolio Strategist* (April/May 1991).

Haut, Arthur N., and William P. Lyons. "Issues in the Valuation of Control and Non-control Shares in Connection with the Acquisition of Stock by Employee Stock Ownership Plans." *Journal of Pension Planning & Compliance* (Winter 1986), pp. 319–326.

Howe, Rex C., and Lee A. Kamp. "Appraisers as Expert Witnesses Before IRS." *The Real Estate Appraiser and Analyst* (Summer 1984), pp. 52–55.

Leung, T.S. Tony. "Myths about Capitalization Rate and Risk Premium." *Business Valuation News* (March 1986), pp. 6–10.

Huggins, Stanley M. "Bank Consolidation: Buy, Sell or Stay Put?" *The Bankers Magazine* (May/June 1990).

McMullin, Scott G. "Discount Rate Selection." *Business Valuation News* (September 1986), pp. 16–19.

Mercer, Z. Christopher, and David A. Harris. "The Perils of Excess." *ABA Banking Journal* (October 1987).

Mercer, Z. Christopher. "Rethinking Bank Capital." *The Southern Banker* (January 1983).

Mercer, Z. Christopher and Kenneth W. Patton. "Building Fee Income" *The Southern Banker* (December 1984).

Mercer, Z. Christopher. "The Adjusted Capital Asset Pricing Model for Developing Capitalization Rates: An Extension of Previous 'Build-Up' Methodologies Based Upon the Capital Asset Pricing Model." *Business Valuation Review* (December 1989).

Mercer, Z. Christopher. "If Deposit Intangibles Exist, Can Uniform Accounting Treatment Be Far Behind?" *ABA Banking Journal* (August 1983).

Mercer, Z. Christopher. "Tailoring Your Capital Plan." *The Southern Banker* (July 1983).

Mercer, Z. Christopher. "Outside Director's Viewpoint Can Be Helpful to a Closely-Held Company." *Memphis Business Journal* (January 31–February 4, 1983).

Mercer, Z. Christopher, and Ronald Terry. "Capital Planning and Capital Adequacy." *The Bankers Handbook* (1978).

Mercer, Z. Christopher. "Personal Planning: An Overlooked Application of the Corporate Planning Process." *Managerial Planning* (January/February 1980).

Mercer, Z. Christopher. "Issues in Recurring Valuations: Methodological Comparisons from Year-to-Year." *Business Valuation Review* (December 1988).

Mercer, Z. Christopher. "Do Public Company (Minority) Transactions Yield Controlling Interest or Minority Interest Pricing Data?" *Business Valuation Review* (December 1990), p. 123.

National Center for Employee Ownership. "Case Study: Phelps County Bank." *Employee Ownership Report* (March/April 1991), p. 4.

Nevers, Thomas J. "Capitalization Rates." *Business Valuation News* (June 1985), pp. 3–6.

Pagano, Mark P. "Uniform Appraisal Practices Are Needed in Leveraged ESOP Valuations." *Business Valuation Review* (March 1991), p. 21.

Patton, Kenneth W., and Z. Christopher Mercer. "Asset/Liability Management Today." *Bank Performance Annual* (1987), p. 85.

Patton, Kenneth W., and Z. Christopher Mercer. "How to Buy or Sell a Branch." *The Southern Banker* (October 1985).

Pettit, Laurence C., Michael D. Atchison, and Robert S. Kemp. "The Valuation of Small or Closely Held Banks." *The Journal of Bank Accounting and Auditing* (Spring 1991), pp. 23–31.

Pratt, Shannon P. "Understanding Capitalization Rates." *ASA Valuation* (June 1986), pp. 12–29.

Reilly, Robert F. "Value Enhancement Through a Valuation Engineering Analysis." *The Journal of Technical Valuation* (August 1990), pp. 41–48.

Roth, David E. "Valuation of Deposit Transfers." *Bank News* (January 1991), p. 16.

Schilt, James H. "Selection of Capitalization Rates for Valuing a Closely Held Business." *Business Law News* (Spring 1982), pp. 35–37.

Schilt, James H. "A Rational Approach to Capitalization Rates for Discounting the Future Income Stream of a Closely Held Company." *Financial Planner* (January 1982), pp. 56–57.

Weiss, Stuart. "Business Appraising: Beware of Amateur Hour." *Business Week* (February 9, 1987), p. 74.

Williams, Julie L., et al. "Mutual-to-Stock Conversions: New Capitalization Opportunities and Post-Conversion Control Developments." *Legal Bulletin* (May 1987).

Representative Fair Value Cases

Armstrong v. *Marathon Oil Co.,* (1987), 32 Ohio St. 3d 397.

Blasingame, Larry R. v. *American Materials, Inc.,* 654 S.W.2d 659 (Tenn. 1983)

Cavalier Oil Corporation v. *William J. Harnett,* Del. Supr. 564 A.2d 1137 (1989)

In re Glosser Brothers, Inc., 555 A.2d 129 (Pa. Super. 1989)

Hernando Bank v. *Huff,* 609 F. Supp 1124 (D.C. Miss. 1985)

Hunter v. *Mitek Industries,* 721 F. Supp. 1102 (E.D. Mo. 1989)

Independence Tube Corp. v. *Levine,* 535 N.E.2d 927 (Ill. App. 1 Dist. 1988)

Kennedy v. *Titcomb,* 553 A.2d 1322 (N.H. 1989)

King, Karen B. Jones v. *F.T.J. Inc.,* 765 S.W.2d 301 (Mo. App. 1988)

In re Valuation of Common Stock of McLoon Oil Co., 565 A.2d 997 (Me. 1989)

New Jersey Sports and Exposition Authority v. *Del Tufo,* 554 A.2d 878 (N.J. Super A.D. 1989)

Pittsburgh Terminal Corporation v. *Baltimore & Ohio Railroad,* 875 F.2d 549 (6th Cir. 1989)

Walter S. Chessman Realty Co. v. *Moore,* 770 P.2d 1308 (Colo. App. 1988)

Weinberger v. *UOP, Inc.,* 457 A.2d 701 (Del. Supr. 1983)

Index